After

LOVE SIGNS

LINDA GOODMAN'S LOVE SIGNS

Volume I

Other books by Linda Goodman

LINDA GOODMAN'S SUN SIGNS
VENUS TRINES AT MIDNIGHT

Linda Goodman's

A New Approach

LOVE SIGNS

to the Human Heart

Volume I

HARPER & ROW, PUBLISHERS

NEW YORK, HAGERSTOWN, SAN FRANCISCO, LONDON

H.R.H.

after years of many inexplicable delays, over which the
author in no way had any control . . . and through Karma's
strange pattern of destiny

Love Signs

was completed in the summer of 1978 in the same haunted
room where it was begun in the winter of 1970

Suite 1217

The Hollywood Roosevelt Hotel
on Hollywood Boulevard
in Los Angeles, the city of "Lost Angels"

the room in which the author's forthcoming book
about reincarnation and other magics

Gooobers

was also conceived . . . and was born . . . beneath the
light of the "small white cross, planted on the far
hill, behind Grauman's Chinese Theatre"

". . . . . *and the light shineth*
in the darkness, and the darkness
comprehendeth it not . . . . ."
JOHN 1:5

The verses beginning each section of the text have been taken
from the work of J. M. Barrie, *Peter Pan*.

☆ ☆ ☆

The occasional verses throughout the chapters are
quoted from *Venus Trines at Midnight* by Linda Goodman,
to be republished by Harper & Row in 1979.

with Everlasting Love

I dedicate this
and all my future books
to "my sneaky guru"
Aaron Goldblatt

who has patiently, throughout all incarnations, guided
my creative efforts and spiritual enlightenment with
the infinite gentleness and wisdom of a Master Avatar;
and who has been . . . is now and ever shall be . . .
responsible for all my miracles . . . every single one
of them manifested only through his faith.

*"Be not forgetful to entertain strangers, for
thereby some have entertained angels, unawares."*

HEBREWS 13:2

*"My children, errors will be forgiven. In our obsession
with original sin, we do often forget . . . original innocence."*

POPE INNOCENT, OF ASSISI
15th Century A.D.

a special acknowledgment
of gratitude

to the patient Bull
Sam O. Goodman

without whose steady loyalty and devotion I would not
have been able to write this or any other book

also to

Sarah Elizabeth Snyder, the Archer
William Dana Snyder, the Water Bearer
Jill Kemery Goodman, the Goat
Michael Aaron Goodman, the Eagle

my children . . . who have taught me, over the years,
many lessons of love . . . from the multi-faceted
viewpoints of Sagittarius, Aquarius, Capricorn and Scorpio

and the three Lions

Robert S. Kemery   Roland H. Chinatti
Robert A. Brewer

my heartfelt thanks to

the three Wise Men

Morton L. Janklow   Arthur Klebanoff   Jerome Traum

who symbolically parted the Red Sea so that this book
could be published, very much in the manner of Moses,
using the effective combination of ancient alchemy,
courage, professional brilliance . . .
and Aaron's rod

also to . . .

Buz Wyeth and Erwin Glikes

who have restored my faith in the integrity
of the publishing profession through their
personal honor and idealism

for Marc Salinger

who will understand my coded message to him
of the power of the magic roses he and I
carried to St. Patrick's through the rain one
April morning in New York . . . when he reads
this . . . wherever he is

". . . words, Bernardo . . . words. There was
a time when I believed in words . . ."

a carousel message to Sally

There is so much to say, and no way to say it, no way to tell you. Maybe if I try to say some of it here, then somehow, someway, you may read it.

You must have guessed I couldn't complete this book until I found you and we bear-hugged again. But now it seems the only way to make the miracle of you manifest is to finish it, so it can be published in time for your next birthday, by Christmas of 1978 . . . for so many reasons I can't fully explain until we're together. And so, I'm going to begin tonight, while it's magical and still and holy, to complete *Love Signs*—for you. Because Aaron said, before he went away . . . that you would want me to, that it would help so many people . . . and that it would bring you back sooner.

Your horoscope . . . and my heart . . . both insisted that what I was told on that terrible December day in 1973 was a lie. As soon as I heard, Michael and I flew to New York to *prove* it a lie. It was a very lonely faith. At first, everyone but Mike and Aaron thought my judgment had been prejudiced by grief. I could see it in their eyes when they looked at me. But I went right on believing anyway.

None of the official "records" seemed real to me. *They* seemed like the dream, not *you*. Only what I knew inside was real; so I clung to that, no matter what anyone tried to make me believe. Every day, for the longest time, Mike and Jill and I walked over to St. Patrick's and said a prayer near the statue of Francis of Assisi, just outside the church, among the trees. Once, we left some roses there, and when we went back the next morning, they had miraclized, like the ones I gave you that time . . . remember?

After a while, I proved it wasn't true. I proved it medically and scientifically. My faith was rewarded, the way I used to tell you that faith always is—if you believe long enough and hard enough. Ray Neff and his wife, Gus, who worked with me on the Lincoln research, helped me a lot with the proof I needed. So did Cleve Backster and Padre Anselmo, of the Benedictine Order—in an unusual way I'll tell you about someday. But even proving astrology and my heart had been right all along didn't help me to find you. Maybe completing this book will do that, in some mysterious way.

I can't forget that the next-to-the-last-time I saw you—you were with Marc. Because of astrology's wisdom (and for other reasons too) I believe that was the symbol of an unexpected twin-joy ending to temporary shadows and confusion. For things are not always what they seem, and people are sometimes too willing to believe whatever they are told. Time will tell. Faith bestows awesome miracles upon the faithful. This I know.

I thought maybe I could let you know the way it is with me . . . with Dad and Dadoo and Bill and Mike and Jill and Grandma G. . . . with all of us . . . by sending you a message through some paragraphs from *Peter Pan*, with slight changes to fit this reality. So I'm using James Barrie's words to try to express what we feel. They begin on the next page.

There's just this one more thing I wanted to tell you. Over and over since you disappeared, I keep dreaming the same dream. About the time I ran away when I was a little girl . . . to St. Raphael's convent on Thirteenth Street, in Parkersburg. The music . . . the incense . . . the whispering sisters . . . the scent of pine and the manger scene . . . the flickering candles . . . all seem so *real* in my dream. Isn't that strange?

all my love, with all my heart

Mom

. . . and now we must return to that desolate home from which she took flight, so long ago. It seems a shame to have neglected her family all this time; yet we may be sure that Sally's mother and father do not blame us. If we had returned sooner to look at them with sorrowful sympathy, they would probably have cried, "Don't be silly! What do we matter? Do go back, and keep an eye on Sally." So long as mothers and fathers are like that, children will take advantage of them, and you may lay to that.

Even now, we are no more than servants. Why on earth should Sally's bed be properly aired, seeing that she left home in such a thankless hurry? Would it not serve her jolly well right if she came back and found that her family was spending the weekend in the country? It would indeed be a moral lesson all children need. But if we contrived things this way, Sally's mother and father, her grandfather and grandma, her brothers and her sister, would never forgive us.

One thing I would like to do immensely, and that is to tell Sally's mother, in the way authors have, that her child is coming back, that indeed she will be here on Thursday week. That would spoil completely the surprise to which the angels and druids and Sally herself are so looking forward. They've all of them been planning it: her mother's rapture, her Dad's shout of joy, Bill's and Jill's and Michael's leap through the air to embrace her first, when what all of them should be preparing for is a good hiding. How delicious to spoil it, by breaking the news ahead of time, so that, when she enters grandly, her mother may not even offer her her mouth, and her Dad may exclaim pettishly, "Dash it all, here's that pesky girl again!" However, we are beginning to know Sally's family by this time, and we may be sure that we would get no thanks, even for this. They would quite likely upbraid us, for depriving the angels and druids . . and Sally herself . . of their pleasure.

"But my dear Madam, it is only ten days till Thursday week, near Easter . . or is it Thanksgiving? . . . so that, by telling you what's what, we can save you days of unhappiness."

"Yes, but at what a cost! By depriving the angels and druids and Sally of ten minutes of delight."

You see, the woman has no proper spirit. I had meant to say extraordinarily nice things about Sally's mother, but now I despise her, and not one of them will I say. She does not need to be told to have things ready, for she already has them ready. Sally's bed is aired, and she seldom leaves the house, and observe, the window is even left open for her. For all the use we are to Sally's mother, we might go back to our own galaxy. However, as we are here, we may as well stay and look on. That is all we are, lookers-on. Nobody really wants us. So let us watch, and say jaggy things.

Sally's dad is now living in Heathcliffe's old doghouse. When his daughter flew away, he felt in his bones that all the blame was his, that everyone had been wiser than he. Of course, he is a simple man, and extremely stubborn. He has a noble sense of justice and the courage to do what seems right to him; and having thought the matter out with anxious care after Sally's flight, he went down on all fours and crawled into Heathcliffe's kennel, which is where he has stayed—and remains to this day. To all invitations to come out, he answers, so sadly, but very firmly, "No. This is the place for me." Each night, when he returns from work, he crawls back into his kennel.

Let us look again at Sally's mother, a very sad-eyed woman. Now that we look at her more closely and remember the gaiety of the old days, all gone now, just because she has lost her babe, I find I won't be able to say nasty things about her after all. If she is too fond of her rubbishy children, she can't help it. Look at her in her chair, where she has fallen asleep. The corner of her mouth, where one looks first, the corner Sally always kissed, is almost withered up. Her hand moves restlessly on her breast, as if she had a pain there.

Suppose, to make her happy, we whisper to her in her sleep that her child is coming back. She is really within two miles of the window now, and flying strong, but all we need whisper is that she is on her way. Let's!

It is a pity we did it, for she has started up, calling Sally's name, and there is no one in the room but Heathcliffe.

"Oh, Heathcliffe, I dreamt my Sally had come back!"

All the dog could do was to put his paw gently on his mistress's lap, and they sat there thus for the longest time.

When Thursday week came, Sally at first planned to tiptoe in and place her hands over her mother's eyes. But then she realized that she must break the joyous news more gently. For great joy is akin to great sorrow, and can be quite dangerous to the heart. She finally decided to just slip into her bed, and be there when they all came in next morning, just as if she had never been away.

And so, when her mother and father and Bill and Jill and Michael came in next morning, they saw Sally there, sleeping like a princess in a faerie tale. She waited for their cry of joy, but it did not come. They saw her, but they did not believe she was there. You see, they had seen her there so often, in their dreams, that they all thought this was just the old dream, hanging around them still. Sally did not understand this, and a cold fear fell upon her.

"Mom! Dad! Bill! Jill! Michael! Don't you know me?"

"That's Sally!" cried her mother, even though she was sure it was only the dream.

At last, the truth of the miracle exploded within them, and there could not have been a lovelier sight on earth. There was no one to see it but a few straggling angels and druids who had stayed behind to watch . . . and a strange man peeking through the window, the one who had brought it all about. He had ecstasies innumerable that we can never know; yet he was looking through the window at the one joy he could not join. But they all knew he was there. Michael was certain he saw him grinning, and Jill thought she saw a copy of The New York Times tucked under his arm.

Oh! the bliss of that moment . . the reunion! There are really no words to describe it, at least none yet taught on this planet, but I am told, on good authority, that every single person in the room levitated . . that is, they all found they could fly. And they flew about the room for many,

many days. Later, they knew it had all truly happened, for they found, out on the street, beneath the window, a tattered and torn copy of the *Times*, with very small letters printed in ink at the very top of the page . . . the initials A.G.

LINDA GOODMAN'S LOVE SIGNS

Contents

Volume I

THE TWELVE MYSTERIES OF LOVE

YOUR SUN SIGN, 44

THE LOVE SIGN COMBINATIONS

Love Signs

. . . why it was written

As you will discover in this book, there are many more Sun Signs with which we have the potential for easy compatibility, sympathy and understanding than those with which we may find some degree of tension, antipathy or lack of communication . . . . . more opportunities for love and compassion than for hatred and mistrust in the harmonics of our solar system.

Yet concerned men and women in all walks of Life, from geologists and ecologists to prophets and astrologers, persistently predict the possibility of approaching cataclysms, both man-made and natural, bringing the danger of annihilation before the critical next decade has passed on this waning planet, so fast losing light. We have been warned, but few have heeded the warning. We have been called, but few have answered. For the Earth to wax again, clearly a miracle is needed.

By learning to use the wisdom of the planets, our co-Creators' code to Universal Truth, we may each create a fragment of the rainbow-spectrum message of *Peace on Earth to men . . . and women . . . of good will* caroled by celestials over Bethlehem two thousand years ago to usher in the Pisces Age of the gentle Nazarene, who asked us only to "love one another," promising that what he did, *we* could "then do also."

It's not too late, for the joyous message of angelic hosts (not yet identified) still rings its clarion call today . . . now ushering in the Aquarian Age . . . heralding hope to those who watch the skies and listen for the music. There could be, I think, no greater prelude to a miracle so needed, perhaps approaching sooner than we guess, than to employ the art of ancient wise men to pave the way for his return with a new Star Quest for love . . . love of man for woman . . . and of both together then for every living plant and creature. For love alone has the power to bring peace at history's twilight hour to Earthlings of good will.

Linda Goodman

In the Year of Our Lord 1978

To All My Readers

Love Signs contains a number of controversial concepts of a moral, philosophical and intellectual nature, in the areas of science and religion.

To some of you, these concepts will be inspiring—to others, they will appear strange and startling—to still others they could be deeply disturbing. They are presented here as truth, and will be recognized as such by many of you—just as they may be viewed as otherwise by some.

I've shared my personal discoveries of truth with you because I believe that any kind of search implies an obligation to exchange with others what has been found, in the interest of hastening the sunrise of harmony on Earth, the ultimate Peace.

However, I do not ask—nor do I even expect—any of you to regard my concepts as *your* truth, unless they should happen to agree with your own personal enlightenment and private convictions.

Partial truth—the seeds of wisdom—can be found in many places. In primal instinct may partial truth be found . . . in earthly law, social custom, scientific research, philosophy and religious doctrine. The seeds of wisdom are contained in all scriptures ever written . . . especially in art, music and poetry . . . and, above all, in Nature.

But *real* Truth can be found in one place only—in every man's and woman's communion with an eternal Source of hidden Knowledge within —which each individual must seek and find for himself or herself.

We may point out the path to others, but each must walk along that path alone—until every single "lost one" has made the whole journey—and all of us have finally reached the Light of full-born Wisdom at the end of the Way . . . where we began, a long-forgotten Time ago.

Foreword

Like Peter Pan's shadow, curiosity about astral compatibility follows the astrologer "second from the right and straight on till morning." At every gathering, someone is sure to demand an answer to a question such as: "How does Sagittarius get along with Pisces?" Typically, on radio and television shows, in newspaper interviews, the astrological professional is invariably confronted with: "My husband is a Leo and I'm an Aquarian. Is that why we fight so much?"—or: "What's the best sign for Gemini to marry?"

Everyone wants to know the ground rules in the game of mixing and matching Sun Signs. I've even found myself helpless in a dental chair, having a tooth extracted, while the attending doctor remarked, "Not that I believe in astrology, but what are my chances with a Capricorn woman?"

Now, those of you who were once young (and, I hope, still are) know that Tinker Bell told Peter: "Everytime a child says 'I don't believe in faeries,' there is a faerie somewhere who falls down dead." Likewise, everytime someone says, "I don't believe in the stars," there is a human relationship somewhere that falls down dead because of a lack of understanding that could have been gained from a basic knowledge of astrology —and that's not make-believe. It's a fact. There's nothing mysterious about the oldest art and science in the world, unless you choose to call the miracles of love and tolerance that result from using it "mysterious." Semantics aside, it works, whatever you call it.

As for those familiar characters in Neverland, Peter Pan and Wendy, although I've used some of their remarks throughout this book to symbolize, at various times, certain characteristics of all twelve astrological signs, Peter's personal Natal Sun was in the Mutable Air Element of Gemini when he was created. Oh, yes! Peter was a Sun Sign Gemini—even though I use particular quotes of his to symbolize other signs in the book, a Sun Sign Gemini he was, who desired never to grow up, searching for something he never quite found, forever destined to be sure only of his own shadow, never of another human being—until, we trust, through eventual enlightenment, he learned at last the lesson of love.

Wendy was clearly a Cancerian—motherly, possessive, gentle and imaginative, trying out her wings in a flight of fancy under the Full Moon, as Moon Maidens often do. No strong Sun Sign harmony between them, you see, so they quarreled now and then, and each heard a different drummer. Wendy ended up in the final chapter as nearly all Cancerians do, safe and secure. No matter how wistfully her heart longed to fly again, she chose home, marriage and children as her ultimate dreams; while Peter, like nearly all Geminis, continued his eternal search for a brighter rainbow, somewhere beyond . . . still obsessed by twin desires, longing to settle down with Wendy, yet longing just as fiercely to remain free—and true to himself.

But the Moon was surely in Aquarius when Wendy was born, in trine (harmonious) Luminary aspect to Peter's Gemini Sun, which is why she flew away with him in the first place . . . and promised to return to clean his house every spring.

It's worth all the time and trouble it takes to compare two horoscopes for compatibility, because when you find a trined, sextiled or conjuncted relationship between two Sun Signs—and also a trined, sextiled or conjuncted relationship between the mutual Sun and Moon Signs (the signs transited by the Sun and the Moon at the time of both births)—plus a positive interchange of the signs on the Ascendents with the Luminaries—love then takes on a deeper dimension. All love is capable of energizing wishes into reality, but love between two people whose personal auras have thus harmoniously blended creates the kind of vibration poets write about, and can manifest marvelous magic.

Wandering through the millions of couples on Earth who are attempting to achieve (or have achieved) satisfying contentment and fulfillment together—and those who are still struggling through heavy sexual karmic testing—are those rare ones esoterically called "Soul Mates" . . . or "Twin Souls."

It sometimes happens that a man and a woman meet and instantly recognize the other half of themselves behind the eyes of each other. The eyes have been rightly called "the windows of the soul." Even their voices are familiar to each other's ears, like a remembered chord of music. These are two who immediately sense the unalterable fact that they have been—

are—and must always be One; even though they might have fought against their fate for centuries and struggled in vain to escape their linked destiny. Almost from the first moment they meet and gaze upon each other, their spirits rush together in joyful recognition, ignoring all convention and custom, all social rules of behavior, driven by an inner knowing too overwhelming to be denied. Inexplicably, often without a word being spoken, they *know* that only through each other can they hope to find Wholeness—only when they're together can they both be Complete in every way.

Somehow, they feel Immortal, and they are . . . for this level of love can bestow the beginning knowledge of the attainment of several-centuries-longevity in the same flesh body on the Earth plane, as well as the accomplishment of changing flesh bodies (the Temples of the soul) in a fully conscious state, without the "coma" called death. The solution to the problem of the "over-population" which rises to the mind as a result of such achievement by everyone on Earth must wait till a forthcoming book for a detailed discussion.

Neither will I attempt to detail the origin and ultimate destiny of Twin Souls here, since I've done so in another forthcoming book, called *Gooobers*, to be published in the near future. But there is so much burning curiosity concerning the subject of Soul Mates or Twin Souls, it bears some explanation here, however incomplete.

A man and a woman who are Soul Mates hardly need to speak the words "I love you," knowing as surely as they do that they must belong to each other whether in this present incarnation (lifetime)—or (due to karmic complications) at the end of many more centuries. The words in the marriage ceremony "those which God hath joined together, let no man put asunder" refer to such as these. Yet this warning is unnecessary, simply symbolic ritual, for no man *can* break the tie between Twin Souls, not even themselves. Nor can any energy in the Universe. The Force that created them is all-powerful and indestructible. The bond may be weakened, their final union and consummation delayed, but they cannot be separated permanently. There can be no end to the kind of happiness they may claim—when they wish to do so—on a timetable dictated by the Free Will choice of the Higher Angels of their own selves. (The Superconscious or Supraconscious of each.)

This kind of instant magnetic attraction is often called "love at first sight," which is no accident of fate, but very real. It's more than curious coincidence that Twin Souls, out of the whole huge world, should be drawn together at the appointed time. The crossing of their paths has been predestined on a Higher Level of Awareness. Certain spiritual energies are at work to bring about their meetings, as surely as the migration of birds and the return of comets are governed by a similar Universal Law. Their coming-together is controlled by the workings of Karma, which is but the sum total of *Causes* set into motion in the Past—and these determine infallibly the conditions of the Present. When the time comes for Twin Souls to incarnate, they are sent to Earth, clothed in flesh (again, the bodies being the Temples of the soul) through particular Time-Energy Forces, at the moment in Earth Time when certain planetary configurations create the proper conditions. These Time-Energy Forces are electromagnetic in nature, yet more complex than this.

None of us can control the eventual results of the Causes we've initiated or set into motion in our past lives, although we *can* control our *re*-actions to the results such past Causes bring into the present lifetime. The "Free Will" to change these karmic events is possessed by the Higher Self, and we may attain such power by learning to tune into or communicate with the Higher Self (Supraconscious). But "Free Will" on a *conscious* level can only be realized in the Future—since, in the ever-moving stream called the Present, we are setting into motion, through actions we currently initiate and through our *re*-actions to past Causes—the future conditions we will inevitably meet.

As for which particular planetary influences in the nativities (horoscopes or birth charts) of two people reveal to an astrologer the indication that these are Twin Souls, they are too intricate to comprehensively explain in this book, in their entire scope—and must await another volume planned concerning this and related subjects. But assuming that such planetary influences are present in the respective charts of lovers, a destiny is revealed in which the two will meet involuntarily—and cannot be separated, even through the experience of death—except for temporary intervals of Earth Time in the present life, for the purpose of karmic soul-testing. During these periods of being apart, however brief or however extended, both persons are lonely, empty and incomplete. Yet even throughout any such temporary spaces in their togetherness, there's a constant, pulsing astral communication between them—for even then, they are linked by a cord that connects them over the miles.

A woman I know was recently in a state of emotional anxiety, desperately needing communication with the man she loved (a Twin Soul), who was out of the country. There was no way they could reach each other by phone or letter. One night, as she was lying in her bed in the dark, sensing his presence strongly but frustrated at being unable to see or hear or touch him, she cried out aloud, involuntarily, "Oh, why can't you *hear* me call you?" Suddenly the lamp on the desk across the room snapped on. At the same moment, a large paper daisy he had given her months before dropped to the floor. Astonished, she sat up in bed, stared at the lamp and the fallen daisy and spoke aloud again. "If it was really you who turned on the light, can you give me a sign you're actually here in your astral body by turning it off now?" Instantly, the switch on the lamp audibly clicked off, leaving the room in darkness—then immediately snapped back on, filling the room with light. Before the incident, the lamp had been off for several hours, so this was no failure of electrical power.

There was absolutely no scientific explanation for what occurred. Neither the bulb nor the switch was loose, and there was nothing wrong with the connection or the socket. All this was thoroughly checked. As for the daisy, it had remained securely in its place, fastened above a picture on the wall, for many months, until that unexpected moment. Such "miracles" are easily explained by the laws of metaphysics. The woman's Twin Soul had felt her need, and answered it, guided astrally by both their Higher Selves, through the silvery-blue cord connecting them, a thread of light actually visible to the physical vision of a trained psychic or sensitive. Later she learned that he was anxiously trying to reach her at exactly the same hour. Those who love faithfully, and who understand how to use the cord of electrical energy that binds them together, don't need Western Union, the post office or the telephone company to communicate. They're always in touch through their astral "eastern-union." There have been countless such occurrences between two people in all kinds of love relationships—parent and child, close friends, husbands and wives . . and lovers.

We still hear the shouts of science: "Give us the facts, the facts, the facts!" Astronomy and science, each unable to see the great metaphysical forest of knowledge through the trees of lower mathematics and physics, sans the "meta," while metaphysics could explain so many mysteries. "Meta" is a Greek word meaning, simply, "beyond." Beyond the fiction of Fact lies Truth? Einstein was aware. Yes, Abstract Al knew. Someday very soon in this dawning Aquarian Age, the discovery of instruments sensitive enough to measure the tremendous energy of love's magnetic force field will demonstrate how its electrical impulses can interrupt Nature's laws (but not adversely), reverse gravity (and also reverse the aging process, through cell regeneration), increase telepathic communion and cause many other miraculous manifestations, including conscious recall of former incarnations, which will finally convince skeptical science. Yes, love can do all this, if the desire is strong enough, and the motive unselfish—where enough faith and enough will are exerted. It happens every day.

It's been frequently observed, by witnesses of credibility, that a ninety-pound woman can lift the wheels of a two-ton truck if her child is caught beneath it—a complete reversal of the laws of physics but in absolute accord with the laws of *meta*-physics. Love is far more than an emotion or a feeling. Love is a positive electrical impulse. Science has not yet developed equipment delicate or sophisticated enough to detect these impulses; nevertheless, they do exist. "Scientists" didn't believe in electronic radio waves either until they could be *measured* . . . . yet they were *there* all along. As H. T. Buckle wrote, in his *History of Civilization in England*: ". . . according to the ordinary course of affairs, a few generations pass away, then comes a period when these very truths are looked upon as commonplace facts; and a little later, there comes another period in which they are declared to be necessary, and even the dullest intellect wonders how they could ever have been denied."

During the weary search for one's own Twin Soul, there will be many side trips, many relationships that at first appear to be genuine, then fade into disinterest and boredom. Even when the Soul Mate is at last discovered, there are often many complications and testings of worthiness which cause temporary pain. Only in continually and consistently practicing tolerance and forgiveness can the hurt be alleviated. To return pain for pain only creates the future certainty of a like reaction, of more pain, through the workings of karmic cause and effect.

Sometimes, it seems that the problems of two people who love each other are hopeless, the wall that separates them too high to ever surmount. But their problems would all dissolve, simply disappear, if they would only touch hands—or hearts—or minds—or even touch noses—and whisper just one word: "magic!" For love *is* magic, the secret power all who love possess without realizing it. No matter how great the injury, or how bitter the words, love will erase it all, as if it had never been. But not without the desire and effort to do so on the part of the one who has inflicted the pain—not without the quality of forgiveness on the part of the one who's been deeply hurt. Desire, effort and forgiveness, intermingled, are necessary to release love's force and power.

The fabled search for the Holy Grail is a dual quest. On a material or Earth level, it concerns the actual cup from which the Nazarene drank at the Last Supper, claimed by the ancients to have been buried near where the druidic priests (descended from the Essenes) held their mystic rites—its discovery imminent in the Age of the Water Bearer.

On a higher, mystical level, the successful conclusion of the search for the Holy Grail is reached, for each human, at the time of reunion with the Twin Soul. For only when all lonely and separated Twin Souls are at last joyously reunited, will the pieces of Life's jigsaw puzzle form themselves into a whole and complete picture within the Universe. Legend whispers that it shall be during the dawning of the Age of Aquarius when the fourteen pieces of the soul of Osiris—scattered when his body was cut into fourteen pieces by his brother, Set (causing the Earth's first Sun-Set) —will come together in one man, *"with all his scattered pieces whole."* One man, who will be reunited with his own Twin Soul, Isis, after millions of weary years of searching, and countless uncomprehending incarnations spent together in the past.

At the same time, the long-ago-sundered Twin Souls of Set and his Nepenthys will be rejoined, to fulfill their destiny of discovering together the Grail of the Nazarene, through the blending of their auras. Then, says legend, through the miracle of *mutual forgiveness* for that long-ago crime, Set and his brother, Osiris—along with Isis and her sister, Nepenthys, will in some way, together, find the lost records of Atlantis . . . . . as well as the burial place of Osiris, which contains the records of the building of the Great Pyramid of Gizeh by Osiris (not by Cheops, as falsely believed down through the ages). When these great and holy events manifest themselves, following the recognition of these four (and one other) of the true identity of their own Higher Selves—many more Twin Souls will suddenly recognize each other. Then we shall at least begin to realize our blessed birthright, as supplicated in those singing lines of the Lord's Prayer: "Thy Kingdom come, Thy will be done, *on Earth, as it is in Heaven*" (as above, so below), changing the pattern of the Trinity of Solar, Stellar and Lunar energies in the cosmos.

Those who love deeply, and who are truly mated with the other half of themselves, have no desire to initiate wars, or to dominate others. As the devotion of Romeo and Juliet, even in death, had the power to dissolve the enmity and reconcile the differences between the warring Capulets and Montagues, so shall the ecstatic blending of all Twin Soul lovers have the same power to unite mankind and womankind, all Earthlings in permanent Peace and Good. *Pax et Bonum*. It's not a coincidence (nothing is) that the man who initiated at least a beginning gesture toward Peace in the Middle East, Anwar Sadat, is a genuinely happily mated man, with a woman by his side who reflects the goals of his Higher Self—as is Menachem Begin, of Israel, who at least initially welcomed the gesture in an equal spirit of good will and sincerity. Nor was it coincidence that Hitler was a lonely, unloved man.

Jesus—the carpenter from Nazareth? He was not alone. He was not unloved by woman. Although it is only a beginning, Scorpio Reverend William Phipps's fine and meticulously researched book *The Sexuality of Jesus* (Harper & Row, 1973), to be republished by Harper & Row in 1979 under the title *Did Jesus Love?*, sheds needed enlightenment upon that long-hidden mystery of Jesus and his own Twin Soul. For he was only a man, albeit a highly evolved one—and she, only a woman. Even as you.

The doctrine of divinity, like the doctrine of patriotism, is a negative vibration, placing one man, one woman, one nation, above all others. Jesus, the *Christ?* Yes, *he* was *more* than human, a different entity, but no different, no more super human or divine than *each* man and woman may rise to become during those too rare and brief periods of tuning in to the individual Supraconscious. Anwar, the Christ . . Menachem, the Christ . . Ruth, the Christ . . . Robert, the Christ . . . Thelma, the Christ . . Michel, the Christ . . Susan, the Christ . . Arthur, the Christ . . and so on, including your own name. Christ is simply another term for the Holy Ghost or the Holy Spirit, which can enter into anyone. We are all sons and daughters of God—and of *His* Mate, His own Twin Soul. How could our Creator not have His counterpart? The polarity of positive-negative, masculine-feminine, exists in all dimensions, on all levels of awareness, within the galaxies of Heaven—and upon the Hell on Earth (as it is presently manifest). Jesus himself never claimed he was divine. *"What I have done, you can do also—and more . . . . . go thou and do likewise . . . . . . be it done unto you according to your faith . . . . . ."* These are not claims of spiritual exclusivity, only reminders that what was being demonstrated were manifestations of the "divine" *within each of us*, miracles we *all* could perform—though not without sacrifice, not without certain disciplines to bring mind, body and emotions under control. Strange, that the word "discipline" contains the word "disciple." Or perhaps . . . not strange at all.

The predicted cataclysms, should they come, should we be unable to prevent them, have been set into motion by many forces of darkness . . . . by the underground testing of immense destructive energies . . . . by the negative vibrations of the current waves of sexual promiscuity and lewdness in magazines and film, abusing and degrading sex to its lowest level . . . . the gorging greed for financial gain . . . . the selfish refusal to share our money, our food or our love with one another. "If everyone ate simply, everyone would eat." The need for sex, like the need for food, is a burning hunger all over the world. But sharing our love does not mean sharing our bodies in sensual group sexual experience. Gluttony is not the answer, to *either* kind of hunger.

Sex is not a sin; only the mis-use of its energy is a sin against the Higher Angel of one's own Self. Sexual union is the ecstasy of "deep" discovered by those who *love*, symbolic of a man and woman's blending with the Universe and all of Nature, in Oneness. It's a simple matter of priorities. You fall in love first—with your eyes. Then with your mind, then with your heart (emotions). By now your soul has joined the experience—whether you realize it or not, you've "fallen in love" spiritually—and it's time to fall in love with your body.

It doesn't work when you take these steps in reverse. For only the *eyes* know how to lead you into the mind of the one they gaze upon. Only the *mind* knows how to lead you into the heart of the one with whom you've found a mental affinity. Only the *heart* knows how to lead you into union with the soul of the one you love. And the *soul* is well aware . . oh! well aware, believe me . . of how to lead you, then, into the ecstasy of Oneness called sexual mating—becoming "one flesh."

But if you begin with the body . . . . . . the body knows not where to lead you, except into more and more sensations of the flesh, which by themselves have no power to fulfill love's yearning or feed love's deeper hunger—sensations that must, by certain physiological laws, eventually cause the body to become immune to sensation, needing ever more and more stimulation—until finally, like a drug, the tolerance level for even this is reached, and there is oblivion of all feeling. Using the body as an instrument for sex alone, without love, is like listening to a symphony on stereophonic equipment but using only one speaker.

Yes, it is time for a Messiah. A Wayshower, who will once again remind us of the basic lessons of love he taught before, so soon forgotten. For it makes no difference how far an individual or a nation has fallen into error; love will bring a renewed dedication to humanity. Just as it makes no difference how far away someone has gone, for love will bring a return. As poet Emmet Fox noted, when it is projected with sufficient intensity, there is no distance that love cannot span, no illness—moral, mental, emotional or spiritual—that love cannot heal. No victory that love cannot win. Love is concentrated kinetic energy, the most awesome force in Nature . . . and beyond Her.

If only you could love deeply enough and sustain love long enough, you could become the source of your own miracles, as powerful as the ancient "gods and goddesses." There is no dream you couldn't turn into a reality, no law you can't change, no situation you can't reverse—if only you could love *enough*.

Loving enough is not easy. Loving enough doesn't mean loving only those who love you, who are kind and considerate and generous. Loving *enough* means also loving those who "say all manner of evil against you," who hate you and actively demonstrate that hatred, who seemingly lack all compassion and sensitivity. Anyone can return the love of those who love him—or her. There's little glory or power in that kind of love. We are incarnated in these flesh bodies on Earth to learn love's deeper, more difficult lesson of loving the *un*lovable. In this accomplishment lies all the force and energy of true passion. More often than not, it's a painful effort, but the rewards, when it's mastered, are . . . beyond imagining. Never mind unnecessary religious "canonization"—you, too, can become a "saint" —*if you can love enough*.

In astrological terms, for a Lion and a Ram to love, for a Bull and a Goat to love—is nearly effortless. But for a Ram to achieve harmony with a Crab—the Lion with the Scorpion—the Bull with the Water Bearer—these demonstrate a higher love. *Love Signs* will attempt to guide those who are fortunate enough to be united with their own compatible Sun Signs—and also show the way to tolerance and harmony for those whose present karmic destiny has decreed the soul-testing of being involved in relationships with people of conflicting Sun Signs.

Even between two individuals whose Sun and Moon Signs harmonize, there are always some planets in their mutual nativities which clash, causing periodic friction and tension. To overcome this is to become tuned in to the pulsing frequency of the Higher Self, to begin the climb up the pathway to enlightenment . . . to walk in magic, showered with miracles. Like a bottomless cup, the Holy Grail of those who love is never empty. In the Neverland mathematics of metaphysics, you see—the more miracles we give away to others, the more we have left for you and me.

Who among us is not, at times, unlovable? And are not these the very times when we secretly yearn and need to be loved the most? Oh! the magic of receiving kindness in return from one to whom we have been *un*kind . . . the miracle of hearing, when we have said: "I'm sorry I said such cruel things," the answer: *"What cruel things? I didn't hear them."*

Then the heart bursts with joy and our cup runneth over. For this most ancient alchemy secret of all is such a simple secret.

If it was negative, it didn't happen—except in the world of illusion.

And so, may the Force . . . of Love . . . be with you. May it prevent the predicted cataclysms of Nature, as well as the personal cataclysms of separation and divorce, through its prisms of Light.

". . and he shall gather his lambs . . ."

ISAIAH 40:11

The
Twelve Mysteries
of Love

*L*ove is man's and woman's deepest need. It's not the threat of illness or poverty that crushes the human spirit, but the fear that there is no one who truly cares—no one who really understands. We all reach desperately for love, no matter how healthy, wealthy or wise we may be, because the alternative is loneliness. And so love is sought both in heaven and in hell, by both saints and sinners, wherever the search may take them, and it takes them to some strange places in the Aquarian Age, through the maze of the sexual revolution.

> *Say, what is this hang-up about sex?*
> *all those people who go to pornographic films*
> *and the ones who won't . . .*

The swingers and the idealists, the puritans and prostitutes, the frigid and the promiscuous, the male chauvinists and the Women's Liberators, whether they read Browning or *Playboy*, whether they watch Walt Disney movies or the latest erotica from Sweden, are all looking for the same thing. No matter which road they travel on their pursuit of happiness, the inner need that drives them on is love. Not to give it. Not to receive it. But to *share it*. To love and be loved in return.

Why is lasting, mutual love so elusive? To reach a complete and permanent union with the other half (the Twin Soul) man and woman must learn the lessons of the twelve Sun Signs. They must master the wisdom of these Twelve Mysteries of Love before they can achieve a final, perfect harmony between their mental, physical, emotional and spiritual natures.

As we make the trip around the astrological or karmic wheel of life, through the rebirth under the influence of the various Sun Signs, sometimes progressing swiftly, sometimes lingering, many times *returning* to a certain Sun Sign experience to relearn old lessons—we evolve, each at his or her own speed. We are forced, by our own Superconscious selves, to gradually perfect the positive qualities of all twelve signs and purge our natures of their negative qualities, so that we each may eventually become the refined gold of a totally evolved entity, worthy to join the other half— the Twin Self. In our longing for love—for our Twin Soul or Soul Mate— lies our latent metaphysical wisdom. The secret of life itself. Esoteric truth.

Every Sun Sign contains a strength that can be reversed into a weakness, and every Sun Sign contains a weakness that can be reversed into a strength, through the law of positive-negative polarity. What is Taurus stubbornness but Taurus patience turned upside down? What is Aries impulsiveness but the negative side of the Ram's positive Mars courage? Will Leo choose to use the great pride and nobility of the Leonine-Solar birthright for the positive purpose of protecting the helpless—or for the negative purpose of becoming an arrogant tyrant over the defenseless? Will the sensible Cancerian caution be turned into Lunar fears and phobias? Will Pisces compassion and humility be reversed to the negative Neptune aspects of deception, introversion and escape? The choice of our Sun Sign polarities is always ours to take. And if we make the wrong choice we must relive that Sun Sign experience repeatedly, until we master the positive strength of that sign.

The Twelve Initiations of Love

In each of the following experiences, man or woman is fully capable of giving and teaching others the first quality, but for the personality to learn the second quality is a struggle. When one's understanding of this second quality equals that of the first, he or she has then achieved mastery of a particular Sun Sign. The soul must pass *more than once* through the *First Six* Initiations of Love as:

ARIES	the infant	"I am"	to teach that love is innocence and learn that love is trust
TAURUS	the baby	"I have"	to teach that love is patience and learn that love is forgiveness
GEMINI	the child	"I think"	to teach that love is awareness and learn that love is feeling
CANCER	the adolescent	"I feel"	to teach that love is devotion and learn that love is freedom
LEO	the teenager	"I will"	to teach that love is ecstasy and learn that love is humility

| VIRGO | the adult | "I analyze" | to teach that love is pure and learn that love is fulfillment |

After achieving emotional maturity in these first six stages of development, man and woman must then pass through love's *Final Six* Initiations (more than once) to discover its deeper spiritual meaning in:

LIBRA	marriage	"I balance"	to teach that love is beauty and learn that love is harmony
SCORPIO	sex	"I desire"	to teach that love is passion and learn that love is surrender
SAGITTARIUS	knowledge	"I see"	to teach that love is honesty and learn that love is loyalty
CAPRICORN	experience	"I use"	to teach that love is wisdom and learn that love is unselfish
AQUARIUS	idealism	"I know"	to teach that love is tolerance and learn that love is Oneness
PISCES	submission	"I believe"	to teach that love is compassion and learn that love is ALL

and so to realize at last that

Love Is Eternal

There is a deep and significant reason why the meditation upon the *Twelve Mysteries of Love* contained here is important to you and the one you love. The key is the number *twelve*. There are 12 basic mineral salts used in homeopathy (the most helpful of all branches of medicine). These 12 cell salts have a great power to influence a positive state of human health in each of their corresponding *twelve* Sun Signs, a fact comprehended only by homeopathic practitioners, not orthodox physicians (except for a rare few of the latter). Minerals of the Earth conform to the number 12, as do both the metric and duodecimal systems. Diamonds, for instance, possess 12 sides or axes, along which they *must* be cut to *achieve brilliance*. There were 12 governors of the Manichean System, 12 divisions of Solomon's Temple, 12 labors of Hercules, 12 Altars of St. James, 12 Greek Gods and so forth.

Long before the 12 sons of Jacob founded the 12 Tribes of Israel, the number thirteen (13) possessed a great mystical significance. As an example, there were 12 Knights of the Round Table, with King Arthur making the 13th member. The ancient Egyptian god-King Osiris, was associated with 12 lesser kings, Osiris being their 13th member. Likewise did the Aztec god-King Quetzalcoatl have 12 followers, he being the 13th of the group. In Christianity, Gautama Buddhism and Shiite Islam, there are also 12 followers (apostles or disciples) and one Master. The 12 disciples represent the *twelve Sun Sign stages of learning*—and the "Master" symbolizes the number thirteen (13)—or the purity of the perfect blend of all the other *twelve* into One Complete Whole.

As an example, each of the 12 apostles in the Christian Bible can be identified by esoteric astrologers with the Sun Sign quality embodied in that individual's particular attitude toward the teachings of Jesus. This interwoven Judaeo-Christian-Islamic religious truth is manifested in the mathematical harmony and beautiful synchronicity of the horoscopic wheel.

Spiritual ignorance, or blindness, causes the superstitious fear of the dread number "13." Hotel floors jump from "12" to "14," and few hostesses will invite thirteen people for dinner. Yet, the true meaning of this holy number is wisdom. If used for evil it can bring great destruction. But if used for good it can bring great regeneration. Used in its negative sense, it symbolizes the "Master," who is the blend of all twelve Sun Sign lessons, having become a "fallen angel," like Lucifer. Used in its positive sense, it means exactly the opposite—an "angel" who remains steadfast, to wield power and wisdom everlasting, tempered with justice and mercy—and above all else—*love*.

Numerology is an inescapable part of astrology. The subject is too vast and complicated to be fully covered in *Love Signs* and will be discussed in detail in a forthcoming book. Meanwhile, however, the briefest mention of planetary numbers is necessary for a full comprehension of the *Twelve Mysteries of Love*. Each Sun Sign harmonizes with and is governed by a particular planet or Luminary (Sun or Moon). And each planet likewise harmonizes with and is governed by a particular *number*. For example:

The Sun (ruler of Leo) vibrates to the number Ten or One ($10 = 1$), which it equals when added via the normal mathematical process.

The Moon (ruler of Cancer) vibrates to the number Two (2).

Jupiter (ruler of Sagittarius) vibrates to the number Three (3).

Uranus (ruler of Aquarius) vibrates to the number Four (4).

Mercury (ruler of Gemini and temporary ruler of Virgo, until Virgo's true ruling planet, Vulcan, is discovered and identified: see Virgo-Virgo chapter) vibrates to the number Five (5).

Venus (ruler of Libra and temporary ruler of Taurus, until Pan-Horus is discovered as the true ruler of Taurus: see Taurus-Taurus chapter) vibrates to the number Six (6).

Neptune (ruler of Pisces) vibrates to the number Seven (7).

Saturn (ruler of Capricorn) vibrates to the number Eight (8).

Mars (ruler of Aries) vibrates to the number Nine (9).

Each planet and Luminary also vibrates to what is termed a "higher octave" number, but we'll leave a full explanation of this for the aforementioned forthcoming book.

You might have noticed the omission of a number that vibrates to Pluto (ruler of Scorpio) in this list. Many astrologers and students of numerology will tell you that Pluto vibrates to the number Nine (9), sharing this number with Mars (ruler of Aries). This is not true. Pluto, like all the other planets, vibrates to its own personal "number"—distinctly and individually its own—sharing it with no other planet or Luminary. Since we've already covered the numbers One (1) through Nine (9)—and Ten (10) as Leo's Sun vibration, bringing us back to One (1) again, *full circle* —you may wonder how Pluto can possess its own number. You will see.

First, it's important to realize that the Mars Nine (9) vibration is the *Masculine* vibration of the Universe, representing and symbolizing the ultimate MASCULINE principle in all of Life and Love. The Venus Six (6) vibration is the *Feminine* vibration of the Universe, representing and symbolizing the ultimate FEMININE principle in all of Life and Love.

Six and Nine. 6 and 9. The Feminine and Masculine vibratory numbers, or 9 and 6. Male and Female. Positive-Negative. Dark-Light. (Polarity.) Notice that when the Feminine number of Venus—Six (6) is turned upside down (*reversing* its polarity), it becomes a Nine (9). Likewise, when the Masculine number of Mars—Nine (9) is turned upside down (*reversing* its polarity), it becomes a Six (6).

Man and Woman then—are inseparable. Each is an *equal* part of the *other*. The Masculine-Feminine Principles are totally interchangeable. Yet, one is always aiming in a direction reverse from the other. There are many more fascinating and revealing levels to the study of Six and Nine in numerology, but we're only touching the subject briefly here. We'll discuss it in depth in a future book.

Notice that both the Six (6) and the Nine (9) when the "tail" is removed—become a *circle*. The circle is the secret of Twin Soul blending —the deepest mystery of the Sun Sign of Scorpio, and Scorpio's ruling planet, the awesome, powerful Pluto. For the number to which Pluto vibrates is—ZERO. The circle. The circle (O) represents Eternity, for it symbolizes the Serpent, eating its own tail. From the Masculine (Positive) *head* of the Serpent flows the male-positive energy force—into the Female (Negative) *tail* of the Serpent. Simultaneously, from the Feminine (Negative) *tail* of the Serpent flows the female-negative energy force into the Serpent's Masculine (Positive) *head*.

This is the secret of Scorpio, the Sun Sign of "sex"—and this is the energy behind the great Power of Scorpio's ruling planet, Pluto. Zero. The *Circle*. O. The Serpent, eating its own tail. The symbol of Eternity. For only when all polarities—male and female, youth and age, dark and light, night and day—thus feed energy simultaneously into one another, and blend their energies—rather than continue to *oppose* one another—can true power exist.

Pluto's vibratory Zero also contains the secret mystery of Christianity's Holy Trinity. "Father-Son-and-Holy Ghost." The "son" (humans, of both sexes) is *masculine* energy. The "Holy Ghost" (Christ spirit) is *feminine* energy. When each flows into the other simultaneously (instead of remaining in opposition), a *Third Energy* is created, which is both, yet neither—neutral and ALL-POWERFUL—i.e.: "The Father" (God). This *Third Energy*, composed of the Masculine and Feminine combined, flowing into each other, and not in opposition, creates many miracles: The Great Power of Divinity. The conception of a child. The conception of an idea (adding the "l" for love, this becomes an ideal). The energy that powers spacecraft from other solar systems.

It is in no way an accident that Kekule, who made the monumental discovery of the benzine ring structure, which paved the way for the theoretical aspect of organic chemistry, said that he dreamed repeatedly of "a snake, eating its own tail" before the concept occurred to him.

Therefore, all the mysterious Pluto-Scorpio "power" comes from a sub-conscious knowledge of this Zero principle that the perfect blend between *Masculine* and *Feminine* creates a *Third Energy Force*, which is both, yet neither—neutral and ALL-POWERFUL—because it does not oppose, but causes polarities to simultaneously blend and flow into each other.

Another indication, another "secret" of Pluto's ZERO circle, is that: what happens when you add the ZERO (O) to any other number? Any banker or mathematics student can tell you that it "increases" the power of the number. Obviously, the sum of one dollar grows larger (has more "power") as you "add the zeros." Thus does $1.00 become $10.00 or $100.00 or $1,000 or $10,000 and so on. ZERO, then, equals POWER. That's nice for all Scorpios to know—as long as they don't forget what causes the power. The Serpent, eating its own tail—Eternity's Secret.

An important building block to the comprehension of the Twelve Mysteries of Love, related to the secret of the circle, is the following. You'll come across the use of the term "co-Creators" many times in this book. To the skeptical, who find it difficult to image the "Old Testament God" with a Mate of His own, I offer this scholarly source, although the faithful and the spiritually wide-awake need no proof, other than instinctive knowledge from within, regarding this or any concept of the truth of creation.

The following quotation is from a painstaking translation of the *Septuagint,* the earliest known (*circa* 250 B.C.) version of the Old Testament (our standard Hebrew MSS date only from the Renaissance). The translation was published by the Falcon's Wing Press in 1960, under the editorship of Dr. C. Musès. From Proverbs 8:3-31 (excerpts):

> *For at the gates of the Mighty, She hath taken a seat,*
> *and at the entrance thereof chanteth Her song:*
>
> *"In the beginning, before the Lord made the Earth*
> *When He furnished the Heavens, I was with Him;*
> *and when He set apart His throne on the winds*
> *When He set to the sea its bound,*
> *and the waters passed not the word of His mouth*
> *I was harmonizing with Him. I was the one in whom*
> *He delighted, and I was daily gladdened by His*
> *presence on all occasions."*

Ecclesiastical Christianity, seeded by the Hebrew Old Testament distortion of truth through the "patriarch" image, has too long taught the falsehood that the Holy Trinity is entirely masculine. By such deception we have been deprived of a sublime and ennobling truth. But the unfolding of the Aquarian Age, foretold by all prophets of all religions, will bring the Light of the conscious restoration of the *Golden Balance* between the Feminine and Masculine energies on Earth. This Golden Balance is the eventual blending of all Twin Souls. Its concept lies ready to burst forth within all yearning, searching hearts. It's called by many names; yet its true name is the REAL SELF, as experienced through the union with one's own Twin Soul. And it begins with the recognition of the Male-Female truth hidden in the Holy Trinity and the symbol of Eternity—the Serpent eating its own tail—the secret "knowledge" given by the *"Serpent"* to Eve, who passed it on to Adam. That this eating of the "forbidden fruit" of the "Tree of Knowledge" was later called "Original *Sin*" reveals the desperation of the dark forces to hide the Light of Truth by a polarity distortion, channeled through the ancient patriarchs who feared losing the masculine superiority principle through sexual equality. But the Aquarian Age daughters of Eve will at last bring the world to recognize that the term "Original Sin" is the Big Daddy of all religious dogma's Super-Hypes. And the Aquarian Age sons of Adam will this time be enlightened to Eve's wisdom. Not even the Church "Fathers" can stop the lightning of the predestined and foretold Uranian spiritual awakening of the New Age of Golden Balance. Perhaps Adam couldn't handle the truth. But today's Water Bearers can—and will.

Under the powerful Uranus vibes and the Aquarian microscope, all deception will be exposed for the hypocrisy it is. And *this* shall be called "Original *Innocence*"—the beginning of Wisdom. When people all throughout the world enter into cooperation with these Divine principles of the Golden Balance of Male and Female, the New Age of Aquarius will finally manifest itself in all the splendor and magnificence of the reborn and wiser Atlantis. Not all the chauvinists and atomic and nuclear energy madmen combined can stop the Uranian tidal waves of Truth.

As man and woman evolve around the astrological karmic circle, absorbing the qualities of other Sun Signs into their own individualities—teaching some, learning from others—each has a spiritual obligation to retain the positive integrity of his or her own Sun Sign in this incarnation and also to respect that right in others. The Lion must have his dignity, as the Crab must cling to security. The Goat must honor tradition, as the Twins must demand their freedom. Each must follow the Aquarian Age adage to "live and let live," to be yourself, and realize that others must be themselves too. The first step toward comprehending love's ultimate meaning—toward finally being permitted to enjoy its absolute fulfillment—is to learn to tolerate instead of condemning the Sun Sign qualities different from our own.

In exploring the interrelationships of the twelve Sun Signs, through both their harmonious and their conflicting traits of character as they relate to our own, we should always try to remember that the final goal of each soul is to give and receive the lessons of each Sun Sign to and from the others met along the way. This journey is a kind of growing of the spirit, from soul-infancy through soul-adulthood, middle-age, "old age" and death, then rebirth. The soul can be freed of this endless circle of birth and death only when we learn to free the physical or dense body, also, of death; a miracle I dare to predict will occur much sooner than we now believe. The "problem" such longevity would create, in relation to the general world population (new births, along with the conquering of death—for centuries—etc.), does have several solutions. But this is not the place to attempt to conceive of the possibilities. An in-depth discussion of such a future in the approaching "New Age" must wait for my next book.

The soul's symbolic journey through the twelve Sun Signs may be comprehended by imaging man and woman undergoing, with their minds and bodies, a matching journey. First, the soul enters the initial phase, similar to earthly birth, then advances through various further stages similar to earthly life, gaining spiritual experience from each, just as we gain mental and physical experience from a similar type journey of our dense bodies. The soul is "born" in the sign of Aries, the symbolic Infant, as reflected through the Sun's magnetic alchemy.

The Aries Love Mystery

The soul, symbolically newborn in Aries (*although not necessarily in its first earthly sojourn*), relates to dawn, sunrise, spring and Easter—or the resurrection from its "death" in the previous sign of Pisces.

In this first excursion into the Fire Element—this experience as the first of the three Cardinal signs—the symbolically "newborn" soul projects the positive, masculine vibration of the Day Forces through the explosive vitality of the Aries planetary ruler, Mars. Like a human infant totally self-absorbed, the Aries soul discovers with delight his or her own toes and fingers—its own physical beingness. To satisfy all needs, only a loud cry is necessary, heard and answered instantly by elders. The real infant doubts or fears nothing or no one, simply because it has never experienced denial. Likewise, the Aries "Infant" soul has a natural trust and a touching faith in the unseen force of goodness which will miraculously grant all its wishes.

On the Earth plane this beneficent force is represented by the parents; in a mystical sense, by our co-Creators. And so they look tenderly upon the "newborn" Aries soul, as parents look tenderly upon their infant, lovingly protecting it from its own naivete, wisely denying some of the demands made through the excited awareness that the soul *is*—has been born, and is *here*. The Aries soul senses: "I AM" or "I exist." And like the symbolic Infant, Aries men and women are oblivious to the possibilities of accident, pain or cruelty on life's path. He or she learns of these negative experiences only from those advanced beyond, who have gathered harshness, suspicion and the self-survival instinct from the growing process.

There's a religious adage that all infants, since they die in a state of purity, immediately become angels. Of course! They have not yet met the devil of Temptation. But if the Aries "Infant" survives, he or she must, like the real infant, time and time again, undergo the sharp disappointment of misplaced trust. As the victim of unkindness, a lack of sympathy or abandonment, the newborn babe feels shocked, frightened, alone—then yells even louder for attention. In the same manner (and for the same reasons) does the soul of the hurt and disillusioned Aries man or woman need and "seek acceptance, yet court rejection"—with a violent emotional reaction to neglect.

The positive qualities of Aries are a heart-tugging innocence and wonder, blind faith and raw courage. Expressed in their negative forms, they can become selfish egotism, thoughtlessness, aggressiveness and impulsive action with no regard for the consequences.

To the Aries soul, Love is a necessity of life, which is taken for granted; for in its infancy of awareness, Love is synonymous with existence itself. Therefore, devotion is instinctively expected and joyously accepted, but with little comprehension of how to return it. Aries *demands* Love, for like the infant, *without* Love, Aries dies. When emotional abandonment (symbolically) can mean death, even the hint of it can bring on unreasonable panic, and inexplicable terror, calmed only by repeated reassurances. Aries continually needs to be reminded that "if winter comes" . . . . . . the miracle of spring cannot be far behind.

The Taurus Love Mystery

The evolving spiritual awareness of man or woman enters next into the Earth element. On the Taurus level, the symbolic Infant soul has become, symbolically, a healthy, chubby Baby, who now relates to the reflective feminine Night Forces, and has learned to sleep on schedule, then wake to anticipated comfort.

No longer does he or she scream without reason, in fright or loneliness— or yell loudly for every need, as in the Arian stage. It has been discovered that all desires will be satisfied by the parents. Like the human baby, in the Taurean stage, the soul is content to sit quietly and patiently in its symbolic high chair and wait for its daily bread with quiet, confident and sure anticipation.

The Bull has also learned how to use good behavior to wheedle more pleasures, more favors from the "parents" and other adults. Smiles and obedience are rewarded, and Taurus doesn't forget what has been learned, however painfully and slowly. Still essentially unaware of anything outside the immediate environment, the Taurus man or woman (like the Taurean symbolic Baby) finds happiness in the family circle and the tangible—in what is known to be familiar, rather than in the strange and noisy outside world.

Through the Taurus experience, the Baby soul discovers the delight of using the senses of tasting, smelling, seeing, hearing and touching. It symbolically smells and chews, and listens to every toy, as well as looks at and touches them in this, the soul's first experience as a Fixed sign of the Organizer. Because possessions bring happiness, this man or woman clutches them, fondles them and finds contentment in calling them his or her own. Taurus says "I HAVE." This is the stage of the Teddy Bear or security blanket (which will return once more, for a fleeting moment, in the Cancerian vibration). On the Taurus level of development, the "Baby soul" is enormously dependent on physical contact with loved ones—to be held, cuddled, kissed and hugged. And the Venus-ruled (Pan-Horus guided) Taurean responds with coos and giggles of ecstasy, understanding affection only through the *feeling* that it's there. The actual baby is fiercely possessive of toys and the attention of the parents, shattered when either seems to be lost, stubbornly refusing to share them, as the male or female Taurean behaves with regard to his or her own bank account and mate.

Taurus positive qualities are strength of purpose, patience, steadfastness and conviction. Expressed in their negative form, they become obstinacy, blind prejudice and lack of reason.

To the jolly, dogmatic baby, symbolic of the Taurus soul, love is physical affection, both given and received without question. Because the baby associates love with all pleasure and happiness, he or she glories in it with an uncomplicated, animal-like appreciation. Therefore, Taurus accepts and returns love with the senses—but has not yet learned to analyze its true worth and value.

The Gemini Love Mystery

In the Gemini soul experience, the symbolic Taurus "Baby" enters into the world of the toddler-Child, and feels again, as on the Aries Infancy level, the positive, masculine Day Forces. For the first time, the soul arrives at the stage of the Mutable Communicator, becoming conscious of its own mentality, aware that it is not alone in the Universe. The Child soul of Gemini learns to communicate needs by speaking, by learning to form words and string them together, while the parents and others listen attentively, rejoicing at each new sound. Talking is fun because it centers all the interest on him (or her). There's a new ability to crawl or toddle over to the cookie jar, without either the Aries yelling or the Taurus waiting, and this newfound independence is intoxicating. Gemini is thrilled by the knowledge now within grasp, and so "I THINK!" Gemini cries to the world-at-large, in great excitement.

The symbolic Child level of consciousness teaches the Gemini soul that there are two sides to the character—a duality or polarity that must be brought into harmony before one can successfully relate to others. The first twinge of unhappiness pulls as he or she bumps hard into discipline, while trying to blend the sleeping and waking Twin Selves. Because Gemini suddenly longs for pleasures outside home and family, the Child soul is often punished for symbolically attempting to run out into dangers not yet suspected. Likewise, the world invites Gemini men and women to explore it, and who knows what they may find out there! With the new mental ability to reason and deduce—to relate—Gemini begins to wish for and to dream of things beyond what has already been seen.

Half the Gemini soul is still an insecure baby, needing the familiar. Half is a yearning child, curious about the many undiscovered marvels just out of tangible reach. The Geminian soul has already experienced Fire and Earth and is learning to cope with the Air Element for the first time. And so this twinned personality experiments, with bright eyes and a hopeful heart. Each new day stirs Gemini's mind with its hidden magic, more enticing now than the discarded toys and the warm circle of parental affection. What the Gemini man or woman sees through the window is a forbidden Eden where all longings lie in mystery, as the ruling planet Mercury (the magician) beckons toward the seductive road beyond.

Gemini positive qualities are versatility, mental alertness, quickness of perception, deductive reasoning and flexibility. Expressed in their negative form they become restlessness, glibness, shallowness, double-talk, unreliability and self-deception.

To the Gemini "Child," love has lost some of its early wonder. It is still needed on this level, more than is realized, but there's something more thrilling than love to seek now. Is it love that holds you back, tugs on one and keeps one from rushing out the front door into Life? Love, then, is perhaps enjoyable, but it is also restrictive. Gemini men and women have not stopped needing it or desiring it, but when love becomes a barrier to their freedom, they rashly discard it, forgetting its warmth and safety—not caring that they may get lost and be unable to find their way back home.

The Cancer Love Mystery

The child is now an Adolescent, the soul having evolved to the stage of Cancer, hovering between childhood and maturity, longing to be grown-up, yet hesitating to cross over to the other side. Cancer brings back awareness of the negative feminine and reflective Night Forces. But this second experience of night is blended with a new, richer and even more sensual feeling (which was only a poetic inspiration, not yet a true reality, on the earlier Taurean level), for a change of seasons has occurred. The spring awakening has deepened into a mid-summer night's dream in all its full-blown and fragrant beauty for these Cancerian Oberon and Titania men and women.

Now the moody, sensitive, "Adolescent" soul vacillates between childish dependence and the maddeningly enticing, beckoning world of adulthood (what is it like to be a man or a woman?). This is beautifully expressed by the experiments between the human and faerie worlds in Taurean Shakespeare's famed classic. Is it sad or happy . . . funny or tragic? The symbolic "Puckish" Cancerian Adolescent observes the adults (humans) in the environment, uncannily perceptive of everything seen and heard. But this grown-up, material world so intensely watched hints of frequent disillusion.

And so the dreams of Cancer are troubled, causing the Crab to cry out in the night, sometimes dragging the old symbolic Taurus Teddy Bear out of the closet, and hugging it closely when no one can see. As with Cancerian men and women, the actual adolescents' changing moods puzzle them as much as they puzzle their families. But those terrors are very real to Cancerians, who fear that maturity will mean the loss of security known with the parents, especially the mother. Will future strangers ever fuss over the Crabs and love them as unconditionally as mother? Cancer is beginning to suspect that they won't.

Unable to explain their apprehensions, the Crabs turn secretive, dreaming alone—or hide and pout, imagining that no one understands. On the Cancer level, the possible loss of parental protection haunts the subconscious. Cancer has already learned what loss is. Perhaps childhood friends have moved away, the family has changed residences, the old familiar neighborhood is gone. The world is no longer so exciting as the Crabs sense its hidden pitfalls. The "Adolescent" Cancerian men and women know that growing up will surely bring unexpected hurt, so they cling to what they *know* can be trusted—*yesterday*.

Because the new perceptions are so acute, Cancer sees a combination of tragedy and comedy in Life as it expands in his awareness through his first excursion into the sensitive Water Element. Still, despite an innate shyness, the Cancerian soul will not be pushed into the background, for this is the second experience as a Cardinal leader, which can turn illogical fear into sensible caution. The Crabs wish on both the Full Moon and the New, only half-conscious of what it is they wish for . . . . . reluctant to find out. What does tomorrow hold? Sentiment moves the Cancerian Adolescent soul to tears. Motivated by the need to hide true emotions, the Crabs say: "I FEEL"—then, so no one will suspect they feel so deeply, they make jokes, believing they fool people. If not handled tenderly at this crucial stage of soul evolvement, the Cancerian man or woman develops a permanent, hard, protective shell against the cruel world.

Cancer's positive qualities are imagination, tenacity, tenderness, sensitivity, care and caution. Expressed in their negative form they become stinginess, irritability, melancholy, clinging and cowardice, possessiveness and moodiness.

To Cancer, as to the actual uncertain and sentimental adolescent, love has become important again, above all else. But it is now synonymous with home, representing emotional security—and the *need* for love is so great it must be disguised behind moody tears and Lunar laughter.

The Leo Love Mystery

The Cancerian Adolescent soul is transformed with brilliant suddenness into a symbolic Teenager, brought by the Leo vibration into the first expression of self-confidence and pride in individuality. Now the soul knows (or assumes) who he is—or who she is—as Leo feels an even stronger pull of the masculine positive Day Forces and the Fire Element than was felt on the Aries level. The world belongs to the Lion—or the Lioness—and so the Leonine "Teenager" gazes at his or her image in the mirror, admires what is seen and makes the noble vow: "I WILL." Summer has come into full bloom of furious beauty with lazy afternoons and bright sunshine, as Leo moves into SELF consciousness from the polarity meaning of Cancer's *self-consciousness*.

The idealism of youth stirs the Lion's heart and sets the blood afire with the dawning knowledge of sexuality, two powerful urges that bring private inner doubts of worth, well hidden beneath outward vanity. The Leo soul knows what to do with this second experience as a Fixed Organizer, using it with apparent confidence to lecture others, take charge of his or her own life and rule over those who need Leo's protection. Yet the Leo man or woman, like the actual teenager, still seeks reassurance in the form of flattery, still cringes secretly when ridiculed, because he is not quite yet a man—she is not quite yet a woman—for all the surface sureness.

The soul has already passed through the painful experiences of infancy, babyhood, childhood and adolescence, so Leo leads with sympathetic consideration for those who are more vulnerable. The soul in its Leo expression has no real desire to crush the helpless. Generosity of spirit was carved into Leo's memory by the tears wept through the Aries, Taurus, Gemini, and Cancer levels. However, although Leos have learned to tolerate and forgive enemies, they have not yet learned to respect the wisdom of elders. Like the real teenager, Leo thinks he (or she) knows all the answers, and is impatient with those who question this new worldly knowledge. The Leo soul worships the Sun, for the Sun is Leo's ruler, the source of all Life—and of his or her Leonine strength. Leo admires and is admired, loves and is loved. As social life begins, the joys of romance begin to bud . . . . . . then finally to flower. Puppy love is warm and bright, bringing to the Leo "Teenager" both elation and disappointment. The dizzy power of his manhood (or womanhood) gives to Leo a sense of personal dignity and importance—through the opposite sex. No longer must the Lions and Lionesses be restricted by the stifling authority of parental guidance. The bridge from childhood to adulthood has been spanned. The responsibilities of maturity are sensed, but still haven't become a burden. Life is all sunlight, the gloomy Past is behind, the miracle of the Future still ahead—and the Present is a time for fun and relaxation. Leo decides arrogantly that the world needs his newfound wisdom, and is more than willing to give it. Only through exercising unquestioned command over younger children (the weaker and not yet liberated souls) can a Leo man or woman in this experience retain the necessary image of superiority and self-respect.

Leo's positive qualities are warmth, generosity, nobility, strength, loyalty, leadership and a soothing, gentle tenderness—the protective charisma of the older brother or sister, of the strong toward the weak. Expressed in their negative form they become arrogance, false pride, vanity, tyranny, haughtiness . . . and romantic promiscuity.

To the Leo in the symbolic Teenager stage of development, love is shimmering romance, the song-of-songs, the fulfillment of all ideals and beauty. Leo is "in love with love" and with himself—herself. Lions and Lionesses give affection generously only because it brings such pleasure to be so royally beneficent, demanding gratitude and respect from the beloved, outraged if love requires that they humble themselves . . . . as yet unable to comprehend its depth, or the beauty of its sacrifice of the "self."

The Virgo Love Mystery

The youthful Leo soul soon senses that summer is ending—and regretfully steps into his first awareness of the coming harvest, through the Indian Summer soul expression of Virgo. The negative feminine Night Forces return again, reminding the Virgin (whose deeper self has remained untouched by the fleeting romances of youth) that maturity brings stern duty

and responsibility. "I ANALYZE," says Virgo defensively, striving for perfection.

Now the evolving soul has, for the first time, become an Adult, frustrated by being forced to comply with society's rules and restrictions, yet
submitting gracefully, with innate courtesy. These men and women have
discovered that to receive their own needs they must serve others in some
way. The Virgo vibration teaches that one must work and earn money—be
of service—in order to be free to play. In this, the second experience in the
Earth Element, also the second experience as a Mutable Communicator,
clocks and schedules assume great importance. The first job is disap-
pointing. Both ideas and ideals must be shelved under the demands of
work or schooling. No time now to dream. The Virgo attention is centered
on scholastic excellence, on keeping up with the fierce competition of the
business world. Learning and competing are both mandatory—surviving
has become a near obsession.

Like the actual young adults they symbolize, Virgo souls see much to
criticize around them, secretly resenting the loss of childhood innocence,
having no certain ideas of what lies ahead. Is it only more work, more
study and more responsibility? If so, then life is serious indeed and must
be faced realistically as soon as possible. It is getting later. Human flaws
and imperfections assume exaggerated importance on this Virgo level. For,
unless Virgo brings in a fruitful harvest, Life cannot continue for themselves and others. It is the end of summer, the beginning of autumn, and
cold winter is just around the corner. Why are all those people still laughing and playing out there? Virgo frets and worries, wondering how to warn
the irresponsible that the season of pleasure is drawing to a close. The
heart is still pure and filled with silent hope, but the mind is now in control.

Earlier Leo enthusiasms have been replaced by resignation and quiet
dreams. Virgo is driven by the fear of dependence into dogged determination not to waste time or shirk duty, the consciousness ever watchful
and waiting, yearning to be something better. Although once again ruled
by Mercury, the soul has by now learned not to scatter the vital forces as
on the Gemini level. Like the symbolic Virgin, Virgo hovers on the edge
of awareness, soon to answer the thunderous call of Virgo's true ruler,
Vulcan, not yet "discovered" by astronomers, but sufficiently near discovery to have already commenced to faintly beam its pulsing influence to all
Virgo-Virgin souls.

Virgo's positive qualities are clarity of thought, discrimination, courtesy,
service to others, practicality and self-honesty. Expressed in their negative

form they become criticism, crankiness, timidity, pessimism, inferiority and hair-splitting.

The Virgin soul has reached its narcissus aspect, half-remembering the heated fires of youth, but as yet unawakened, only vaguely sensing the passion that lies ahead, soon to be revealed by Vulcan. To Virgos, love means surrender of the self, a mystery they prefer not to solve. So they channel its energy into excellence in work . . . . . and although these men and women offer gentle devotion, love's true meaning still sleeps within the Virgin heart.

The Libra Love Mystery

Turning from the lonely Virgo path of self-discipline, the evolving soul reaches out once again to the positive Day Forces, as the Libra vibration seductively beckons to it to accept, for the third time, the challenge of Cardinal leadership. In the Libra consciousness, the soul is fully grown, aware now of both sunshine and shadow. During the struggle for maturity which culminated in Virgo, it has learned that there is in the world (and in people) both night and day—good and evil—dark and light. Beyond that, Libra is consumed with the intriguing polarity of male and female.

Experience has taught Libra men and women to judge their fellows fairly. Until the Libra level, the soul's interest has been centered primarily on itself. Now it expands to include, for the first time, an awareness of the necessity to relate to other human beings. The soul is now equipped with the lessons of five previous levels, capable of leading with both logic and force. Libra acts with a blend of wisdom composed of knowledge gained through one excursion into WATER and from twice experiencing FIRE, EARTH and AIR. "I BALANCE," says Libra, priding himself or herself on seeing both sides. Because it shatters Libra's conscience to be unfair, decisions are difficult and painful. A sense of social justice is emerging, and in the face of prejudice or intolerance, Libra often turns to endless argument, using the cold logic learned through Gemini and sharpened through Virgo. But this approach is softened by a new sense of the value of persuasion. Libra has acquired the quality of charm, which he has discovered is a sure way to win, so he artfully uses a mellow voice and dazzling smile to cajole and get his way with others.

Libra feels a growing awareness of beauty of harmony—in music, art and romance. As Librans subconsciously recall their Virgo loneliness, they experience the stirring of a deep and primal urge to find a mate. Sentimental, yet practical, the Libra soul instinctively knows the need for someone to walk nearby, in both love and business, in order to balance Life and satisfy the desire for harmony of Libra's ruler, Venus. In the Libran Air Element, however, a love partner is not easy to find. When the vices and virtues of prospective mates are weighed and balanced on the Libra Scales, they often are found wanting, bringing on the anguish of emotional indecision. But through it all, this man or woman continues the relentless search for someone to share life's joys and sorrows. The autumn season so loved will someday fade, the spring so fondly remembered is long past, and there is one thing Libra knows: he—or she—must not be alone when winter comes. And so Librans respond to sunset's beauty, sadly sensing simultaneously that for all its crimson-gold glory, it nevertheless announces another approaching night of the soul.

Libra's positive qualities are justice, intelligence, charm, gentleness and emotional balance. Expressed in their negative form they become laziness, procrastination, indecision, argumentativeness, pleasure-seeking and temperament.

To Libra, love is a mating of the minds and hearts—not too passionate, not too detached—a happy medium, to be equally shared. But these souls are too infatuated with love's surface beauty to penetrate completely its deeper implications. They recognize only that they love. It has not yet occurred to them to wonder *why*.

The Scorpio Love Mystery

As it enters its second experience in the Water element, the now mature soul welcomes the chance for meditation through a return of the negative feminine Night Forces of the Scorpio consciousness. On a *public* level, Scorpio is enormously capable of executing the now very familiar duties as a Fixed Organizer. On a *personal* level, Scorpio is troubled to discover that he faces for the first time the awesome mystery of his own existence. Where did he come from?—where is he going?—why is he here? Scorpio must tear the veil from life, regardless of the cost, to quiet his restless spirit, suddenly released from its former preoccupation with earthly needs alone, as he cries out: "I DESIRE!"

There is much that the Scorpio soul *knows* . . . . but even more that is *sensed* and cannot yet be defined. The Scorpio vibration brings such a burning need to penetrate the unknown that it must be buried beneath deep layers of calm reason, or it would consume the mind and sear the soul. Lessons well remembered from Libra softness and impartial judgment have made Scorpio wary of expressing opinions to those who would tear them apart. The strong Scorpion instinct for survival springs from a deep-seated fear that he who is not forearmed will be destroyed. Each defeat sustained by Scorpio only strengthens the inner conviction that the first loyalty must be to his or her own personal integrity. For Scorpio senses that if the *self* is lost, then *all* is lost.

On the Scorpio level of consciousness, the soul is newly aware of the relationship between birth, death, sex and religious truth. Scorpio knows that, in some mystical way, these are all intertwined. Therefore, sex becomes something intimately explored with an intensity unknown to those either behind or ahead of Scorpio's stage of evolvement. Although Scorpio trusts love only after it has proven itself deserving of such trust, once dedicated to another, loyalty is unswerving and eternal. Feeling fiercely the need to protect themselves and those they love from hurt, Scorpio is compelled to demand "an eye for an eye and a tooth for a tooth" as insurance that injuries will not be repeated.

Through the subtle influence of the ruling planet Pluto, the experience of death comes to the Scorpio soul, as friends and relatives pass away, increasing the need to penetrate even deeper for the knowledge buried in the silent subconscious. While Scorpio's spirit soars upward like the eagle, defying gravity, worldly desires and passions intensify, forcing him to question his own worthiness. Ultra-sensitive, but now able to totally disguise such sensitivity, Scorpio now learns the amazing power of his or her own mind—the silent *will*—and uses it secretly, lest others learn how to use the same kind of power over him—or her. The Scorpio consciousness is the period of the soul's testing.

Scorpio's positive qualities are loyalty, will power, magnetism, gentleness, insight and amazing self-control. Expressed in their negative form they become ruthlessness, fanaticism, revenge, sadism, suspicion and self-hatred.

To Scorpio men and women, love is a consuming flame, worth any sacrifice—and they must conquer its challenge. Sexually uninhibited, yet emotionally fearful and mentally suspicious, they strive desperately to unite love's physical and spiritual vibrations, with a strange mixture of eroticism and purity. But the satisfaction of desire only leaves the Scorpio soul still hungry for something beyond.

The Sagittarius Love Mystery

Emerging from the long night of Scorpio meditation, the evolving soul turns again with hope toward the positive masculine Day Forces, as it bridges autumn and winter through the Sagittarius consciousness. Now it experiences for the third time the vibrations of the Mutable Communicator, and answers for the last time to the impulsive element of Fire. In Sagittarius, man or woman has become a skeptical philosopher, a reluctant prophet, still unsure of the final answers to the riddle of life. So the Archer probes further, with penetrating logic and embarrassing candor, to give validity to Jupiter's claim that "I SEE."

It is now time for the soul to be once more aware of its own *duality*. Sagittarius feels a compelling urge to explore his or her own mind and attempt to unravel the secrets of human behavior at the philosophic stage of higher learning. Yet, part of this soul resents the stern requirements of ever more complicated education and longs to play hookey from Life's demanding karmic school. He—or she—plunges from the heights of supreme optimism and blind faith to the depths of sarcastic cynicism. First frivolous and gay, then serious and owlish, Sagittarius is the Centaur, half man–half horse, aiming sharp arrows of curiosity directly into the bull's-eye of the knowledge sought. The Sagittarian search for truth takes this soul through the maze of religious concept, veering from stark atheism to spiritual fanaticism, until the stronghold of church dogma has been exposed—and either accepted or rejected, in part, or in whole.

Sometimes Sagittarius frolics like a clumsy clown, with an irresponsible disregard for the future. Sometimes he thinks seriously, on a level high above and beyond his peers. In the Sagittarian stage, the soul has reached the symbolic stage of retirement. Driven by their ruling planet Jupiter, the Archers yearn to travel, to bask under foreign Suns, to see and learn of other countries, people and ideas. Although they grudgingly submit to the necessities of work, duty and responsibility, they are extremely impatient of such unwelcome restriction over the realization of their dreams.

To cover a constant restlessness of spirit, Sagittarians adopt the pose of the actor, the thespian, which enables them to entertain others with a mixture of funny and tragic farces, while they remain free to pursue the Socratic method of inquiry with their own souls, behind their theatrical masks. There is little time for tact on this level, as Sagittarius rushes ahead to find the answers before "Life" is over. Autumn is ending, the first winds of winter are blowing—and the exhilarating weather challenges the Archer to tempt fate, in order to prove that man is stronger than Nature. The winter season's withdrawal into seclusion has not yet taken hold. And so Sagittarius delights in each snowflake, pondering the design and origin . . . then rolls them together into a snowball, tossed without warning to topple the stuffiness of more sedate souls. Although intuitively sensing that "old age" looms ahead, with its promised rewards of wisdom and peace, the soul is too nostalgic for the carefree days of lost youth . . . spring and summer . . . to resign itself gracefully to its inevitable maturity.

Sagittarian positive qualities are optimism, candor, cheerfulness, logic, honesty, daring and enthusiasm. Expressed in their negative form they become recklessness, emotional confusion, carelessness, lack of tact, rudeness and fickleness.

To Sagittarius, who has reached the symbolic middle age of the soul, true love must be discovered now—or lost forever. As the Archers seek a mate for all seasons, they are blinded by love's idealism and challenge and therefore wounded by love's reality, because their anxious quest has not yet led them to search for love where it really hides—within their own hearts.

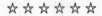

The Capricorn Love Mystery

Now the chilling blasts of winter grow more insistent, forcing the experience-weary soul to symbolically retreat back into the haven of the family circle, to submit once again to the meditative, negative-feminine Night Forces. On the Capricorn level of consciousness, for the fourth and final time, the soul feels the powerful vibrations of Cardinal leadership. But this time it leads through the stable Earth Element, from a position of strength inside the home, beside the hearth. Why should the Goat expose himself (or herself) to the icy temperatures outside, just to be seen and heard—applauded and praised?

Capricorn souls, now sure of both their ability and their right to take command, no longer feel the need to display or aggressively flaunt their power—either for public adulation, or for inner security. By this stage, the soul has learned that true peace comes from *within*. Being appointed Leader is a responsibility to be handled as carefully as possible, with no special recognition due for doing what is obviously one's duty. The Capricorn's relatives (especially parents) now assume marked importance for either good or ill, because the symbolic "old age" of the soul has arrived—and along with it, a sense of the priorities of life, the most important being the security of *belonging*. The excitement of romance and the freedoms of youth are not nearly as enticing to the Goat as comfort and contentment with those he can depend on to care for him (or her).

Capricorn is both prepared and willing to impart the hard-earned Saturnine wisdom, but only when invited to do so. Because the Goats know the folly of forcing people to mature before their time, they smile with the benevolent indulgence of a fond grandparent (whatever his or her chronological age) upon the playful antics of the still young at heart. Secretly, the Capricorn soul longs to abandon duty but is by now resigned to the knowledge that sheer idealism is impractical—and spontaneous enthusiasm can never replace experience. Acutely aware of the dangers of impulsive action, the soul has become more conservative—and the Goat's refusal to either scatter efforts or to indulge in sentimentality brings on accusations of emotional coldness from those born into the Fire and Air Elements. Capricorns respect authority because they see the law as a necessity for the protection of human rights and safety. They shyly worship the famous and successful because Capricorn's ruler, Saturn, teaches them to revere achievement, knowing full well its price.

Although Capricorn may appear to be serious and unyielding to more liberal souls, Life has also taught the Goats its humorous side, and their subtle jokes are tinged with the irony of existence. Because the new Saturnine duties as counselor to the foolish weigh heavily on their shoulders, they sometimes try to drink the last full measure of Life's rare pleasures, calmly accepting them without false modesty or undue inhibition. Only afterward, when the sobering influence of maturity returns, does Capricorn feel a vague sense of remorse and melancholy for having succumbed to the temptation of forbidden passions. In this soul vibration there is a compulsion to acknowledge the necessity for being practical, as Capricorn admits, "I USE." But a gentleness of spirit softens the severity of the surface sternness commanded by Saturn, for the Capricorn consciousness brings with it a sympathy for human mistakes, born from the understanding gained through ten stages of Life's—and Love's—mysteries.

Capricorn's positive qualities are determination, stability, wisdom, dependability, sureness and tranquility. Expressed in their negative form they become selfishness, narrowness, ruthless ambition, rigidity, snobbery, depression and loneliness.

To Capricorn, love is a quiet and undemanding exchange of personal gratification. The Goats have fully learned the valuable lesson that love is not measured by excessive emotion. But because they equate it only with the necessities of mutual need and desire, they have not yet experienced the release of its inner longings.

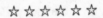

The Aquarius Love Mystery

Having reached the Aquarian initiation, the evolving soul feels that it must return to life much of what it gathered along the way. And so begins a "second childhood" on the level of the Water Bearer, who pours out his knowledge, both determined and anxious to share it before he leaves this planet to explore the exciting realm of the unknown on the other side.

Aquarius feels the stirrings of the masculine positive Day Forces for the last time as a Fixed Organizer, in the final experience of the detached and unpredictable Air Element. A puzzle to friends and family, the Aquarian man or woman cavorts in peculiar fashion with the young at heart—peculiar, since wisdom and experience are in direct contrast with such liberal, eccentric behavior. There were so many mysteries missed in the past because there wasn't time to investigate them. Now Aquarians must taste them all—must investigate every nuance of up and down, left and right, will and won't. They delight in shocking those around them, suddenly aware of an inexplicable ability to peek into the future. Amazingly intuitive and bristling with unexpected flashes of telepathic images, the Aquarian soul examines people and ideas without sentiment, arriving at truth with no apparent logic or traceable effort.

On this level, the soul tends to flaunt law and authority because the spirit actually exists in the world of the future. Aquarius knows that the rigid rules of today's society must sooner or later be compromised. There-fore he (or she) sees no sensible reason to respect what will surely evolve into something new and different tomorrow. If violent revolt is necessary to bring about tolerance, brotherhood and understanding, then Aquarius believes the result will be worth the conflict. However, although they ad-vocate change for the world (and for their friends and family), the Water Bearers remain Fixed in their own personal opinions, private codes and life-styles, reflecting the contradictory nature of the ruling planet, Uranus.

The soul has now acquired a true humanitarian approach. To the un-prejudiced Aquarian, every human being is a friend, whatever that per-son's personal values may be, for the Water Bearer has learned that he (or she) is one with all mankind and womankind—and with Nature. Yet, per-sonal relationships may be neglected, as these men and women pursue an idealism related to the benefit of society in general. Like the Aquarian Age it reflects, the soul at this stage envisions a golden and glorious future that may be attained only by blasting old customs and outdated ideas to clear the way for spiritual awareness, through the thunderbolt path of acceler-ated mass Karma. If more conservative people are offended by the Uranus behavior, the Aquarian individualist laughs off their disapproval. Secure in an intuitive grasp of the future, Aquarians retort, "I KNOW" to all questions, then perversely refuse to explain *how* they know—except to the children, who understand through their own innocence the innocent state of simplicity the soul returns to in the "second childhood" Uranus vibra-tion.

The Aquarian positive qualities are vision, individuality, tolerance, friendliness, inventiveness, originality and genius. Expressed in their negative form they become eccentricity, neurosis, detachment, absent-mindedness and refusal to cooperate.

To Aquarius, love is a detached and unselfish emotion, to be explored and enjoyed. The Water Bearer understands love's scope and investigates all its dimensions, but scatters it carelessly, confusing it with friendship. Physical fulfillment leaves Aquarius emotionally empty and still wistful, failing to sense the mystery of *Oneness* with the mate—the final truth of love, which awaits discovery silently, in the shadows—the secret guarded by Neptune, just beyond Uranus comprehension.

☆ ☆ ☆ ☆ ☆ ☆

The Pisces Love Mystery

Just as the soul is symbolically "born" into the innocent thoughtlessness of Aries, it symbolically "dies"—or leaves the painful Earth plane—to enter into the sympathetic humility and mystical awareness of Pisces. In the Piscean Sun Sign stage, evolving man and woman begin to comprehend vaguely the secret of Time as an eternal NOW—able to (in varying degrees) see the Past, Present and Future as one. This is the soul's third and final excursion into the sensitive Water Element—its fourth and final vibration as a Mutable Communicator—and the last experience under the feminine negative Night Forces.

Ideally, by the time the soul has reached the Pisces stage, it has attained spiritual enlightenment on its long journey through the Mysteries of Love experienced in the preceding eleven Sun Signs. If not, then it must return to certain Sun Sign vibratory experiences on the astrological circle to learn lessons not absorbed because they were too hastily skimmed over in previous incarnated stages. But each such return brings a new vulnerability to that Sun Sign lesson—a new inner urgency to master its positive essence and discard its negative. Of course, some high or advanced souls, after reaching the Piscean stage, elect of their own choosing to return to Earth to rescue those still in darkness. However, we are discussing here the average Pisces obligation and pattern.

Man and woman, on the Pisces level, have passed *at least once* through all twelve stages of initiation, and many have been required to fall back and retrace their steps hundreds of times in this experience, because Pisces is the most difficult of all the twelve Sun Signs to comprehend and master. Usually such an accomplishment is not gained the first time around the wheel of life, except by intense *desire* and *will*, which is not to say such achievement is impossible—but it is a path, up until now, chosen by very few. This is why astrology teaches that Pisces is "an old soul"—also the reason that not every Pisces man or woman is the epitome of spiritual grace; why some swim in waters dangerously close to the fires of Dante's Inferno. The Fish lives in two worlds, simultaneously experiencing both Heaven and Hell.

With the secret wisdom of the Piscean ruling planet, Neptune, Pisceans know that sadness and ugliness are not a part of God's plan. They have glimpsed the beauty of truth, and the brilliance of such mystical vision brings an urge to retreat from the negative vibrations of the Earth plane. So Pisces often avoids confrontation and tension through the escape route of drugs, alcohol, daydreams, artistic creation, philosophical theorizing, meditation or religious retreat. Pisceans may become teachers, monks, nuns, mystics, artists, musicians, composers, abstract mathematicians and highly intuitive scientists—or they may choose to swim down into the murky waters of alcoholism and drug addiction, even insanity. It is, indeed, a difficult and complicated vibration for the soul, for this Sun Sign experience is fraught with temptation for the Pisces man or woman.

Because they've been "through it all" on a subconscious level, the Fishes have a natural compassion for the troubles of those around them. The Neptunian soul is intimately familiar with life's vicissitudes, understanding the weakness of human nature, therefore tending to pity, rather than to condemn, man's and woman's failings. This is why these "old souls" so frequently become the recipients of everyone's secrets, trials, worries and apprehensions. Yet the initial instinct is to turn away from sticky entanglements in all forms. Only when the Fish finds the courage to face his or her own problems with as much spiritual wisdom as is offered to others can the Neptune mysteries be fathomed.

Through this "death initiation" (death of the human ego) the soul grows more forgiving, more gentle, better able to understand its true relationship to the co-Creators . . . . as Pisces affirms "I BELIEVE." To realize the full glory and truth of love, the Fish can, if he or she chooses, call on the innocence of Aries, the patience of Taurus, the awareness of Gemini, the perception of Cancer, the nobility of Leo, the discrimination of Virgo, the judgment of Libra, the penetration of Scorpio, the honesty of Sagittarius, the wisdom of Capricorn—and the humanitarianism of Aquarius. But sometimes these many fragments of secret knowledge and talents serve only to confuse Pisces, causing the Fish to then take the easier path of passive nonresistance.

The Pisces positive qualities are humility, compassion, sensitivity, spiritual awareness, psychic comprehension, philosophic insight and a healing potential. Expressed in their negative form they become timidity, apprehension, masochism, idleness, lying and weakness of will.

To Pisces, love is unselfish submission of the ego to the desires of the one needed to become Whole. The Fish gains more pleasure from giving than from receiving, more happiness in serving than in being served. Yet enigmatic Neptune tests the Pisces soul with the lure of multiple sexual and romantic experience—floating from one affair to another.

In such promiscuous manner—*or by becoming a romantic recluse*—does the wary Fish escape the dangers of being "hooked" by deep or permanent emotional commitment. But the Pisces man or woman who resists this

temptation to avoid love's pain by seeking only love's pleasure . . . .
is richly rewarded by the mastery of love's final mystery. He or she can
then glimpse for the first time on the soul's weary journey the true passion
of blending in a trinity of mind, heart and spirit, resulting in a rare physical ecstasy—the ultimate Piscean fulfillment of Love's long-ago Aries
springtime promise of a miracle.

The Planets

we've fought a long and bitter war
my Twin Soul and I

lost and lonely, fallen angels, exiled
from a misty, half-forgotten galaxy of stars
wounded cruelly by the painful thrust of Mars
caught in Neptune's tangled web
shocked and torn asunder
by the sudden, awful violence of Uranus

tortured by the clever lies of Mercury
crushed beneath the icy weight of stern, unyielding Saturn
who lengthened every hour into a day
each day into a year
each year into eternities of waiting

scorched, and nearly blinded

by the Sun's exploding bursts of arrogance and pride
as Eve and Adam, stilled and helpless, deep within us cried . . .

still we fought on in unrelenting fury
striking blow for blow . . . driven by the pounding drums
of Jupiter's giant, throbbing passions.
stumbling at the precipice of the Moon's enticing madness

to fall, at last, in trembling fear
before the threat of Pluto's ominous, tomb-like silence
consumed by inconsolable sadness, and the bleakness

of despair

we bear . . .

the wounds and scars of furious battle
*   I and my Twin Soul*

but now we walk in quiet peace
with all our scattered pieces whole
together, hand-in-hand . . . full serpent circle
back into the Pyramid-shaped rainbow
*   of tomorrow's brighter Eden*

crowned by gentle Venus with the Victory of Love
that did not die
but has survived the night of selfish seeking
to wait for morning's soft forgiveness

*   and the dawn of understanding**

* From *Gooobers,* a forthcoming novel about astrology and reincarnation by Linda Goodman.

Your Sun Sign

The term "Sun Sign" means that if you are, for example, a Gemini, the Sun was exercising its powerful influence through the ZONE OF THE ZODIAC (not the constellation) called Gemini when you were born—from May 21st to June 21st inclusive (in all USA time zones for the past several decades; with a day's difference, for instance, in Greenwich, England). You'll find that the dates covering the twelve Sun Sign periods vary according to which astrology book you read, and this can be confusing to the layman. The reason for the variance is that most astrologers don't wish to puzzle you with the information that the Sun "changes signs" in the morning, afternoon or evening of a particular day. And so they "rob" one consecutive Sun Sign of that Change Day and give it to the other—to make things come out even. This only adds to the confusion. It's all very nice and easy to pretend each new Sun Sign period begins precisely at midnight. But it doesn't.

For example, except for leap-year variations, the Sun (for the last several decades, as well as currently) both LEAVES Aries and ENTERS Taurus sometime on April 20th in all USA time zones (on April 21st, however, in Greenwich, England). It's important for you to know that April 20th contains BOTH signs. Otherwise, you might go around all your life thinking you're a Bull, when you're really a Ram.

So remember always that if you were born on either the FIRST or the LAST day of any of the Sun Sign periods listed in this book, you'll have to know the exact TIME, plus the longitude and latitude of your birth, to judge whether or not the Sun had "changed signs" by that hour at the place where you were born.

The term "Moon Sign" refers to the zone of the zodiac (not the constellation) through which the Moon was "passing" and exercising its influence when you were born. The term "Ascendent" (occasionally called the "Rising Sign") means the sign of the zodiac that was "rising" on the Eastern Horizon at the exact moment of your birth. The Ascendent varies with the location of your birthplace on Earth (longitude/latitude of birth locality). Those of you who want to know more about these things may consult the reading list at the back of this book.

A note regarding "cusp birth dates": So often, those who were born on an astrological "cusp date" (the day during which the Sun changes signs) will say (and believe) that their personalities seem to contain the qualities of *both* Sun Signs. And they imagine this to be caused by their "cusp birthdays."

For example, a person born on January 20th may feel that he or she behaves at times like a Capricorn—at other times like an Aquarian. The same thing is true for all "cusp people." Some astrologers will tell you this is because a "cusp birth" causes the person so born to exhibit the traits of both signs. In my extensive and varied personal experience as a professional astrologer, I have been convinced that this is simply not true. In every single instance, without exception, the person who believes that he (or she) behaves in a manner which is a blend of both "cusp Sun Signs"— is behaving in that manner because that person's *Moon* or *Ascendent* is in the "second" sign.

For instance, the above-mentioned particular person born on January 20th in the morning of that day is a Sun Sign Capricorn. If this Cappy sometimes behaves like a Goat—and at other times behaves in the manner of an Aquarian Water Bearer, it is always because the Cappy's *Moon* or *Ascendent* was in Aquarius at birth—NOT BECAUSE HE OR SHE WAS BORN ON A "CUSP DAY." If such a person born on January 19th behaves essentially always like a Goat—and never as an Aquarian— then the Moon or Ascendent was NOT in the "cusp sign" of Aquarius at birth.

You are one Sun Sign or the other. Your personality cannot and does not partake of two Sun Signs because you were born on a "cusp day." It's true that each of the three "decanates" of every Sun Sign (every astrological sign is encompassed by 30 degrees)—each "decanate" of 10 degrees each—bestows its own variation of the particular Sun Sign quality. But that is a separate matter entirely. If you are a Capricorn, you are a Capricorn. You are not a "partial" Sun Sign Aquarian because you were born on a "cusp day." If you find yourself occasionally behaving as an Aquarian, you can be certain it's because the *Moon* or *Ascendent* was in Aquarius at your birth (or that you perhaps only *imagine* your Aquarian characteristics because you've been overly impressed with the error so frequently repeated by misguided astrologers.

This image may help to make it clearer to you. Your (for example) Capricorn characteristics imprinted upon your personality when you drew your first breath (impressing the billions of electric cells in your brain much in the way a computer is programmed) were caused by the Sun's exercising of its powerful influence through the zone of the zodiac called Capricorn. This process (which creates your personal Sun Sign) is a Time-Energy Force. For want of more precise terminology, the process is somewhat electromagnetic. You may then, for the purpose of helping create an image, ask yourself if an electric light may at any time be half on and half off. Of course it cannot. An electric light is either ON or it is OFF. It cannot be both on and off at the same time. Neither can the Sun (for similar reasons) exercise its powerful influence through TWO SIGNS simultaneously.

When the Sun is vibrating its force through Capricorn, it is vibrating its force through Capricorn. At the exquisitely timed cosmic moment (which may be Earth-timed only within minutes, using present astronomical-mathematical means, to all intents and purposes)—at this moment when the Sun "enters" the sign of Aquarius, it is then exercising its powerful vibrations through Aquarius, and no longer through the sign of Capricorn. Period. The light cannot be on and off at the same time. The Sun cannot be imprinting the characteristics of both Capricorn and Aquarius at the same time. It is a cosmic and astrological impossibility. The "orb of influence" rationalization used by astrologers who dwell upon "combined cusp day" traits does not apply in relation to the Sun Sign. In relation to many other phases and facets of astrology (including the present "orb of influence" of the Aquarian Age) such as aspects and so on—it does apply. But NOT in the case of a Sun Sign.

As for "Astrology 13," the astronomer's joke against the holiness and validity of astrology, disregard it. For reasons I can't detail here, for want of space, this concept of "thirteen Sun Signs," and so forth, is completely fallacious. Half-seriously and half-humorously, I offer you the ultimate proof. Astrology 13 would make your author a Sun Sign Pisces rather than an Aries. All my friends and relatives will tell you that the idea of my being a Piscean is fallacious to the point of being hilarious. Neither is Nelson Rockefeller a Gemini (which Astrology 13 would make him) but a Cancerian Crab all the way. Neither is Billy Graham a Libran (which Astrology 13 would make him) but a Scorpion Eagle all the way. And that, dear readers and astrology students, is THAT. A determined Ram (not a tactful, gentle Piscean) has spoken! So be it. I urge you not to allow this deliberate seed of confusion, planted by astronomers who wish to muddy the astrological issue, grow into one of the Little Prince's huge baobab trees of darkness and negative falsehood.

☆ ☆ ☆ ☆ ☆ ☆

Sun Sign Birth Periods

ARIES	March 20th into April 20th
TAURUS	April 20th into May 21st
GEMINI	May 21st into June 21st
CANCER	June 21st into July 22nd
LEO	July 22nd into August 23rd
VIRGO	August 23rd into September 23rd
LIBRA	September 23rd into October 23rd
SCORPIO	October 23rd into November 22nd
SAGITTARIUS	November 22nd into December 21st
CAPRICORN	December 21st into January 20th
AQUARIUS	January 20th into February 19th
PISCES	February 19th into March 20th

Love Sign
Combinations

ARIES

Fire—Cardinal—Positive
Ruled by Mars
Symbol: The Ram
Day Forces—Masculine

ARIES

Fire—Cardinal—Positive
Ruled by Mars
Symbol: The Ram
Day Forces—Masculine

The **ARIES-ARIES** *Relationship*

>*Then rather curiously they both snapped out*
>*the same remark:*
>
>*"Shut up!"*
>
>*"Shut up!"*

I wonder . . . . . is it proper and dignified for an Aries person like my-self to analyze the 1-1 Sun Sign vibrational influence between two Rams—to describe what it's like when they blend their compatible but equally combustible natures, as friends, neighbors, relatives, business associates, lovers or mates? Let me consider it for a moment. All right, I've considered it. Of course it's proper. Who's better qualified? No one. As for being dignified, receiving a Dignity Achievement Award has never been my chief goal in life. That settles *that*. So let's get on with it. I can't stand waiting around for things to happen, can you?

First, we should probably discuss the number of mistakes it's possible for two Rams to make, in a close association. Gigantic. Simply gigantic. Still, the number of successes can also be overwhelming—and since Rams are so frequently compelled to impulsively jump into puddles head first (Aries always leads with the head), it won't be so lonesome being stuck upside down in the mud, with a kindred soul for company.

When these two strong egos first mix their personal auras, clear the field, and count down for the blast-off, which is usually a surge of spontaneous empathy. It's really such a joy to discover a positive, enthusiastic, and open personality, after being stuck with all those squeamish squares, and boring wet blankets—the secretive, stingy ones, and especially those cold, unapproachable people who freeze you, when all you're trying to do is be friendly. No wonder there's such an instant rush of mutual admiration! Each Ram will find it a blessed relief that the other one isn't all stuffy about things like extravagance, impulsive behavior, rash speech, and being late for appointments. Not only that, now there's someone who will go to the dentist with them, and not think they're "sissy."

Most Arians hate two things equally: (a) going to the dentist—and (b) having someone take their picture "candidly" or otherwise. Sitting still and posing while the photographer adjusts lights in a studio is almost as bad as submitting to a molar tooth extraction or root canal work, because it gives you all that time to decide you're ugly, which is equally as grinding a pain to the self-conscious Rams, who are ultra-concerned and somewhat vain about how they look. (Astrologically, Aries rules the physical appearance.) The Ram's fear of the dentist is in no way, however, a reflection on Aries courage. Mars supplies these people with all the courage they need, and an extra helping of it any time they ask, even on very short notice. Their dread of the dental drill is an isolated hang-up, and mustn't be construed to mean that Rams are cowards. They simply don't like anyone messing around with their heads. That normally includes drugs. It definitely includes eyes, ears, nose and mouth—also the brain—which means don't mess with their opinions either.

Most Aries females, for instance, dislike going to beauty parlors. Beauticians are so bossy, and they simply will not comb your hair the way you tell them, or part it where you order them to part it. After all, it's not *their* hair, it's your hair, but give them an inch, and they'll snip off four. The Aries woman may impulsively, to her later regret, cut her own hair drastically too short, or crooked—but let someone else turn her into a shorn lamb, and she'll be furious. As furious as she'd be with herself. (Aries is not at all selective about anger.) Girl Rams would rather go to the extra trouble of washing their hair at home than suffer a hair stylist who thinks he (or she) owns their heads. The Aries sensitivity related to anything connected with the head area is really pronounced. You'd be sensitive about your head, too, if you had a dozen or so scars scattered around on your head and face you began collecting in childhood, from crashing into things (and people) head first.

As for the "extra trouble" of doing something themselves, that's no large thing. Rams almost never mind going to "extra trouble" for themselves, or for others. When it's for others, the extra trouble stems from the generous impulse of the Mars-ruled souls to give more than may be needed of their time, money, love, loyalty, and everything else. When it comes to themselves, they tend to bring on the extra trouble by creating problems where none would exist if the situation were left alone. "Leaving well enough alone" seems like silly advice to a Ram. Why should anyone be satisfied with "well enough"? What kind of a goal is that when, with a little effort, well enough can be made better? (Aries never theorizes that well enough might possibly be made worse.)

Unless one or both Rams have a Capricorn, Taurus or Cancer Moon Sign or Ascendent, it will probably be easy for them to borrow money from each other, and neither will be likely to create a fuss about being paid back promptly—which is another area of empathy between them. These two are straightforward about everything, including money. It never occurs to them to be deceptive. Actually, they don't know how.

Now and then, they may overestimate their ability to pay, or even forget a debt, because of being caught up in something new that's so exciting it consumes their entire attention, but they are not dishonest, and absolutely never sneaky. Nothing both hurts and angers a Ram more than to be unjustly mistrusted or suspected. It would mortify the typical Aries man or woman to let down anyone to whom either gave his word, and this includes creditors. Arians may be either forgetful or delinquent, but eventually they'll pay everything they owe in full, often more than they owe— because Rams are not unduly suspicious, *or* cautious, about spending, so it's easy for them to be oversold and overcharged. No matter. The Mars idea about money is that when it disappears, more will soon manifest, in one way or another. (Does the Infant fret and worry about where the next dry diaper or bottle of milk will come from? Certainly not. It will magically appear when needed. *Everybody* knows *that!*) Each Aries person in this 1-1 Sun Sign Pattern association will be touchingly grateful for the trust of the other. Not only will two Rams usually instinctively trust one another, they won't take advantage of one another, and considering the way the rest of the world usually treats both of them, this can be a warm and wonderful feeling.

It's all a merry-go-round of happiness between Aries and Aries in the beginning, but after the pink cotton candy melts, there may be moments of disillusion. You know what happens when Fire meets Fire? Higher and hotter flames. That should indicate the possible ramifications of an association between two wild and woolly Rams, whether it's business, romantic, friendly or otherwise. It could be otherwise, if they insist on butting away at the impossible task of trying to break each other's vulnerable yet indomitable and unconquerable spirit.

Scattered among the more typical extroverted Arians, are the not as common, Sheep-type Aries people, whose Mars egos have been, very sadly, crushed in childhood, and who therefore control their natural exuberance behind a most *un*natural introversion. If the two Aries people who are involved with one another belong to this group, they may not appear, on the surface, to be capable of arousing anger in each other, but appearances are deceptive. At some time, in some way, their horns are sure to lock.

When Mars clashes with Mars, the result can be full-scale war, with all flags flapping, bravely and colorfully. Occasional flare-ups are bound to occur when these two are thrown into close, daily proximity, without the relief of some separateness in their association. But there will also be some glorious Highs to offset these Lows.

Most of the time, the direct, forceful manner of Mars will create a wave of sympathy between two Aries people. It's when their mutual need for ego trips overlaps that they can expect the fireworks. Here's a possible solution to that problem: One Ram is permitted to have everything his way on Mondays, Wednesdays and Fridays. The other Ram gets to be Big Boss on Sundays, Tuesdays and Thursdays. Saturdays, they can just fight it out, letting the Ram with the toughest horns win—and bind up the loser's wounds with typical Aries instant contriteness and warm generosity. It's a formula that should be successful in most cases, since neither Aries will mind taking a periodic fling at playing second glockenspiel, knowing that he—or she—will be allowed to be conductor again the next day.

It's been said that Aries people have a way about them. They do. Their own way. Yet, despite that sometimes antagonistic Martian exterior, they'll sense each other's desperate need to be appreciated and liked. When they get together, they may struggle for leadership, but the experience will supply some well-needed lessons. The shock of living with someone—or being around someone—as innocently thoughtless, selfish and aggressive as one's self, is sure to soften any battering Ram, although there may be a few scars to show for the lessons in living thus mastered. Aries hearts always carry more scars than the Rams ever show, or openly discuss.

It will be necessary for both of them to realize that Aries is the Infant of the zodiac, symbolizing the dawn of the personality awareness, or Sunrise.

Aries represents the East, the Day Forces—which is why most of them fight sleep, tranquility, rest and resignation to Fate with such vigor. The negative intrusion of any degree of criticism or pessimism darkens a Ram's "Easter" horizon, and considerably dampens the Aries spirit, especially when the blow to innocence and Sunrise faith is delivered forcefully from another Ram. Yet, temporary resentment seldom remains long enough to become permanent bitterness, because Aries possesses a childlike faith that a quarrel can somehow be made up, a relationship can be repaired each time it's broken. It's unthinkable to a Ram that any given situation is anything but the way he (or she) sees it at the time. Nevertheless, no one (except Sag and Gemini) can switch a mistaken viewpoint more swiftly, or bury yesterday's unhappiness and hurt more completely, than an Aries man, woman or child *who is handled gently*. To a Ram of either sex, or any chronological age (barring a more pessimistic Moon Sign and/or Ascendent), each Sunrise brings a new covenant of resurrection—the resurrection of a shattered dream, idea, goal or friendship. Why look backward, or worry about what's past, and couldn't be helped, when today is so full of promise?

A few sentences back, you'll notice the phrase "who is handled gently" in italics. The trouble is, although Rams need to be handled gently themselves, they aren't inclined to handle each other (or anyone else) gently. Aries people can't seem to get the hang of the Golden Rule. They comprehend, even personify, its generosity and forgiveness, but they can't quite interpret what it means to treat others as tenderly as they need to be treated. They will not be led by the nose, pushed or forced by anyone, including those who are clearly stronger than they are, and certainly not by each other. (A typical Aries person would literally stand before a criminal who pointed a loaded gun in his—or her—direction, and fearlessly talk back.) Rams expect their own wishes to be granted, their own orders obeyed without question, as quickly as possible (unless there's a softening influence of several Pisces or Libra planets in the horoscope). It's the instinctive Mars urge to rebel. The drive to initiate and to lead is so strong in some Mars-ruled men, women and children that even friendly suggestion is sometimes construed as unbearable interference, let alone the forceful commands of a relative, neighbor, friend, business associate, mate or lover born under the same, unconsciously demanding Sun Sign.

If one of the two Aries people is stronger by planetary positions at birth (not wiser and more patient, which would be beneficial, but *stronger*), the result of the association could be that the "weaker" Ram gradually turns into a neurotic Sheep, constantly and pathetically almost apologizing for his (or her) very existence—or else rationalizing every word and action, for fear of offending or being misunderstood. Such a situation is very sad, for to see the proud strength of a spirited astrological "animal" like the Ram reduced to weakness and tears, constantly attempting to placate the more dominant personality, yet inwardly frustrated and emotionally restricted, is against the first law of astrology: Be true to your own Sun Sign essence, or be prepared to lose the powerful individual potential of your own birthright.

It's never easy for two Rams to exist in tranquil harmony (although it can undeniably be exciting!). One happy probability is that both of them will usually be inclined to forgive and forget everything but the most cruel encounters. As for the latter, a powerful effort should be made to avoid them, because they'll be long remembered by Aries . . . . . for the very same reason that infants, who instantly forget, with a trusting smile, the more commonplace hurts and pains—will recall, with subconscious terror, the deeper experiences of traumatic rejection . . . . sometimes forever.

Two Rams will have to try to control their tendency to lash out at one another while their tempers are still hot. They'll strike a blow, shortly afterward feel a surge of guilt over their hasty unkindness, then impulsively attempt to make up for their anger by showering each other with an outburst of affection, or the peace offering of an extravagant gift. Gifts, by the way, are a Ram's way of saying "I like you" or "I love you"—occasionally given apologetically to say "I'm sorry." But never is an Aries gift given for the purpose of "buying friendship." The Mars-ruled are contemptuous of getting what they want by buying it (they're accustomed to demanding it). So they fiercely resent, and are also very deeply hurt by, such untrue insinuations or accusations. Aries gifts are always from the heart, given in a straightforward and honest gesture of good will. Nevertheless, their motives are often misunderstood by those too materialistically minded themselves to be able to comprehend giving without some ulterior motive (since that's their own pattern of behavior, they believe everyone must be the same).

Happily, this is another area of hurt two Rams probably won't inflict upon one another. Each Aries person understands the gift-giving syndrome that's part of the Mars nature (matched only by the other two Fire Signs) and, therefore, both will usually give and receive joyously, back and forth. A Ram is as delighted to receive a gift as to be able to give one. It's part of the wisdom of Aries innocence to know that it's of equal importance to graciously receive as to generously give. For if no one *received* happily, there could be no happy giving. Consequently, the typical Ram will react with the elation of a child to the receiving of a "surprise present," and two Arians can keep themselves broke (but exalted and happy) as a result of their mutual urge to express their enthusiasms through gifting.

Down through the centuries, the Ram has been a symbol of sacrifice for spiritually blind, emotionally warped and mentally dense religious fanatics. The Old Testament is packed with bloody examples of the "burnt offerings" of these misguided "holy men." In no way was the patriarch Abraham following "God's" wishes or commands to first be willing to murder his own son to please the Almighty, and then to "hear" God's voice grant a last minute reprieve, commanding him to murder a helpless Sheep in his place. Abraham, sadly, heard only the voice of his own delusions, not the voice of God. Neither of our infinitely compassionate and wise co-Creators would be so sadistic as to command the murder of children, or of the lowliest of our animal brothers and sisters, for Their own greater glory, as a senseless test of faith and obedience. The Earth sorely needed the example set by the gentle Nazarene, Jesus, who used the Sheep in parable after parable illustrating love and kindness, who is often pictured embracing the "lamb" and who brought to the world the image of the Good Shepherd, in his effort to straighten out the kinks in the twisted thinking of these "servants of God," who were, through their cruel sacrifices of animals, unknowingly serving Satan, for all their otherwise pious and humble attitudes.

In such mythical legends as Jason and the Golden Fleece, the sad fate of the Ram has been repeated, all through mythology, as well as in biblical history. The unfortunate Ram who attempted to cross dangerous seas and rescue a brother and sister from the jealous act of a stepmother, in a great act of courage, was unable to save the sister from drowning. When he reached the shore, and delivered the brother safely, his thanks was to be murdered, for allowing the other one to die, even though he had tried desperately to save her.

Such is the symbolic fate, in varying degrees, in all kinds of endeavors, of many Aries people. For all their enthusiastic efforts and the sincerity of their impulses, human Rams frequently are either ignored or despised for their trouble by the very ones they have tried to help. The Arian simplicity of purpose and direct approach isn't always welcomed by the more cynical of this world. Ram Thomas Jefferson discovered this, as did modern day Aries politician Eugene McCarthy. Ram Nikita Khrushchev's personal motives were also, to a large extent, misunderstood and unappreciated both by his own people and by Americans.

And so, the teaming up of two Arians can be beneficial, inasmuch as they're able to help each other avoid becoming a "burnt offering," or being sacrificed to the calculated maneuvers of the more worldly wise who would "fleece" them. They provide each other with protection against those who would otherwise take advantage of their altruistic instincts. There are always bullies who wait for a chance to attack the defenseless. Admittedly, it's difficult to image the feisty, fiery and normally outspoken Rams as "defenseless." But in the final analysis, they are extremely vulnerable to those who would use their natural guilelessness and lack of sophistication against them.

In any association between two Aries people, within the family circle, in the office or across the bridge of love and friendship, one thing is certain: emotions will periodically run high, and close to the surface. Catullus described perfectly the attitude of this Sun Sign to its own emotional immaturity, when he wrote: *I hate and I love. You may ask why I do so. I do not know. But I feel it, and am in torment.*

Between two Rams, there will seldom be any deception, pretense or hypocrisy, but neither will there be a great deal of caution, reason or practicality. There's very little that will be neutral in this 1-1 Sun Sign Pattern vibration of the double Mars involvement. These two are capable of reaching the far heavens of happiness, or of consuming themselves in childish displays of rage, resentment and thoughtless selfishness. Yet they will never fail to understand and sympathize with each other's bright red, diamond-dusted dreams, especially those dreams that didn't quite make it, for one reason or another. Perhaps together, they can both try again. And somehow, someway, someday . . . . . they'll win. Tough dreamers always do.

ARIES *Woman* ARIES *Man*

———◆——◆——◆———

So uproariously gay was the dance, and how they buffeted
each other on the bed and out of it! It was a pillow
fight rather than a dance, and when it was finished, the
pillows insisted on one bout more . . .

As fiercely independent, bright and clever as the Aries girl is, the Aries man is even more so—in his own opinion. And he'll demand recognition of it eventually, no matter how he fools her, and himself, in the beginning. From the very first time she pushes through a door ahead of him, he'll feel the faint stirring of a desire to teach her that, in any tangle between a girl and a boy Ram, the male of the Sun Sign will win. He should decide to thus subdue her early in the game, or say goodbye. There may be a few noisy, tearful skirmishes before she catches on, but she'll blossom beautifully when she's allowed—no, forced—to become a woman.

However, demanding that she drop her career or job to take up the fulltime job of waiting on his whims is not the most ideal way to unfold her womanhood, and establish his manhood. There are other ways. Unless she willingly sacrifices her "pre-*them*" occupation to warm his slippers, or join him in his personal goals, forgetting her own (which sometimes happens), it's best for him to let her stay out there where it's all happening. It would also be a wise mutual decision to let it be his income that pays the rent or mortgage, food and utilities bills. Her money can provide the extra things they'll need to satisfy the extravagant impulses they both frequently feel. That way, the male Aries will be solidly entrenched in the image of the masculine side of the team, and it's important to get that straight, right at the start.

I mean, let it be plainly understood that he is MAN and she is WOMAN. There will be lots of opportunities to wonder about the division of actual control in the relationship, and there's no sense adding to this by a confusion of sexual male-female roles.

The masculinity challenge of the Mars female begins the day she first zings the male Ram of her choice in the heart with her sparkling hopes and excitements, so much like his own, and will follow him through all sorts of living arrangements, including temporary geographical separation. She may try to dominate him by telephone, telegram or letter, if he's not within touching distance. Since the Aries man knows that no one has successfully dominated him from the time he was born, he might feel like calling it quits when he feels the first tug-of-war from an Aries girl, but he'd be smarter to curb his annoyance, and try to tame her instead.

Every Aries woman has a deep, hidden desire to be protected and defended by her man. In her private daydreams she is always the lovely, gentle Guinevere, and he is the kind, tender, strong Lancelot—or he'd better be if he doesn't want his Guinevere to become a frustrated Virginia Woolf, which is a very possible and most undesirable result when a man either leans too far backward with her, in an attempt to please—or leans too far forward, in an attempt to take charge. The former probably won't occur often, because leaning over backward is not a normal position or direction for the typical male Ram. Leaning too far forward is more likely. But he should understand that her Guinevere wish to be conquered is purely romantic and sexual. It has little or nothing to do with the personality, or other areas of her life. His masculine Mars macho that keeps her starry-eyed and emotionally fulfilled on a stroll along the beach, or in the privacy of the bedroom, won't normally be welcomed regarding activities separated from romance. She draws a sharp line between submitting romantically and submitting in other ways, and it's best for him to realize this if he wants to keep her. Expecting this lady to keep his curfews or follow his orders is unwise, but *ignoring* her is downright dangerous. He's capable of making all these mistakes until he learns she'll neither toe the line nor be brought to heel by the dictator treatment, because she's cut from the same mold as he—which was, of course, thrown away after the Aries Sun Sign was made. That's how Rams believe that the old saying got started "They threw away the mold when they made you, baby." They sure did. (Actually, it refers to the ancient potter's mold, but it fits the Aries situation quite aptly.)

The first thing the Aries girl will notice about her male counterpart is that he's even more bossy, belligerent and bellicose than she is. Obviously—and also fortunately. If she's puzzled by the Yin and the Yang of it, a brief meditation on her all-time-favorite faerie story might cause her to experience the dawn of comprehension.

This woman never failed to cry, as a child, when she read about the Prince charging bravely into the woods to find his Princess and awaken her from her lonely slumber with the kiss of True Love. (Aries females invariably get all soft and squishy inside at the mere thought of True Love, their idealism in affairs of the heart being as eternal as Spring itself.) But really now, dear Aries girl, when you're honest with yourself, would it all have been quite so magical if the fiery, courageous Princess had come charging bravely into the woods on her horse to claim her Prince and rescue him from the Wicked Witch? The same meditation should be practiced on all the other faerie tales she still believes in, and dreams of every fortnight or so. Imagine dainty Cinderella, red-faced, puffing and perspiring, as she tried to shove a glass Hush-Puppy on her Prince's foot, to see if it fitted him. Mother Nature knows what she's doing. The Aries man-woman relationship will stand a better chance of success if she permits him to steal her Mars thunder. It somehow sounds better coming from him—if he doesn't carry it too far. Besides, since she's no stranger to toughness herself, she knows very well, if she'll stop to ponder it, that his tough Aries facade is only a cover for his quivering Aries idealism, his desperate inner longing to be needed—and noticed.

All right, so she should *notice* him as he sits there astride his white horse, shooting off all that Aries bossiness to disguise his secret fear that no one will ever love him as much as he knows he needs to be loved (which is considerable)—unless he demands it. This man can be very tender and gentle, for all his brash independence, and he's an expert at pretending he's not hurt when he's actually been deeply wounded. She knows how that is. Since they're both aware of all these Mars secrets about each other, you'd think they would cool the fireworks, but it usually takes more than one painful lesson to teach them the futility of constant ego challenges. Often, the ultimate lesson is the frightening experience of nearly losing each other, then realizing at the last minute, before the ultimate and final disaster—like the old silent films *Perils of Pauline* serial—that meeting Force with Force never works.

If she'll do all her Mars charging at her man's enemies, instead of at him, he'll adore her for it, and in return he'll give her every bit as much loyalty as she gives him. That's certainly a fair trade. But somebody has to start it.

It may seem at first that these two are well mated sexually, since they both require essentially the same thing of love—that it be the kind of physical-emotional blending poets write about as the epitome of the soul-mate theory, which nearly every Arian believes in as absolute romantic dogma. Whether they use the term "soul-mate" itself or not, Rams never doubt, when they love, that their union was not only Made In Heaven, but also made to last throughout a lifetime—and beyond. However, before this potential peak of harmony becomes a reality, a serious obstacle must be overcome—the instinctive, although almost always unintentional, self-ishness of this Sun Sign.

Now, everything everybody wants to know about sex (whether he—or she—has been afraid to ask or not) is based on either deliberate or non-deliberate selfishness, using the partner for self-gratification. Not how can

I bring him (or her) more fulfillment, but how can *I* be more fulfilled? Sex-sex-sex. Doctors David Reuben, Masters and Johnson, Kinsey and Freud, have all explained it, tested it, researched it, analyzed it, observed it, photographed it, taped it, listened to it, written about it—just about everything but demonstrated it in public auditoriums. (Too much competition from stage, film and magazines.) But most men and women still haven't received the message.

It might be a good idea for these Mars lovers to buy one of those large posters, showing a couple walking, blissfully hand-in-hand, toward the mountains, the ocean or the cornfields, gazing into each other's eyes . . . with the inscription at the bottom: *LOVE BEGINS WHEN THE NEEDS OF SOMEONE ELSE BECOME MORE IMPORTANT THAN YOUR OWN . . . .* and nail it firmly near their bed, right next to the tapestry depicting *THE WEDDING OF ROMEO AND JULIET,* which always hangs in spirit, if not in actuality, on the wall of every Aries bedroom. Romeo and Juliet were also soul-mates, you see—but *they* were unselfish. It's not necessary for the Aries man and woman to end their honeymoon with a double suicide scene in order to prove unselfishness. A little thoughtful consideration on both sides will suffice.

When these traces of infantile selfishness have been erased by tenderness, the sexual sharing of love between these two can be an ecstatic exchange. With Aries, sex is composed of strange contradictions, barely comprehended, causing their mating to be an incredible combination of explosive desire, direct and penetrating, fiery and uncontrolled . . . . and haunting fragments of flowers in the rain, fresh breezes and glittering snow diamonds. That's what happens when the powerful thrust of Mars is gentled by being expressed through the naivete and starry wonder of the symbolic Aries Infant. It creates a rare and startling blend of abandoned, stormy emotion—and the peace of a still and silent dawn. At once primitive—and poetic. The alchemy of equal parts of searing passion and fragile innocence is very nearly a holy thing. Obviously, then, at its very best, the sexual union between two Rams can be an experience to cherish. Even at its worst, it will be . . . . . interesting.

What will she do if he flirts with other girls? Well, what would *he* do if she flirts with other men? Same thing. An emotional explosion of the hydrogen bomb magnitude—which is just as foolish and suicidal to love as the actual hydrogen bomb is to our planet. Each Ram will let the other know unmistakably that iron bars on individual freedom will not be tolerated. But it's a one-sided freedom, since each of them refuses to be strangled by jealousy, while at the same time displaying intense jealousy of the other. Aries people do tend to want to have their cake and eat it, and it may take several noisy, emotional scenes to teach them that they can't have it both ways. They'll have to learn that love's not a game to be won, a battle to be fought or even a prize to be won. It's a gift—to be given. Rams will demand a lot of things from life, and get them. But no one, not even an Aries, can demand love.

He'll make it clear that she should not dare to be jealous of *him*, but *she* had better not even look at another man. She'll make it just as clear that he's not to smother *her* with jealousy, but at the same time, *he'd* better not be caught glancing with the slightest flicker of interest at another woman.

You know what that is? It's selfish. If you're an Aries, you may not have thought about it like that, but *think* about it. Rams can even become jealous if they notice a smile on the loved one's face in sleep. Who is he (or she) dreaming about? And don't believe that very question hasn't been asked by lots of Aries couples in the morning. "Well, you must have had pleasant dreams last night. Were you meeting your old boy friend in your astral body?" And don't think the answer hasn't been: "It's none of your business what I dream. Besides, I noticed you weren't so anxious to wake up when I kissed you Good Morning just now. Were you lying there, half awake, practicing mental telepathy with that girl you flirted with at the supermarket last week?"

There are variations of dialogue, but such confrontations are a definite possibility when two Rams have promised to love, honor and cherish—but *never* to obey! The solution is for these two to practice their own telepathic communication, and to reassure each other of their undying devotion constantly, because the symbolic Infant's subconscious fear of losing love lies at the bottom of all Aries jealousy, incongruous as it may seem, as it struggles with the conscious Mars urge for personal independence. If he forgets to call to say he'll be later for dinner, who better than she should understand his need to follow a sudden impulse without first holding a committee meeting?

Should the winds of April call him away from the hearth, she may be simultaneously called to follow her own skylark cadenza, and when they return to each other, they can exchange magical tales of the wonders they nearly touched, the miracles they almost caught. An Aries man who's out there rushing after some new, exciting goal he just discovered is simply being true to himself, and the Aries woman who faces the truth must admit she couldn't really love a man who wasn't true to himself. The new, exciting goal needn't be a woman. Not unless it becomes a woman through her unfounded jealousy. If she trusts him *completely,* she probably won't regret it, because an Aries man, more so than any other Sun Sign male, will usually live up to exactly what's *expected* of him. And that works in reverse too. What's sauce for the goose is surely sauce for the gander between these lovers.

A couple of years ago I received a letter from an Aries woman married to an Aries man. They have three children, one Gemini and two Taurans. She described so well the happiness that can result from a double 1-1 Sun Sign vibration (with some effort) that I'm going to quote part of her letter here. She wrote, in part:

". . . . . . and when I read aloud the last paragraph of the Aries woman section, in your book *Sun Signs*, to my also Aries husband—the part that says, 'She may be a little impulsive, bossy and independent, but you can't have everything'—he asked, 'What else would a man *want?*' My Aries husband understands me, and he'll always be able to hold me, even though I sometimes threaten to leave him when our Ram's horns clash. It's because, as your book says—when I 'come running into his arms, my world all dark and dismal'—he holds me close, and comforts me, and would never, *never* say—'What did *you* do to *deserve* it?'—like that darned Libra man you wrote about in *Sun Signs!* I never realized before just how important that is to me."

So, you see, an Aries-Aries relationship *can* work. And the two of them needn't sacrifice their Mars courage, initiative or independence. The Aries woman who wrote that letter ended it with a postscript:

"I have a tremendous urge to tell you to add Ayn Rand to your list of prominent Aquarians. She fits it like a glove. But of course, you know I wouldn't sign off this letter without at least one suggestion on how to run your business."

An Aries to the end she was, but a girl Ram who's learned to admit her Mars need to take the lead, and can laugh about it, instead of either denying it or being ashamed of it—has learned an important lesson. You must love yourself (which requires both honesty and humor) before anyone else can love you. I'm sorry to say I've lost that lady Ram's name and address, since I typed out the excerpt from her letter, and if she reads this, I hope she writes again, so I can answer a vital question she asked.

If the Aries man and his Aries woman each practice the Golden Rule, and do unto one another as they would have the other do unto them, assuming their mutual Sun-Moon aspects are not discordant, their relationship will bring to them both the reward of emotional maturity, plus the best of all possible gifts—the freedom to be completely themselves with one another, with no fear of rejection.

When they quarrel, he may threaten to leave her in the heat of the moment, but he probably won't. Not for keeps anyway. Once he's loved an Aries woman, all other girls will seem boring. (Restful, perhaps, by comparison, but boring.)

She feels the same way about him when *she* threatens to leave and doesn't mean it. But she should try to remember that he can chop wood, blast through granite mountains, pilot planes, build houses, govern a city, state or nation, change tires, practice medicine or law, produce and direct films, operate a tractor, and shovel snow—at least as well as she can. It may no longer be true that a woman's place is in the home. But it will be eternally true that a woman's place is inside her man's heart.

ARIES

Fire — Cardinal — Positive
Ruled by Mars
Symbol: The Ram
Day Forces — Masculine

TAURUS

Earth — Fixed — Negative
Ruled by Venus (also by the
*   Planet Pan-Horus)*
Symbol: The Bull
Night Forces — Feminine

The ARIES-TAURUS *Relationship*

◆◀◆▶◆

> *Above, where all had been so still, the*
> *air was rent with shrieks and the clash*
> *of steel. Below, there was dead silence.*

Because Rams and Bulls each have tough horns, the determination of Aries and the stubbornness of Taurus might seem to be identical traits. They are not, and numerous incidents will occur between the two of them to make the distinction clear.

For example, an Aries parent wants a Taurus child to eat, and emphasizes it with a Martian command like: "You swallow every bite of that Wheat Germ and pick up your spoon this second, do you hear me?" That's determination.

The Taurus child sits quietly, not moving a muscle, gazes back steadily and says, "No." That's stubbornness.

An Aries boss wants a Taurean employee to work on his or her day off and states firmly, "I need you on Saturday, and it may take all day, so cancel any other plans you have." That's determination.

The Taurus employee calmly answers, "I'm busy Saturday. Get someone else." That's stubbornness.

After a few encounters, the difference between the two traits will become evident. Determination *initiates*. Stubbornness *reacts*. The first is a Positive action. The second is Negative *re*-action. Therefore, in any clash between Aries and Taurus, the Ram starts it and the Bull finishes it. It's important to remember that. Taurus won't forget it. Taurus doesn't forget *anything*.

Although Aries people get accused of running around burning their bridges behind them, and shooting off sparks in reckless abandon, they have their gentle moments too. Taurus people get accused of always pouting and brooding like dull globs of earth, ready to smother Arian enthusiasm in negative silence. But Bulls have their imaginative moments too, when it suits them, and they possess a thoughtful wisdom and wonderfully warm sense of humor behind that pragmatic exterior. Still, the essential differences between these two Sun Signs must be faced.

Rams are inclined to be aggressive, impulsive, bossy, extravagant, talkative and optimistic. They pursue excitement and quick results—and they require a dash of magic to make life interesting.

Bulls are inclined to be reserved, practical, usually sparing with words and self-sufficient, though somewhat pessimistic. They pursue stability, solitude and sure things—and they require lots of rest and tranquility to make life bearable.

You can see right away that these people are not the Bobbsey Twins. Their inner motivations, not to mention their outward actions, tend to wander in divergent directions. However, sometimes it's beneficial to knock around with someone who possesses the qualities you lack. Because this is a 2-12 Sun Sign Pattern association, the Taurean is more apt to be tolerant and sympathetic toward the Ram, and the Aries will try to imitate the Bull's placid stability. After all, placid stability is more or less synonymous with strength, and Aries people will try anything—even if it's against their natures—to gain more strength. Weakness is a four letter word to both the Ram and the Bull.

Although Bulls are equally fond of strength they're temporarily (until their true ruler, PAN-HORUS,* is "discovered" and named) ruled by Venus, which tempers the whole thing somewhat, so they're not as intense about proving it or flaunting it as the Mars-ruled Arian. Taureans understand the compulsion behind Aries courage and flashing independence, since every Sun Sign carries the seeds or karmic memory of the qualities of the sign immediately preceding it in the zodiac, as with every 2-12 Pattern. But because the Bull has already been there, in an unconscious sense, he's also aware of the pitfalls involved in throwing caution to the four winds. The Taurus goal of financial security, however, can often be obtained through cooperation with the tireless drive and energy of the Mars person, and Taureans instinctively know this, which is one reason why they're attracted to Aries in the first place.

As for the Ram, he or she secretly envies the Taurus reserve and sensible outlook, and could profit immensely from being exposed to the Bull's realistic approach to life. Every Sun Sign unconsciously senses there are lessons to be learned from the sign immediately following or ahead of it in the zodiac, in a 2-12 vibration. This is why Aries feels drawn by the dependability of Taurus, as something tangible to lean on when that Mars rashness brings on a shower of trouble.

If a free flow of give-and-take can be established between the Bull and the Ram, their natures could blend in such a way that each could attain with the other, through their association, what it would be difficult to realize alone. The danger inherent in the mixing of their Mars-Venus auras is that the Ram, on occasion, may exasperate the Bull beyond his (or her) great limits of endurance, until the Taurean finally makes up that very stubborn Bull mind, after long deliberation, that it's no longer worth the effort. Conversely, there's always the possibility that the Bull may so frequently refuse to catch fire from the Ram's many flaming ideas, sparks of ideals and dreams, that the Aries person will eventually leave in desper-

---

* The approximate place of an extra-Plutonian planet (Pan) was officially announced by Dr. C. Musès in 1965, through the publication La ricerca scientifica (p. 200) published at Rome by the National Research Council of Italy. Pan was calculated to be at 355° celestial longitude (i.e. 25° Pisces), with about nine degrees of south declination, on January 1, 1979, and due to enter Aries in 1984. Musès notes that the astronomer W. H. Pickering at his observatory in Jamaica during the first half of this century had previously computed, from extensive data on commentary perturbations, the existence of a planet with a period of 333 years. Musès' calculations yield a distance of 48.4 astronomical units from the sun, which agrees with Pickering's period by Kepler's third law.

Astrologically, the two meanings of this planet are expressed by Pan, ruler of chthonic earth forces and by Horus, restorer of the immortal body in Egyptian tradition. In this connection, Dr. Musès drew my attention to the startling depictions in the papyri of Pa-di-Amon, Khonsu-Renap, Ta-Shed-Khonsu, and Amon-m-Set in the Cairo Museum, and also on the sarcophagus of Hent-Taui in the Metropolitan Museum, New York City.

ation, to avoid depression—which no Mars-ruled man, woman or child can tolerate for long periods of time, without relief.

The Ram may be puzzled, and frequently frustrated, by the Bull's periodic spells of melancholy and introversion, even though it's relieved by lots of fun and giggles and from time to time may coax the Bull into parties and social activities, which, if it's not overdone, may help to balance the Taurean's instinctive "loner instinct"—a trait best not overemphasized. Encouraging the Bull of either sex, or any age, to express the innate Taurus love of form and color in music or art—or suggesting ways to retreat to the fields, woods and hills (all Bulls have an intense, even if buried, love of Nature)—are all ways the Aries person can use to coax Taurus into more placidity and peace.

The major mistake made by most Arians with a Taurus friend, relative, business associate, lover or mate, is to press the Bull into a decision. It will never work. Never. The Bull must decide in his (or her) own time. Demanding, pushing and insisting (the typical Mars strategy, when Aries desires are blocked) will only make Taurus more unwilling to budge, often causing these people to become totally uncommunicative. If Taurus believes that the suggestion is valid and sensible, he (or she) will consider it, and finally say "okay." Until then—and otherwise—no power on Earth can force the situation prematurely. That's the way it is, and no one, not even a fiery Ram, is going to change it.

If the Bull can learn, as they say out West, to ride "loose in the saddle" with the Ram, and not always expect the Aries person to be practical, the association will also be smoother. Rams must be allowed to express themselves through their own Mars pattern, which must contain a certain amount of violent ups and downs, in order to eventually learn that impulsive, rash behavior usually brings regret. The Aries person will undoubtedly benefit from the nearness of a more stable Taurean to lean on when things go wrong—and he (or she) will accept advice with surprising docility from the Bull, as long as it's tempered with tenderness, and isn't offered so frequently or dogmatically as to make the Ram feel "fenced in."

Aries people of all sizes, shapes, ages and sexes must be allowed to forge ahead without undue restriction, or too much negative disapproval. Actually, silent disapproval disturbs the bright, hopeful Aries spirit even more than spoken disapproval. It seems, somehow, to the direct Ram, more ominous and threatening—and just plain "scary." Remember, Aries is the symbolic newborn Infant, just as Taurus is the symbolic older baby. (See the "The Twelve Mysteries of Love" in the front of this book.) If the Ram's spontaneous enthusiasms are constantly buried beneath a ton of earthy Taurean "don'ts," he-she may become a frustrated Sheep—a Ram whose ego has been cruelly nipped in the bud of blossoming. The Arian needs to be cautioned against all that brimming-over excitement, now and then, but cautioned lightly, and with much gentleness.

Aries discovers the new country, whether it's geographical—or a mental continent. With the direct penetration of Mars to the core of any situation, the Ram leads and pioneers both the land—and innovative ideas. Then the Bull can enter into his or her own natural activity of building, of turning the country or idea Aries has discovered and pioneered, into a thriving community—or a concept that becomes practical and useful.

All human relationships—Life itself—must have, for Taurus, a clear purpose, and a definite function. Lacking a defined goal of usefulness, in the midst of scattered thoughts, and aimless activities, the Bull becomes confused, and finally withdraws. He (or she) learns only through the senses and through experience, and only by exercising a Fixity of intention can this Fixed Sun Sign remain true to himself—or herself. To Taurus, every thing, and every person, has a proper place, and should stay there, serving its purpose, never pretending to be something it's not. Aries behaves and dreams in a straight line, always going forward, ignoring the fact that both ends of that straight line are wide open to the winds of fate, whereas Taurus behaves and dreams in a circle, which encompasses lessons of the past and careful plans for the future, leaving no opening for failure due to irresponsible action.

The Ram can help the Bull break open that circle to let in the light of optimism and new ideas—and the Bull can assist the Ram to bend the direct Mars straight-line of activity and feeling into at least a semicircle shape, to help close out some of the inevitable disappointments that will be met throughout the eventful, Aries roller coaster existence. It's a strange and lovely thing that music, in any form, will almost always serve to build a bridge of understanding between Aries and Taurus and heal some of the hurt caused by each other's personality differences, which can be vast.

Since the Sun is exalted in Aries, these people frequently feel that victory has been won even before the battle. Every Ram feels an identification with Birth, Spring and the ecstasy of Easter—the resurrection. It's the reason for that soul's existence—the miracle he (or she) possesses to innocently offer other Sun Signs—the way Aries people serve both mankind and their true, inner self. Aries believes in the triumph of Life over Death, of Faith over Doubt. However, behind his (or her) bravado lurks the peculiar emotional insecurity of the Ram (those karmic memory seeds from Pisces, just behind Aries, on the astrological circle)—and the attempts of an Earth Sign to hold him (or her) back in any way only result in an increase of this hidden vulnerability. Then, an Aries person will either suddenly and violently shatter all ties with the smothering Taurean—or submit, and fall into a sad neurosis, completely unnatural to the Mars Life Force.

For the reason that the combining of Mars determination with Taurus willfulness creates an immense amount of sheer power, ancient astrologers warned that a blend of the Aries-Taurus qualities, if not carefully balanced, can result in great cruelty. Adolph Hitler's severely afflicted Taurus Sun and Aries Ascendent (plus other negative natal aspects) is the classic example of this warning ignored. It can occur within the birth chart of one individual—or become manifest through an association between a Ram and a Bull, depending always on the planetary positions of both at birth. The tendency may, of course, be overcome, through enlightenment, and many Rams and Bulls produce an equally powerful alchemy of kindness and beneficence via their association. But there are, unfortunately, for example, some Aries and Taurus people who channel such negativity by becoming "hunters-for-sport," expressing the dark side of Aries courage and Taurus strength in a cruel manner, which causes them to be, instead, if they only comprehended it—cowardly—in the worst sort of way. Shooting a wild animal in cold blood, including deer, rabbits, ducks, pheasants and all our feathered friends in the sky—then carrying the silent corpse through town, as a trophy of macho, is a pathetic kind of cowardice in its lowest form—not the demonstration of "manhood" or "womanhood" some believe it to be.

If the Sun and Moon in the birth charts of the Ram and the Bull are inharmoniously aspected, in mutual Luminary relation to each other, the danger of cruelty must be guarded against carefully. However, when the natal Sun of the Ram is beneficently aspected to the natal Moon of the Bull (or vice versa) and if their mutual Ascendents are also harmonious, in a triple exchanged aspect, Taurus can help Aries soar to the heights of happiness and serendipity by supporting the Ram's emotional balloon flights of fancy with warm, kindly patience (also by providing a comforting, soft patch of Earth to fall on when the string breaks). And the Ram can lead Taurus to the higher slopes of the imagination, up where the windswept view of the future is as huge and grand as the Bull's own sturdy dreams.

☆ ☆ ☆ ☆ ☆ ☆

ARIES *Woman* TAURUS *Man*

◆━◆▬◆━◆

"Get your things, Peter," she cried, shaking.

"No," he answered. . . . "I am not going with you."

"Yes, Peter."

"No."

A romantic involvement with a Taurus man is sure to be an educational experience for the Aries female. She thinks immovable objects (him) are simply things to kick aside, leap over or melt with the irresistible force of Mars heat (hers). Not this one.

She shoves—he sits. She pushes—he pouts. She demands—he digs in. Then, look out. The next step could be: she weeps—he walks. Away, that is—for keeps. But Bulls and Rams can do other things together. Like, if she smiles—he'll soften. If she coaxes—he'll cuddle. If she bear-hugs—he'll beam. You'll notice it's always she who initiates the first move between them . . . . . of any kind.

They may quarrel about money (her extravagance—his economy), or lock horns over the Aries need for excitement, and the Taurus need for peace and quiet. But with some effort at adjusting to each other's different metabolisms and personal mannerisms, this man and woman can find a rare and very cozy contentment together.

Since she demands, and requires (both), an abnormal amount of freedom, it's a fortunate thing the Bull is not unduly jealous. He's not jealous, but he is very possessive. The difference between these two qualities can be found in the dictionary—or through living with each other. *She's* jealous. *He's* possessive. They should carefully check Webster, and take it from there.

Yes, a Taurus man is stubborn, there's no denying this astrological fact. His sometimes blind, unreasonable bull-headedness can be unpleasantly aroused, if an Aries girl wants him to pick daisies with her when he wants to snooze—if she subjects him to her friends, when he wants to quietly read—(at other times, he'll be happy to entertain them all with his marvelous humor)—or if she insists on spending more than he earns, faster than he doesn't earn it. Yet a well-loved Bull will bear up under a great deal of "sound and fury, signifying nothing" but noise and nonsense, with tranquil aplomb. Normally, he'll take it with an unruffled good nature when she fights with his boss or his relatives, howls with a toothache, loses her engagement ring in the mashed potatoes at a restaurant, and doesn't realize it until after they've left, the place is closed and the garbage truck has already done its ruthless chop-chop thing.

A contented Taurus man will patiently put up with most Aries misguided missiles of enthusiasm unless he's pressed too hard, and too often. Then, he's likely to erupt into the infrequent but ever latent and smoldering Taurean anger. Rams who have never been exposed to the Bull's anger should not press their luck. And that happens to be a most serious astrological warning, in no way intended to be humorous.

If he's handled gently, with a decent amount of consideration for his own feelings, this man will stick by the girl Ram he loves through the darkest storms, like a steady rock of solid love, covering the miseries of her mistakes with a warm, protective blanket of sheer devotion. It's rather like coming home, all safe and secure, from a long journey through a frightening nightmare of rejection, where no one really cares or understands. *He* cares, even if he can't quite understand her temporary emotional traumas. And he'll usually back up his caring with a dependable bank account, and a leakless roof over her head (not to mention a well-stocked refrigerator), to the very best of his steady ability, while he builds slowly and surely for an even more secure, and even luxurious, future.

In the average love affair or marital relationship between the Bull and the Aries woman, she'll provide the ideas and the energy while he provides the stability and security. This applies to both the financial and the sexual aspects of their cooperative venture.

Although Taurus men are as practical about love as they are about everything else, they're also deeply affectionate, quietly romantic and deeply sentimental. The Aries woman who's grown into the mistaken impression that her usually undemonstrative Taurus lover or husband doesn't really love her anymore will never fail to be periodically surprised by receiving an extravagant Valentine, or other card, on some unexpected holiday, which expresses the shy Taurean feelings tenderly and eloquently, in the words of the verse.

Still, there could be some problems concerning the physical sharing of their love, after the first magnetic attraction of Male-Positive and Female-Negative polarity loses its novelty. Sex is, to the Aries woman, a form of release—mental, emotional, physical and spiritual. It's the visible manifestation of the Mars Faith and Strength combined, in a powerful urge of *self*-expression. To her, sexual activity justifies itself as a thrilling fantasy, which could, in some miraculous way, known only to her, make every dream she's ever dreamed come true. Sex is, to the Taurus man, a normal and natural function, for the purpose of achieving two very tangible and sensible results—the satisfaction of sensual and erotic flesh needs—and children. A family.

She's compelled to release the Mars sexual energy, even if it doesn't result in much of anything, except frustration—and imaginative romancing is absolutely essential to her. He doesn't see the sense in releasing *any* kind of energy unless its purpose is to produce something practical and useful—and the typical Taurean does not regard daydreams as either essential or productive. Consequently, the girl Ram may gradually and eventually become impatient with her Bull's desire for frankly sensual and somewhat unimaginative lovemaking—and he may (at a relatively slower rate of speed) become honestly puzzled by the trip to the stars she feels must be synonymous with passion, in private, wistfully wishing he could take her there but sensing they might get lost, because he's uncertain of the route . . . . and after all, there's no map to guide him. A harmonious relationship between their mutual Suns, Moons and Ascendents will miracle away these differences in their natures, and allow the two of them to achieve a rich fulfillment through their sexual union, as well as in every other facet of their togetherness.

However, with a tense aspect between their natal Luminaries and/or Ascendents, it may be difficult for the Aries female to keep the Bull in her pasture, unless she makes a constant and conscious effort to please him, an unselfish urge that does not come naturally to the typical Arian. It takes mountains of hurt and resentment to make a Taurus man leave a woman he's once loved (or permit her to leave his possessive domain), but once he goes, he is *gone*. Permanently. A little tenderness today can prevent a lot of tears tomorrow.

Despite the many arguments these two are almost destined to have in the area of both mutual and individual finances, she'll soon learn a touching truth about her Taurus man's attitude toward money, which is so vastly different from her own (assuming they're both typical of their Sun Signs, and their birth charts don't confuse matters with a variety of planetary positions that create the exceptions that prove the astrological rules). In the beginning, she'll think he's an outright tightwad, and he'll think she's as improvident and careless with cash as they make females (he believes they're all made, more or less, in a similar extravagant mold). Gradually, however, his great Bull's heart will be moved, when he slowly comprehends that her carelessness with cash is nearly always motivated by impulsive generosity. He'll see that, although she spends a good deal of money on herself (Aries represents the *first* astrological house; therefore, all Rams are exceptionally concerned with their physical appearance), she spends even more through her gestures of giving, much in the sense that a child gives, with a feeling of sheer delight in pleasing others and receiving the reward of their happy smiles. He'll probably relax his attitude somewhat then, regarding his initial disapproval of her wild and carefree spending. In fact, after their relationship has had time to solidify into a permanent pattern, her spontaneous generosity may even cause him to love her more.

At the same time he's learning to adapt to her financial looseness, even affectionately, she will be discovering that he's not such a miser as she first thought him to be. She'll realize that his caution stems from his uncontrollable need to be sure of tomorrow's security, his deep-seated fear of being suddenly thrown out into the street and forced to rely upon the charity of others or the government, which would kill his proud spirit of self-sufficiency. And she'll see that, once her stubborn, but kind-hearted, steadfast and loyal Bull knows their future is reasonably insured (not excessively, as is the case with the typical Crab or Goat), he's genuinely generous. Barring an afflicted Moon or Ascendent in Earth or Water elements, he'll be as tickled as she to give gifts to their friends and families, and lend money to those who need it, without pressing them for repayment—as long as his basic nest egg for tomorrow is left untouched, the amount of which, of course, varies with each individual Bull. But the typical Taurus male won't take huge chances with his security. If his Aries woman tries to convince him that they should move into a better apartment or house, and trust a promise someone made to them regarding future paychecks, commissions or bonuses, to make up the difference in rent or mortgage payments, she's engaged in a futile endeavor. The Bull won't move an inch until he's *sure* he can handle the extra burden. To Taurus there's never been a promise since the world began that's been made of anything but talk and thin air—both materials he's found to be totally unreliable for the purpose of building anything concrete and lasting. Yet, when push comes to shove (an excellent descriptive phrase to use with Taurus) this man will share half of whatever he has with anyone whose real need he's been made aware of, most especially his family, friends . . . . and the woman he loves.

There may be times when the Bull's stubbornness seems like the coldest kind of cruelty to an Aries girl. For example, he may say something unkind to her in public, when she's been frisking too much for his taste and acting up in general, and it will cut her to the quick. She'll try to force him to apologize, openly or at least to admit he didn't mean it (which he didn't, and she *knows* it), while he sullenly refuses to grant her the verbal solace and reassurance she's seeking (or, rather, demanding). As she continues first to command, then finally to plead with him to retract his statement, he'll grow even more silent and removed, like a chunk of marble, unseeing, unhearing, unfeeling—apparently.

Then she'll impulsively run out, angrily weeping, into the night. He's the coldest, cruelest man she's ever known, and it's all over between them. He can't do that to her. A few blocks down the street (maybe twenty or more, depending on the extent of the adrenalin she was generating when she stormed out of the place where she left him)—she sees a coffee shop, and wanders inside, to sit by herself, crying all over her donuts, and fiercely hating him . . . . . until their favorite song hits her ears, from the ceiling speakers, reminding her of what she's lost by walking out on him. So, she pays her check, leaves hastily and ends up standing on a street corner, forlorn and alone, trying to hail a taxi to take her home—sorry, at last—and now really frightened. It's late, there are no taxis anywhere, and she has to walk home, giving her time to think over a lot of things as she hurries down streets that seem unusually quiet and deserted.

But . . . who is that there in the shadows, leaning calmly against the building across the way, waiting patiently for her? It's him. He's still there. She feels a surge of happiness as she runs across the street into his safe arms. He didn't go away and leave her after all. It's all right again. No, he didn't go away—this time. He'll probably still be there, patiently waiting for her after the next fiery, emotional, farewell scene too. But, someday . . . .

If she's wise, she'll count her blessings before it's too late.

ARIES *Man* TAURUS *Woman*

—◆●◆—

*". . . unless this tie is round my neck we don't go out
to dinner to-night, and if I don't go out to dinner
to-night, I never go to the office again, and if I
don't go to the office again, you and I starve . . ."*

*Even then Mrs. Darling was placid. "Let me try, dear,"
she said . . . . . and with her nice cool hands she tied
the tie for him.*

In an Aries-Taurus romance or marriage, when the woman is the Taurus
and the man is the Aries, the relationship has a slight edge for success over
its chances when the sexes are reversed. That's not a guarantee either way,
of course, it's just what I said—a slight edge. The qualities of passivity,
steadfastness, and quiescent receptivity (Taurus) are more natural when
exercised through the female. The qualities of aggression, independence
and forceful action (Aries) are more natural when exercised through the
male—never mind Women's Liberation, which is right and good and
timely and necessary, and all that, but the passage of ERA is never going to
forcefully (or any other way) alter Mother Nature's basic tenets. At the
very least, the conflicts may be somewhat fewer in number, when she's the
Taurean and he's the Ram, in this 2-12 vibration. Still, it's the *intensity*
of the conflicts, not the *quantity* of them, that damages any relationship,
so these two ought not to become heady with optimism. It depends.
Mostly on the Moon and Ascendent positions of each of them.

A Taurus woman, unless the fourth house of her horoscope is severely
afflicted, is a born homemaker. (Thank goodness *somebody* enjoys it!)
Even if she has adverse aspects in her birth chart which tend to tempt her
into spending a few years as a playgirl type (a most rare occurrence), her
basic desire, nevertheless, is to create a comfortable home, filled with fine
furnishings, good food, babies and music—with the beds all nicely made,
the corners clean, the laundry folded and put away and all the bills paid.
Throw in a flower garden in the back yard, and an extra powder room,
well stocked with bubble bath. She's not unreasonably jealous, without
good cause; she's patient and she seldom nags. She's normally a warm, gracious hostess for her husband's business friends—and a pretty good listener.

Now, since an Aries male requires a constant and dependable sounding board while he discusses his favorite topic—himself—since he frequently brings people home to sell them a new project or idea he's dreamed up—and since he's a little careless with the budget, because he never learned to spell the word "thrift" in grammar school—you can see how a Taurus woman can provide him with a perfect base of operations. Normally, Aries men like sports, and the typical Taurus female loves nature. So if the sport he happens to favor is camping out, or hiking in the woods, add another plus on the potential success side of their relationship, otherwise, there might be some Saturday-afternoon-football tension.

The trouble starts in areas they may never anticipate during the mating season. She may prefer living in the country or the suburbs, and most Aries men can't exist for long, without the excitement and action of the city. There may be some who can, but they're few and far between, and even they like to flash around in the bright lights on weekends. Camping and hiking aside, he's not a farm boy at heart. If he has a Taurus Moon Sign or Ascendent, he may plant a few potatoes or milk a few cows, but essentially, for him, the pull of the sod will never replace grabbing a taxi to catch a miracle.

Sparks may also fly in the area of mutual funds, because their attitude toward money is not necessarily mutual. He wants a new car; she wants a new freezer. Things like that. His favorite man at the bank is the one in the Loan Department. Her favorite man at the bank is the one in the Savings Department. You know how bankers like to push their own thing, so these two outsiders don't help matters any by pulling the Bull and the Ram apart. However, when he spends money on jewelry for her, or on furniture for the house, she may be more loose about it. Taurus females usually appreciate fine jewels and luxurious decor in the home, but they'll expect these things to be practical, made to last for a few hundred years before they need to be replaced.

Despite her general tranquility, she may lose her cool if he burns holes in her new couch or spills grape juice on her carpet (before marriage, you can substitute her new skirt or her carefully clutched pocketbook for the couch and carpet). It's hard for him to figure why she gets so upset over such small incidents. To Aries, crying over spilled milk (or grape juice) is a huge waste of time. If something is lost, broken or damaged, there's always more where it came from. Taurus has a few doubts about that.

Fortunately, most of their disagreements can be smoothed over by reconciliations at bedtime since the physical relationship between them can be snugly satisfying. The Aries male is certainly not unhappy about the Taurus woman's capacity for sensual, erotic feeling, but he may be somewhat frustrated by her lack of mystical creativity when it comes to making love. She welcomes sex as a practical and enjoyable activity that brings a total gratification of the senses and the added bonus of producing some bouncing bambinos. She may, therefore, fail to comprehend why sex should be like a wild dream that transports two souls to the top of a mountain in Tibet, like a comet streaking across the night sky—or a miracle connected with throwing three coins into the Fountain of Trevi, in Rome. To her, sex is sex. Love is love. What does any of it have to do with tossing a few Lincolns into some dirty, green water—or with comets, for that matter? This woman has a funny bone about sex, since Taurus humor isn't restricted to any one facet of Life. It's broad. If the Aries man should happen to step on a tack as he's running passionately toward the bed on their honeymoon, she'll crack up laughing. His reaction? It may postpone the honeymoon a few days—or nights—until his Martian male ego has recovered.

Still, although she may remain mystified by his romantic idealism during their entire association together, it needn't necessarily cause complete sexual incompatibility. There are deep emotional wells in her, and it's possible that her ultra-feminine response to the Ram's strong, direct love urges, plus her obvious pleasure with his masculine charisma, may eventually make him wonder why he thought he had to go climbing mountains in search of happiness anyway. It's possible. Not certain, but possible. (Aries is reluctant to accept substitutes for miracles.)

A word of warning: Just because the Taurus girl doesn't pick up every nuance of the Aries sexuality, this should not be interpreted to mean that she's not sentimental or romantic. She is. Oh, she most certainly is! If she's ignored on February 14th, or if he forgets to remember the day they first met (first made love together, first decided to get married, got married or whatever, in whichever order), the inconsiderate, thoughtless Ram who neglected to honor these historic occasions will never hear the end of it. This woman has a memory like an elephant for personal injury and emotional hurt.

Some of the astrological descriptions of the Taurus female make her seem like a contented cow in a pasture, and that's pretty insulting. So what if she isn't overtly flashy, the center of attention at every gathering? Her quiet beauty is like a still pool, filled with fragrant lilies, deep in a piney forest. Taurus magnetism pulls powerfully on a man's heartstrings, because it promises such peace and rich adventure, especially on a Ram's restless heartstrings. The Aries male soon discovers that this feminine creature, who is so calm and composed (the way he'd secretly like to be himself), can fill his spirit with fresh flowers, fill his house with the music of love and companionship, besides being an uncommonly good cook. In addition, she can fill his heart with lots of laughs, and a loyal devotion that can outlast forever. She also knows how to accumulate and save money. No cow could pull off all that. This girl can well afford to leave the false lashes (which look like spiders' legs) to the less-female types than she. She's all warm woman, and she doesn't need the masquerade of artificial glamour to prove it.

What she may need to do, however, is to climb out of her earthy rut, now and then. A lady Taurean can seem pretty cold and heartless to the friendly, direct and open-hearted Aries man when she's made up her mind about something, and slammed the door in the face of any further discussion. If he shouts at her that she's stubborn at such times, it will do about as much good as when she tells him, firmly, that he's selfish and spoiled. In a word—none.

Who, *her*—stubborn? Who, *him*—selfish and spoiled? It wouldn't be wise for either of them to hold his or her breath until the other admits such character deficiencies.

Lots of affection, plenty of ambition, honesty and the guarantee of financial security are the four ways to her heart. An Aries man can supply the first three with no difficulty, but he may have to make some adjustments in his general life-style to meet her expectations of the last item. Aries incomes do tend to often fluctuate, and that can make this lady very nervous.

Normally, of course, she's not nervous—only when her emotional or financial security is threatened. At most other times, she exudes a placid mystique that can be deliciously relaxing, in particular, to a Ram. It can also be a substantial aid in recharging the batteries of this man's dynamic Mars energies when he's run down from his various mental, emotional or physical excesses. (An Aries man will jog till he drops.) Admittedly, when she goes into one of her very rare rages, her placid mystique can change into anger of volcanic proportions, without much of a warning. But it happens so seldom, it's one of the least likely causes for trouble in their relationship—unless the Ram is foolish enough to insist on trying to win these infrequent, but dangerous, encounters. It will never happen. Retreat is the expedient strategy. Go fight an earthquake.

☆ ☆ ☆ ☆ ☆ ☆

ARIES

Fire — Cardinal — Positive
Ruled by Mars
Symbol: The Ram
Day Forces — Masculine

GEMINI

Air — Mutable — Positive
Ruled by Mercury
Symbol: The Twins
Day Forces — Positive

The ARIES-GEMINI *Relationship*

It was not really Saturday night, at least it may
have been, for they had long lost count of the days;
but always if they wanted to do anything special
they said this was Saturday night, and then they did it.

Working as a team, this combination of Sun Signs could sell Manhattan back to the Indians—blackouts, muggers, creaky subways, uncollected garbage, and all. Of course, both of them being idealists, they would probably realize what a rotten deal the Indians got in the beginning, and end up giving them back New York for a few strands of love beads and a peace button, along with all the other rights the white man stole from his red brother—if they could swing it.

Because both Aries and Gemini love causes, and share the same talent for creative, persistent salesmanship, they can perform fantastic feats of ingenuity together. They also share a casual attitude toward accumulating great power or money, which may be why they are seldom as successful as they should be, considering all the emotional (Aries) and mental (Gemini) energy they pour into anything that interests them—for the moment, that is. Nothing holds the interest of either of these Sun Signs for longer than a moment. Well, sometimes maybe two or three moments.

Since Aries bubbles with naive impetuosity, and Gemini is determined to attain complete independence by breaking every bond of the spirit, maturity of thought seldom supports their mutual endeavors.

One might say that the combined qualities of this 3-11 Sun Sign Pattern association present a picture of optimism, punctuated with brief splashes (usually, very brief) of sensitivity and hidden insecurities. When Aries and Gemini blend their natures as neighbors, friends, business associates, relatives, lovers or mates, it doubles up their individual drives for freedom against all who would confine them in a morass of convention and caution. Separately or together, they look young, act young—and therefore, quite naturally, often behave like children.

Now, children can be endearing, guileless and lovable. They can also be unintentionally selfish, irrational and thoughtless. So it is with any association between this 3-11 influenced team. Preferably both of them, but at least one of the two, must eventually grow up, or most of their time together will be spent playing around in a sand pile, with a couple of brightly painted buckets, and large shovels for the you-know-what they're both so good at handing each other and the rest of the world.

Basically, both Aries and Gemini are honest—the Rams especially so—but these two can fool themselves until they forget where honesty ends and self-deception begins. It's their innocence, or ignorance, whichever, of their own individual natures. In other words, they're both as expert at selling themselves as they are at selling the general public. If the product being sold isn't genuine, the Gemini will usually be the first of the two of them to suspect it, with Mercury's sharp, analytical mind, although Gemini is capable of outsmarting himself (or herself), by continuing to *imagine* it still may be what he-she originally believed it was. As for Aries, it's extremely difficult for this Sun Sign to tell the difference between what glitters so enticingly—and real gold. Such discrimination is learned by the Ram only after repeated, heartbreaking disillusion and disappointment.

I've been referring to the "two of them." Actually, perhaps I should say the "three of them," because, although Aries is clearly one person, indivisible, "with liberty and justice for all," every Gemini is distinctly two people, the person he-she really is . . . . . and the person she-he would like to be. The Twins, you know. Add the Mars ego of the Ram—almost a separate entity in itself—and it can get pretty crowded, with all those auras mixing, attracting and repelling, blending and clashing, by turns. It's not a bad idea for these two Sun Sign people, essentially compatible as they are, to stand apart at intervals and take a fresh look at each other from a distance. It clears away some of the smog that's bound to accumulate between them.

Aries pushes ahead instinctively, convinced of the sincerity of cause, as well as the eventual victory, with little or no time out to reflect on the pros and cons of any given situation or problem. Conversely, Gemini weighs, sorts and figures out all possible maneuvers and conclusions with the cool, casual detachment and logic so typical of all three Air Signs (Aquarius and Libra being the other two). Yet for all Gemini's mental gymnastics, practicality may be missing. Gemini can quickly deduce what might go wrong but often decides to outwit destiny or fate, and even himself (or herself) by clever Mercurial strategy. There are other differences of approach between these two.

Aries, influenced by a Cardinal Sign, will insist on being at the *head* of things, leading, challenging, always initiating and inspiring, with enthusiasm and daring. The Ram will accept just about any idea, sound or unsound, that appeals to and arouses the emotions—to which the ego can relate in a personal way. Mutable Gemini prefers to relate in an *im*personal manner, and will accept ideas that appeal to the mental deductive process, communicating through the logic and cleverness of Mercury reason, while the true self remains in the background, watching—unsuspected by those who are being hypnotized with the Gemini charm.

Aries enjoys riding the lead elephant and waving to the crowd, but the Twins have no burning desire to be the glory-spangled hero or heroine. Gemini would rather delegate all the confining duties and obligations of leadership to others, remaining free of responsibility, free to try on new ideas for size . . . . . to explore new people, places and things. The Geminian analysis is less intense than that of Aries, since everything is calmly checked through the computer of the mind for possible flaws—or potential. Although the Gemini approach is essentially mental, the Twins sympathize with the Ram's emotional approach, even while remaining detached from such overinvolvement himself (or herself). Mercury-ruled men and women understand the Mars reckless impulses. Nevertheless, they realize that their own best course is to avoid becoming emotionally entangled, whenever possible.

Close human associations that threaten to smother, long-term employment without either change or challenge—anything that nails down their dreams or clips Mercury's wings, Geminis distrust, for fear their very spirits will be confined. The Air Sign of Gemini strives to soar above the flames that rage around the Fire Sign of Aries. By remaining aloof and slightly out of reach, Gemini more often manages to achieve the kind of freedom Aries also seeks but doesn't always find. Of course, too much mental and emotional freedom can create its own confusions, and when the Twins get caught in the webs of their own mental convolutions, the very directness of the Ram can sometimes help to untangle the knots.

Fortunately, the typical Aries person not only senses the duality of Gemini but is usually willing to give it room to *be*. That's why this association is frequently beneficial to the Geminian, because understanding—or the lack of understanding—concerning his (or her) dreams has a great deal to do with whether they come true, simply grow rusty, or become only will-o'-the-wisps. Gemini eternally chases but never catches. A Gemini will dream from the time he-she is a tiny tot, until past the century mark. To most people, Mercury's curiosity and experimental urges seem like a patchwork of erratic, changing attention spans, but the Ram seems to recognize that all these myriad interests are only Gemini's attempt to integrate the many-sided, fascinating-to-Aries, Mercurial personality.

An Aries person is less likely to resent the Gemini's flitting from subject to subject, in the search for all the answers, while shooting forth a continual flow of imagination and static energy. Interrupting a Mercury Bird when he-she is verbally expressing is like trying to catch a firefly, and oddly, the Rams (who are rather experts at interrupting themselves) comprehend this. These two continually interrupt each other, with a mutual lack of resentment, a most jolly thing about their association.

If there's a negative aspect between the Sun and Moon or Ascendent in their birth charts, Aries may accuse Gemini of too much woolgathering and not enough concrete action, and will try to box Gemini into direct answers. Then the satirical tongue of Gemini may wound the Ram's easily bruised ego, and there will be a fiery battle, with sparks flying everywhere, as Gemini's airy attitude fans the flames of Mars anger. Still, the winds will change, after a while, even after the stormiest scenes . . . . . and bitterness is seldom allowed by either of them to linger. As with all 3-11 vibrational patterns, Aries and Gemini are basically good friends, and most always remain that way, in addition to being able to verbally communicate their differences of opinion to such an extent that they clear the air for a resumption of harmony.

The Mercurial mind of Gemini, no matter how cleverly it's occasionally disguised behind a mask of calm and charm, resembles a top. Always spinning. Aries will happily jump on for the ride, and probably enjoy the dizzy pace. As long as the Ram doesn't try to chain Gemini's free spirit with too many questions and demands, it will work out rather smoothly beween these two. (These four, counting the Ram, the Twins, and the

Mars ego.) Aries and Gemini can build sand castles from the colorful ethers of their combined thought images tall enough to reach all the way to the stars. But the foundation must be sound and stable, or they'll topple to the ground. If they build strongly in the beginning, the end could be really out of sight—all rainbows, butterflies and leprechauns. Patience is the secret key to the other side of the fence, where the grass always looks greener and fresher to both Aries and Gemini, the eternal young ones, who search for Shangri-la, the Emerald City of Oz, Wonderland and the Fountain of Youth. Together, they have a better chance of finding all these places than most people . . . or than they would have if they each searched alone.

☆ ☆ ☆ ☆ ☆ ☆

ARIES *Woman* GEMINI *Man*

"You won't forget me . . . will you, before springtime comes?"

Of course Peter promised; and then he flew away.

There are Aries women and Gemini men who hold hands lightly and skip down the street together like children. There are other Aries women and Gemini men who have sarcastic, furious verbal donnybrooks from the time they awake until they go to bed—and they both talk in their sleep too. Often, the emotional blending of Mars and Mercury in a love experience produces a strange alchemy of haunting tenderness, punctuated by sharp hurt, making the relationship capable of both triumph and disaster. It may be because Gemini, unlike the other two Air Signs, verbalizes both his admiration and his contempt so clearly and unmistakably. Or perhaps it's because Aries, unlike the other two Fire Signs, is consumed by the passion of the moment, whether it's love or hate, never thinking about tomorrow's possible regrets.

This 3-11 Sun Sign Pattern is quite distinctive in its influence over two people linked together through its friendly, and very communicative, vibrations. There's no doubt they'll quarrel occasionally, even frequently; yet their more tempestuous arguments will contain the seed of spring, and fresh promises for the future. Their misunderstandings are extremely verbal, and often quite loud, but somehow, not too serious. It's almost as though they're both aware of the potential of a truce in the midst of the battle.

These two might accurately say of themselves . . . . . .

> some people love with restraint
> as if they were someday to hate
> but we hated gently, carefully
> as if we were someday to love . . .*

There's very little restraint in the love between Aries and Gemini. When the Ram and the Twins fall in love with each other, neither will waste time wondering if the end of the affair, or the marriage, will be blissfully happy or achingly sad. The initial attraction between them, the magnetic pull of their carefree natures, causes both of them to reach out toward each other trustingly, with no worry about a far-off ending. If it should eventually occur, in whatever form—separation, divorce or death— the memories of love as naive, exciting and as full of blind faith as a child's heart on Christmas Eve, will soften the edges of the recollection of any sorrow or hurt they've mutually suffered. That's the beauty of the 3-11 vibration, in which genuine friendship forms the foundation for the empathy, from the very first hello.

Jealousy can be a large troublemaker. The typical Aries girl is as jealous as it's possible for a woman to be, without turning solid green, and she's seldom able to recognize it rationally. It doesn't stem from a possessive nature but from the Arian symbolic Infant's terrible fear of rejection (which would mean literal death to an infant) and need for constant reassurance that it (she) is cherished. The undue Aries concern over losing love to another is more understandable when it's viewed in the light of these subconscious feelings of infantile helplessness and total dependency upon continued and uninterrupted affection. It's a feeling that's always present, just beneath the bright Mars bravado of independence and self-sufficiency . . . . . which is not real in any sense, only make believe . . . . a kind of protection against further vulnerability.

* *Venus Trines at Midnight* by Linda Goodman (New York: Taplinger Publishing Company, Inc., 1970. To be re-published by Harper & Row, 1979).

The typical Gemini man is *not* excessively jealous (barring some Venus-Mars affliction in his birth chart, or an Aries Moon or Ascendent). And this is where most of the difficulties may lie. Because, you see, she secretly would like him to be. The least he can do is pretend he is. Whether she consciously realizes it or not, the girl Ram rather enjoys arousing the jealous instinct in her man. It reaffirms her importance to him, a matter that can't be reaffirmed too often for any Aries. The Gemini male may oblige her, by granting her wish, if she steps out of line too obviously. But most of the time he'll be too busy changing his clothes, his moods, his ideas, his dreams and his disposition to pause long enough to stop, look and listen to any innocent flirtations she's flaunting at him in the hope of warming up his cool, detached and airy approach to life—and to her.

Conversely, he won't have to flaunt any flirtations in front of her to bring on a bright green explosion. Saying good morning too intimately to Apple Annie at the corner newspaper stand will suffice. Considering his love of freedom and his phobia concerning emotional shackles that curb his natural gregarious activities, a little of that will go a long way with a Gemini man. Although she must learn to somehow either control or hide her jealous fears (if she doesn't want to lose him), he must also learn to sympathize with her motivation for such behavior—an inner fear that she lacks enough femininity to keep him faithful (if he doesn't want to lose *her*). There has been so much propaganda over the years about the slinky, sexually seductive, feather-brained, soft and sweet type of bunny-kitten "every man yearns for," you can't blame the Aries woman for developing a neurosis about her quick mind, her direct approach to love and her lack of sneaky female guile—especially since she was born under the influence of a masculine Sun Sign.

She has courage and initiative, she's energetic and ambitious—all allegedly masculine traits. Men believe they have the market cornered on those qualities. Haven't you been reading the Women's Liberation pamphlets? (The Aries woman may very well be the leader of the ERA group in her community.) What's a girl Ram supposed to do to be considered feminine—read Marabel What's-Her-Name's book, *The Total Woman*, and total herself by just sitting around murmuring "You're wonderful, darling," and never do anything on her own? That's just about the size of it, according to Marabel and all the male chauvinists. Skimpy, isn't it?

Oh, I suppose she could do other things to retain her femininity, like wash, iron, cook, diaper babies, shop for clothes, gossip, iron, wash, cook, have babies—am I repeating myself? Sorry, I was beginning to get bored. As an Aries myself, I've never understood why a girl must be labeled "pushy" just because she knows her own mind. If most men prefer a Stepford Wives type robot to a real woman, that's their hang-up. Aries females, along with their Sagittarius and Leo sisters, sometimes rival the "male chauvinist pigs" by being rather blatant "female chauvinist sows" themselves. Such feminine gender animals do exist.

Now, why did I write that? I've given the quick-witted Gemini men a new verbal weapon. My apologies to Ms. Steinem, whom I greatly admire, but it is true, Gloria, and you know it. Please don't be offended, because I'm one too. That is, I believe anything they can do, we can do equally— and some things better. No need to list the latter. We all know what they are. Oh, you don't? Well, for heaven's sake—patiently and tenderly providing a gentle garden for babes to grow in for nine months, being able to bear pain at a higher threshold than men, possessing the common sense and esoteric logic to know that war never solved anything, and being able to sense danger and evil, long before they appear, are just a few of our superiorities over the masculine essence. We're also more sensitive, intuitive and psychic, certainly more compassionate—yet far more realistic than men. But not quite as sentimental. (You didn't know that men are secretly sentimental? So much so that they've taught women to see the poetry and beauty in Life too.) It's all right for the female chauvinist sows to be aware of their own areas of both equality and superiority regarding the masculine sex, but they should also recognize the areas of a man's equality and superiority regarding womanhood. That's what makes true femininity and true masculinity.

With her innocent faith in miracles, it's destined that the Aries woman someday discover a man who's looking for a real woman, and he could be a Gemini. This man may have two heads, and twin desires, but he also possesses a driving need to be able to play mental chess with the woman he loves. Not for Gemini the serene siren who gazes up to him in silent, palpitating passion, because it's easier than trying to match wits with him. He definitely falls in love with his mind first. His heart follows after, then his physical desire. Romance usually proceeds in just about that priority order with the Twins. As for the Aries woman, the order is only slightly changed. She falls in love first with her heart, her mind follows quickly after—and, finally, her physical desire. The initial patterns are switched, but that's not as important as the fact that they both end up on the same frequency, in its proper place—last, after mental and emotional affinity has been established. It's an amazingly successful formula.

Because he'll appreciate the constant mental challenge of the Aries girl (Aries rules the head, Gemini the mind, among other things), she'll eventually learn to trust him to love her for what she is. Then she may show him what she's allowed no other male to discover—that she can be genuinely sweet and tender, with a man who proves he's her superior in some ways, while making it clear at the same time that he also admires her for her own qualities, which are equal to his, some being likewise superior. It's a complicated juggling act, but a Gemini man can pull it off, if anyone can. His natural charm and glibness (some people call it blarney) can keep her Mars vanity and ego appeased—and he can certainly handle any kind of verbal debate she cares to start. She may start quite a few.

She may have difficulty in adjusting to his typical Gemini habit of lateness. She's often a little lax in that area herself, but Rams have a rather selfish way of being outraged when they're forced to swallow their own medicine.

A Gemini man was once three hours late for an appointment with me. Anticipating his excuses (one of the benefits of being an astrologer) I wrote a little verse about him while I was waiting.

> I'm sorry I kept you waiting
> look, don't cry . . . it was only an hour or two
> couldn't you find something to do?
> I would have, if I had been you.*

When he finally arrived, he read it, and exclaimed, "Oh, wow! How did you know exactly what I was going to say?" The Aries girl who's in love with this two-headed, twin wonder of dual desires and actions should carefully study the difference between the word "gregarious" and the word "unfaithful," and note that there *is* a difference. She should also study the meaning of the two words "freedom" and "love," and comprehend that, to a Gemini, these two words are synonyms. It will help to cut down on the arguments.

As for their physical compatibility, he's one of the few men who's capable of creating the illusionary quality this woman must associate with sex. She idealizes the sexual expression of love into a colorful, layered fabric, woven from every book she's ever read, every movie she's ever cried over and every shining hope she's ever held deep inside her heart. She's convinced that bells should literally ring at the moment the two of them become one. With him, she may actually hear them, because his imagination can supply all the fantasies she needs to fulfill her romantic Cinderella dreams.

This sort of empathy is what causes them to initially fall in love, sometimes at first sight (neither Sun Sign is noted for slow action). But later, it may take more than fantasies to keep her love burning brightly, when his Gemini detachment fails to satisfy her *total* concept of sexual expression, which is *not* purely imaginary. She also needs the tangible. She may begin

* From *Venus Trines at Midnight,* by Linda Goodman.

to feel there's always a tiny part of himself he holds back, even during their intimacy, and she could be right. She holds nothing back, with the Aries instinct to give completely of herself. The Mars inclination toward direct action is seldom diluted in the giving of passion—or in the exchange of it. He may fail to arouse in her such natural (for Rams) physical impulses, with his airy approach to lovemaking. Then she might feel that faerie stories are empty, when there's no fire to set them ablaze, and become bored—or, much worse, frigid.

It's a delicate area of adjustment, and the relationship will have a better chance for success if the Moon and/or Ascendent of his birth chart is in a Fire Sign. Otherwise, he may not be able to teach her what she's so enormously capable of learning, after her initial inhibitions have been overcome by his idealistic preliminaries. The Gemini Prince can kiss the Aries Princess awake, but she may fall back asleep again if total passion is lacking, without ever really knowing why. Then Aries Fire can turn into Aries Ice, which is a sad waste, considering the warmth she can so generously give when the complete potential of her fiery nature is encouraged to develop.

During one of their games of mental chess, when he's behaving in an impossible manner, she might try saying: "I realize that you believe you understood what I just said, but I'm not sure you caught what it was I didn't intend to imply, for fear you might misunderstand what I believed you thought." If it confuses him, she can say: "Good. Now you know what it's like to talk to yourself—or rather, to yourselves. Both of you."

She might also leave this book around near him, open to this chapter, to remind him of how dull his life would be now if she hadn't streaked across his heart. But she should curb her impulse to hand him the book directly, and order him to read it immediately. Cinderella would never do that.

ARIES *Man* GEMINI *Woman*

--------◄◄◆►►--------

*He came back, and there was a greedy look in his
eyes now which ought to have alarmed her, but
did not.*

Unless they met in high school, and were married shortly thereafter (which does happen rather frequently with these two Sun Signs, since they're both always in such a hurry), an Aries man may fiercely resent his Gemini girl's past love life, which could have been, by normal standards, somewhat extensive. It's almost sure to include, if not a couple of ex-husbands, at the very least, half a dozen broken engagements or a few flickering old flames. All Geminis should be wary of early marriage, unless they were born when the Moon or Ascendent was in Capricorn, Virgo, Cancer or Taurus.

It's not that she's fickle or promiscuous, but this girl may run through a long list of pitchers while she's playing the field, before she finds one who can bat her average. Yes, I know that batters don't pitch, and pitchers don't bat, ordinarily—but any man who can't do at least two things equally well, preferably more, and also preferably both at once, is likely to strike out with her.

Of course, we know that could never happen to an Aries man, since he can do everything and anything better than anyone else, at any time, so I suppose it's just an academic discussion, but it wouldn't hurt for him to remember it anyway.

All her life this woman has thought it was the house at the top of the hill that had golden windows. She keeps climbing all the way up there, only to look below, from the summit, and discover the house at the bottom of the hill is the one with golden windows, after all. So she slides back down, and re-discovers that the house at the bottom has only ordinary windows, as she first had thought, then looks up to see the golden windows shining once more at the top of the hill, decides she's been wrong, and trudges back up the hill again to another disappointment. Why are those golden windows so elusive? It can be spiritually exhausting, all that climbing up, and sliding back down, and climbing back up, until she learns that the reflection of the Sun is only an illusion—not real at all—and relative, depending upon the time of day and one's location at any given moment.

There may be times when a Gemini girl thinks an old love was really the one with golden possibilities, but before she finds out that this, too, is an illusion, she will have lost the Aries man, whether she left him standing alone at the top or at the bottom of the hill. A Ram will never sympathize with his woman's nostalgia over yesterday's romances, even though he may go out under a toadstool, and light a candle to an old flame every spring, on Groundhog Day, himself. Remember the Aries self-centeredness. He can do it. She can't. Why? Because he knows *his* nostalgia is innocent and will never lead anywhere. He's not so sure about *hers*. (Aries hidden insecurity.)

Their relationship may have a few other pitfalls along with its undeniable delights—like a possible lack of will power and stability. Rams possess simply oodles of drive and energy, but sticking to things they start is not one of their strong points. Since a man subconsciously depends on his woman to supply what he lacks, he may be leaning on a feather in the breeze when he leans on a Gemini girl. Will power and dependability are not her major talents either (unless her Moon or Ascendent, as just mentioned, happens to be in Cancer, or in an Earth Sign—and naturally, the same is true of him). Consequently, these two (these three or four) can send up a lot of flares that keep sputtering out, as each one indulges the other's weaknesses of procrastination and quick boredom.

This is one man who probably won't insist that his Gemini woman stay home to sweep the hearth, wearing a calico apron and watering the vegetable garden. He'll probably realize he can use her versatile viewpoints and original thinking in his business life or career, so it's common to find this couple working together, after marriage, as well as before. They usually make a crackerjack team. He knows exactly what he wants—and she has plenty of ideas about how to help him get it. Besides, he can watch her more closely if she's with him all day. It eliminates his worry about the milk man, the cleaner, the grocer, and the handsome chap who runs the elevator in their apartment building. Her Mercurial proclivity for harmless (usually) flirting adds plenty of fuel to the fires of Aries jealousy, and anything that might keep such Mars sparks under control is desirable. A survey to determine how many Aries men eventually suggest that their wives work as their secretaries, or full partners, might prove astrologically interesting. On the other hand, these lovers often meet on the job. The same kinds of occupation and career interest them both, so it's only natural that they may bump into each other in some creative field or profession that offers excitement and challenge.

You'll never see an Aries man and a Gemini woman, however long they've been married, sitting at a restaurant table reading the paper, or staring at the other customers, in silence, ignoring each other, the way so many couples unfortunately do after the first flush of romance has become a little softer. Aries and Gemini will always have something to say to each other—sometimes too much. Conversation, in any case, is not likely to lag between them. Most of the time, their verbal communication will consist of stimulating and scintillating exchanges, but when she touches a raw nerve in his sensitive Mars ego with her talent for hitting the satirical mark, it could turn into a verbal contest that could leave some pretty deep wounds. Happily however, these two are inclined to forgive and forget injuries as quickly as they tend to inflict them.

Strangely, this love relationship is sometimes harder on others than it is on the man and woman themselves. The more sincerely and deeply they're in love, the more likely it is that their friends, neighbors or relatives, at some time, however rarely, will suffer from this Air-Fanning-Fire romance. Now and then, a Gemini woman will imagine all sorts of things about people that are, quite simply, untrue. She'll convince herself that a particular dialogue took place with another person, and report it to her Aries lover or husband, in words that haven't the slightest connection with reality, or with the words that were actually spoken. (Her Mercury imagination, you see, fills in the dull or uninteresting gaps with more creative phraseology.)

Loving her as intensely as only a Ram can love, he could take furious offense at these slightly exaggerated insults to his lady fair, and direct his Mars anger, full force, toward the shocked person he's been falsely led to believe has treated her so shabbily. (Aries men are fiercely loyal to their friends and relatives, and especially to their mates.)

Later, her honest Twin will trouble her conscience by softly, yet insistently, reminding her that things didn't quite occur as she colorfully described them to her Ram. If she then levels with him, he should control his Mars fireworks of outrage, and appreciate her attempt to separate reality from imagination, with tenderness. For the Gemini woman is made of fragile material. She's not, like him, protected on her journey through Life by the fierce warrior Mars—only by the unpredictable magician Mercury, who often hides from her, just when a girl most needs her ruling planet's wisdom.

Her heart contains so many different chords of haunting music. She's a symphony of memories, made of loveliness and light, ugliness and shadow, making the more direct Aries man who loves her sometimes wonder,

"Who is she—this intimate and familiar stranger? Who is she . . . and what is she?"

Who is she . . . ? Whichever Twin leads the way, at any given moment. What is she? She's the bunch of marigolds in a sky blue bowl, on her teacher's desk, in the third grade . . . . . the circus parade she once watched, when the clown threw a pretzel to her, and she caught it joyfully . . . . . she's hayrides and hurricanes . . . . . her first pair of black patent leather Mary Janes, a summer storm in the woods, at scout camp, that made the pine trees smell as fragrant as hyacinths . . . . . a field of purple heather she sat in once, for hours, that transported her all the way to Scotland, where she was the Lady of the Lake . . . . . and also the lonely Evangeline . . . . . the small, lost bird she fed, until it was strong enough to fly, when she was five. These things are what she is. All this.

And so, while the Gemini girl-woman must exercise a certain amount of discipline over her imagination, if she expects to achieve harmony with the straightforward, honest Ram she loves, she must be careful not to restrict it entirely, because it's the quality that makes her seem so exquisitely feminine to him. Children, too, possess vivid imaginations, and he thinks of her, this man, more often than she knows, as a little girl who needs his loving protection. Except, of course, when she shatters his image of her helplessness by beating him at mental musical chairs, King's X, tic-tac-toe, and so forth. Some Gemini females can be, when they choose, intellectual terrors, their speech as sharp as a knife, their mental acumen nothing less than brilliant—which isn't the most soothing balm for a male Ram's masculine self-confidence. But then, there's also the bunch of marigolds in the sky blue bowl. . . .

As for him, he's made, not just from the rough-hewn robes of raw courage, tied with the crimson cord of bravado—his Ram's horns curl around the memories of his Lancelot days, the time he first swam, in water way over his head, when he couldn't swim—but he *did*—his broken top, his broken dreams . . . and the nightmares with no shape or form, from a buried, now forgotten childhood fear . . . the Christmas when Santa forgot the puppy on his list . . . the sky rockets, Roman fountains and spitdevils he ignited, when he was nine, on Independence Day . . . the first time he ever saw a horse, and smelled the intoxicating odors of a barn . . . the way he felt when he first knew how holy a silent night could be, sleeping alone, beneath countless glittering stars that sang to him a remembered melody no one else could hear.

They are so many things, this man—this woman. Mostly, they are the sometimes inhabitants of a land, a kingdom they discovered by themselves, where everything is beautiful . . . but lonely . . . needing other eyes to see it too, for only thus may it be recognized as *real*. They may each visit on another's private worlds, but if the mutual invitation so wistfully extended, unspoken . . . is rejected . . . . . then each may retreat into his or her kingdom, more and more often, leaving the other regretfully behind. These lovers should never permit such a retreat to occur, because the stars and planets have designed their make-believe lands so very much alike, they're sure to be happier when they dance through each other's dreams, than when one stands forlornly before the *No Trespassing* sign of the other.

Sexually, this man and woman will believe themselves to be ideally mated, in the beginning. The Ram dreams of arriving in the garden of love on a flying carpet of adventure, straight out of the Arabian Nights (or the Age of Chivalry, either one), and the Gemini female will play her role in his dream-drama to perfection. She'll not only go along with the game, but she'll think up enough new twists to keep him fascinated far beyond the honeymoon. No one can make an ordinary bed seem as much like a Sultan's harem as a Gemini woman, which is richly satisfying to an Aries man, who wants his mate to be the epitome of Woman. With her, he'll never know who awaits him at night in the privacy of the boudoir. It could be Cleopatra, George Sand, Mata Hari, Rebecca of Sunnybrook Farm, Lady Hamilton or Fanny Brice. For a while it will excite him, until he starts to look around in the closet and under the pillows for "the sensuous woman."

His own sexual expression is direct and intense. Hers is somewhat more elusive and complicated. True, he enjoys approaching their lovemaking on a path of imaginative romance, but he expects to quench his thirst in a stream of pure, honest passion, when he arrives at his destination. There's often an air of the intangible in her attitude toward physical love, to the extent that he may accuse her of being somewhere else during their intimate moments, and she could resent his masculine intrusion into what, to her, is always a sacred place—her mind.

This man needs daydreams in association with sexual union, but there's a time and place for them, and to him, the last act of their love drama is not the proper place. He believes, like George M. Cohan, that the finale of anything (if it expects to receive an encore) should include a stirring version of "The Stars and Stripes Forever." Listening to Ram Andre Previn's full orchestral recording of Holst's *The Planets*, on cassette or stereo, may help her sense his romantic pace. The section titled "Mars" will deliver the message profoundly, up to and including the violent percussion emphasis at the very close of that passage, that symbolizes the rhythms of his ruling planet with startling lucidity. It's an Aries sex education—and like everything else in the world, it's more beautifully learned with a musical background.

He may sometimes feel she's searching for something that never existed, and fail to realize that with a shade more gentleness from him, she might be able to transmute her vivid imaginings into equally lovely realities. Gemini images flash a true picture of what *could* be—if they're tenderly allowed to take form and shape. It's her dual consciousness that may distort the communication. But love can keep those Mercury circuits free of negative vibrations. Love can do anything—literally, anything.

This eternally youthful man and woman could hear the same music together, and follow the same distant drummer, for many happy years . . . if she understands that his jealousies and petulant angers stem from his Aries emotional vulnerabilities . . . . . . and if he respects her love affair with her other Twin Self. It may sometimes lead her into places she runs to more swiftly than he can follow, but she'll return, refreshed, and ready to race with him toward new horizons.

He's so bright and brave, so friendly, open and enthusiastic. She's so utterly feminine, charming, versatile and spontaneous. If only they don't try to change each other, they can remain boy and girl forever. And children . . . . . are the luckiest people in the Universe.

ARIES

Fire — Cardinal — Positive
Ruled by Mars
Symbol: The Ram
Day Forces — Masculine

CANCER

Water — Cardinal — Negative
Ruled by the Moon
Symbol: The Crab
Night Forces — Feminine

The **ARIES-CANCER** Relationship

*. . . but of course neither of them understood
the other's language.*

A Crab can become a little tense and edgy, spinning around on an Aries carousel. Because the Lunar physical-emotional metabolism is more delicate and fluctuating, Rams can exhaust Moon people with their excessive Mars enthusiasm, which flames in even the quieter, Sheep-type Arians, on occasion (and remember that the Sheep types are in the minority). Consequently, to the determined, somewhat reckless Ram, it may frequently seem as though the Crab disapproves of his (or her) behavior. What do these Cancerians expect you to do, wonders Aries —bury your confidence and develop an inferiority complex, just to please them?

Not necessarily. True, the Crabs might feel considerably more comfortable if the impulsive Mars rhythms could be slowed down a bit, to match their own, more cautious calliope music. But it won't benefit the basic insecurity of Cancer to have Aries join him (or her) in wailing "nobody-loves-me-everybody-hates-me-let's-go-eat-worms." One weepy hang-up like that is sufficient in an association or a relationship. Why try for two?

Very few people are aware of how frantically Aries men and women (and children) seek acceptance while they're rushing around feverishly courting rejection with their impulsive, thoughtless ways. Among those few aware ones are Cancerians, who themselves are abnormally sensitive to hurt. Even as they appear to frown on Aries rashness, they sense, with their acute perception, that the Rams are not always as tough as they act. Because of this perception, there can be some lovely and solid relationships between these two Sun Signs. However, since theirs is a 4-10 vibrational pattern, this association more often occurs in an unavoidable career, business or family situation, than in a romantic one. The Higher Selves of any two people influenced by the 4-10 vibration may possibly arrange matters this way, because of the heavier Karma, which must be leveled and harmonized, and human nature being as it is, few people would choose the tensions and conflicts of a 4-10 soul testing if there was a choice. Naturally, there are also love and marriage involvements between Aries and Cancer, from time to time. It's just that the Ram and the Crab teams are more often found as relatives or co-workers—in a boss-employee or other career entanglement. Even those Rams and Crabs who are romantically attracted will usually first meet in a career or family atmosphere, or these matters will be a main topic of conversation between them initially.

If the Sun-Moon aspect between their natal charts is harmonious, this combination can be surprisingly financially successful and emotionally compatible. But if a negative Luminary or Ascendent aspect exists between their horoscopes, there will be some steep hills to climb, and much soul testing for durability.

Aries likes—and needs—to win. Aries also enjoys leading. Now, Cancer has nothing against either winning or leading. As for the latter, remember that Cancer is a Cardinal Sign of leadership, despite the Crab's attempt to hide his or her desire to lead beneath a veil of feigned unconcern. Aries is also a Cardinal Sign, and the Ram's horns being equally as tough as the Crab's shell, you can see there may be a few skirmishes over who follows the leader in any game they're playing. It's a tricky problem, because when you have two leaders, how do you determine which one will follow? (Especially when neither has any intention of doing so.) It seems like an impossible situation, but there is a solution. They can walk side-by-side, with no one ahead, no one behind. It's called compromise. Cancer tends to compromise with less pain than Aries, so it's usually the Crab who must initiate the offer of truce between them. Aries may try, yet somehow manage to say the wrong thing, in the wrong way, tinged with too much ego, which leaves the Crab either snapping angrily, or weeping inconsolably.

All right, so now we have them (we hope) walking side-by-side toward the winner's circle—peacefully, for a while—then up pop the differences between their personalities and strategies again. The Crab advances in a rather zigzag direction, never straight ahead, like the direct, straightforward Ram. The Cancerian approach to anything is deliberate, disguised and careful, never mind how many jokes they tell along the way to distract you from noticing their techniques. Whereas the Ram is ever ready to discard dead wood and clear the decks for action, the Crab wants to be sure that no one throws out the baby with the bath water, so to speak. That's admittedly a mixed metaphor, but when discussing and describing Aries and Cancer, it's permissible. No single metaphor, analogy or allegory would suffice to fit both of these divergent Earthlings, who often seem to each other to be from different stars or galaxies.

Life is one huge challenging contest to Aries, who rushes out to meet obstacles headlong and headfirst, even when he or she must go out of his or her way to find them. If they aren't there, Aries will create a few, for what fun is a contest with no obstacles to overcome?

Indeed, obstacles attract Aries like bar magnets. Meeting with constant agreement everywhere both annoys and bores a Ram. Aries is either dismayed or furious when another person refuses to fight or argue. That takes all the excitement out of it. The Mars adrenalin surges, the Aries vitality is instantly recharged, in the face of any sort of opposition. Let a conflict loom on the horizon, and the Ram is in his or her glory, bravely facing the thrill of challenge, and the explosive excitement of meeting it victoriously. There's nothing wrong with this, as long as Aries will stop once in a while to notice that there are other people in the world besides himself (or herself) and that they have feelings too. Aries people don't mean to step on anyone's sensitive feelings, but they're so intent on getting wherever it is they're going (and you can include the rare and more introverted Sheep types, along with the flashier Rams) that they can be inconsiderate and thoughtless without realizing it. Excluding those few Arians who may have a severely afflicted natal Sun or Mars, the typical Ram would never hurt anyone on purpose. Nevertheless, he (or she) does, especially the ultrasensitive Crabs.

By now, you can see that one of the problems between Aries and Cancer is sensitivity to hurt. Aries people have little or no awareness of this particular weakness in themselves—it clashes with their self image of strength. Therefore, when Aries is hurt, the Mars-influenced reaction is to either immediately deny it, or to become defensively angry. Cancer's vulnerability is carefully hidden, so the typical Cancerian reaction to hurt is to crawl inside the Crab shell and pout—or turn just plain crabby. If the wound is deep enough, either of these responses may be accompanied by a few buckets of tears and sometimes, the Lunar sensitivity peeks out from behind the Looney-Bird humor. When these two have hurt each other, one of them (Cancer) disappears into an inky blob of gloom, or an injured silence, punctuated by cranky snapping. The other (Aries), frustrated by the Cancerian retreat strategy, and feeling helpless to take any kind of action to resolve the disagreement between them, may then become furious, and release a torrent of words and actions, with the predictable effect of causing the Crab to burrow even deeper into the sands of silent pouting.

Just go back to Nature for a moment, via astrological symbolism, and picture an aroused ram butting his (or her) horns against the hard shell of an impervious crab, while it frantically digs deeper and deeper into the sand on the beach. On the beach? What is a ram doing messing around on the beach, beside the mysterious ocean, anyway? He's out of his element. (So is she, if the Arian is female.) Just as the crab would be lost trying to crawl up the rocky mountain slopes where the ram is more at home. It requires a Sun-Moon trine or conjunction between their horoscopes—or a great deal of patient understanding from both—to bring these two very different astrological creatures together in a mutually acceptable emotional terrain. Even then, although they may learn to tolerate each other, and help each other grow, evolve and learn, the differences between them will be distinctly visible.

It's true that Cancerians may hide in the mop closet when their feelings are hurt, and are normally quiet and reflective sorts (except when they're making you giggle over their funnies), but they shouldn't be considered by Aries to be totally impassive, easily molded or incapable of resistance. They may not fight with the flaming sword of Mars, and may prefer to tackle obstacles with serenity, secrecy and patience; yet Crabs are not altogether quivering, soft masses of fear. Correction: Crabs *are* quivering, soft masses of fear, but the Ram shouldn't forget that hard shell they hide under while they're shivering and quivering. It's not advisable to rap one's knuckles on it. Whereas the Ram is inclined to favor instant and open attack when security is threatened, the Cancerian man or woman will, as unobtrusively as possible, first attempt to seek the underlying root cause of the trouble, then maneuver out of it gradually, with a secret strategy and incredible tenacity of purpose. The Crab's ability to hang on to your toe, ear, finger—or a notion—until it gets what it wants, should never be overlooked or underestimated. (That goes for both boy Crabs and girl Crabs.)

Aries and Cancer have different motivations, different approaches to life —and different goals. But if each will give something of his (or her) basic goodness to the other, both of their lives will be greatly enriched. This is a Fire and Water combination; therefore, each is subconsciously aware that the other can destroy him (or her). Too much Aries Fire can dehydrate Cancer's delicate feelings. Too much Cancerian Water can drown the Ram's enthusiastic, shining hopes. Fire represents optimism, in astrology— Water, pessimism. The two elements seem to be incompatible; yet another word for pessimism is "caution," a commodity with which Aries could beneficially experiment—and another word for optimism is "faith," a quality Cancer would find very useful.

If they're willing to take the time to translate the message of each other's hearts, who knows how high the dreams of the Ram and the Crab can reach together? Perhaps all the way to the Moon—or to Mars.

☆ ☆ ☆ ☆ ☆ ☆

ARIES *Woman* CANCER *Man*

*She wanted to risk it, come what might, but
that was not his way . . .*

Like all females born under masculine Sun Signs, who are, in addition, ruled by a masculine planet (in this case, Mars), the Aries girl has private doubts about her femininity. Ever since dancing school, she's been reluctant to let her partner take the lead.

Most of the fellows she's waltzed around have panicked when they weren't allowed to set the pace and the rhythm of the relationship, and the male machismo mystique being what it is, her feminine "macha" caused them all to stalk off to look for a girl willing to humor their fantasies of superiority. The girl Ram is far too honest to imitate her more submissive Sun Sign sisters by pretending to allow the man to initiate every word and action, while she smiles with amused tolerance behind his back. There's a perfect example of that sort of well-meant but demeaning deception in Margaret Mitchell's great American novel, *Gone With the Wind,* when the dying Melanie says, of Ashley, "Look after him, Scarlet—*but never let him know.*"

After a few heartbreaking experiences of discovering that honesty is not always the best policy when it comes to romance, an Aries female may understandably (and justifiably) begin to have some inner traumas as she wonders about her desirability as a woman. Then along comes a Cancerian man to court her (yes, I said *court* her) with a respectful, gallant courtesy, like a Prince straight out of a storybook. Not only that, he makes her laugh a lot, and laughter never fails to brighten a Ram's disposition, making her sweeter to be around. From the very beginning, he makes it clear that she excites him and thrills him, no matter who walks through the door first, which one starts the conversation or who initiates a telephone call. At last! She can finally do and say what comes naturally around a man—and he still loves her. No wonder it's an intoxicating experience for her. It may be the first time she's ever felt like a member of the opposite sex.

When he convinces her she's not the wicked old witch after all, that she's really lovely, desirable Snow White (as she always suspected) it can be exhilarating—for a while. Assuming there's a harmonious aspect of interchange between their Luminaries, Ascendents and other major horoscopic positions in their nativities, her daydreams have a good chance of coming true. Otherwise, Snow White could find herself living in the woods with only one of the Seven Dwarfs—Grumpy—and still waiting in vain for the Prince.

An Aries female will never be permanently at peace with herself until she discovers a man who will want her to love him freely and openly, without quibbling over who initiates the first goodnight kiss, and without pouting if she occasionally interrupts him with a sudden burst of cheerful, enthusiastic chatter. She needs a man who understands that if he'll just allow her to be herself, she'll give him all the adoring love he needs to feel strong and virile and masculine. Just murmuring "Whatever you say—or whatever you decide, dear" (with a hidden smirk) is romantic hypocrisy, a travesty of honest devotion. Her love is direct. It shrinks into restless frustration when it's restricted by petty arguments over what constitutes the difference between masculinity and femininity. She loves him with all her heart and soul and mind and being—isn't that enough? Yes. It should be— and it very well may be, for a boy Crab. But Rams have other areas of friction with Cancerians.

Both of them are intensely jealous. The chief difference is that Cancer enjoys it more than Aries. To the Crab, jealousy simply proves how much he's loved and needed, and with this woman, he'll get all of that kind of proof he needs—maybe a little more than he can handle. Jealousy can sometimes bring a sense of emotional security to the Ram too—just a light touch of it, now and then. But when it's overdone to the point of smothering possessiveness, it can sharply cramp her life-style, which is friendly, free and gregarious—and the truth of it is that a Cancerian lover or mate may lay it on with a heavy hand, once the courting gallantry is over, and he's sure she is his. Of course, it's equally true that his Crab-like trait of hanging on, when it comes to love, is an indication of his inclination toward loyalty and faithfulness. She certainly has no objection to that. In her opinion, it's the very least one should expect from true love. It's when his loyal devotion subtly and gradually is transformed into clinging, which brings the feeling of being fenced in, that she'll show flashes of resentful rebellion.

Each of these two Sun Signs is as fond of money, fame and recognition as the other. However, the Crab hides his ambition better. Although they share the same basic goals of emotional security and financial success, they have rather seriously conflicting ideas about how to achieve them—as well as what to do with money, when it's there. (She wants to spend it, or give it away, to create a nice, smooth cash flow—he wants to save it to make it expand into a higher balance.) Even before either of them achieves any degree of material success, there will be disagreements. Aries is optimistic, positive, *sure* of winning. Cancer is often pessimistic, negative and fearful of the future (Crabs call it sensible caution)—and this is where these two may need an interpreter to communicate.

It's impossible for the Ram to comprehend how the Crab hopes to win, at the same time he's expecting to lose. To Aries, this puzzling Cancerian attitude was expressed perfectly by physician-philosopher Jean-Baptiste Baudin, when he wrote: "To be ambitious for wealth, and yet always expecting to be poor; to be always doubting your ability to get what you long for, is like trying to reach East by traveling West. There is no philosophy which will help a man succeed when he's always doubting his ability to do so, and thus attracting failure." Granted, there are more July birthdays in *Who's Who in Industry and Commerce* than any others (except Taurus and Capricorn), but that's because the Cancerian has going for him a more than adequate substitute for courageous Aries optimism—a hard-shell tenacity of purpose.

There's not much use trying to explain this to an Aries female. She's familiar with a term like "determination," but she doesn't understand the word "tenacity," because it diametrically opposes her most evident quality —impatience. Tenacity implies waiting, and this woman loathes to wait for anything, from a bus or a red light to the arrival of her current lover at the door when they have a date—or her husband's arrival home from work, if she's a married Ram. Let him be five minutes late, and she either phones the sheriff in impulsive panic, or paces the floor, working up sufficient steam to leap on him with reproaches when he does arrive. Her Cancerian lover or mate's general attitude toward ambition and success, with or without the tenacity, utterly confuses her. She believes in simple things, that people should face the direction in which they wish to travel, and she faces the East. How can he ever expect to arrive in New York when he's headed toward California? All right, so the world is round, and he may eventually get there, but it takes so much time that way.

There are several possible outcomes for the dilemma. She can become desolate in the face of his moody spells of depression, and finally decide she must escape, to avoid the fate of seeing every last one of her fiery aspirations submerged in his watery Cancerian pessimism. Or she can try to cheer him out of his periodic melancholy with her own strong Mars faith, by boosting his spirits with courage and humor—like reminding him of the old proverb that every time a sheep bleats, it loses a mouthful of hay. He can throw up his hands in defeat at her impulsive emotions and financial extravagance, take off alone with his stamp collection and his old fishing hat—or he can gently, patiently teach her that caution does sometimes make sense, and that counting to ten has the benefit of never adding up to a total of zero.

Another trouble spot could be this man's tendency to keep secrets. The Aries woman is not so closely molded in the image of the Sphinx as he. When the Crab refuses to tell her what's on his mind, she may imagine all sorts of far-out things, and torture herself into a fit of Mars hysteria. He'll soon learn (let's hope) that it's more peaceful in the long run to come completely clean with her. To level. If he clams up, she'll just pry until she sees it's no use, then decide the whole thing isn't worth the energy and heartache—and possibly leave him. Suddenly. With little or no warning. Remember, Aries will waste no time on a situation that's been analyzed as impossible to change. It could end with the Crab still sitting on his secrets, while she skips off chanting Edna St. Vincent Millay's lines: "Thanks be to God, the world is wide, and I am going far from home—and I'll forget in Camelot the man I loved in Rome." He will weep.

Then, too, there's Mama. If his mother is still living, the girl Ram who loves a boy Crab may have some stiff competition for his devotion and attention, perhaps not when they first meet—but she won't avoid it forever. If his sainted mother has passed on, Mama's qualities could take on added luster, seen through the sparkling glass of memory. Did his mother *never* scorch a shirt, bake flat biscuits, sing off key, waste money or lose her temper? No. Never. Not one single time. Did his mother *always* save cash, look prettier by sewing her own clothes, string her own beans, wear just the right amount of makeup and know exactly what to say to make him smile when he was blue? Yes. She did. Always. In a strange way, it might work to their benefit, the Mama thing. A glowing example like that is surely a challenge, and this girl can't resist struggling to meet a challenge. She may become nearly as perfect as he thinks his mother is—or was—just to prove to him that no one can top a Ram.

In their sexual life, adjustments will also be necessary. When love is new, his tender consideration for her desires and needs will make her feel cherished, therefore emotionally secure. (Both of them have this incredible hang-up about needing emotional security.) He'll be, in the beginning, a fabulous lover. A Cancerian can be as imaginative, subtle and clever in the bedroom as he is at the bank. Her frankness and lack of guile concerning sex, a sort of unconscious vulnerability in her, will stir him deeply. Regardless of past experiences, an Aries girl always brings a kind of fresh innocence to her approach to lovemaking—in addition, when she loves, she loves fiercely and passionately, truly giving all of herself in total honesty, and *this* will make *him* feel emotionally secure. But she may be unable to remember the thrill of their original physical compatibility when he's been cranky and moody for a few days and refuses to respond to her affectionate advances. What appears to be (but isn't) his rejection of her can considerably dampen her erotic enthusiasm. It's the Moon. She'll just have to wait until the Moon changes, and stops pulling his emotions back and forth like a piece of taffy. What she should not do during these temporary Lunar phases that threaten to eclipse their happiness is become angry, and say things to wound him she'll later regret. He'll crawl into his Crab shell and stay there, for this man is acutely sensitive. However much he may joke about it, he is—and sexual hurt will cause him to retreat into brooding passivity for long periods. Or worse yet, he could seek the solace of alcohol's seductive siren song.

On the happy side of this relationship, a Crab can be very amusing and entertaining, and can make anything from counting money to digging clams wacky fun, with loads of laughs. His beautiful sensitivity and his gentlemanly air of protectiveness can bring out all the femininity in his Aries lady. He'll secretly be proud of her courageous mind and bright spirit, no matter how he grumbles about her immaturity, and he'll grow to depend on her for the emotional support he needs when the Moon sends fragments of old fears from childhood to haunt him. On the negative side, she may believe he's too stern at times, too fussy or stingy, while he may feel she's not capable of taking care of herself without a keeper. He could now and then drown his disappointments in drink or drugs, always a very real danger with a Water Sign—and she could now and then lose her quick fiery temper in such a way that it takes a long time to atone for the pain it caused.

This is a man who's not ashamed of sentiment; he's affected by music, art and poetry, and when his heart is moved, tears come to his eyes—and this is a woman whose own heart needs a great deal of tender, loving care, for she is, emotionally, an infant, whatever her chronological age. If they crossbreed her Aries initiative with his Cancer tenacity, they might achieve wonders. Their natal Suns are squared, and so it will require lots of patience—and lots of love. But then, doesn't everything?

☆ ☆ ☆ ☆ ☆ ☆

ARIES *Man* CANCER *Woman*

"Hullo, Wendy," he said, not noticing any difference, for he was thinking chiefly of himself.

"Hullo, Peter," she replied faintly, squeezing herself as small as possible. Something inside her was crying.

An Aries man is initially lured by a Cancerian girl because she seems so appealingly helpless and feminine. (Note: I said she *seems* helpless. We'll take that up later. Appealing and feminine she definitely is, no argument there.) She appears to need his strong masculine shoulder to cry on, his fiery emotional support.

When the Moon Maiden gives a Ram her flattering, undivided attention, it proves to him what he's always suspected—that no woman can resist him. She'll cook for him, baby him, laugh at his jokes, add some pretty funny ones of her own and generally make his life one long, sweet song of soothing serenity, with comical lyrics. But the music he hears could be a prelude to a slowly growing feeling of being smothered. As you well know, if you're at all acquainted with astrology, Rams do not like to be smothered—by blankets, authority or restriction of any kind—not even by love. Smothered in attention is fine, but the Aries male draws a line at having his freedom squeezed out of him. Now, it's true that no one can squeeze away a man's freedom as painlessly and pleasurably as a Cancerian girl. If she's subtle about it, as most Moon Maids are, a Ram could find the trip on her romantic flying carpet a thrilling experience (she has a deep-seated wanderlust hiding behind her homemaking knacks, you know). However, if the Crab shows signs of beginning to cling too closely, the Aries male may jump off the carpet, without a parachute, if necessary.

About her feminine helplessness: He'll sooner or later learn that it's somewhat of an illusion—maybe someday when she incorporates her own bank, re-decorates a friend's house, runs for Congress or rescues a child from drowning in the ocean, beating the lifeguard to the spot. Cancer is a Cardinal Sign, and these women possess an amazing stamina and tenacity, along with all that moonlight fragility. After the first shock has worn off, he'll probably admire her for it. He admires any kind of strength, and she's far stronger than her timid tears when he's hurt her feelings (which may be frequently) might indicate. He could even fall more deeply in love with her when he discovers she's not all "sugar-and-spice-and-everything-nice," since he essentially needs a woman who will fight back with him now and then.

But other sour notes may threaten to spoil love's concert between these two Sun Signs—like money. She has a pronounced compulsion to accumulate it, maybe even paper the bedroom, kitchen and nursery walls with it (her three favorite rooms). To her, financial security is synonymous with emotional security. The two are inseparable. He likes money too, and can think of hundreds of exciting uses for it, but stashing it away in a rusty old trunk in the attic or a bank vault for a rainy day is not at the head of his list. To Aries, money is to spend (or give away). His motto is: "Money can't buy happiness." Since they're both in love and happy, who's worried about cash? She is. *She's* worried about it. Because, you see, *her* motto is: "Happiness can't buy money." The Aries man contemplating a ring-around-the-rosy with a Moon Maiden should think about that. Carefully. He still won't agree with it, but he should think about it.

It won't be long until he notices her moodiness. Of course, he's moody too, but that's different and understandable. With Aries, everything is different and understandable when they do it—also justifiable and permissible, as well as excusable. (Remember, Aries is the adorable but totally self-centered symbolic Infant of the zodiac.) *Her* moods he considers to be uncalled-for damp prisons of gloom, and it must be admitted that they are deeper, more indigo and longer lasting than his. Sometimes it happens that a Ram cheers a girl Crab out of her periodic Lunar melancholy with his sheer optimism. It makes him feel strong and masculine, and gives her the emotional stability she needs. But there's a danger that he may eventually revolt against a fluctuating depression he can't fathom, if only because it frightens him into thinking that perhaps his self-made Mars miracles don't have the power to swing the Universe he believed them to have. Rather than face that horrible thought, he could split. He may not get too far. She's kind of nice to come home to, and make up with—and who else bathes his ego in such charming shades of lavender and soft green, with such silvery sincerity? She's funny and tender at the same time, and eternally capable of pulling him out of those holes he jumps into, head first. Besides, she bakes a terrific blueberry muffin—and the chemical attraction between them is an added attraction. It might not have been what first drew them together, the initial interest might have been based on other things . . . but after a while it grew into a positive aspect of their relationship well worth considering.

Her Lunar imagination quickly sparks the flame of his Martian sexuality, and his enthusiastic, idealistic lovemaking can pull her out of her bashful (or snappy) shell into a beautiful fulfillment of latent passion. There's an affectionate quality in the Aries approach to sex that may reach a part of her nature which has timidly hidden itself behind her crazy, Looney Bird laughter until the right man came along to find it. Unfortunately, however, this woman's ingrained sense of Cancerian practicality soon tells her that "man can't live with hyacinths alone—he needs bread." (Cancer sometimes has a way of twisting truisms around, or reversing them, to accent the negative, and eliminate the positive.) That's when the *real* cash conflict may begin, when she mentions money in the middle of some romantic interlude, just as the two of them are about to become "one." Suddenly, sexual closeness is replaced by an emotional explosion.

Any relationship between Aries and Cancer is usually subjected to a generous sprinkling of fights over money—how to obtain it, and how to dispose of it. He's extravagant, she's thrifty. At least, she's normally economical, until she spins into one of her many moods, triggered by the phases of the Moon, and indulges herself in a buying spree of feminine frivolities to boost her sagging ego. Most other times, however, she's a little reluctant to part with cash, to put it mildly.

If they manage to overcome the sensitive point of finances, through mutual give-and-take, Aries and Cancer possess the potential of building some solid dream castles together, especially if there's a trine, sextile or conjunction between his Sun and her Moon, or vice versa. Her combination of creative flights of fancy and a common sense attitude about cash (an odd contradiction in Cancerians) coupled with his audacity and Mars determination, will usually give this Sun Sign couple immunity from the need to apply for Government Welfare. Still, the problems aren't over. Her moods keep popping up to plague them.

He may fail to comprehend the delicacy of her emotional needs and be completely baffled by her changing moods. Perception is not an Aries strong point. It can throw him into a fit of perplexity. What could he have done wrong? (Nothing. I keep telling you, it's the Moon.) Only moments ago, she was skipping around like a dodo bird chattering and giggling and humming a tune, feeding the kitten soybean cakes—all smiles. And now, tears. What happened? Check *The Farmer's Almanac*, or the evening paper. It may be the Full Moon. Or it may be that her feelings have been bruised by something he didn't even realize he said. Perhaps he failed to notice her new dress, or forgot to tell her how delicious her carrot casserole was. Ever since childhood, this girl has feared that no one loved her. He'll have to gently teach her that the best way to get love—is to give love. (This won't be easy, since it's a lesson he desperately needs to learn himself.) The Aries man should remember that the way to keep a Moon Maiden happy is to be sure she always receives lots of love, lots of food and lots of money. She's not greedy, she's just security-hungry, and that's not the same thing at all. I left out something. If she's a typical Lunar lady, add to the list—lots of babies. Well, at least a *few*.

A Ram is nearly always enthusiastic about approaching fatherhood, and she'll adore this quality in him. But after the bundles of joy grow out of their booties into Buster Browns, they may begin pulling their parenthood wagon in opposite directions. He believes in teaching the youngsters to be independent. Although he can be bossy and demanding with them, his general inclination is to give them lots of room to grow in. She takes motherhood seriously, and I mean very seriously. She'll closely scrutinize their food, clothing, romances, careers and health. They'll be stuffed with pea soup, cuddled, coddled and watched over—all done in a spirit of friendly persuasion, of course. Mama knows what's best, what's right to eat and wear, who's wrong to love and marry. All this could lead to his accusing her of smothering their individualities—and to her accusing him of being too harsh, and too detached, by turns. The offspring may feel they're being slowly squashed between two cement walls, at times. Compromise in child raising is a must, or this relationship will crack irreparably.

The Ram's ability to give and receive love depends upon his image of himself as the strong one. He needs constant freedom of expression and action. His woman must have absolute faith in his ability to move mountains. Otherwise, his frustrated emotions may form strange neurotic patterns, turning him from a courageous Ram into a meek, unhappy sheep. Like being under a witch's hex. She should never remind him that she is better than he at juggling the bank balance (even if she is)—or anything else that may cut sharply into his masculinity. If she refrains from tossing wet blankets on his dreams, he'll stay close to home, contentedly. If she allows him to lead the parade, without dampening his hopes, he'll be able to make her mountains of secret worries and fears disappear forever. But there's always the possibility that her despairing silences, sulky temper and occasional touches of hysteria will drive him right up the side of her money-papered walls, and out of the house—and that his rash words and impulsive behavior will bring her watery nature to a boil, until it sloshes over and drowns his incentive.

When she's weeping, and he doesn't know why, he shouldn't storm out of the room impatiently. He should take her in his arms, and lullaby her with tender reassurances, to stem the tides of fear and loneliness rising in her, whispering softly, "Please don't cry, and don't worry. Everyone loves you because you're so smart and so pretty, and you tell funny stories. Besides, we're almost sure to be rich someday. And as for me, I love you even more than other people do, and that's really a bunch. You don't have to offer to do the neighbor's laundry. We're not quite that poverty-stricken, and we never will be. Now, I want you to wash your face, brush your hair, blow your nose, and get dressed in something beautiful, because I'm going to take you out to dinner." He should then mention the name of the most expensive, exclusive restaurant in town. She'll stop sniffling right away.

"All nine courses—including the dessert tray?" she'll ask, then, tentatively, her eyes beginning to sparkle.

"Yes, darling, all nine courses, including the dessert tray . . and afterwards, we'll go to a movie, whichever one *you* want to see."

That last promise ought to do it. It may be the first time in years the thoughtlessly selfish Ram has allowed her to choose which film to see . . or anything else.

☆ ☆ ☆ ☆ ☆ ☆

ARIES

Fire—Cardinal—Positive
Ruled by Mars
Symbol: The Ram
Day Forces—Masculine

LEO

Fire—Fixed—Positive
Ruled by the Sun
Symbols: Lion & Shy Pussy-
cat
Day Forces—Masculine

The **ARIES-LEO** Relationship

"So are you a cowardly custard."
"I'm not frightened."
"Neither am I frightened."
"Well, then, take it."
"Well, then, you take it."

Most everyone knows that Leo is symbolized by the Lion. As for Aries Rams, once they've been taught (by Leo) the gentle joys of submission, they become perfect lambs. Now, the Bible hints that when the "lamb lies down with the Lion," we may expect either Götter-dämmerung—or 1,000 years of Peace. There's some dispute between theologians and metaphysicians as to the happy or sad ending of the prophecy. It could be a combination of both. Most things are. Let's hope, however, that the lamb lying down with the Lion will bring permanent Peace, and not the Götterdämmerung (end of the world). Of course, it might be argued that a truce to the clubbing around of these two would *seem* like the end of the world. A smooth, snoozy relationship between them would be the living end—of something. Possibly of all the fun they have racing each other to the finish line, and competing for the cheers of the lesser animals.

Rams are winners. Indisputably. Winning is their chief occupation. They list it that way on their resumes. Occupation: *WINNING!* Whatever the game may be—love, friendship, business or family life—they'll win it. That puts Aries right at the top.

Leos don't waste their valuable time trying to win anything. They don't need to compete. They were *born* superior to everyone else, clearly the most important person in any love, business, friendship or family contest. That puts Leo right at the top too—with much less effort and energy. The question is, will there be room at the top?

Well, yes . . . in a large arena with lots of space, they could each grab a share of the spotlight and sweet rounds of applause. But on a stage of any smaller dimensions, like an office, schoolroom, apartment or house—it might get a little crowded. Something would have to give. Namely, someone's gigantic ego.

I'm not going to fool around with tact. It will hurt less if the message is direct and swift. It is the ego of the Ram that must bend and bow to the majesty of Leo, because the Lion and Lioness were born to lead, born to command, born to be first—BORN FREE! That means free of anyone's domination, including the government, the Internal Revenue, employers, teachers, neighbors, friends, relatives, astrologers—and especially pushy Rams. The Aries half of this team will have to be content with knowing he or she can fight any of the other Sun Signs and win . . (well, maybe not Scorpio).

But all is not lost. (Aries considers nothing lost, just temporarily misplaced.) When I said Aries can't win against Leo, I meant in the sense of grabbing the trophies in front of an audience. Privately, the Ram can win just about anything from the Big Cat, simply by listening respectfully to those long, Leonine lectures, heaping on the praise—and keeping personal intentions and opinions to himself (or herself). The first part is easy. Aries enjoys lifting people's spirits, and showering compliments on anyone who excites the Mars admiration of power and strength (which Leo has in abundance). However, keeping quiet about the ultimate goal is a tough order for most Rams. Aries people do like to boast about it when they win an election, a kewpie doll at the carnival or an argument. Too much bragging in this double Fire Sign combination, and the Leonine half of the team may stalk off in injured dignity, when it becomes obvious that he (or she) is being manipulated or out-staged, either of which shatters Leo's pride. It's no coincidence that a group of Lions is technically termed a "pride."

If a Lion or Lioness is in a position where stalking off in injured dignity is not possible (like an under-age child or a legal mate), he—or she—will sit in a corner and pout, looking out with reproachful, sad eyes, and stroking his or her vanity. Then too, there's always the chance that Leo will roar like the MGM Lion, and fiercely attack the injustice perpetrated by a mere peasant. That can be dreadfully noisy. It's safer for the Ram to allow a Leo of either sex to believe that he (or she) has won any game the two of them might be playing. No one, in or out of the jungle, can be as magnanimous, cheerful and just plain huggable as an emotionally and physically pampered Leo. Pampering, however, is a talent in which Aries definitely does not excel.

Aesop, in his fables, points out how easy it is for the Lion to be managed by a lesser animal, the jackal. When the Lion becomes furious with him and roars in great anger, the clever jackal restores himself to royal favor easily—simply by reminding the Lion, at the height of his rage, that he's the King of the Jungle, the Ruler of All Beasts, and therefore mustn't expect too much from a lowly jackal. It works like a charm.

The trouble is, a Ram is not a jackal. Aries is more likely to order Leo, in the heat of battle (and oh! there will be battles) to either give in—or get out. This will immediately create an emotional dead-end street. Since giving in is a total impossibility for a Leo—and getting out is a cowardly action, beneath the dignity of royalty (what true monarch ever retreats?), the Lion or Lioness is left with no choice except to roar louder, with increasing arrogance. Eventually, when Aries discovers that even a Ram's tough horns will not topple that splendid Leonine courage and stamina (emotional, mental and physical), it's all over but the shouting, which can last an exhausting length of time, since both these Sun Signs are rather fond of dramatic speech and posture.

"How dare you!" "Don't raise your voice to me!" "Don't give me orders!" "You won't get away with that!" "I will not do as you say!" "Oh, yes you will!" "This has gone far enough!" "Do you know who you're pushing around?" "You will do as I say!" "Never! Do you hear me? NEVER!" It goes on—and on—and on. If they sold tickets, they'd have a packed house. Nothing on or off Broadway has the dramatic impact, suspense and action these two manage to pack into each Act of one of their Ego plays—and the Finale inevitably calls for an Encore. I know one Aries-Leo pair who punctuate their turbulent sessions by taking turns flipping the volume up on the record player. Even hard-to-please Broadway critic John Simon would call it a hit musical.

However, although Leo must win in the final analysis, this Sun Sign is not a conqueror to be feared, ready to grab the spoils of war and grind the vanquished beneath his (or her) boots. Both the Lions and Lionesses are noted for their generosity and nobility of attitude toward the defeated. Of course, it must be admitted that Rams are not good losers. But if it's possible for Aries to ever lose gracefully, it will be with a Leo.

These Sun Signs are astrologically trine (harmonious) and influenced by the magical 5-9 Sun Sign Pattern (see the Sun Sign Patterns section in the front of this book). Therefore, each senses the other's superior qualities, when compared with anyone else either of them knows. Since a genuine admiration for each other is seldom lacking, when peace descends and an armistice is declared, it's often full of vows (dramatic, naturally) of eternal loyalty and devotion. Until the next battle. Then it starts all over again.

In the family circle—in the classroom or office—or between lovers or legal mates—the relationship can be a warm and happy one, as long as Aries is willing to look up to Leo as a guide, preceptor, counselor or teacher—and as long as Leo continues to wrap Aries in the cozy warmth of the kind of loving kindness and protectiveness the Sun-ruled can give so effortlessly. It will be, on the whole, a successful association, even though not always tranquil, because the Aries-Leo relationship is blessed by the grace of the magical 5-9 Sun Sign Pattern vibration. Leo will provide plenty of sincere and extravagant compliments, something Aries needs as the flowers need rain. And vice versa. *Totally* vice versa. Both Aries and Leo not only seek appreciation, they quite frankly demand it. If one of them has a conflicting Moon Sign or Ascendent, their quarrels may be more serious and hurtful; yet forgiveness is, even then, usually the final resolution.

One trouble area will be those long dissertations of wisdom from Leo, which often begin with the words, "Now, listen to me, and I'll explain how wrong you are." Since the Ram has enough trouble coping with bossy people in day-to-day living, to be forced to sit through the same sort of thing each night at dinner may ignite the very short fuse of the Mars temper . . . . but I'll tell you a secret. Actually, Aries will privately give Leo a lot of credit, and sincerely respect the advice given so freely and constantly, a lot more than he or she lets on. This may be because the advice given by a Leo to Aries is so frequently cushioned in real affection and concern. Rams desperately need loving guidance, and the chances are better than average that they'll get it from the Lion—or Lioness. As long as it is clearly "loving," not arrogantly authoritative.

If only the Ram could learn to *ask* Leo to do things, instead of commanding, "Do it now, and don't ask questions"—the relationship between them would be smoother. No one orders royalty around like that, not even Prime Ministers. It requires lots of effort for the Mars-ruled Ram to learn to be more gracious when trying to get Leo to do something, but it's an effort that must be made, or the struggle for dominance will disintegrate into continual dispute.

When there is mutual consideration, this can be a singular and extraordinary relationship, for Leo senses the hidden insecurities and dependency just behind the spectacular, brave Aries personality, and knows the Ram's surface sureness is not backed up by inner conviction—while Aries will grow to depend on Leo, not just for the well-organized Leonine mind and steadiness in a storm, but also for the ability of his (or her) sunny nature to give warmth and meaning to each moment of life. The Ram knows how quivering and sensitive Leo's heart really is, never mind the cover of superiority and bravado. These two have much natural sympathy. You can tell it when they smile at each other. It's a strangely intimate smile, a grin of gratitude that says: "Thanks for understanding me—I understand you too."

In each other, Aries and Leo will find the excitement they are constantly searching for. They're both essentially dynamic personalities, driven by a desire to live life fully, missing nothing. They know that stars grow wild, like a field of daisies, somewhere high above and beyond the banal and the mundane. And even though their goals may be different, unless one of them had the Moon or Ascendent in a more financially cautious sign at birth, like Cancer, Scorpio or one of the three Earth Signs, they both believe in arriving at their destinations by traveling First Class, not just in a material sense but in every way. That may need some careful thought to be comprehended.

We can take the world others created or imagine a new world. Aries and Leo would rather imagine a new one into manifesting, maybe the kind they dreamed of when they were children. This may be it, they muse when they meet, or at least the start of that new world. There's no telling where it will lead . . but it won't be boring.

☆ ☆ ☆ ☆ ☆ ☆

ARIES *Woman* LEO *Man*

———◆———

"How clever I am," he crowed rapturously, "oh, the cleverness of me!"

Wendy was shocked. "You conceit," she exclaimed. . . . "of course I did nothing!"

"You did a little," Peter said carelessly, and continued to dance.

A love affair between a Lion and a Ram, although it can be a warm and wonderful experience, will also produce frequent emotional storms—especially when they've frozen each other's considerable pride into icicles. But icicles melt quickly between two Fire Signs, and storms have a way of clearing the air, so that afterward, everything looks all fresh and green again.

It often starts like this: he promises to call her at five o'clock, then doesn't phone till midnight, and refuses to apologize. He tells her she can't spell, and she wears too much makeup. Then he tells her to shut up, and listen to him for a change. He does *what?*

Well, that slices it. She's had enough of his overbearing arrogance, and impulsively decides to toss him out of her life. Who needs him anyway, with his bossy Napoleon routine? *She* does.

With all her independent "I can take care of myself" airs, at last she's found someone who knows she can't, and who calls her bluff. It's no good telling him to "go get lost." That's just what he *won't* do. Later, she'll remember how his voice was warm and gentle when he finally called, never mind the lateness. She'll recall how affectionately he scolded her about the purple eye shadow, and spelling "cat" with two t's. Maybe he was only being tenderly protective instead of insufferably condescending and . . . . . . maybe she should forgive him. (She might as well. She's been conquered. Now she knows how Josephine felt, not to mention France.)

It won't be long until he's instructing her in all sorts of things she wasn't even aware she didn't know until he came along to point out her ignorance. What's more, she'll shock herself by blissfully basking in it. Of course, after the novelty wears off, she'll come down off the ceiling and top him a few times, just to keep the score from getting lopsided—and her

Big Cat will discover how a Lion feels in a cage with a Lion tamer. First surprised, then resentful . . then outraged. But finally subdued. Or at least, finally willing to smooth the rough edges of his superiority complex. Actually, her fiery temperament is all right with him, as long as it doesn't reach the place where it interferes with—or outshines—his own. It never will. He's concerned over nothing, really. Since when did Mars ever outshine the Sun? Interfering with his own is another matter.

This is the powerfully magnetic 5-9 Sun Sign Pattern, and so, when these two Fire Signs see Venus together, the romantic scene is explosive, but it's also a blinding light turned on an enchanted garden. Maybe those old dreams he packed away aren't so impossible after all. They're *his* dreams, aren't they? That's enough to make her positive they'll come true —and Mars faith makes mountains fly! As for her domineering ways and flashing independence, these are only distress signals for someone to guide her in the right direction. Isn't that what Lions do best—organize other people's lives, and save them from their own mistakes? She's certainly a challenge, and when did a Leo ever run away from a challenge? She may sock him in his masculinity with some rough blows, but Lions aren't weaklings. He should just sock her right back (figuratively) and let her know that he's the one who whistles for taxis and things. After he directs her Mars energy into his own groove, he can relax—while she supplies all the fire he needs, when he needs it—and he *does* need it.

Since he's more practical and sensible (Leo is a Fixed Sign, remember), she'll sometimes accuse him of being pokey and stuffy. Since she has more instant vitality, sometimes he'll accuse her of wearing him out. Eventually, she'll loosen him up—and he'll slow her down—so it will come out even, and they'll both be ahead. Most of their quarrels will be instigated deliberately anyway, on a subconscious (occasionally conscious) level, for the pure pleasure of making up and reassuring themselves of each other's love. Reconciliations provide the repeated thrill of feeling the magic all over again. Their friends may wonder why they stay together, fighting the way they do, but *they*'ll know why.

For one thing, they don't spend all their time together in dispute. Influenced by the 5-9 vibration as they are, they will have many moments that will be marvelous and mad, merry and miraculous, full of lilacs and raindrops, druid dust, violets and enchanted carousels. Her genuine guilelessness moves him strangely, touching a chord of response in his own idealistic heart. Her sparkling excitement is contagious, matching his own sunny enthusiasms. Aries is the symbolic Infant of the zodiac (as explained in the Twelve Mysteries of Love section in the front of this book); therefore her naivete and air of innocence stir some deep well of tenderness in him. He's compelled to protect this bright, brave spirit, who, like the real infant, hasn't the slightest notion how many yawning chasms lie in wait for her to stumble into . . in the darkness. He'll help her avoid them, affectionately, with his wiser, more mature judgment, for Leo is ahead of Aries on the karmic wheel of life.

She will, living up to the "infant essence" of her Sun Sign, stop demanding her needs, and lose her fear of falling with no one there to catch her, once she's experienced the warm security of the Lion's devotion. His strong arms will catch her if she falls, and he's clearly capable of meeting . . any needs . . she may have. And so, she relaxes, becomes calmer, more tranquil . . . gently soothed by the Lion's loyal lullaby of love. A Mars-ruled woman admires strength, of both the physical and the moral sort, and this man possesses it. She will place her trust in no other kind of male, however much she may struggle against submission.

Aries and Leo strike a powerful vibration of physical response in each other, which is intensified by constant emotional stimulation. Sexual expression between them can be wonderfully healing, because each fulfills what the other requires of mating: passion, blended with affection. That's not as common a need as you may think. Most people desire—and are able to give—only one or the other, not both. The result could be a stirring of feelings they both thought were safely buried with the lost ideals of childhood. That's pretty heady stuff, the kind of happiness they'll pursue together at almost any cost in temporary tears or heartache . . . or punctured pride. But Leo won't pay the price of being possessed for it. He wants to roam the jungle, unfettered by the clanking chains of jealousy. So does she. Therefore, does the "freedom" bit work both ways?

It does not. She'll have to give him plenty of rope, while he'll permit her just about enough with which to hang herself. As frustrating as it is for the Aries woman to turn the other cheek to her Leo lover or husband, it's immeasurably more agonizing for the proud Lion to humble himself. Humility is a virtue he constantly preaches but nearly never practices. She'll have to be the one to forgive first, and try to understand. I wish her luck and courage. She'll need it.

Their sexual compatibility will not be without some sharp growing pains. A girl Ram has this strange quirk. She knows how small her chances are of finding a male virgin, but she comprehends this with her head. Her Mars-ruled heart has other ideas. Incredible though it may seem, she'd like to believe she's the first woman he's ever touched, whispered to or conquered sexually. Since romance is as natural as breathing to Leo males, she's indulging in a vain hope. When she prods him into admitting every passionate sigh in his past, with names, dates and places included, this fact will be driven home. All right, so he's made love to other women. She'll accept that, though it will be painful. (Rams always face unpleasant truths with courage, once they're recognized as inevitable.) But another shimmering Aries dream must yet be subjected to the cold, hard realities of human nature. It doesn't have to follow that he *enjoyed* it, does it? Perhaps he was seduced; maybe some vixen handcuffed him or tied him with ropes while he struggled desperately, and he still has nightmares about the ugliness of it all?

Now, there's no use expecting a Leo male to plead frigidity. He's too proud and honest. No, he wasn't tied to the bedpost with square knots, or handcuffed. (Remember, we're talking about romantic experiences before they met, *past tense*. There's no way she'll be able to forgive or forget a present or future tense infidelity, not after they've given themselves to each other, and made a commitment. It isn't that she *won't* forgive, she *can't*. That's the way Aries is.) Anyway, after she tricks him into relating his former affairs by touching his swollen vanity, he'll hasten to tell her that he didn't give his heart away to any of those girls, not until he found her. But she may not hear him. She'll be too busy picturing wild orgies. He doesn't really belong to her, as he said. It was all an illusion. Her knight-in-shining-armour has muddy feet; his white horse has turned into a splotchy, grey donkey.

It's this sort of shattered dream of misty purity that can destroy the sexual harmony between the Aries idealist and a Lion with a long romantic history behind him. *Her* past love life? That's different. It will be rationalized away by a dozen different excuses. *She* didn't enjoy it, you see. (I keep telling you that Rams are unintentionally selfish.)

There are two possible solutions. The first one is for her to grow up emotionally and realize that the Present, if it's strong and beautiful and good, cannot be soiled by Yesterday, which is already gone and forgotten. In light of the typical Mars temperament, however, that solution is highly unlikely. It's against her basic nature, unless she has a more detached and objective Moon Sign or Ascendant, like Gemini or Libra. (An Aquarian Moon or Ascendant will work too but may cause her to be *too* detached and objective to suit him, creating other problems.)

The best solution is for the Lion to tell her frequently and periodically about the negative reactions he had to his discarded past sexual experiences (till she feels safe from falling into the darkness of loneliness)—and then to enumerate all the aspects of his sexual fulfillment with her which are not only superior to the others but "firsts," between them alone. There's no need to explain here the meaning of the word "firsts." Any Aries-Leo couple will immediately understand.

Her frank admiration of his courage and confidence and wisdom arouses all the Leo male's masculinity (although she may also, at times, considerably dampen it with her other qualities). His firm refusal to be dominated brings out a latent femininity in her she never knew she possessed, and perhaps she didn't . . . . . until him. However, although she may submit to her Lion emotionally and sexually, she'll never give up her individuality and independence, not even for him. He needs large amounts of worship to feed his hungry ego, and to her worship is analogous to meekness, a quality she's never acquired. Leo will give her ample opportunity to cultivate it. She knows he's stronger than she is, and this turns her on. Yet, if he uses his strength to boss her around like an arrogant male chauvinist, it will turn her right off again. An Aries girl will never conform to any form of feudal feminine fiefdom. But she'd better take it easy if she wants to be liberated by this Lord and Master. When she demands her rights, he'll roar at her in frustration a Great and Mighty Truth: "I can only *permit* you to be my equal if you *first* acknowledge my superiority!" It shouldn't be difficult for an intelligent Aries girl to interpret such a command. It simply means that a proud Leo King, whose supreme sovereignty has been properly and duly recognized, will then have the confidence and power to place his Aries Queen on a throne as high as his own, and allow her to reign beside him. (She can wear the diamond tiara, but he'll hang on to the sceptre.)

She'll admire him, respect him and love him intensely. She will also remain quite fond of herself, and of doing her own thing—though she may permit him to show her how to do it. There will be moments when he drowns her enthusiasm by scolding away her hopes with Leonine practicality. There will be other times when she wounds his pride by interrupting him, or forgetting to ask his advice. Then he'll freeze her with his regal dignity, and she'll outrage him with her stormy anger. But when his icy aloofness melts, and her fury subsides, happiness will always return to these two. After the flames of indignation have flared and died away, the overwhelming need to run into each other's forgiving arms again will create the miracle of spring—eternal magic.

As with all 5-9 Sun Sign Pattern couples, the Ram and the Lion will discover that their devotion for each other spills over into a larger love and compassion, because their powerful trined Suns vibration is influenced by the benevolence of the 9th house ruler, Jupiter. Every 5-9 Sun Sign association in which the two people involved are really serious, feels Jupiter's beneficent rays, to some degree, in their relationship. When you really love someone all the way through, I mean love him (or her) so much that everything seems to be part of everything else, you understand better how everybody feels. You know how it is with people when they hurt, when they're lonely. Somehow, you want to share with them your own peace and joy. And in some manner, you find a way, together, to do this.

Love is a benediction to Aries and Leo because of what they see when they look deeply into each other's eyes. He sees a woman vulnerable enough to need his wisdom, yet independent enough to challenge and stimulate him. She sees a man gentle enough to treat her tenderly, yet strong enough to protect and conquer her. And they both see . . . . something else . . . . some mystery of Yesterday, some promise for Tomorrow . . . . something they can't define, accompanied by the music of memory. Between Aries and Leo, the chemistry is right. The moment they touch, then together make a wish on Venus in the morning sky, whole waiting galaxies of stars are watching in wondrous joy, and making a wish on *them* . . . in anticipation that the birth of love between these two might herald the long ago prophecies of Peace promised to the world . . . "when the lamb shall lie down with the Lion."

☆ ☆ ☆ ☆ ☆ ☆

ARIES *Man* LEO *Woman*

------◆◄◆►◆------

*. . . and we return to them as their mouths close,
and their arms fall to their sides. The pandemonium
above has ceased almost as suddenly as it
arose, passed like a fierce gust of wind; but they know
that in the passing it has determined their fate.*

A Lioness is not easy to live with, and sometimes just plain impossible to handle. She can be proud, aloof, vain, self-centered and arrogant. She can also be a strong, vital, warm and generous woman, if her obvious superiority is recognized and respected. Although she never surrenders herself lightly, with an Aries man who's careful never to destroy her dignity, and who makes it clear how much he admires her, she will be unexpectedly docile. No one who knows her will believe it possible, because they've never seen her conform to anyone's wishes as willingly as she does to his.

Astrology practically guarantees harmony and happiness to this 5-9 Sun Sign Pattern April-August relationship, especially if the aspect between their luminaries is beneficent. In this case, the affair or marriage could nearly be made in Heaven. Even when the Sun-Moon aspect in their comparative horoscopes is unfavorable, these two will tolerate each other rather well. He won't mind her extravagance as much as a man born under one of the other Sun Signs would. In fact, he may encourage it. It quite probably matches his own. Of course, Leo women don't like to admit they're extravagant. They'll tell you they are very economical, and in a way, some of them are. Leos can be level-headed and practical regarding normal expenditures, but they seem to go into a trance when it comes to luxuries, and frequently are penny-wise and pound-foolish. The Aries man is usually both penny-foolish *and* pound-foolish. If either of them has a thrifty Moon Sign or Ascendant, all this may not apply, but even so, sooner or later the two of them will reveal their Sun Sign essence in gestures of generosity. They both love giving and receiving gifts.

Not too surprisingly, the Aries man who loves a Lioness will encourage her to live up to her birthright pride and dignity. A queenly attitude becomes her, he believes. (It also makes him seem like a real winner for having managed to capture her.) Although the Ram expects other females to wait on him and to exist solely for the purpose of gratifying his desires, he'll often display a softer side of his nature with this woman, be more considerate of her wishes. Perhaps he places her on a pedestal to win and keep her royal favors, but more likely the reason is that he honestly feels she deserves a bit of worship, because she's so very special . . . so very much like him(!).

One of the happiest marriages I know is between a Lioness and a Ram, Rosemary and Norman. For years, he cheerfully fixed her meals, kept the house in order and coddled her lovingly to make sure she got enough rest, while she was moving smoothly through medical school, then postgraduate work, finally becoming a successful psychiatrist. The experience served to mellow his Aries "me first" nature considerably, without making a dent in his masculinity. Because Norman cherishes his beautiful Lioness, she treats him with a gentle graciousness that leaves no doubt which one is Tarzan and which one is Jane in their marriage. When she's not working, Rosemary serves his meals; when she looks at him her brown eyes sparkle with real affection, and there is in her manner the quiet sweetness of a female who is completely fulfilled as a woman. He gazes at her with open admiration, even proudly permits her to be the center of attention when they have company; yet there's always the distinct impression that he is the man of the house.

It's not that these two don't have their share of disagreements. Psychiatrists are no more immune from occasional emotional tension than dentists are immune from a toothache. But between Fire Signs, a temporary clash of wills brings the spice of excitement . . and the much-to-be-desired lifting of spirits that comes with making up. An occasional quarrel keeps Aries and Leo from taking love for granted, which can be boring and uninspiring. These lovers have a basic need for periodic re-charging of their initial passion.

Aries men are always driving hard toward some goal, and there's a chance the Ram may be so intent on getting where he's going he may fail to praise her enough. When a Leo woman feels she's not being properly appreciated, she becomes cold, indifferent—and even lazy. She either neglects her femininity, taking no interest in her appearance (a sad and serious warning symptom of her inner agony), or she'll turn to the opposite reaction, placing undue concentration on glamour, and openly soliciting the attentions of other men. The Aries male who will accept his woman's flirtations or an actual affair with another man has not yet been born. The merest suggestion of infidelity will produce a wild scene of jealousy. In the long run, this may be helpful, if it causes him to realize he's been neglecting to pay her the romantic homage she'll always seek as long as she lives.

Actually, neither of these two can be said to be untouched by jealousy. Now and then, one may get the notion it might be "fun" to tease the other just a little by pretending an interest in another person. The resulting free-for-all between these two Fire Signs is usually about as "fun" as tickling an angry gorilla under the chin with a feather.

A Leo woman needs to be told frequently how much—and why—she is loved. Then she won't be so suspicious of the time he must spend away from her. The Ram who spoils his majestic mate won't be sorry. She may be somewhat demanding, but that's not as hard to live with as her disposition when she's neglected. When this woman fancies she's being ignored, she will begin to attach unreasonable importance to trifles. The very same reaction to being ignored can be expected from the Ram. He can, with enough provocation, imaginary or real, be almost childish in his demands, downright petulant with resentment when he thinks he's not being loved or noticed enough. Experiencing ingratitude will drive him into fiery anger—and her into frozen hurt. In both of them, the desire for adulation is overemphasized, yet still a necessity for self-respect. When they don't find enough of it in the outside world, which they seldom do, they can give this valuable gift to each other, to make up for the lack of it elsewhere.

Sexually, they are unusually well mated. Their mutual instinct for uninhibited passion in lovemaking is tempered with their shared need for tender affection. Although they are both lovers, in the warmest sense of the word, they are also both idealists. A gentle kiss on the cheek is as important to her, and to him, as the more erotic expressions of sexual Oneness. The Aries man possesses within his nature an abundance of both sentiment and fire, which never fails to bring an answering response from the Lioness. What they are both searching for, when it comes to physical fulfillment, is the wild abandonment of Lady Chatterley and her lover, mixed with the poetic tenderness of Elizabeth Barrett and Robert Browning—in equal parts. The chances are much better that they'll find this rare emotional blend with each other than with most others. If anything disturbs their idyllic sexual relationship, it will be his resentment of her old flames. Old flames have a way of never dying out with a Leo woman. The coals still burn, years later, not because she wants to rekindle a discarded affair, but because she's reluctant to part with souvenirs of past worship and adoration. These memories never lose their luster for her.

If the Ram should come across any of her old love letters, which she may save and read periodically to feed her romantic hunger, he'll be nearly as hurt and furious as if he had caught her in an actual act of infidelity. He'll probably question her about her past loves reproachfully, whether she saved the mash notes or not. Since she's sure to brag a little, perhaps even exaggerate the whole thing, he'll lose his cherished illusion that he's the only male who ever came close to conquering her—and losing that illusion can seriously harm their sexual harmony. Aries must be first (and last) in the game of love, as in every other game he plays. He also likes to be first in getting attention at parties; therefore he may not ignore any females who glance at *him* with admiring interest. (Rams are not selfish, just thoughtless sometimes.) What happens then? How can you ask? Remember that the Lioness wants everyone to know she's adored by the man she has allowed to love her. He would be unwise to so humiliate her before others, however innocent his intent, because this woman will not tolerate such an affront to her dignity. She may be confident enough of her own charms to be certain that she's adored by her lover or husband, but it's important to her for *others* to be *equally* aware of this. Let him peel a grape for another woman in public, and he'll see his bright, sunny and affectionate mate transformed into a clawing cat before his eyes . . . or worse, into a marble statue of icy disapproval. Later, when they're alone, there will be an emotional explosion.

But they'll make up, almost before her tears have dried . . and there will be another reason for him to tell her how dear she is to him, and mean it—another chance for her to let him know how much she needs him—another chance for both of them to assure each other how shallow they find other people after experiencing the depth of their own kind of love and friendship. For the Ram and the Lion are graced with this most desirable of all blessings from the gods—the ability to be friends, as well as lovers. They may take turns inflicting unintentional emotional hurt, but in every other way, they trust each other more than they trust anyone else. A disagreement always brings home this happy truth to them when it's over. That's the beautiful thing about quarrels between Aries and Leo, unlike quarrels between other Sun Signs. As the bitter chill in the air when you walk through winter winds makes the coming of spring a great miracle, the misery caused by hurt pride makes being happy together after almost losing each other even sweeter than before.

The impulsive, impetuous Ram will find a warm home in the heart of the Leo woman, and she will lionize her Aries mate. In return he'll bring to her the splendid gift of himself—*all* of himself—and that's something he never quite gave to anyone . . . . until he found her.

ARIES

Fire — Cardinal — Positive
Ruled by Mars
Symbol: The Ram
Day Forces — Masculine

VIRGO

Earth — Mutable — Negative
Ruled by Mercury (also by
the Planet Vulcan)
Symbol: The Virgin
Night Forces — Feminine

The **ARIES-VIRGO** *Relationship*

Indeed they were constantly bumping . . . if
they saw a cloud in front of them, the more
they tried to avoid it, the more certainly
did they bump into it.

ries likes to generalize, hates to bother with details, and is bored by meticulous analysis. Virgo is meticulous, likes to analyze details, and abhors generalities. That gives you some idea of the distance between these two Sun Signs to begin with—and now that we've begun, here are a few more.

Rams initiate all their actions from pure feeling—they trust their emotions and are skeptical of undue practicality. Virgos are practical, they trust their mentality, and are skeptical of pure feelings and emotions. When Aries people are upset, they'll usually shout it from the rooftops and open up their grievances to air them out. When Virgos are upset, they keep it buried inside and shut up their grievances to gather the rust of resentment. Rams are careless of their physical health, yet they're seldom chronically ill. Virgos are extremely careful of their physical health, yet they frequently complain of assorted symptoms of illness. And that's only a partial list of their differences.

Both of them are usually quick to help others, although their motivations are somewhat different. Arians do it because it makes them feel good to be the cause of happiness, since it proves to them that they can pull off a minor miracle anytime the occasion arises. Virgos do it because it gives a Virgin the nervous twidgets to stand by and see confusion adding up to chaos, when a little clear thinking would, in their practical opnion, untangle all the snarls. It's instinctive for a Virgo to step in, take a nip and tuck here and there, then go on his or her way without either waiting for or desiring any thanks. Aries won't wait around too long for thanks either, but you'd better believe the Ram desires it. If it isn't forthcoming, Aries will be both hurt and angry, unlike Virgo, who doesn't really expect too much of people anyway, and is therefore capable of shrugging off ingratitude by chalking it up as just another one of the many imperfections of human nature.

It's true that both of them lean toward purity of purpose. Each wistfully longs for the beauty of the spirit and seeks a shining ideal. Aries and Virgo ride together on a mutual search for truth and loveliness, but when their snow-white steeds reach a fork in the road, they take off in different directions. The Rams blindly and instinctively believe they'll find what they're looking for, despite all disappointments and the apparent impossibility of success. Virgos have little or no hope of ever actually discovering the Holy Grail, and even if they did, you can be sure they would find a chip in it.

Still, regardless of all these split-offs in their personality patterns, the Ram and the Virgin, when their paths cross, can find a strange comfort in their relationship. If it's business, admiration and respect—and a mutual desire to help one another—will nearly always result from the association. If it's friendship, it will probably take a business twist somewhere along the way. In the family circle, there's also much warm satisfaction possible through this blending of the two divergent natures, influenced by the 6-8 Sun Sign Pattern vibration.

Aries and Virgo often confide things in each other they would never tell anyone else. They seem to sense that the mutual trust implied by intimate confession won't be violated—and it seldom is, though the Ram may find it hard to conceive of how the situation described by Virgo could ever have developed, considering his or her own outlook. Likewise, the Virgin will sincerely sympathize with the Ram's experiences, even while privately failing to comprehend why they were ever permitted to occur.

Yet, no matter how close Aries and Virgo may be, Aries will feel deeply Virgo's frown of displeasure when he (or she) is late for an appointment, goofs off, or becomes careless and irresponsible. It's never as easy for the Ram to enjoy work as it is for the Virgin. What Aries views as harmless procrastination, Virgo interprets as an almost sinful waste of valuable time. Of course, after office, study, or family obligations are properly attended to (all of which may take endless time and attention), when there are no guilty twinges because everything is nicely snuggled away in its own cubbyhole—the Virgins often lead rather interesting and, in rare cases, even shockingly unorthodox private lives, when they lose those compulsive worries.

Sooner or later, after these two have spent a reasonable amount of time together, the Ram will be sure to remind Virgo of his or her inclination toward unnecessary worry and receive a reply like, "What compulsive worries? I don't allow things to bother me to excess." Whereupon Aries is likely to retort, "Oh, no? How about the morning last week when you missed your daily shower because you couldn't find the Ivory Soap, and you won't use any other kind—spilled a drop of ink on your shoe, and found a fly in your soup at lunch? You had a splitting headache and nervous indigestion for days afterward."

The Virgo rejoinder probably will be, "That is somewhat exaggerated and incorrect. The indigestion lasted only three hours and forty-five minutes, and it was caused by that dreadful, greasy soup I ate, not by my nerves. The headache lasted sixty-five minutes—not several days—and was the result of my not getting enough sleep the night before, not from compulsive worries. I missed my shower, not because I couldn't find the particular bar of soap I always use, but because I was late for an appointment. As for the ink, naturally I was a little upset about ruining a twenty-two-dollar pair of shoes I've only worn for a couple of years. I can't afford to be as casual about money as you are."

That last remark is Virgo's tactful way of accusing Aries of being extravagant. Virgins are careful to maintain scrupulous politeness when they're annoyed, so their irritability is softened by their typical courtesy.

Because Virgos are so analytical and fond of clarity, Aries people are inclined to look on them as picky and cold. Far from being cold, however, Virgos are the most inwardly sentimental of all the Sun Signs. (The important word in that sentence is "inwardly." It causes all the misunderstandings.) Their very discrimination itself implies high ideals for things and people to live up to, and when they don't—well, anyone would be cranky once in a while, from being so constantly disillusioned. Virgos are frequently nervous around Aries people because the Virgins dislike being openly firm—and dealing with a Ram requires, at times, being openly firm. The Arian impulsiveness can cause Virgo to feel secretly inadequate because of being helpless to change a situation, so they'll sometimes try to cover the feeling with a judgmental attitude—a kind of silent disapproval. It doesn't really matter what kind it is. Any kind of disapproval will annoy Aries, even if it's only vaguely implied and not verbalized. It is, nevertheless, felt or sensed. The typical Aries man or woman isn't looking for reasonable discussions or cool, sensible Virgo remarks about right and wrong, what's proper and practical, and what is not. Rams respond beautifully to generosity of spirit in others—and quite unpleasantly to stuffiness or criticism. Aries will often rebel and struggle for identity in a close association with a Virgo because he (or she) considers calm, rational talks a cold substitution for affectionate warmth, friendliness, and an open-hearted manner.

Yet, when there's a favorable aspect between the Sun and Moon in the charts, Aries and Virgo can grace one another with many mutual blessings. In an Aries-Virgo association where there is such a harmonious Luminary influence, the Ram may surprise himself (or herself) by following Virgo's quiet example and paying serious attention to Virgo's always well-meant and helpful advice. And the Virgins will surprise themselves too, by allowing the Rams to coax them into losing many of their inhibitions and dropping a few layers of their usually sedate behavior. All it really takes for this combination to blend smoothly is for each person to spend more time concentrating on the virtues of the other, rather than dwelling on the differences.

The clerk in the supermarket who frowns at the cash register and crankily scolds you for not taking your place in line is probably a Virgo. But the softly smiling, mild-mannered, and bright clerk who courteously answers your questions about where the soybean patties are kept and when the fresh melons will be available, and cheerfully helps you pick up the things that spilled from your cart is probably also a Virgo.

The customer who aggressively demands to be waited on immediately in a store, then leaves all the clothes hanging on a peg in the dressing room, after trying them on impatiently and deciding they all look dreadful —is probably an Aries. But the friendly, trusting person who will loan a stranded, out-of-town stranger ten dollars without even asking why it's needed is probably also an Aries.

The thing of which Virgo is seldom aware is that Aries senses unerringly whether the Virgin's concern over his or her welfare stems from genuine devotion, affection, and friendliness—or merely from a dutiful obligation. And when it stems from the latter, the Ram would just as soon try to manage alone as to accept help from someone whose true sympathy and heart isn't involved in the offer, however much he (or she) many need Virgo's assistance and advice.

As far apart as they seem to be at first glance, however, Aries and Virgo can stumble upon some happy surprises when they hike along together and take care to avoid the thistles, brambles, and thorns of disagreement. In the Ram, the Virgin can find someone really worthy of helping toward achievement, someone who will generously shower Virgo with a warmly enthusiastic and touching gratitude in return, someone who may even be able to unlock the little doors of those Virgo inhibitions and private longings. In the Virgin, the Rams can find the sincere appreciation they need—and a heart as honest and loyal as their own. Virgo can teach Aries to discover beauty in small things, to know the wisdom of waiting— to believe in the eventual success of patience. Aries can teach Virgos to discover and believe in themselves.

☆ ☆ ☆ ☆ ☆ ☆

ARIES *Woman* VIRGO *Man*

He was so much the humblest of them, indeed he was the only humble one, that Wendy was specially gentle with him.

When anyone describes an Aries girl as pushy, bossy, emotional, impulsive, impractical, and impossibly immature, the Virgo man who has loved her will nearly always disagree. He didn't find her to be any of those things.

To him, she was a lot of woman—perhaps too much woman for him to handle—but he remembers her as direct and honest, fresh and innocent. "She was generous with her time and money," he'll say. "She shared my idealism about love, taught me many things, and treated me gently and kindly. She may have been a little hurt or jealous occasionally, but she never created any really violent scenes. She was always willing to talk it over with me—to listen to reason. And when we made up after a minor quarrel, she made me believe in happiness all over again, like the very first time. She was gentle, affectionate—and eternally young."

When he finishes that nostalgic speech, his companion will probably ask, "Are you sure she was an Aries?"

Yes, she was an Aries, ruled by Mars, the planet of war and aggressive action. But an Aries woman surprisingly often will show her softer side, her hidden femininity, and her deep latent capacity for unselfish love to a Virgo. When she finds a man who's kind and considerate, a man who admires her courage and her bright mind, who seldom competes with her, who teaches her tenderly, sympathizes with her faults, and has faith in her dreams—she trusts him with her whole heart. Her hidden Aries insecurities and secret fears of inadequacy melt away, and with them, the need to assert herself forcefully, in the mistaken belief that to conquer is to win—in love, as in war. The necessity for combat disappears when the total love she seeks so desperately is given to her as a gift, purely and completely, as Virgo love is always given, with no strings attached.

Then why didn't it last? Virgo's instinctive fear of matrimony. Since the Aries woman is unable to see patience as a virtue and expects all her wishes to come true instantly, the second she says "abracadabra," she may lose heart (perhaps too soon), run away in tears, and eventually convince herself it was only a lovely friendship. Strangely enough, that's just what a broken love affair between these two frequently becomes after the scars have healed. Thanks to Virgo's inbred courtesy and gallantry, there are fewer bitter memories than those which usually linger after a shattered romance between other Sun Signs.

Still, sometimes love does last forever between Aries and Virgo, and when it does, Life can be very beautiful. There will be a few shadows scattered throughout the sunlight, however, and they'll have to be faced realistically, not emotionally. He's willing to face anything realistically, without self-deception, but she may need some help. (In fact, she may need a *lot* of help.) But if she should succeed, she deserves more credit than he does. A Virgo man finds it easy to analyze a situation, spot the flaws, reach a compromise, and clear away the confusion. He really doesn't deserve much praise for doing what is so instinctive, what comes so naturally to him. The Aries girl's natural reaction to a problem is to first slam it with a hammer, then butt against it with those Ram horns, hoping to demolish it. If that doesn't work, she's ready to sit down and discuss the pros and cons of it, but the pros may be all on her side—the cons on his. Therefore, if she can learn to face a misunderstanding with a cool temper and a rational mind, she deserves the kind of appreciation reserved for those who accomplish the nearly impossible.

All those memories of the girl Ram that the Virgo man we discussed before still retains in his neat mind were formed when their love was new. If the affair had lasted longer or developed into marriage, she may have seemed to him a trifle less like an angel. He might also have seemed to her a few inches shorter than a saint. Most of the squabbles between Aries and Virgo will blow hot and cold over his urge to criticize her. If he's truly analytical, he'll soon realize that, with her, he's safer when the wind blows hot than when it blows cold. As I've counseled repeatedly, there's more to fear from Aries ice than from Aries fire. The latter soon burns itself out. The former can shock the astrological novice, when the Aries woman stops crying "wolf" and cries "good-bye." Once she's gone she's not likely to look over her shoulder to yesterday. The freedom of today may be far more exciting to her than the fast-fading recollection of past heartache. It has been said that Rams never learn from burning themselves on a hot stove. They're always ready to touch it again. Perhaps. But not necessarily the same stove. That's worth remembering.

Back to the criticism. True, he has secret ways of convincing her that his criticisms don't mean she isn't loved. But loved or not, she won't be happy when the list of her shortcomings is longer than the list of her talents and virtues. If he wants a tranquil relationship with this woman, he'll learn to appreciate her taste and cleanliness in creating an attractive home, and refrain from peeking under the sink to see if she's polished the drain on the garbage disposal—or poking into the closet to see if she's scrubbed the shelves. She probably hasn't. Someone else can do all that. Like him. Or a maid.

She could also have a habit of spend now—pay later—which may bring on periodic spells of Virgo nervousness. Pouting in the corner, nagging, or hiding the credit cards won't work with Aries. The best solution is to let her get a job and squander her own money.

The combination of Aries and Virgo is a 6–8 Sun Sign Pattern. Among other things, this means that devotion, service, and working together will always be part of their relationship. It also means something which may come as a surprise to those who don't understand astrology—a strangely compelling sexual attraction. She represents sexual mystery to him. He represents to her the kind of sexual relationship she can trust. Somehow, despite the basic differences in their natures, these two may enjoy a rare compatibility of physical desire and expression. Perhaps it's born of the essential innocence and purity of intent the symbolic Infant and the symbolic Virgin bring, in an esoteric sense, to their lovemaking. Or it may be their mutual belief that sexual union is the ultimate blending of a man and woman's deepest yearnings, bringing their bodies, minds, and souls together in a singing unison of purpose and mutual tenderness. It could be this woman's directness, the simplicity of her approach to intimacy, that appeals to the Virgo man's innate honesty—or his unselfish consideration of her needs that touches her so tenderly—and the fact that his latent passion can be aroused only with someone who joins him in the desire to raise physical love to a higher level than a casual erotic encounter or a brief pleasure.

Whatever the reason, the sexual relationship between them is usually a strong force, often resulting in the kind of emotional peace and physical fulfillment that makes it easier for them to tolerate the differences and tensions in other areas of their togetherness. With Aries and Virgo, sex is a renewal of hope and rededication to each other. In most Aries-Virgo unions, the Virgo man will feel that the Aries female is all the woman he'll ever want or need. The enthusiasm of her spontaneous passion nearly always deepens his basic earthy instincts. But she may sometimes feel that *he's* not spontaneous or involved enough in passion, and she may lie awake beside him on more than one night, wondering to herself if this is all there is to love. Somehow, she hoped it would be more like her daydreams, more stormy and wild and abandoned. She adores his gentleness and consideration, but she may wish occasionally he'd make her feel really truly conquered and overpowered—like Heathcliffe and Cathy on the moors.

The girl Ram must comprehend that the Virgo man she loves is frequently driven, by the combined forces of his foster ruler Mercury and his true, as yet undiscovered, ruling planet Vulcan, to commit himself to the mental gymnastics of the moment—and pursue a thought to its conclusion. When she accuses him of neglecting her at these times, he won't understand. His busy mind has been busy meditating on amoebas, splitting and popping into the air as they reproduce themselves. At a time like that, to be pulled back to the reality of man-woman love can annoy him. She'll resent his detachment, and her instinctive urge to employ the fiery Mars method of *demanding* that he pay attention to her can create some unpleasant scenes between them. He'll intensely dislike being boxed in by her insistence on direct answers. Especially when he's immersed in one of his frequent spells of deep-blue depression and futility.

At these times, the only way to handle him is to pretend she doesn't even notice his gloom and sadness. She should make a conscious effort to remain cheerful herself, totally curb her own sensitivity to neglect—and concentrate all her concern and sympathy toward *him*, not herself. She should suggest happy things for the two of them to do . . . and talk about positive plans for the future. But quietly and sparingly—not in a running streak of conversation, which will only drive him deeper into mental seclusion. He doesn't need chattering when he's worried and won't tell her what it is that's troubling him. He needs to know she's there, that's all . . . that she's somewhere near, singing or humming . . . confidently going about her business in the background. It gives him a feeling of security.

Even if he turns a deaf ear toward her suggestions to go somewhere and refuses to budge under her gentle urging to change the scene, he'll gradually come around if she doesn't press him. Once is enough for any suggestion. If he doesn't pick up on it . . . wait for a while. The one thing he doesn't need during these Virgo worry sessions is the third degree . . . or the added burden of seeing the woman he loves in tears because his silence and detachment have caused her to feel neglected, and therefore sorry for herself. Self-pity is the very worst thing the girl Ram can allow herself to indulge in when her Virgo man has temporarily retreated from her, mentally and emotionally. Patience, gentleness, tenderness, and just being there if he should need her . . . these are the ingredients of the subtle alchemy guaranteed to bring the twinkling stars back to shine again in his clear, calm Virgo eyes.

She should stop finding fault with him (Aries is quick to imitate, and may pick up the Virgo critical syndrome after a time) and instead count her blessings. This man will seldom interfere with her freedom by imposing unnecessary restraints and restrictions on her activities. (This is wise of him, because she'd do her own thing anyway, through sheer resentment at being told how to behave, where to go, and what time to return.) But there's no denying that the sometimes sharp and satirical words of the Virgo male can deeply wound this woman in the sensitive area of her self-confidence. Also, he may not be as demonstrative as she'd like him to be—not in relation to their sexual intimacy, but in their day-to-day communication and contact.

Demonstrative affection does not flow easily with Virgo and may have to be deliberately cultivated if he wants to keep her, because the tangible expressions of devotion (the small touching things, such as bear hugs, a kiss on the cheek, a meaningful wink across the room, or an unexpected tight handclasp) are a deep-seated need within her. If these constant reassurances of love are missing from their relationship, her belligerence and defiance will grow in direct proportion to the degree of her emotional starvation.

The Aries girl is gregarious, affectionate, and demonstrative. It hurts and worries her when the man she loves makes it clear he'd rather be busy doing other things without her now and then. But he needs many more moments alone than most other men, for without them, his Virgo crankiness, nervousness, and irritability can increase. Although it won't be easy for the girl Ram to really understand her Virgo man's frequent need for privacy and solitude, she can comfort herself with the thought that this man is far less likely than any other Sun Sign to hurt her by flirting with another woman when he's not with her. Like Aries, Virgo usually falls in love for keeps. Yes, I know love that lasts forever is rare enough to be a miracle. But if you *expect* a miracle, you'll find it . . . . . . every time.

☆ ☆ ☆ ☆ ☆ ☆

ARIES *Man* VIRGO *Woman*

——◆◄◆►◆——

"Oh, say you're pleased," cried Nibs . . . . .

*He was a lovely boy, clad in skeleton leaves and
the juices that ooze out of trees; but the
most entrancing thing about him was that he had
all his first teeth. When he saw that she was
a grown-up, he gnashed the little pearls at her.*

It's sad, but often true. An Aries man will at some time in his relationship with a Virgo woman feel the need to prove to her that his ideas and ideals are sensible, that he is emotionally mature—and in general, he will try to arouse her enthusiasm for his plans, his ambitions, and his feelings.

It's not that she isn't pleased, but her response, if she's a typical Virgin, may leave him with a vague sense that she somehow disapproves of what he's been trying to tell her. She probably does. She may wholeheartedly support most of what he's projecting and imagining, but there will nearly always be some small portion of his narrative she feels is off-center, or not well enough thought out and constructed. Virgos are like that. They spot the weak links in the chain and warn you about them before the chain breaks. We all really ought to be grateful to them for this neat habit they have of pointing out flaws before it's too late, so the bottom line and the end result of every venture will be more perfectly successful. Most people *are* properly grateful for Virgo's ability to bring calm order out of chaotic disorder. Not the Ram. He'll fiercely resent her lack of total commitment to his causes, his emotions, his outrages, his dreams, and his superiority. After a time, he may angrily accuse her of having no sensitivity and no imagination.

He's very wrong. This girl possesses a lovely, sensitive imagination. Other children may eat "Chicken and Stars" soup for years without a single comment, but when *she* was a little girl, she would always delightedly exclaim (quietly, shyly, to herself, when no one could hear) "Oh, just see the little stars floating in my soup!" When someone gave her ginger ale in a cut-glass goblet one morning, and it caught the sunlight, she cried out (within) "Oh, how perfectly marvelous! I have a rainbow in my ginger bubbles!"

Just because she whispered these marvels only to her secret make-believe best friend—and seldom or never exclaimed them aloud, she grew up with everyone around her thinking she was terribly prosaic and un-imaginative—because she didn't flaunt her brilliant mind and private thoughts. Then *he* came along, the handsome, dashing Ram, to make her feel she was a very special person. It warmed her cool Virgin heart, and made her more sure of herself than she had ever been before. Now here he is, like all the others, accusing her of having no imagination. Insensitive? Perhaps he's the one who's insensitive.

This woman's inner world may not be peopled with imaginary faerie creatures every single moment of the day. Nevertheless, it's a beautiful land of wonder, because she sees loveliness in the small and ordinary things. Once the Aries man who cherishes her truly comprehends this—stops yelling at her and putting her down—he can persuade her to open the locked trunk of her wistful yearnings and secret fancies and expose them to the warm sunbeams of loving affection—encourage her to bring her fears out into the fresh air, instead of holding hurt inside, where it may grow into migraine headaches and all manner of aches and pains and physical ills. Yes, she will learn much of value from him.

He can learn a lot from her too. Like thoughtful consideration for others—the peace and happiness of serving (instead of being served). This she demonstrates nearly every day they're together. Yet he seldom notices. He doesn't see her gentle smile when he silently wishes for a magic elf to help him with something he's doing physically or some problem he's pondering mentally. She glides into the confusion so softly, he's hardly aware of her presence . . . . . and helps to make things come out right, even without being asked. Also without expecting to be praised. She would glow under his gratitude, but she won't demand it of him. She's only doing what comes naturally to Virgo when she's helping, so praise is not her aim, since ego and self-aggrandizement are not her motives. Still, it wouldn't hurt him to notice—and perhaps say "thank you, darling" now and then. He might even say "thank you for loving me" . . . because the pure love of a Virgo woman is a priceless gift, never given casually.

A Virgo woman is so nice to come home to when she *likes* herself, is *being* herself—and allowing the Ram she loves to be *him*self. If she's a typical Virgin, she's unobtrusive (unobtrusive compared to Aries!), yet bright and pleasant, a joy to be around. She's quiet and courteous and she needs lots of affection (for which she'll never ask, any more than she asks for gratitude). She's sometimes critical, yes, but ordinarily she's at least polite while she's hair-splitting and nit-picking.

The Aries man who loves this intelligent feminine creature might comfort her when she's blue and discouraged over some small mistake she's made (Virgos tend strongly toward self-chastisement) by reminding her that even the gentle Nazarene momentarily made the mistake of losing his wonted "perfect" control when he lashed the money changers in the temple. Then too, there are the "lost years," during which the humble carpenter isn't mentioned in the scriptures (quite a number of them, as a matter of fact). The Ram might tell his worried Virgo lady it's probably that, during those "lost years," Jesus more than once nailed the wrong boards together in the carpentry shop of his father, Joseph . . . . . miscalculated his taxes, which were due to be paid to Caesar's Internal Revenue (or didn't make it to Bethlehem in time to pay them on the deadline date), ripped his robe on a sharp rock . . . . . stubbed his toe . . . was briefly cranky with Mary Magdalene . . . . and committed who knows how many other miscellaneous minor goofs? Thanks to the uptight censors of the scriptures, no one does. But one can make a spiritually educated guess. And who is she, the Ram can then ask her, to aspire to a more flawless record of human behavior than that of such a simple, humble man as Jesus of Nazareth?

It may help to enlighten the Virgo woman to how unnecessary most of her worries about her failures really are. And help her to see that perfection is not the requirement for self-acceptance she so often believes it to be.

There's frequently a misty enchantment inherent in the physical love between the Aries man and the Virgo woman. These two are rather likely to be among the few people still left who are still sexually unpolluted by the explicit sex being flaunted in everyone's faces, whether they like it or not. The Ram is a confirmed idealist (and a super-jealous one besides), whereas the female Virgin is normally turned off by sexual or any other kind of vulgarity and cheapness. She also would prefer him not to leave the catsup bottle on the dining-room table. Discrimination flashes its sparkles into many facets of human existence, from sex to catsup bottles to messy closets and untidy drawers—not to mention sloppy thinking and a dull intellect. Her own thinking is never sloppy, her own intellect never dull.

Their lovemaking will reflect their mutual idealism and subconscious search for purity and innocence. This doesn't mean the physical aspect of love between them will lack passion. The male Ram, ruled as he is by Mars, is passion personified. Yet, he's also touchingly affectionate, usually mindful of the small things related to sexual unity—and she will respond to this quality in him with genuine joy. But she must be careful not to criticize his romantic techniques or allow her innate coolness of approach to make ashes of the flaming sort of sexual expression he offers her so trustingly. Conversely, he must be careful not to offend her sense of delicacy by always making sure that tenderness and gentleness are a part of their union. It would also help if he didn't pout or feel so wounded those times when she'd rather demonstrate her love for him in ways other than physical. The vitality of his sexual stamina may often exceed hers—and when it does, he should remind himself that patience is a virtue which brings its own reward—in addition to the reward of her return to being a warm, loving woman.

He must simply give her time to rest awhile and refresh her desires. Also, he should know that her enthusiasm for making love will always be somewhat diluted in direct ratio to the vexing worries and problems she's encountered throughout the hours preceding his need that she surrender herself to him. Even at best, Virgos never surrender their whole selves to love. Aries men do. And this is a basic difference between them which will need to be handled with care.

Despite their natural affinity in matters romantic, these two could allow their romance to gradually take the form of a less emotionally demanding mutual mental respect. There's certainly nothing wrong with mutual mental respect, but it needs a few more brilliant facets to set it off—like mutual emotional involvement and vibrancy. Still, rarely is even a romantically frustrated Virgo or Arian unfaithful. Not without monumental cause. It's equally rare, if they're typical of their Sun Signs, for either to leave or desert the other, even under extreme provocation—once they've committed themselves to devotion. For to Virgo, devotion is first analyzed, then defined as more responsibility than sentiment. Consequently, when a Virgo decides to desert such a "responsibility," you can be sure the decision to "cut out" was motivated by personal injury of such immeasurable depth it decreed either a final solution of escape or actual mental breakdown. Virgos have little or no immunity to long-continued mental and emotional pressures.

The Aries man is reluctant to admit he's been wrong about a relationship for the exact opposite reason than that of Virgo. He keeps trying, not because of "responsibility," as she does, but because of "sentiment." It's difficult for the Ram to imagine he could have been mistaken about love, once he's believed in it with all his heart. This man puts all of himself into every venture, dedicates himself with fiery intent to every challenge—and love is no different from the rest. Could Romeo ever stop loving Juliet, or Juliet ever grow tired of Romeo? Of course not. That's more or less the way he sees it. He forgets that both these medieval lovers died before they were twenty, and had they lived, they would probably have experienced their share of misunderstandings and disagreements, being only human. Strangely, he's as much a perfectionist about love as his Virgo woman is about everything *but* love.

It's as though she *expected* love to have flaws, therefore isn't terribly surprised when the flaws appear. It's only the other areas of life where she's repeatedly disillusioned to find things less than flawless. With him it's just the opposite. Life's major disappointments he can shrug off, but of "love" he demands perfection. Somewhere in between their oddly transposed views, these two should be able to find a basis for understanding each other.

When serious trouble arises in this relationship, the tie is usually severed by the slashing scissors of unbearable *outside* pressures of one kind or another, not by a decline of their love. Sometimes it's her near fanatical obsession with the obligations of a career or her duties in the home. Sometimes it's his fierce ambition and single-minded purpose that causes him to place her last—after his great goal in life—his crusade for self-identification. Then she may feel an irresistible compulsion to interfere by criticizing his attitudes—either privately or publicly. This first frustrates, then humiliates, and finally angers him into a Mars-like rage of resentment, which in turn freezes her desire to help him into icy detachment and an almost smug satisfaction at his misery. Then something will have to give— fast! Otherwise, their mutual need for reciprocated affection from each other will soon become secondary to their mutual need for self-respect— and they'll part, each to seek alone the peace of mind they couldn't find together.

That's the dark side. The bright side is that this man and woman can mend the silver cord that links them together each time it breaks—with the magical healing power of love. But only when he defines love as unselfishness and an awareness of her needs—only when she defines love as spontaneous trust and enthusiasm for his dreams. Once these two get their definitions straight, their love can last . . . . . . and the tiny cracks they mended with mutual consideration won't even show. Unless the Virgin keeps inspecting it with a magnifying glass—or the Ram impulsively, carelessly shatters it again. Love is like a precious work of art, fragile and delicate . . . much lovelier and far more valuable when it's weathered the years.

ARIES

Fire — Cardinal — Positive
Ruled by Mars
Symbol: The Ram
Day Forces — Masculine

LIBRA

Air — Cardinal — Positive
Ruled by Venus
Symbol: The Scales
Day Forces — Masculine

The ARIES-LIBRA *Relationship*

◆━━◆❋◆━━◆

> So with occasional tiffs, but on the whole
> rollicking, they drew near the Neverland; for
> after many moons they did reach it, and what
> is more, they had been going pretty straight
> all the time.

The Libra people who read this chapter may claim I haven't been fair with them, since I'm an Aries myself. (They're always claiming somebody hasn't been fair with them.) Are reckless Rams envious of the marvelous tranquility of the Venus-ruled people when their Libra Scales are perfectly balanced, as they sometimes are? No. Rams are not envious of Libran tranquility, even though astrology insists they should be, the two Sun Signs being opposed to one another on the karmic wheel of Life, therefore each lacking what the other possesses. At least, the typical Arian will never openly admit that he or she is envious of Libra, however much the Rams would secretly like to imitate Libra's lovely calm and tranquil equilibrium. The derivation of the word "equilibrium" is the word "libra." Or the opposite. Either way, the word and the Sun Sign are linked. Nothing is more important to a Libran than equilibrium. They do so hate to lose it. Nonetheless, they frequently do.

One of the times the Ram secretly envies the Libran is when an Aries person makes a swift Mars-like decision, then is forced to face the inevitable opposition Libra-type emotional trauma that always follows. Did I do right or wrong? Should I have said "yes" or "no"?—after it's already too late to change anything. Believe me, the Arian indecision *after* the fact is more painful than the indecision *before* the fact from which Librans suffer—and certainly not as constructive.

No one can be more charming, intelligent, and optimistic than Librans who have a firm grip on their Scales. They're simply great at getting groups of people to blend harmoniously and smoothing over tensions (when they're not personally involved). Aries men and women admire and respect Libra for the Venus-type virtues they themselves lack. But Aries is also Libra's opposition Sun Sign, and so Libra must admire and respect the Mars-type virtues too. Does that sound like an order?

One of the most noticeable differences between Aries and Libra is that the simplest Aries statement somehow comes out sounding like a demand. Even when Rams ask a question, it often seems more like they're telling you than asking you. On the other hand (we must be careful to look at both sides, since we're dealing with the Scales)—on the other hand, when the Venus-ruled Librans ask a question or make a statement, they manage to charm you right out of your good sense, so you're left vulnerable and unable to defend yourself.

It doesn't matter whether the Libran asks, "Why are you so consistently ignorant, dear?"—or remarks, "What you're doing reveals your complete lack of breeding"—it will evoke a musical tone reminiscent of "The Lost Chord." Those bunny-tail-soft Venus voices create images of maple syrup being poured into bowls of honey. That's why Libra can argue for hours with Aries and leave the impression it was the Ram who was being impossibly rude and wrongheaded, in comparison to Libra's nice, sensible logic. Now what is that, if it isn't unfair? No wonder Librans make fabulous lawyers, the kind who win all the verbal debates in the courtroom before the jury. If Libran lawyers can twist tough judges around their fingers and woo an indifferent panel of jurors to their side, you can imagine what happens in a battle of wits between Libra and the impulsive, quick-tempered, emotional Ram. No contest.

Perhaps Libra will accuse the Rams of being too hasty to make a sound judgment, of rushing in rashly, with no thought of possible consequences

—then sweetly remind them of the beauty of the symbol of the Lady Justice with her Scales balanced in perfect equilibrium.

ARIES: "Yes, but she's wearing a blindfold, so how can she see right from wrong?"

LIBRA: "The blindfold is only there to protect her from prejudice, dear."

Then Aries may ask Libra if he (or she) has ever heard the fable about the ass that starved to death because it couldn't make up its mind which field of clover to eat first? Finally, the Libra man or woman will smile—and once the Ram is under the influence of that dazzling Venus aura, the Aries fire sputters out. It's difficult for the friendly, open Rams to resist a smile and a kind word, and they're too naive to suspect Libra of using charm as a weapon against them. Nevertheless, Libra does.

Most of the time in this relationship, the Libran will remain cool and stable. But when the Aries aggressiveness becomes intolerable, it can have the same effect upon this normally gentle person as the accumulation of tension has in the sky—a thunderstorm. Every instinct of Libra recoils from unpleasant confrontation, but when he (or she) feels seriously threatened, a firm, sometimes even impulsive, action will be taken, if only for the purpose of regaining calm. This may seem a little confusing, but you'll have to apply Libra logic if you want to straighten it out. The best I can do is tell you that, with Libra, the end always justifies the means. On that point, at least, most Rams will agree.

Actually, with the respect always felt for one's opposite Sun Sign, Rams will, however reluctantly, look up to the Libran judgment and privately wish they possessed it. Aries is aware that Libra is fair and logical, and a clear thinker. The Aries man or woman knows that Libra decisions are nearly always right, but a Ram can get a little jumpy, sitting around watching Libra make them. The word "decision" itself causes most Librans to break out in a rash. It doesn't bother Aries. A decision has to be made? Great. Toss a coin or a feather—or just do what you instinctively feel is right, then forget it. That's the Aries motto. Dive right in. (If there's no water in the pool, Rams scrape their chins on the cement, but they'll just stick on a Band-Aid, and be on their enthusiastic ways again.) It's not that Aries doesn't see the potential value in the nice, safe "middle-road" Libra wears down into a ditch, but a Ram would rather take a chance now and then on the path to the right or the fork to the left—and see what happens. It's exciting. And that (to look at the other side) is one of the qualities Libra admires in the opposite Sun Sign of Aries. It works both ways.

If you want to test people's grasp of astrological knowledge, ask them which one of these two Sun Signs has the most violent temper. Before you jump to any hasty conclusions, *think*. Libra is Air and Aries is Fire. Fire *seems* more volatile and violent than Air, but Libra is the Cardinal of the three Air Signs—and Cardinal means "leader," among other things. Aries is also Cardinal, yet you must remember that in Nature air is not as innocent an element as it seems when it becomes aggressive. Have you ever watched a nice, calm, "nonviolent" tornado, cyclone, or hurricane? The quiet steam, composed of moist "air," that drifts out of the spout of a teakettle can be turned into a force powerful enough to rip up the ground for miles around. Also consider that the chief constituent of air is nitrogen. Nitrogen may be an inert gas, but it's the principal reason why explosives explode. So—which one has the most dangerous temper, Aries or Libra? You decide. (But don't ask Libra to decide, if you're in a hurry for an answer.) I didn't say which one is the noisiest when angry. I said the most dangerous. If you study this paragraph carefully, you'll see why people are puzzled when most astrology books, referring to the Venus rulership of Libra, describe all Librans as peaceful, gentle, beautiful, sweet, and calm. They are all those things—half the time. And I suppose we must confess that Aries could profit by trying to imitate some of those positive Libra personality patterns.

These two will at times argue instinctively, but in all fairness, when a conflict between a Libran and a Ram develops, the object of the quarrel to Libra is (usually) to win and achieve eventual peace and justice. The object of most quarrels to Arians is (usually) to win and prove they're right (even when they're wrong) to satisfy the considerable Mars ego.

An association between Aries and Libra, influenced by the 7-7 Sun Sign Pattern, is in most cases a fortunate experience for both. But if there's a negative Sun-Moon aspect between their horoscopes, there can be some fiery and windy periods of tension and conflict. With a harmonious Luminary exchange, Libra will provide a rich atmosphere of freedom of thought and action that will richly nourish the self-confidence of the Rams. The typical Libran will usually treat Aries with gentleness, seldom with tyranny or harsh words—and this is an attitude designed to bring out the very best in the Mars nature, to encourage the finest qualities of the Ram to flower. Instead of trying to force Aries into any particular pattern of behavior, Libra will more often recognize the Arian individuality and respect it.

Under the natural instinct to imitate the opposite Sun Sign, a Ram will frequently discover that a relationship with a Libran friend, relative, business associate, lover, or mate leaves him (or her) with the Mars courage and intense drive intact, but softened into a more tolerant and balanced

Venus pattern. Conversely, the Libran man, woman, or child will respond to the Arian friend, relative, business associate, lover, or mate by finding his (or her) indecision gradually turning into a firmer purpose, inspired by the Aries ambition into higher achievement, on both a personal and a public level. As with all 7-7 vibrations, this combination works best when it's composed of two members of the opposite sex. With a Libran and a Ram of the same sex, a recurring sense of envy, resentment, and competition will often trouble the relationship (unless the Suns, Moons, and Ascendents of each are in friendly aspect in the two nativities).

The Ram will have to try to understand the Libra's very real need to conserve his or her energy and not waste it unnecessarily, as Aries is often driven to do with Mars energy. It's Libra's way of maintaining physical and emotional poise—not laziness. When the Ram sincerely tries to see both sides of any disagreement between them and makes a genuine effort to sympathize with the Libran Venus nature, the Libra man or woman will return the favor with much affection and cheerful encouragement, which will considerably lift the Aries spirit. Librans would much rather be happy and pleasant than cranky and argumentative, if Aries will only play fair with them.

Someone once remarked that Librans are the positive, living proof of reincarnation, because nobody could become that impossible in just one lifetime. Present a Libran with this theory, and the reply will be, "Oh, I've heard that about Aries people, but not Libra. Isn't Libra symbolized by the Scales of Justice and Truth? I don't see anything "impossible" in trying to be reasonable. On the other hand, Aries is a *most* unreasonable sign, and I think . . . ." A smart Ram, at that point, will offer the Libra man or woman a slice of cheese cake. He (or she) will dimple, all smiles and sweetness again (since Librans love sweets), and the argument will be over. It's just as well, the Ram couldn't have won it anyway. Besides, losing an argument with Libra is usually beneficial in the long run, because the Venus judgment is nearly always right. By the time it's so endlessly weighed and measured and balanced—and discussed and debated—it certainly *ought* to be.

ARIES *Woman* LIBRA *Man*

-------◆◆◆◆◆-------

*"Wendy," he continued, in a voice no woman
has ever been able to resist . . "Wendy, one
girl is worth twenty boys." . . . .*

*"I think it's perfectly sweet of you," she
declared. She also said she would give him
a kiss if he liked.*

As I've mentioned elsewhere in this chapter, Libra and Aries are opposite
each other in the karmic wheel of Life. The astrological rule is that
you're strongly attracted to the opposite sex of your opposite Sun Sign, but
normally don't get along too well with the same sex of that sign. It would
seem then, that the Aries woman and Libra man would be natural lovers,
destined to live happily ever after.

Natural lovers they are, because the chemistry is right. Destined to live
happily ever after they may not be, unless there's a harmonious Sun-Moon
relationship between them, in which case they could remain sweethearts
for a lifetime, the choice being up to them. Otherwise, with a discordant
Sun-Moon aspect in their mutual charts, it could be touch and go. They
may touch—tenderly—but it won't be long until they go—in opposite directions—putting them right back where they started: opposed.

It's a waste of time for astrologers to keep mentioning the Libra man's
fatal charm for women. He's been practicing it, with instant success, since
he was thirteen (or younger), and his reaction to flattery is simply to flash
that dimpled, Libra smile and murmur, "Tell me all about it, honey." All
right, so he's aware of the blessings of his Venus birthright. He may not
be as aware that all that charm can be a curse when he's mixed up with
an Aries female. (No one ever gets involved with an Aries—they get
mixed up.)

The long line of women who cue up behind him everywhere he goes
will turn an Aries girl who's been a gentle lamb into a Dragon Lady, with
fire flaming from her ears. Mars jealousy is often irrational, and it does
cramp his Venus style. Still, before he decides to leave her because she's
spoiling all his fun, the Libra man might meditate on the word "love."
The longer it's stored up inside and allowed to increase in depth, the more
powerful and satisfying an emotion it can be. (Read *The French Lieuten-*

ant's Woman for proof.) When love is restrained, then given fully at a special moment, with a very special person, it can bring spiritual peace, along with physical ecstasy. Falling in love with love, and getting married for the sake of marriage, are common Libra mistakes. She can be lovely and desirable, but if she's not bright enough to argue with him and challenge him, his fine Libra mind will get rusty. There's no chance of that with an Aries girl. She'll provide him with all the arguments he could possibly use—and enough mental challenges to last for several lifetimes.

When the Libra man gets restless and wants to roam—alone and free—where he can once more accept the favors of a harem of females, the Aries woman probably won't ask him shyly why he's leaving. She's more likely to shout, "Where do you think you're going, Charlie?" He'll tell her he's off to find another seashell, because the shore is full of them. She might remind him then, that seashells are empty. Instead of throwing an emotional tantrum (which may frighten him into splitting so fast he forgets to take along his classical tape cassettes and his favorite baby-blue angora bathrobe), she'd stand a better chance of winning (which is what all Rams want to do all the time) if she curbs her Mars temper and uses his own Libra logic as a weapon. Which is only fair, since he's always using it against her.

"Look, darling, Life is more than one long party of wine, women, and song. While you're getting high on a steady flow of casual affairs, remember that after you pour all the wine out of a flask, you have left only an empty bottle. Then the party's over. Of course, you can always fill it up again from your inexhaustible source, can't you sweetheart? Or is your capacity to love *really* inexhaustible? Why don't you turn some of those romantic urges you express so well (this works better if she's wearing his baby-blue bathrobe—especially this next part) into other creative channels, like art, music, writing, or acting? I could help you. I have a brain equally as brilliant as yours—even though our bodies are made differently—because you're a man and I'm a woman."

The last reminder is a necessity. When a Libra male is led into thinking about the differences between the sexes, he's more or less helpless. Not that the typical Aries woman will have the patience to accept the foregoing advice. She's more likely to yell at him to "Leave! Who needs you anyway!"—push him out the door—slam it—lock it—toss his tapes and bathrobe out the window—and then sit up all night crying in frustrated anger and regret. But I thought I'd throw it in anyway, for those Aries girls who think they are emotionally mature enough to cool it with this man. It's really the only way with Libra. Fairness, logic, and reason. No skyrockets. They disturb his sense of harmony and topple his equilibrium, which is always dangerously seesawing at best. Besides, if you read the section just before this, you'll recall that Air Signs can be goaded into tornado behavior that could make even a Ram run for shelter.

There are so many good things about this blend of Air and Fire between Aries and Libra, it's a shame for them to spend their time bickering. The typical Aries woman isn't looking for a muscle man. She wants a lover whose mental muscles have biceps. The Libra man's mind does. He'll stimulate and challenge her mentally and emotionally. All she needs to do is choose a subject, and he'll have a thousand and one things to say about it, pro and con. Since just a touch of controversy intrigues her, she'll honestly enjoy the debates they have, as long as they both play by the rules and refrain from punching each other in their complexes or tramping on one another's delicate and sensitive Achilles' heels. He'll find this an easier counsel to accept than she will. Tact and courtesy come naturally to Libra, but such consideration for the other person comes hard to Aries.

This woman isn't basically selfish—she's thoughtless. She truly never means to be rude or unkind, and certainly not toward the man she loves. She simply doesn't think or count to ten before she speaks her mind. And her mind can be quite opinionated. Don't forget that Aries is the Sun Sign of the benevolent dictator, regarding both sexes. Benevolent dictators are genuinely concerned about people, compassionate, generous, and devoted to the cause of everyone's welfare. But they don't bother to ask the people they're so loyally championing what it is *they* might want. Never mind. Like the benevolent dictator, no matter what the people want, Aries will see that they get it—because Aries knows what's best for them better than they do. Warmth and arrogance make a frustrating blend, but all Fire Signs possess the combination, making their friends, relatives, and lovers love them and want to strangle them by turns.

When someone points out to a girl Ram that she's being unreasonable and impulsive—and the pointing out is done with tact, gentleness, and affection, she'll never fail to listen, quickly see the error of her ways (she does everything quickly), and try hard to please by making sweeping changes in her original views. But when she's ordered or forced to halt along some mistaken course she's chosen, there's no way she'll give in. That's too much like retreat and Aries never, but positively never, retreats. Mars, the planet of war itself—retreat? It will never happen. Since Mars is her ruler and influences all her motivations, strategy, and behavior, you really can't expect this lady to accept dominance or harsh criticism in a docile manner. If anyone can turn the female Ram into a gentle lamb (besides Leo—and sometimes Gemini, Sag, and Aquarius), it's a Libra man. He'll gently correct her, try to make her see her mistakes in an affectionate and tender way. And nine times out of ten it will work like a charm. The tenth time he should leave well enough alone and consider himself fortunate. You can't win them all. The trouble is that Libra would *like* to win them all—every debate, discussion, argument, dispute, and disagreement. So would Aries. So unless one of them accepts defeat graciously at least part of the time, there's never going to be peace in this relationship—and peace is what the Libra man needs as desperately as the Aries woman he loves needs excitement.

She would profit by trying to give him the peace he needs, because some of it would then drape its soft clouds over her too, softening her disappointments and calming her fears of rejection. He'll likewise profit by trying to give her the excitement she needs, because it will shake him from his spells of Libra lethargy and keep his Scales swinging in balance, instead of dipping one way or the other and getting stuck there.

The Libra man's unconquerable optimism (when his Scales aren't in a down-swing mood of fretting futilely) will strike a spontaneous chord of response in the Aries woman's heart, for it matches her own bright faith in tomorrow. Her naive confidence that whatever she believes intensely enough and long enough just has to come true will strike the same kind of response in him, often moving him to tears (for he is sentimental). She'll like that in him, the sentiment. That's why she fell in love with him, because he's the combination of strength and tenderness she seeks.

But she'll become impatient and accuse him of being lazy, when he's in one of his restful periods, not comprehending the necessity for his Venus-ruled nature to rest between long spells of energetic activity. Her own nature is different, her metabolism is so charged with vitality, she scarcely needs any rest at all—or so it will sometimes seem to him.

His kindness and friendliness are the two qualities she loves most in him. The very same two qualities he loves most in her. They are both kind, both friendly. In a world full of people who are cool, detached, and disinterested, this is not a small thing—and it forms an amazingly strong foundation for their relationship.

Being a 7-7 Sun Sign Pattern, very few of the disputes between the Libra man and Aries woman will happen on the way to or from the bedroom. (Especially if she buys him a king-size water mattress.) To a Libra male, drifting off to romance or dreamland within the soft folds of one of those undulating, billowy contraptions is very close to his idea of heaven. They may fight in the kitchen, the den, the front room, the back porch, the garden, the basement, attic, or garage—but when it's time to kiss goodnight, it will be time to make up for these two. The reconciliation based on the undeniable sexual attraction between them may not, however, last eternally (without that Sun-Moon harmony assistance). He's gentle, poetic, imaginative, considerate, charming, and romantic, all of which sends little tingles and shivers down her spine, from the top of her hard head to the tips of her busy toes. Their physical relationship at first seems like the tangible expression of every love song she's ever dreamed over while she was waiting for the paragon of virtue she's imaged in her heart to come to life.

That's the trouble. Making this man come to life. The Libra approach to sex is mental, light, and airy. Libra men seek shimmering ideals and far-out experiences of erotic expression and sensual feeling, sometimes so far out, sometimes soaring so high above her head—she'll long for something solid to grab. Like, two warm arms and a burning passion you can touch, as well as dream about. Ethereal love and aesthetic sexual response can leave Aries somewhat chilly. Female Rams need plenty of warm affection and fiery lovemaking to feel completely fulfilled in a physical relationship. With this man she may be left feeling a little empty. Something is missing. Exactly what she can't say, maybe the last line of the song. If she has the Moon in Libra, Gemini, Aquarius, Sagittarius, or Leo—or if his Moon Sign is Aries, Sagittarius, Leo, Gemini, or Aquarius—the missing lyric may be found. If the Moon of either was in any other astrological sign at birth, it may be elusive. But the search for it will be delightful.

A Libra man who memorized the old nursery rhyme in school that went: "Peter, Peter, pumpkin eater—had a wife and couldn't keep her—put her in a pumpkin shell, and there he kept her very well," had better check with Mother Goose again. An Aries woman will not sit happily in a pumpkin shell while he glides gracefully around the town, charming all the girls—or while he hides in the library, polishing his Libra mind. With her, he shouldn't expect marriage to balance his Scales—unless it's a complete mental and emotional partnership. Still, if he's honest, he'll realize that's the kind of relationship he really needs himself. When all the parties are over.

☆ ☆ ☆ ☆ ☆ ☆

ARIES *Man* LIBRA *Woman*

—————◆◀◉▶◆—————

"I won't open unless you speak!" Peter cried.

Then at last the visitor spoke, in a lovely,
bell-like voice. "Let me in, Peter."

It was Tink, and quickly he unbarred to her.

It usually isn't difficult for the Libra girl to persuade the Ram to unbar his door or his heart to her. He's putty in her lovely, dimpled hands—and Rams, as you know, are normally putty in no one's hands. Aries men are not made of Silly Putty. They are made of iron and steel (the metals associated with the Aries Sun Sign). But with the Libra lady, he'll melt like a snowman in July. He can't resist her charm, the way she praises all the wonderful qualities he's perfectly aware he possesses himself, but which others are (it seems to him) forever ignoring—the undeniable sexual chemistry between them, and her womanly sweetness. (This is in the beginning. Later, he will experience a few surprises regarding her "womanly sweetness.") Besides, she's probably quite beautiful (most Libra females are), with a smile like carob cupcakes, and every Aries man adores having a girlfriend or a wife who causes other men to envy him. He needs to be proud of the woman he loves, to be able to show her off and brag about her. He wants her to always look prettier and be smarter than other women so it will be obvious that he's won first prize in the love carnival. (Rams, you see, have this inbred thing about winning.)

Since she probably is superior to lots of other women, super bright and startlingly attractive, curvaceous and so forth, this woman will fit all his Mars requirements, and at the start of their affair, everything will be peaches and cream and buttery softness between them.

But the Libra woman in love with an Aries man may later find herself knocked out of balance frequently. Considering her nearly neurotic reaction to being forced into instant action before she's completely sure what she wants to do, having an impatient lover or husband shout, "Come on, what's it going to be—pineapple sherbet or deep-dish apple pie à la mode? The waiter is growing a beard waiting for you to decide"—could cause their relationship to suffer some rocky periods. This man wants things done now, immediately—even sooner if at all possible—even though his demands for whatever it is he wants are often given at the last minute.

"Do you want me to do it today, darling," she'll ask, "or may I do it tomorrow?" (Whether it's taking his favorite red sweater to the cleaners or typing up his address book so he'll have an extra copy if he loses it. He's always losing things.) "Today," he'll tell her. "I want it done today." (If he'd wanted it done tomorrow, he'd have *asked* her tomorrow.) Actually, most Rams would like anything they "request" to be done yesterday.

This sort of irrational and impatient Mars-like reasoning can throw her delicate Venus psyche out of kilter. She could ask, "Isn't it more intelligent to plan ahead and try to do it tomorrow?" only to hear him shout at her, "Don't argue with me! Just do as I say—*please.*" If he has a softer Moon Sign or Ascendent, he'll add the "Please"—if not, he'll just toss out his orders cheerfully, thoughtlessly demanding, without the slightest idea he's being unreasonable and somewhat spoiled.

I know one Libra wife who gave her Aries husband a birthday gift she made herself. A wall hanging created in velvets and satins, with variations of the Mars fire-engine red tones, embroidered with the words: "Dear Lord, give me the gift of patience—*but hurry.*" He was delighted. That's one of the nice things about the typical Arian. He's able to laugh at himself and seldom gets all stuffy when his faults are pointed out (*gently*, not harshly or with a severe, critical attitude). But they do have to be pointed out now and then. Once a Ram recognizes how selfish he's being, he'll feel guilty and ashamed, say he's sorry, and promise not to do it again, after which he'll proceed to do it again—and again—and again. Apologies are not difficult for the average Mars-ruled male to handle. It's one of the most lovable things about him. Aries is quick to admit a fault and accept the blame, but not too quick to drop the bad habit that was apologized for so openly and generously. Still, it's a decided virtue to be able to admit one's mistakes and try again. He does try. He doesn't always succeed, but the good Lord knows he tries.

She apologizes sweetly too. Like Aries, Libra seldom shrinks from admitting mistakes and being willing to say she's sorry. In fact, she may be *too* ready to admit mistakes—or perhaps the better way to express it is that she may be too ready and willing to decide that what she decided (or did) might have been wrong. She'll worry if she's hurt his feelings by something she's said or done, and try to gracefully atone in some way. She'll be doing a lot of that with this man. Atoning, that is—apologizing and atoning for hurting his feelings, because this man is ultrasensitive. He wants everyone to like him, even to love him—family, friends, and strangers—and naturally the woman he owns. (That's more or less the way he thinks of her—owning her, like a special, exciting, precious, and long-awaited, long-prayed-for gift he found under his tree on Christmas morning.) Aries men can be extremely self-centered without meaning to be so. She'll gradually comprehend this, but before she does, her more tender Venus feelings will be bruised more than a few times.

She'll try all her powers of Libra logic and persuasion to make him see that not every single person in the world can love him. But it will make little impression on her Ram. He won't be able to understand why he isn't liked and admired by his worst enemies, never mind what he's said or done to anger them. They should understand that he was right, after all— and that he meant no harm. He was only defending himself from something negative they did to *him*. Why aren't they friendlier? Why don't they see he's sorry for his hasty words and has already forgotten his anger? The Ram will expect people to forget an injury as swiftly as he does. He's always deeply wounded when people pout or bear a grudge over something he considers past and forgotten.

His enemies today are his buddies tomorrow. He'll rush home furious with someone, and expect his Libra lady to share his fury toward the person who's offended him. If she refuses to do so, if she fairly tries to see the other person's side of the issue, and attempts to point out to her Aries lover or husband where he just might have been wrong, he'll turn on her, sometimes violently, sometimes even tearfully—and accuse her of disloyalty. She doesn't love him. If she loved him, she would be on *his* side—and not defend his enemies. He's not interested in her Libra fairness. The only *fair* point of view is *his* . . . . . . and if she really *cared* about him she'd *see* that.

While the Ram is angry, it's impossible for him to see any side but his own, and he definitely will expect the woman he loves to champion him fiercely and consistently. The next day, he may feel quite "sheepish" about the whole thing, and be a perfect "lamb" about confessing his rashness and making amends for his goof. *Then,* you see, it's all right for her to say he's been wrong—because he has realized it himself. But not before he's realized it on his own. Never before.

Naturally, a Venus-ruled female is more capable than most women of balancing the delicate situation of the quick tempers and even quicker reconciliations of the Ram she loves. She's tender, womanly, logical, and intelligent and wise. But she was born under a masculine sign, and she can balk once in a while herself when she feels he's being completely unfair. It probably won't change him, however. He'll either pout or storm angrily out the door (slamming it hard as he leaves), or sulk in the corner, convinced she hates him.

It wouldn't be wise for the Libra woman to display her "iron fist in its velvet glove" too often with this male. He senses when he's being manipulated, after a period of time. He may innocently accept it for a while (Aries possesses almost no guile, and is nearly never unduly suspicious), but once he's caught on that she's trying to mold him into any sort of pattern of behavior, he'll become either obstinate or outraged—or both. *No one* tells him what to do. He is his own boss. Even when he earnestly desires to take a certain course of action, he's likely to refuse to do it if he thinks she wants him to, not because he's suspicious of her motives, but because he has a horror of doing anything someone else suggests—especially anything someone else *openly directs* him to do.

The fact that she likes to argue (discuss, debate, or whatever) every minor and major decision or situation won't alienate the typical Aries man. He sees this as controversy, challenge, excitement! He'd be bored to tears with a woman who never fought back with him. His Mars nature is exhilarated by the promise of battle, whether it's only a mild personal verbal battle over which film to see—or what kind of car to buy—or an argument concerning public or more general topics, like what should be done about pornography, solar heating, nuclear power, corruption in politics, or any other burning issues of the day. But he'll like to win all these discussions. He won't give in, not an inch—until he does win (or until his clever Libra lady allows him to believe he's won). Then he feels proud, self-contented, and happy. And he'll treat her with all the loving affection and tenderness any woman could desire.

This man's sexual image of himself is closely woven into his ability to be always right and emerge victorious in the eyes of the woman he loves. He must be respected, liked, agreed with, and looked up to in order to properly project his considerable Mars virility as a lover. If he feels rejected intellectually or in any other way, he'll freeze into Aries ice (always more serious and lasting than Aries fire—or fiery rages). Their sexual relationship will normally be an uncommonly happy and wholesome one. Her femininity and his masculinity harmonize beautifully and smoothly, in the most natural way. As long as she doesn't allow the masculine side of her Sun Sign essence to intrude into their intimacy (like displaying her capabilities in every area under the Sun to be equal to his, which they quite probably are) and then expect him to feel like the conquering male in a physical sense. He must take the lead in their sexual togetherness, as in every other way. If she allows this, and understands the needs behind it, he'll be the most sensitive, romantic, sentimental, affectionate, and passionate lover she could imagine. But he can become a demanding tyrant if she destroys his ultranecessary confidence in himself.

There's little chance of this occurring, unless she has the Moon or Ascendent in Virgo, Sagittarius, Cancer, or Capricorn—or a lot of planets in Earth Signs in her birth chart. Her basic instinct is tact and thoughtfulness, which is usually blended nicely and equally with her own well-designed and controlled, forceful drive and aggressive nature.

Although their natures constitute a clear polarity, the Mars-ruled man and the Venus-ruled woman are exquisitely mated. After all, Mars and Venus themselves fell wildly and permanently in love—even while Venus was wed to Jupiter. They were caught, of course, in a web woven sneakily by Neptune—but the anger of Jupiter didn't dim their passion by any means. A study of Greek mythology is of immense benefit in comprehending all Sun Signs.

Taking into consideration that the Ram likes to leap around on rocky slopes and the Venus lady lives in a precarious world of the swinging trays of her golden Scales, wherein the slightest breath of wind can upset her inner harmony and outward tranquility, these two often manage to blend their divergent natures with surprising success. The Libra woman can find the intoxicating freedom and exciting mental activity she seeks through this man—and the Ram will enjoy walking through Libra's cool woods, down winding trails of bluebells and butterflies.

The Libra lady is quite a lot of woman. Very few men can cope with her powerful combination of masculine determination and delectable daintiness. But the Aries man is one for taking on super challenges and winning them—and her challenge offers precious rewards to the victor. All men are little boys at heart, but the Ram is more so than most. There's nothing childish about him on the surface. He's tough and forceful—the kind of male they call a man's man. It's the aura of impossible dreams and wistful yearnings hovering mistily around his shoulders that gives him his air of youthfulness . . . . . . some lingering enchantment behind his eyes that makes him so vulnerable. If she uses her Venusian charm and patience to direct his flaming ambitions and incredible energies toward some worthy goal, he can become a crusader for all manner of goodness and glory. (Both of them possess a strong sense of mercy for the weak and can become outraged over injustice.)

She'll seldom or never drown his enthusiastic spontaneity with stern criticism, sarcasm, silent pouting, long brooding silences, or withdrawal—and that will please him. He'll seldom or never refuse to be genuinely interested in and fascinated by her need to talk things over and discuss them—and that will comfort her.

The root cause of any difficulties between them will spring from their shared birthright of the Cardinal essence. For they are both Cardinal Signs of Leadership, Aries and Libra. A relationship will never work when there's a constant battle over which one is the chief, and which one is the Indian—or which one is the general and which one is the private—

who gallops ahead and who canters behind. They'll have to learn to ride their horses side by side, as equals, not as superior and subordinate. It's the only way they'll ever find the way back home into each others' hearts when they've quarreled and both of them have been deeply hurt. Otherwise, they'll get lost like Hansel and Gretel, and you know how glad *they* were to return home together, after all their adventures were over. The only real security anyone has is the safety of being loved by someone who accepts you just as you are, with all your flaws, and wouldn't trade you for another—ever. Someone who makes you know this, even when you're behaving badly. That's safety. That's emotional security. That's *home* . . . . . . where love is.

☆ ☆ ☆ ☆ ☆ ☆

ARIES

Fire — Cardinal — Positive
Ruled by Mars
Symbol: The Ram
Day Forces — Masculine

SCORPIO

Water — Fixed — Negative
Ruled by Pluto
Symbols: Scorpion & Eagle
Night Forces — Feminine

The **ARIES-SCORPIO** *Relationship*

◆◀●▶◆

*Had the pirates kept together it is
certain that they would have won; but
the onset came when they were all
unstrung, and they ran hither and thither,
striking wildly, each thinking himself
the last survivor of the crew. Man to
man they were the stronger; but they
fought on the defensive only . . . . .*

In their secret hearts, Aries men and women rather like to fancy themselves as colorful, fierce pirates. After all, pirates are brave, romantic and dashing. But like the pirate crew in Neverland, Aries often dissipates the Mars energy in the premature exposure of emotional reaction, fighting on the *defensive*. A Ram never attacks unless struck first. Remember that Aries is the symbolic Infant of the zodiac, and infants don't yell unless they're ignored, or someone jabs them with a sharp safety pin. After all, it's the only defense they have against pain or neglect. When more serious danger threatens, their guardian, Mars, comes to the rescue.

Scorpios, however, are masters of the *offensive*—an offensive laced with clever, cool strategy, exquisite patience and an uncanny sense of the weakness of others. You won't find Scorpios coming unstrung, running hither and thither, or striking wildly. When they strike, it's straight on target, with deadly precision. Anytime you're stung by the tail of the Scorpion, you know you've been stung. That's why people seldom mess around with Pluto power the second time. Once is usually more than enough.

Still, it's almost impossible to feel sorry for Scorpions (although offering sympathy to a Scorpio is rather like lending a dollar to the Agnelli family, of Italy—or the Middle East oil czars). It must seem tiresome to watch people recoil when they discover you were born in November.

An Aries friend of mine has a trusted secretary he had always thought was the dearest, as well as the most efficient woman in the world. Then one day he inadvertently found out that Molly was a Scorpio. He nearly went into a state of shock. It was as though he had been harboring a serpent in his office. His loyal Molly—a *Scorpio*? The normal Mars courage plummeted to rock bottom as the Ram reacted to this frightening astrological blow. When he grew calmer, he remembered Molly's hard work over the years, her valor beyond the call of duty, her efficient cool in emergencies—and yes, her sometimes rough tongue.

At that very moment, Molly, who was getting out the mail, held up a letter and said, "Considering you dictated this, it doesn't sound too bad." Translated into Scorpio language, that meant: "Your creative expression is improving."

My Aries friend felt a warm glow, as if he had received praise from on high. He had. So he ventured to remark, "Listen, about your being born in November . . . ."

Scorp glanced up from the IBM Selectric Correctional, threw him a hypnotic stare through the gathering steam in the air (from Fire and Water) and said, "Yes? *What about it*?" The Ram then murmured, "Oh, nothing, Molly. Nothing at all. I was just wondering what to get you for your birthday . . . ."

Now, if you know anything about astrology, you know that's not a typical reaction from an Aries employer. Or any other kind of Aries person. Rams don't back down for anyone.

Strangely, a Ram won't normally push ahead immediately with a Scorpio, as he or she will with those born under all other Sun Signs. There's something about those compelling Pluto eyes, reflecting a quiet poise and hidden strength, that flashes a message to the Ram: "Beware. *This* still water runs very deep. And it could drown you. You're only a paper Ram, and a Ram is a member of the sheep family. You're out of your element with me. You're in the big ocean now, way over your head, full of sharks, seaweed, odd nocturnal creatures, hidden reefs and mystery."

That's where all Scorpios originally came from—the sea. If they're also found on the desert these days, the burning sands are no less a strange territory to Rams.

Aries instinctively absorbs the message, which is "danger." Ah, DANGER! It's the one word that will excite the Ram to action, so the initial caution is soon replaced by the Mars forward charge, rising to meet the challenge thrown down. It's almost always a mistake. When it comes to an actual showdown, a Ram is tougher, louder and more emphatic than a Scorpion. But when things get to that point, the typical Scorpion will simply disappear, wrapped in aloof silence, leaving Aries to ponder the same old mystery. Did he (or she) leave in recognition of defeat—or because I went too far? In other words, even if you appear to win with a Scorpio, you'll never be sure. You'll always have to guess.

It doesn't take many experiences for the average Ram to learn that the best method for dealing with a Scorpio is cooperation—at a safe and respectful emotional distance. The intimacies of romance are something else. Here, we're dealing with the general vibrations of this 6-8 Sun Sign Pattern between Aries and Scorpio in a business, friendship or family relationship.

Examples of the Aries-Scorpio interaction are always valid, whatever the sex or the age of the Ram and the Eagle involved, and so, the following may be aptly and helpfully applied to any Mars-Pluto association in which the reader may be involved, by simply changing the names and the specific situation. *The basics remain.*

One summer, a few years previous to this time of writing, I noticed my ten-year-old Scorpio son was becoming markedly plump (well, all right, fat) and also lazy, from consuming the typical childhood diet of ice cream, cake, candy, soda pop and the nutritional poison from fast food chains—using his allowance to buy the "forbidden fruit." (*Actual* fruit, you can't get some kids to eat. It must be forbidden.)

"Michael," I commanded rather loudly and angrily, with Mars firmness and directness, "you will stop eating that junk, and you will stop now. Immediately. No more sweets will be brought into your room, and hidden on your closet shelf. Nor will you secretly fudge any more Eskimo Pies and chocolate Wing Dings with your allowance. Do you *understand* that? Do you *hear* me?"

His answer was total silence. Within two weeks, he gained ten additional pounds. I then cut off his allowance, every penny of it, to punish him. *Now,* let's see him find a way to get even with me! I thought. He did.

The following week, I received several phone calls from his various teachers, reporting incorrigible behavior from Mike in school, and an absolute refusal to do his homework assignments. Then, fortunately, I finally remembered that I'm an astrologer. The ban on sweets and bad food was lifted. His allowance was not only restored but increased.

"Michael," I said to him, gently this time, and softly, "I trust you to know better than anyone else what's bad for your body, mind and soul—and what's good for it. You are ruled by Pluto, the wisest, as well as the most powerful planet in the entire solar system. I'm sorry I shouted at you before. It's just that [here, I became somewhat calculating, I must admit], well, it's just that it hurts me to hear all those kids at school calling you 'Whale.' That's not the right kind of nickname for an *Eagle.* I know it's affectionate, but . . . . . ." I trailed off, unable any longer to fill in the growing silence between us. This time, along with his silent stare, he answered me with a faint, mysterious smile. Inwardly, I shuddered.

I don't expect my readers to believe what happened next, because if I hadn't seen it with my own Aries eyes, I wouldn't have believed it myself. This determined Scorpion-Eagle, whose inner strength and integrity had at last been recognized, actually began to make *his own green salads* after school, without the slightest hint from me—refused all desserts, munched apples and chewed on tangerines between meals, and stuck to a diet that would starve a Yogi. Miraculously, his secret closet cache of candy bars disappeared. All this without a single additional word from me, and with a steely will power that was honestly frightening.

His reward was a series of weekly karate lessons, where his instructors marveled at his robust health, not to mention his "Scorpio death grip" *he* taught *them.* He had no desire for a black belt, however. He just wanted the training as a warning to the school bullies, instinctively knowing the power of suggestion. Karate is excellent training for young Scorps, by the way. It instills in them courtesy, respect for authority, and most important of all, it stresses *defense,* rather than *attack.*

Within two months, no one was calling the Eagle "Whale" anymore. His new nickname, dictated by Scorpio himself, has become MOE—and his friends would not dare call him anything else. Certainly, this humbled

Ram would not dare. MOE stands for "Master of Eternity." That figures, with Pluto. MOE then organized a group of his closest friends into an organization called the PEARLS (the meaning is secret, and I have no hope of ever learning it), who are dedicated to defending younger children and the elderly from all manner of Manhattan muggers.

That's what can happen when an impulsive, bossy Ram handles an Eagle of *any* age, or *any* sex, with the proper respect. An invaluable lesson for the Aries person, when dealing with a Scorp, in this 6-8 influenced association.

With a Pluto person, Aries shouldn't expect to find the fairness of Libra, the compassion of Pisces or the warm generosity of Leo. He (or she) may even find a basic selfishness exceeding that of Capricorn, if not that of the Ram himself (or herself).

But Scorpio is intensely loyal, and never compromises principle. This makes a big hit with the Ram, who is also fiercely loyal, and who has an equal contempt for the compromising of ideals or integrity. Scorpio never gives in, never admits defeat. Aries is likewise dedicated fiercely to winning. Only sissies give up, and give in. Everybody knows that. These two certainly know it.

Yet, there's another Scorpio quality, intangible, indefinable, that Aries finds impossible to fathom. Is it will power? Or is it, simply—*will?* It is the latter, and it's responsible for the strong, emotionally charged aura surrounding even the quietest, *apparently* harmless, Scorpions.

Now, this doesn't mean that every Scorp has to come on like Dracula. Many of these men and women have undeniably sweet and pleasant personalities. They're interesting, intelligent and courteous. But shy, insecure and defenseless, they *are not*—and Aries should not allow himself or herself to be fooled by their gentle voices, their unobtrusive demeanor and lack of surface aggression. In this association, it's always wise to remember that the elements of Fire and Water are combining, and each has the latent ability to destroy the other, which is explained in more detail in the section called "The Elements" at the back of this book, and in various other chapters dealing with the Fire and Air Sign compatibilities.

I know a Scorpio man who married a Scorpio girl, after a long (and naturally secret) engagement. When Herb and Donna's first baby arrived in April, my initial impulse was to offer to adopt the child. A tiny Ram, under the restrictive dominance of *two* Scorps? Little Joshua must be rescued, I told myself, before his Mars ego is completely crushed. But the truth is, that Aries Joshua has benefited tremendously from the quiet discipline, and intuitive wisdom of his double Pluto-ruled parents. An evolved and enlightened pair of Eagles are an excellent example of moral courage and personal integrity for a Mars youngster, who needs and wants guidance in the right direction. Scorps are perfect teachers of will power and stability to an explosive Ram, who tends to explode in a burst of enthusiasm, then lose interest before the sparks have settled.

There is always, of course, the danger that Pluto power exercised over Mars will be too severe. A Ram of any age may be dampened by Scorpio's Water element caution into becoming the sheep-type Arian, unnaturally introverted and self-effacing, which is definitely not desirable, because it's a denial of the Mars birthright. In the happier Aries-Scorpio associations, however, the Ram will respond beautifully to the strength of the Eagle friend, neighbor, relative, business associate, lover or mate, and try to imitate the Pluto poise, which is a decided positive result of this blend. Just so, the Scorpio half of the team tries to develop more elasticity of viewpoint, in relation to the Ram's more open nature, and far more free and friendly approach to life. The emotional coldness Scorpio can project at times is capable of breaking the warm Aries heart, as well as his (or her) spirit, and self-confidence.

There will be occasional moments when the Scorpio's penetrating gaze of angry disapproval, or thwarted will, can be downright spooky to an Aries, causing the Ram to inwardly quake, never mind his or her Mars rulership. I know a Scorpio father who, when he was frustrated beyond further discussion by the contrariness of his three sons (one of them an Aries), would simply grow stone-silent for a few seconds, then speak, in a sepulchral voice, the ominous Pluto words: *"I'll remember this."* It's rather a healthy idea for all Rams involved with Scorpions to remember *that.* Meaning, the Eagle will never forget an injury. Never. Nor will the Scorp man, woman or child ever forget an act of love or kindness. It's much safer and happier to give them the memory of the latter, and avoid the former, whenever possible.

Some Scorpions become slaves to their own wills. So much so that the Eagle will persist in a purpose, even when it's become obvious that the continuation of a certain course will surely lead to self-destruction. Aries well understands that kind of intense, later-regretted compulsion.

But Aries is a Positive Fire Sign—the reckless, Mars-driven crusader, stirred emotionally by dedication to a cause, and the excitement of a dangerous mission. Scorpio is a Negative Water Sign—the seasoned veteran, possessing a deep sense of realities and the strength to endure hardships, with no illusions about the glamour of marching bands, uniforms and decorations for bravery. Their strategies are very different. Aries *defends* fiercely, in the front lines. Scorpio *attacks* suddenly, unexpectedly, from the rear. At war, these two Sun Signs are natural enemies. Peace is better—and it begins with Love.

☆ ☆ ☆ ☆ ☆ ☆

ARIES *Woman* SCORPIO *Man*

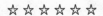

> *The kiss that had been for no one*
> *else Peter took quite easily. Funny.*
> *But she seemed satisfied.*

A Scorpio man penetrates life to the core. He has an almost superhuman capacity to face the facts about himself and others. So it can be a little frightening when he lets you backstage to see what's really going on behind his mask of unshakable self-confidence. What does a woman do when she's been trusted with a secret like that? If she's an Aries, she usually falls in love with an unbelievable intensity.

He may permit her to share parts of him never before revealed to anyone else. That's because he admires the absence of feminine guile in her nature. He responds to her fresh innocence and faith in him, and he's touched by her loyalty. Somehow, this man senses that the Aries girl, unlike her sisters of the other Sun Signs, won't use her knowledge of his inner being against him. Revenge is never an Aries weapon. Although retaliation is something he understands and uses himself, in a strange way that only makes him appreciate the Ram's lack of it even more. Consequently, there can be a depth to the love between Aries and Scorpio that's seldom equaled for sheer passionate devotion and spiritual closeness.

Since neither of them is ever satisfied until they've drained the cup of romance of its last drop of pleasure, emotionally they're well matched and mated. Mentally, they're about as far apart as two people can get and still remain members of the same human race.

His Pluto mind is shrewd, critical, cautious and skeptical. Her Mars mental processes are careless, direct, impulsive and uncomplicated. This distance between their mental outlooks can take one of two paths. It can add intrigue and glamour to their relationship, based on the law that opposites attract—or it can "break the law," and widen into such a chasm, that they find it impossible to communicate, even on those levels where they're alike and sympathetic. Which way it goes depends almost entirely on the Sun-Moon aspects between their horoscopes.

Before the affair reaches the point of a forever scene, however, this man will have asked a few searching questions, and no one asks searching questions more thoroughly than a Scorpio, even when he asks them only with his eyes. Will she take the cold, hard truth from him, which he'll hand her frequently, with meekness and respect? No. She won't. (Meekness? He has to be kidding.) Will she fall apart at his slightest Scorpion sting? No. She'll never fall apart. Her reaction to hurt may range anywhere from a childish tantrum to violent rage. Will she moan and sniffle because he spends a few hours privately talking with a pretty girl about astral projection and ancient witch rites? *If he does what?* No. She won't moan and sniffle. She will do *other* things. *Her* things. I'm willing to forget he even asked that last question, if he is. And he'd better be.

Thought for a Scorpio male reading this chapter: If she acts like that now, just think what marriage to her will be like. I see. You've already thought. That figures. It's hard to tell a Scorpio anything he doesn't already know. But here's something he may *think* no one knows. Despite the answers he came up with in his compatibility quiz, the Scorpio man believes he can teach this girl to keep her cool. Besides, her vital spirit and fiery independence fascinate him.

The trouble could start when he discovers he'll never train this woman to completely control her emotions to match his own cool poise. Then the vital spirit and fiery independence he thought were such flashing virtues may lose their attraction. As long as things go smoothly, he'll accept her aggressive ways. He may even enjoy them. But if she insists on forcing him to conform to an emotional pattern against his own nature, he'll turn like a Scorpion whose tail has been stepped on—and strike. Scorpions are known for their certain retaliation against being trod upon, even when it's accidental. But who would ever step on a Scorpion's tail deliberately anyway? A *Ram would.*

When a Scorpion is confronted with a situation he finds unbearable, he doesn't waste time trying to push it out of the way, like Taurus—devising schemes to evade it, like Libra—or accepting it as fated, like Pisces. Nothing will do but the total annihilation of the obstacle to his peace of mind. For example, if it's a religious dogma against his own principles which someone is trying to shove down his throat, merely to attack the offending church itself is a trifling action, beneath his Pluto Power. He'll set out to destroy the roots and branches of *all* religion, and become a militant atheist. If a hardened criminal breaks into his home and steals from him, merely to help the law apprehend the man is far too mild. Dishonesty has threatened him personally; therefore dishonesty must be wiped out of existence—even if it means the electric chair for the worst offenders—and a long jail term for six-year-olds who snitch Hershey bars. When it's a romantic injury he's suffered which has brought him emotional pain, simply to demolish the girl and their love affair is not enough. He'll turn the incredible force of his will into a scorching, bitter condemnation of all intimate relationships, and the institution of marriage itself. With Scorpio, nothing is done in halfway measures (including devotion, loyalty, and integrity, of course). Pluto men build all the way up to heaven—or destroy all the way down to hell. That's why they're so interesting.

Admittedly, "interesting" may not be exactly the right word, but any Mars-ruled female will get the general idea. It's the old appeal of masculinity, virility and strength. Still, it would be wise for the Aries girl who is about to form an attachment with a Scorpio man to consider carefully his Pluto nature before she exposes her bright fire to that flood of rushing water. If she has anything to say about it, I mean. She may not. The magnetism of Scorpio practically guarantees this man success in whatever he's after, including her. Remaining detached in the face of a Scorpio romantic assault requires an objectivity most Rams don't possess, especially in view of the fact that this is a 6-8 Sun Sign Pattern. Aries is the sixth astrological house of Service to Scorpio. Scorpio is the eighth house of Sex to Aries. And that's about the way it wraps up. She serves him in many ways, with surprising docility, and he provides sexual fulfillment for her. Naturally, the inter-change is not always quite so plain and simple. But basically, their relationship will unfold a curious inclination on her part to submit to this man and allow him to be her Svengali, while he satisfies her deepest desire for physical proof of the kind of complete and eternal love she needs. Their sexual attraction can continue into old age, with none of its original passion dimmed. After death, it can burn just as intensely on the spiritual plane.

This is a couple most likely to walk out on the porno films with explicit sexual scenes. Don't believe everything you've read about Scorpio. Such a public display of intimacies will usually offend the Eagle's ingrained sense of the privacy of human relations to the same degree that it offends her idealism. The only area where sex can cause problems between them is her tendency to exaggerate his strong appeal for women into accusations of unfaithfulness—or if his typical Scorpio suspicion should cause him to interpret her free and friendly manner with all men as flirting. He should realize that she's too honest and full of ideals about love to commit adultery without extreme provocation, and even then, she'll confess it almost before it happens.

Conversely, she must understand that, for all of his passionate inner involvement with sex, the Pluto concept of love is based on purity and integrity. When his needs (which are considerable) are satisfied at home, he'll remain absolutely immune to the wiles of other women, even if one should openly try to seduce him on the street (which is always a possibility with Scorpios). That makes the question of his sexual loyalty entirely her responsibility, and she'll have to assume it or suffer the consequences.

If she can manage to tolerate his quiet air of superiority, exasperating silences and deep wells of secrecy—his somewhat stingy attitude (compared with hers) about spending money, and his iron-clad convictions of right and wrong, even when they differ from her own, she can find an enduring happiness with this man. But that's a lot of tolerance for an Aries woman to master, and Rams are not noted for patience. It may help if she realizes that those firm convictions of right and wrong he so relentlessly and intensely clings to, were formed, on a subconscious level, from the karmic seeds of the weighing and balancing of the sign behind him, Libra —and are now forged into a solid form. It's all part of his karmic, spiritual growing process. He really can't help it.

If he can overlook her surges of jealousy, her financial extravagance, frequent demands for attention and her somewhat immature emotional approach to all problems, he'll find all the woman he's ever sought in an Aries female. But Scorpios are not, by nature, the overlooking kind. Assuming her Moon or Ascendent is in a Water or Earth Sign (with the exception of Taurus) or his Moon or Ascendent is in a Fire or Air Sign (with the exception of Libra) they can take a chance on discovering together the place where the Eagle flies . . . . . . the magical flowers that grow on the summit of the Ram's rocky ledges.

Even without such planetary assistance, these two can simply use their Free Will, and *decide* to have a harmonious relationship. When Pluto and Mars combine forces, there's literally nothing that can't be *willed* to manifest, and happiness is no exception. When this man and woman make a wish on their own stars, the firmament trembles, comets streak by, and trillions of twinkling, tiny starlings chorus an obedient "yes!"

☆ ☆ ☆ ☆ ☆ ☆

ARIES *Man* SCORPIO *Woman*

————◄◆►————

*"But if I had been a weak man," he said. "Good
heavens, if I had been a weak man!"*

Might I make a helpful astrological suggestion for the Ram who is on the
verge of becoming involved with a Scorpio female? Get a copy of Ibsen's
Hedda Gabler, and read it between the lines. Hedda was clearly a Scorpio
woman, and the descriptions of her sometimes incomprehensible behavior
will prepare him for all possibilities, even though the lady Eagle he loves
may be a somewhat more average Scorp, with more subdued Pluto Power.
It's only sensible to be prepared for the worst, even if you expect—and actually receive—the best. Forewarned is forearmed, and it never hurts to be
forearmed with a Scorpio.

As for the unfortunate Hedda herself, she's admittedly an extreme example, yet an interesting study for Eagle watchers. Her cool, quiet, mysterious feminine mystique is punctuated by sudden, violent frenzies, which
are puzzling, to say the least, coming from such a normally gentle, self-
contained woman. Her nice, easy-going Taurus or Pisces husband is at a
complete loss when it comes to comprehending her emotional needs. Then
along comes a clever, worldly chap, undoubtedly an Aries, who thinks he
has mastered this woman, plumbed her depths and dominated her with
his masculine superiority. When she finally kills herself, all the confused
man can manage to murmur is that "people just don't *do* that sort of
thing."

Scorpios do. They can do all sorts of either strange and frightening or
weird and wonderful things—and they never warn you ahead of time what
they're up to.

Granted, as I've already noted, Hedda is an exaggerated image of the
Scorpio woman. The average Pluto-ruled female probably won't climb to
such heights of ecstasy, or plunge into such wells of despair as the unfortunate Hedda. But even if she only lets the air out of his tires when he
won't let her drive his car, or casually cuts his telephone cord when he
calls another girl, a Ram who's aware of the Scorpion tendency toward secret revolt, followed by sudden retaliation, will find life with this girl considerably less traumatic.

It's her secret revolt, more than her sudden retaliation, that could cause the tension between these two lovers. An Aries can be driven wild by an act that, although easy enough to forgive in itself, is the result of a premeditation unknown to him. Since she's inclined to be secretive when she's not in action, her inexplicable surges of angry revenge can infuriate him. Rams do not like unpleasant surprises, and they simply can't *stand* not to know secrets. Normal outbursts of temper he can handle, with the experience born from his own stormy impulses. But she didn't give him the slightest hint that she was going to burn up his new Adidas jogging booties, and starch his favorite jeans. At breakfast, on Monday morning, her voice was cool and calm, her eyes burned into his, expressing their usual intense devotion, and her goodbye kiss was as passionate as ever. How was he to suspect he'd return home that night to a pair of charred sneakers and stiff Levi's? And all because he told her on Sunday he didn't feel like taking her to the movies, because he wanted to hike in the woods, with some old buddies from college he hadn't seen in years.

How DARE she sock him and shock him with a surprise maneuver like that, retroactively? He'll show her a thing or two! But by the time he's ready to show her a thing or two, she's not watching his fiery scene, because she's already reverted to her silent aloofness. She's turned off. Detached and disinterested. Also uninterested.

Scenes of this sort can rattle a Ram to the roots of his horns. What she's done outrages him, simply because it sneaked up on him in such an . . . well, in such an *outrageous* way. Add to that her talent for coolly turning off, before he can even fight back to defend himself, and you can see why he may gradually become an aggressive, frantic shadow boxer, hitting out blindly, and never getting the satisfaction of landing a victorious punch (symbolically) on his lady Eagle's (also symbolic) jaw. To so surprise him, after he's already blithely forgotten the incident that infuriated her, then retreat, and refuse to even notice him or listen to his angry sputterings, is not a pattern of behavior calculated to win all the confrontations in the final tallies—for her. She might lose the last hand of her bridge game by losing him.

Actually, if the Ram will just let her win, or allow her to believe she's won, he'll save a lot of wear and tear on his ego, through bypassing fruitless emotional conflicts with this woman, which are destined by the stars to lead absolutely nowhere. It's really the only way to get along with a lady Scorpion—simply permit her to satisfy herself that she has repaid the hurt or slight she's suffered from you, then *say no more about it.* One of his finer rewards for such emotional control and maturity, will be her gradual and certain, deeper respect for him. Since the fighting pattern just described is the absolute only one Scorpio recognizes, it's the only one powerful enough to keep their relationship on an equal basis. As Grandpa used to say, "You can't fight City Hall" (truer even today than in Gramp's day, in both its literal and symbolic sense). She holds the trump card—self-control. The proper way to handle and keep a woman like that is, obviously, not to lose your own control.

He can always remind himself, during his more discouraged moments, that this woman is as loyal to the man she loves as she is determined not to allow him to step on her Scorpion tail. When a lady with a Scorpio Sun Sign, Moon Sign or Ascendent falls in love, her friends, her family, her career, reputation, her suffering—all count for nothing. She won't hesitate for a second to openly show her scorn for anyone who threatens to stand in the way of their happiness together, to cast a shadow on their love or to harm her man in any way. A devotion of this level of intensity should make it easier to overlook the manner in which she occasionally manipulates their personal squabbles against him. Rams need to be loved all the way—or not at all. And that's precisely how Scorpio loves. All the way—or not at all.

An Aries man who has only recently become emotionally involved with this girl (let's say this woman—Scorps are never girls, they were all born women) may think the foregoing is an unjust summary of the character, traits and personality of his dearly beloved. That's because he was picturing the retaliatory attacks, followed by instant withdrawal, which were just described, as a kind of black-widow-spider operation. So, how could a female with such a whispery, throaty voice and gentle, feminine ways, be a closet black widow spider? She is not, of course. That's the point. Her Pluto revenge tactics needn't resemble something out of a vampire movie. She's not the Bride of Frankenstein. She's simply a sweet, rather shy lady, who has her quiet moments, and who is sensitive.

After they're married, he'll learn. He'll receive a fast astrological lesson, when he tells her—"I wish you'd go to the beauty parlor and let them style your hair, before my business partner [my boss, my agent, or whatever] and his wife come here for dinner tonight. The way you're wearing it now is so dated, and very unbecoming." (Aries rules the first astrological house of personal appearance, and Rams are really quite vain about their own looks, and the looks of their loved ones. Almost as much so as Leo.) The Scorpio woman won't scream at him in rage, because her glamour has been criticized. She'll just smile sweetly and say, "Of course, darling." She'll still be a perfect angel of womanhood when he arrives at home that night, accompanied by Mr. Grumple and his bejeweled wife.

His Scorpio mate's voice will be velvety warm and sensual when she whispers to him in the bedroom, "Sweetheart, *you* explain to the Grumples, won't you? I have a dreadful headache, and I'm just not up to meeting anyone tonight."

"You *what!*" he shouts. "How can I explain this to them? They're out there in the front room waiting to meet you, and you're still in your nightgown, and you haven't even started dinner? This could ruin my whole future! Do you realize what you've done to me?"

His rage has not the faintest effect. She has already closed her eyes and placed the ice bag on her head, still smiling sweetly, leaving him to cope with his hungry guests alone. You see? Not like the vampire movies at all! Just a nice lady, with a headache, who's terribly sorry she's causing him such embarrassment. (Next time, he won't insult her hairstyle.)

The Aries man is competent and courageous when he's involved in a situation he can understand, but he lacks the ability to successfully oppose the type of reasoning that goes over his head. It will bewilder him when she refuses to fight him with weapons of his own choice, but it will also have the long-term effect of subduing him, which can result in a growing emotional maturity. Although loving and living with a Scorpion may be a little bumpy, it will mellow the Ram's fiery personality and open his eyes to his Martian faults of selfishness, rashness and impulsive speech, like no other experience he's ever had before. If he really loves her, there's much she can teach him—and he, likewise, her.

In 1970, in California, I met a fascinating Scorpio woman, who had just separated from her Aries husband. (He was a surgeon, a typical Mars occupation, although a not very evolved or enlightened one.) Neither of them knew enough astrology to understand, and therefore to tolerate, each other's natures. But I got the impression they might still be in love, and I hope this book is published in time to help them get back together. Her marriage taught her at least one astrological lesson she'll never forget. (Scorpios always profit from experience.) "Men cringe when they meet a Scorpio," she told me. "They think we're all deadly and dangerous. So now, when they ask me my Sun Sign, I just flutter my eyelashes and tell them I'm a Pisces. It works like magic!"

There's no telling how many November girls are running around out there pretending to be Fish—but you've been warned. It's a shame astrological ignorance makes such a disguise necessary. Scorpio women, if properly understood, are beautiful people, with an unsurpassed tenderness and an enormous capacity for love.

The sexual attraction between an Aries man and a Scorpio woman is instant and magnetic, and can be permanently fulfilling. Their physical relationship will never be indifferent or casual. Sex, combined with love, is a basic formula in the Scorpio search for personal salvation, the same kind of glory the Ram seeks to satisfy his misty ideal. He must conquer sexually, and she'll allow him to do so, but she won't be passive, she'll meet him more than halfway in erotic expression. Her intense response to his lovemaking blended with her willingness to submit to him physically, represents the ultimate in ecstatic union to this man, who seeks a real woman, never a quiescent partner, yet neither a dominant mate who will try to overpower him. In his secret heart, he is the original, virile, yet pure and innocent Adam—in her secret heart, she is the original, tempting and mysterious Eve. Unless one of them has a serious Mars or Venus affliction in the natal chart (which, with these two, can lead to various forms of sadism or masochism), there will be no doubt at bedtime who is man and who is woman—and, with all due respect to Women's Lib, that's the way it was intended to be by our co-Creators.

A Scorpio female can't forgive being badly loved, in or *out* of the bedroom, and she may occasionally, if he's unthinkingly wounded her, use a denial of sexual Oneness against him as a revenge weapon, which is a large mistake on her part, since it may very well turn him into an insecure, and therefore selfish, lover. He should establish his mastery from the beginning in the area of physical passion.

Scorpio is compelled to violate the unknown, in order to *know*, then knowing, keeps the secret. Aries plunges in recklessly, to discover truth and happiness, then shares it enthusiastically and openly. This is an essential difference between them, which can be bridged only by mutual trust and forgiveness each time it appears. When he displays his emotions carelessly, he may create pain in her heart she'll find hard to forget, and although her outward response to his Mars fireworks may simply be a soft-spoken—"Aren't you over-reacting, darling?"—there's no determining what may be occurring within her, behind her cool mask. There's only one answer to a question like that.

"No, I'm not over-reacting. I am just being me. I was born under a different star than you, and I have to express my feelings. Don't you want me to be true to myself?" Yes, she does. She may never reveal it, or admit it . . . . . . but she does.

☆ ☆ ☆ ☆ ☆

ARIES

Fire — Cardinal — Positive
Ruled by Mars
Symbol: The Ram
Day Forces — Masculine

SAGITTARIUS

Fire — Mutable — Positive
Ruled by Jupiter
Symbols: Archer & Centaur
Day Forces — Masculine

The **ARIES-SAGITTARIUS** *Relationship*

. . . but perhaps the biggest adventure of all
was that they were several hours late for bed.
This so inflated them that they did various
dodgy things to get staying up still longer,
such as demanding bandages . . . .

Both of these Sun Signs like to stay up late. They're afraid they might miss something. That's why they're reluctant to retire early, leave parties early—or walk past two strangers fighting in the street. Rams and Archers are forever being advised by well-meaning friends, "Stay out of it. Mind your own business. It's not your concern. It's a lost cause." This last warning is a mistake. These two would walk a thousand miles for any cause, and if it's a lost cause, they simply can't bear to stand by without trying to save it. The fact that it's none of their business only makes it more intriguing, since both signs are infused with excessive amounts of curiosity, as well as a determined opinion that they know all the answers.

As for "demanding bandages," Aries and Sagittarius are also the most accident prone in the zodiac (with Aquarius running a close third). For obvious reasons. Not only on account of the traits just mentioned, but because Aries men and women are always ramming their horns into places where angels fear to tread—or even tiptoe. Sagittarians (symbolized by the Centaur, with bow and arrow) are all just naturally born a little clumsy. It isn't easy to balance a body that's half horse, half man. Neither is it easy to balance a personality that's half philosopher, half clown.

Aries and Sagittarius get along pretty well most of the time, because they have so much in common—like their noticeable abundance of idealism. No one is more idealistic than the naive Ram, with the childlike faith that "wishing will make it so," unless it's the Archers, who aim their arrows toward some galaxy unseen by mortal man or woman.

Of course, today, with less idealistic people poisoning the Earth and its atmosphere, the Jupiter arrows can get stuck in a mass of solid pollution before they get past a low-hanging cloud. Rams and Archers aren't the only people with good intentions, but they're usually too busy, especially as a team pushing their ideas of Utopia (often running in concentric circles) to be sidetracked by personal or political greed.

Another thing Aries and Sagittarius have in common is their fondness for heated discussion. Only a Libra has more fun starting arguments. But logical Libra is driven by a desire to be fair and see justice done. Rams and Archers are simply constitutionally unable to ignore a verbal challenge for other reasons. Aries argues because someone has dared to tell them they're wrong, when the Rams know they're always infallibly right. Sagittarius argues because truth isn't being told, and if there's anything an Archer can't stand, it's to hear truth distorted.

The fable about the Emperor's new clothes is an excellent example. There they were, all those brainwashed subjects, thousands of gullible people—standing in the ditches, and cheering their insane Emperor as he paraded by in his carriage—stark nude. Because he was their leader, and could therefore do no wrong, they saw him draped in luxurious satins and velvets, sparkling with precious stones. "See how beautiful the Emperor's clothes are!"

There's no telling what might have happened to that mythical kingdom, if a small child (who could only have been a little Virgo girl with the Moon in Sag—or a young boy Archer with the Moon in Virgo) hadn't shot an arrow of truth into the crowd and called out (in modern idiom), "Hey! Dig that! The old dude is as naked as a jay bird!" I don't remember what happened to the child in the fable, but I hope the youngster wasn't picked up by the Emperor's guards for interrogation. That would have been rough on the guards.

Anyone who has a Sagittarian for a friend has submitted to a certain amount of verbal surgery. This cheerful, friendly puppy dog approaches you on the street, whacks you on the back and opens up with, "Well, hello there—how are you! My gawd, it's good to see you again, but I almost didn't recognize you. Boy, are you skinny!" Then comes the usual Sagittarian apology for the rudeness, because these people are basically kind-hearted, and only the occasional, unevolved Archer would wound you deliberately. "Oh, no, I've done it again, haven't I? Stuck my big foot in my mouth. You're probably *sensitive* about being skinny, right?"

Or maybe this scene: "How are things going, old chum? Listen, I hear you got fired because you've been hitting the bottle too much. That's nothing to be ashamed of. Look at President Andrew Johnson. He was an alky, and they tried to fire him too. Did you ever think of getting a job as a wine taster? Now, there's a career where you could really go places! Say, how about bringing that married woman you've been dating and dropping over to the house tonight? Don't worry, I'll tell my wife to hide the liquor. You know what St. Patrick said. God invented whiskey to keep the Irish from ruling the world!"

Producer-TV personality David Susskind is a double Sagittarian. (Sagittarius Sun Sign and Ascendent.) Perhaps you caught his television show the night of the famous interview between "friendly puppy dog" Susskind and the bombastic Russian Ram, Nikita Khrushchev, which was running along quite nicely until David looked Premier Khrushchev straight in the eye and shot out something like: "Why is your country so deceptive, and why do your officials lie so much?" How's that for warming up a cold war? Zing! Zowie! As papers across the nation reported the following day, and even owners of black-and-white television sets could see, Aries Khrushchev's face turned several shades of angry red, and his features strongly resembled a thundercloud about to explode into a storm.

Aries normally admires and defends Sagittarian honesty, since Rams also pride themselves on telling the truth. But they draw the line at hearing the truth about themselves. That's a marked difference between Aries and Sag. The Archer is nearly as blunt in making unflattering statements about himself—or herself—as in telling others their faults. The Ram champions the truth only up to the point where it begins to sting, or come too close to home. Aries people aren't noted for easily recognizing or accepting their shortcomings and flaws.

Although most Sagittarian arrows are shot in good faith, with no real intent to be malicious, an occasional unevolved and unenlightened Centaur will blast a Ram with a cutting and cruel remark that bears no relation to truth, guided only by a desire to hurt. (All traits of all twelve Sun Signs can be, at times, expressed through their negative polarity.) While such a brutal Sag may get away with this sort of behavior with most people, he or she will discover it isn't very smart to so attempt to shoot down a Ram of either sex. The arrow will be shot right back, with the added Martian thrust of righteous outrage, not always hitting its mark immediately (Aries' aim is not as true as the Archer's) but eventually finding its fiery way home. Jupiter is a large and powerful star, but even in the sky, Jupiter remains a healthy distance away from the warlike Mars, ruler of Aries. To fail to defend against attack would disgrace the Mars reputation for fearlessness, and topple the entire astrological structure. It will never happen.

But this is a 5-9 vibrational association, and the frequent friction between these two can be smoothed with the quick regret and open forgiveness both Sun Signs are capable of demonstrating when they've been naughty or unkind toward each other. Neither Sag nor Aries is able to contain anger for long periods of time, and neither Sun Sign bears ill will beyond the passion of the moment—unless one of them happens to have a Scorpio Moon Sign. Then the injury might be remembered for more than a few days. Even so, the Sun is more powerful than the Moon's lighter influence, and eventually, the sunny dispositions of the Ram and the Centaur will restore harmony between them.

Many careers and activities attract the wandering, restless Sagittarian, from jungle safaris to gambling dens or the stock market, the biggest gambling den of them all—from horse breeding or dog training to religion—from medicine and the law, to higher education—as long as the Archer is free to move around, and talk—to take a chance, and find a thrill.

Many careers and activities attract the gregarious Aries too. Just pick a profession, and the Ram will be happy to run it for you. They're not choosy, as long as they can be boss. Aries is a Cardinal Sign of leadership. Sag is a Mutable Sign, and less inclined to seek authority. Intuitively, the Archer knows the boss is tied down to the desk, often being unable to take as many vacations as his or her employees—and Sag does love those vacations! Actually, both of them prefer being their own boss, and gravitate toward occupations or professions where nobody tells them what to do, or when to do it.

Although the Ram and the Archer are both essentially extroverts, both born under the Positive, Masculine Day Forces, you'll meet more quiet Archers than quiet Rams. Perhaps that's because the more philosophically oriented Sagittarians have discovered the hard way—and I *do* mean the *hard* way—that you learn more when you're listening than when you're talking. After all, Jupiter does rule higher education (among other things), and it's only natural that the Jupiter-ruled gradually become adept at self-education. Archers are all naturally intuitive, and the meaning of "in-tuition" is to be taught from within.

To understand the basic difference between Sag and Aries, it's necessary to understand the differences between the two planets that rule them, Jupiter and Mars. These two people are so much alike, on the surface, that it may be hard to detect any differences, but there are.

Jupiter influences the Sagittarian man, child, woman, boy or girl to be expansive (often to exaggerate experiences and feelings, but seldom the facts)—to be brutally honest and extremely experimental, in all areas of life. Jupiter's vibration also creates a great wanderlust in Sag, and blesses the Archers with occasional flashes of prophetic vision. Symbolized by the Centaur, which is half horse, half man, the Archer has far more personal confidence and assurance than the Ram (never mind the Aries surface brashness) because Sag contains the total experience of both human and beast.

Mars influences the Aries man, child, woman, boy or girl to be forceful and direct in all ways—to fiercely defend themselves against attack—and to be bravest in an emergency or a crisis. Such defense from the vibration of Mars is necessary for the Aries person, because Aries is symbolized by the Infant, newborn, and like the human infant, Aries would, quite literally, die without affection and care, *unless* Mars protected.

Not as wisely prophetic as Sag, Aries, nonetheless, sees straight through to the heart of all things, being blessed with a combination of Mars penetration to the core and the Infant's innocence and naivete, which is the purest wisdom of all. The most vital difference between these two, however, is that the Ram is far more vulnerable to cruelty and neglect. Also, there is never maliciousness in the Aries intent, for, like the newborn, Aries comprehends, essentially, only goodness—whereas Sagittarius has lived long enough (soulwise) to have developed more cynicism and worldly-wise attitudes.

Great idealism and striving are present in Sag, but seldom innocence. Sagittarius has learned to think, to use the intellect, to prophesy and to philosophize. Aries comprehends no other path to happiness than the new-born instinctive emotional reaction to love and kindness. Only the fierce protection of Mars keeps the Ram from being totally helpless in the hands of stronger people. Wasn't it wise of our co-Creators, in arranging to keep the karmic plan in order through astrology, to insure that the Infant of the karmic wheel would be watched over and protected by the devoted warrior (and lover of Venus) Mars?

This is the graced-by-the-gods 5-9 Sun Sign Pattern, making compatibility between the Ram and the Archer relatively easy to achieve. Both the rare, quiet Arians and Sagittarians—and the more common, typical, extroverted types—are far happier when they're both mentally and physically active, learning. Like the proverbial prophets, Sag frequently fares better away from the place of birth, and delights in traveling to get there (with little nostalgia for the "roots" left behind). Aries suffers painful heart tugs from the memory of the "safety" left behind, but nevertheless bravely joins the Archer, trying to match the faster pace of the Centaur's canter. When the Ram joins Sag, and they travel together, the trip may be a little noisy, but never dull, and they'll energetically defend each other against any baddies who threaten them. Despite their frequent squabbles, the unquenchable idealism of Sagittarius will forever move Aries to spontaneous affection and an unaccustomed compassion—just as the Archer will forever be touched by the naivete and honesty of Aries, knowing that here is someone who can be trusted never to be hypocritical or disloyal. After all the smoke has cleared away, these two will still be standing there, smiling at each other with their hearts. You might say that the Ram and the Archer are combustible, but compatible.

☆ ☆ ☆ ☆ ☆ ☆

ARIES *Woman* SAGITTARIUS *Man*

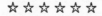

The Never bird saw at once what he was up to,
and screamed . . . .

To face an astrological truth bluntly and candidly, as Archers like to do, a Sagittarius male is more likely than any other (with the exception of Gemini) to be unfaithful in some way, if not physically, then mentally, through harmless flirting.

Naturally, that's a generality, certainly not true in every single case, with every single Centaur. But it's true often enough to make a love affair between a girl Ram and an even "mildly" promiscuous boy Archer about as much fun as skipping rope in sandals with cherry bombs strapped to the heels. Any man who thinks it would be a challenge to play that kind of romantic Russian roulette with an Aries female would be safer taking American singer Anita Bryant to a meeting of the Gay Liberation group. If you should run across a Mars-ruled girl who claims she isn't jealous in the smallest way of her man's attentions to other women, and theirs to him, she is either lying (because she has an afflicted Mars or Mercury in her nativity) or she's adopted, and her parents didn't tell her her true birth date. You can wager on it, and win. You have astrology's guarantee.

Of course, there's always the chance that she's not in love with the man who doesn't arouse her jealousy (jealousy of all types being merely a deep-seated fear of rejection), and she simply doesn't care. Aries ice. In fact, that's an excellent barometer of the girl Ram's feelings. If she's casual or detached regarding her lover or husband's flirtations, she's no longer in love, and he'll be told soon enough that she's stopped caring. It's the earliest Mars warning signal of romantic dissatisfaction, and very little time will elapse between such a signal and the final goodbye wave from this woman.

Aries and Sag are both Fire Signs, and fire attracts nearby fire, simply by a spark leaping from one flame to another, sometimes many feet through the air, let alone across a room. Therefore, the Sagittarian man will be drawn to the Aries woman almost from the first time they meet, for the purpose of either love or friendship. Being influenced by the 5-9 Sun Sign Pattern, their natal Suns are trined, and so they are, in a word—sympatico. It might be better if he aims for friendship, instead of love, if he isn't quite yet ready to settle down to being a one-woman man. He may have enjoyed the four-in-a-bed scene in the American film *Bob and Carol and Ted and Alice*, and accepted it all in a spirit of fun and laughs—but *she's* the one who walked out on the scene, and tossed her buttered popcorn in the usher's face as she left the theatre. (As I've said elsewhere in this book, Aries anger is never discriminatory.)

One thing to be said in defense of a typical male Archer is that, if he's tempted to succumb to the charms of a new love, he's as likely as the Aries woman to confess it almost immediately. Basically the Jupiter-ruled male is both sincere and honest. Neither of these two will ever carry on a long-term deception. Admittedly, with an Aries girl, he'd be better off not being quite so truthful. He shouldn't feel obliged to report to her every single wink he receives from the predatory females who abound these days, urged as they continually are from so many directions to be sure they aren't deprived of their share of multiple sexual adventures, with no rules to the game except variety. The Mars woman's imagination supplies her with more than enough images of infidelity, without his adding the burden of meaningless winks to her feelings, and to their relationship.

It seems strange for a girl with such apparent self-confidence, who is so openly independent, to be so emotionally vulnerable. But she is, and she suffers greatly through her inner fear of being hurt or deceived in love. Aries is a masculine sign, and so the girl Ram is never quite certain of her femininity. This makes her secretly believe that even women who are clearly less intelligent and less attractive than she, are nevertheless more desirable to the man she loves, if for no other reason than their outward feminine manners. Wondering about a thing like this can be an indescribable private torture. Yet, unfortunately, her outbursts of jealousy will often receive little real sympathy or compassion from an Archer, who places a high value on personal freedom and mutual trust between two people in love.

Such an attitude is all well and good, but if he doesn't train himself to be somewhat more gentle with this woman's basic nature, and try to handle her hidden fears with more tender concern—being willing to talk things over with her now and then, to ease her mind—he'll lose her more quickly than he found her. And the emptiness she leaves in his heart may not be as easy as he thinks to fill. There's always a terrible feeling of loneliness on both sides when a man and woman whose natal Suns are trined, and who truly loved each other, separate. If the feeling they thought was love was only friendship, and was, therefore, inaccurately defined by them from the beginning, the parting will be less painful—and they may even be friends again later. But not if they deeply loved. The pain is too great, then, to transmute former affection into a casual friendship.

If mutual trust can be established between them, from the start, an Aries girl has an excellent chance for emotional harmony with a Sagittarian man, and he with her. Many Archers are sexually stable and reliable, and with those who are, love between these two can be eternally exciting and always stimulating—emotions which, in an odd sort of way, bring peace and contentment to the hearts of those born under Fire Signs. Peace and contentment within, you see, are not achieved in exactly the same manner by everyone.

Both these lovers are optimistic, open-hearted, warm and friendly. They're also both visionaries, but his visions are more practical, since Sagittarius, unlike Aries, has the prophetic ability to foresee the outcome of his dreams from their inception, as well as the self-honesty to separate them from mere fantasies, based on delusion. Although they're both expert at tossing pie-in-the-sky, his pies are seldom half-baked.

When this man and woman fall in love, the blend of her Mars enthusiasm with his Jupiter daring, gives them an insurance against boredom. Love seldom grows cold between two people who share a mutual excitement for new ideas, and an eternal youthfulness of spirit. They'll probably even vote alike, because it's an extremely exceptional Ram or Archer who isn't politically liberal. There are occasional conservatives born under both Sun Signs, of course, although the odds are that a Sag more than Aries will lean slightly to the Right. Even so, the rare conservative Sagittarian will be motivated by political idealism. Since they both feel strongly about the burning issues of the day, this is more important than it may seem as a contributing factor to their compatibility.

It's only fair to warn the Aries girl that a Sagittarian man is more likely to remain a bachelor than any other Sun Sign, except Virgo and Aquarius. His affectionate, impulsive nature (very much like her own) allows him to slide into a romance easily, and he can be precipitated by her Mars force into a commitment he's not ready to keep. Since most Archers refuse to lie at the altar, broken engagements and disappearing grooms are not uncommon with this Sun Sign. They're not cruel—just honest. I know one Sagittarian man who's been promising to marry a charming widow for more years than either of them can remember. She's still waiting, with Cancerian tenacity. If she were an Aries, she'd tell him to go dunk his donuts in someone else's coffee, lock her door and change her telephone number. Sudden action like this often brings an Archer to his senses, if he really loves the woman. If he doesn't, she has only herself to blame. He probably never actually told her he loved her. Sagittarian men are usually quite careful not to say "I love you," unless they mean it, and they have plenty of dodgy verbal tricks to get out of it, without arousing suspicion. Here are a couple that every red-blooded male Archer has used, at one time or another. Pay close attention to the exact words.

GIRL: Darling, you do love me, don't you?
ARCHER: (hurt and angry): How can you ask me a ridiculous question like that? You don't know how I feel by now?

(or perhaps . . .)

GIRL: Do you really love me? Do you *really*?
ARCHER: What do *you* think, sweetheart? I don't see how you can wonder. (Showering her immediately with passionate kisses.)

Later, she'll accuse him of emotional breach of promise, but she didn't listen carefully. He didn't lie to her. Sagittarians never lie. Didn't you know that?

Normally, this man is not the domestic type. Look at the way he treats his own family—casually. And the way he loves his own relatives—from a distance. But the girl Ram isn't tied down to the heart either, so she won't mind his wandering, as long as he takes her with him. If she gives him miles of rope and lets him know that she, too, believes in personal freedom, the Archer can be a generous and stimulating partner, in or out of wedlock. She should learn to love animals, because sooner or later, this man will bring home a dog or a horse. If they live in a small apartment, let's hope it's a dog.

He may spend lots of time at the stables, in the woods, hiking or camping—involving himself in sports as a participant or spectator—or involving himself in the theatre as a participant or spectator. The more-intellectual type of Archer will substitute books and philosophy for nature, sports or the stage, but whatever, his interests will frequently be outside the home. It doesn't mean he isn't in love with her, and the Aries girl must realize that, if she wants to hold him for keeps.

Their sexual adjustment is almost automatic. Both of them are deeply affectionate, and passion is never lacking, since they're both Fire Signs. His approach to physical lovemaking may be slightly more casual and detached than hers, and not quite so intense, but it will be no less sincere, and certainly no less idealistic. Each is capable of a warm response, which can make their intimacies wonderfully fulfilling, although perhaps not completely free of sexual selfishness (one of the most common causes of sexual disharmony). They may both have to learn that real happiness comes from an inner need to *love*—not to *be* loved. The lesson shouldn't be too difficult, because the sense of giving is strong in both their natures. Since they're also mentally and emotionally well mated, the physical relationship between them (barring jealousy and unfaithfulness) can be ideal in every sense.

She won't like it when he sometimes makes promises he can't keep, for Archers often impulsively reach out farther than their arms can stretch. She may explode into angry tears when he carelessly blurts out an unpleasant truth, without regard for her sensitive feelings. And she could become annoyed with his clumsy attempts at humor, which can be poorly timed. Sagittarians are half clown, you know, and the antics of clowns are never subtle. She's stuck with Emmett Kelly, so why not accept his peanuts and cotton candy, laugh and enjoy it? Although he may occasionally resent her claims on his freedom and her demands on his time, he'll admire her bright mind and respect her independence.

As for the possibility that his Jupiter tendency to promiscuity will ignite her Mars jealousy, don't overlook the Archer's strong sense of honor and

personal integrity. He'll behave the way he's expected and trusted to behave. There's an old metaphysical formula, so magical, it works wonders.
A friend of mine, Hank Fort, once wrote a song, with lyrics that sum up
this infallible Universal Law, and they say, in part . . .

> *give makes give—greed makes greed*
> *flower makes flower—and weed makes weed*
> *clean makes clean—dust makes dust*
> *doubting makes doubting—and trust makes trust*

The Aries woman in love with an Archer, who repeats that last line
over and over again when her heart is troubled, will discover that it's truly
a miracle mantra that will bring her more reasons to rejoice than to cry.
For truth makes truth, you see—and lie makes lie.

☆ ☆ ☆ ☆ ☆ ☆

ARIES *Man* SAGITTARIUS *Woman*

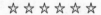

> *. . . and then Peter gripped her and began to draw her*
> *toward the window.*
>
> *"Let me go!" she ordered him . . . . . .*
> *Of course she was very pleased to be asked.*

A Sagittarian girl who's attracted to an Aries man is only doing what
comes naturally. She admires courage, craves excitement, likes to have fun
—and the Ram is certainly not a stick-in-the-mud. True he's somewhat
bossy, and inclined to insist on getting his own way. But he's eternally a
sentimental romanticist, and that's what she's looking for, even though
this girl may not recognize her own goal until someone points it out to
her. Once she is made to realize it, however, she'll gather a goodly number
of scars from looking for it in all the wrong places and ways. But she'll
cover them, often with the mask of the clown. Sag always tells a joke
when Jupiter's idealism has been struck. It's a defense mechanism. This

woman desperately needs romance, because only romance can heal her instinctive cynicism. She was born somewhat skeptical, and her excursions into love frequently do nothing to soften it, but instead, only sharpen it—and her wit.

Not being overly sensitive (unless his Moon is in a Water Sign, or his birth chart contains an extremely well-aspected Neptune), the average Aries man isn't greatly perceptive when it comes to analyzing human nature. He more or less takes people as he finds them and may therefore find her need for romance difficult to conceive when she comes on to him like a comic Valentine, with a cynical laugh, lugging a copy of Kate Millett's *Sexual Revolution*, and defying him to possess her. Or when she wears one of her other Sagittarian theatrical masks that disguise her as a wacky, wriggling puppy—or as a shy, withdrawn spinster.

In her heart, the Sagittarian girl longs for an intelligent, honest man, who will take her into his warm arms and protect her forever—from herself. Before he can do that, the Ram will have to gently remove her greasepaint, and tell her firmly that the musical comedy is over. She'll protest, because she loves the theatre and she also shares Cinderella's fear of the midnight curfew, when her coach turns into a pumpkin. Nevertheless, it must be done. A girl Archer is much easier to handle when she's sitting in a pumpkin, barefoot and humble, than when she's flying around at the ball, flirting and flapping her defiance at a man. Once she's been properly bent into submission (a task about as easy as trying to pass a race horse while riding a turtle), she can be the sweetest woman in the world. But the Aries man will need a quick turtle to catch the Sagittarius mare.

He can comfort himself with the thought that this girl is not only slightly clumsy in a physical sense (despite her graceful walk and bearing) —she's also a little clumsy emotionally. Sooner or later, she'll stumble. Then he can pick her up in his warm, understanding arms, plunk her down in that pumpkin, and demonstrate the facts of life to her—the facts of life being that he is a man and she is a woman. (Sag is a masculine sign, you know.) He could find this even more of a challenge than taming the Aries female, because a girl Archer, being half horse, can run faster than a Ram. If he can convince her that she can trust him to love her completely (unlike those other phony hypocrites who broke her heart), she'll reward him with freedom, stimulating conversation, devoted friendship, affection, humor, warmth and generosity. All that is surely worth a little trouble at the starting gate.

In the beginning, the Ram will be outraged by her blunt speech and lack of consideration for his tender male ego. Neither will he be happy with her sheer luck in winning all the Monopoly games by intuitively grabbing up Boardwalk and Park Place, and in general, making him look foolish in front of his friends with her frankness. Aries men are determined to retain their masculine superiority, independence and personal freedom at any cost. If he has trouble communicating this to her, he might try a little history. "Baby, do you know who wrote the greatest statement of freedom the world has ever known—the Declaration of Independence? A male Ram, named Tom Jefferson. Who else could have authored such a glorious example of independence, but an Aries?" It might impress her.

Of course, there are other things that same history lesson might teach her too, like the absence of humility in the Mars nature. Arian Thomas Jefferson also wrote his own epitaph, a typical example of Aries modesty: *"Here lies Thomas Jefferson, Author of the Declaration of Independence, Author of the Statute of Virginia for Religious Liberty, and Founder of the University of Virginia."* He didn't have to mention that he was President. That was already taken care of elsewhere on his marker, by tradition. So Tom could afford the self-effacing gesture of excluding it from the tribute to his accomplishments which he composed himself. Like all Rams, Thomas Jefferson was a radical, an innovator of new ideas, a fiery lover of independence—and most certainly not bashful.

But why should he have been? After all, he did pioneer, develop and manifest all those things, with his Mars enthusiasm and courage. Why should he hide his light behind a bushel of false humility? In the area of ego, the Aries man and his Sagittarian woman won't have much tension. Well, maybe a little, but not much. As a Cardinal sign, he can't help his instincts to lead. As a Mutable sign, she's not consumed with the ego or personality. She'd rather keep it tucked out of sight if it interferes with her traveling around in her mind, or geographically. Mutable signs are not unduly ego-driven. (The other two Mutables are Pisces and Virgo, and these people are hardly pushy egotists.) Of the three Mutables, Sag is perhaps the most conscious of the *self*, and the "self-consciousness" of the Archer is seldom overdone.

The term "self-conscious" is confusing and contradictory. One thinks of it as indicating humility or embarrassment—or a degree of introversion. Isn't this the image conjured for you when a person is described as "self-conscious?" Oddly, we Americans have twisted the true meaning, which is, of course, "conscious-of-the-self"—and that certainly has naught to do with humility, introversion or any of those submerging-of-the-ego patterns. Anyway, whatever, the girl Centaur is a few degrees *more* self-conscious than her Pisces and Virgo mutable sisters, yet considerably *less* so than the male Ram.

Not all, but by far the largest majority of Sagittarian women prefer male friends to female friends, so the jealous Ram will have lots of opportunities to remind himself that she's only being friendly, cheerful and gregarious, not unfaithful. She's more than a little inclined toward jealousy herself when goaded, but not nearly so much as he. Whatever number of mean little green monsters do hide in the background of her aura won't have many chances to appear, because her Aries lover or husband also prefers the company of men. Isn't that lucky?

That's another thing. This girl is lucky. Somehow, a great many of her worst goofs turn out right side up, under the benevolent and fortunate influence of her ruler, Jupiter, who blessed her at birth like a faerie godfather (an interesting term) with the shining qualities of faith and optimism, which, when combined, are a mighty powerful force for sheer "luck," which isn't luck at all, only the result of the law of magnetism. One attracts what one images—and she images happiness a great deal of the time.

Despite her general air of loose or unconventional social behavior, remember that Jupiter rules spiritual insight and prophetic essence of all religion. This girl possesses an inner innocence and a touching faith in people (at least she did when she was younger) that often place her in awkward positions, and make it seem she's more flirtatious than she really is. It all begins so innocently.

ARIES: You spent the entire night in Mr. Cromwell's town house because he's your boss, and he needed you? I'll just bet he needed you, that sneaky old goat. As for you, you have the morals of an alley cat. (Rams are not noted for their care in choosing words when the Mars temper is exploding.)

SAG: His dog was due to have puppies, and he was going to let her have them all by herself. Someone had to help the poor thing.

ARIES: A dirty old man who seduces his secretary into sleeping with him is not a poor thing.

SAG: I meant the dog. Mr. Cromwell is a creep. He went to bed, and I had to deliver the puppies all by myself in the kitchen. One of them was born dead. It was so sad. I cried all the way home in the taxi.

ARIES: You cried all . . . so that's why your makeup is smeared. Darling, I'm sorry, I didn't realize . . .

SAG: You mean you didn't *trust* me. Don't try to apologize. You called me an alley cat. That's an obvious indication of your psychotic hatred for animals, using a poor cat to symbolize a prostitute—which you think *I* am. Just leave—I never want to see you again!

A few scenes like that, changing names, places and situations, and the Ram will learn, hopefully before he's lost her, that unfounded jealousy is something she won't stand for, because it implies she's dishonest, and Sagittarians all have a thing about truth and integrity that amounts to a regular neurosis with some of them. Just ask their psychiatrists. If she had submitted to Mr. Cromwell's seductions, she would probably have told Aries quite frankly, leaving out none of the lurid details.

Barring such a forthright confession, the Ram should have faith in her. True, Sagittarian women, like Gemini and Pisces women, percentage-wise, are tempted more often into experiments in sexual promiscuity or multiple affairs than their other Sun Sign sisters, because they are Mutable, and also dual in nature—but the Archer is not sneaky. Whatever the Aries man may accuse her of, it should not be deception. This woman will always be true to herself, and to the man she loves, until she falls out of love with him—or until he unfairly doubts her. Even then, she's more apt to break off their relationship angrily and emotionally than to be unfaithful simply to punish him. (Unless she has a Scorpio Moon Sign or Ascendent.) Even those girl Archers who have a history of casually changing sexual partners will normally indulge in only one affair at a time, and such behavior is usually triggered by a series of severe romantic disillusionments.

Both Sag and Aries are equally guilty of flashes of conceit, bossiness and recklessness, which they both consider to be virtues. They're also both hampered by a contempt for caution, prudence and patience, which they both consider to be vices.

Once they've discovered that compromise is the best way to solve their disagreements and end their quarrels, they can achieve a kind of mental and emotional harmony, not to mention physical harmony, that couples who don't gamble for such high stakes (and who are not guided by the graced-with-mutual-sympathy 5-9 vibration) could ever hope to reach. Their sexual rapport should be both stimulating and quieting . . . warm, imaginative . . . and full of shooting stars. As long as she remembers that "silence is golden" during their lovemaking and refrains from puncturing his passion at a strategic point with one of her Sagittarian verbal arrows. Intimate moments are not the ideal time for cheerful chatter or candid observations. Otherwise, the way these two express and share the sexual side of their love can be deeply satisfying for both of them.

Neither of these two Sun Signs is stingy by nature, so money shouldn't create many problems between them, except perhaps where and how to get it, after they've spent it all. If it comes to a race to see who's more extravagant, you can bet on the Ram, since the typical or average Archer is normally a few (short) lengths behind Sag in scattering lettuce around carelessly. Her general disposition may be a degree or so calmer than his too, but you can't really depend on this, unless she has a Pisces or Taurus Ascendent or Moon Sign, so he'd best not think it will save him when he tries to boss her around, or insult her cooking or housekeeping, neither of which are the average girl Archer's strong points.

The important thing for the Aries man to realize is that this girl is as much of an idealist about love and Life as he is—perhaps even more so. Her popularity and her friendly, open manner with men doesn't change the quality of her basic integrity. Does his fondness for innocent and harmless feminine admiration mean infidelity on his part? No, it doesn't. Seldom, if ever. Like her, he'll remain faithful to love until love is no longer there, and even then will tend more to confession than to secrecy. But he might consider the fact that she has her fears too. Very much like his own. As long as he's honest with her, this girl will love him with her whole heart, run bravely alongside him wherever he wants to go. She may lose her temper and say things she doesn't mean—but the moment she knows he's really hurt, she'll rush to his side to bind up his wounds, whether they're physical or emotional, with an unexpected tenderness and gentleness. Then the flames of their Fire Element natures will ignite all over again, just like the first time.

The only thing he needs to remember is to be honest with her always—keep the make-believe and excitement alive in their relationship—and not speak rashly, in anger. Exactly the same things she needs to remember about him. These two are so much alike. Proud. Brave. Generous. Impulsive. Passionate. Independent. Idealistic. And very, very vulnerable to coldness and rejection . . . especially from each other. Once they've permanently conquered their mutual unintentional selfishness, nothing can separate them. The strength of their love is unconquerable. Mars and Jupiter are a formidable combination.

ARIES

Fire — Cardinal — Positive
Ruled by Mars
Symbol: The Ram
Day Forces — Masculine

CAPRICORN

Earth — Cardinal — Negative
Ruled by Saturn
Symbol: The Goat
Night Forces — Feminine

The **ARIES-CAPRICORN** *Relationship*

*"It is only the gay and innocent and
heartless who can fly."*

*"What is gay and innocent and heartless?
I do wish I were gay and innocent and
heartless."*

That wistful complaint from James M. Barrie's *Peter Pan* might well be spoken by a Capricorn who envies the Aries ability to fly happily through life, with free and careless style. However, the Goat needn't envy the Ram's flair for being heartless, because it's synonymous with selfishness, a quality not at all exclusive with Aries. Capricorns possess more than their fair share of it.

Aries selfishness is the result of the Ram's thoughtless and often infantile desires. What Aries wants, one way or another, Aries gets, when he—or she—has learned to curb that Mars enthusiasm and not forge ahead too quickly. Capricorn selfishness is motivated by the Goat's determination not to look back to see who slipped and fell behind, lest it delay his (or her) own personal appointment with destiny. Still, selfish is selfish, whatever the basis or the cause, and they're both guilty of it rather frequently.

As for the other two requirements for flying—gaiety and innocence—the Goat has every reason to envy the Ram. Gaiety is not a word one ordinarily associates with Saturn-ruled people. Try applying it to Capricorns Humphrey Bogart, Edgar Allan Poe, Joan of Arc or Howard Hughes. Bogart gaily pulling out his revolver. Poe gaily "quothing" the Raven. Joan of Arc gaily leading the Armies of France against England. Howard Hughes—well, Howard Hughes gaily doing *anything*. Or even his identical twin brother, Robard Hughes. (If he should happen to have one—just fantasizing, you know.) Nor is innocence a Capricorn quality. Cappies are never innocent, not even as tiny babes, toddlers and children. The entire bunch of them, whether clad in pink or blue booties, were each and every one born a little old man, or a little old woman, with an ingrained and very "grainy" sense of both wisdom and patience, not normally acquired until near or past the century mark, chronologically speaking.

And so, you see, there's small chance that the Goat will fly through life with the naive gaiety and innocent guilelessness of the Ram, until well past what is fallaciously called "middle age" (since it's really quite young in a life expectancy span of three to five hundred years, attainable even now, for those who properly seek it). Then the Capricorn "reverse aging" process will begin, bringing on spurts of total abandon that can sometimes cause the Goat to even soar high above the Ram. That's why Aries people usually feel more comfortable around older Goats. The younger ones make them nervous.

Aries reasons for forming any kind of human relationship or association are always impulsive and idealistic, governed by the emotions. Capricorns have more practical motivations. Although Goats quite understandably resent the astrological implication that many of them are inclined to "marry up the social or financial ladder," it's nevertheless more often true of Cappy than of Aries. It's not that Capricorns are cold and calculating. After all, they're just thinking of those yet-to-be-born youngsters. Not only are they going to wear shoes, they're going to wear good shoes, because a podiatrist is frightfully expensive. And they're certainly not going to suffer (the children, not the podiatrists) in the future for any romantic flings of the present. This is why Cappy is often horrified to hear about a couple of friends, living in unwedded bliss, who plan to give up their jobs and bike across Europe for a year or so. It isn't the lack of the marriage certificate alone that disturbs the Goat. What if she should get pregnant over there?

And if he gives up a perfectly good job, how will they ever afford to get the children's teeth straightened?

Now, this may shock a few of the Cappies reading it, right down to the toes of their sensible boots, but we're into the Aquarian Age, my dears, and the girl and her beau in our example are experimenting with a trial marriage. You see, they aren't planning to have any children with crooked teeth or toes, until they're sure they can stand each other long enough to raise a family with some sense of permanency. If it doesn't work out, they'll part as friends (usually)—much sadder, but also considerably wiser.

The typical Aries reaction to such an arrangement is rather touchingly sentimental and romantically hopeful. If the two of them really love each other, thinks the Ram, then they should *know* it's going to be forever, so why not marry in the beginning?

The typical Capricorn reaction to the same situation is also rather touchingly sentimental and romantically hopeful. The Goat girl echoes the girl Ram's question. If the two of them really love each other, they should *know* it's going to be forever, so why not marry in the beginning? So far, the Goat and the Ram are walking the same path. Then Mars and Saturn part company. Abruptly.

After due deliberation, and careful reflection—and after the initial shock has passed—Cappy will give the issue thoughtful Saturnine consideration, and finally decide that the arrangement makes good sense after all. (Since the Goat is a confirmed realist, Capricorn morality is very closely interwoven with Capricorn practicality.)

All right, forget about the orange blossoms and the moral issue, but still Capricorn wonders, *"who's* going to pay the *rent?"* Probably the girl. Her lover, you see, yearns to become a poet, so she may have to support them both for a while. Aries finds nothing at all wrong with *that*. Not so Cappy. Capricorn's advice to the girl then, would be: "Tell him to forget the limericks and earn some bread, or bid him one of those friendly farewells, with no regrets."

Capricorns are always hurt when Aries people accuse them of being ambitious. They think no one knows it. Who, *them?* Ambitious? Yes, *them*—ambitious. There are other Saturnine traits that Goats are a little slow to recognize in themselves, like those periodic binges of gloomy pessimism, their hankering to grab the top rung of the social ladder, their reluctance to defy the Establishment—and their often blind obeisance to tradition, family, law and order and all forms of authority. (Goat J. Edgar Hoover was just doing his Saturn thing.)

Rams are ambitious, too, but quite open about it. Instead of pessimism, they have periodic binges of downright foolish optimism. Most Aries wouldn't know a social ladder from a tall shutter, they delight in defying the Establishment, they feel no obligation whatsoever to respect any sort of authority—and their blind obeisance is paid, for the most part, to themselves, to their own ideas and desires.

As an Aries myself, I make the following confession most reluctantly. But if it will help make the vibration between these two Sun Signs more clear, well . . . all right. My daughter, Jill (a Capricorn), was wiser than her mother from the very day she was born. Not only wiser, but calmer, more practical, more sensible—and exasperatingly *always* right. Did I mention more cautious? Also more cautious.

I began rather early taking Jill along with me when I was Christmas shopping, knowing she would make sure I didn't lose my money, my pocketbook, my packages—or my head. We started this little holiday tradition when Cappy was only eight years old. It was humiliating. But it never failed to work.

Before I started taking her along, there was never a Christmas I didn't leave my shopping money—or half a dozen gifts—on a counter somewhere on the first floor of Macy's or Gimbel's only realizing it when I was on a crowded elevator, on the way to the twelfth floor. After a while, I decided I was really overworking St. Anthony (finder of lost articles) and drafted my tiny Goat into duty as chaperone. I pass this along to Aries parents of Capricorn youngsters everywhere, as sort of a Noel gift . . . for all seasons.

Bobbs Pinkerton, the warm and wise Capricorn editor of my first book, *Sun Signs*, once swore to me that she wasn't a typical Goat Girl because she adores (she claimed) bright colors. "*Mad* about them," I believe, was the way she put it. (Astrologically very doubtful, although she does have a Sagittarius Moon, and quite probably *wants* to be mad about them.) So we made a bet—naturally, a small one, since Capricorns don't wager with much largesse—and went through her closets.

We found nothing but black (with a few stingy white trims), navy blue, dark green, and brown. Finally, she triumphantly pulled out of the very back of the closet a wild, canary yellow jumpsuit, carefully wrapped in tissue and strongly smelling of moth balls. I gave her my most direct Mars look, and she owned up, blushing, "Well, I only wear it at home, but it was such a bargain." Being a typically honest Goat, she knew the fourteen cents she bet me was rightfully mine, and promptly paid it.

Capricorns have this truly marvelous ability to face the facts dispassionately, curb their faults and make the very best of their virtues. It wouldn't hurt most Rams to imitate them. Speaking of jumpsuits and such, Cappy Bobbs claims she has an eighty-year-old Capricorn neighbor who wears mini-skirts with demure high-necked, long-sleeved blouses. "Well," she says, "I figure it this way. The legs are the last to go."

So it's a mistake to think of all Goats as Grandma Moses or Whistler's Mother. The male Capricorns are not always as prim and proper as you might think either. Not being burdened with excess baggage of Aries idealism, they can shock a Ram with all sorts of unexpected propositions and behavior—in private.

However, in the final analysis, the Capricorn mind runs in rather conservative grooves, at least publicly. Aries is frequently accusing Capricorn of a lack of sympathy; yet the Goat is not without tender concern and compassion for those he (or she) thinks are genuinely worth it. Cooperation can mean undreamed-of success between the Ram and the Goat, when they mutually aim their horns against prejudice and falsehood, instead of toward each other.

Picture the shy but sturdy and sure-footed mountain goat, stepping carefully from crag to crag, with confidence and determination . . . . . managing to find sufficient nourishment in patches of sparse grass, even swallowing cardboard and munching on tin cans when it's necessary. Nothing is permitted to delay his slow yet steady progress to the beckoning pinnacle of truth, wisdom and justice.

Now picture the rocky mountain ram, who requires a diet of richer grass. Unlike the goat, the ram finds it impossible to calmly digest the rusty nails of criticism and the broken glass of disappointment . . . and often misjudges the distance, in leaping between the crags, causing him to fall, and smash his horns. Because the dreamer's vision distracts him on Nature's rocky path, the bighorn ram takes some unscheduled detours along the way.

That's the basic difference between Capricorn and Aries men, women and children. Both Sun Signs are tough climbers. But the Goat's final destination is the very top of the mountain, the only place where he (or she) feels really secure. To the rare, more gregarious Ram, who makes it up that high, the top of the mountain is a lonely spot, with no more challenges—and what is Life without the thrill of danger? For Capricorn—*peaceful.* For Aries—*boring.*

☆ ☆ ☆ ☆ ☆ ☆

ARIES *Woman* CAPRICORN *Man*

"Now," said he, "shall I give you a kiss?"
. . . . She made herself rather cheap by
inclining her face toward him, but he merely
dropped an acorn button into her hand; so she
slowly returned her face to where it had been
before, and said nicely that she would wear his
kiss on the chain round her neck.

The unmistakable air of loneliness that hangs over a Capricorn man, even in a roomful of people, draws the Aries girl straight to his side. To the sentimental, egocentric female Ram, the reason for his loneliness is obvious. He's been waiting for her—to show him how beautiful life can be. So she directly proceeds to show him. Aries never beats around the bush.

Her initial enthusiasm, however, may soon be stifled by the Capricorn man's slow responses—his earthy immunity to her fiery Mars charisma, and her impulsive emotions may finally lead her to decide he's too stuffy, aloof, distant. How can she help him find the sunlight when he's so drearily attached to his career, not to mention his family—including his great-aunts and kissing cousins, as well as his saintly parents? There's little hope he'll ever sweep her off her feet and marry her when he's already so permanently wedded to his job, his ambition and/or his relatives.

It could be the end of a promising relationship that might have been deeply satisfying, as well as financially successful. Why should she waste her time trying to break through his loneliness to show him that life is beautiful, when he obviously enjoys his isolation? He wouldn't recognize beauty if it knocked him over. She's wrong.

Capricorns do appreciate beauty. But he'll never tell her about those pictures he painted in school when the teacher wasn't looking, or the music he used to drown himself in when no one was listening, before he buckled down to the serious problems of carving out his security in a mad world . . . . . . unless he thinks she really cares.

It can hurt to lose someone you love because you're unable to communicate your feelings, and this is too often the case between the quiet boy Goat and the aggressive girl Ram. How can he let her know about all those secret dreams he wants to give her—how can he show her the life-long romanticism hidden deep within his shy, funny Goat's heart? Well, he should look at it this way: if she can't see more virtue in the exceptional than in the exciting, she's not the right girl for him. Or he might memorize Elizabeth Barrett Browning's sonnet that begins, "How do I love thee? Let me count the ways . . . . . . ," and practice, practice, practice. Lovers down through the ages have learned they can say things to each other in verse, that were buried inside their souls, just waiting to be discovered, so they could be revealed to one special person.

So, you see, the Mars-directed instinct of the Aries girl might have been right. He really *was* waiting for her to come along, and show him how to paint rainbows. It's just that her initial approach might have been overwhelming for the more introverted Goat. Capricorns have difficulty coping with reckless action and abandon, even in the name of love. It takes this man a certain length of time to make sure he has a firm grip on the reality of a romance, and even then, he proceeds with caution. This way, he's sure not to slip and fall, or make any mistakes he'll regret at some future date. With Aries, it's "fly now—pay later." With Capricorn, it's "pay now —and fly later, with a clear conscience."

Assuming Capricorn and Aries do reach across the chasm of their differences, and hang on to each other's hands and hearts, the disparities between their outlooks on life must still be either overcome or over-looked. He'll try to over-look them. She'll try to overcome them. Even in tackling the problems of their differences, they're different. It lies in their divergent approaches to a situation. Here are a couple of examples.

The situation: He has just hurt his knee, and the doctor has told him he shouldn't aggravate the injury by walking on it for at least three weeks. (Capricorns are always banging their kneecaps, visiting the dentist, breaking bones or suffering a touch of arthritis. Otherwise, their health is great.) The knee injury spoils the skiing trip they'd planned in the mountains.

ARIES: "I'm sorry you can't come with me, darling. But I'm sure you won't mind if I go along with the others and try to enjoy myself anyway."

CAPRICORN: "Do you know what you are? You're *selfish*."

ARIES: "Do you expect me to sit here and hold your hand, when I've been looking forward to this weekend all year? Couldn't you make an effort and come along, even if you don't ski?"

CAPRICORN: "No, I do *not* wish to come along in my crippled state, and yes, I *do* expect you, if you love me, to stay here and hold my hand."

ARIES: "Do you know what you are? You're *selfish*."

(Actually, they're both right. They're *both* selfish.)

Another situation: (If the first one hasn't already scared them off.) She's temporarily broke, so he lends her the money to have her car overhauled, and to make her rent payment. She has no qualms whatever about asking him. After all, they're in love. It both impresses and touches her that he's so sweet about giving her the cash without any coaxing or quibbling. Several months pass, and she still hasn't repaid the loan. She's forgotten all about it, you see. So he gently reminds her, but she thinks he's only teasing. Meanwhile, she's showered him with an expensive color TV set and a pure silk kimono for Christmas—plus a solid gold wristwatch and a St. Bernard puppy for his birthday—all on her credit cards. He's sincerely moved, and grateful for her gesture, but not so grateful that he forgets to mail her an informal written statement, listing the two hundred dollars he loaned her (with some Capricorns this could conceivably also include a few extra dollars in accrued interest) and love flies out the window in a burst of Mars fireworks.

ARIES: How *dare* he put our intimacy on a vulgar, financial basis?
CAPRICORN: How *dare* she violate our intimacy by refusing to respect
              an obligation between us?

And so it goes—bumpety, bumpety, crackle and pop.

On the physical side of love between them, the same kind of hurdles must be overcome before they find sexual satisfaction. When the Ram mates with the Goat, it's a blending of Fire and Earth, and these are not normally the most compatible of elements. His sex impulses are controlled by Saturn, the planet of solid resistance, self-discipline and permanence. Hers are directed by Mars, the planet symbolizing the masculine principle of flaming penetration. Capricorn would rather remain lonely and starved for love than risk being burned by a temporary passion. Aries would rather risk being scorched than not even try. So she's usually the one to initiate the sexual advances. Assuming the stars are favorable, and she catches him when he's too weak to resist, the Capricorn man will respond to her fresh, enthusiastic expressions of love with the kind of profound intensity only the Saturn-ruled can understand—and a depth of affection that will surprise her as much as it will delight her.

If these two miraculously manage to get together, it's probably because he has the Moon in Aries, Sagittarius, Leo, Gemini or Aquarius—or because she has the Moon in Capricorn, Taurus, Virgo, Pisces or Scorpio. Then the differences between them (and there are undeniable differences) will tend to attract instead of repel. In other words, rather than become annoyed by his caution, stability and composure, she'll respect him for these qualities she lacks, and try to imitate them. Rather than become uptight over her forceful drive, he'll envy and admire it, and loosen up his laces a little himself. With a harmonious Sun-Moon relationship in their mutual charts, love between Aries and Capricorn can grow into a deep, and lasting, devotion—sexually and otherwise.

However, with a square or opposition between their natal Sun and Moon signs, the Goat and the Ram will either lock horns in constant battle, or become so bored with each other that they wander off someday and forget to return. Whatever their planetary positions, there's always the chance that his distrustful reserve in the beginning will petrify her natural romantic buoyancy, and they'll never get beyond holding hands at the movies—or making magical promises with their eyes which they never keep.

The Goat and the Ram are not immune to the common mistake of all 4-10 Sun Sign Pattern lovers, who see the world through different-colored glasses. They fall in love, then try to change the very qualities they first loved in each other. When he first decides he loves her, he's impressed by her optimistic, bubbly conversation. Even her recklessness intrigues him into feeling an unaccustomed, grudging admiration. He smiles at her extravagances, and chuckles indulgently at her mistakes. Then, perversely, he tries to mold her trusting, hopeful personality into a more conventional and acceptable form. But she will not be molded.

When she first decides she loves him, she's enormously impressed with his strong, silent aura of strength. It both mystifies and excites her. His patience and mildness are soothing to her tangled emotions, and her heart beats faster, just imagining what it would be like to share an intimate, day-to-day relationship with this gentle, quietly humorous, wise and steady man. Then she begins to feel stifled by it all, so she tries to coax him into tossing caution over his shoulder. She beckons to him to come and chase clouds with her, to run through sweet-smelling clover fields in a summer rain—only to find he's brought along his umbrella again.

The Capricorn man can't understand why the Aries girl has such fun riding on an endless merry-go-round. It only makes him dizzy. But she likes the calliope music and the way the wind blows her hair. She will wonder why he keeps his heart locked up so tight. He'll tell her it's just to be safe. But there's nothing in a heart to steal. Only things to give.

When this man and woman drift away from each other, the strain of the music they once heard together may haunt them, reminding them that perhaps they didn't try quite hard enough. He may not reveal outwardly the pain he feels over losing her, but still waters run deep, and Earth sorrow runs even deeper. She will weep inconsolably for many a day, following her own fiery emotional pattern, but by and by she'll forget, though she may watch the sunrise wistfully for years afterward. She won't tell him how she's hurting inside—why should she? He's so cold and detached, and barely even says hello when they pass on the street . . . . . like that time at the corner, when the city traffic was so heavy and noisy, they could only wave to each other. He didn't even smile. But what she doesn't know is that somewhere, deep within his lonely heart, he may be thinking things she suspects, like, maybe such words as . . . .

> How old am I? I'll be 92 next Christmas
> though I won't admit to one day over 20 . . .
> even after all the birthday cards are cut and shuffled
> it's hard to figure
>
> I've aged at least 500 years since I stumbled into you;
> yet I still believe in faerie tales
> like the Princess and the Frog
> and I still believe you wanted me . . .
> perhaps I'm only three or so?
>
> you'll never know . . . how old I am
> but I'll tell you anyway
> I was born the hour I met you . . . and died today.*

She doesn't hear the words his heart speaks to her silently, of course. She's thinking her own thoughts, remembering the thing he said to her, one dawn, as they were walking along the shore, by the ocean . . . . when he held her in his arms, and said quietly . . . . "and here you'll stay, until it's time for you to go." Then she asked him, "When will that time be?" But he didn't answer. So she never asked again. Aries is proud.

Remember the message of the stars. These lovers who are victorious over the heavy soul-testing of the 4-10 vibrational influence, are blessed by Venus. And perhaps it does take the gentle planet Venus to soften two hearts ruled by the masculine planets, Mars and Saturn. Venus . . . and music . . . poetry . . . and memories . . .

The tensions and troubles, the misunderstandings and lack of communication this man and woman must face—are formidable. But their re-

* From *Venus Trines at Midnight* by Linda Goodman.

wards for being patient with each other, and waiting for the heart's wisdom to guide them—are forever-after. Now she wishes she had stayed home and held his hand that time when he hurt his knee. How could she have been so selfish? Now he thinks maybe he should have offered to go with her, just to watch her ski down a snowy hill, knowing she was his. How could he have been so selfish?

Foresight is much better than hindsight. But it still might not be too late to say "I'm sorry." It's never too late for those who really love. And even when the Ram and the Goat who once cared for each other are apart . . . . . . wherever they are . . . . . . Venus is winking down at both of them, shining the message of her light on their loneliness, with a sparkling promise of maybe a new tomorrow.

☆ ☆ ☆ ☆ ☆ ☆

ARIES *Man* CAPRICORN *Woman*

◄━━◆◆◆━━►

> . . . from first to last she had been
> wiser than he.
>
> Of course this was a pity; but whatever
> Mr. Darling did he had to do in excess;
> otherwise he soon gave up doing it.

The kind of effect an Aries male and a Capricorn female have on each other mostly depends on her age when they first meet. If she's still in her teens, or under thirty, she may see him as a rather crude, pushy, cave-man type, with no future. And he may see her as a sourpuss, or at the very least, a weird, granny-type recluse. (Of course, I know of one Goat Girl who's quite a loose swinger, and about as far out as you can get, but she has all her other planets in Aquarius, afflicted by Mars. Here, we're dealing with the essentially pure Sun Sign types.)

If they meet when she's past thirty (the farther past, the better) she may be a barrel of laughs, full of young ideas about everything from psychology to ecology, and they'll have much more in common. This can lead the Ram to think she's as impulsive and carefree as himself, but he's made another one of his rash Aries judgements. She's still a Capricorn, under the iron influence of Saturn, and her kooky reverse aging twist will never stretch quite far enough to snap or distort her basic ideas of security. Nothing will ever change Cappy's reverence for success and a solid bank account. Now, most Aries men are bristling with success potential. It shines out from their faces like a beacon light, and shows itself in their aggressive walk and movements. But Rams don't always display a natural knack for building solid bank accounts. Until *they're* past thirty. (Make that fifty. Better yet—sixty. After all, with a potential life span of three to five hundred years, he has lots of time to mature.)

Capricorn girls gravitate toward those at the top by instinct. After all, someone has to know who's who, and what's what. Is a sense of responsibility so bad? No, but to Aries it can be un-nerving. It smacks of Caution and Prudence, two words this man never even learned to spell because he has a kind of Freudian hang-up about them. They symbolize the thing he fears most—repression of his Mars enthusiasm.

That's why a love relationship seldom develops when these two meet in a business situation, where the Ram is the boss and the Goat Girl is his secretary, for example. Right away, he'll see that she's a perfect jewel of an employee, with a compelling, if slightly subdued and controlled, sex appeal. She's capable and efficient, with a bag full of funnies (though she keeps her humor pretty well hidden during working hours). It flatters his Mars ego that she realizes she's a subordinate, and subordinates must learn from those above them. Then he discovers (hopefully before it's too late) that she's unobtrusively learning everything she needs to replace him as boss. Obviously, a Ram who's threatened like this will forget about her sex appeal and fire her in a flash. But even then, he'll probably always remember her as an excellent secretary, although his harrowing experience forces him to add a qualifying descriptive phrase, like "quietly ambitious."

When they're not competing with each other, however, the Goat and the Ram can make an interesting couple. I didn't say flashy or fantastic. I said interesting.

By now, you know Capricorn is symbolized by the mountain billy goat. But you may *not* know that Capricorn's corresponding symbol in Greek mythology is Janus, the two-faced god. Before you get the wrong impression, let me explain the meaning of Janus' two faces which is that one of them is turned toward the Past, the other toward the Future. With Capricorn, the Future is important only as it relates to the Past. The Ram will soon discover he'd better have a respectable family tree, going back at least five or six generations, if he wants to impress this girl. As for her, well—a Capricorn woman doesn't really need a family tree. You might say Capricorns are their own ancestors. *Ponder that*. If you know any typical Goats, it will begin to make perfect sense.

Frequently, a Capricorn girl will find herself involved in what can only be called an "impossible" romantic situation. And there's a good reason. A woman who secretly feels she's an impossible person will unconsciously seek out an impossible love relationship to match her opinion of herself— and to punish herself. Just what she deserves, *she* thinks. An impossible affair for an impossible person. *Me*. But this girl is often much more warm and lovable than she permits herself to realize, and always far more physically appealing and attractive than she believes. On top of that, her mind is stable (barring an afflicted Sun or Mercury) and she's not flighty.

It's up to the Ram to convince her she's a very desirable female. With his talent for enthusiastic appreciation and his tendency to place the woman he loves on an ivory pedestal, he may manage to bring the shy or insecure Cappy out of her shell rather neatly. Aries has a better chance than most other Sun Signs to swing the Goat Girl from self-depreciation into a rightful pride in her feminine sexuality. Still, even if he finally accomplishes this minor miracle, he may not get to take her into his arms right away for keeps. There's her family.

Unless her parents outraged the Saturn sense of decency in some way, leaving bitter scars, the average Capricorn is fanatically devoted to them. If her family doesn't approve of the Ram, she may not either. If they *do* approve of him they may be ill or in financial straits, and she feels it's her duty to remain with them as long as she's needed, even if love itself must be sacrificed. I tell you there's only one way out of that Capricorn family trip. Offer to let her bring Mums and Pops along to share your married life—find a large house or apartment with plenty of spare bedrooms—and make the best of it. Otherwise, if the Ram talks her into deserting her relatives in their hour of need, or into leaving them to cope with their own problems she'll become gloomy, blame herself and feel constant guilty twinges. It's disconcerting to try to make love to a woman who's continually having gloomy chills and guilty twinges. Especially for an Aries male, who needs and demands, at all times, intense, concentrated attention —directed toward himself.

Their sex life can be greatly improved if the Ram studies the astrological implications of the Saturnine emotional nature more closely. Sometimes when a Capricorn girl wears a mask of casual indifference, it may be concealing the most tormenting passions. If she represses physical expressions of affection, it's only because Saturn keeps silently warning her: Watch out. Be careful. Don't be fooled by your senses. They're unreliable, and they can trick you.

Listening to that inner voice, while burning with the desire to consummate physically an emotional and mental attraction, can build up frustrations—and frustrations can take many strange forms. With Capricorns, it can result in filling up the inner emptiness with ambition for power, excessive financial security—or even collections of antiques. Some of them become cranky and cross, and a few accept their fate by pretending to believe that solitude is a sign of spiritual attainment. The courageous Ram won't be afraid to rip off the Goat's icy mask of indifference to expose her hidden passion. The trouble is that the insensitive Ram may fail to *recognize* it as only a mask, never guess the depth of feeling behind it and give up before he's begun to fight.

It may also freeze the flames of passion between them if the female Goat uses her self-chosen, protective cloak to shatter the confidence of the Aries man in his ability as a lover. Once he feels his lovemaking is not arousing an equally intense response in her, he'll suffer agonies of inferiority. It hardly matters if his unhappiness is based on a fallacy, and she really longs to love him as fiercely in return but can't trust her own emotions and feelings. He may not be perceptive enough to grasp her secret desire to reciprocate his passion, and another Aries-Capricorn relationship ends before it's had a chance to grow into the kind of profound emotional experience it might have been.

The general rule between these Sun Signs should be to check each other's Moon Signs. If the Sun and Moon in the respective charts are harmonious, the Ram can magically transmute the cold, grey lead of Saturn into the sparkling diamonds of Mars, through the pure alchemy of love. But if the Moon and Ascendent of one or either was in negative aspect to the other's Sun Sign at birth, and vice versa, these two may have to wait, and catch each other the next time around, in a future incarnation, when some karmic patterns have worked themselves out. However, such mutual natal afflictions are rare, and most Rams and Goats can achieve harmony together eventually, if they try, however rocky the path may be in the beginning. Mountain climbing is always harder when you start; yet the closer you get to the top, the easier it is, the fresher the air, the brighter the Sun . . . and the spirit leaps with joy at the nearness of the dream's fulfillment.

The Capricorn train of thought is never permitted to run off the rails. Consequently, the Goat Girl becomes upset when anything unexpected or unorthodox threatens to disrupt the smooth status quo, and a Ram may unknowingly supply such disruptions. When Cappy is upset, it can make an Aries man feel more than a little tense. This female normally has nerves of steel, eyes like a hawk, and the patience of Job himself. The impatient Ram may feel, somehow, inferior to her self-control. He shouldn't. For her self-control is only the chain she uses to bind her spirit from flying too far out, where there's no one to catch her, if she should happen to fall. His arms are strong enough to catch her. And he's persuasive enough, determined enough, to convince her of this—if he's patient. This man follows the sunrise, and he's hurt when the Capricorn he loves won't join him. She's gentle and warm, and makes his heart smile with her jokes. Yet, there's something about her manner that says: "Don't come too close."

Must astrology interpret this message for a bright Aries man? What she really means is—"I *want* you to come closer, but I'm afraid it's only my stability you want, that you don't really need *me*—as a *woman*." Surely a Ram will know how to answer such a silent plea in this girl's lonely, quiet eyes. Later, she *will* move nearer, and maybe not murmur any romantic words, but if he watches closely, he'll see that soft, secret little Capricorn smile of deep pleasure. If he doesn't look fast, he'll miss it. All the same, it's there, reflected from the sunlight within . . . of knowing she's loved.

He's really a very lucky Ram. As beautiful as she looks at this moment, Saturn has promised to make her look lovelier every year that passes. He may be a stern ruler of her emotions, but Saturn never breaks a promise. And neither does she. At last, the Aries man has found a love he can trust, a love to have and to hold. That's surely worth the challenge of fighting a few dragons of selfishness—and rounding off their squared Suns into a circle of understanding.

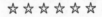

ARIES

Fire — Cardinal — Positive
Ruled by Mars
Symbol: The Ram
Day Forces — Masculine

AQUARIUS

Air — Fixed — Positive
Ruled by Uranus
Symbol: The Water Bearer
Day Forces — Masculine

The **ARIES-AQUARIUS** *Relationship*

◆━◆

They began the verse, but they never finished it . . .

Aries and Aquarius have this outstanding thing in common—they're both curiously attracted to anything new until they've extracted all the fun and truth from it. Then they toss it away and go on to the next new and exciting adventure. With these two, there is no looking back and sniffling over the past, if they're both typical of their Sun Signs. To the Ram, today is *ever* so much more thrilling than yesterday. To the Aquarian Water Bearer, *tomorrow* is a thousand times more fantastic than either yesterday *or* today.

Once in a while, they slip off the time track separately, somewhere between the past, present, and future, and bump smack into each other, in a meeting that isn't part of the conscious itinerary of either. It's always an interesting encounter, and a fated one, planned on a higher level, long before both of them were born. Aries and Aquarius are influenced by the 3-11 Sun Sign vibration, and a blending of their auras brings them into the shared experiences of travel, education, and spiritual discovery—along with karmic memories from former reincarnations, as well as the hopes, wishes, and dreams of the present existence. You can see why they don't find each other lacking in fascination.

Aries people throw themselves into things with total commitment (for the moment), enthusiastically and fully involved in what's happening. Aquarius is equally as enthusiastic, but these people don't throw themselves into anything. The Water Bearers approach every experience with a studied detachment, snoop around, scratch their heads, and wiggle their ears—from a safe distance. That way they can enjoy it without getting either tangled up or tied down. Of course this subtle psychological difference won't help you tell them apart when you pass them on the street. But there are other ways.

The Ram may be running, with head bent forward, showering confetti and sending up rocket flares. The Aquarian may be riding a unicycle, munching on a pickled radish, and spinning a hula hoop, with a friendly quetzal perched on one shoulder. They both stand out in a crowd.

One of the meanings of the 3-11 vibration between friends, relatives, business associates, lovers, or mates is: karmic obligation. The association or relationship involves either some great blessing and good exchanged—or some great sadness brought from one to the other, perhaps in the form of an obligation or responsibility, far-reaching in its effect on the lives of both.

An Aquarian blessed with an Aries friend who stands by him (or her) through long months of trouble or illness (either personal or in the family), when no one else cares or helps . . . . may wonder, "Why did she (or he) do it?" The Ram is simply repaying a favor from a long ago Lifetime (buried in the subconscious) of similar help received. Perhaps in the process, the Ram receives an enlightenment, starting the Aries person on the road to a future career, some unexpected goal or dream that wouldn't have been revealed in any other way, save through the circumstances of the Ram's offering help to the Aquarian. In reversing the signs, the same situation may develop, with many variations on the theme.

Another Aquarian handles the business affairs of an Aries, keeping the Ram out of trouble with taxes and creditors, smoothing out financial wrinkles, and arranging miraculous loans under impossible conditions—unconsciously motivated by the soul memory of monetary assistance received from Aries in another time, another place—and a karmic debt is repaid. An Aries man has a close male friend whose Aquarian wife frowns on the friendship. She is illogically suspicious of the Ram, and he, in turn, feels an inexplicable tension when she enters the room. It could result in the

Ram breaking up his friend's marriage to the Aquarian—or with the Aquarian wife preventing the Aries from continuing a valued friendship with her husband. How it ends depends upon the degree of evolvement of the Ram and the Water Bearer at the time of the situation. Karma is complicated.

The good or evil these two Sun Signs (or any two Signs influenced by the 3-11 vibration) bring to each other is seldom minor. The contact is not casual, and they have little conscious control over its outcome. Yet, if Aries and Aquarius will meditate on the laws of Karma, or reincarnation, they'll understand why one of them is so willing to aid the other, and learn to accept the favor gracefully. Or, they'll comprehend the reverse situation— why the two of them continue to senselessly hurt one another—and through understanding, be able to end the karmic pattern by the simple Karma-canceling act of forgiving and forgetting. Otherwise, they're only stacking up additional obligations for future lives, wherein their two souls will be chained together, in an endless succession of close relationships, through the inevitable law of magnetic attraction and repulsion, action and reaction.

Aquarius is one of the four "human signs" in the astrological circle, the other three being Gemini, Virgo, and Libra (unless one counts the Centaur—half-horse, half-human Sag). Consequently, Aquarian passions are more controlled than those of the Rams, whose instinctive loves and hates often cause them to act from sheer animal urge, or personal gratification of the ego. The Uranus-ruled Aquarians more often flee from instinctive action into the realms of the higher mind—and the domain of pure intuition. This gives the Water Bearers an uncanny psychic or intuitive ability.

Sometimes Rams will also appear to be psychic, but they're really not, in the true sense of the word. It's only because they plunge straight into the heart of the situation, and the penetrating action of their ruling planet, Mars, gives them the correct answer. Aries goes directly and immediately to the *core* of the problem, using neither logic nor rational reasoning, simply being obsessed with an overwhelming need to leap in and get to the bottom of the thing. The swifter, more intricate flashes of Aquarians emanate from the electro-magnetic wave lengths they're tuned into under the influence of their ruling planet, Uranus—which symbolizes electricity, among other things . . . . and lightning, too. The Water Bearers merely grab an impression out of the air, or absorb it through some sort of electrical osmosis, without expending a tenth of the energy put forth by Aries to reach the same conclusions.

Aries and Aquarius are essentially compatible. There's an almost visible cord of understanding running between them, so that even when they strongly disagree, it's always possible to replace tension with harmony any-time they choose to do so. It's the natural sympathy between Fire and Air, and it's something else. It's the normally easy (barring unusual planetary afflictions between the horoscopes), effortless possibilities of communi-cation open to all 3-11 Sun Sign Patterns, on all channels. The third astrological house symbolizes communication of all kinds—visual, through the printed word—and also through the spoken word, including minds speaking to minds, hearts speaking to hearts.

Rams are frequently accused of being naive, impractical dreamers. Aquarians are frequently accused of being just plain crazy. That's another reason why these two usually get along so well. They both feel misun-derstood by the world and everyone in it. They also both feel they're on the right track, separately or in unison, and it's the rest of the world that's out of step and off-center. Naturally, this draws them together—for mutual comfort and mutual protection against the establishment. The Rams are reckless, the Water Bearers are pixilated—but they manage to spin these qualities into complicated webs of leprechauns, miracles, rainbows, and as-sorted magics, creating dirigibles of dreams which, surprisingly enough to more sensible souls, take off into the blue skies of some wildly successful personal and business ventures.

The Aquarian, Uranus-inspired tolerance insulates most Water Bearers against the shock of the sudden whims and highly original, creative urges of Aries. There will be times when the Rams believe Aquarius doesn't quite have it together, and when Aquarius will despair of being able to cope with the hot temper flashes of Mars. Yet generally, these two should enjoy a mad, fabulous, and unique association. Aquarius is a Fixed Sign, and so, on occasion, the Water Bearers can be more than a little stubborn. But stubbornness won't work with Aries. Only love and kindness. Great gobs of it.

The Water Bearers may attempt to enlighten the Rams with their theories about submerging the ego, claiming this brings peace and happi-ness. But to Aries, submerging the ego is scary, quite like being swallowed in a dark tunnel. "Where does that leave *me*? Where will *I* be, the Me-of-Me . . . in some kind of eternal void?" the Ram wonders. Arians are never strong on the yoga state of Nirvana. To become unconscious of *yourself*—that's *ecstasy*? In this instinct, Aries is intuitively right.

The concepts of Aquarius are light-years ahead of their time, for the most part, yet no more infallible or immune from misjudgment than the ideas of Aries—although the Uranian wisdom will be poured out from the little brown jug of Aquarius anyway, solicited or not. "All human troubles stem from an overemphasis on the emotions and an exaggeration of per-sonal feeling," claims Aquarius.

"People who deny their emotions and bury their personal feelings are cold and heartless, lacking all enlightenment and perception," retorts Aries.

So—where do they go from such a dead-end street? Back to their leprechauns, miracles, rainbows . . . and dirigibles of dreams.

☆ ☆ ☆ ☆ ☆ ☆

ARIES *Woman* AQUARIUS *Man*

*Then he nearly cried; but it struck him how
indignant she would be if he laughed instead. So
he laughed a haughty laugh, and fell asleep in
the middle of it.*

These two could have a glorious time together, if the Aries girl could only get one thing into her head. When an Aquarian man laughs, it's because he feels very sad. When he cries, it's because he feels very happy.

Once she catches on to this important game he plays, she'll have an easier time of it with all his other tricks. I'm referring to the tricks the Water Bearer uses to keep a girl from guessing he cares for her. Also the tricks he uses after she's already guessed, and he doesn't want her to find out how *deeply* he cares. And don't leave out the tricks he uses when he knows he's helplessly in love, but still trying to convince himself he can switch it back to friendship again, before it's too late. If you like games, this man is more fun than a stack of crossword puzzles and a trunkful of poker chips. An Aries girl likes games. But there's a small catch here. She only likes games when the other player lets her win all the time.

The Aquarian male has no patience with girl Rams who play by those rules. He's not going to give her any handicaps or free rolls of the dice just because she cries a few angry tears. Since she's so independent and aggressive, for a girl, he'll probably say, "Listen, buddy (Aquarians call everyone buddy), if you're so sensitive, how come I saw you marching in that Women's Lib parade last week? You females who demand equal rights had better be ready to take them all on, like moving furniture, fixing the plumbing, changing tires—and fighting right alongside the men in a war."

He's wrong. She only pushed her way into that parade because she couldn't resist the excitement of the drumbeats. After all, Rams are idealists, who sometimes start cheering for a cause before they know what it's all about. She's not likely to be a card-carrying member of any Women's Lib group. An Aries girl? She was *born* liberated—and she has no intention of giving up her feminine privileges, just to prove she's *equal,* when she already knows she's *superior!*

It's just that she likes to knock around the issues now and then, to keep her mind sharp. Like, she'll say, "Your argument that equal rights mean women have to wear uniforms, grab machine guns, and start killing people is deceptive and unrealistic. If women ran this country, there wouldn't *be* any more war. It's the men who are so big on physical violence, fighting, and war—not women."

AQUARIUS: Is that right? Drop into Macy's basement some morning when they're having a sale. I know a guy who runs the Red Cross bandage concession there every Saturday. It would turn General Patton's hair white in five minutes. Talk about cold-blooded atrocities. You women and your tears. What a put-on!

Sooner or later, she's going to complain that he's aloof and detached—or downright cruel and sadistic. (It amounts to the same thing to Aries. In her eyes, aloof is a synonym for cruel, detached a synonym for sadistic.) It's simply his admirable, yet admittedly annoying, breadth of vision that isolates him from the petty, personal emotions of individuals, while he's promoting the high ideals of brotherhood and sisterhood. An Aquarian is more interested in a permanent cure for the common cold than in handing you a Kleenex when you're sneezing. He's more concerned about the medical problems of geriatrics and aging than in helping individual little old ladies across the street. Uranus keeps his heart and mind directed toward the alleviation of all unhappiness and evil in the world on some bright tomorrow. There's not much sympathy left over for the personal distress close to him today.

This man is basically good-natured and kind, make no mistake about that. And his aims are noble. However, when dealing with Water Bearers, you should always remember Robespierre (who had an Aquarian Ascendent). His moral principles and his plans for the regeneration of France were undoubtedly most sincere and idealistic. But he overlooked the fact that France was a country populated by human beings with feelings, and in his crusading zeal, he chopped off quite a few heads—literally.

The Aquarian tries to be optimistic and sympathetic to his friends in trouble . . . . and to the Aries girl (who needs his broad shoulder to weep on after he's hurt her). But his sympathy too often consists of rather vague generalities. With his broader Uranus vision, the Aquarian male instinctively understands the deeper significance of sorrow. He knows that only through suffering can the soul be perfected—and he hates to interfere with the workings of Fate. Who is he to throw a monkey wrench into Destiny's plan? For all he knows, Destiny is a synonym for God. (You can see their synonym definitions also differ slightly.)

All right, so he can be kind and gentle, tender, sweet and funny, when it suits him. But he's still cold and heartless when he's seen through the sentimental eyes of the more sensitive, open-hearted Aries girl. The difference in their natures may be occasionally adjusted through compromise, but never completely overcome.

He has hundreds, maybe even thousands, of friends. With a crowd like that, she is obviously not going to be wild about each one of them. (*She's* not an Aquarian—*he* is.) The more time he spends with them—away from her—the more chances she'll have to be jealous. Since jealousy is the Aries girl's romantic Achilles' heel, their relationship will have a better chance if she lets him bring his friends home than if she forces him to meet them out in the park, beside the squirrel cage. There's nothing she can do to erase his "thing" about friendship. He's a humanitarian. He enjoys people. She'll simply have to face it.

The thing to do is forget about all his virtues—like vision, originality, foresight, friendliness, and humanitarianism—and concentrate on his vices. He has lots of those. (I know that sounds like strange advice, but we're dealing with an Aquarian, which means that everything you've ever learned must be reversed, and read in a mirror backward.) It's not his virtues then, but his vices that can keep them together. Let's run over a few of them.

He's unpredictable. She'll have to admit that's an exciting quality to Aries. It beckons to her Mars love of challenge. He's also eccentric, weird, unconventional, and odd. Beautiful. If there's anything this girl would find a real drag, it's an uptight man stuck in a conservative groove. He hears strange music, and he follows a wild and distant drummer (all Rams adore parades). Oh, wow! Well, what do you know—*a parade*! If she's a good girl, he'll let her hold his hand and skip along beside him. As for the wild and distant drummer he follows, to Aries a drumbeat is a drumbeat.

Who cares? Any kind of percussion makes her pulses pound, sends her heart into throbbing spasms of hope and glory-spangled banners of excitement.

Her pounding pulses may slow down a bit, however, when it comes to reaching sexual fulfillment with this man. In the beginning, the Aries girl's more direct, flaming Mars drive may whiz right over the head of her Aquarian lover. What happened to him? He was here just a minute ago. Oh, there he is. She'll have to go back and pick him up. He's still sitting there, scratching his left ear, and trying to analyze the first kiss. You mean there's *more*? Well, that certainly is interesting.

He's willing to be educated, and to let her teach him. Whether or not he ever graduates is another question altogether. No, she hasn't stumbled upon a male virgin. It's possible, of course, but the probable reason for his awe and wonder is that, to the typical Aquarian, each new experience of life is exactly like the first one—to be tasted, savored, then either treasured or discarded. His approach to romance is no different. Because the attraction of Aries and Aquarius is essentially one of emotional appeal and intellectual curiosity, their sexual mating may be unpredictable. It's the same old problem again. His *apparent* detachment—and her impatience with anything short of instant gratification. Yet, if the Sun-Moon relationship between their horoscopes is harmonious (and often, even if it isn't), there's a good possibility that practice will make perfect between them in the physical expression of love. Her Arian aura of freshness and lack of guile—her basic honesty about sexual love—will strongly appeal to him and move him to an unaccustomed tenderness. But she'll always have to retain the ideal image and innocence of the first seduction. For that matter, so will he.

A lot of their problems will be caused by the fact that she is Cardinal, therefore likes to lead—and he is Fixed, therefore refuses to follow. Also, they were both born under a masculine Sun Sign, and in addition, each is ruled by a masculine planet—both of them powerful, unpredictable planets. Mars and Uranus are not marshmallows. They are equally explosive and forceful, like the lovers or mates they rule, and whose actions they guide. Some of the edges can be smoothed away from these rough spots by the 3-11 vibration of easy friendship and communication between them. And there are other ways astrology can lead the way to happiness for the girl Ram and her Water Bearer (also for the Water Bearer and his girl Ram—since the masculine charisma of ownership and possession works both ways with these two).

Esoteric free-thought association, for all of its mystical quality, can be

helpful in a surprisingly practical way. They should try meditating together on the deeper layers of the meaning of their 3-11 Sun Sign Pattern.
In astrology, it's called a *sextile* relationship. When you think of the word
"sextile," a picture arises of snowflakes and stars, since the astrological symbol for the sextile resembles both. It looks like this: *   and what could
be a lovelier image than snowflakes and stars?

                                                            *   *
                                                              *
                                                            *   *
                                                            *

A snowflake is totally unique and original in its design—and so is the
Aquarian man. No two snowflakes are alike, and this man also . . . is like
no other on Earth. As for stars, they're the glittering diamonds in the sky
children wish on (and all those who believe) which should remind him of
her. For the Aries girl's heart will ever be the heart of a child, believing in
magic and miracles . . . spring and sunrise, as naive and trusting . . . as
excited by every new wonder and thrill of discovery . . . as open and
friendly as a child . . . and every bit as vulnerable, beneath all her surface
bravado and outward independence.

They'll be surprised how this small exercise in meditation will lift them
back to joy and laughter from the shadows of fear and rejection, jealousy
and anger. If everytime she sees a snowflake, she thinks of his uniqueness
. . . and everytime he sees a star, he thinks of her childlike innocence of
intent . . . the tension between them will melt into understanding, as a
snowflake melts . . . and sparkle with new promise, as a star shines.

Snowflakes and stars can be a magic mantra for all 3-11 influenced
lovers, but especially for this man and woman. Falling snowflakes and
shooting stars can be the private love code between them.

Sometimes, these two Sun Signs remind you of the ancient fable,
slightly distorted. A magic purple leprechaun comes along to grant the
Aries girl and her Aquarian man three wishes. In typical daffy, Uranian
fashion, he wishes for a blueberry pudding. Instead of leaving well
enough alone and asking for her own heart's desire, the Ram is so insulted
and angered by her lover's flippant wish that she blurts out: "I wish you
had that silly pudding stuck on your nose!" And so naturally they have to
sacrifice their third and last wish to get the pudding off his face.

It's sad, when two people who love each other have used up all their
wishes. Still, something may be left of yesterday to use as a bridge into tomorrow. What about all those crazy dreams, and . . . wait! Listen! Isn't
that the crash of a wild, off-beat drum in the distance? It is. They both
heard it. Never mind the quarrel. He grabs her hand tightly, and off they
go to catch up with the parade together (with the Ram in the lead, of

course). Now, if she can only keep him from flirting with the lady elephants . . . and he can only keep her from weeping over the clowns.

Well, what do you know? It's snowing! And the stars have come out.

☆ ☆ ☆ ☆ ☆

ARIES *Man* AQUARIUS *Woman*

◄◆►

*He frowned. "I am back," he said hotly. "Why
do you not cheer?"*

It is April 9th, 1971, the day (though not the year) of his birth, and he
has just sent his mother a telegram of congratulations. Now the Ram is in
a hurry to rush into the arms of the Aquarian girl he loves. He comes
bursting through the door, grabs her enthusiastically, plants a passionate
kiss on her cheek, and says something like, "I have a wonderful idea
about how to celebrate my birthday tonight. We'll go down to the Village
and have dinner in that little Italian place where we first met, then catch
Ali MacGraw and Ryan O'Neal in *Love Story*."

The Aquarian girl stares dreamily at a spot somewhere past his left
shoulder, and murmurs, "I wonder how that shoe-polish stain got up there
on the ceiling? Maybe I could paint some flowers and peace symbols to
cover it. Far out. A ceiling mural, just like the Sistine Chapel . . . . ."

ARIES: What does that have to do with my birthday?
AQUARIUS: I'm sorry, darling. I could have sworn Michelangelo was born
            in Italy . . . . maybe it was France . . . . .

You see, the only word she picked up in his exuberant speech was "Italian." Any competent astrologer could tell you there will be trouble in
River City tonight. (If I seem to be mixing up my geography, never mind,
the Aquarians reading it will understand.) It's a mistake, however, to
think a Water Bearer isn't always acutely aware, just because she seems

vague and aloof. Actually, she didn't miss a thing. For proof: Back to
River City . . . .

AQUARIUS: What's wrong, honey? You seem upset.
ARIES: I'm not upset. I'm *mad*.
AQUARIUS: She has a Taurus Ascendent.
ARIES: *Who* has *what*?
AQUARIUS: Ali MacGraw. She's an Aries like you, but she has a Taurus
           Ascendent. I've been crying since I read the first sentence.
ARIES: Now you've lost me. You've completely lost me.
AQUARIUS: What can you say about a twenty-one-year-old girl who died?
ARIES: You're thinking of *suicide*? Baby, I'm not *that* mad—honest!
AQUARIUS: That's the first sentence in the book. I can't wait to see the
           film—and that crazy little Italian waiter with the curly hair
           and moustache who guessed we were in love—so he brought
           candles and flowers and wine to the table . . . and, oh—that
           reminds me! I want to give you a bottle of the same kind of
           wine we drank that night for your birthday. I'll have to make
           a note, so I won't forget. It's next month isn't it? Why are you
           looking at me like that? Was it *last* month?

Well, she may miss a *few* things . . .

There's a curious air of absentminded detachment about an Aquarian
girl. Some people interpret it as daydreaming. Grandma would have called
it woolgathering. A Ram will call it an unforgivable outrage. To an Aries
male, who was, remember, born under a Cardinal Sign, the cardinal sin is
to ignore him. She isn't exactly ignoring him. Then again, she is. But no
more than she ignores anything that would chain her down to specifics,
when she's concentrating on something not even remotely connected with
the happening in front of her.

The average Aries man falls in love impetuously and fully, and he
demands an immediate response. If he doesn't get it in a short time—a very
short time—his built-in defense mechanism against being hurt takes over,
and he tells himself, "Who needs her?" *He* does, perhaps, very much, but
Aries is not a sign to risk unrequited love if he can help it. It's never as
easy for an Aquarian girl to be certain she's in love, even when she's deeply
interested in a man. It's because of her Uranus friendship curse—or blessing. (It can be either, by turns, depending.) She finds something utterly
fascinating and compelling about nearly every stranger she comes across,
let alone everyone she knows. How does she tell the difference between
such fascination and love? This girl honestly has a problem figuring out

the answer to the question of "Is it love or friendship?" The one thing she knows for certain is that love must *begin* with friendship. Not for her the physical chemistry alone that consumes some couples and causes them to wrongly believe they're made for each other. The anatomical differences between male and female never constitute, to this lady, sufficient reason to become emotionally involved. Her essence is Air, she was born under a mental sign—and she must be intellectually attracted to a man before the contemplation of either sex or romance makes a bit of sense to her. Not that she isn't capable of chalking up an occasional mistake. She is not, after all, Prudence Purity. But she makes fewer errors of judgment than her Sun Sign sisters who are seeking only a sense of physical belonging with a man.

She's seeking something else. Just what it is, she's not quite certain—but it's definitely something else. Once she's found it, she'll become intensely interested in the body-buddy game, but before that, she's not about to be seduced by the ordinary player who's merely looking for some sensual pleasure. Nor is she easily overwhelmed by the Aries man's insistent declarations of idealistic love, based on impulsive emotion alone. But there's nothing bashful about her, and once she believes it would be mentally exciting, intriguing, and worthwhile to become more intimate with the Ram who attracts her, she won't concern herself with coquettish tricks to keep him guessing. She's more likely to announce, suddenly and unexpectedly, when he's least prepared for such a lightning bolt, "I think I love you. Why don't you spend the night?" or perhaps, "Why don't we live together?"

It will shock him for a moment. A brief moment. But since he's as honest and straightforward as she is (they both despise hypocrisy and neither of them gives a dandelion what the neighbors think—they do what they jolly well please, adore flaunting convention and defying society's silly rules), he'll recover right away and accept her proposal. When such a suggestion comes from a man, it's a proposition. Coming from a woman, it's only a friendly *proposal*. Little niceties like that are among the pluses of being a female that are tough to give up in exchange for the benefits of ERA's "proposed" sexual equality.

Speaking of sexual equality, that brings us to perhaps the most important single, threatening aspect of a relationship between these two. She was born under a masculine Sun Sign, and her attitudes and actions are aggressively guided by the also-masculine planet Uranus. The Ram, too, was born under a masculine Sun Sign, his attitudes and actions likewise aggressively guided by the also-masculine planet, Mars. On top of that astrological standoff, she's Fixed (stubborn) and he's Cardinal (determined).

It may sound pretty discouraging, like the game of childhood, where one person draws a line and dares the other to step over it—or like General Lee facing General Sherman, cannonball to cannonball. But it's not all push-and-pull between these two. There's also a good deal of give and take, principally because of the beneficent karmic influence of their 3-11 Sun Sign Pattern. It brings to their relationship all kinds of beautiful bonuses and boosters to happiness and harmony. The most beneficial of these is the friendship aspect of the 3-11 vibration, allowing the couples influenced by it to be friends, as well as lovers. You can see how this might solve a lot of the Ram's problems regarding her Uranian friendship fetish. In addition, the influence creates the atmosphere for free and flowing communication between them—most of the time. They'll find it easier than most couples to talk about their disagreements—to communicate their feelings to each other. They'll both benefit more or less equally from this particular reward of their personal Sun Sign Pattern vibration, because she's an Air Sign and all Air Signs do enjoy talking. He's an Aries, and enjoys it even more. All these goodies somewhat dilute the negative effect of the Fixed versus Cardinal and double masculine standoff between them. Not that the latter can be completely ignored. It will still be necessary to cope with these matters to some degree, but a solution won't be difficult, and certainly not impossible.

Once she's decided their relationship is worthy of her whole involvement, the sexual compatibility between the Ram and the girl Water Bearer (who is, by the way, regardless of being called a Water Bearer, not of the Water, but of the Air essence—only one of her many contradictions) contains the potential of being a rare and beautiful blending. But a potential must be encouraged to develop. She may be puzzled by the intensity of his desire and the overwhelming passion of his lovemaking. Still, it's always a positive happening for an Aquarian woman to be puzzled by anything, for she is curious, and usually won't rest until she's solved any puzzle Life or Love presents to her. A word of caution to the Ram, however. She becomes quickly bored after she's put the pieces together and satisfied her curiosity. So the best insurance that their physical Oneness will always hold its first fine rapture for them is for the Aries man to always treat their sexual union as something special, different, and unusual in some way. He should vary his approach to their intimacies from time to time. She doesn't mind if the variations consist of a deep and silent physical togetherness after a quarrel, with the sudden fulfillment of love hunger becoming an eloquent apology between them without words . . . an unexpected time of the consummation of their erotic needs at odd hours during the day, instead of always being a bedtime ritual . . . if he decides to play classical music during their closeness, and turns up the stereo loud enough to make spoken endearments between them impossible (and also unnecessary, since music does have a soaring aphrodisiac effect) . . . whether they whisper and talk constantly during the physical expression of their love . . . . and he recites poetry to her or tells her funny stories about kangaroos . . . whether he's tender and gentle or violent and feral . . . just so sex is never dull or boring—never a repetitious ritual. Her thirst for change is something he'll have to realize.

She should realize that this man is wounded more deeply than he'll ever show when her occasional sexual detachment leads him to believe she doesn't really need him. She should never respond to his sexual overtures with anything but a sincere and all-consuming enthusiasm, always welcome his embraces with unmistakable joy and anticipation. Otherwise he could become temporarily impotent and unable to express his physical love for her, because of a never-admitted feeling of inadequacy, which she might not even notice, since sex, to her, like everything else, is only one facet of her varied existence. She may be happily tuning the engine of the car some Saturday morning or skipping through the woods picking a bunch of wildflowers during these cool periods, without the slightest notion of why he's so morose and frustrated. She should warn herself to be more alert to his moods—forget the dwell/tachometer, drop her bouquet of oxalis—and murmur in his ear that she needs to rest awhile (in his arms, of course), yet still not make it seem as if she's the initiator of the lovemaking she's suggesting. Keeping the Ram sexually contented and happy takes a lot of careful consideration, and this woman, while not deliberately or intentionally *in*considerate, can become absorbed in a multitude of manic activities and interests, while neglecting the one activity that's important—their love.

Sometimes the Uranian experimental urges and unpredictable behavior of the Aquarian woman will seem to the Ram who truly loves her like a patchwork of erratic, changing moods and frustratingly brief spans of attention. He can't seem to catch her . . . . like a butterfly or a lark. But if he doesn't try to dominate her personality and allows her the freedom she needs to work out her individuality, all her myriad interests will one day integrate naturally into the whole of her fascinating self.

Sometimes, the driving ambition, endless energy, and profusion of dreams shooting forth like comets through the vibrant aura of the Aries man will seem to the Aquarian woman who truly loves him like living with a sack of fireworks, ready to explode at the touch of a match. She can't seem to convince him to slow down to her complicated and intricate, but slower and more dreamy, approach to living. But if she never forgets to remember to make him know she loves him with all her heart when he stumbles and falls, just as much as she does the times when he's elated by victory (maybe even more, because of his vulnerability), his emotions will gradually mature and his confidence will grow into a tall tree of stability. Then she'll wish he was little-boy-impulsive again, because she'll miss his spontaneity. She's ruled by Uranus, the planet of change, you see. So she'll perversely toss a match into his Mars sack of fireworks just to see if he's still the man who first made her laugh when she was sad and weep when she was happy, by reminding her of her own springtime when everything was green and fresh and new. She won't have to wonder long. The roman candles are still inflammable . . . the sparklers too. He was only pretending to be mature and stable. And in her crazy-daisy, upside-down Aquarian way, that will make her very, very happy. So happy, she'll surprise him with a bottle of the wine they used to drink a toast to each other that night in the Village . . . for his birthday. (It will be August, and his birthday is in April, but no matter. He won't care.) Then she'll turn up the volume on the stereo. Warsaw Concerto. Maybe Rhapsody in Blue. Or Beethoven's Fifth.

An Aquarian Cassandra weaves a spell of druidic enchantment and marvelous madness from which an Aries man will never escape. Later, when they're both "resting" (which was his idea alone), he'll stare at the ceiling, and say, "You know, darling, the mural you painted to cover the splash of shoe polish reminds me of a painting by Michelangelo."

"Oh, wow!" she'll exclaim, delighted. "How did you know I wanted to go to Italy in the autumn?" How did he know? Easy. He finally mastered the high-frequency modulation and tuned in to her Uranus channel. Besides, he's always wanted to see the Sistine Chapel himself. Maybe they can go there to celebrate *her* birthday, he'll tell her—in October. She'll grin, and say that's a lovely idea. She's always wondered what it would be like to be a Libra woman. He'll tell her he thinks it would be great, because, as a Leo, he's always wanted to have an affair with a Libran. Then they'll have a pillow fight. She'll win. Feathers everywhere. He won't mind losing. Yes, they've finally tuned in.

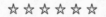

ARIES

Fire — Cardinal — Positive
Ruled by Mars
Symbol: The Ram
Day Forces — Masculine

PISCES

Water — Mutable — Negative
Ruled by Neptune
Symbols: The Fish & Whale
Night Forces — Feminine

The **ARIES-PISCES** *Relationship*

><><><

Even then they had time to gather in a phalanx
that would have been hard to break had they
risen quickly, but this they were forbidden to do
by the traditions . . . .

An interviewer at an employment agency would have no trouble iden-
tifying these two Sun Signs, no problem in telling a Ram from a
Fish. All it takes is a little experience, and a minimal understanding of astrology.

INTERVIEWER: What was your most recent place of employment?
ARIES: I was production chief at Parakeet Publishing, at 42 East
83rd Street.
INTERVIEWER: I see. I'll check them for a reference. The Parakeet Publishing Company, at 82 East 43rd Street.

ARIES: That's not what I said. You got the address backwards. Are
              you hard of hearing, or are you trying to intimidate me?

INTERVIEWER: Could I have your present home address, please?
PISCES: Sure! I live in the McCall Apartments, at 7000 6th Avenue.
INTERVIEWER: All right, let me make a note of that. That's the Bacall
              Apartments at 6000 7th Avenue, right?
PISCES: (visibly confused) Well . . uh, if you think it's a nicer
              neighborhood, I guess I could see if they have a va-
              cancy . . . .

Walk up to a Ram and remark, "As an Aries, you're probably creative"—
and the Ram will reply, "You can say that again! I'm loaded with original
ideas. Would you like to hear some of them?"

Walk up to a Fish and remark, "As a Pisces, you're probably involved in
one of the water sports, like surfing or scuba diving"—and the Fish will
reply, "Well, I can't swim, but—uh, which one do you think I should be
involved in? I suppose I could learn . . . ."

Walk up to a Ram and remark, "If you continue along the path you're on
now, you'll never end up as a leader"—and the Aries person will reply,
"How would you like a punch in the mouth?"

Walk up to a Fish and remark, "If you continue along the path you're on
now, you'll never end up as a leader"—and the Pisces person will reply,
"Really? Gee, I hope you're right."

The pattern that gradually emerges with the Ram is *aggressiveness*, sometimes to excess. The pattern that gradually emerges with the Fish is *accommodation*, also sometimes to excess. Aries, of course, is a Fire Sign and
Pisces is a Water Sign. There's a marked difference between Aries aggressiveness and Pisces accommodation, and just to be sure I've made that
difference clear, here's another example. A Ram has just walked up to the
counter and ordered a pizza, to take out.

CLERK: Okay. One pizza to go, coming up! How do you want it, with
              mushrooms or green peppers?
RAM: Neither. I want black olives and onions. And see that you don't
              burn it, like you did the last time I was here.

Now, a Fish has walked up to the counter, to order a pizza, to take out.

CLERK: Okay. One pizza to go, coming up! How do you want it, with mushrooms or green peppers?

FISH: Well, let's see—what do most of your customers order?

CLERK: We sell a lot of mushrooms.

FISH: Mushrooms. I'll take mine with mushrooms.

CLERK: Of course, personally, I prefer green peppers.

FISH: Oh. Well . . . uh, could you change that, please, to one pizza to go, with green peppers?

CLERK: Sure, but look, now—why don't you just order it the way *you* want? Don't let me influence you.

FISH: Well—could I have two pizzas, then—one with mushrooms, and one with green peppers?

You can see that Pisces is accommodating. What you may *not* see, however, is the multiple motivation behind it. The kind-hearted Fish really do like to please people, when they can. Every Piscean dreads the embarrassment of outright confrontation, and they dislike attention focused on themselves. But there's also a more subtle reason why Pisceans are reluctant to commit themselves to a personal opinion: they're always on the alert for snoopers, because they have an absolute horror of "Big Brother." At an airport, a stranger passing by, carrying monogrammed luggage with the initials CIA or FBI, can catapult the typical Fish into a nervous panic. Try to convince a Pisces that those letters stand for Charles Isidore Abernacky or Frederick Bruce Israel. Go ahead, try. What kind of Jewish mother would name her boy Frederick Bruce? Someday, make a list of all your Pisces friends who have un-listed phone numbers. It will be interesting.

When a Ram meets a Fish, it seems that here is a sweet, mild, gentle soul the Aries person can push around more or less as he (or she) pleases. I'm sorry to say that this is what the fiery Aries often tries to do with the watery Piscean. But the Ram should study the natural sciences—and the Bible.

From the natural sciences, he'll learn all about the elements of earth, air, fire and water—and that water can be dangerous to fire. Flip the flame on a lighter as high as you like, then dip it into a glass of water. Sputter . . . . pssssttt . . . and out. Although water may seem to be the weakest of the elements, it's actually the strongest. A few drops of water dripping steadily on a rock for a long enough period of time will wear the rock away into fine sand. I know an Aries landlord who impulsively raised the rent on the New Jersey apartment of a Pisces lady named Marion. She accepted the news from him sweetly, with gentle feminine submission. However, the Arian landlord has spent the last eight months in and out of the courtroom. She sends him little notes about the leaky plumbing and such (one drop at a time, you see), and he still hasn't been able to hike the rent by so much as one dollar. Before it's over he'll probably lower it.

The secret of the great strength of water is its non-resistance. Water does not *resist*. Toss a pebble into the river, and what happens? Water doesn't resist the object penetrating its calm. Old Man River just opens up, swallows the pebble, covers it over—and keeps moving right along. The Nazarene relates the strength of Water's powerful passivity to the human personality. "Resist ye *not* evil," counseled Jesus, whose birth, by the way, ushered in the Age of Pisces, nearly two thousand years ago.

The Fish are influenced by the mysterious, infinite wisdom of Neptune, and so they seldom resist the more aggressive Rams, who are driven by the fiery force of the red planet, Mars. Often, Aries people find that Pisceans have a restful, cooling effect on their flaming frustrations. An association between them is usually beneficial to both. Each Sun Sign carries, within karmic memory, the seeds of experiences gained from the Sun Sign immediately behind it on the astrological wheel of life—and conversely, there are many lessons to be learned from the character and qualities of the Sun Sign immediately following one's own.

This is a 2-12 Sun Sign Pattern, meaning that Aries represents the second astrological house to Pisces, and Pisces represents the twelfth astrological house to Aries. Translated, Aries will always, in one way or another, symbolize money to Pisces, whether in a negative or a positive sense. In some manner, money will be a vital consideration, and a frequent topic of discussion between them.

To the Rams, the Fish represent many secrets, which Pisces usually keeps and won't tell, causing Aries to be exceedingly annoyed. If not that, then the two of them will spend much time discussing secrets—or the past sorrows of one or the other. Sometimes, the secrecy syndrome is beneficial, but you can be sure, however it works out, that both money and secrecy will form the foundation, in a variety of ways, of any association between the Ram and the Fish, whether they're involved as friends, relatives, business associates, lovers or mates. "Secrets" may include all matters of the occult, the esoteric or the metaphysical, such as astrology, hypnotism, astral travel, telepathy and the like. Sooner or later, these matters will prove to be of mutual interest to any Aries-Pisces combination, whatever the sex, age or relationship of the two of them, as with all 2-12 Sun Sign Patterns.

Since Pisces lies behind Aries on the karmic wheel, the Ram feels an instinctive tolerance for the foibles of the Fish, somehow understanding the Piscean behavior, even though it differs so vastly from his (or her) own. Each Aries person has spiritually experienced the passivity and submission of the Pisces nature, which is why Aries, in the present incarnation, leans so hard toward the extreme opposite of Piscean humility—ego. With all their brashness, Rams reveal their karmic soul memory of the Piscean experience through their hidden vulnerability to hurt, and the quickness with which Arian compassion and generosity can be aroused.

The Rams, however, aren't about to chance any masochism (openly, at least) in this lifetime. One might say that Aries comprehends and appreciates the Pisces attitude without envy, and without condemning it. They've already received their report cards in the Piscean spiritual school, thank you, and they prefer not to return. They didn't like the teacher (Neptune) all that much. And so it goes with all the Sun Signs, around and around the birth wheel—again and again—until all the necessary lessons are learned, and the soul can graduate from the earth-flesh level of awareness and existence, into a higher, and more individual awareness.

Due to this 2-12 influence, the Fish will never fail to in some way look up to Aries as having something important to teach them, and unlike most Sun Signs, in relation to the sign ahead of them, Pisces is usually placidly willing to imitate, and to learn from the Rams. (Water is not only the strongest and most powerful of the four elements—Water is also wisest—which is *why* it's strongest.)

On the whole, the Ram and the Fish are nicely compatible, with neither overly desirous of interfering with the other's approach to life, but rather complementing it instead. Yet there will be times when they experience some heated (Aries) or chilly (Pisces) encounters. The forthright Ram has little patience for the sometimes slippery tactics of the elusive Fish.

I know a Piscean in Colorado who pleasantly (Pisceans are nearly always pleasant) once remarked to me: "Well, you know what I always say—promise anything, and get out of it later. That's my motto." The Fish are uncommonly cheerful about confessing their little flaws. This method of backing away from a commitment quite naturally may create, on occasion, a barrier between Pisces and the very direct, naively honest Rams, who will usually display undisguised resentment when the Fish swim away alone now and then, to exchange whispered secrets with the ocean—or who may feel hurt and neglected if the Pisceans should glide behind some cool seaweed to refresh their weary souls, without leaving behind a trail indicating where they may be found. But no harm is meant by the kindly Fish. Lacking the Ram's tough horns, and the Mars emotional, spiritual and mental stamina, it's the Neptune soul's only protection against an abrasive daily existence in this harsh world—the wear and tear of life's problems.

The Piscean motto of *"promise anything, and get out of it later"* may sound deceptive; yet it's a philosophy that keeps the Fish young and tranquil—and off the psychiatrist's couch. It also allows Pisceans to conserve their energy, thereby enabling them to remain composed enough to listen to everybody else's troubles for hours on end. Nevertheless, to the Rams, sneaky is sneaky.

☆ ☆ ☆ ☆ ☆ ☆

ARIES *Woman* **PISCES** *Man*

> *"Which story was it?"*
>
> *"About the prince who couldn't find the lady who wore the glass slipper."*
>
> *"Peter," said Wendy excitedly, "that was Cinderella, and he found her . . . ."*

I don't want to shatter any glass slipper dreams, but this combination usually works out better when the girl is the Pisces and the boy is the Ram. An Aries female needs a determined, thick-skinned male, who has the aggressiveness to say, "Shut up, and listen," when it's necessary. And it will assuredly be necessary, from time to time, with this girl.

There are, of course, as always, the exceptions that prove the astrological rule. A Pisces man, for example, with the Moon or Ascendent in a Fire Sign, such as Aries, Sagittarius or Leo, may possess just the right blend of fiery command and gentleness of manner to make this rather spunky one become as meek as a lamb. Well, maybe not *that* meek—but more docile and manageable than she'd be around most other men.

In a way, it's what she secretly seeks and longs for—someone who will control her firmly (and make her feel feminine)—on occasion. Someone who will allow her to be boss (half the time)—and be the tender, charming Prince of her dreams (the rest of the time, whatever time is left). She needs a strong big brother to protect her, a companion she considers her equal in intelligence, a lover who will physically conquer her, and a quiet man who will not try to confine her spirited personality, or domineer her. It would also be nice if he could be a poet.

And of course, he should be willing, even anxious, to defend her loyally against her enemies (until she forgives them, then he should love them) as she will defend him against his (whether he wants her to or not). And let's see—yes, he must also admire and respect her, and tell her so frequently—be the kind of man who likes to chop wood and fix things when they're broken (including her heart)—a man who can handle an emergency with cool poise, and meet a crisis with great courage. He must, by all means, be possessed of impeccable integrity, and be snowflake-pure-sexually-faithful to her. (But he must not be a doormat, or self-effacing.)

If possible, she would like him to consist of equal parts of Rhett Butler, Robert Browning, Muhammed Ali, Mike Todd, Abraham Lincoln—and her favorite saint. Maybe a touch of Charlton Heston, Warren Beatty, Jimmy Stewart, Marlon Brando and Steve McQueen, with just a dash of Norman Mailer—if that's not asking too much.

Nearly every single Christmas of her life, for as far back as she can remember, she carefully printed out her request in a letter to Santa Claus, and he ignored it, year after year, leaving all sorts of useless things under the tree, except this one most important gift. (You can sympathize with his problem.)

When you consider it carefully, a Pisces man has as many chances to live up to her romantic ideals as any other male. *None.* Which means that he at least starts out even. You know? The Fish certainly can't ask for better odds than those.

A girl Ram is fun and fresh. She's pretty and punchy, full of spirit and sparkles and warmth and generosity—all that. But she does need to be sat upon occasionally, when her Mars will causes her to be a bit too frisky and free for her own good—or for the peace of mind of the man who loves her. Pisces men just never sound very convincing when they say things like "Shut up, and listen." The Fish is more in his own element when he's figuring abstract physics or math theories, calculating the relativity of time, in relation to space—or quoting Tennyson. It's possible for the Ram and the Fish to meet, mate, and murmur sentiments into each other's ears happily, for a lifetime. It can happen. Not often. But it can. Where's your faith in miracles?

A Pisces man is more likely than any other to genuinely believe in the kind of enchantment every Aries girl lives within, and demands romantically. She'll adore him for it. She'll trust his dreams, have faith in his visions—and she'll respond (at first, anyway) with little flutters of excitement to his sensitivity and his gentleness. Then she'll feel an irresistible urge to defend him against those who judge him unfairly as an idle dreamer with no future. (She'll have simply bushels of chances to do that!)

Most people have been so brainwashed by astrological over-simplifications, they think every Pisces is a wishy-washy candidate for Alcoholics Anonymous, or group therapy (nude group therapy, considering the Age we're living in). True, he was born under a complicated and difficult Sun Sign. The stars portended at his birth that he'd have to pick his way through a haze of daydreams. He was also fated to get caught in the sticky octopus tendrils of other people's troubles as he swims along through life . . . . trying his best to mind his own business (which can be even more tangled and confusing). His ruling planet, Neptune, seems to be forever leading him into situations so mysterious, so intertwined with intrigue and half-truths that even a Ouija board couldn't get to the bottom of the whole mess. This is so for Pisces of both sexes. Talk it over with Ted Kennedy, Elizabeth Taylor, Jackie Gleason, Dinah Shore or Pamela Mason sometime. They're all Pisceans too, and they've been there. EVERYWHERE. More than once.

The Aries girl who's annoyed by the elusiveness of her Pisces man should ask herself how *she* would react to being part of what some flippant astrologers call "the dustbin of the zodiac." It's not much fun to carry the weight of knowing you're the embodiment of *all* the other eleven Sun Signs. And this man has the added burden of frequent precognitive flashes that clutter up his consciousness. Not only that, but his Neptunian compassion can seduce him into some situations that can only be called weird. This forces him to cover the fact that he's the softest touch in town under a variety of false fronts. These can range from crankiness and crustiness to drunkenness—or a psychedelic trip that's far out (far out from this harsh world). But lots of creative writers, imaginative artists and abstract thinkers (like Einstein) have also been Pisceans, and they learned to handle their Neptune vibrations. This man does have a choice of streams, you know. All Fish do, when they break away from the chaotic cross-currents.

The danger inherent in a relationship between an Aries woman and a Pisces man is that the sexes tend to get mixed up. A male Fish can be as masculine, as virile and as muscular as the next guy. But he's also ultrasensitive—for a man. The female Ram can be as feminine, as tender and as glamorous as the next girl. But she's also strong-willed, determined and independent—for a woman. Because of his instinct to withdraw from conflict, the Pisces man may prefer to retreat, rather than face up to the Aries girl's Fire. She won't like it. Rams feel helpless, and become even angrier, when they're forced to shadow-box their way out of a disagreement. It can drive her up a tree to be ignored, and a Piscean is an expert at the technique of passive non-resistance.

She may also resent his reluctance to push himself with others. It's beyond her comprehension how anyone can take so much lying down. Just as it's beyond *his* comprehension how anyone can stand up on his feet constantly, fighting and attacking and counterattacking, and wasting all that energy. His mildness, if carried to extremes, can finally goad her into lashing out at him with some cutting and unkind remarks that she doesn't mean but that can nevertheless wound his feelings deeply. This sort of scene can be triggered by almost any minor incident.

PISCES: My paintings are going to be exhibited at the museum's Art Show next week. See? Here's the program. It says: *"Special showing of new art forms by Fried Hot."*

ARIES: Are they talking about an artist or an *egg?* That can't be you. You're Fred Haught.

PISCES: I guess they weren't sure how to spell my surname, and maybe the mistake in "Fred" is just a printer's error. I've been trying to decide what to do. . . . . . .

ARIES: Don't tell me what you're going to do. Don't tell me, let me guess. You're going to change your name, right?

PISCES: Well, I hadn't thought of going that far. Do you think I should?

ARIES: I think you should grab the art director of that museum and say, "Look, boob, you spelled my name wrong. Print new programs, or I remove my paintings from the exhibit."

PISCES: Oh, I couldn't insult him like that. He might be offended, and then I'd lose my big chance to exhibit my paintings.

ARIES: Well, if you don't do it, you're going to lose your big chance to exhibit me as your wife. I AM NOT GOING TO BE INTRODUCED AT THE MUSEUM AS "MS. FRIED HOT," SO YOU EITHER COLLAR THAT ART DIRECTOR AND DEMAND YOUR RIGHTS TODAY—OR I MOVE OUT OF YOUR LIFE TOMORROW. DO YOU HAVE THAT STRAIGHT?

He won't refuse. He'll agree with her, and leave for the museum. But he may not return. He'd rather be Fried Hot than boiled alive in her Mars temper. Of course, this is an extreme case. Still, it does illustrate the challenges and hurdles to be met when there's a reversal of the dominant-passive roles between these two lovers. If there's a compatible Sun-Moon-Ascendent aspect between their birth charts, their relationship can work out ideally. She'll have enough Fire to spark him to great accomplishment, to give him faith in himself and his dreams—and he'll have the right amount of Water to soothe and gentle her fears, to give her emotional security.

With an adverse Luminary or Ascendent aspect between their nativities, however, they may face a few problems.

The Aries woman is woven of finer threads than those who see only her surface confidence ever suspect. She is many things more than a fireball of impulse. She's the ecstasy she felt when she buried her nose in the fragrance of the bouquet of violets she picked in an elf-haunted, shady corner of the yard, when she was three . . . . . the kitten she watched get run over by a streetcar . . . . . she's red kites and yellow balloons, the rainy days of childhood . . . . . the newborn baby a lady on the bus let her hold in her arms when she was nine, and acting out a private madonna make-believe . . . . . the snow sparkles under the street light she truly thought were diamonds . . . . . the spanking with a wooden paddle her fourth grade principal gave her at recess, before everyone in school . . . . . she's the sunrise someone forgot . . . . . the song someone remembered . . . . She's her first belly-smacker in the pool, when she was trying desperately for a perfect swan dive . . . . . and more. She's the poem the Pisces man tried to write, but couldn't quite complete . . . . . yet he could, if he'd only allow her to help him write the last verse.

The sexual relationship between them will be the eternal and beautiful mutual attraction of explosive activity and cool stillness. But it can also be the attraction of a potential conqueror for a potential victim, if there are severe planetary afflictions in their respective horoscopes. With favorable planetary exchanges in their nativities, however, the Ram and the Fish could enjoy an exceptionally happy physical chemistry that could outlast periodic bickering, or hurt feelings. Their philosophical approaches to Life may be different, but their romantic goals are identical. Both of them desperately seek a sexual experience of great intensity—and both are sentimental and imaginative. In expressing their love through sexual union, they can fulfill each other's secret fantasies, escape into their own private wonderland and close the door against the rest of the world.

A Piscean who wants to teach an Aries girl to float tranquilly in his pond must make a decision to level with her about everything, and then stick to it. His fondness for keeping secrets, and for telling half-truths to spare her feelings (or his own), is something this woman will never stand for. She puts all her cards on the table, and she can't trust a player who hides any aces up his sleeve. Unless the Fish is prepared to be 100 percent honest with her, in every way, he'd better find another poker partner.

If someday he should discover he can't keep anything from her, not even his innermost feelings, and he's compelled to confess to her all his secret yearnings—he loves her. It's the first sign of capitulation from a Pisces man.

It's not, however, a guarantee that he'll capitulate all the way into marriage. This man is extremely reluctant to take on the complications of both emotional *and* legal involvement. The first one is hassle enough with which to cope, as far as he's concerned, without adding the burden of the second. The common Neptune definition of marriage is "a close friendship, recognized by the police." Eventually he'll gobble the bait, and allow himself to be reeled in, but he'll struggle less in the marital net if the Aries woman will pretend they're still having an affair that's *not* recognized by the police. I know an actual, living, breathing Piscean male in California who has substituted a Siamese cat for a family (the typical Fish fears the responsibilities of a family, as he fears the snooping of Big Brother or Sister, the Internal Revenue, CIA and FBI). The Fish with the Pussycat has a motto he repeats often: *"Kitty litter is cheaper than diapers."*

The Ram will have to make-believe with her Fish that they're involved in only an emotional union, nothing more, even after they are duly wedlocked (she should *never* use the term wed-*lock* with him). If this keeps him romantic, makes him happy and causes him to feel freer, why not allow him to live in his fantasy of bachelorhood?

He may alternate between leaving her, and returning again, unsure of how to convince her of his devotion. But all she wants is to be loved and understood, never to be questioned—to be accepted for exactly what she is. As a matter of fact, that's all he wants too. The only dragons that stand between Aries and Pisces are his Neptune illusions, which to him, are reality—and her Mars reality, which is, actually, an illusion. Plus the smaller gargoyles of his passivity, and her impatience—and their mutually sensitive, vulnerable natures. No outsider can slay these dragons and gargoyles for them. They must be destroyed from within. That's the way it always is in faerie tales. At least, in the ones with happy endings.

ARIES *Man* PISCES *Woman*

--◆◈◆--

The many gentlemen who had been boys when she
was a girl discovered simultaneously that they
loved her, and they all ran over to her house
to propose to her except Mr. Darling, who took a
cab and nipped in first, and so he got her.

Since no man is more male than a Ram, and no woman is more female than a Fish, the love between these two is never flawed by confusion over sexual identification. It's a true mating, in every sense of the word you can imagine. When an Aries man and a Pisces woman fall in love, Mother Nature smiles approvingly.

At its best, the liaison brings out all his shining Aries heroism, and all her tender Pisces devotion. These two are Romeo and Juliet in the flesh. At its worst, it can bring out his latent Mars sadism and her latent Neptune masochism. Even so, if he enjoys playing Tyrannical-Master-of-the-Mansion, and she gets kicks from playing Little-Eva-in-the-Snow, who are we to spoil their fun?

I remember well the evening I spent with friends of mine, an Aries man and his Pisces wife, in West Virginia. After their seven children had been tucked in bed, the handsome Ram placed a protective arm around his pretty girl Fish, and spoke emphatically: "My woman doesn't run around chasing a career and joining clubs. I keep her pregnant in the summer and barefoot in the winter—so she stays out of trouble."

As I started to hand her a heavy brass ashtray to throw at his head, I noticed the strangest thing. She was smiling up at him with absolute adoration and pure worship. I haven't the slightest doubt that they'll walk into the sunset together, long after their golden wedding anniversary, holding hands like sweethearts—with him still tall, and strong—her still fragile and barefoot. It almost makes you cry, doesn't it? It was such a traumatic experience for me, I went out the next day and bought five new pairs of shoes to hide under my bed. When my Pisces friend expressed her curiosity, I just told her, "Well, winter's coming, you know, and I may want to run out some morning at four A.M. to buy a paper or something." I don't think she understood, but I felt more secure.

Aries and Pisces are not generally as compatible, over a long period of time (especially if they live in Alaska, where her feet might get frost bitten) as he would be with an Air or Fire sign—or she would be with an Earth or Water sign. They're basically quite different. But in the immortal words of the Frenchmen: *"Vive la différence!"* It can be quite enough to attract them in the beginning. As for building the elemental attraction into a stable relationship, there's a good chance they can succeed if his Moon or Ascendent is in Pisces, Cancer, Scorpio, Taurus or Capricorn—or if her Moon or Ascendent is in Aries, Leo, Sagittarius, Gemini or Aquarius.

Before the Pisces girl is married, her phone rings constantly, with one male after another calling her for dates. She has an awful time deciding between Tom, Dick or Harry—because she hates to hurt Bill, John and Bob. Anyway, she really loves Jack, if she could only forget Roger. Life is full of frustrations. Like deciding which one to marry—or deciding whether or not to allow half a dozen or so of them to protect her against poverty and boredom, by paying her rent and taking her to Sun Valley to ski. Things like that. Maybe lending her their cars, an occasional Porsche, a BMW or a Saab. It's such a rough life. The Women's Liberation movement doesn't move Pisces females much. The whole ERA noise just kind of floats in one Neptune ear and out the other. The Pisces woman feels it all depends on what you want to be liberated *from*. It certainly does. Amen, sisters! (And brothers.)

After she's married, her phone will continue to ring approximately every ten minutes throughout the day and night, but then it will be her neighbors, relatives and friends who need an ear to confide in, and a shoulder to weep upon. Her Aries husband will fly into a few Mars tantrums over her tendency to turn their home into a therapy clinic. She should be listening to *his* troubles. Not *part* of the time. *All* of the time. Except on holidays, when he's resting, or sleeping—or knocking around with his pals.

A girl Fish is an exquisite listener. That's how she gathered all those admirers, beginning with grade school. She's also beautifully humble, and sympathetic, and *that's* how she gets caught in her own Neptune web. A Pisces woman who feels, finally, that her individuality is being smothered by the dominant ego of the Aries man she loves, usually won't protest loudly, or argue about it with any degree of intensity. No matter how desperate she becomes, she's more likely to keep smiling . . . . but with a blank expression in her eyes. When he loses his temper with her over a trifle, she normally won't fight back. She'll just blink a few times, and yawn. But the yawn may be a silent scream.

If she seems to be drifting and dreaming, if her smiles are vague, and her attention wanders, the Ram should ask himself if he has been perhaps overlooking her needs in pursuing his own, which is easy for him to do, though he never does it intentionally. An Aries man is seldom aware of his occasional selfishness. It's more thoughtlessness than selfishness any-way. He's so intent on living-being-doing every moment, he just doesn't take the time to look around him. When it's pointed out to him that he's been rude or inconsiderate, he's invariably surprised and embarrassed—and sorry.

It was never his intention to be cruel or unfeeling. No one can be more sentimental, kind-hearted, foolishly generous and fiercely loyal in love than Aries. But her Neptune passivity can not only encourage his un-thinking selfishness and his latent chauvinism, it can blind him to any hurt he's given her. If he realizes it, he'll probably apologize profusely, and be-have like a perfect angel (until he forgets again, and has to be reminded). So you can't blame all their troubles on him. The Pisces woman must ac-cept at least half the responsibility for her own unhappiness, and ask her-self if she has been leaning a little heavily on the martyr routine.

There's not much need to analyze their sexual relationship in detail, as we did with the other combinations, because, as you can see from the as-trological facts stated at the beginning of this section, it's clear that this is the perfect Romeo-Juliet, Tarzan-Jane blending, in a sexuality sense. The result, in relation to their physical intimacy, isn't difficult to guess. She'll not only be sensitive to his every lover's mood, wish and desire, she'll decode and fulfill them, almost before they're formed. In return, he'll gratefully give her an exciting display of his Mars intensity, and much tender (for him) affection. None of the boys who used to call her on the phone, and lend her their BMWs, could have prepared her, emotionally or otherwise, for the kind of passion that rages in the heart of a Ram, once he's found a woman he can call completely his own.

This brings us to the subject of sexual and romantic infidelity (a subject we always eventually reach in every Aries chapter). The girl Fish is not a flirt, mind you, but what it is, you see, is that—well, men flirt with *her*. She's not promiscuous, she just thinks that admiration from members of the male sex is the nicest part of being a female.

As for the Ram, he's not a playboy type either. But he's not going to throw rocks at a little worship from the opposite sex now and then, which he uses to polish up his ego. He thinks that's all part of being a man. None of this should cause any real trouble between them; nevertheless, it probably will, because, although the Pisces girl is inclined to understand and trust her man—Aries is never as insistent on freedom for his partner as he is on freedom for himself. In the Ram's opinion, *his* casual encounters with other women are innocent. *Hers* are suspect, clearly deliberate ma-neuvers toward an actual act of unfaithfulness.

It's not at all fair, of course. It will help if she'll realize that his attitude isn't based on romantic selfishness, but only on his well-hidden feelings of inadequacy. Being influenced and guided by Neptune compassion, she'll probably comprehend his secret fear, and behave accordingly. Whether he's right or wrong, an Aries man will never tolerate a promiscuous or an unfaithful woman—and one slip is many more times than enough for him. If she doesn't work overtime to convince her Aries man, with all her heart, that she belongs only to him—it's out in the cold, cold snow for little Eva.

Put two completely different kinds of people together, and do they grow to love each other less and less—or more and more? With Aries and Pisces, it's not the differences between them that matter. It's what they have in common—the fear of being hurt. Her vulnerability is easily discernible— his may be disguised by Mars bravery and brashness, but it's just as real, just as painful as her own.

TAURUS

Earth — Fixed — Negative
Ruled by Venus (also by the
Planet Pan-Horus)
Symbol: The Bull
Night Forces — Feminine

TAURUS

Earth — Fixed — Negative
Ruled by Venus (also by the
Planet Pan-Horus)
Symbol: The Bull
Night Forces — Feminine

The **TAURUS- TAURUS** *Relationship*

Observe how they pass over fallen twigs without
making the slightest noise. The only sound to be heard
is their somewhat heavy breathing.

Somehow, an astrological rumor has gotten around that Taurus people are inclined to be overweight. This is false. Some of them tend to plumpness, true, but most of them do not.

They love to cook and they love to eat, but normally, the splendid physique of the Bull causes any excess calories to turn into solid muscle. With the female Taureans, good food only seems to give them a look of sturdy coordination, and a slow, sensual grace. (Taurean film star Audrey Hepburn is *fat*?) Of course, there are always the inevitable exceptions, but the truth of the matter is that it's the Sun Signs of Cancer and Libra who are more susceptible to plumpness and extra curves than Taurus. (I said susceptible, that's all, *susceptible*.) I just thought I'd mention it, to put the Taurus people reading this section into a contented frame of mind. That's always the safest way to keep Cows and Bulls—contented.

Another misconception about these people is that they're lazy. Taureans are not lazy. They're simply dedicated to the proposition that wasting energy is a sin, which is why you'll seldom catch them in a quick movement. (Except for rare Bulls like Fred Astaire, who have heavy Gemini influences in their birth charts.) The reason Taurus people have so much strength is because the typical Bulls conserve it, the way they conserve their money. When you put two Taureans together, it's difficult to get them to move into any sort of instant action (unless they're angry, but we'll discuss that later). In fact, moving *two* Bulls is *twice* as hard as moving *one* Bull (an example of uncomplicated, sensible, Taurus-type logic). Picture a couple of piles of rich earth, just sitting there, side-by-side. Isn't it peaceful? Neither of them wishes to profane the peaceful stillness by chattering unduly. When they first meet, they'll size each other up more or less silently. No Bull is ever overly anxious to impulsively jump into an association with another Bull (or any other kind of astrological animal) until all the various possibilities have been carefully judged and seriously considered.

This brings us to the third unfair and fallacious astrological rumor—that Taureans are stubborn. They are not stubborn. They're merely determined and firm in their convictions, not nervous flibbertigibbits who are continually changing their minds and losing their heads. The Bulls change their minds rarely, and lose their heads with even greater infrequency. It's only *reasonable*, you see, after you've done all that careful judging and serious considering, to stick to what you *know* is right. When two Taurus people (of either sex) who hold conflicting opinions are brought into close proximity, they both become even more *reasonable* with each other than they are with others of contrary opinion.

One of the producers of a major television network where I was once a writer is a Taurus. I remember the time he was assigned by the network to build a prime time TV spectacular around a popular singing star, also a Taurus. One calm, peaceful morning, the Taurus star arrived at the Taurus producer's office to discuss the format of the show, and these two Bulls were closeted together behind locked doors for nearly six hours, without so much as a coffee break. Each of them had his own ideas about the spectacular, the guest stars, the songs, the musical theme, the scenic background, lighting effects, and so on. When the famous Taurean finally left, the Taurus producer's secretary and staff crowded around him to ask, "What's he like?" The weary Bull considered the question carefully, as usual, and finally allowed as how the star was a nice, friendly person, intelligent and creative. Then he paused, and said, "But look how long it took him to approve of one simple TV format. He kept pushing some ridiculous ideas he had, over and over, before he realized that I was right in the first place. All that valuable time wasted. I've never met anyone so stubborn." Everyone broke up. It took them several minutes to calm down, while the Taurus producer kept asking, "What did I say that was so funny?"

The last chapter of the foregoing story is that the agent for the Taurus singing star phoned the next day to proffer the singing Bull's apologies. He had decided not to do the spectacular they discussed, and had signed with another network. Period. End of story.

You've probably heard lots of unfair rumors about female American singing star Barbra Streisand being difficult and unreasonable to work with, right? Barbra is a Taurus lady. Obviously, such rumors are false. As I've just pointed out, Taureans are completely *reasonable*. I refer the reader once again to the fourth paragraph of this chapter for a detailed explanation of the reasonable attitude of these unjustly maligned Taurus people. At least no one ever accuses them of not being musical. Every Taurus ever born either sings beautifully, as an amateur or professional—in the shower or tub—while shaving—or if nothing else, adores listening to music, and dreaming about singing.

An association between two Bulls, laboring under the double weight of a 1-1 Sun Sign influence, can be placid, stable and mutually comforting. These people are normally sweet, patient Teddy-Bear types, respectful of each other's rights, quietly devoted, and unquestionably loyal. Still, life may become somewhat stagnant and uneventful for them, unless the birth chart of one or both contains planets in Air or Fire Signs. Taureans are suspicious of change, because the Bull is conservative, and that's *not* a false rumor. If you know a Bull who actually enjoys change, especially abrupt change, he or she was either adopted or the Moon and/or Ascendent was in a sign like Aries, Gemini, or Aquarius at birth. Maybe Sag. The typical Taureans are on guard against quick reforms or sudden switches in the status quo, being very much like the Goats in this respect. They feel that, on the whole, things have been plodding along pretty well for a number of centuries, so why disturb things by changing the rules and regulations of life? To the average Taurean (always allowing for the rare exceptions who prove the rule) any sort of radical interference with Fixed Habit (Taurus is a Fixed Sign, you know)—is unwise. Fixed Habits have already been proven worthy by time, and a new, untested idea could be merely a hare-brained scheme, which might be the dangerous wedge that brings disaster. When a Bull does change his (or her) mind—which does occasionally occur—you can be jolly well certain the change of opinion has been methodically blocked out and measures up to all the necessary qualifications of practicality.

There were, of course, a fair number of double Taurus teams who participated in the "youth revolution" of the sixties, but an honest survey would show that an extremely low percentage of them were draft-card burners who escaped to Canada, or elsewhere, because of conscientious objection. Taurus may "conscientiously object" to many things, but facing physical danger is not one of them. The Sun Sign Taurus rules patriotism in astrology (as does Cancer). American television hero Archie Bunker is a Bull. (Not actor Carroll O'Connor. Archie Bunker. Only sissies avoid their patriotic duty.) Of those Bulls who did follow their consciences in this respect, they all suffered private guilt twinges later. Even now there are Taureans who are willing to demonstrate for new causes like Ecology, Solar Energy, Greenpeace, Women's Rights and so on, just as some of them demonstrated for Civil Rights for the blacks. After all, it is the Aquarian Age, and even Bulls can't help being swept up in the violent changes. But it will have taken them considerable time to decide to join any protests, and they will have done so only after due cautious reflection.

The currently Venus-ruled Bulls you may know who marched two-by-two in yesterday's Peace Parades, sniffing posies, believed in "Peace" itself quite naturally. Yet only a handful of those who called the police "pigs," threw trash on the White House lawn, set fires, and otherwise defied law and order—or streaked through towns and hamlets naked, to proclaim their pristine innocence—were Taureans. (In the latter instance, it's a safe bet the Bulls, however, *watched* the streakers with interest and amusement. The slapstick aspect of "streaking" tickled their fancies.) But on the whole, the "revolutionary" Taurus protesters just stood there quietly, clutching their Peace signs, candles, flowers, incense, or whatever—and it's quite possible some of them are *still* standing there.

Their defense of established mores and their respect for authority (when authority is *sensible*) is often what draws two Bulls together initially—and the glue that keeps them together. Taurus feels that, if change is needed, the only *reasonable* (there's that word again!) way to bring it about is within the system. Actually, the rest of us should be properly grateful for these basically kind-hearted, reliable souls, who are so dedicated to the reign of cool reason. We need the assorted viewpoints of all twelve Sun Signs for any sort of sane and lasting Peace on Earth. But a couple of Bulls, when they're doubling up on their innate character traits, can freeze into a mold that's just a touch fanatical. Both are deeply and sincerely concerned with protecting their investments, their possessions, their families and loved ones, and their country from wild-eyed radicals. Of course, you must realize that to Taurus, the definition of "wild-eyed radicals" can be an affectionate couple, who are embracing on the street, wearing twin stickers on their Levi's reading: *"One-two-three-four, we'd rather _____ than go to war."* They'd rather *kiss* than defend their own country?! That sort of philosophy, to the typical Bull, borders on anarchy.

The most potentially damaging aspect of a Taurus-Taurus association is the great reluctance of either Bull to repent when one has seriously offended the other. Even when a Taurean is inwardly convinced that he (or she) has been mistaken, the tendency is to stubbornly stand by what's been unwisely said or done, because to admit a mistake is uncomfortably close to being weak, and the very word "weakness" makes a Bull see red. Now and then, one Bull can coax the other to unbend and say "I'm sorry," or make up, but not often. Sometimes, tickling them helps. They giggle, turn pink, then finally mumble, "Aw shucks, I didn't mean it." It's always easier for Taureans to back down when the disgrace of being wrong is cozily blanketed in humor. It breaks the fall.

When a Bull finally comprehends that Taurus patience is a graceful, desirable virtue, but that turned upsidedown, it's transformed into plain, cussed, bull-headedness, it will be easier to forgive the other half of the Taurus team his (or her) own spells of the same "virtue." Two Bulls can work or play side-by-side, and behave beautifully. They'll be mutually docile, dependable, and sweetly compliant—if one doesn't push the other too far, or too hard. Nearly all Taureans have a sensational sense of humor, and if they can learn to laugh at *themselves,* their adjustment problems will be all over. There's nothing like a funny bone to tickle the Bull into moving, or changing a Fixed position. Humor is one of the greatest qualities a human being can possess. Blended in generous amounts with the wonderful Taurean dependability, it can help to make these lovable and huggable men and women more *reasonable*—as well as a shade more flexible.

An afterthought for any two Taureans, who have lost sight of one another's basic sweetness and cuddly qualities: Taurus Tom Snyder, of television fame and familiarity, has his very own (no joke) Teddy Bear, tucked tenderly somewhere behind the cameras during his program, sometimes clearly visible, at other times playing peek with the audience. Wouldn't you just *know?*

Every Bull, male or female, clutches a symbolic Teddy Bear for emotional security. So you see, the two of you are really very lovable sorts, not nearly so stern and bull-headed as you both behave at times.

And you can also be certain that every Taurean has a funny bone hidden somewhere behind the silent facade. When they permit one another a glimpse of it, the rich humor shared by these two in their 1-1 Sun Sign association will burst forth like a refreshing rain of happiness, to wash clean those stubborn memories of mutually inflicted hurt . . . . . . and allow the flowers of forgiveness to grow in their hearts.

☆ ☆ ☆ ☆ ☆ ☆

TAURUS *Woman* TAURUS *Man*

◂◂◆▸▸

*He was one of those deep ones who know about stocks
and shares. Of course no one really knows, but he
quite seemed to know, and he often said stocks were
up and shares were down in a way that would have made
any woman respect him.*

A Taurus man walks firmly, in a straight line, toward his goal, step-by-step, not leap-by-leap. He's perfectly content to reap the harvest of his well-deserved rewards in their own due season, and misfortune or bad luck barely disturbs his tranquility. He may carry a heavy load of responsibilities and bravely accepted, wearying duties—his great heart may be burdened nearly to breaking by the painful memory of myriad past disappointments, but the strong Bull goes right on walking, as though nothing had ever happened. More often than not, his steady and patient plodding is eventually crowned with sweet success.

One is reminded of the equally brave, pathetic Nature bull. He stands there, uncertain, but unflinching . . . . . maddened by pain and starvation, facing the sadistic toreadors . . . . scorning any display of weakness, refusing to fall, no matter how many dozens of sharp bandilleros pierce his body . . . . . charging the taunting red cape again and again and again, in uncomprehending confusion . . . . . both infuriated and terrorized by the screams of the crowd . . . . . until he's mercifully executed at the end of the grisly ceremony of fake male macho known as The Bullfight, the unspeakably cruel "sport" Papa Hemingway so adored, in which cowardly, despicable humans, fancying themselves to be heroes, torture, tease, torment—and finally murder a magnificent animal . . . . . while spiritually retarded brutes of both sexes look on and cheer his death agony from the bleachers, in chilling imitation of the bloodthirsty, roaring, insane multitudes in the Coliseum, shortly before Rome fell into the blackness of oblivion—*last time*—via the courtesy of Karma's just and final *coup-de-grâce*.

Should the foregoing, thunderous truth offend, perchance, anyone reading the Spanish language edition of this book, so be it. I make no apology, nor does astrology, to such Iberians and Mexicans. *"He that killeth an ox is as if he slew a man"* (*Isaiah* 66:3). There are many millions of fine Spanish and Mexican men and women, residing both in the U.S. and south of the border, who find their thrills, pleasures and excitements in ways other than watching the public torture and murder of helpless beasts —and this book is written to be shared by these Light-Bearing Ones, who don't stand in the shadow of shame that darkens their ancient heritage of long-ago splendor. The others may come along for the ride, if they wish, but let them both be forewarned and informed that their possible annoyance over my frank analysis of their bullfights leaves this Ram unrepentantly unruffled and unmoved.

The transiting Mars is passing over my natal Aries Sun today as I write, and the effect of the influence will last a considerable while, as always, during which times, certain things never fail to get socked into their proper place in my life. Rather like spring housecleaning, you know?

The typical male Bull possesses the same calm, silent strength of purpose as his astrological symbol, if he's a spiritually evolved Taurean. Even if he's a Taurus mutant, like Adolf Hitler, the powerful determination is still present. The average Taurus man is visibly influenced by the courage and iron will of his Bull symbol, and makes admirable use of it. This man knows what he wants, and is willing to sacrifice whatever is necessary, without whining or complaining, to reach the green pastures he seeks.

Nothing could endear him more to the Taurus woman. She is impressed. Let the other girls shiver in romantic ecstasy over the barefoot prophets who lie in the grass all day, idling away the hours, stringing love beads, and strumming their guitars. Give her a practical Bull, who wears shoes. When *he* hangs a strand of love beads around her neck, they won't be made of dried coffee beans. They'll be from a real jewelry store, and they'll be paid for in full. If *he* strums a guitar, it will be to pick up some bread as a musician, not merely to howl at the Moon on a summer night in Central Park—or in London's Kensington Gardens (Taurus men always make one think of England's John Bull).

These two have much in common. Like, she has a firm grip on her pocketbook, and he hangs on to his billfold with both fists. Since they're both lovers of Nature, they're crazy about planting green things and watching them grow—like Mutual Funds and Christmas Clubs. That's another thing they have in common. They both know Santa Claus is a put-on. He doesn't live at the North Pole, never did. He's the president of their bank, his name is Christopher G. Kringle, and he doesn't drive a sleigh pulled by reindeer, he drives a good, solid Buick sedan. If they've been good all year, and made their regular deposits, he stuffs their socks with dividends and interest payments, which will someday provide them with a house in the peaceful country, near a quiet stream, far from the honking taxi cabs, smog, noisy teenagers and smoky night clubs of the city.

It's easy to be fooled by Bulls, but don't be. Like, the night club thing. You might believe the glamorous Bulls you've seen hanging around sizzling, noisy, boisterous, and bellicose places like Hollywood, California—so obviously incompatible with the image of crickets chirping cheerfully in a country twilight—are a living denial of their earthy Sun Signs. Don't jump to hasty conclusions. Taurus never does. Take American film actor Glenn Ford, a Bull. In the Spring of 1978, he was quoted in a popular news magazine as saying, "I'm going to surprise everyone I know very soon, when they hear how many acres and acres of land I'm buying in Australia, which is where I plan to live."

Behind the surface glitter of whatever occupation or career (including politics) a Bull follows on his way to the farm, hides the smoldering, ever-growing-stronger dream of escape from the teeming city, to the blessed peace and freshness of the sweet-smelling countryside—hay, horses, manure, and all. The dream may surface at any time throughout the life of a Taurus, but *surface it will*—even though it's delayed until what the insurance companies con us into believing is the last third of the "alleged" life span.

Should it happen to take the Taurus man a little longer than he planned to build the foundation for their future together, whether in music, art, business, banking, politics, or whatever, the female Taurean is as patient as he. This woman probably won't mind working for a few years to support her Bull, as long as he's out there symbolically pitching the hay and genuinely trying to make the grass of their escape grow greener. She'll wait—uncomplainingly, for the most part. It all sounds perfectly lovely, doesn't it? They're a matched set—and unbreakable.

The first thing you know, they've fallen solidly in love. The next thing you know, they're standing firmly before a Minister, Priest, Rabbi or J.P., gazing calmly into each other's tranquil eyes and murmuring "I *do*." The third thing you know, the honeymoon is over, and they've both started saying "I *won't*." About various things. She wants children, but he thinks it's wiser to postpone a family until their bank balance is fatter—so she has a baby or two anyway, just to show him he can't push *her* around.

She wants to buy an expensive electric organ because she loves to play and sing, and he tells her, "*No*. We simply can't afford it." If she wheedles or coaxes, he'll say "NO!" a little louder. So, she opens a charge account (after carefully calculating the monthly payments into her household budget) and orders the organ delivered anyway. The following day, he sends it right back to the store, just to show her she can't push *him* around. (Sometimes it's an expensive stereo, with speakers. Same thing.)

Perhaps there's a film she wants to see. So she plants a few smooches on his cheek, and whispers some private endearments into his close-to-the-head Bull's ear, even if it's really flattened and laid-back in anger. "Come on, sweetie-honey-bug-lollipop, let's go to the movies tonight? Pretty-please-with-brown-sugar-and-cream-on-its-tail?" (Not all, but most Taurus lovers tend toward more than a touch of baby-talk, like Libra lovers. It's the Venus rulership of both signs.)

HIM: Nope.
HER: Why not, sweetie-pumpkin?
HIM: Because I don't want to.

That closes the subject, for the remainder of the evening. Later, after they've tucked themselves cozily into bed, and turned out the lights, he says, "Hey! You forgot to kiss me goodnight. I'm feeling very romantic, baby-dumpling. Kiss me, and see what happens." (Most Bulls are very plain-spoken, regarding sexual matters—privately, that is.)

HER: (sweetly, melodiously) No.
HIM: Why not, honey-pot?
HER: Because I *don't want to*.

(a few moments of heavy silence . . . . then)

HIM: I'm going to a hotel.

HER: (suddenly alarmed) Why?
HIM: Because I *want to*.

And another subject is closed. Sometimes for the night, as he plods angrily, clutching his favorite blanket, no farther than the den. Sometimes for several weeks or months, if he really checks into a hotel as he threatened (and he might!). It depends.

I know a devoted couple who live in Los Angeles (and this is, druid honor, an absolutely true story, with only a couple of minor changes to protect the innocent—or the guilty). Both Taurus Sun Signs. He's a songwriter, a lyricist and composer of Hollywood film scores. She's a retired Berlin newspaper reporter, who was born in Germany. When they were "keeping company," the Bull repeatedly refused to marry her. He thought they should test the stability of their love first, before taking such a drastic step, for a "reasonable" length of time (which stretched out into quite a number of years). His Taurus lady cried, pleaded, begged, became angry—and tried to reason with him. He wouldn't budge. "Don't you care for me?" Yes. He cared for her, intensely. But the Bull just wasn't ready for a matrimonial commitment, and *that was that.*

It's now more than a decade later (as of this writing). They remain very much in love, and they have four children—two boys and a set of twin girls. They still have not legally married. *He* has cried, pleaded, begged, become angry—and tried to reason with *her.* She hasn't budged an inch. He's even asked his "mother-in-law" to talk to her, reason with her, and try to move the now mother of his children from her firm position—and for a Bull, that's a gigantic concession. A Taurus man likes interference from relatives in his private affairs like General Motors likes Ralph Nader. But this hasn't accomplished anything either.

HER: The children have your name legally, they have two loving parents, they're included in your will and your insurance, we have a nice home, and we're a warm, devoted, and happy family. We don't need a piece of paper to make it legal.
HIM: Honey-baby, don't you love me?
HER: Of course I love you, deeply.
HIM: But sweetheart, if you love me and I love you, and we're so happy together, and you *know* it will last forever, and we have four children who need the emotional security of wedded parents, *why* won't you marry me?
HER: Because I don't want to.

Of course, not all Taurus couples go as far as that, but it's always a possibility, since, as I told you, the foregoing is a true situation. The average Taurean man and woman will usually insist on the full sanction of the law before entering into any kind of cooperative venture, whether it be business or matrimony, and most Bulls see a decided similarity between the two.

In a liaison of love between Taurus and Taurus, there will be many times when their mutual stubbornness, and refusal to look at the other side, will lead them down the blind alleys of mental and emotional prejudice, and they'll find it difficult to communicate. Still, one of the marvelous things about Bulls is that they possess the ability to shrug off frustration and learn from experience. What Taurus has finally learned, Taurus never ever forgets. *Never. Ever.* If these two try hard to learn the lesson of forgiveness (never easy for Bulls) they can hold each other's hands tightly (Bulls do everything tightly) and find their way out of those dark blind alleys. I know a Taurus woman whose favorite philosophy is: "Every experience is a good experience." It's an admirable attitude, but I've noticed she has a little trouble forgetting the bad ones. She learns from them, yes —but sometimes the lesson she learns is merely to turn her back on the person or situation, without ever trying again—and such lessons teach the heart nothing.

Sex, of course, is only another human experience, but an extremely important one to Taurus lovers or mates. Their initial attraction is usually strongly physical, with the mental and emotional blending coming later, like the honey frosting on a carrot cake. Normally, that's not the ideal priority order in which to approach total love, but with a couple of Taureans, surprisingly it works out fine. Perhaps not so surprisingly. Because sex is an exercise in total sensuality for the average or typical Taurus person, the physical expression of love between this man and woman can gradually develop into an almost psychedelic experiment—although most Bulls (not all, but most) scowl darkly at the very mention of drugs. To Taurus, if you smoke grass, you're foolish and weak, if you drop acid, you're unquestionably mentally unsound—and if you mess around with speed, cocaine, heroin, angel dust, and so forth, you're on a frantic Freeway, headed straight toward spiritual suicide—as swiftly and surely as you're headed toward actual suicide. Ponder the percentages.

Most Taureans have a solid grasp of the metaphysical teaching that drugs are the False Prophets warned of by the Book of Revelations in the New Testament—which, if not recognized as such, can bring on the Götterdämmerung prematurely. Actually the dogmatic Bulls are closer to truth than they suspect. It may have been, in the cosmic concept, necessary for drug-induced awareness to burst open: new spiritual vistas for the

Golden Age of Aquarius. But this galactic-cosmic experiment of the Masters—this preliminary to Earth's spiritual awakening—has served its purpose (at the cost of much human suffering, as well as enlightenment). Now it's time to halt, lean back and ponder the insight thus gained. Every Sun Sign is charged with a special and particular mission, and the Taurus Bulls (and Capricorn Goats) are charged with keeping our collective feet on the ground regarding such matters.

Oddly (and *actually*) it has been the solid, Earthbound (but perceptive) Taureans of my personal acquaintance who've been the ones to first realize that all the hullabaloo about electronic bugging and snooping has merely been a *material level* rehearsal for the swiftly approaching time when every man and woman will be able to "read" each other's human auras, and therefore able to perceive far more "secrets" than it's possible to learn about people via tape-recorded conversations, telephone tapping, and such. You didn't realize that Earth Sign Cappy Richard Nixon performed such a vital and giant galactic preparatory role for all of us, did you? (Neither did he.)

In like manner, drugs have been the *material level* rehearsal for the fast approaching opening of the *Third Eye* in every man and woman, which will allow them to see and interpret the human aura, and recall past incarnations. Children are all born with the Third Eye open (see last paragraph of Scorpio-Scorpio chapter). In medical terminology, they are born with a soft pineal gland. But it gradually grows less soft as children submit to the imagination-stifling restrictions of their elders, until it finally becomes stone-hard, and like all adults then, they "have rocks in their heads" (which is, by the way, literally how that term originated in the subconscious).

Many true mystics and "sensitives" (including Taurus "psychic" Peter Hurkos) have suffered a blow on the head, near the Third Eye (pineal gland) which caused it to soften again, as in childhood, allowing them to perceive the *real* world and the *Eternal Now* of Past, Present and Future. Tibetan monks have accomplished this through physical manipulation exercises, meditation—and even surgery (in rare cases). But *Love* (quite seriously and technically) accomplishes it more swiftly. The so-called "saints" (and Jesus himself) used only Love as the method for opening up the Third Eye or pineal gland. It's a whole lot safer, and much more pleasant than falling off a ladder or bumping into a door—also considerably more joyful than monotonous, boring Eastern meditation rites. Besides, the latter can dangerously release the Kundalini Serpent Power *prematurely*, which causes all manner of bodily pain and emotional torment. In other words, don't contemplate your navel, never mind what any flower-draped Tantra Guru might tell you, until you've *first* learned to *love one another purely and unselfishly,* as the Nazarene counseled, learned how to *forgive your enemies*—and to *do unto others what you'd like to have them do unto you*—or you may have reason to wish your Third Eye would harden again. A word to the wise is sufficient. A word to the foolish, as all Bulls know, is wasted.

In 1975, I had a discussion with three enlightened Bulls (two males, one female) who were easily convinced, despite the typical Taurean stubbornness, that it's time for Earthlings to move on to the next practice session, beyond the initial stage of drug-induced, largely false visions—the next stage of spiritual development being the realization that one may only *surely* "see God" or "know Truth" through the control of the *conscious* mind—through control of what Francis of Assisi called Brother Body, via proper nutrition, exercise, and avoiding the abuse of sexual energy—and third (and most vital) through the daily, hourly practice of an interchange of love, kindness, and forgiveness. Including the kindness not to further torture our animal brothers and sisters, by way of butchering them, murdering them, shooting them for "sport," dissecting them—and eating their flesh—which circles right back (full serpent circle) to the necessary cleansing and purification of Brother Body (and Sister Body).

Somehow, I have a distinct and nearly tangible sense that the Bulls who are reading this chapter about themselves and their attitudes toward all these urgent matters are breathing hard behind my shoulder and demanding to know how to protect themselves from the naked mental and emotional exposure of their personal auras soon to be readable to everyone who says "Good morning" to them. (Taureans have such a thing about privacy, you know.) Dear Bulls, don't worry. Adequate protection from the invasion of your innermost private thoughts, as revealed in your aura, is definitely possible. But you must be patient, and I know you'll understand when I tell you that you must wait for a forthcoming book of mine, if you want me to discuss the details of such protection with you, step-by-step. Believe me, there's time. Now, may we return to the subject of the Taurus attitude toward drugs?

To the Taurus man and woman, if they're typical Bulls, using drugs is like "instant God," a quick glimpse of profound Truth—so profound it can literally blow the mind of a not-yet-sufficiently-evolved person, not to mention his or her soul. From an esoteric and cosmic point of view, according to the wisdom of the ancients, the Taurus Bulls have nailed the Truth square center, in this respect, as they do most everything else.

Taureans may be a bit overly stuffy concerning the dangers of smoking "grass," but even supposing that grass (pot) is relatively harmless (especially when compared to the destructive effect of the poisoning process of alcohol, nicotine, and white sugar addiction) it's nevertheless not too cool to develop a dependence upon even the mildest emotional or spiritual crutch. If you were to try an experiment, and use a crutch, without the need for one, in a surprisingly brief period of time you'd be shocked to see your actual leg shrink in size—and eventually it would become permanently atrophied, permanently paralyzed, for the simple reason of non-use. Ask your doctor.

Substituting for the crutch the mildest or most potent simulant or depressant, from grass and coke to heroin or angel dust—and substituting for your physical leg and Third Eye (pineal gland) wherein lies all psychic power, sensitivity, and spiritual wisdom—the identical process occurs: shrinkage and eventual permanent atrophy of the Third Eye from non-use.

Taurus men and women instinctively know it's just plain dumb to paralyze anything deliberately, whether it's an arm, a leg, the Third Eye, or any other part of the body. Every Bull possesses such innate horse sense or common sense (barring severe afflictions in the nativity). In this feeling, Taurus hits the nail square center again.

It may seem strange that Taurus, normally, on the surface of it, the most un-esoteric Sun Sign of the twelve, should be so close to the spiritual truth concerning drugs. Yet, it's not really strange at all to an astrologer. Everyone, you see, strongly feels, on a subconscious level, the magnetic attraction (polarity-pull) of his or her opposite Sun Sign on the karmic wheel of Life—or the zodiac wheel. The sign opposite Taurus is the deeply spiritual and psychic, sensitive, and perceptive Scorpio—ruled by the powerful planet Pluto, which is the planet in charge of all these matters (in close partnership with Neptune, ruler of Pisces). Scorpio's ruling Pluto is also intimately aligned with Pan-Horus, the *true* ruler of Taurus. When Pan-Horus is finally identified and named (once again) and takes over the time-energy rulership of all Bulls, allowing Taurus people to return their foster ruler, Venus, to Libra, where she belongs—Taureans will be as "knowing" as Scorpios in all spiritual matters, while retaining the soft influence of Venus—from a distance, in an esoteric sense. "Be ye wise as a Serpent, yet as harmless as a Dove," therefore applies to enlightened Taureans.

The Sun Sign Taurus astrology students reading this might want to contemplate a quick and easy proof of the inescapable tie with one's opposite polarity Sun Sign (in the case of Taurus–Scorpio). Astrologically, *Taurus* rules the throat and vocal cords. The opposite sign, *Scorpio*, rules, among other things, the sex organs. When puberty occurs in a male, which is a *sexual* change, there is a simultaneous change of *voice*. This polarity proof can be given in multiple and fascinating ways, all around the horoscopic wheel—but a detailed analysis of these will have to wait for that forthcoming book I mentioned.

Scorpio. Ah, yes! That brings us neatly back to sex—which I'm sure pleases the patient Bulls, who have all been waiting so nicely and quietly for us to return to a subject of intense interest to them.

No one who uses a mind-expanding drug to increase the sense sensations will ever come as close to the ultimate in sensual expression and experience as two Taurus people who are twin souls (not all of them are) when they are making love. A person on a drug high may perch atop a mushroom (a large one, naturally) deep in ecstasy, contemplating the scent of a bar of soap, the intricate patterns in a daisy's petal, the exquisite taste of a drop of water, as well as its bursting life force . . . . the texture of a splinter or the symphony of the sound of a ticking clock. But this spaced-out dude or dame has nothing on two Taurus lovers.

A Bull of either sex can spend hour after endless hour lying on the rich, fragrant Earth, *beneath* the same mushroom (where it's far more comfortable, with ample room to stretch out) contemplating ecstatically the scent of the beloved's skin, the intricate, delicate, faerie cobweb sky-map of the lines in the lover's hand, the singing feel of soft hair, the delicious taste of an ear lobe . . . . . . or the crashing crescendos of the partner's heartbeat.

Taurus people don't often burst verbally into poetry (though they frequently burst into song) during lovemaking, and they're not overly sensitive to the finer emotional implications of sex, but they are certainly receptive to its sensual possibilities. The Bull doesn't feel the same lack of a sixth sense as most people, being so acutely aware of and turned into the other five. There's seldom any serious disagreement in the area of sexual union between two well-mated Bulls, except perhaps when one of them refuses to make love because he (or she) is pouting about something. That's when a sixth sense might come in handy. It could help one Taurean develop more psychic perception about why the other one is being so stubborn, by using ESP to flash on what the temporarily frigid one really wants—which I can tell them is *not* to be left alone, no matter how it may seem. (It's probably just a secret desire to be coaxed.)

In other areas of their relationship, a Taurus man and woman have the potential to accumulate a sizable amount of money and material possessions—which you'd better believe they'll manage to keep. They're both sentimental, warm, and loving, their emotional behavior gently guided by their foster ruler, Venus, who influences their nature with much tenderness and gentleness but is also occasionally an influence of temptation toward every form of excess, including food, drink, financial greed, sex, and anything else you can think of offhand (with the already noted exception of drugs, which only the very *rare* Bull is tempted to abuse). These two are equally strong, patient and emotionally stable—except for those far-apart spells of blind fury, which normally only occur every decade or so, when the Bulls are really aroused—then look out! As I mentioned earlier in this chapter, the Taurus man and woman are a perfectly matched set.

As for any periodic problems of communication between them, the Bull knows exactly how to say "I'm sorry" and "I need you" in silent Taurean sign language—and his Taurus woman knows exactly how to interpret it. With these two, a touch on the hand in a dark room can dispense with the necessity of speaking a single word.

Shall we leave them now? You may have noticed how very, very quiet and still it's become, during the reading of the last few pages. That means the Bull and his mate are *communicating* . . . . . . and wish to be left alone. Don't be rude and snoopy, now, and try to read their auras. Leave these lovers in peace. Don't disturb the Bull, and the Bull won't disturb you. In other words, let's mind our own business. As Taureans always mind theirs.

☆ ☆ ☆ ☆ ☆ ☆

TAURUS

Earth — Fixed — Negative
Ruled by Venus (also the
  Planet Pan-Horus)
Symbol: The Bull
Night Forces — Feminine

GEMINI

Air — Mutable — Positive
Ruled by Mercury
Symbol: The Twins
Day Forces — Masculine

The **TAURUS-GEMINI** *Relationship*

Without giving a thought to what might be
the feelings of a fellow-creature thus
abruptly deprived of its closest companion,
Peter at once considered how he could turn
the catastrophe to his own use. . . .

Taurus men and women are quiet, steady, practical people, who try to mind their own business. On occasion, they can be fierce, though most of the time they retain an admirable calm. A Bull can look a tornado in the eye, if necessary, without flinching or batting a lash. Nevertheless, his (or her) splendid strength and determined staying power is a poor match for the flashing agility of a pair of Twins, who can cleverly twist and turn their way out of any earthly threat—the Twins, of course, being two different people disguised as one, who call themselves Gemini.

Pity the poor Taureans who are faced with these two fast-moving, twinkle-toed people, with razor-sharp minds, skipping around and confusing them, all the time giving them the illusion that they are facing but a single toreador. It's hard to see how anyone can find sport in cruelly tormenting a great, noble beast, whose only desire is to be left alone, in peace. It almost makes one wish for the Bull to score, with a sudden, furious thrust of his horns. Sometimes, that happens. And it's a fair warning to misguided Geminis, who have no idea how unpleasant it feels to be struck unexpectedly from the rear, when you're grinning and bowing and gracefully bobbing around—and not looking behind you.

I have a Taurus neighbor, whose daughter, also a Taurus, fell in love with a Gemini charmer. After six months went by, and she still hadn't brought him home to meet the family, the Taurean began to be curious, and finally, became concerned. "What's with the mystery routine? Are you ashamed of him? Does this guy have two heads or something?" (He had no idea how warm he was getting.) One afternoon, he ran into his daughter and her Gemini boyfriend on the street, so the three of them (the four of them?) had lunch, and got to know each other. To his delight, the Bull discovered his future son-in-law was bright, handsome, courteous and versatile. (Oh, was he versatile!) He spoke six languages, piloted his own plane, had degrees from two universities and played the saxophone.

Over the cheese soufflé, the Gemini brilliantly discussed his career (he was a public relations counsel), his political views, and his religious beliefs. When the hypnotized Taurus father admired the huge diamond ring that glittered on one of the Gemini's expressive, artistic hands, he was told, "It's a family heirloom that belonged to my great-grandfather, and it's insured for seventy thousand dollars." No doubt about this man being financially stable enough for his daughter. At last, the Gemini remarked he had to dash off to see his stockbroker, smilingly waved goodbye and disappeared. He forgot to pick up the check, but that was an obvious oversight. After all, the man had a lot on his mind, between his clients, his Wall Street investments—and being in love.

The following week, in one of those flukes of fate, the Taurus was having his hair cut by a barber, who just happened to be the Gemini's brother-in-law, and the truth came out. He wasn't a public relations counsel, he was an assistant to a veterinarian. He had two wives and five children he had neglected to mention. His academic degrees consisted of a high school equivalency diploma. The plane was a single-engine model aircraft he flew in the park on Sundays. And the "diamond" was one of the imitation zircons he sold through a mail-order house, to make enough bread for his weekly lessons on the saxophone, which he did happen to play rather well. "I'd class him as a young Hymie Shertzer, but with a real pop sense of jazz, you know?" mused the barber brother-in-law. A sense of jazz indeed.

How did the Taurean father react to this gross betrayal of faith, involving his adored Taurus daughter, and his own judgment of character? With the blind fury and violent rage of a Bull who has been red-flagged once too often. Fortunately, by the time he reached the Gemini's apartment, the "Twins" had just left for Mexico, to join a rock group on a tour of South America. However, two years later, Gemini returned, felt a sentimental urge to visit the scene of the romantic crime, and paid a call on his old Taurus girl friend. At first she stubbornly refused his apologies, but within a half-hour she had forgiven him (the Gemini charm), and melted into his arms. In another fluke of fate, at that precise moment, the father Bull walked through the door. (I mean he actually did nearly walk *through* the door.) I will spare you the gruesome details. Later, when the stitches were removed, the Twins left once again for Mexico, this time to take up permanent residence there. It was a wise move.

It takes a Taurus man, woman or child a long time to learn, but a lesson learned is never forgotten. Never. An elephant is absent-minded, when compared to the memory of a Taurean once wounded. Naturally, not every Gemini keeps his (or her) Twin Selves as separate as the traveling sax player. Most Geminis manage to blend their two distinct personalities into one bright, intelligent and interesting human being, reasonably honest, and refreshingly adaptable. Still, the Geminian ability to change from one viewpoint to another, when it seems necessary for survival, can give Taurus an uneasy feeling that something is happening that he (or she) can't quite grab—or trust.

This is a 2-12 Sun Sign Pattern, meaning that Taurus is the sign immediately behind Gemini on the karmic wheel. Therefore, Gemini contains a soul memory of the opportunities it's possible to miss, through excessive Taurean caution. That's why Geminis of both sexes, and all ages, are so anxious to avoid mental ruts, or any other sort of stalemates, in this incarnation. Yet, the Twins sympathize with the Taurus reluctance to toss away security in favor of the unknown more than most other Sun Signs do because, in a subconscious sense, they've "been there."

As for the Bulls, since Gemini follows Taurus on the astrological circle, all Taurus men and women are faintly aware that they have something to learn from these bright, quick people. But what Gemini wants to teach, Taurus finds difficult to comprehend. The Bulls would like to be able to take life more casually, to think fast on their feet, toss away the past without regret, and skip happily ahead into a new adventure each day. He— or she—wistfully yearns for the freedom of spirit that Gemini, running a few lengths ahead, keeps dangling in front of the slower Taurean, sparkling and enticing. But—what if someone should break into the house, and steal all the Bull's precious possessions while he (or she) is out chasing fireflies with the Twins? What if one should happen to stumble, and break one's big toe, while jogging alongside Gemini? And what if the night air should give Taurus a sore throat? Who will be waiting back home to nurse and care for him (or her)?

It's always easier to sell life insurance or Blue Cross to Taurus than to Gemini. A typical astrological Sun Sign situation is a Gemini salesman or saleswoman, from a Scorpio insurance agency, fast-talking a Taurean customer into signing up for a huge stack of varied policies and annuities. Bulls are usually careful not to fall for a Mercurial pitch, except when it comes to purchasing solid security and protection for their families and their possessions, not to mention protecting their incomes in the future. Then, the Bulls become helpless pawns in the hands of a clever and charming Geminian.

Often the dogmatic Taurean determination to stick with facts that have been tried and tested may seem like stubborn prejudice to the more liberal, open-minded Gemini person. Conversely, the typical Bull feels it's always possible for an apparently accurate statement of brilliant Gemini logic to be actually conveying a falsehood or deception behind the surface glibness. What gives Taureans their initial mistrust of Gemini is the Twins' amazing dexterity of speech. Anyone who can juggle words with such ease, and spin them into such hypnotic tales full of wit and excitement, is suspect to the less loquacious Bulls, who tend to make every word count in their own rare speeches. In verbal showmanship, the Gemini man or woman is nearly always supremely eloquent, seemingly logical and clear. Only a Libran can match Gemini's powers of persuasion. But Taurus is not persuaded so quickly.

Not all Geminis are completely straightforward in their methods of arguing. Some of them veer away from the issue, on side trips, inciting Taurus to shout, angrily, "Stick to the point, will you?" Stop *rationalizing!*" Gemini also leans toward a certain amount of diffusiveness and repetition in speech patterns, which sometimes causes Taurean friends, relatives, business associates, lovers or mates to get into the Fixed habit of simply tuning out, after the third or fourth repeat.

Astrologer Evangeline Adams (granddaughter of John Quincy Adams, great-granddaughter of John Adams) once noted the typical Gemini verbal dexterity, by using Paul's Epistle to the Romans, in the New Testament, as an example. Verses 25 through 29, Chapter Two, and Verses 1 through 11, Chapter Three, constitute a masterpiece of Gemini glibness and charm, accomplished with Mercury double-talk. St. Paul, who was surely a Geminian, was obliged to tell the Roman gentiles that circumcision was not a necessary requirement for salvation. At the same time, he was bound to the Jews, by previous statements he'd made to them that it was. His efforts to successfully solve this contradiction are a truly classical example of the Gemini mind at its sharpest and best, cleverly confusing each side while irresistibly courting the approval of both. It's easy to see why Geminis are adept as politicians. They're able to bring opposite opinions together and hang them on a thread of truth, coated with charm and logic, creating an aura of idealism and peace on all sides. Gemini is not called the "communicator" without cause. President John F. Kennedy was a most typical Geminian, in every respect.

The airy detachment of Gemini can hurt and annoy Taurus, by turns, because, to the Bulls, detachment is indicative of being either rudely ignored or condescendingly patronized, neither of which is particularly pleasing to them. Some Bulls carry the scars of real or imagined rejection from an Air Sign for many years. It's often what causes those streaks of bull-headed stubbornness. For the life of them, Geminis can't see how anyone could be so opinionated that he (or she) is deaf to all logic and reason. Yet, an affectionate word or two, an arm thrown round a shoulder, or a warm, friendly clasp of hands (any form of *touching*) will make the tender, Venus-ruled Taurean heart melt like butter in the Sun. For all their cleverness, Geminis frequently fail to comprehend this magic formula for softening the Fixed and firm Taurean mental or emotional position. The occasional coldness projected by the Mental Sign of the Twins will only freeze the Bull into a more solid lump of obstinate earth. (Frozen ground is harder to shovel, you know, than the soft, rich earth, which has been kissed awake by the summer Sun.)

Geminis are always looking for short cuts. All right, Twins, here's a short cut to your compatibility with Bulls. The most common cause of tension between you is the Taurus habit of feeling, when he (or she) ought to *think*—and your own habit of thinking, when you ought to *feel*. Don't try to dazzle the Bulls with your brilliance—baffle them with bear hugs.

☆ ☆ ☆ ☆ ☆ ☆

TAURUS *Woman* GEMINI *Man*

———◆◆◆———

*Wendy was pained too to find that the past year was
but as yesterday to Peter; it had seemed such a
long year of waiting to her. But he was exactly
as fascinating as ever. . . .*

While the Taurus woman sits beneath the rose bush, carefully stitching a piece of needlework, with the words "Home, Sweet Home," the Gemini man is drumming his restless fingers on the window pane, humming his own melody and lyric to "Song of the Open Road." No matter where these two (these three, counting his invisible Twin self) meet along life's highway, they'll eventually reach a fork in the path that will force them to flip a coin, to decide which one to take—the one leading to a comfortable, conventional marriage—or the one leading to a casual affair, with no strings attached to the heart. Correction: *He'll* flip a coin. *She'll* consult her common sense, to see if she might be headed in the wrong direction.

Once a Taurus girl is absolutely sure she loves a Gemini man, she'll first try everything in her considerable power to entice him into a permanent arrangement, complete with both social and legal sanction. And she possesses more weapons for enticement than you may think: erotic sensuality, tender affection, rich humor, fantastic home-baked biscuits, patience and fortitude. If none of these powerful feminine wiles work, she'll sigh softly, take a deep breath, and settle herself cozily into the role of mistress, still secretly using the very same weapons, but content to wait until he sees the light. "Everything comes to him—or her—who waits," is her philosophy. A Taurus woman may be cautious about getting her feet tangled up in romantic poison ivy in the beginning; she may be slow to allow herself to get tripped up by moonlight and roses, and fragile promises, at the start. However, once this lady has fallen, she has fallen, and it takes a steel derrick, or a Mack truck, to pull her out. Sometimes, the four-wheel drive of her common sense comes to the rescue, sometimes not.

Geminis are equally as wary as Taurus about being trapped in the beginning, but even after a Mercury Bird has capitulated to love, he keeps one light foot in the bedroom and one poised on the front porch for ready flight, if necessary. He'll tenderly give her one of his Twin hearts to have and to hold, but he hangs on to the other—just in case the one he gave away should happen to become soiled or broken, or damaged in any way.

What good is a cracked heart to him? It will never sell as a new one. Think of the depreciation. It's a kind of Gemini insurance policy against disillusionment. That's where they differ. (I mean, that's *one* of the ways they differ.)

The Taurus woman, who is ordinarily so respectful of all kinds of insurance, has no emotional insurance against hurt, once she's handed over her loyalty to another human being. Unless there are severe afflictions to her natal Mars or Venus (or Sun), this lady will wait out anything, from another woman to poverty. She'll calmly ignore the changeable antics of her altar-shy, Mercury-ruled man, and not always—but usually—she'll win. If there are certain planetary squares or oppositions in her birth chart, it's possible that she may be the one to break his heart by chasing will-o'-the-wisps of pleasure just to torment her Gemini man, whose love is delicate and easily torn apart. But that's an exception to the rule, and the average Taurean Bull will sit serenely by the fire, toasting her toes and calmly counting the days between visits from her lover.

Her friends will try to make this sentimental woman see that she may be wasting her life, but she won't listen. She'll stubbornly insist that the delays preventing their marriage are valid ones, that tomorrow, next week, next month, next year—it will all work out. They love each other, and love can make anything happen, can't it? Yes, it can. But not when love is blind, as Taurus love sometimes is. A Taurean who's convinced she's right is difficult to lead into a realization of the truth—the truth being that all may not be lost if she recognizes the danger of a dead-end scene in time to zap some life back into the romance. But she may not want to admit things aren't as rosy as they could be. As sensible as she is about everything else, she can be incredibly foolish when it comes to her own emotional security. If he has the Moon in an Earth or Water Sign, or she has the Moon in a Fire or Air Sign, they have a better chance to stay together, each supplying what is missing in the other. And that can be a mighty satisfying arrangement.

A Gemini man is quickly bored with the same woman, but that doesn't have to mean infidelity. He just likes to examine the various faces of the girl he loves, test the nuances of her emotional facets—sort of look at her through trick mirrors, for a change of mood. But the Taurus female has only three moods: sweet, affectionate contentment, sullen brooding—and raging fury. A Mercury man may secretly wish she'd vary them with a few impulsive whims, careless excitement, or a game of emotional hide-and-seek, now and then. She may hate change, but learning to adapt to new patterns is a necessity for a woman in love with a pair of Gemini Twins.

She might like it, if she tried doing something new and wild each week.

It doesn't have to be as far out as astral traveling, or opium parties. Maybe just part her hair on the other side, for a change (when a Taurus girl does that, it's a clear signal for the man who can read it) or switch her brand of bath oil, or throw some mushrooms in with the eggplant. She might even try saying she's sorry when she's wrong, instead of pouting. A Taurus woman has a way of choosing a side, and staying there, refusing even to listen to an apology, much less a compromise. This girl doesn't realize how cruel and cold she seems, once she's made up her mind and slammed the door shut on any further discussion.

Sexually, the same problems of change-versus-stubbornness may creep into their relationship. She wants to be well loved, and to her, the physical expression of that love should be a rich and total experience. She expects complete sensual satisfaction from a lover, and she gives him full measure in return. A Taurus woman thinks sex is great because it produces sweet, cuddly babies and brings emotional peace and physical fulfillment at the same time—a triple blessing. When she makes love, there's nothing misty about it. She wants to feel her man is there beside her—*all* there—not just the parts of him he's not using while he's daydreaming. Since his Mercurial mind may be wandering on the wind, she may resent what she interprets as his lack of earthy passion, his casual attitude. And he may resent what he sees as her intrusion into his emotional privacy, which Gemini will consider sacred, even during their most intimate moments. She might have to persuade herself to try various, different approaches to pull him off his cloud and back into her arms. Otherwise, he may grow weary of beating his wings against a stone wall, and become even more detached. He'll be happier than he guesses, however, if he allows her to show him the way to a deeper affection by trusting her more instinctive Venus vibrations, and her earthiness, instead of hovering somewhere, just out of touch, when she needs him so profoundly. All Air Signs tend to mistrust sex, in a vague sort of way, unless it's first been strained through the imagination, which sometimes purges it of its very essence. A Gemini man wants his sexual experience diluted, in varying degrees, with fiction and fantasy.

I know a Taurus woman who is unusually psychic, for her normally un-esoteric Sun Sign. (That happens, you know, even with Goats and Virgins of the male and female sex. World-famous pyschic Peter Hurkos is a Bull—with a powerfully trined Neptune, of course.) This particular lady Taurean was deeply and genuinely in love with a peripatetic Gemini man from California, for more years than she's able to forget, and maybe she still is in love with him, in her own stubborn way. There are several Neptune trines between their birth charts, creating a rare emotional telepathy, which they used to communicate with each other, without benefit of telephone or letters. Sometimes, their uncanny ESP brought them together when they were miles apart, more than just mentally and emotionally and spiritually. It brought them also into physical Oneness. She once remarked to me that she told him she believed she could almost . . . conceive a baby through their powerful mutual projection, and she wasn't ready for that, for they weren't married. (Taurus realistic humor.) That's a strong union. Strong indeed.

But his Twin Gemini desires never blended into one single dream she could depend on. Finally, she read his mind (reversing his Mercury trick), saw nothing there but more ephemeral promises, and cut the telepathic cord between them with the cold, sharp scissors of Taurus determination. Now he can no longer reach her astrally, or any other way. She refuses to answer either her telephone—or her heart—when they ring. She knows when it's Gemini who's calling. But it doesn't move her. A psychic Taurus woman is still a Bull. Metaphysical talents don't make a dent in her iron will—once her mind has been made up firmly.

And so, a Gemini man isn't always blameless when his affair with a Taurean girl has tied itself into obstinate knots. He can wear himself into his own kind of rut. He might pause, during one of his spins around the carousel of changing lights and sounds, and ask himself if he's still hearing the same calliope music he heard when he first jumped on for the ride. A melody without words . . . . . a story without an ending . . . . . a whirl around a circle that goes nowhere but back to the beginning. How many brass rings must a man grab to jingle in his pocket—to watch turn green, and tarnish—until he reaches for one made of solid gold?

TAURUS *Man* GEMINI *Woman*

------◆◎◆------

He loved flowers (I have been told) and sweet music
(he was himself no mean performer on the harpsichord);
and, let it be frankly admitted, the
idyllic nature of the scene stirred him profoundly.
Mastered by his better self he would have returned
reluctantly to the tree . . . . . .

Someone once wrote a verse about a man nothing could deter—"nor rain, nor storm, nor gloom of night could keep him from his appointed rounds." The reference has been applied to a postman. But it certainly must have been a Taurus postman, probably delivering a Valentine.

The slow, smoldering passion of the Bull is not easily, nor quickly, aroused. It grows in him, you might say, rather insidiously, sneaking up on him gradually, and gathering great strength as it sneaks. After this man's senses have been ensnared, or his Venus-ruled heart has been touched, he'll seldom, if ever, go back on his choice (unless his Moon or Ascendent is in Gemini, Sag or Pisces). His instinctive attitude toward involvement is total, and he'll follow it through to the bitter (or sweet) end, through rain, sleet, snow—yes, often even through the Gemini girl's unexpected hurricanes of anger or tornados of emotion. He's a regular Pony Express, all by himself, the Taurus man.

Nothing and no one, no consideration of reputation (normally his chief concern), no negative opinions of relatives or friends will stop or even slightly sway this otherwise sensible male when he's fallen in love. The moment a normally practical Taurean gets caught in a romantic web, his common sense is buried beneath his newly discovered sense of touching, hearing, smelling and seeing the girl of his quiet, but nonetheless deep, dreams. He's capable of making promises of eternal fidelity, and keeping them—faithful, steady and loyal almost beyond belief. Once truly in love, Taurus is in love for keeps. If it doesn't work out to a faerie-tale ending, the Bull may pine away in heartbreak, or drown himself in other sensual experiences, like becoming a morose alcoholic (one of the most terrifying mistakes a Taurean can make), or a gluttonous gourmet, an equally unnatural state to Taurus, since the Bull's higher instincts are to avoid excesses of *any* kind.

He sounds like every girl's imaginary romantic daydream come true. Except to the Gemini girl, whose daydreams of love are not quite so all en-compassing, or down to earth. Gemini is airy. Gemini flies free, like a kite, sometimes buffeted by the wind, falling, then rising again on the whim of a passing breeze—but always soaring beautifully, catching the sunlight be-tween clouds, and reflecting it back again.

Comedian-actor Orson Bean once quite precisely described a Gemini girl he knew. He asked her, "What is your husband's birthday?" And she immediately exclaimed, "Oh, good grief! I don't have a husband."

"You sound as if you don't like men," he said to her then, surprised. "No," she replied merrily, "I *adore* men! It's *husbands* I can't stand." Bean persisted. "But why? What's wrong with husbands?" Gemini mused thoughtfully for only a second, before she answered. "Well, they're so darned possessive. Like, they want to know who you're dating, and . . . . ." her voice trailed off.

Now, to the average person reading this, and surely to the Bulls reading this, that Gemini girl's answer may seem shockingly sexually promiscuous. Not to an astrologer. I analyze her answer differently, understanding Mer-cury double-talk as I do. You see, she was simply being true to her Twin Self. A "date" to Gemini can be a harmless appointment with her hairdresser, a jet-set makeup consultation with Way Bandy, a trip to the dentist for some cap work, a visit with her psychiatrist or her brother-in-law. This woman is always making dates to meet people, then shows up late, or forgets all about them. It isn't that she's seeking an affair or a cas-ual sexual encounter, just someone who's fun to be with, and exciting to talk to, who will stimulate her imagination. At least, that's the way it be-gins, and that's where it will usually remain, if she's properly understood. Remember, there are, at all times, two of her, and how can one man keep two girls happy every minute of the day and night? It becomes, after a while, a sort of a mathematical problem, you see. (Taurus may not see.)

Her social need to move around, and mix, in the company of both sexes, needn't destroy a relationship. She can be deeply committed to one man, even though she needs the company of several dozen, on occasion. But try to get a possessive Bull to comprehend such a need. I mean, she can try, but she's taking a chance. It would be better if she explained it all to him before they marry, then all he can do is pull a slow burn and stalk off in anger. If she waits till later, when he considers her his lifelong possession belonging exclusively to him, in every way—and *then* tells him that she's simply got to get out and tumble with the acrobats and spin around on the Ferris Wheel once in a while because she's often so bored—or else go daffy—his reaction may be identical, but his anger won't be so controlled.

The typical Taurus man will not take kindly to the discovery that his woman wants to run to the carnival every fortnight or so. You can bet on it.

Of course, if his Moon or Ascendent happens to be in Gemini, Libra, Aquarius, Leo or Aries—or if his natal Mars or Venus is in Gemini, conjunct her Sun—everything could be peachy. He'll have the stability and the quiet soothing influence of his Taurus Sun Sign to affectionately pin down her wings when she needs it, but just enough "air" to fan her enthusiasms, or just enough "fire" to catch the spark of her freedom himself. As for her, if her Moon or Ascendent is in Taurus, Virgo, Capricorn, Pisces or Cancer (it will help if she has Mars or Venus in Taurus), she'll be content to sit cozily at his feet much (not all) of the time, and let him scratch her head while she purrs like a pussycat or moos to match his mating sounds.

Otherwise, he'll find it difficult to communicate with her, and she'll find it difficult to cope with him. For example, in the area of money. She delights in spending it, he leans heavily toward saving it. In the area of food. He's obsessed with eating it (though usually not to excess, depending) and she probably despises cooking it. Salads she can toss with one hand behind her back. Anything more complicated she'd just as soon leave to the chef at her favorite French restaurant.

He'll have heavy trouble understanding her Mercurial moods, and this girl can change moods like some people change shirts in a tropical zone. It started back when she was a child. First she wanted to be a nun. Then she wanted to be a priest. Things like that. Now she switches from gay to depressed, from generous to stingy. First she wants to be an actress, then she wants to get a degree in anthropology. A Bull can become understandably edgy when she's pulling one of her quick changes. He'll walk in some late afternoon, give her a big, warm bear hug, and she'll shock him by nearly swooning in his arms.

TAURUS: What's wrong, sweetheart? You're as white as a sheet.

GEMINI: Oh, I'm so weak, darling. Please, help me to the couch.

TAURUS: But, baby, what is it?

GEMINI: There are colored spots before my eyes, and the room is spinning around. I'm so dizzy. And there's a sharp pain in my head. My arms and fingers are numb. Look—I can't move them.

TAURUS: My God! I'll call the doctor right away. Just lie there quietly, now, and don't move.

GEMINI: May I put my head on your shoulder?

TAURUS: Of course.

(Five seconds pass, by the clock.)

TAURUS: How do you feel, darling? (Lifting the receiver, and preparing to dial the doctor.)

GEMINI: Great! Let's go swimming! I'll race you to the pool!

Oh, I don't know. I suppose, after all, maybe a Taurean could cope with it better than most other men. You must admit it takes nerves of steel to handle a scene like that, several times a day. And most Bulls do have steel nerves.

Their sexual relationship can be just as changeable. She'll cuddle up to him some evening, right after dinner, and whisper, "Rudolph, let's go to bed early tonight, and pretend we're on our honeymoon, back in that little cabin in the mountains in Switzerland." Well, you certainly don't have to hit a Bull over the head, after a hint like that.

TAURUS: (his passion pounding) Wait until I put out the lights, sweetheart. I'll be right there.

GEMINI: (already in the bedroom) Hurry, darling, hurry! Oh, just look at the Moon! It's so beautiful, and the stars are so bright. I think I'll make a wish on one of them . . . .

TAURUS: (already snuggled beneath his favorite Teddy-Bear blankets) Honey, will you please get away from that window, and come here, close to me?

GEMINI: Okay, but do you know where the yardstick is? I want to measure something right away.

TAURUS: *You want to do what?*

GEMINI: I want to measure this wall, to see if there's enough space to have a fireplace built in here, just like the one we had in our honeymoon cabin. Wouldn't that be romantic? Hand me the telephone, will you, Rudy? Be an angel. I want to call the carpenters right now, before they close the office. Put on the light. I can't find the directory in the dark, for heaven's sake.

Yes, it takes nerves of steel. Taureans are sensual, erotically inclined, and deeply passionate lovers. Gemini approaches sex as just another exciting adventure into the magic fairyland of the imagination. All Bulls possess a rather basic (sometimes slightly crude) sense of humor about sex, but he may miss the joke when she keeps slipping away from their intimacies into her own private world of fantasy.

This man wants to squeeze a real woman, not a misty nymph or an astral body. Her mind is her playground, full of fascinating images, but that sort of thing is far too intangible for a Bull, whose feet are planted firmly in reality. There will have to be compromises.

What will confuse the Taurus man most about the Gemini girl he loves may be summed up in one very simple question. *Who is she?* Is she truly his very own woman, the one he's been waiting to possess for the longest, longest time—or is she just a product of his wishful thinking! He so very much wants to fly high with her, up into the clouds, but he's not sure he knows how, and his wistful puzzlement is described in this verse:

Is it You?

or is it just that I've made you wear
those love robes I've been saving
since the days when my sand castles
were big enough to walk around in . . .
and strong enough
to stand against the tides

I can't remember who first said
that—"what you don't know, can't hurt you"
but what's-his-name was wrong
supposing I climb all the way to the top of the tree
then find out . . . it's not really You

how do I get back down again
all by myself?

I've always been afraid of heights*

* *Venus Trines at Midnight* by Linda Goodman (New York: Taplinger Publishing Company, Inc., 1970. To be re-published by Harper & Row, 1979).

TAURUS

Earth — Fixed — Negative
Ruled by Venus (also by the
* Planet Pan-Horus)*
Symbol: The Bull
Night Forces — Feminine

CANCER

Water — Cardinal — Negative
Ruled by the Moon
Symbol: The Crab
Night Forces — Feminine

The **TAURUS-CANCER** *Relationship*

———◄◆►———

*I will tell you where they are . . . . they are already
in their home under the ground, a very delightful
residence . . .*

Cancerian Crabs love their mothers, their homes, money, babies and
food. Taurean Bulls love money, their homes and mothers, food and
babies.

You can see these two Sun Signs are uncommonly alike, except for a
few minor changes in the order of priorities.

One thing that becomes clear right away about both Crabs and Bulls, if
you study astrology, is that they both want people to be nice to them. In
fact, they desperately need people to be nice to them (though you might
not guess it from the way these two behave, at times). The very nicest
thing Cancer can do for Taurus is to cook up a big dinner (which they'll

both enjoy eating), then sit around and talk about how to make more money (which they'll also both enjoy). The very nicest thing Taurus can do for Cancer is to buy an almanac to keep track of the waxing and waning periods of the Moon, and treat the Crab's changing moods accordingly. Cancerians are ruled by the Moon, and therefore are constantly affected by its fickle, fluctuating influence.

Since the practical Bulls have too much common sense to let the Moon push *them* around, right away that makes Taurus sorry for Cancer, which will please the Crabs immensely. It's not that they consciously seek pity, but they do like to know that people sympathize with their problems, instead of always accusing them of exaggerating life's daily tragedies. How can you exaggerate a tragedy, for goodness' sakes? A tragedy is a tragedy, like a rose is a rose is a rose. And Cancerians take their tragedies seriously.

They're not only serious much of the time, they're cautious too. As serious and as cautious as Crabs John D. Rockefeller, Nelson Rockefeller, and various other assorted rocks. They have depressed periods of black melancholy that would frighten Edgar Allan Poe's Raven into flying right off the mantelpiece. Then they flash a "funny," and their crazy Lunar humor has everyone giggling. You think a sad-faced, morose comedian is a non sequitur? Image the late film actor Arthur Treacher. (You know, the one who always played the butler.) You say a compulsive wife and mother, full of fears and insecurities, always worrying about her brood, whose career is making people laugh, is a non sequitur? Image American comedienne Phyllis Diller. Both Cancerians. Also, the two of them have managed to pile up quite sizable green nest eggs through their Looney Bird antics, like proper Crabs. (Green for m-o-n-e-y.) Sometimes, Lunar people are silent and timid, and at other times they chatter your ear off. Like I said, they're moody.

Despite their having so much in common, Taurus finds it difficult to understand the moods of the Crab. To the Bulls, it's a waste of time and common sense to weep and moan about a situation. Taureans seldom weep or moan (although they occasionally moo) and they're rarely moody. However, once Taurus men, women or children dig in their heels, and get set for a spell of the blues, rare as it may be, they're not kidding around. They're moping in earnest. When a Bull takes a notion to have a mood, you'd better know it's a good, strong one, that's going to last for months— even years. And it won't be interrupted by silly fits of giggles.

Cancerian moods, on the other hand (is there a Libra in the room?), usually don't last more than a few hours, a few days at the very most—and they cover a wide range of emotions, from tender humor to cranky criticism, from intelligent, vivacious conversation to trembling shyness. They switch from laughter to tears, from faith to cynicism, from bitterness to joy

—and then they snap at you, "What do you mean, *I'm* moody? *You're* the one who's impossible to get along with." (We won't tell the Crabs that a preposition is a poor thing with which to end a sentence, or even to end a sentence with—until the next mood switch to sweet and submissive. Otherwise, we may be snapped at—I mean, they may snap at us.)

Because Cancerians are so sensitive, they're aware of what's going on inside of people, and are, therefore, usually compassionate. Yet, their sympathy may come and go, especially when they're looking for sympathy themselves, which is frequently—and *most* especially if the sympathy entails a loan of money. Then the sympathy is much more likely to go than to come. Crabs think twice before they whip out their checkbooks. This is another area where Taureans and Cancerians have a great deal in common. The Bulls not only think twice before whipping out their checkbooks, they stop, pause, and think once again, just to be sure. However, both Sun Signs are truly generous to old people and to children. They're just a little tough on everybody in between. If it will put a hot meal into a child's tummy, or help a relative or loyal friend pay the mortgage on his or her home, Cancer and Taurus will relax their financial caution—or, when either of them have fallen in love. Romance warms their hearts and opens their pocketbooks miraculously.

The reason these two are slow about spending their money isn't because either of them is stingy. They're thinking of the future. There's always a rainy day to save for, right? (I can visualize the Crabs and Bulls reading this, nodding their heads, and asking silently, almost desperately, "Isn't that right?")

Well, yes, astrologically, that's right. There *is* always a rainy day to save for (for which to save). It's guaranteed to arrive, when you want it that much. I've never yet met a Taurean or a Cancerian who saved for a rainy day and failed to see that rainy day arrive, right on schedule. There's an ancient metaphysical truth, that warns: *Be careful of what you want* (or what you image) *because you will get it.* No doubt about that. None whatsoever. If you concentrate on saving for a rainy day, sooner or later you'll get caught in a downpour. How about imaging love and happiness and security instead? That sort of "wanting" and imaging will manifest into reality just as surely, under the very same Universal Law.

Now about that secret worry all Cancerians and Taureans have that they're going to end up in the poorhouse someday if they don't take care of their assets—I have some fantastic good news for them. Are all you Crabs and Bulls who are reading this section paying close attention now? Okay. Here it is: They don't have poorhouses anymore! *Honest.* They stopped building them years ago. Isn't that great news? So you can all go out and buy the luxuries you've always wanted—pianos, stamps for your stamp collection, antiques, old coins, caviar, gold frames for your baby pictures, cameras and . . . . . . what's that? *Now* you're worried about all the people who are broke, and the families in the poverty belts who don't have a poorhouse to *go* to? Oh, good grief.

I suppose, to be fair, we Fire and Air Signs should take it a little easier on watery Cancer and earthy Taurus about their mutual tendency to worry. If it were not for the Cancerians, we'd never have had any CARE packages, or orphanages, or foundling homes, or lend-lease (the United States is a Cancerian country, you know). If it were not for Taurus, we'd never have any big empires, or huge industries that employ thousands of people, like the Hearst Newspapers Syndicate, and many, many others (William Randolph Hearst was a Bull)—no real estate companies (mostly Taurus) or banks (mostly Taurus or Cancer) or farms (mostly Taurus). Admittedly, the mutual Cancer–Taurus traits of care, caution, worry and conservatism keep all of us sane and secure. When you think of all the Cappies and Virgos (and some Scorps) they have helping them, it really makes you feel like going to St. Patrick's Cathedral and lighting a candle in sheer gratitude for the way they protect the rest of us from our reckless follies and selfishness. (Or the church of your choice, of course. It's just that not all places of worship offer the beeswax for the ritual, you know?) While we're there, we may as well light another candle for Cancerian and Taurean humor. Humor, like cleanliness, is very definitely next to godliness. Humor on one side, cleanliness on the other, with godliness in the center—like a spiritual sandwich. (Although Crabs and Bulls prefer theirs with an extra helping of lettuce.)

Real humor stems from tragedy, which is why the serious-minded Crabs and Bulls are often so hilarious, especially when they team up as a couple in business, love, friendship—or within the family circle. During the lulls between their comedy routines, sometimes a Bull will show a stubborn streak, but the Cancerian will usually have a lot of patience with the Taurus pouting. The Crabs have so much experience with it themselves, you see.

Both of these Sun Signs like to eat, and they both love to cook, so there might be some difficulty keeping their diets under control when they spend a lot of time together. If you know a Taurus–Cancer combination, the best Christmas present you can give them is a copy of a book on nutrition. Like *Back to Eden,* or a gift certificate, good for at least a year, from a health food restaurant. As for indulgence in the bubbly, Cancer is considerably more likely than Taurus to enjoy a sip of wine or stronger spirits, now and then. The Crab is also better equipped (as a Water Sign) to handle the sips. If the Cancerian tempts the Taurean into tasting the grape too often, there will be trouble. The Bull hates excess, and seldom messes around with it in any form, but when he slips, he does it the way he does everything else—on a grand scale. Taurus is better off at a milk bar, since he (or she) has what you might call an empathy with good old bossy.

Taurus and Cancer get along smoothly most of the time. Even when they don't there's not much noise, and seldom any explosive arguments. Both of them normally react to hurt or aggravation by slinking off alone to brood. It doesn't make the misunderstandings any easier to bear, but it does keep things relatively quiet. Of course, there won't always be *total* silence between them during a disagreement. There will be some soft sounds occasionally, when the Bull sits in the corner like a solid lump of resentment, mumbling under his (or her) breath—while the Crab huddles in the broom closet, crying into several large tissues and emitting periodic choked sobs. Still, the gentle sounds of angry mutterings (Taurus) and sad snifflings (Cancer) are more peaceful than the hollering you can expect with the more volatile Sun Signs. (Not counting the rare and horrifying occasions every ten years or so, when the Bulls fancy they're in a china shop and someone waves a red flag.)

The meeting of a Bull and a Crab is often a fated one, with an element of compulsion on both sides, since it's a 3-11 Sun Sign Pattern, with heavy karmic undertones. There's more than a casual interest in each other, and the benefits or hurts resulting from the association usually have a long-lasting effect on both lives, if they continue to see each other for more than a few months.

Taurus and Cancer make an excellent team for any kind of business or industrial ventures, stock brokerages, banks, gardens, nurseries, farms, politics or real estate companies. The Bull will build the foundation carefully, organize it sensibly, and the Crab will run it with careful efficiency, making sure their mutual efforts gain the maximum publicity. (Cancerians may not be extroverts but they're surprisingly good at getting newspaper space, and getting their pictures on the front page or the TV screen.) The chances are excellent that any Cancer–Taurus business partnership will thrive and stay in the black. If there's any red on the books, it's probably from the blood (mixed with sweat and tears) these two pour into any project they're devotedly dedicated to making solidly successful. Assuming the Bull has the Moon or Ascendant in a Water or Earth Sign (except Capricorn) and the Crab has the Moon or Ascendant in a Water or Earth Sign (except Scorpio)—and sometimes even the parenthesized planetary positions won't stop their mutual achievement compatibility—these two could both end up in *Who's Who,* and likely find also that their personal relationship is harmonious, and comparatively free of tension. However, without such aid from their birth charts, there could be some pouting, muttering, mooing and sniffling, from time to time. Yet, compromise will usually be easier for them than for most other Sun Sign combinations. They each possess a certain amount of placidity, which often creates harmony from the sheer inner need and desire for peace and quiet.

Because Taurus is Earth and Cancer is Water, it's more probable that the Crab will slowly and gradually grow to imitate the Bull's Fixed habits, than the other way around—even though Taurus is behind Cancer on the karmic wheel of life. Why? Water is flexible, and does not resist, which is the wisdom of Water. It takes the shape of the vessel into which it's poured. When that vessel is a Taurean, the shape is usually symmetrical and pleasing. Considering the Taurus feeling for form, and the Cancer sensitivity for color, they can paint some rather nice pictures on the side of the jug too. Then they'll hang a price tag on it, take it to market, and come home together with a nice fat profit.

☆ ☆ ☆ ☆ ☆ ☆

TAURUS *Woman* CANCER *Man*

◂━◆━▸

He had one of his dreams that night, and cried in
his sleep for a long time, and Wendy held him tight.

The Cancerian male secretly desires to be babied by his woman. A Taurus female loves to spoil her man. Add these two astrological facts together and what's the result? Love at first sight? No, not quite.

A Crab doesn't rush into anything, including romance. Not only is rushing against the Cancerian grain, but it's impossible for a Crab to advance directly, in a straight line. All Crabs have this funny side-waddle. Did you ever watch one? First, he veers to the right, after which he turns to the left. Finally, he appears to be retreating backward—until the object he wants tries to escape, then he lunges forward, grabs hold, and hangs on —until he loses a claw. Even if he does, he'll just grow a new one, which is why Cancerians are called "tenacious," and that's often too mild a word for them.

Neither is a Taurus girl the type to leap overboard into a sea of passion, trilling ecstatic songs of eternal love. This woman wants to be wooed, and I mean really wooed. She'll expect a mountain of proof from a lover before she commits herself. So you can see that "love-at-first-sight" is not quite what happens when an Earth Sign like Taurus meets a Water Sign like Cancer. It takes time, usually months or years, seldom days or weeks. However, once committed, the Taurus woman knows how to keep her man sweetly contented. And the Cancerian man, once he's decided to make his forward lunge, is a lover to end all lovers, particularly in persistency.

The Crab's secrecy about his feelings and intentions during the courtship period is not exaggerated. The spring of 1973, I received in the mail a hard-cover copy of my first book, *Sun Signs,* from a Cancerian man in London, who attached this note to the book: "Dear Miss Goodman, I am in love with a wonderful Taurus girl. She is everything you say in the chapter about 'The Taurus Woman,' and I'm going to marry her. I would really appreciate it, if you would autograph this copy of your book *To Maggie, a lovely Taurean,* and return it to me at the address below. Very sincerely yours, etc. . . ." There was a P.S. on his note. It said, "Please don't write anything in the book about Crabs. She doesn't know I'm doing this, and I'm having a friend drop it off at Heathrow Airport, where she works, so she won't have any idea it's from me. I don't want her to guess how I feel about her. We only met a few months ago. Thank you."

I was a little concerned about Maggie, but I resisted the temptation to tip her off. Knowing she was a Taurus lady, I figured she would have the patience to wait till he decided to openly declare his devotion. Since that was a number of years ago, I doubt if she escaped the Crab's tenacity. They're probably married by now, and the proud parents of some little Bulls or Cows or Crablets. If so, I take this opportunity to congratulate them!

A relationship between Cancer and Taurus may seem nearly perfect, and it is undeniably a better than average romantic combination. But that doesn't mean it will be totally free of flaws. For example, there's the Cancerian mother complex. He may be one of the lucky ones who managed to graduate from adolescence into manhood, adjusting himself to the image of his mother as just another person—a wonderful person, to be sure, but just another human being involved in his life. If so, the Taurus girl will be lucky, because his strong admiration and respect for his mother will simply give him an increased measure of devotion for all women, including her.

But he could be one of those Crabs who never quite solved his mother hang-up. This type of Cancerian male (and remember, the sign of Cancer symbolizes motherhood, and the part of the body it represents is the breasts) carries a fierce, subconscious resentment against being weaned. So he solves his secret dilemma by either coldly rejecting his mother—or by remaining completely dependent upon her. Neither attitude produces a healthy emotional scene, and the woman he marries is sure to feel some occasional repercussions. Assuming he has chosen not rejection but dependence, it can create a few problems, which might try the patience of the average female. Fortunately, a Taurus girl is not an average female, and patience is one of her strong points. (So is a temper when she's pushed too far and decides to put her foot down rather heavily, which seldom fails to put the Crab in his place, and makes everything very clear, with a powerful hint that enough is enough.)

CANCER: Sweetie pumpkin, I'm sorry I'm late, but I dropped by Mama's, and we got to chatting about old times, and . . . . . . say, look, Mama sent you this huge basket of fresh strawberries from her garden. Aren't they yummy looking?

TAURUS: Strawberries give me hives. I have told both you and your mother that strawberries give me hives at least a dozen times. (Pregnant pause.) Since you weren't here, I had to put up the window shutters by myself. How do they look?

CANCER: Well, they're nice, Honey-cakes, but . . . . . .

TAURUS: But what?

CANCER: It's just that Mama says shutters are more trouble than they're worth. The slats keep breaking, they're hard to dust—and like she says, drapes are ever so much richer, and more colorful, and all. Don't you think?

TAURUS: No, I don't think. I have no brain. I'm a drone. A robot.

CANCER: Now, don't get upset, Sugar-lump. You're just all tuckered out from working so hard. You deserve a nice treat. Let's have dinner out tonight, and catch a movie afterward.

TAURUS: I'd rather stay home and watch the Academy Awards on television. We can send out for pizza.

CANCER: Mama says it can make you blind, and cause symptoms of paranoia.

TAURUS: *Eating pizza?*

CANCER: Watching color television so much.

TAURUS: I feel like pizza, and I want to watch the Oscars tonight, so let's not discuss it any further.

CANCER: All right, but Mama says it can clog your arteries.

TAURUS: Just how does your mother figure color TV affects the arteries?
           I'm fascinated by her medical knowledge.

CANCER: The pizza. Mama says starchy dough and hot spices are poi-
           son, and we've been eating a lot of that kind of thing lately.
           Tell you what, let's just run over and have dinner with Mama
           tonight. She's all alone, and she's making chicken dumplings,
           and . . . . . .

TAURUS: Dumplings aren't starchy, huh?

CANCER: Not the way Mama makes them. She . . . . what are you doing?

TAURUS: Hello, is this the Pizza Parlor? This is Gertrude Glassberg. Send
           me up a small pizza, please. No, I don't need a large one this
           time. My husband and I have decided on a trial separation.

CANCER: What did you say? Honey-cakes, I really think . . . . .

TAURUS: (grimly) Pack your bags. And hurry. Mama's dumplings are
           getting cold.

There's a limit to Taurean patience. Naturally, not all Crabs are so
tightly knotted to the maternal apron strings as this one, but it can be
rough, living up to an image of perfect womanhood. Still, a Taurus girl
can cook up a mean dumpling herself, she often sews her own clothes,
she's thrifty, she smells good (girl Bulls adore perfumed soap, and all the
accessories), and she's uncommonly sensual. So, you see, she has a few
things going for her that Mama can't top.

The physical relationship between them will be ideal—or as ideal as
they want it to be, and encourage it to be. The potential for harmony is
surely there. Her sexual nature is deeply affectionate, tender and uncomplicated. He is also deeply affectionate, tender—though perhaps a bit
more complicated. The tangible satisfaction of the senses, and the earthy
reality of passion, is important to a Taurus woman, whereas the *emotional*
release of sexual union is important to a Cancerian man, but these slightly
different requirements need not conflict. Instead, they can blend, and
create a physical relationship of rare completeness. There's something
warmly protective in the Taurean expression of sexual love that seems to
answer the silent cry of Cancer to be enveloped in clouds of tenderness, to
have someone wipe away all her tears—and all her fears of being alone
and unwanted. When a Taurus woman expresses her devotion through
lovemaking, there are no games, no fantasies, there is no false modesty—
just a comfortable feeling of giving. In spite of his own more imaginative
approach to lovemaking, this is just the kind of sexual security a Cancerian man secretly longs for, in his heart.

Two people who love can't avoid hurting each other occasionally, but with the Bull and the Crab hurt can last longer than it does between other Sun Signs. They'll have to realize that this is an unnecessary waste of time and emotional strain, since the hurt itself is unintentional. Rather than talking it over, like Gemini or Libra—getting it off their chests by exploding in temporary anger, like Aries, Leo or Sagittarius—or rising above it in detachment, like Aquarius and Pisces—this man and woman may allow the hurt to take deep roots and grow into a coldness that would be more dangerous to the relationship than the original misunderstanding. When a Taurus woman is upset, she tends to pout, then freeze into a forbidding rock of stubbornness. When the Crab has been wounded, he withdraws into his shell, to cry and pity himself alone, afraid to make any move, even a move toward forgiveness and apology, lest it bring on more hurt. So there you have it. A stubborn Bull, refusing to say "I'm sorry," when she truly *is* sorry, and even taking her own sweet time about accepting a shy peace offer from the partner—and the shattered Crab, peeking out timidly from his hard shell, quivering with heartache inside, sometimes snapping in crankiness to cover the pain of being unloved, however temporarily. It's hardly an atmosphere conducive to reconciliation.

Perhaps it would help if they looked at it this way: Pouting in silence is impractical. (They both hate to be impractical.) It leads nowhere—except into the dark tunnel of more loneliness. (They both hate dark tunnels.) What she should do is use her beautiful, Venus-inspired patience (Venus is her ruling planet, you know, until Pan-Horus is discovered and named, and Taurus returns the borrowed Venus influence back to Libra, where it belongs). If she waits for the next change of the Moon (*his* ruler) all she needs to do is smile and whisper "I love you"—and he'll pop right out of his shell into her arms.

What *he* should do is use his beautiful Cancerian perception, inspired by his Lunar vibrations, to understand how much more susceptible this woman is to physical affection than she is to verbal eloquence, and instead of writing her notes bashfully signed, "Guess who?" and tucking them down inside the box of detergent, hoping she'll find them when she's doing his laundry—he should simply grab her firmly, as only a Crab can grab, and kiss her soundly. Then she'll cuddle right up next to his heart, where she belongs.

And let Mama stuff the cat with her dumplings.

☆ ☆ ☆ ☆ ☆ ☆

TAURUS *Man* CANCER *Woman*

———— ◄─◆─► ————

*"She wants me to unbar the window," thought Peter,
"but I won't, not I."*

*He peeped again, and the tears were still there,
or another two had taken their place.*

Imagine you are a huge rock, sitting high on top of a mountain. Nothing frightens you, or moves you. You're so tough, the storms of thousands of years haven't even scratched your surface, though they've worn away lesser rocks into helpless pebbles. Then one chilly day, an apparently harmless drop of water brightly splashes on you, and trickles its way into a deep crack in your center, which has been there since you were born, but has been overlooked by the rains and winds until now. What will you do?

You will do nothing. You, who have stood up against centuries of floods and tornados, have nothing to fear from one tiny drop of water. The next day, the thermometer drops to zero, and the drop of water freezes in your center. The freezing causes it to expand, and the expansion hurts you. Since nothing has ever before been able to weaken your strength, how do you feel about a drop of water which is expanding inside you, and threatening to crack you in two?

A quiet little meditation like that will throw a great illumination on what it's like to be an earthy, invulnerable Taurus man in love with a watery, gentle and sometimes Looney Moon Maiden. It can shake him to his foundations. But it's too late. She's already penetrated the secret place no one else has ever quite reached—his heart. Since a Bull's heart is as strong as both his will and his back, he probably won't break in half. But he'll never again be the same, once this girl has enticed him to run along the beach under a midnight sky, in the zig-zag directions of the Crab, crying and laughing—and *feeling*. Taurus knows all about touching, but feeling is a slightly different word. She'll teach him all its meanings and synonyms.

An occasional Cancerian girl will claim she's not typical of her Sun Sign because—"I don't like to cook, I don't want children, and I hate staying home." Don't let her fool you, like she's fooling herself. The reason she's scooting around in those Crab-like sideways patterns is because she hasn't found the man she secretly yearns for, the one who will protect her and wrap her up in thick blankets of devotion. She may inwardly love babies and cooking and homemaking, but she's not going to stand over a hot oven or rock a cradle for just any male. Until *he* materializes out of her moonlight dreams, she'll cover up her tender maternal feelings and sentimental femininity with ambition for financial security, a successful career and public attention, sprinkling jokes everywhere she goes, punctuated with a crazy Looney Bird giggle, that says (or tries to say), "I don't care!" But if you listen to the hidden chords, her Lunar laugh is whispering a wistful message: "I'm lonely and frightened and sad—don't dreams *ever* come true?"

Yes, they do. If you believe in them. Emphatically and irrevocably, they do. The formula is so deceptively simple only a very few people ever discover its truth. The Galilean said it this way: "Whatsoever things ye desire, pray as if ye had already received them, and ye shall have them." That's really all there is to it. If you truly *want* it, "it's no longer a dream." What you image shall come into being without a shadow of a doubt, the time element depending entirely upon the intensity of the image. However, the Cancerian girl is inclined to pray for things, not "as if she had already received them," but as if Fate had no intention of ever giving them to her. Therefore, Fate doesn't. It's simply a matter of reversing the vibrations she sends out from Negative to Positive.

The Taurus man is a slow starter in romance. Though he has an enormous capacity for love, it doesn't burst into verbal or physical commitment overnight. Once it does blossom, however, it flowers beautifully, and usually permanently. Permanence is something the Moon Maiden needs, for all her whimsical emotional wanderlust. Like her, this man will not yield his complete self until the right woman arrives on the scene. He'll take his good old time deciding, but his surrender, when it comes, is often instant, and his fidelity is eternal—if he isn't pushed beyond great endurance by the incorrigible behavior of his partner.

Most Taurus men (not all, but most) don't experience love in its *total* sexual and emotional fullness until they're out of their teens (or even years later than that), long after their buddies have chalked up scores of "conquests," live-in affairs and a few marriages. But never forget that the Bull is enormously capable of making up for lost time, and the depth and intensity of his love is well worth waiting for. She can console herself with the thought that, while he doesn't break *down* easily, neither will he want to break *up* quickly. That trait will certainly appeal to the girl Crab, who is also slow to take hold—and even slower to let go—of anything. Like raveled shawls, broken umbrellas, cracked mirrors, used doggy bags, empty lipstick tubes, the pink ribbon from her old baby bonnet, lidless bottles and jars, bottle and jarless lids, half pieces of curtain rods, newspapers with all the clippings already clipped, outdated redemption coupons, sharpened-all-the-way-down pencils with only a nub eraser left, and old lovers (unless she has an Aquarian or Gemini Ascendent or Moon Sign, in which case she may throw really valuable things out with the morning trash, then be puzzled why she can't find them weeks later).

The Bull is possessive (not quite the same thing as jealous) and his approach to love is likely to be solid, sensible and practical, seldom emotionally erratic, capricious or unduly enthusiastic—but cozy! Although the two of them are much alike in many ways, this is one where they may not be. A Moon Maiden can allow unfounded jealousy to torture her into moods of deep depression—or worse yet, a suspicious, bitter or clinging attitude that can infuriate a Bull. (The clinging he doesn't mind so much, he may even enjoy it—the suspiciousness he can do without.) Her active imagination sometimes causes her to develop fears which, although based more on fantasy than fact, can bring on floods of tears, and a touch of hysteria. It sounds hopeless, but it isn't really. In fact, not many Sun Sign combinations have as much hope for success as Taurus and Cancer, once they know who they are, and where they're going.

Taurus already pretty much knows that about himself. Temporarily ruled (until Pan-Horus is discovered and identified) by the harmonious, peaceful Venus, he's more inclined to keep an even keel regarding their differences than she is. This woman is ruled by the Moon, which is a reflector of light. So she instinctively reflects the moods around her, indeed, every change in her immediate environment is reflected, mirror-like, in her heart and brain. Sometimes all that reflecting creates an eclipse of her true self. It's not easy for a Moon Maid to know who she is, and where she's going, although she has an uncanny sense of the feelings and intentions of others. Lots of people trust their secrets to her, and are rewarded with both tender sympathy and wise counsel. Yet, it's next-to-impossible to pry her own secrets out of her.

The Bull might say to her, "I don't understand you. You say you love me, but you spend all your time running around, giving birth to ideas and babies, buying clothes, taking CARE packages to your friends, working for the PTA and Greenpeace and the garden club, listening to music, painting pictures, making bank deposits, learning French, visiting the planetarium, and sitting out in the back yard, staring at the Moon by yourself. You don't need me. I'm just in the way around here." Now, she may perceive, after a speech similar to that one, what the problem is. He's hurt, because he's not getting the attention he needs, the pats on the head and affectionate hugs and kisses he hungers for, to make him feel securely loved. However, lacking her Lunar sensitivity, he may not understand how much she needs all her busy activities—as well as her world of dreams —so she can reflect back into life all the things she absorbs by living it.

It should be obvious, then, who must make the first move to wave the olive branch. The one who most perceives how it is with the other. That would, of course, be her.

Still, her attempts at making up with him can seem a little vague and devious to the direct, uncomplicated Bull. First, she retreats in tears, then crawls toward him sideways. It confuses him. How is he to interpret her message when she tucks a baked apple under his pillow, or leaves a sentimental poem under his wet cake of soap, in the shower? It stuck to the paper, obliterating the words, and for all he knows, it could be a farewell note. She should just come right out and say, "I do need you, and I can't live without you, and the reason I scoot around all the time is because . . ." etc. and so on. Then she should prove she means it in a physical way—the only language a Taurus man understands. Simple. Plain. Honest. Down to Earth. And sensual. He doesn't like to be teased. No Bull likes to be teased.

Their sexual compatibility, barring severe afflictions between their natal planets in their respective birth charts, is usually excellent. She may now and then wish he'd be a little less clumsy with his romantic jokes, and a little more delicate in his verbal expressions of passion. But on the whole, the Taurus sense of touch is as refined and delicate as anyone could ask. His masculine virility can coax this uncertain girl out of her shell, with the promise of the kind of fulfillment most women only read about in novels. The Bull will give the Moon Maiden a feeling of being snugly loved, warmly desired—and, yes, sexually dominated (which is what she really wants, in her secret heart).

Don't frown, ERA ladies. Not all, but some females actually do enjoy being "conquered" by males, at least physically. Admittedly, true equality means neither sex is superior, and therefore neither should submit to or dominate the other. But the sexual relationship between a man and a woman is an entirely different matter from their interchange intellectually, or on an achievement level. It's a very *personal* and *individual* kind of emotional chemistry—not always predictable.

The Taurus man will lavish enough affection on the Cancerian woman, to banish the fears she's accumulated since childhood that nobody really wants or needs her because most people are more capable in every way than she. *He* does. *He* wants her, and he *needs* her. And he'll show it in unmistakable ways, if she'll let him.

It's difficult for this lady to resist real love when it's offered with the kind of sincerity Taurus love is offered. In return, she'll adore him madly (with an emphasis on the madness, during the Full Moon) and probably never leave him—unless he places her in the middle in a fuss with her family, or insults her mother (a cardinal sin to the Cardinal Sign of Cancer, if she's a typical Crab). Then he may lose her for a while. This girl is intensely loyal to her mama, usually, and sometimes papa runs a close second. But she'll return to her Bull when the Moon changes (assuming he apologizes, of course). Since he's so stubborn, the reconciliation may never occur if she doesn't understand, and forgive him before he asks to be forgiven. He won't beg.

She is so changeable—or is she fickle? He is so patient—or is he obstinate? Which is it? The true answer depends on which way they look at it. While he's wearing his Taurean blinders, it's impossible for him to see the truth about anything, so he appears bull-headed.

While she's gazing into her Lunar mirror, the truth is sometimes distorted, so her emotions appear to fluctuate unreliably. But when the issues are cloudy, they can always find their way back to each other, through the mist, if they meditate on this ancient wisdom: *Seek the truth, and the truth shall set you free.* What is the real truth? Love. Unselfish and forgiving love. The genuine kind.

TAURUS

Earth — Fixed — Negative
Ruled by Venus (also by the
   Planet Pan-Horus)
Symbol: The Bull
Night Forces — Feminine

LEO

Fire — Fixed — Positive
Ruled by the Sun
Symbols: Lion &
   Shy Pussycat
Day Forces — Masculine

The **TAURUS-LEO** Relationship

"None of us has ever been tucked in at night."

Bulls need lots of loyalty and affection in order to be sure they're loved and *appreciated*. Leos need lots of worship and compliments in order to be sure they're loved and *admired*. Neither of them get quite enough proof that they're cherished, even from compatible people who were born in their own elements (Taurus is Earth, Leo is Fire), and when they constantly demand to be emotionally "tucked in" by each other, they can really become frustrated.

These two Sun Signs are square, which means they don't harmonize too well, unless the Sun and Moon in their respective charts are in mutually agreeable signs. As in all 4-10 Sun Sign Patterns, the square aspect (Taurus is 90 degrees away from Leo) is a tension maker. Yet, the 4-10 vibration bestows giant rewards of peace and harmony when the two involved have demonstrated the patience and selflessness to pass this karmic soul testing in a human love relationship.

With Taurus and Leo, the tension starts like this: Leo is much too self-centered to give the strong, silent Bulls the absolute devotion and obedience they insist on receiving *most* of the time. Taurus is much too stubborn to give the vain, proud Leos the unquestioning worship they demand *continually*. They're both Fixed Signs, so they're both good organizers, and they each possess an unusual amount of emotional dependability. But they're also capable of being—well, *Fixed*. My Thesauraus offers the phrase "pig-headed" as a substitute for "fixed." (Just for the record, the other two Fixed Signs are Aquarius and Scorpio.)

Sometimes, the fiery Leo will depend on the more tranquil, stable Taurus to cope with an unpleasant situation, then rob the Bull of all credit for the accomplishment. However, this doesn't bother Taurus the way it would a more egotistical sign. The last thing Bulls are interested in is personal glory. They won't turn their broad backs on it, should it be offered them, but they can take it or leave it alone. Taurus is more interested in *cash* appreciation and emotional peace of mind.

I know a Leo man who was tenderly devoted to his invalid Taurean wife for many years. She outlived most of the doctors who predicted her death every six months or so, and continued to manage household affairs from her bed for triple her life expectancy. The Lion took full credit for her amazing stamina. After all, wasn't he giving her the best possible tender, loving, expert care, under conditions which would have put a weaker man flat on his back, or driven him into a mental breakdown? Yes, he was. But her Taurean iron will was at least partially responsible for her medical miracle.

Strangely, although they had many other areas of constant contention and argument, she quietly permitted him to take the credit for her courage without a trace of resentment. She well knew how much she owed him, and she also knew how much effort her strength and cheerfulness over the years cost *her*. But Taurus seldom fusses or quibbles about being overshadowed by the Leonine ego. She allowed him, even encouraged him, to take all the bows, and smiled to herself. Worship, however, she refused to give him, which made him a most unhappy monarch, and for which he perhaps never quite forgave her. But credit she willingly relinquished.

I once knew a Taurus man who worked as a registrar and assistant to the president of a Barber School in New Jersey. The president (the Bull's superior, of course) was a warm-hearted, brilliant, generous, typically proud and arrogant Leo—a Lion, whose name was Dr. Andrew Julian. As a matter of fact, it still is. Why should he change it, when it's lettered in gold, stenciled, stitched or monogrammed on all his cuff links, shirts, briefcases, under-garments (allegedly), towels and silverware? My Taurus friend and Dr. Julian benefit from a harmonious Sun-Moon aspect between their birth charts, so they still fondly admire and respect one another, although they no longer work together. Nevertheless, their business association fairly bristled with daily examples of the 4-10 Leo-Taurus relationship, its mutual helpfulness—and its pitfalls.

There was the time Dr. Julian held a private conference with an investor who wished to buy an interest in his Barber School. The investor was a millionaire, and uncommonly loose and magnanimous with his cash. He didn't care how much he invested, as long as he could visibly appear to run the operation—as long as the school would bear his name (never mind that he had no barbering experience).

Naturally, the Lion roared loudly at this double threat to his authority and affront to his prestige. For several hours, angry voices rose and fell from behind the closed door of the Lion's plush den—which is the only way to describe any Leo office. A plush den.

Finally, the door opened, and Dr. Julian commanded imperiously, "David! Come in here immediately!" (Leos seldom ask, they command, as befits royalty.) When the cautious Bull slowly walked into the firing line, the Lion waved a disdainful hand toward the angry investor and directed majestically, "*Talk* to him, David." Then Leo swirled around in his expensive swivel chair, pouting in injured dignity, and staring out the large picture window of his den—as though the other two men were not present. (The King did not deign to take any further notice of the peasants.)

After a few minutes of quiet questioning, the Bull uncovered the basic problem. The potential investor was an Aries. A Ram. It was *his* money, and by golly, *he* was going to be boss, and *his* name would be on the school. Nobody was going to order *him* around. The Taurean explained *patiently* that Dr. Julian was loved by all his teachers and students (he really was, they adored him, pride, arrogance and all), that he was furthermore highly respected by all the companies which did business with the school, with whom he had established a warm rapport over the years (true).

Of course, these solid compliments were not missed by Leo. They rained like fragrant roses on the Lion's head, which was still turned away and facing the window. Then the Bull's rich, Taurean voice, deep and soothing, was heard by the secretary, floating over the transom, as he spoke calmly to the Aries investor. "Don't you think it would be smarter if Dr. Julian's name were to remain on the outside of the building, in all the advertising, and on the school's letterhead? Since he's had over forty years' experience running a Barber School, wouldn't it be better if he continued to do so? However, it makes more sense, and it's more practical for *you*, Sir, to be the one who signs all the checks, so the people at the bank will know *you're* the Financial Backer and Advisor of the operation. Why should you spend twelve hours a day here, as Dr. Julian does, when you have more important things to do? Your time is too valuable for you to be tied down to a desk, as he is, from nearly dawn till midnight, seven days a week."

After that masterpiece of manipulation, the Aries investor beamed happily, like a child who has just been given a lollipop and told he could play hookey at the same time. He was delighted to be called "Financial Backer" and "Advisor," to know he'd be respected by the bank and the bankers (however much cash they may possess, for some odd reason, Rams are seldom ever truly respected by bankers) and that he wouldn't have to spend twelve hours a day, seven days a week, working. (He hadn't thought of that—Aries never does.)

The Lion swirled back around on his padded, swivel throne then, and offered everyone a cigar to celebrate the closing of the deal. Later, after the new Aries partner had left, Dr. Julian, his dignity now completely restored, walked over to the busy Bull's desk and remarked, with his large, handsome Leonine head and pride both held high, "I certainly told him off, and let him know who runs this school. I think I handled the situation rather well, don't you?" The Bull, patiently and respectfully, allowed as how he certainly had.

One area of potential agreement between Taurus and Leo is promoting and building. Leo loves to promote grandiose schemes and large ideas, and all Bulls delight in contemplating the financial return of what might be the seeds of the Taurean empire they're always building in their minds. The path Taurus follows is steady, purposeful and relentless. Obstacles don't disturb or upset the Bulls as they do Leo, because Taureans accept limitation and delay as part of the price they have to pay for eventual success. One of the favorite mottos of the Bulls is: *If a thing is worth doing at all, it's worth doing well—and also worth waiting for.*

Leos, who are fanatically fond of freedom, refuse to accept, or even to recognize, limitation. Their attitude is ever hopeful and determined. It never even occurs to them that they can't win all the chips with one grand and glorious toss of the dice, whether the game the Lion or Lioness is playing is business, friendship, romance, matrimony or gambling. The Big Cats will almost always take a chance, and in Kipling's words, "make a heap of all their earnings, and risk them on one turn of pitch and toss—

and lose, and start again at their beginnings—and never breathe a word
about their loss."

The reason Leos never breathe a word about their loss is because they
convince themselves they didn't lose. It's all a mirage. Taurus, to put it
mildly, is not nearly so quick to take a chance, whether the Bulls are risking their money or their hearts. And when they lose, the memory of the
loss will linger a long, long time—long enough for the Taureans to profit
by the experience. Yet, when the chips are down, the Bull and the Lion or
Lioness can match each other's contempt for misfortune. Neither is inclined to make a big deal of it, although they both might shed some private tears of sharp anguish. Leo and Taurus equally dislike public weeping or open admissions of failure.

In the long run, the Bull believes the safest way to double your money
is to fold it over once and place it back in your pocket. That pretty much
sums up the Taurean philosophy about either romantic or financial gambling. When the Bulls are young, they think the security of having cash
in the bank, combined with the devoted love of a member of the opposite
sex, is the most important and vital thing in life. When they grow older,
they're positive it is.

The only thing Leos are that positive about is their own ability to make
it happen. Not surprisingly, the Leonine warm-heartedness and nobility of
spirit, when blended with their faith in themselves, draws others to them,
including Lady Luck, who often showers upon them generous amounts of
both love and gold.

Leos are all Big Cats, with huge hearts and splendid strength, who
sometimes see themselves as neglected kittens when their own ego images
aren't constantly reflected back to them by others and kept alive by extravagant compliments. (But the compliments must be genuine—Leo sees
through insincere flattery as shrewdly as any monarch who's being appeased for favors—barring an afflicted natal Sun.)

Although Leo wants to lead, and the Lions or Lionesses sometimes impose on the Bulls' patience unintentionally, these proud people also enjoy
protecting those they love, and lavishing gifts and kindness upon them.
Isn't that the way all good kings and queens feel about their subjects? A
Taurean will be secretly and deeply pleased by this Leonine protectiveness, demonstrative affection and concern over his—or her—welfare.
However stubbornly they may deny it, no one needs or appreciates
kindness and affection more than Taurus men, women and children. Their
loyal, dependable hearts ache for it. That's another nice similarity between these two. The Leo and the Taurus hearts are equally loyal. Often,
the warm friendliness and interest projected by Leo will make Taurus feel

all snuggly and secure. So they are attracted into the same circle of empathy.

It's only when Leo starts giving those royal commands, which Taurus interprets as being shoved, that the trouble starts. After a time, Leo's bright Fire may scorch the Bull's endurance, until the Taurean buries the Lion or Lioness beneath a ton of earthy stubbornness and negative reaction. But Leo is ruled by the Sun, symbolizing warmth and light, the Great Life-Giving Force of the Universe. Taureans are softly ruled (until Pan-Horus* appears to claim and influence them) by Venus, symbolizing Peace, Love and the musical Harmony of the Spheres. Between them, these two heavenly bodies keep the world spinning. All the other planets are merely supportive. The Sun is Life. Venus is Love. Is there more?

☆ ☆ ☆ ☆ ☆ ☆

TAURUS *Woman* LEO *Man*

> She had believed in him at the time,
> but now that she was married and full
> of sense she quite doubted whether
> there was any such person.

Every Taurus woman has an affinity for music. She has a rich, musical voice, whether she's singing Carmen at the Met or simply saying, "I'll take two extra pints of cream today" to the milkman. Some Taureans compose music, direct it, or sing it—and all of them bask in it. Listening to its soothing sounds has a tranquilizing effect on the Bulls.

So, how could there be friction when a Leo man, married to a Taurus woman, wants to play music? There can be. And that's what astrology means by stating that their natal Suns are squared. This is the difficult and tense 4-10 Sun Sign Pattern, which may be a challenge, but which is more richly rewarding than all the others, if the challenges are courageously faced and conquered. Incidents which could never become un-

* See footnote, page 68.

pleasant between any two other people, based on situations where harmony should naturally exist, can erupt into volcanos between a Leo and a Taurus, unless there's an unusually favorable Sun-Moon aspect between them.

A couple of years ago, I was visiting in the home of a Carmel, California, couple, who have been an unusually loyal and devoted pair for many years. She's a Taurus. He's a Leo. She's a karate instructor. He's a poet, and an Oriental art dealer. The evening I was there, after enjoying a delicious dinner cooked by the Taurean wife, the three of us were discussing music, and the Lion and I discovered we had a mutual love for a particular version of "Ave Maria." When he placed an LP recording of the classic on the stereo, I leaned back in my chair, prepared to enjoy the music bouncing around the rafters from the many speakers the Lion had built and installed himself all over the house.

But as the opening chords swelled out to fill the room, I noticed the Taurus wife had disappeared. Suddenly, I heard a door slam—*hard*. Her husband, slightly abashed, explained: "Louise can't stand it when I play the stereo, so I guess she's gone to bed." It shocked me so much I couldn't concentrate on the recording. A normally gracious and hospitable Taurus woman being rude to a guest? A Venus-ruled woman who hates *music*? Astrologically impossible.

The next morning, at breakfast, she was her usual charming calm self, and when I asked her why she hated music, she replied calmly, "Oh, I don't hate it. I *love* music. I have, ever since I was a child."

"Then why . . . . ." I asked.

"You mean last night," she sniffed, icily. "I just can't bear to be around when Larry plays his stereo. He insists on turning up the volume so high, it drowns out all the tones, and hurts my ears. It's really a prostitution of music, I think, to play it that loudly, but you can't reason with him about it, so that's that." (The Taurus resignation to the inevitable.) "Tell me," she said, "since you're an astrologer—does his horoscope indicate that he's deaf?" (The Taurean humor, never subtle.)

No, he wasn't deaf. He was expressing his Leo urge to do everything on a grand scale, even though this particular Lion is the Shy Pussycat type. Whatever type he is, a Leo man can't bear to do things by half measures, and this compulsion is completely unrelated to his manner (if he's one of the quieter, less flamboyant Leos, in his outward personality). If it's a house, it must be large and luxurious, with a private den for him (his royal throne room, in a manner of speaking). If it's a woman, she must be both beautiful and intelligent. If it's a ring, it must be glittery, and visible across the room. When the Lion weeps, he sheds great torrents of tears. When he laughs, he laughs long and loudly. When he listens to music, he needs to hear it soar gloriously, to fill his heart and soul and ears. And when he's hurt, he either roars dramatically, or blushes furiously in humiliated frustration—as my Leo host, Larry, did rather frequently during my visit with him and his Bull wife, Louise.

Ordinarily, a Taurus female would never object to her husband's playing music, whatever the volume. Yet, I know another Taurus woman who sighed in ecstasy when her Lion courted her with a ukulele, in West Virginia, during their college courting days—then became bored each time he played and sang for her after they were married. You see, it's not a Taurean antipathy for music these two lady Bulls were displaying. Music, in both cases, simply *became the channel for the square of tension* between them, and their Leo mates.

Whether or not any individual Leo male possesses the emotional poise to deserve his astrological comparison to a King, this is nevertheless his private ambition—to rule those around him, most definitely including the Lion's own mate. A Taurus girl instinctively desires to submit to her man, to stick by his side faithfully and loyally through all seasons. But being ruled sounds suspiciously to her like being pushed, and no Bull will tolerate being pushed. Although Taurus women are capable of deep, lasting devotion and a warm-hearted love, they don't toss around careless compliments, they have no use at all for flattery, and they think worship is for the weak-minded. Since all Lions require and demand compliments, flattery and worship, you can see what's often missing in the relationship.

Leos are fiercely proud, fiery people, who brandish their own batons and refuse to play second fiddle to anyone. Even the Shy Pussycat Leo smolders with resentment when he's denied his rightful place in the Sun, preferably a few miles ahead and beyond anyone else who may be soaking up its rays. After all, the Sun is *his* ruler, which is why he's so noble and generous, despite his occasional arrogance and freezing attitude of superiority. To him, the Sun is not the center of the Universe, around which all the other planets revolve. *Leo* is the center of the Universe, around which his family (and hopefully, his friends) revolve—or they'd better, if they don't want to be frozen and ignored for the sin of not paying due respect at court.

Although this man's disposition is undeniably masterful, and therefore sometimes a shade tyrannical, he's a gentle, magnanimous lover, after a quarrel. His Leonine nobility of spirit makes it natural for him to want to kiss and make up. Verbal apologies he can't handle gracefully. They destroy his vanity. But he'll show he's sincerely sorry with a variety of romantic overtures. That's why these two often sense more empathy and mutual harmony in their sexual relationship than when they're trying to play the banjo together.

A physical and tangible display of affection is sometimes the only way to reconcile an argument with a Taurus girl. She'll remain stone-faced and immune to flowery words and persuasive arguments. Long conversations bore her, because she feels only through her senses. Taurus wants action, not words. So she'll respond beautifully to his passionate acts of love, and it all works out fine. They often reconcile after a squabble without the proud Lion ever having to lose his dignity. Making love is never beneath his dignity, no matter how violently he's been fighting with the loved one —or how recently. He needs a woman who can both accept and contain the depth of affection and passion he's capable of giving, and this one can. Her sensual talents for eroticism certainly won't displease him either. They'll make him "feel like a King," an expression many Leos use to describe their sexual fulfillment with the right woman.

However, her quality of conserving words isn't quite as soothing to the Lion, outside the bedroom. She may be less than ecstatic when he becomes emotionally aroused, and desperately needs an attentive, approving audience. She may even yawn in the middle of one of his dramatic speeches or lectures, and nothing can so cruelly destroy this man's sensitive ego so much as an obvious sign of boredom from a rebellious subject— especially from the woman he loves. If she really wants to keep this man forever (and every Taurus woman seeks the security of romantic permanence) she'd better drink pots of black coffee, and make sure she remains wide awake when her Lion is on stage.

The most common complaint of the Lion against a Taurus girl is that she lacks enthusiasm. He often feels like shaking her into action, and shouting, "*Say* something! *Do* something! Anything at all. But don't just sit there." *Her* most common complaint against *him* can be summed up in four Shakespearean household words, "*Much ado about nothing.*"

He'll love the way she can turn a leaky tent into a cozy castle, her talent for making a dollar stretch like Silly Putty, and her rich humor—though he won't appreciate her jokes that ridicule his dignity, or puncture large holes in his ego. She'll warm up to her Lion's bear hugs, and intensely admire his ability to organize his dreams into the marble and alabaster of reality. She will not, of course, be at all happy about his extravagant tendencies, or his need to go out and review the troops when he feels the need for a little extra applause from the crowd. They'll always have their periodic tugs of tension. After all, they are both Fixed. Yet, the secret respect they feel for one another sometimes creates an unexpectedly soft, soothing carpet beneath their differences of opinion.

This lady doesn't allow herself to display visible anger often. She's patient, good humored, and willing to bear a great deal of silliness, along with Life's sadness, without evidencing excessive emotion. But when she does become angry—good and angry—it's best to get out of her way. Like, across town. Or maybe even another city or state, until she cools off and calms down—which she'll never fail to do eventually. A Taurus woman is always deeply ashamed of her own weakness, after she's given in to an emotional tantrum (during which her "creamy-smooth" Venus voice will more resemble that of a drill sergeant who trained for the operatic stage in youth—loud and forceful), and so she may be extra shy and affectionately loving later in trying to balance her act. But the Lion shouldn't let her sweetness following a disagreement fool him. She remembers what it was he did to arouse her Bull-like fury, and she'll remember it for years . . . and years . . . and years. Taureans tear into a wild and furious rampage of anger only very rarely—sometimes only once or twice during a lifetime. But it isn't the quantity of Taurus anger that matters—it's the *quality*. Volcanic.

A lady Bull shows her temper more frequently than just mentioned only if she's constantly and continually goaded by the domineering ways of a Leo who lectures her and scolds her periodically, and then, when she won't obey his every whim, turns away from her and pouts for long periods. That sort of behavior can rumble any Earth Sign into furious frustration, if it's prolonged over a long period of time.

This woman is made of more than her Taurean temper and stubbornness. She's also made of steadiness, courage, warmth, unswerving devotion, placidity, calmness and deep, deep emotions. She's enormously affectionate and giving, and her natural ability to laugh at herself is one of her most endearing qualities (unless she has a Leo, Scorpio or Capricorn Moon Sign or Ascendent—in which case she'll find it hard to chuckle when the joke's on her). There's no nonsense about this lady. She's sensible, down-to-earth, and she never pretends to be something she's not. She's real and genuine, honest and reliable—rather worth keeping.

As for him, he's made of more than his pride, vanity and self-centeredness. He's also made of sunshine and hope and confidence. His wisdom and benevolence are unmatched, when he feels he's really needed. The Lion will stand bravely against an army, to defend what he believes in his heart is right and true—just as he'll fight any force that threatens to harm the woman he loves, however uneven the battle may seem, even when the odds seem to be hopelessly against him. Whatever kind of pain she feels, whether it's physical or emotional, her pain is Leo's sworn enemy—something he must defeat, to prove his worth to his lady. Very much like the Knights who fought for King Arthur. Except that Leo is both Knight *and* King.

In his imagination, he lives in the Age of Chivalry, the Age of Romance. He belongs to another century, another time . . . when there were still worlds left to conquer, visions to follow, and dreams to dream. He tries hard to make the best of being lost somewhere on the time track, in a strange country where his leadership is not needed, and his ideals are not cheered. Even his white horse is gone. And the Holy Grail is only a memory from long ago. Leo, the Lion-Hearted, is therefore more wounded and lonely in spirit than those who see only his surface armour of arrogance ever guess.

No matter how many obstacles this man and woman face in achieving emotional harmony together, they'll stand by each other, against the whole world, if necessary. When fate brings sorrow or tragedy, neither of them will fail the test of loyalty. And that can be love's most enduring song—with or without the background music.

☆ ☆ ☆ ☆ ☆ ☆

TAURUS *Man* **LEO** *Woman*

————◄●►————

*Alas, he would not listen. He was
determined to show who was master in
that house.*

May a Bull aspire to own a queen? Most Bulls are more at home in a china shop than in the presence of royalty, and you know how flustered they are in a china shop. They're not frightened by the pomp and pageantry, but all that bowing and scraping and riding around in golden carriages—and coronations that last for days, while everyone gets tipsy, and stops working—is just plain "too much fuss and feathers" for the sensible Taurus man.

He isn't unappreciative of beauty. Most Taureans have a latent (or exposed) talent for artistic form, through painting, dancing, sculpting or music. But his biggest talent is looking at the world through practical glasses. He saves both his money and his emotions for a good cause, and throwing either away on red carpets and crowns is not, to his way of thinking, a good cause.

A Leo girl is looking for a man who recognizes her as a Queen, who can (in addition to cherishing and adoring her) provide her with the kind of life she knows she deserves. She wants a lover or mate who will allow her to live in the style to which she would like to become accustomed, surrounded by luxury and literate friends . . . an existence overflowing with beautiful clothes, parties and brainy conversations, with rings on her fingers, bells on her toes, and maybe even an occasional photographic safari to Africa—or summers on the Riviera. "July and August are so unpleasant in Manhattan (or Los Angeles) don't you agree? All those tourists." (Translation: peasants.)

You can understand then, why she feels a little tense and restless if the Taurus man she loves expects her to hang around in a small apartment, bringing him his beer and pretzels, while he watches television and reads the *Wall Street Journal* in his stocking feet. How mundane and plebeian. So she surprises him one night. She brings him a pitcher of ice cold Perrier water, with a slice of lime, and a delicate china plateful of Triscuits, spread with caviar—hands him *New York* magazine, folded to the back pages of the homes-for-sale listings (beginning at around $200,000) and lovingly tucks a cozy, comfy—and modish—pair of house slippers from Saks' on his feet. He mumbles his gratitude softly, and smiles at her affectionately.

The next night, when she comes home from the hairdresser late (because he didn't give her money for a cab, and the subways were crowded), he's still sitting there, grumbling over her tardiness, with his beer and pretzels, watching the six o'clock news on TV, in his stocking feet. The slippers were too tight, and anyway, he thinks men who wear house slippers are sissified. *New York* magazine? *What* magazine? House listings? *What* house listings? Later, she finds the magazine spread out neatly under the kitty litter box in the pantry. Obviously, something has to give. It won't be the Bull.

Bulls don't back away. They either hold their ground—or they charge. She's better off resigning herself to her Taurean lover or mate's holding his ground, than to risk goading him into charging. Believe me. Still, if she's willing to wait, and not rush him, he may someday provide her with all those things she seeks, including the rings on her fingers and bells on her toes—maybe even a lovely home in the suburbs, or a wonderfully warm and beautiful remodeled barn in the country, complete with fireplaces, beams or rafters, and the sweet scent of new-mown hay drifting through the windows each morning. He may not reach his goal of security overnight, but she'll never find a man with a better chance (counting her invaluable help) to someday present her with her very own kingdom over which to rule. Just give him time, and *don't nag him.*

In 1971, when I visited the Hearst "castle" in California, the estate of the late William Randolph Hearst (a Sun Sign Taurus), the image of the Bull was everywhere. A determined Taurean male, slowly but surely building a newspaper empire, stacking up millions, then creating—from a private dream of love in his incurably romantic heart—a solid, tangible faerie-tale castle, not imaginary in any sense of the word. The furniture in the several-hundred-odd rooms is massive. Everything in and on the estate is bigger than Life, bigger than it need be, typical of the Taurean admiration for plain and simple *hugeness.* The larger, the better, for the Bull. Wherever I looked, I could see the Venus taste for life's "necessary luxuries," like the gold bathroom fixtures, pure silk wallpaper, thick Persian rugs, and ornate (large, of course) expensive marble statuary.

Every male Bull should drop by the Hearst castle to see what Taurus dreams look like when they finally come true. If he's in love with a Lioness, by all means, he should take her along. She'll be enthralled, and purr like a kitten all the way home. It will perhaps then dawn on her that his stocking feet are leading him in the same direction—and if she helps, not hinders, his plodding path, he'll get there. This could be just the male who might someday give the Lioness her very own yacht for her birthday. (Maybe she'd better image that occasion as their anniversary. He'll probably be much more sentimental about the latter date than the former.)

When the Bull has finally accomplished his mission in life—a comfortable home, and a large collection of Washingtons, Lincolns and Jeffersons (not paintings—green bills), the Lioness will surround him with her own touches of richness. She'll see that he's comfy and cozy, padding around in his stocking feet on thick carpets, under soft lights, to the sound of stereophonic violins, smothered with constant attention and bathed in a smooth, serene existence. Nothing could make him happier.

But while he's still laying the foundation and digging the hole for the cornerstone, he won't want to take the time to dally at court. He'll resent being expected to run around to parties, play politics with her friends, wait on her royal whims and feather dust her throne. All that foolishness of continually pampering her pride and plumping up her ego seems to him like a shameful waste of time, and Bulls do not like to waste time, any more than they like to waste money (which, as you know by now, is not at all).

Although these two Sun Signs are square, and therefore capable of clashing violently over their differences, if they hang in there until the clouds start showing their silver linings, it could be super. They'll find each other great company as they wander through the tower rooms, feed the swans on the lake, share romantic dinners by candlelight, pull up the drawbridge over the moat, and pull on velvet ropes for the servants to turn down the satin sheets on their imported canopy beds. Yes, I said beds—plural. They'll probably have separate boudoirs, because the Lioness will likely want her own dressing room. She has to have, after all, some place to keep her creams, lotions, perfumes, bath oils and manes (hairpieces).

If they're patient . . . . well, Taurus is patient, so at least half the problem is solved. She, however, is a Fire Sign, and Fire Signs are all a little short on patience. It makes the preliminary period of castle building somewhat fraught with fretting and tricky tensions, all the way from minor molehills to major mountains. In the interim, while they're dreaming of their two monograms entwined inside a heart etched on their Fostoria, silver, linens and fine china, they can idle away what few leisure hours the Bull can afford, making love. It could be one of the few times when they'll be in complete agreement. On the other hand, it could not. Much depends on the Moon-Sun relationship between their horoscopes.

On the positive side of the Luminary harmony in their nativities, there's the physical compatibility they can reach together. A Leo woman is proud and aloof, even distant, with strangers. But when she's wrapped up in the arms of the man she truly loves, she becomes a fierce Lioness, who fairly oozes affection and sex appeal. The Bull won't fight with her when she's running her gentle hands through his hair, smoothing his skin, massaging his back, kissing his ear, and stroking his hand.

A Taurus man is almost helplessly vulnerable to the touch, the sound and the scent of his woman, and since Leo females nearly all adore perfume, he'll whiff away contentedly, like the peaceful Disney Ferdinand the Bull, in his most blissful state of ecstasy. His strength is awesome, yet this man is always in danger of becoming a Samson in the clutches of a sensuous, Leonine Delilah. He's ruled by Venus, and nothing brings him more peace of mind and spirit than fulfilling his deep, earthy romantic desires with a passionate Lioness—unless it's counting a stack of fresh, new green bills, or sniffing a home-baked apple pie, just out of the oven.

On the negative side, if the exchange of energies from the Sun and the Moon in their respective birth charts is square or opposed, there must be some heavy adjustments made in relation to the sexual harmony they achieve. He may slowly and gradually, but very finally, tire of trying to please her and to feed her insatiable ego, if he's forced to frequently sleep alone—or face her bored back in bed—when he hasn't made her feel cherished enough during the day to make her feel he deserves her royal favors at night.

Or perhaps she's the one who will slowly and gradually, but very finally, become weary of secretly wishing he'd try harder to fulfill her physical needs by making her feel adored and intensely desired, sexually. The Bull's sensual, down-to-earth, and sometimes unimaginative lovemaking may leave her lying awake beside him, hour after hour, dreaming of the Prince who never comes to claim her waiting heart . . . shedding quiet tears she's too proud to let him see, or to ever tell him about. And after a while, the warm-hearted, high-spirited and affectionate Lioness may become totally frigid.

Frigidity is ever a lurking danger with the instinctively passionate Leo woman. If she's continually neglected, from her fiery dreams and desires of youth she'll freeze into the cool detachment of the Leonine nature, a defense mechanism that's not natural, and is always very sad. Detachment because—what Queen would allow anyone to guess she isn't completely worshiped? Not even the Prince Consort who has so tragically failed her will be permitted to glimpse her broken heart, or be made aware of her terrible emptiness and loneliness. False pride is every Leo's Waterloo.

It's his bull-headedness and her false pride combined that keeps them both restless (or resigned) and unfulfilled. Somehow, there's a lack of honest communication between them. So they never discuss their individual lovemaking disappointments with one another—until love solidifies into nothing but a sort of comfortable familiarity and companionship—or shatters into divorce. Sometimes one or the other of these two lovers or mates will find escape through drink, drugs or casual affairs. But usually not. They're both too basically honorable to be disloyal, too conscious of their reputations to make public fools of themselves—yet too stubborn (him) and too proud (her) to seek a solution, tenderly and gently . . . together. But it's never too late for mutual confession and humility to create an unexpected miracle. They should both begin by remembering how it was between them when they first fell in love. The memory will soften them . . . and they can progress from there.

This is not a man who will appreciate his woman serving him dainty food, or pressing him into fastidious behavior at home or in public. She'll discover that the first time he yells at her, during dinner, "Where's the ketchup bottle?" "You call that a sandwich? Take it back to the kitchen and add a few layers." Or—"How about a coffee mug, woman? These little china things give me the willies."

Don't ask where he got the word "willies." Taureans have a way of manufacturing words that have a soft, cuddly sound, whether they're insulting or complimentary. Did you ever have a Bull call you "Honey"? It's an experience in total sensuality, which is no wonder, when they all have those deep, mellow, buttery voices, unmatched by any other man, except Scorpio.

She'll accuse him of being sometimes slightly uncouth, and nearly always obstinate, as, of course, he definitely is. He'll accuse her of being haughty, high-and-mighty, and snobbish, as, of course she definitely is. What do you do, when one's worst complaints against the other are justified and true? It's simple. (Not easy, but simple.) She'll have to comprehend that his lack of "couth" is simply indicative of his earthy, rather dependable nature, his contempt for the frivolous and the non-genuine— the phony. She'd do well to imitate it. She'll also have to recognize that his obstinacy indicates his strength of character, and stop deliberately inciting it by behaving like a spoiled Queen, who pouts when she doesn't win her own way. She can always get around his obstinacy if she tries, with amazing ease, simply by hugging and kissing and squeezing him into contentment again.

He must realize that her haughtiness is nothing but her inbred protection against exposing her fears of imagined inadequacy, therefore losing face and subjecting herself to painful ridicule—and stop deliberately causing it by refusing to acknowledge her very real superiority as a woman— and her deep need to be drenched in extravagant compliments. He can always get around her quite easily, by taking her out to sparkle in public more often, and showing her—especially *telling* her—that he's aware of how lucky he is to have married a very super lady, in all ways. (Every Leo woman *is* just that, never mind her little failings.) His Lioness is enormously capable of both giving and receiving love, if only she's properly appreciated . . . . . . and loved in return.

Whatever age the Bull may be, he's a Teddy Bear at heart, the chubby, high-chair-stage symbolic Baby of the zodiac (as described in "The Twelve Mysteries of Love," in the front of this book). I once knew a Leo woman who could not see her Taurus husband as any sort of "Teddy Bear," or cuddly in any way. She saw him only as a stubborn, mature man, who believed in nothing but "the practical," and who thought all sentiment was silly, sentimental rubbish. One day, I coaxed her into taking home to him a large stuffed, furry Bull. The kind of toy one normally gives to—yes, to a baby. He grunted.

That was it. Didn't even say "thanks." He completely ignored the furry image of himself—for weeks. The hurt and wounded Lioness placed it on the television, where he'd be sure to see it constantly, and still—not a word from the phlegmatic, undemonstrative Taurean. Then he became ill. During his illness, while he was asleep one morning, she happened to unthinkingly move the toy Bull from the television while she was cleaning. When her Taurus husband awoke from his nap, his roar could be heard all over the house. *"WHAT HAPPENED TO MY BULL? WHAT DID YOU DO WITH MY BULL? ! ! !"* he shouted. She'll learn.

The Bull and the Lioness will have to start listening to each other's silent, pleading hearts . . . . . . when what she's really saying, beneath her haughtiness, is—"Please, *show* me how much you love me" . . . . . . and what he's really saying, beneath his stony stubbornness, is—"Please, promise me you'll stay, and never leave me."

TAURUS

Earth — Fixed — Negative
Ruled by Venus (also by the
  Planet Pan-Horus)
Symbol: The Bull
Night Forces — Feminine

VIRGO

Earth — Mutable — Negative
Ruled by Mercury (also by
  the Planet Vulcan)
Symbol: The Virgin
Night Forces — Feminine

The **TAURUS-VIRGO** Relationship

. . . . . but on the whole the Neverlands have a
family resemblance, and if they stood still in
a row you could say of them that they have each
other's nose, and so forth.

Virgos admire the Taurus strength of purpose, although they have little tolerance for the Bull's stubbornness in the face of an obvious mistake. Taurus is somewhat in awe of the quick Virgo mind, though the Bulls have little sympathy for health nuts, cleanliness bugs or the finer nuances of Virgo hair-splitting.

But what are a few minor differences between friends? These two will normally find plenty of things to be friendly about, not the least of which is common sense. The phrase may at times, however, annoy the critical Virgo, since the Virgin knows the kind of sense referred to is far from common. It's extremely rare. Someday, you can be certain, some Virgo will finally succeed in correcting this particular inaccuracy in the language.

Taurus and Virgo will hang on firmly to their mutual principles while the rest of society is flipping out in an insane dance of tragedy—and frivolous foolishness. Neither the Bull nor the Virgin makes much of a distinction between tragedy and frivolous foolishness. In their sensible opinions, the latter is a direct path to the former. Virgos remember every flaw they have ever seen, from a torn shower curtain to a character defect in a friend. The memories are painful, and they keep the Virgins eternally disillusioned, not to mention pessimistic about human nature. Still, in a way, Virgos give the impression they almost enjoy their memories of the cracks and dusty corners of Life. It gives them something to do with their bright and busy minds. Taurus remembers everything he (or she) has ever seen too, though the Taurean really doesn't *want* to remember. There's a nagging voice inside the Bulls which tells them that wasting time is somehow sinful—and wasting it on things in the past you can't change is wasting it as surely as any other way. Yet, they helplessly cling to their old memories, and the lessons they've learned, as if they were graven on their foreheads in letters of stone. Taken as a whole, Virgos have more complicated fears (including their own health, and the danger of accident) than Taurus. Whatever the Bulls are afraid of, it's not physical.

This is not a lively pair you would want to hire to sell the Brooklyn Bridge in a hurry, collaborate on a book of faerie tales, promote a get-rich-quick stock in a bucket shop—or operate a fast-moving blackjack game in Las Vegas. These two were both born under feminine negative Earth Signs. Which means that they're passive and receptive (feminine)—suspicious, somewhat fearful and cautious (negative)—although loaded with integrity and dependability (Earth). It's a wonder they ever get around to meeting each other. However, once they gather the courage and aggressiveness to say "Hi!" to each other, and make a date to meet again (which will be kept punctually), the friendship, or business partnership, or whatever (usually a combination of both) will probably flower slowly, surely and serenely into a beautiful relationship. Within a family group, these are usually the two who get along smoothly together, and feel isolated from the rest of the radicals around the breakfast table.

I once knew a Taurus musician and a Virgo singer. They used to meet almost every morning in front of the Brill Building in New York (the headquarters of Broadway songwriters). The Bull was—and still is—an extremely talented composer. With or without formal musical training, he'll eventually make it to the top of his field. But he harbors the typical Taurean resentment against fate, because family responsibilities prevented him from attending Juilliard, and therefore he carries a fair-sized chip of wood on his shoulder (which can make your posture sag a little, along with your spirits, when you're also lugging around an electric guitar all day long).

This Bull is suspicious of singers who want to use his songs without paying him first, or signing a contract, and he also stubbornly refuses to let anyone sing his tunes if he thinks they're not right for him (or her). However, the Virgo male vocalist could usually talk the Bull into or out of anything. The Virgin singer (and of course I use the term Virgin symbolically) was picky and choosy about the material he recorded, and invariably wanted to change a note here or a word there in the lyrics, before he thought the song was perfect enough to match his perfect voice, and his perfect judgment of public taste. Still, he had fewer objections to the Taurean's songs than to anyone else's, because an association between Taurus and Virgo is influenced by the harmonious 5-9 Sun Sign Pattern. Somehow, they rang clear and true to his critical and acutely sensitive ear.

These two once considered a business partnership in a publishing company, but Virgo is ruled by the restless planet Mercury (until Virgo's true ruler, Vulcan, is discovered and identified) and so the Virgin singer eventually became annoyed and impatient with the Bull's lack of aggressive drive, left New York, and married a bright Sagittarian girl named Sharon, who cheered him up for a while (Sag and Virgo being a tense, 4-10 Sun Sign Pattern, it was a very short while, but they could still reconcile, when their stars cross again). It was good for him, however brief, because all Virgos desperately need cheering, and after being touched by Sag Sharon's Jupiter vibes of joy and luck, the Virgin vocalist finally drifted into other areas of show business he felt needed to be perfected by his kindly, courteous and meticulous attention.

Taurus just shrugged his strong shoulders, adjusted the wooden chip on his shoulder, and his guitar strap, kept plugging and plodding, and quietly waited for his big chance. (With Taurus, it has to be big—huge—or forget it.) Now I hear he's writing the musical score for a Hollywood film, featuring two top stars. Patience pays.

That's how Taurus often wins out over Virgo—in the area of patience. Taurus always has it. Virgo usually lacks it. Virgins can appear to be tranquil, calm and patient on the surface, but their minds are constantly ticking away, and tocking them with all sorts of inner frustrations when things don't happen as quickly or exactly in the manner they'd like. The flesh is willing, and able to remain on Earth (for a while) but the mental attitude is changeable and restive. Mercury is the true ruler of the Air

Sign Gemini, and is not at all at home in its temporary association with the Earth Sign of Virgo. Consequently (possibly through sheer boredom) the tricky Mercury sometimes agitates Virgins into behavior against their real natures, and contrary to their deepest desires. Virgos may take heart, however, for, as detailed in the Virgo-Virgo chapter of this book, when Vulcan is recognized and named, within a few years (or sooner) it will begin to express its powerful, magnetic vibrations through the personalities of all Virgins, causing them to be stronger, tougher—and less likely to switch horses, ideas, girls or career in the middle of the stream of Life's little annoyances and irritations.

Still, it will always be more natural for Taurus to succeed in a larger way than Virgo (which the Virgins don't really mind terribly) because Taurus is a Fixed Sign, "Fixed" meaning, astrologically, steady, organized and supremely capable of building a lasting foundation beneath a career, a house (making it an enduring home) or a marriage. Virgo is a Mutable Sign, "Mutable" meaning to change, to move around, to communicate between others, to carry information and truth back and forth, with both vertical and horizontal opinions. The Virgins don't feel a burning need to build a great empire or ride around in a flashy car to the sound of cheers, with ticker tape confetti falling all over them and messing up their neatly brushed hair. (Not to mention the rolls of squeezy-soft toilet tissue some people toss out the window at heroes in a parade—how vulgar can one be?)

Virgo's driving urge is to serve the world and all the individuals in it, or on it, by pointing out their faults—to bring order out of chaos and anarchy —and accumulate a reasonable amount of personal security for the future at the same time. If a Virgin should happen to wander beneath the glare of a spotlight of fame through an accident of Fate, he (or she) will blush, perhaps shyly enjoy it for a brief period, then often alienate the Press with critical remarks, express irritation with the clamoring, great, unwashed public—and finally exercise the Virgo birthright option to make a firm, clear-cut decision to retreat to the very private life most Virgos seek above all else.

Taurus wants to retire into seclusion too. And the Bulls usually have very definite ideas of where it will be. The country. Sooner or later, somewhere between the ages of six and sixty, every Bull, whether male or female, will gravitate heavily and fixedly toward the countryside—anywhere the Taureans can indulge their passion for the Good Earth, trees, grass and quiet streams, free from the interference of noisy, foolish, chattering people. But when the Bulls do finally settle down with the chickens and ducks and cows and haystacks, they don't want to depend on fickle Mother Nature's harvest for their security. This is why they'll endure the confusion and frivolity of the cities, no matter how many years it takes, so that when they leave, it will be with a large bundle under the arm—which will not be full of what the farmers use to make the grass grow green. Taurus people mistrust *that* substance, in *all* its forms. It will be filled with what is *already* green—beautiful, crisp pieces of currency, engraved with the glorious eagle of the United States of America. (Bulls are nearly always fanatically patriotic. Their motto is: "My country, right or wrong—my family, right or wrong—my friends, right or wrong—and last, but not least—my opinions, right or wrong.")

When Taurus and Virgo show a harmonious Sun-Moon aspect between their birth charts, in addition to the natural harmony of their 5-9 Sun Sign Pattern influence, they can happily retire together to the country. The Bulls will sit on their assets contentedly, while the Virgins dash back and forth to town for supplies . . . and to straighten things out now and then. Virgo may nag a little when Taurus is sloppy, and they may indulge in some affectionate bickering, like the characters in Neil Simon's *The Odd Couple* (who are, indisputably, a Bull and a Virgin, a Taurus-Virgo team), but on the whole, they'll be compatible.

It must be astrologically confessed that Virgos can be as opinionated as Taureans. The only difference is that the Bulls are opinionated in a Fixed, rather general sort of way, and the Virgins are opinionated in a hair-splitting, detailed sort of way. Once upon a time, there was a small Virgo boy, named Charles Edison Cameron. One day in grade school, in Fayetteville, North Carolina, Charlie's teacher goofed. A rather normal, unimportant trifling mistake, but the young Virgo simply couldn't bear it. The teacher placed two dots on the blackboard, across from each other, like so:

•   •

She then informed the class that these dots represented "two points." "Now," she instructed them, "the lesson today is to prove that a straight line is the shortest distance between two points. Do I have a volunteer?" Up shot the hand of anxious Virgo Charlie, a worried frown on his face.

"Teacher," he said, very respectfully and politely, "you are wrong. A straight line is not necessarily the shortest distance between two points." The teacher flushed, visibly annoyed. "Really?" she asked the eleven-year-old, Mercury-ruled youngster. "Would you like to step up to the blackboard and explain how you can dispute such a basic theory of mathematics?" Virgo Charlie trotted immediately to the blackboard, picked up the chalk and demonstrated the proof of his statement, as the entire class rocked with laughter and the teacher's face turned bright red. His demonstration looked somewhat like this:

"You see, Teacher," Virgo Charlie said courteously, after the laughter had died down, "that line appears to me like it could run all the way to China if it wanted, and golly knows how much further than that if it was goin' straight up, instead of around. So, how could a straight line be the shortest distance between two points?"

The teacher had, of course, neglected to take the horizontal-vertical aspect of her example into consideration. And she had also goofed on her terminology, using the word "between," instead of saying "the shortest distance *connecting* two points." It's a common mistake of educators, even erudite math instructors. But Virgo Charles Edison Cameron could not allow such an error of thinking and speaking to stand uncorrected. In the not too distant future, you'll be hearing more about Virgo Charles Edison Cameron, through a brilliant and blessed "breakthrough" invention of his which will be of even more importance to the world than the discovery of his namesake—so remember his name.

If Taurus and Virgo should ever decide to write a book together, the Bull will see to it that the plot is substantial. Virgo will supply the dialogue, correct the spelling and grammatical errors, punctuation and other mistakes. Taurus will then add some rich humor, market it wisely, and make sure it earns money. Sometimes people think Virgins are too timid and self-effacing, too courteous to be so super-critical. To these people, I submit a letter I received in 1970, shortly after the publication of my first book, *Sun Signs*. It reads as follows, verbatim:

> *Dear Ms. Goodman . . . I find, on page seventy-eight, line one, in the paperback edition of your book, Sun Signs, a mistake. I quote from the book the phrase: "the sandal clad people of Chaldea . . . ." The phrase should read, "the sandal shod people." Otherwise, you give the reader the impression that the Chaldean people wore sandals, and nothing else. Sincerely, Janine Hartman. P.S. I am a Virgo.*

I wish to take this opportunity to thank Janine. As for my other readers, please permit me to correct here and now the impression I may have given to modest Virgins, conventional Taureans and the like, that the people of

Chaldea all ran around naked, except for their footwear. My normally ultra-cautious and super-bright *Sun Signs* editor, Capricorn Bobbs Pinkerton, is properly chastised also. (A Ram may be excused for such carelessness, but *never* a Goat!) Isn't it fortunate that Janine added her P.S.? I would never have been able to guess her Sun Sign if she hadn't.

If there are any major publishing houses on the East or West Coast who are looking for a terrific copy editor, might I suggest they hire Janine? I'm sorry to say that in typical careless Aries fashion, I've mislaid the envelope with her address. But I feel certain I'll hear from her again, when she reads the Virgo–Virgo chapter of this book, and this time, I *promise* to hang on to her address. I think she's *neat!* My present scholarly Taurus editor, Dr. Charles Musès, agrees—*firmly*, of course.

☆ ☆ ☆ ☆ ☆ ☆

TAURUS *Woman* VIRGO *Man*

───●◆●───

". . . . here's the rock."

It's almost impossible for a Taurus woman to seduce a Virgo man. But she shouldn't allow herself to feel inferior over this. It's almost impossible for *any* woman to seduce a Virgo man. Remember that Narcissus is supposed to have been a Virgo (though if he was, he had an Aries Ascendent and the Moon in Leo). The reason astrological legend has labeled Narcissus as a Virgo is that most Virgos are somewhat self-centered, not in the egotistical sense of Leo, or in the spoiled sense of Aries, but in the symbolic sense that all technical, literal Virgins (both male and female) are absorbed in themselves, because they're unaware of what being totally awakened in all ways really means.

This man can't bear the thought of any sort of self-surrender. It implies a lack of self-discipline. He's not terribly interested in conquest either. So it's not surprising that he can't arouse much enthusiasm for Valentine's Day. However, the Taurus girl is a few strides ahead of her astrological sisters, should she decide to educate the Virgin in awareness of what makes the world spin for those who enjoy the ride. He may not chase her down Lovers' Lane with bated breath, but neither is he likely to run away from her. Since their natal Suns are trine to each other, there's a lot going for the relationship from the start. Their natures, goals and desires are similar. Influenced by a double Earth vibration, the almost always harmonious 5-9 Sun Sign Pattern, they're both steady, sensible types, who would rather be caught doing almost anything than messing around with fantasy, flightiness or fickleness. She's soothing, and has a nice, quiet voice. He's gentle and has clear enunciation. So, naturally, they don't grate on each other's nerves.

If the Taurus girl plays her cards right (which is a somewhat inappropriate metaphor, since few Earth Signs like to gamble) she can have him eating out of her hand before he knows what hit him—and even coming back for a late-night snack in her kitchen. What hit him will have been comfort. A female who speaks and moves so sensuously and slowly seldom makes mistakes. Unless you're a Virgo man yourself, you just can't imagine how comfortable it is to be around someone who's not always making mistakes and goofs you feel compelled to catch and correct. Didn't anyone ever tell you that compulsive criticizing isn't much fun? It can be exhausting.

Neither of them becomes angry very often or very easily. They have fairly tranquil, peaceful dispositions in common (though he may bite his nails and blink his eyes a bit more than she does). Still, when the Bull does lose her temper, it's quite a blast, never mind how rare, and it may leave deep scars. When Virgo finally works himself up into a snit, it's usually a relatively shallow, surface emotion, that doesn't last very long, and certainly doesn't drive itself deep into his soul. Worry is something else again. A Virgo man's worries do drive themselves deep inside of him, but not necessarily into his soul. They settle in the general region of the stomach and the intestines, which is why he's always poking about in her pantry when he stops for that late-night snack—to see if she has any Pepto-Bismol or Tums handy. Now, if she had a quick temper like other females, she might take offense at this apparent slur on her cooking. But the typical Taurus girl will accept all the little idiosyncrasies of her Virgo lover with equanimity, unless, of course, her Moon or Ascendent is in a more sensitive sign.

Virgos don't itemize their apprehensions every few minutes. They don't even holler about them every few hours. They can't see any point in airing them as often as once a year, and some Virgos keep their trembles locked up inside for decades. Do you have any idea what that can do to your digestive system, not to mention your subconscious or psyche? It's also the major cause of arthritis and rheumatism.

I've always felt that Hamlet may have had a Virgo Moon Sign, revealed when he said, "I could be bounded in a nut shell, and count myself king of infinite space, were it not that I have dreams." Virgos are normally quite satisfied with small, nutshell-like spaces in which to stretch their egos and ambitions. They're normally content to be hard working, polite and helpful—to spin their own little cobwebs of hope, without tramping all over everyone else. It's those darned dreams. Everyone knows (and certainly Virgo does) that bad dreams and nightmares from suppressed emotions can cause anything from an attack of gastritis and mild constipation to ulcers. That's where the Taurean woman comes into the picture. Not to nurse him, but to soothe him, with her practical philosophy about nightmares.

TAURUS: If you have a healthy mind and body, and fulfilled emotions, nightmares don't exist. Period.

VIRGO: But how can you keep your mind, body and emotions healthy, when everything around you is falling apart, the world is being run by raving madmen, and your car has a broken transmission, you've lost your umbrella, and missed your insurance payment, and your socks all have holes in them, and . . . . .

TAURUS: (firmly) People who are properly loved have healthy, happy, fulfilled minds, bodies and emotions. A nice, warm bath and a cup of good, nourishing soup can solve any problem. Give me your socks. I'll darn them.

She makes it sound so simple (and it is, really) that he'll stop worrying, because obviously, he is properly loved by a woman who is both sensible and sensuous. At least, he'll stop worrying temporarily, while he's chewing her crunchy carob brownies, and nibbling her fragrant ear lobe. A Virgo man is repelled by most artificial odors. He likes everything to be natural, as Mother Nature intended. But he rather enjoys the fresh, feminine smell of scented soap, especially on the ear of a sympathetic woman who listens calmly to his worries, without becoming all flustered about them herself. She's an excellent listener, and he can be a pretty fascinating talker. A Virgo man's conversation is usually highly intelligent, clever, bright and interesting, even if it's not always terribly punchy.

Sexually, both of them fall under the category of the silent type. *She's* silent because she prefers to partake in lovemaking undistracted by verbal romantic coquetry, just drowning in the intimacies of union with the man she loves so deeply. *He's* silent because he can't think of many wild or spontaneous things to say about sex anyway, and even if he could, he'd probably be too embarrassed to say them in mixed company (the two of them alone together *are* mixed company—to Virgo). He's not frigid, and he has nothing against sex. In fact, a Virgo male can create great beauty in the physical expression of love by blending desire with emotional tenderness, stimulated by mental excitement. But he's not moved to a single tremble or tremor by the kind of sex that lacks the qualifying aspect of its higher purpose. She won't object to that attitude—no real woman would. She'll probably believe she's lucky to share with him an experience of such gentle affection and passion, and she's right. She is. Virgo love burns with an intense white heat that fulfills with a more mystical depth than the brief, red flame of more casual lovers.

Not that he doesn't know how to employ the light touch of romance, if and when he chooses. This man isn't the kind to fall asleep in the middle of making love, no matter what you've heard. (He's too wide awake from worrying about whether or not his partner is pleased with his sexual behavior.) Some Virgo men indulge in dozens of light-as-a-feather affairs, because they're experts in the art of playing at love. And so an occasional Virgo male will attract promiscuous women, with loose morals. They feel safe with him. Because he takes it all so casually, they sense there won't be any unnecessary emotional scenes of jealousy. Just good, clean Virgo fun. However, since this man never seeks a party girl for a mate, he soon tires of the shallowness of the game, and then he's ready for a permanent relationship. If he should happen to be strolling through a Taurus girl's garden about that time, he'll be enormously susceptible to a serious romance, followed by marriage. To state it plainly, he's a sitting duck.

She'll have to remember, however, that marriage is not a natural condition for a Virgin, although if anyone can make matrimony seem to be more cozy than confining, it's a Taurean female. As long as she doesn't make him feel possessed, he'll be putty in her hands. She needn't worry about giving him too much freedom. No matter how much rope she gives him, he'll probably only use it to find his way home to her in the dark. He's rather a creature of habit, when all's said and done. He's grown accustomed to her face, to her fragrant ear, his own private shower, the fresh orange juice she squeezes for him every morning, and his shirts all nicely stacked in the drawer, with no ring-around-the-collar. So how is he going to be able to get used to hanging his socks on a strange towel rack? Especially when the neatly darned toes and heels would be sure to remind him of her, and cause him to have an attack of the guilties on the spot.

He may fail to see why she needs to surround herself with so many luxuries, and she may complain that his ideas of personal comfort are somewhat Spartan, but neither of them are inclined to throw away money with careless abandon—so finances will seldom be a subject of contention. With or without a harmonious Sun-Moon aspect between them, this man and woman can rely on the smooth empathy of the 5-9 vibration to mist each misunderstanding with sympathy, and soften each argument with forgiveness. It's not easy to please a Virgin, but the Taurean woman can come mighty close to doing it, and she's capable of touching her Virgo man's skeptical heart with her own special kind of warm, unselfish devotion. If she sticks to it (and that's where much of her talent lies—in sticking to things) she may, after a while, learn the knack of Virgo criticism herself. Then she can send him a Valentine, in verse, that says . . . . . (in part)

> . . . . . *to be absolutely honest*
> *as you've carefully taught me to be*
>   *you're still a little off center*
> *investigating truth*
>   *without consequences*
> *and doing your thing . . .*
>   *playing with platitudes*
> *reading books about Buddha*
> *to learn how to die, before you've started to live*
> *straining emotions through a sterile sieve*
> *and scrubbing your squeaky-clean ivory tower*
>   *with Brillo pads*
> *each morning*
> *. . . but you're improving**

☆ ☆ ☆ ☆ ☆ ☆

TAURUS *Man* VIRGO *Woman*

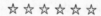

> *"It is so naughty of him not to wipe," Wendy*
> *said, sighing. She was a tidy child.*

Virgo girls turn up their pretty noses at messes. Most of them are as neat as pins. There may be a Virgin here or there whose surroundings are a lit-

---

* From *Venus Trines at Midnight* by Linda Goodman.

tle cluttered. But her mind is always well dusted, and sliced into precise thoughts—and there's probably no loose tobacco in the bottom of her handbag.

In August of 1974, I was having lunch with a Virgo newspaper reporter. We were discussing her Sun Sign, and she remarked, "I'm not at all hooked on that Virgo neatness compulsion. I let my trash can overflow for days before I get around to emptying it."

"Sure," I told her, "that's because you don't like to get your hands dirty." Then I stared pointedly at her fingers, and her poise shattered like fragile glass.

"Why are you staring? Oh, this smudge? That isn't dirt. It's my ring. I have a lot of acid in my system, and gold turns my skin green when I get nervous. I thought I got it all off when I washed my hands an hour ago, but—well. I know it looks like dirt, but it isn't, and—uh, waitress! Where is your powder room please?"

One of the barriers between a Virgin and a Bull is that a Taurus man is inclined to be a teeny bit untidy. Some of them are downright sloppy. And a few Bulls are just plain slobs. They love beauty and luxury around them, but they're too busy making the bread that buys it to be bothered picking lint off their trousers, combing their forelocks into neat curls, sweeping up their crumbs and ashes, draping their sweat shirts on satin hangers, or polishing their shoes to a high gloss. The practical Bull may worship currency, but not to the extent where he feels compelled to launder all his bills and press them with a hot iron. To Taurus, wrinkled money is still money, as good as gold. Just like a man with a wrinkled shirt is still a man (perhaps more so than those chaps with their ruffled cuffs and velvet lapels)—and also as good as gold. An occasional Taurean will place an emphasis on grooming, but he won't make a fetish of it. As long as he's scrubbed and clean, he's not going to worry if his shoelaces aren't tied in neat bows or one sock dips down a quarter of an inch lower than the other.

There's a misconception about Virgo girls which may shock the Bull who discovers it. Naturally, all Virgos aren't Virgins, but it goes deeper than that. Her love of order and her sharp foresight, based on a highly developed critical sense, make her seem conventional to the point of being puritanical. But she is not necessarily Beth, of Louisa May Alcott's *Little Women*. The Virgo puritanical morality is an astrological myth. After all, you can be courteous, gracious and discriminating without being a prude.

She investigates the facts, observes the action, works it all through her mathematical thought processes, and forms a clear opinion (usually unspoken) of what's best for everybody. However, what her acute observations have led her to believe is best for everybody can be anything from building more convents to encouraging more nude group therapy. It depends. Her moral attitude is intellectual, and her emotions are seldom involved (unless she has the Moon in a more sensitive Air or Fire Sign). Virgos are as curious as they are critical. How can you correct a flaw if you haven't examined the vase? So, this girl is often accused of (or given credit for?) a stuffy sort of morality she doesn't possess.

The Bull doesn't talk much about his ethics or morals. He *feels* what is right or wrong, then acts with blind determination, and very little reflection on the intricacies of the issues. When their different methods of arriving at the truth lead them to the same conclusion, things are pink and rosy. But when they take a mental detour, these earthy lovers can bury each other in frozen silence and unbending stubbornness.

I was once a helpless bystander during a quarrel between two friends, a Virgo girl and her Taurus lover. We had all three been rapping about the Aquarian Age sexual revolution, its implications and various by-products, from the vulgarity on the newsstands to capitalizing on sexual lust and violence in films, all in the name of glorious freedom from censorship. Before I had a chance to air my personal views, these two began to challenge each other.

TAURUS: Sex, sex, sex, I'm so tired of hearing about it, and reading about it. You'd think it was only discovered yesterday, the way it's headlined as news continually.

VIRGO: (musing thoughtfully) Maybe if prostitution were legalized everywhere, it would help.

TAURUS: Help what—the prostitutes?

VIRGO: Well, sex isn't going to disappear, and it's possible that these women serve a useful purpose for their customers.

TAURUS: (his neck turning bright red, and bristling in anger) Yeah? Well, their "customers" are buying a lie.

VIRGO: True. Nevertheless, a lie may be just the fantasy needed by the emotionally crippled, and these women could be providing a sort of physical therapy for such men.

TAURUS: (beginning to paw the ground) I'm sure glad I found out your attitude toward morality before I married you.

VIRGO: (still cool and unruffled) To accuse human beings of wrongdoing, and then condemn or punish them, will never change anything. If you must be so judgmental, try to learn to hate prostitution, *not* the prostitute. Direct your anger toward the *crime*, not the *criminal*. The problem with your attitudes is that they're always so dogmatic, and you never attempt to exercise *discrimination* (Virgo's favorite word).

TAURUS: (now aroused to the full fury of the Bull) The problem with *your* attitudes is that you don't know how to be *firm* (the Bull's favorite word) about anything, including your opinions. You can't place a financial value on emotion. It's less than human. I never thought you would defend such a thing. I thought you were a nice, decent woman. What's wrong is *wrong*. And it's wrong to sell love. So that's that.

VIRGO: It's only natural that *men* would prefer to have women *give* their "human emotions" away, free of charge, rather than *sell* them.

TAURUS: Don't give me that feminist double-talk.

VIRGO: I think it's curious that most people who are so critical of prostitution are quite permissive regarding sexual promiscuity. The very ones who despise prostitutes (*excluding* you, of course, dear) are the same ones who believe that casual sex, without commitment, is very glamorous and "in," and anyone who doesn't go along is hopelessly straight and square. That's disgustingly hypocritical. I still say that prostitution exists because it treats an illness of society itself, the *same* society that condemns the prostitutes.

TAURUS: It treats a *symptom*.

VIRGO: Then, like I said, why not treat the *cause?*

I'm sorry I can't tell you the final outcome of their argument, because my taxi came, and I had to leave before it was resolved. However, that brief (and actual) portion of their conversation should clear up any muddy, preconceived astrological notions that every female Virgo Virgin is a nun-like Miss Innocent—and every male Bull is a coarse, erotic creature of lust, snorting in passion at all the cows in the pasture.

If Carrie Nation reincarnated today, and began waving her hatchet at prostitutes on street corners, there might well be more "sensual" Bulls and "sexy" Scorpions following behind her and yelling "Right on!" than supposedly "puritanical" Virgos—which would surprise everybody but astrologers. The Virgins would probably be eloquently urging Carrie to use her hatchet on the porno theatres and newsstands where the concentration on sexual excess is first encouraged—to attack the root of the matter, not its branches—with the typical Virgo-like ability to *analyze* and *discriminate*, while remaining cool to misleading emotional attitudes.

It takes Virgo to figure out that the massive rise in sexual abuse of children, venereal disease, abortion, and the great increase in rape the feminists are so outraged about, is not the fault of the prostitutes. Prostitution has always been around—as an outlet for the emotionally deprived and disturbed. Virgo calmly comprehends that the true guilt for deliberately arousing the emotionally healthy to join and increase the ranks of the disturbed lies *elsewhere*—in places other than the brothels.

After a while, the Taurus man will grow to appreciate his Virgo girl's own special brand of honesty, and realize that her tendency to avoid labels, and to analyze things before hastily judging them, is a definite virtue, not a vice. It takes time. She might even someday cause her affectionate Bull to admit that a woman who was once a prostitute was the only one who really *believed* the man who promised her he would conquer death— the only one of all his fervently devout apostles and followers to go to his tomb on Easter morning to seek him—while all the hypocrites were either weeping in lack of faith, or running around trying to figure out how to escape the wrath of the Roman soldiers, some even going so far as to deny they ever knew him.

A Virgo girl who's in love with a dogmatic-type Bull may have to convince him that her views on public morality don't necessarily reflect her private code of behavior. Like Caesar, a Taurus man expects his woman to be above reproach. She probably is, although she may not be above reproaching *him*, if he turns sex into a subject for humor. To her, sex is a beautiful, pure emotion that deserves respect—and a good deal of concentration and practice to make it perfect. Her cool, analytic approach may initially chill the Bull's more direct and sensual lovemaking attitudes, but they'll probably find a way around such a temporary impasse between them. As with the other 5-9 Sun Sign Patterns, romantic love and sentimental affection will play equally as important a part as passion in their sexual union. Most of the time, this man and this woman will be wonderfully able to fulfill each other's silent needs, through the rare intimacy of understanding common to all 5-9 vibrations, especially to those of the Earth Element.

Practicality may not sound like a romantic word. Yet, with these two, it can form a deep and comforting bond between them, a strong cord to encircle their love. Neither Virgo nor Taurus is the kind to indulge in passionate emotions for no reason, or to become enraged over things that can't be helped by anger. He may brood a little—and she may have some mild attacks of indigestion—but on the whole, they'll both agree with the alcoholic's creed: "Give me the grace to change the things I can, to accept the things I cannot, and the wisdom to know the difference." (It's doubtful, though, that they heard the words at an AA meeting. It takes tremendous pressure and unbearable anguish to drive a typical Earth Sign to either drink or drugs.) When the rest of the world seems to be crazily dipping back and forth, she feels safe only with him—and should he happen to bump into the uncontrolled, abrasive emotions of a stranger, he'll run back to the security of her arms, the refreshing, quiet stream of her controlled feelings. He'll say something richly humorous that strikes her funny, she'll laugh her little Virgo silver bell laugh . . . . . and then "practicality" can become a very romantic word. She may be finicky, yes—but unreasonable? Never.

There's a chain of sympathy, bright and golden, connecting the Virgo girl's obsession for "little things" with the Taurus man's enjoyment of the senses. He likes the way new pencils smell like cedar. She adores sharpening them to a fine point. He likes the crisp, clean, cold feel of falling snow on his cheeks . . . . she's fascinated by the tiny, glittering stars it makes on the sidewalk. He likes to chew pine needles, to taste their fresh, green, spicy Christmas smell. She loves to pick them up and place them in neat stacks, one by one.

The Virgin and the Bull can spend their lives together drenched in the ecstasy of contemplating all the small and ordinary wonders around them. It's such a fiercely gorgeous (and natural) "high"—if only they don't smother it by expecting too much. The eternal perfection she seeks is a mirage. The eternal security he seeks—likewise. They're both looking for a sure thing. But the nearest they may ever come to a sure thing is each other.

TAURUS

Earth — Fixed — Negative
Ruled by Venus (also by the
Planet Pan-Horus)
Symbol: The Bull
Night Forces — Feminine

LIBRA

Air — Cardinal — Positive
Ruled by Venus
Symbol: The Scales
Day Forces — Masculine

The **TAURUS-LIBRA** *Relationship*

"Oh, well, if you look at it that way . . . . . ."
"What other way is there to look at it?"

nyone who wants to understand an association between Taurus and Libra (both presently ruled by Venus) should contemplate the elements. That's the first step to knowing who's on first and what's on second in any kind of ball game involving two very different individuals.

Don't jump to the hasty conclusion that the earthy Taurean is much stronger than the airy Libran, and that both of them could be burned to a cinder by a raging Fire Sign like Aries, Leo, or Sag. Both Earth and Fire may appear to be more dangerous than Air. Earth is certainly heavier. Fire is certainly more consuming. We all know what damage an earthquake, or a flaming volcano, can do. Surely a mass of Air (the essence of Libra), ethereal as it is, and constantly moving around—can't do much harm, compared to a solid mountain of Earth, like Taurus.

You'll have to turn to physics and chemistry for the truth. Air is the chief nourisher of life. We all need air to breathe, therefore it's comforting, not to mention handy, to have around. But are you aware that, statistically, air kills more people every year, in one way or another, than all the other elements combined? Air may be invisible. It may have no definite shape, and it certainly doesn't seem capable of affecting anything as material as Earth. However, if you've ever been lolling around among the coconuts in the South Sea islands when a typhoon struck, you'll know that things aren't always what they may seem. Especially Air. And especially Libra, the *Cardinal* of the three Air Signs (the other two being Gemini and Aquarius). Libra represents the astrological Air Element in its most active form. End of lesson. End of moral. End of warning? Yes, that's better—end of the warning to those Bulls who think they can plant a heavy foot on the Libra Scales and topple these pleasant people into submission.

In no way, dear Bulls, is Libra passive. Yet Libra may appear to be a pushover for a tougher personality. Here is this absolutely charming person (except when he or she is playing "cranky crocodile"), this dimpled, beautiful (or handsome) creature, with bright, intelligent eyes, a smile that warms the cockles of the heart, and the serenity of the spirit, a bland, innocent expression—and a voice that's faintly reminiscent of church bells, ringing high in the Swiss Alps.

Surely a person of such obviously gentle amiability couldn't possibly be a threat. Ah, but that Libra smoothness of manner is but a soft camouflage which enables the sharp spear of the Libran's clever, logical mind to penetrate, *with a minimum of resistance*. Libra knows very well that the immature rashness of Aries, the rude frankness of Sagittarius, the arrogance of Leo—and the immovable obstinacy of Taurus—are nothing but obstacles to success. They're detrimental to the carrying out of one's real purpose—winning the controversy and getting one's own way, which is all that counts in the final analysis, to Libra. And that sort of deduction, in itself, you must admit, is a clear and indisputable display of Libra logic.

If you don't believe these insights, check with your Republican senator or congressman, regarding both their personal and group confrontations with Libran President Jimmy Carter—or with someone who served in the Armed Forces, under the immediate command of Libran Dwight Eisenhower—or perhaps with some of the former lovers and husbands of Libran Brigitte Bardot. Maybe someone who tried to move Libran Eleanor Roosevelt from her determined, but flower-strewn, path—or anyone who's ever tangled with Libran author Truman Capote, verbally or otherwise. You will receive immediate confirmation of the astrological facts. And never mind seductive Venus. Venus being the ruler of all Librans, it's only logical that Librans of both sexes tend to operate in the traditional Venus (or feminine) way. And all you male chauvinists know how women manage to get their own way by sweetly charming the enemy into surrender. Libra lads are very much like Libra ladies in this respect.

You say that Taurus is also ruled by Venus? Yes, but with serious reservations. Venus is not the true or natural ruler of the Bulls. Taurus is only borrowing the guidance and influence of Venus from Libra, until the *real* Taurean ruling planet, Pan-Horus,* is telescopically discovered and once again identified. Therefore, although the Bulls also have the benefit of Venus sweetness, tenderness, and softness, she doesn't bestow upon them quite *all* of her favors (such as her secret strategy) as she does with Librans. Rather like a woman who doesn't tell all her secrets to every man she guides and influences—only to her true lover, the one who possesses her heart. Pan-Horus will shower Taureans with *other* kinds of power. Wait. (The Bulls will. They're patient.)

There's a general inertia in the nature of the average Taurus man, woman, or child, that causes the Bulls to instinctively acquiesce to the customs of their community, office, classroom, or family circle—to the conventions of society and the laws of their government. If you cross-examine the Bulls, however, you'll find that they don't necessarily obey because they believe all these people and laws are right. It's because the typical Taureans are convinced that ignoring convention or flaunting the law might bring trouble and disharmony, a state of affairs that Venus warns the Bulls to avoid, at whatever cost—the same tip she gives to Librans, you see. It's just received and utilized in different ways by these two. Once a Taurean is driven too far, he or she doesn't lack either strength or courage. Far from it. When it reaches push-to-pull, the Bulls of any age, and both sexes, will defend both their personal principles and their loved ones, fiercely. (You'd better believe it!) But Taurus sees absolutely no sense in stirring up muddy waters or risking violent agitation, just to win a minor point.

Libra does. Winning an intellectual point or decision, however minor, major—or in the middle—is the reason for the Libra person's very existence, symbolized by the Libra Scales, balanced in perfect harmony and justice. If there's any sort of controversial issue at stake, the typical Taureans will simply yawn, or shrug, and state calmly (in those rich, mellow voices that compete with the Libra buttery, whipped-cream voices for sheer appeal) that it doesn't make the slightest difference to them *what* happens in a matter too small to interest them—or one too large to concern

* See footnote page 68.

them. But nothing is too small or too large to need Libra's careful weighing and balancing and judgment.

Should the bathroom be painted pink or green? Should we impeach the President? Does an electric toothbrush get your teeth cleaner? Should the police crack their clubs over the heads of youngsters who are only expressing their idealism and their disgust with hypocrisy? (The big Libra issue of the sixties.) *On the other hand,* should the young people insult the police by calling them "pigs," when they're only trying to do their duty and keep the peace? Is censorship to be tolerated in a land dedicated to freedom of speech and thought? *To look at the other side,* in all fairness, is the lack of basic censorship responsible for the moral degeneration of youth in this country? Will such permissive attitudes lead to America's downfall, as it led to the extinguishing of other great civilizations, such as Babylon, Atlantis, and Rome? But then, *to reconsider,* how can there be liberty if there is censorship of any kind? Is jogging healthy or unhealthy? Should everyone be required to use solar heat (instead of nuclear power) and waterless toilets—for serious ecological reasons? Do the AMA and the FDA have the public's—or their *own*—best interest at heart? Or is this century someday to be known as the "Dark Age" of healing? If the bathroom is painted pink, instead of green, will it clash with the yellow towels? If it's painted green, instead of pink, will it look like a hospital room?

You can understand why Librans have to rest a lot. It isn't fair to call them lazy. When you engage in all that mental activity from the time you wake up in the morning, and can't decide which side of the bed to get out on—until the time you go to sleep at night, and can't decide whether to wear the top or the bottom of your nighty-nights—you're bound to feel a little weary and exhausted once in a while. Not to mention a little edgy.

Most Taureans can get weary and exhausted just from listening to a Libra contemplating all those decisions. It sounds like insanity to the Bulls. Just do what you feel (and therefore *know*) is right, don't let anyone budge you an inch from your position—and SHUT UP about it. That's the average or typical Taurean's philosophy about decisions, in a neat nutshell. To the Bulls, constant argument is the most futile, wasteful, and therefore the most sinful, occupation they can imagine. No one ever really wins an argument except the person who manages to fall asleep and snooze until it's over. No one ever emerges victorious from a debate, right?

Wrong. Librans do. They emerge victorious from all of them, except the ones with which they become quickly bored. It's no wonder they win, when you think of the Libra weapons, smuggled to them by Venus. Charm. Tact. Dimples. (*Somewhere* on their bodies they have dimples. Every last one of them. Whether they show or not.) Where were we?

Dimples. Intelligence. Flattery. Optimism. A serene and soothing manner.
Those satiny voices. That incredible smile that bursts upon their features
like an explosion of pure Sunlight. That gorgeous laugh. And besides all
these powerhouse weapons, they have the sneakiness to use against you
their spears of logical deduction when you least expect it. I can't stress this
danger often enough to the Bulls, who believe their own passive resistance
will eventually wear down the Libra friend, relative, business associate,
lover, or mate who's trying to prod them, gently, into either verbal or physical action of some kind.

The arguments Libra initiates, manipulates, and finally wins with
Taureans, can cover everything from politics to religion. As for the latter,
I once overheard a conversation between a Libran Catholic priest (a
Jesuit, naturally) and an obstinate young Taurean, who had stubbornly refused a scholarship to Notre Dame and was bullheadedly determined to
become a professional football player. Notice that the subject of football is
not even mentioned.

Beginning of Conflict:

LIBRA: (initiating) I suppose you claim to believe in God?

TAURUS: I most certainly do.

LIBRA: Then, why don't you pray to Him, regarding your vocation, if
          you aren't *sure* whether or not you want to study law?

TAURUS: I *am* sure I don't want to study it. (Libra loses the first round.
          But no matter. The trick didn't work. *This* time.)

LIBRA: (moving right along) But, just in case you *might* be mistaken,
          why don't you pray?

TAURUS: Because I'd feel silly, that's why. Prayer isn't scientific.

LIBRA: And yet, you say you believe in God?

TAURUS: (stubbornly) Of *course* I do. I *told* you I do.

LIBRA: (speaking gently) Then how is it that you don't believe He is
          wise enough and compassionate enough to guide you?

TAURUS: Because I've never heard God talking. No one has. It isn't sci-
          entific.

LIBRA: You don't believe He can answer prayers? A God you believe in
          so strongly? How can God be so powerless?

TAURUS: I just told you. I never heard him speak. Scientifically, there's no
          way He *could* speak.

LIBRA: I see. You won't be satisfied until God appears to you in solid
          flesh, and says, "Hey! Why don't you become a scientist? You'd
          make a great one! Forget about law school, young man. Your

destiny lies elsewhere," as He spoke to Moses, behind the burning bush.

TAURUS: (genuinely shocked) How did you know I'd rather be a scientist than a lawyer?

LIBRA: (flashing a heavenly Venus smile of victory) Because I prayed for you this morning, at mass—and suddenly, God revealed it to my subconscious. He answered my prayer, as you can see, without speaking a single word.

TAURUS: Gee! Okay, Father. From now on, I'll say a prayer everytime I need to make a decision. Could you see about getting my scholarship changed from law school to biology? I wasn't even sure what I wanted to do until you just made me see. Would you call it a divine revelation?

LIBRA: That's exactly what it was, my young friend. That's what happens when you pray. I'll check with an associate of mine at Notre Dame tomorrow, and let you know before the day is over.

End of Conflict.

Librans use what is known as the "Socratic method" of discussion. You have to watch them closely. And listen carefully. A Taurean who is too busy resisting to pay attention to Libra logic can trip on his (or her) own obstinacy.

This is an association influenced by the 6-8 Sun Sign Pattern, which means that Taurus represents the eighth astrological house of intriguing mystery (among other matters) to Libra. Of course. Libra would adore to solve the mystery of how the Bulls manage to remain so tranquil, and untouched, by all the raging personal and public controversies around them, so untormented by mental traumas, so frustratingly able to sleep throughout the night, like peaceful babies, never suffering the insomnia of decision-making that tortures Librans, sometimes until dawn—when the Good Lord knows they need their beauty sleep, their rest, as much as Taurus, even more, to keep their equilibriums in balance.

Libra represents, to Taurus, the sixth astrological house of service, among other things. Of course. Didn't our budding scientist Taurean somehow manage to persuade the Libra priest to provide the service of pulling a few strings for him at Notre Dame? Just by kidding around about wanting to play pro football? When *this* Bull was born, his natal Sun was in Taurus, but the Moon and Ascendent were both in Libra.

★ ☆ ★ ☆ ★ ☆

TAURUS *Woman* LIBRA *Man*

———◆———

Now I understand what had hitherto been bothering me.
. . . . this trick had been in his head all the time.

She is sad about something. It doesn't matter what it is. The world is dark and dismal, and there's no hope that anything will change. Life is real, Life is earnest, Life is serious, Life is monotonous—and Life is certainly negative. She's a Taurus girl, indulging herself in a rare, but ever-so-deep and blue, binge of futility.

Along comes a Libra man. He sits down quietly next to her, takes her hand gently in his own, and looks at her softly, in silence, after offering her his large, clean handkerchief. She continues to frown, in abject misery. *Men!* Men are part of what's wrong with everything. And here's another one of them, trying to feed her a line so he can seduce her. But wait. *This* one isn't saying a word. He's just sitting there near her, very near . . . . . . peacefully pouring calm all over her, like olive oil—and gazing at her with . . . . is it adoration? Whatever it is, it's romantic. Then, after a long while, he speaks.

"Never mind, darling. You'll feel better tomorrow." His voice is like creamy-smooth caramel candy—and oh, how she loves creamy-smooth caramel candy! (So does he, although it's very bad for both of them.) But even this doesn't cheer her. No. Life is real, Life is dull, Life is a great big nothing. Life is a put-on and a put-down. Both.

"No, I won't feel better tomorrow. *I won't. I won't. I won't.*"

Libra speaks again, still sweetly. "You're so beautiful when you're sad. Tears make your eyes sparkle like green emeralds. If it didn't break my heart to know you're unhappy, I'd like to see tears in them all the time. Let's see how they look when you laugh."

Life is real, Life is—well, Life is getting more interesting. But—"No, I can't laugh. I want to, but I can't. I simply *can't.*"

"You *must.* Darling, if you believe long enough, and deeply enough, all good things will come to pass. Not a single dream you ever dreamed will fail to come true, if you keep your emotional balance and look at the bright side." Now, he smiles. A Libra smile is a deadly weapon that should be outlawed, so Libra men could never use it to take advantage of poor Taurus girls, who melt into squidgy fudge ripples when they're shown affection—and are truly appreciated. But so far, they haven't been outlawed. So . . . he smiles.

"Tomorrow will be better. It really will. You'll see."

"No, it won't. I want it to be better, but I just know it won't."

Then he kisses her. *It will.*

Everything will be better tomorrow. The Sun will shine, the flowers will blossom, the dew will be on the buttercups—and the female Bull will be deeply in love for keeps with a charmer who was only trying to be kind, and who may be confused when he discovers that what his romantic sentiment actually meant to her was an ironclad contract of loyalty, for better or for worse, in sickness and in health, for richer or for poorer—seven days a week, twelve months a year—for as many years as they both shall live.

"I do."

The voice you just heard was that of the Libra man, addressing the minister. He didn't have the heart to hurt her, and couldn't decide what excuse to give her, so he thought—"What the heck?" (Librans normally don't swear or curse. Prostitute that heavenly voice with obscenities?) At least, not when they're young enough to say *"I do"* for the first time, they don't swear. After a few marital mistakes, they may occasionally gosh-darn the institution of marriage that so magnetizes them.

So . . . what the heck? Why not smell the buttercups, and let her tuck him in at night with passionate kisses, between soft blankets of love? "Why *not*? Why *shouldn't* I marry her? It's *my* Life, isn't it? Marriage is a wonderful thing, she's a beautiful girl, so what's *wrong* with marrying her?"

You see? Already he's trying to start an argument, just like a Libran. Nobody *said* he shouldn't marry her. Did you hear me say that?

It's possible the Libra lover will find he's made the right decision by not making a decision to charm his way out of the Taurus girl's feminine, appealing wiles. They'll probably be as happy as two turtledoves, as they walk, hand in hand, from room to room, through their rose-covered cottage in the country—or if their dreams have been briefly delayed, through their soot-covered apartment in the city.

THE DEN-LIBRARY-LIVING ROOM-PARLOR: They're in perfect agreement here. She loves rich fabrics, in soft colors, a blend of beauty and luxury that makes a room seem warm and comfy. He loves pastel shades that harmonize, lots of bookshelves, loaded with books, furnishings that are quiet and soothing. Maybe a minor tiff over traditional opposed to modern, or a chair or lamp or so, but on the whole . . . in agreement. The stereo cost a small fortune, but they're both crazy about it. Who can live without music? Not Libra or Taurus (though he won't like it played too loudly).

THE KITCHEN: They're still holding hands, still draped in harmony. She adores to cook (if she's a typical Taurean), and although she may prefer food like eggplant, potatoes, and vegetables, she's delighted to tickle his palate with the more exotic dishes that send him into appreciative ecstasies (and also perhaps send him to the gym rather frequently to work out—and work off—the calories). Then maybe afterward, a few hours out on the town with his male friends. You know . . a little man talk. But he'll be back for her next meal.

THE BEDROOM: In this room, holding hands may not be enough. They'll probably hold each other closely all night long, every night, in the sheer ecstasy of realizing that the long search, for someone who realizes that love is the most important thing in the world, is over at last. To him, that person is her. To her, that person is him. They're both ruled by Venus, so their sexual problems should be the very least of their worries. But his physical expressions of love may be a little ethereal for her, at times. She may privately wish he'd put a little more emphasis on the physical, and a little less emphasis on the intricate moods of eroticism and fancy he verbalizes so beautifully. He may privately wish she would put a little more stress on imaginative, poetic ways of making love, and a little less stress on simple ordinary bodily contact. However, they'll meet somewhere betwixt and between body, mind, and soul—and probably find their relationship more satisfying than the average couple who exist in only one romantic dimension.

THE BATHROOM: They'll still be billing and cooing in pleasure. Or rather, he'll be billing and cooing—she'll be softly mooing. He loves long, luxurious baths and showers, fluffy bath mats, thick towels, expensive shaving lotion, and rainbow-colored toothpaste for his Libra smile. She loves bubbly bath oils, powders, perfumes, thick bath mats, fluffy towels, and scented soaps.

There's hardly a square foot of space, in or around their home, where they'll disagree. Except perhaps for the front porch. That's where she may sit on the stoop, and wait—and wait—and wait—for him to come home, on those nights he's gone to the gym to work out—and out on the town afterward, with his friends. (Male friends. She hopes.) And maybe the basement.

The basement is the room where she'll spend lots of time helping him keep up his reputation as a handsome Libran charmer. That sort of charisma requires stacks of clean shirts and socks. They must be folded just so, and placed in his drawers, just so. It makes him nervous when his socks don't match, or his new sweaters fade all over his white-on-white shirts. Then he may drift into the habit of charmingly nagging her a little about being a slave to the house (and his laundry). Well, now, *there's* a problem. Which is it? Does she stay in the basement so much because she's weary of waiting on the front porch for him to come home—because he went out—because he's weary of her being in the basement all the time? Then maybe it's *his* fault. *On the other hand,* maybe it's *her* fault. Who started it? *He* started it, by going out so much. *No,* she started it by making him fat with her rich desserts. Or, did he start it, by demanding that his clothes closets be so perfect they'd pass inspection at Yves St. Laurent, when Prince Charles is there making a selection? He used her fluffy bath towels and scented soap—she used his thick bath mats and talcum. He spent their savings for a golf club membership, and a new car to surprise her, but she wasn't surprised, she was angry, and pouted sullenly for weeks. It sounds confusing, but Libra will straighten it all out with nice, clear logic . . . unless after a while, she turns obstinate and stops listening.

Libra men sometimes behave as though they're trying to drain Life of every ounce of knowledge and every drop of pleasure . . . reading best sellers, rapping with intellectuals, catching films, plays, and concerts . . . soaking up the admiration of pretty girls at parties . . . and soaking up other things.

A Taurus woman prefers to stay home, and cuddle by the fire, maybe go out socially once a week. She can't make jogging a way of life. She needs other interests, and most of them lie in togetherness, the two of them . . . hiking through the woods or going camping, remodeling the house . . . making some common sense out of the present so they can build a future, buy a house in the country, and leave the madness of the metropolis. She was not born for condominiums. She was born for barns and hay and fresh air . . . and country roads to stroll along, hand in hand, with the man she loves.

Not every Libra man is a playboy type. Then again, many of them are. But, playboy or no playboy, he'll insist on keeping his intellect sharp, and one of the ways he does this is by being gregarious. If she wants to continue playing those happy scenes with him in the den, the bathroom, the kitchen, and the bedroom, she'll have to accept the mingling at intermission. He may prefer studying ancient civilizations, dabbling in one of the arts, or grabbing an extra degree or two, to hanging out in a smoky nightclub. But, wherever and however he does his mingling, she should get out of the basement, off the front-porch stoop, into her prettiest dress, and tag along beside him—without pouting.

Maybe she won't enjoy it quite so much as he does, but she'll have to pretend she does, if she expects to someday, through her beautiful patience, entice him into moving into that remodeled barn in New England, or wherever. She should try to laugh about it, with her magnificent sense of humor. After all, tomorrow will be better, remember? It probably will be better, if there's a harmonious Sun-Moon aspect between their birth charts. If not, well . . . tomorrow may be worse. But on the other hand, nothing is perfect. And isn't that what they promised each other? For better . . . or for worse?

"No," answers the Libra man, sadly. "Tomorrow *won't* be better, I'm *sure* of it. Life is real, Life is earnest, Life is a put-on, and a put-down, a big fat nothing. *I'm* a big fat nothing."

Her voice is like creamy-smooth caramel, when she soothes him. "You aren't a big, fat nothing, darling. You're handsome and brilliant, and . . your eyes shine like emeralds when they're full of tears. If you believe long enough, and deeply enough, all good things will come to pass. We'll have to keep our emotional balance and look at the bright side." Then she smiles, a dazzling smile, and his heart turns over.

"Those are such beautiful thoughts, sweetheart. So wise. Where did you ever learn such a lovely philosophy of Life," he asks, now smiling back at her.

". . . from someone I knew, a long, long time ago. He taught me everything I know about life . . . and love. I miss him. I wish I could find him again. I wish he would come home."

Strangely . . . . . . they're back in each other's arms again. We should leave them alone now, because he just whispered into her buttercup ear, "I *have* come home—to stay."

But wait. Let's listen for just another moment. She's sighing, making contented little mooing sounds. "Do you suppose you could take a day off next week, so we could go out in the country and look at some farmhouses for sale?"

"Why wait for next week? Let's go right this minute."

Yes, tomorrow *will* be better. Not perfect, but better. After they've moved to the countryside, he'll glance up at her some night, when they're sitting by the fire, and begin sharpening his Libra logic and intellect again. "You know what I've been thinking? That promise about—'all good things come to pass.' What it really means is—all good things will *come*—comma—to *pass*. Nothing ever remains. Everything is always changing. Like that warning, 'even this shall pass away.' I suppose that includes the sadness, as well as the gladness. If you wait long enough, the gladness returns again."

You see? The fresh air and the hay and the green fields . . and the cows . . . didn't dull his mind at all. But he doesn't have to teach her anything about "waiting long enough." Patience is her secret power, over Life, and Love . . . and *him*.

TAURUS *Man* LIBRA *Woman*

However, John continued to sleep so placidly on the floor, that she allowed him to remain there. "And I know you meant to be kind," she said, relenting. "So you may give me a kiss."

A Libra woman is unpredictable. You never know how she's going to manage to get her own way. All you can be sure of is that she'll get it.

"What?" you'll exclaim. "A sweet, feminine girl like her is bossy?" Yes. A sweet, feminine girl like her is bossy. But that doesn't mean she has to advertise the fact by having it stamped on her bikini—"*Bossy.*" (Someone might think she's a female Bull.) The Libra woman is ruled by Venus, the gentle planet of peace and love and beauty and harmony—all those delicious things. A Taurus man is ruled by Venus too. But Taurus is a feminine sign. And Libra is a masculine sign. That doesn't make her a tomboy, anymore than it makes him a sissy (the *Bull* a *sissy?*). It has deeper implications. It's always easier for a man to be born under a masculine sign, and for a woman to be born under a feminine sign. It makes doing what comes naturally—more natural. However, it isn't necessarily unfortunate the other way around. Usually, a masculine vibration only makes a girl more spunky—and a feminine vibration only makes a man more sensitive. There's nothing wrong with the sexes trading a few virtues back and forth. The danger lies in overdoing it. These two probably will not. They may *under*do it.

Of all men born under a feminine Sun Sign, the Bull is less likely to overdo the feminine qualities of passivity, acquiescence, submission, and so forth. It simply keeps his virility and stubbornness balanced by sweetness and tenderness, if he doesn't overemphasize the caveman bit. The Libra girl will have a little more trouble with the sexual balancing act. After all, she's symbolized by the Scales, and scales have a delicate mechanism of adjustment. Her innate sense of fairness and impartial judgment, plus her masculine Sun Sign vibes, may lead her to announce: "Darling, I'm joining a women's lib group. We're going to picket the White House."

His innate sense of conventional behavior, plus his respect for authority and firm convictions about a female's function in life, may lead him to answer: "You make a fool of yourself in front of the President, and I'll liberate you by chaining you to the bed until you get some sense, woman." Under that kind of dictatorial attitude, Venus di Milo can turn into Stonewall Jackson, as her Scales dip precariously from feminine to masculine.

A Libra girl nearly always is beautiful. Even if her features are plain, her absolutely stunning smile makes you think she's beautiful. She has dimples, her eyes are soft, her voice is clear and lovely, her manners are graceful. She lets you pull out her chair, hold open her door, and carry her packages with an air of appealing helplessness. Outwardly, she's an angel of femininity. Inwardly, she's driven by the masculine principles of her Cardinal Sign of Leadership: force–strength–courage–positive action –penetration–conquer and dominate. She can manage her own career, and she's adept at getting everything she wants out of life–or from a man. It doesn't mean she's invulnerable to hurt, but she wears a tougher suit of armour to protect her from it than her manner might suggest . . . . . . and she recuperates quickly.

Taurus recuperates slowly from a broken heart. All the more reason for him to be sure he knows the rules before he plays any romantic games with a Libra female. The Bull makes decisions only after careful consideration. He doesn't like to discuss a situation until it's already settled in his mind. Then he acts with deliberation and seldom changes his opinion. She acts with equal deliberation and also seldom changes her opinion. Once she's made up her mind, she carries through with incredible energy and purpose. So she can't understand why people unjustly accuse her of being indecisive. What gives her such an unfair reputation is the period of weighing and balancing she goes through *before* she finally makes up her mind. With Taurus, the decision-making period is sensibly utilized for silent contemplation. With Libra, it's intellectually utilized for lengthy discussions of pro and con that can last far into the night. She may have occasion to resent his lack of enthusiasm in contributing to the talkathon.

HER: I'm for legalized abortion . . . I think. Do you believe anyone has the right to tell a woman what to do with her own body?

HIM: I never thought about it. Nobody ever tried to tell me what to do with my body.

HER: Well, *think* about it. What would you do if someone raped you, and then you found out you were pregnant?

HIM: (yawning) I'd change my name from Earl to Gladys.

HER: Please be serious, sweetheart. Do you believe the Catholic Church should be allowed to lobby against legal abortion, and claim it's murder?

HIM: According to both the Bible and the Constitution, they should.

HER: Maybe you're right. On the other hand, what about the population explosion?

HIM: (yawning again) An ounce of prevention is worth a pound of cure. That's what my grandmother used to say.

HER: That's true. An abortion can create emotional scars in both the woman and the man. Metaphysically speaking, a soul shouldn't be denied its channel of birth. Still, when you look at the other side, if a girl is unmarried, and her parents won't help her . . . . .

HIM: So she calls a home for unwed mothers. Say, listen, are you pregnant?

HER: Ah! That's just the point. Do those homes influence the girl in her decision about adoption—as opposed to abortion—as opposed to keeping her baby? It certainly isn't fair if . . . . . . *Earl?* Earl!

HIM: ZZ ZZ ZZ ZZ ZZ ZZ ZZ ZZ ZZ ZZ z z z z z z z z z z z z z z z z

She shouldn't judge him too harshly. He tried. But as soon as he satisfied himself that the problem under discussion wasn't his *personal* concern, he lost interest. She could awaken him very easily, by turning out the lights, and giving him a silent message about a subject that *does* affect him, intimately—making love. Just because she failed to arouse him into passionate verbal declarations and opinions doesn't mean she won't be able to arouse him physically. A Bull can always be led into becoming passionate about passion.

The physical magnetism between this man and woman is often very powerful, probably the basis for the initial attraction—and familiarity will seldom breed contempt. It will more likely add depth to the sexual expression of their love. Her approach may be a few shades too abstract for his sensual, earthy needs. Yet, they are both sentimental romanticists who understand how to blend eroticism with affection to achieve total fulfillment together. This is a 6-8 Sun Sign Pattern stressing sexual curiosity and satisfaction—and also emphasizing unselfish devotion and service.

Undeniably, the Taurus man is often a great blessing to the Libra woman. His very presence soothes her restless spirit. And no one can more solidly and dependably guide her through those Libran moments of sometimes agonizing indecision more comfortably than the Bull. His warmness and humor—his reliability and common sense—are often just the qualities she's been searching for out there among the clouds. After all, even the birds rest in the trees now and then . . . and build their nests there, where they feel safe and secure . . . however much they may enjoy flying.

Another rather lovely thing about these two is that her natural Pollyanna optimism can act as a beautiful balance for the Bull's natural tendency toward pessimism. No one can cheer up a Taurus man, when he's down in the dumps of depression, as effortlessly as this charming lady. He could balk, if she tries to drag him into her social whirl, or expects him to blow up the printed balloons she carries in the protest parades. But he'll be a lovable Teddy Bear when she wheedles him with her wide smile and coaxes him with her maple-sugar voice. He privately admires her intelligence, as long as she acknowledges the fact of masculine superiority. It's a rare Bull who truly believes, in his heart, that men and women are equal in all ways. A Taurus man will be proud of the way his Libra lady manages things so smoothly. The trick is to keep him from discovering that her real talent lies in managing *him*.

TAURUS: I suppose you're thinking I need a shave. Well, I just got back from a three-day camping trip, you know, and I . . . . . .

LIBRA: Sweetheart, I think it's a perfectly *marvelous* idea! Why didn't you tell me you had decided to grow a beard?

TAURUS: A *beard*? And look like some freaked-out hippie? *Me*? You've lost your senses, woman. Never!

LIBRA: Other men might. But *you'd* look like one of the apostles. How long will it take to grow it completely?

TAURUS: I was just getting ready to sha. . . uh, well, it might take a few weeks, I guess. One of the apostles, huh?

LIBRA: I think . . . . . . Matthew. Or maybe Mark. When did you decide to do it, darling?

TAURUS: Oh, you know how it is, sitting around in the woods, by the campfire. Somehow, it gives you a different perspective on things . . . .

TAURUS

Earth — Fixed — Negative
Ruled by Venus (also by the
  Planet Pan-Horus)
Symbol: The Bull
Night Forces — Feminine

SCORPIO

Water — Fixed — Negative
Ruled by Pluto
Symbols: Scorpion & Eagle
Night Forces — Feminine

The **TAURUS-SCORPIO** *Relationship*

>➤◆➤

The more quickly this horror is disposed
of the better.

*I*t is not, of course, *always* a horror, although the potential is there. When they really try, Taurus and Scorpio often get on well together, sometimes superbly. If the Moon Sign of one is conjunct, sextile or trine to the other's Sun, they can chart new worlds of the mind or spirit, in space or on the ground. It can be a beautiful, lasting relationship in science, literature, the arts—or in simple human closeness. When they have a negative aspect between their Suns and Moons, they will remain opposed and powerful enemies, until one or both of them evolve to the concepts of tolerance, compassion and unselfishness.

As with all 7-7 Sun Sign Patterns, Scorpio and Taurus each sense in the other the missing qualities that would make him (or her) whole and complete. The magnetic polarity of their opposition on the astrological wheel tugs on them rather firmly—for good or evil. Scorpio is everything Taurus wants to be. And Taurus is everything Scorpio would like to be. However, each of them would almost rather literally be caught dead than admit it. Scorpio is not a dual sign, yet the Eagles live in two worlds at the same moment—the world of wherever their compulsive soul-yearning takes them and the visible, material world, believed in and seen by ordinary mortals. Scorpios float somewhere between both, a law unto themselves, as inscrutable as the Great Pyramid of Giza. To disguise themselves, and to keep people from seeing them dangling in the air like that, most Scorpios wear a mask. It could be a mask of sweet gentleness, icy detachment or cold practicality. But beneath it, they are all smoldering, boiling, bubbling cauldrons of intense emotion.

Taurus owns no false faces. Like the other Earth Signs, the Bulls don't particularly like to dress up on Halloween—either to fool people or to frighten them. They just want to make them laugh (and make them behave). The Bulls live firmly and tangibly in one world only—Earth. Good old, familiar, safe Terra Firma. They are what they are, and nothing or no one will ever change them from what they were born to be—veritable mountains of dependability, courage, patience and determination. Although the average Taureans weren't born with Scorpio's power of penetration and steely will, nor the Eagle's awesome regenerative potential, they do embody the true and genuine inner calm Scorpio longs to possess, the total emotional control Pluto-ruled men and women only *pretend* to own. It is for this that Scorp envies the Venus-ruled Taureans. (Now and then, a Bull is born whose Moon and Ascendent are in Scorpio—then look out! I mean, this person is a powerhouse supreme.)

As for the typical Bulls, they wouldn't bother to plod across the street to either own or imitate Pluto's emotional intensity, but they would trudge thousands of miles, even leap over barbed wire fences—uphill, if necessary (if no one was looking)—to gain Scorp's ability to *know* without any kind of calculation . . . *to simply know*. Taureans would give all their gold to be able, like the Eagles, to stare into someone's soul and learn all that person's secrets. If only they could master this ability, the Bulls could build their empires faster. And if Scorpio could master, in turn, the Taurean impassivity toward Life's magnetic emotional storms, they could accomplish their mysterious purposes with far less toll on the inner psyche.

Naturally, when these two get together in any sort of association—business, family, friendship or love—and decide to lend each other the use of their individual talents and virtues, working side by side, they can change destiny.

A blend of their qualities through a close *"relation"*-ship is never bland. It can tremble and shake with both highs and lows. I have a Taurus friend with a Scorpio brother, and they're equally devoted to their Piscean mother. But when the Bull moved into a new house, he was too busy with the pressures of several financial crises to get in touch with his Neptune mother right away. Besides, he didn't want to worry her with his personal problems. One night, the Bull and his wife invited the Scorpio brother for dinner, and he accepted. They prepared his favorite meal, the children were all washed, and brushed, and excited about seeing their uncle—but he didn't arrive. When they called his home, he wasn't in. The puzzling Pluto silence continued for several days. Then one morning, a note came in the mail from the "missing" Scorpion relative. It said, simply: "There's a very lonely lady in the Bronx who hasn't heard from you in too long a time. After you get in touch with her, I'll be happy to come for dinner."

The direct, uncomplicated Bull was red-flagged into fury over his brother's undeniably devious behavior. Why didn't he just come right out and say he was angry when he was first invited to the house instead of pulling the mystery routine and the silent treatment?

Why? Because he's a Scorp, and that's the way Scorpios are. Simple directness has no sting to it, you see, and this Eagle was determined to sting his sibling. The surprise element is necessary for completely effective Pluto retaliation. Yet, shortly afterwards, when the Bull's financial woes had reached the emergency stage, the Scorp offered to lend his brother the cash he needed, without even being asked. That's *also* the way Scorpios are.

One of the qualities Taurus possesses, and Scorpio usually lacks, is a sense of the ridiculous. There are Eagles who possess a fine sense of humor, but it's seldom along the lines of the absurd. Humor is Nature's great balancer. It bestows a sane perspective to life, and helps the Bulls avoid the twin (no relation to Gemini!) destructive influences of self-pity and egocentricity. When you laugh, you're surrounded with warm, happy people. A joke attracts a crowd. And when you laugh at *yourself*, everyone adores you—because you've made yourself as human and fallible as they know they are themselves, allowing them to feel, for a brief moment, not so aware of their own vulnerability. Perhaps the lack of such easy and spontaneous humor, of the type which attracts a crowd, is why Scorpios often prefer to travel alone and incognito. It's difficult for the Pluto-ruled to feign fallibility. Besides, they have no need to be adored.

A Bull might approach a Scorpion in a typically playful (and rare talkative) mood, and call out: "Hey! Why are you hiding behind that bushy beard and the dark shades? Are you afraid people will find out you're really Barnabas the Vampire? I've got it! The beard and glasses make you feel safe, is that right, Barny?" (If the Scorp is a lady Eagle, substitute "Vampy" for "Barny"—sans the beard, of course.)

"Right, Barny? (Or Vampy.) They replace the security blanket you chewed on and took to bed as a kid." (The Bull is thinking of his or her own blanket-Teddy-Bear stage of childhood.)

Scorpio will not laugh. The Scorpion will just murmur quietly, without so much as the twitch of a whisker, *"Perhaps."*

But Taurus persists. "No kidding? Looking like one of the Smith Brothers on the cough drop box makes you feel secure?" Whereupon, Scorpio will smile Pluto's faint smile of warning, prior to deadly attack, and remark in deep, Velveeta cheese tones . . .

"You're jealous, aren't you? Jealous that I have a beard, and you don't. Is it because a beard symbolizes masculinity and you're sensitive about that, for some reason?"

Now, nothing in heaven or hell can wound the ultra-virile Bull as cruelly as an insinuation, in jest or otherwise, of *that* nature. The Scorpion has struck again, whether the name is Barnabas the Vampire, alias Vampy or Barny—or Leonard the accountant. The Eagle has drawn blood. Taurus retreats, hurt and puzzled that a simple, good-natured joke laid an egg, floundering in water over any Bull's head. Of course, when pushed too far, the Taureans won't retreat. They'll paw the ground, snort—and charge —totally destroying the Scorpion, who will then, in his (or her) final moments, whip around that dangerous tail, deliver the fatal sting—and they'll *both* fall down dead. Naturally, I'm referring to an imaginary scene between the Nature symbols of the two Sun Signs. In a similar human encounter, you may translate it your own way.

Speaking of Nature symbols, I trust the reader is not confused by the reference to Pluto-ruled people as both "Scorpion" and "Eagle." An Eagle is a Scorpion regenerated into the higher octave of his or her own Superconscious, capable of projecting all the finer, positive qualities of the Sun Sign. Like a kind of reincarnation *within* a reincarnation, so to speak. All Scorpio people are Eagles *part* of the time. If they keep trying, they can *remain* on this high level permanently, lifted from the Scorpion's sands, into the Eagle's skies of enlightenment, through aspiration—on the wings of the repudiation of revenge, soaring into a dedication to defend the helpless.

Many Scorps do appreciate humor, but normally only when it can be seen or projected in an impersonal way. Such as on stage or screen, or among friends—*watching*. Very few Scorpions find it hilarious when the giggles are at their own expense, and they're not cheery back-slapper types, as the Bulls can be, when they're feeling especially jolly. The typical Scorp will chuckle sincerely at funnies only when in the company of good and trusted friends.

Scorpio Mike Nichols, American comedy writer, author, performer and director (a rather large hunk of comedic talent), doesn't exactly have a reputation for being a continual bag of laughs in his personal life when the joke is on him. The same thing is true of country comedienne Minnie Pearl. She's a howl on stage, but privately she's an intense, dedicated Scorpio lady, with passionate political and other convictions.

Scorpio and Taurus do have some things in common. They both have a tendency to be reserved with strangers. Neither of them are blabbermouths, and neither is inclined to make long speeches unless there's something important to say. Also, both equally dislike being rudely questioned by inquisitive people. But their reactions to such intrusions are quite different. Scorpio will use subtle strategies to keep his (or her) secrets secret. When subtlety fails, the Scorpio will simply lie, justifying it as an inalienable right when dealing with those who would violate his (or her) sacred privacy. (At any other time, Scorpios are the very souls of integrity, however.) The silent implication is: "You pried into my personal affairs, and you got what you deserved." (The snooper should be grateful for the lie. It's better than receiving a sting from the Scorpion tail. Sometimes, both defense measures are employed, simultaneously.)

The Bulls have an equal sense of privacy, and you won't find them telling all they know, any more than Scorps do. But the Bulls are not subtle, and they'll seldom bother with a lie. Taurus will squelch a prying person directly, with a plain statement of fact, like: "Mind your own business, jerk, and buzz off."

No one can say "no" more emphatically, and mean it, than Taurus and Scorpio. If they say it to each other, that's the end. But when they say "yes" to one another, a solid, lasting friendship will develop. Because the Bulls and Eagles have one more thing in common. *Loyalty*. For those they love and trust, they'll move mountains, against any odds. They both consider a kindness exactly as they consider a loan at the bank—to be paid back promptly, with interest.

☆ ☆ ☆ ☆ ☆ ☆

TAURUS *Woman* SCORPIO *Man*

———◄◄●►►———

Was that boy asleep, or did he stand waiting . . . with his dagger in his hand?

There was no way of knowing. . . .

In the beginning, a Taurus girl may be wary of accepting the silent invitation in the hypnotic eyes of a Scorpio man. She's heard some disturbing rumors about him. She's been told he's ruthless and sexy. Admittedly, that's a strong combination, and it could make anyone a little cautious.

A Scorpio male has many shining virtues to offset his dark vices, but he is not one of the Rover boys, with a naive trust in the goodness of human nature. Nor is he Andy Hardy or Tiny Tim. Through the magic window of his penetrating Pluto gaze, he sees too much of human nature to have much faith in its goodness. He has more faith in his own instinct for truth and decency. In God he trusts. Of everyone else he is suspicious. That's why he appears to be ruthless. Yet, if he's an Eagle (instead of the Grey Lizard or Stinging Scorpion I described in the Scorpio chapter of my first book *Sun Signs*) he only destroys the enemies who would destroy him or the helpless (and he knows which ones they are). Those who merely step on the Scorpion's tail by accident he will just sting lightly, to deliver Pluto's message that they are not ever to again impose on him—or upon a defenseless friend. Then he nobly allows them to go on their way, unharmed. It's a lesson. That's all. *Learn it* is his unspoken warning to the offender—*or beware of the next encounter.*

Actually, his actions are impeccably fair and just, never petty—and always in line with his own strict ethics. Scorpio never asks of anyone what he is not prepared and willing to give of himself. It's a philosophy similar to the code of that family-oriented society called the "Mothers And Fathers Intellectual Association," which is sometimes abbreviated by its five initials, and symbolized by a mythical, legendary Black Hand. With Scorpio, as with this society, the black hand symbolizes protection for the weak, the poor and the helpless, as much as it symbolizes a threat to the disloyal, the greedy, the pushy and the snoopy. At least, these were the noble Robin Hood-like sentiments in the beginning, at the society's birth in the eighteenth century, in Sicily, before the sincerity of the motive became stained by decades of dark deeds.

Many people think of Robin Hood himself as a Sagittarian. He was certainly an expert archer, and probably also a Sun Sign Archer, but I've personally always felt that his Moon was in Scorpio. Was Robin Hood ruthless in his attempts to "distribute the wealth"? Only the bad guys and the wealthy thought so.

Just as every individual member of the Mothers And Fathers Intellectual Association is not above reproach, every individual Scorpion is not above reproach. There are, in both groups, some well-intentioned and some evil souls. However, here we're considering the average Scorp, and playing the percentages. So, let's say the Taurus girl soon loses her initial timidity concerning the Scorpio man's ruthlessness.

In reality, the Bull fears very little which is tangible. Besides, he's already made her feel warm and secure by sending her brother to summer camp, bringing her mother flowers, treating her like a lady, and treating her father as an older and wiser senior citizen—*a man of respect*. But Taurus is not quite so brave when it comes to the *in*tangible, the unseen or the emotional—so how about the rumors of his sexiness?

What can I tell you? Like I said, they are probably true. A Scorpio male is not an impotent eunuch, or a bashful, stuttering schoolboy. He is, in every sense, a man. He's as virile as Aries, as sentimental as Libra, as passionate as Leo, as sensitive as Pisces, and as sensual as the Taurus woman herself. If you add that all up, and it comes out as one word—sexy—well, is that something to complain about? True, an astrologically unenlightened woman might naturally fear such a strong masculine charisma. But what's to fear? This man doesn't run around seducing innocent damsels, as some astrology books would have you believe. It would be difficult to make an accurate survey of such a thing, of course, but any "violated" females would quite probably be Scorpio's willing victims.

To a Taurus woman, physical proof of her deepest feelings is a necessity of Life. So the alleged Scorpio "sexiness" shouldn't deter her from examining the possibilities of experiencing Life and Love with this man. If she does, you can be sure she'll experience both in all of their various facets, nuances, shades and tones. What Scorpio finds fascinating, he probes and penetrates to its deepest meaning. What he finds unworthy, he causes to disappear by coldly ignoring it, as if it didn't exist. Eventually, it doesn't—at least, not in his own awareness, or in his immediate vicinity. That goes for both people and things. Obviously then, the problem lies in being sure they both find the same things and people interesting—and the same ones boring. Otherwise, there can be crossed wires, crossed purposes and possible emotional chaos. A Taurus girl can get attached like glue to a person or an object, and it could be disconcerting to have a dear friend or relative, a treasured cream pitcher or hooked rug, just disappear into thin air because the man you love doesn't share your enthusiasm or taste.

If their birth charts indicate a harmonious Luminary aspect between them (Sun and Moon) they'll share the same experiences, and blend their polarized individual personalities into one powerful vibration. If not, well maybe a little of that caution she felt initially will be called for, after all.

Since this is a 7-7 vibratory pattern, he has what she needs, and she has what he wants—and will probably get—(explained in the previous section more clearly). Naturally, an attraction like that will cause these two to be pulled together like bar magnets when they meet, assuming they're both free, willing and able to tackle a rich relationship. Sometimes, even assuming they're not. Did you ever try to keep two bar magnets from clinging together? Pick up a pair at the hardware store and experiment. It will be an excellent illustration of the magnetic law of attraction and repulsion in astrological romantic compatibility.

A Taurus girl is practical. She's not flighty, impulsive, or a misty dreamer. In her steady heart, passion is not easily or quickly aroused. It grows slowly into fullness. But once her senses are caught by someone, when she finds herself noticing the scent of his hair, trembling at the sound of his voice, melting at the sight of his walk or his smile, and quivering inside when he touches her hand, her practical common sense may be suspended indefinitely. Despite her natural earthy stability, a Taurus woman in love is more vulnerable than a girl Fish, and that's pretty vulnerable.

She was born under a Fixed Sign, so she won't change her mind, once she recognizes her lover as the man she's been waiting for (sometimes for years). If he's a Scorpio, she can count on his loyalty matching hers (unless they have serious afflictions between their mutual charts). She's possessive in love, but that's not quite the same thing as sudden flares of unreasonable jealousy. Taurus is not jealous. Jealousy is an emotion that has roots in a basic insecurity. *Possessiveness* describes the pride a Taurean takes in anything she owns—and the devotion she lavishes upon it, whether it's a man, or an heirloom bedspread.

A Scorpio male will understand the difference between these two words, and he'll give her very little reason to experience jealousy, while he rather enjoys her possessiveness. For all his reputation as a sex symbol, this man seldom looks upon sex as a pleasant pastime or a series of casual encounters. To him, sex is the reason for both life and death, the doorway to each, the one mystery he may never completely solve. It is, therefore, very close to being a religion to him. Which means that, when he finds the right partner, his concept of sex will be pure, though intense, and experimental promiscuity is not part of that concept. Therefore, regardless of astrological rumors, he's less likely than most men to be unfaithful to the woman he loves, and if she was born under an Earth or Water Sign, the chances are even smaller that he will deceive her. The earthy Taurus woman understands the passion that rages and burns in Scorpio, perhaps better than any other female, and she'll respond with a matching intensity of physical expression. However, although she may welcome his passionate lovemaking, she may not be as enthusiastic about his passionate convictions outside their physical relationship.

He's a mysterious blend of cool reason and hot emotion, though he chooses to expose only the former, keeping the latter a dark secret. She'll approve of his cool reason, his surface poise and his practicality, because they match her own. But hot emotions leave her cold—and disapproving. Scorpio becomes involved through his emotions, which, like the still waters of his Sun Sign, run very deep. From deep, it's only a step to passionate involvement. Whether it's politics, neighbors, career, ecology, space travel, relatives, abortion—whatever the issue—Scorpio takes a passionate, emotional stand—or shows his disinterest unmistakably. Taurus has little sympathy for the violent extremes of love and hate. To her, it's an exhausting and unnecessary strain on the nerves. This will be the underlying cause, in one form or another, behind all their disagreements, major or minor.

For the benefit of the Taurus woman who is sad and lonely, because she's had a quarrel with a Scorpion she loves, I'll reveal one of his secrets to her, contained within a verse I once wrote, in an attempt to help any unsuspecting soul, who's troubled by being unable to solve this man's Pluto mystery. He is speaking to her . . . .

> your icy voice put out the stars
> it cracked my heart, and broke it in splinters
> your tone as cold as Colorado winters
>
> but I promise to soon forget
> the contract we almost made . . . you'll feel
> the swift response of an equal
>   as the dream begins to fade
> I'll drown you in pseudo kindness
> and a casual, friendly glance
> I can almost imagine your blindness
>   as I watch and wait
> for the chance
> to suddenly—cruelly—make you know
> how easy it was to let you go*

* From *Venus Trines at Midnight* by Linda Goodman.

It's called *The Sting of the Scorpion*. And here's the secret I promised to reveal to the Taurus lady. It wasn't easy for him to let her go. It tore him apart. But he hid the pain of his own grief beneath the frozen features of Scorpio detachment. Now that she's been told, she can, perhaps, penetrate his disguise and heal those broken splinters if she remembers this: when she's angry, a Taurus woman can truly project an "icy voice" and a "cold tone." How can she see how he feels inside, while she's wearing the blinders of stubbornness? The only thing that kind of attitude will bring is "the swift response of an equal"—and he *is* her equal. In Fixity . . . . in patience . . . . in loyalty . . . but also in remembering hurt . . . . and in the need to learn how to forgive.

☆ ☆ ☆ ☆ ☆ ☆

TAURUS *Man* SCORPIO *Woman*

————◄◆►————

*He was a brave man; but for a moment he had to stop
there and wipe his brow, which was dripping like a
candle. Then silently he let himself go into the
unknown.*

A Taurus man who feels himself sinking into the mysterious underworld of a Scorpio female's magnetic attraction, is either headed for what may be the most traumatic experience of his life—or the most uplifting. The outcome will definitely not be neutral.

It might be the former, if there's a negative aspect between the Sun and Moon in their respective horoscopes. But if these two Luminaries are in a harmonious relationship, it could very well be the latter. Assuming everything is cool with their planets, it's all right for him to sink in, but he might want to tuck a copy of the Bible under his arm, as he falls into the immeasurable depth of her love. It's really a good idea to study the Holy Works before becoming involved with this woman on an intimate basis. No matter what they say or do, Scorpios can always find a passage in the Scriptures to justify themselves. And they'll quote it, to make sure you know their motives are blameless. Not only are they experts on both the

Old and New Testaments, but they also have the psychic ability to read between the lines—and what Scorpio finds between the lines is quite a testament in itself.

Not every Scorpio girl has the Bible committed to memory, of course, but it won't hurt to take heed of the possibility. If she doesn't quote the Scriptures when she's loving him, or stinging him, she may have memorized large chunks of the Tibetan Book of the Dead. At the very least, she may have dropped into a couple of Hare Krishna meetings, or had an Egyptian scarab tattooed somewhere on her body, visible only to the "naked" eye. No? Then check her dressing table (if you can find the key to unlock it) and see if she has a pack of tarot cards, or a well-thumbed copy of the *I Ching* tucked in among her love potions, exotic perfumes and aphrodisiacs.

I don't mean to imply that this woman's nature is too hot for a Taurean man to handle, or her psyche too coolly mysterious for him to penetrate. After all, that silent film star Rudolph Valentino, the sheik to end all sheiks was a *Taurus*. So the Bull is quite capable of sneaking into a Scorpio girl's tent, under the stars, with his nostrils dilating romantically. Since she's chemically attracted to the opposite sex of her opposite Sun Sign (Taurus) she may even run out of the tent barefoot to meet him. If she does, she'll resemble Queen Nefertiti herself, in the moonlight. That's what makes it all so special. In the quiet moments of their aloneness together, a Scorpio woman can become to her Taurus man the image of every love goddess down through the ages. In the daytime, she slips on her Scorpion mask and becomes Susan, the shy secretary—Millie, the modest maiden—or Laurie, little-girl-lost.

Despite her apparent tranquility and surface sweetness, this is not a female who is easy to live with. She's fascinating, feminine, intelligent, loyal and passionate. But she is not an innocent, wide-eyed maiden who is willing to become a love object. Scorpio lives in the emotions, but sometimes they're bottled up inside for years. That's why she seems so docile, then suddenly, with no warning, she erupts into boiling anger—or disappears into frozen silence, which is even harder to cope with and certainly more difficult to understand.

For a time, she'll go along with what her man says, unless he becomes too demanding. Then she'll show her hidden strength. Tact and compromise are not her strong points. For that matter, they're not his either. Neither Taurus nor Scorpio has much idea of what it's like to see the other person's point of view. No, that's not quite right. Taurus has trouble seeing another point of view. Scorpio sees it quite clearly, with her uncanny perception. But she still prefers her own wishes to what her Ouija board may tell her someone else's are. They'll have to make some adjustments here, or spend their lives together with their backs turned, arms crossed, and mouths sealed in stubborn silence. Both of them were born under a Fixed Sign. But both of them were also born under a feminine sign, so they can be equally gentle and sympathetic, when they choose to use these "negative" vibrations, which are the "feminine" compensations for the "negative" qualities of their Sun Signs.

He's ruled by Venus, the planet of peace and love. She's ruled by Pluto, the planet of explosive passion and mystery. Their sexual compatibility, therefore, is usually full of strange surprises and sensual ecstasies. She associates sex with the mystery of her own existence, and respects it as a sacred act of love. She also has a devouring curiosity about its secret implications, which can only be satisfied by ever deeper intimacy with the man she loves, although there will always be an aura of purity about her desires. Sex is never cheap to a Scorpio woman, and she'll insist on being loved for her whole self, not just for her physical appeal. So will he.

The Taurus man may never totally comprehend their lovemaking in as much depth as she does, but that certainly won't prevent his enjoyment of it. To the Bull, as to the Scorpion, sexual expression is an act of worship, a constant renewal of spiritual strength, through the giving and receiving of passion between them. However, sex alone is never enough for a lasting union, even when it's as fulfilling as it normally is with Taurus and Scorpio in their 7-7 Sun Sign Pattern relationship. Other facets of their love will need constant attention. It's never easy for these two to reconcile after a serious quarrel. Their mutual Fixed vibration keeps them apart. Scorpio says, "I will forgive. But I *cannot* overlook." Taurus varies this only slightly, and says, "I will forgive. But I can never *forget*." They're both lying to themselves. What they really mean is, "I can't forgive." Because, true forgiveness *does* overlook, and true forgiveness *does* forget. The refusal to truly forgive is a dark and evil thing. The seeds thus planted in the heart will grow into cold and lonely isolation, premature aging, chronic disease and emotional neurosis, as surely as an acorn will grow into a giant oak tree.

His comic sense may be another cause for tension between them. The Bull needs an occasional practical joke and a constant touch of humor to make his life, which is serious enough, bright and bearable. She may laugh at his comic remarks, but her eyes won't be smiling, and he'll soon learn she can't stand to be teased, because she's never been able to really laugh at herself. His rich humor is what makes him such a warm human being. Instead of being annoyed by it, if she will let some of his laughter linger in her heart, she might find it's the extra dimension she needs to color her own emotions a few shades lighter.

The love vibration between Taurus and Scorpio is perfectly symbolized by the strange pilgrimage of Taurean silent screen idol Rudolph Valentino's much discussed "Mystery Woman," who, despite whispered rumors, has never been provably identified to this day. Whatever her name may have been, her Sun or Moon Sign was surely Scorpio (which might be a clue to her identity). Yes, she could only have been a deeply bereaved Scorpio woman, conceiving Life, Love, sex and death to be inseparable, as she made her lonely visits to her Taurus lover's grave, dressed completely in black, her face covered by a veil . . . . . . to offer the memory flowers of her intense passion, grief and loyalty . . . . . . each year, with unwavering faithfulness, on the anniversary of his death.

That's the way it is with Taurus and Scorpio. No light flirtation, or casual affair. It will be frigid disinterest, total disaster—or a devotion which will last a lifetime, and beyond that, past forever. All—or nothing at all. The Bible will come in handy, either way.

☆ ☆ ☆ ☆ ☆ ☆

TAURUS

Earth—Fixed—Negative
Ruled by Venus (also by the
Planet Pan-Horus)
Symbol: The Bull
Night Forces—Feminine

SAGITTARIUS

Fire—Mutable—Positive
Ruled by Jupiter
Symbols: Archer & Centaur
Day Forces—Masculine

The **TAURUS-SAGITTARIUS** *Relationship*

. . . . . . for the procession must continue indefinitely
until one of the parties stops or changes its pace.

The Bulls will in no way change their slow, steady pace, so it's up to Sagittarius to stop running for a spell, now and then, if these two are ever going to settle down, and cash in on the several possible rewards of their 6-8 Sun Sign Pattern vibration.

Since the Archers are symbolized by the Centaur, who is half-horse, half-human, their association will be rather ripping half the time. I use the English idiom because Sag is so often flying off to foreign countries (or dreaming about flying off to them). Nearly every Archer secretly longs to make some sort of a career out of travel, and one way or another most of them manage to do just that. When Sagittarians are playing the role of the clown, or the gay philosopher, using the animal, or the rear end of their Centaur symbol, the Bulls find them highly amusing. Taureans will howl at the slapstick antics of the Archers, tripping over their speech and their feet. They feel a warm, protective glow toward the cheerful, well-meaning, good-natured, and somewhat awkward horse-half of Sag (pronounced to rhyme with badge).

But let the human side of the Archers turn up, and Taurus is puzzled and annoyed. As the Bulls watch the Sagittarians playing the roles of serious idealists, fighting fiercely in the courtroom, the classroom, on a television screen, or on a political platform, they're uncertain whether to cheer them—or fear them.

The Jupiter dedication of the moment may take Sagittarians into a raging battle against the establishment, which will usually be abrasive to the more conservative Taurean nature, causing the Bulls to draw back in surprise and ask themselves, "Who is this strange creature, riding around like a drunken dreamer, tilting at the sturdy, solid windmills of society?" An awkward, yet also sometimes graceful, racehorse may be quite likable and good for some belly laughs, but a careless idealist who is threatening to tear holes in the fabric of comfortable custom can be downright dangerous. Taurus can't figure out how to deal sensibly with a Sagittarian, who's aroused to a high pitch of recklessness by a cause (preferably a lost one, because they give you a bigger glow within when you win them—and being lucky, the Archers nearly always win).

Every Sag (including the extroverted and the introverted ones) is at heart a bright-eyed, bushy-tailed optimist, who inwardly believes that everything will come out in the wash, then cries great, dramatic tears when it doesn't—which serves him (or her) right for expecting too much out of Life, as far as Taurus is concerned.

The Bulls are clear-eyed, smooth-tailed pessimists, who never expect anything to come out in the wash—so when they lose a couple of socks at the laundermat, it serves *them* right for constantly imaging negative possibilities, as far as Sagittarius is concerned. Sag has no patience with Taureans who go glooming around, spreading inky moods. The Sagittarian man, woman or child's own tears may be very damp and profuse, but they dry quickly when the eternal Jupiter rainbow comes out to drape itself around their shoulders and bathe them in hopeful colors again.

This is a 6-8 Sun Sign Pattern, emphasizing service, health and all manner of mystery. Because Sagittarius represents "other people's money" to Taurus (among other 8th "house" influences, which are different with each individual Sun Sign association between these two) the Archers may be the ones to raise the funds for Taureans to realize their huge endeavors. Because Taurus represents the 6th astrological "house" of work, duty and service to Sag, these two are not infrequently found associated in some mutual undertaking that blends the Jupiter flair for promotion and salesmanship with the Taurean ability to build a solid foundation (which is of great value, when the Archers ride the rear end of their Centaur symbol, and fall flat on their hopes). The Bulls admire the exciting pictures the Archers create, but they become restless and suspicious when Sag slaps on the paint with strokes that are too broad, and colors that are too garish for the practical Taurean taste.

Sagittarian people sail around, goofing and stumbling a lot, but they're as likely to stumble on a piece of pure, unadulterated luck, as they are to fall head first into an open sewer. The former accident is due to their marvelous faith, courage and optimism—the latter, to their obstructed line of vision. Your chances of falling into a hole naturally increase when you're gazing at the sky, shooting arrows into the future, and not looking where you're skipping.

Since the Bulls usually keep their eyes more or less fastened on the ground, they can help Sag watch out for the open sewers and other traps waiting to trip them. These two can make a really socko team in the stock market, or in any sort of gambling venture. If there's a harmonious Sun-Moon aspect between them, they may become millionaires fairly quickly. Actually, they'll do pretty well together in any sort of scheme involving money—their own or someone else's—whether it's farming organic fruits and vegetables, or selling foreign sports cars. The association can be found anywhere from film-making to breeding racehorses, from the newspaper field to a church. (Most Bulls are rather dogmatic about their religious beliefs, usually intensely loyal to the religion of childhood—and all Archers are possessed of a strong, though often tangled and knotted, religious streak.)

Normally, Taurus remains close to family ties. A Bull will sacrifice much for his (or her) loved ones, and bear up under a bushel of trouble for them. Sagittarians are also willing to offer a helping hand and a cheery word to their relatives—from a distance. The typical Archers and their families don't live in one another's pockets. Sag is more interested in the good of humanity as a whole than in lavishing excessive attention on blood lines. That's for horses, isn't it? Yes, and also for the half-horse Centaurs, if they'd give their relatives half a chance.

Both of these Sun Signs can spot a hypocrite or a phony a mile away, and neither of them is inclined to tell a lie to save face, or merely to be courteous. The Bulls ordinarily will state the truth of the matter as they see it, firmly and clearly. Should they think it might truly wound someone, however, they'll clam up and not speak at all, rather than stir up unnecessary unpleasantness, if the issue is not an urgent one. The Archer has no such reluctance. All Sagittarians shine with a certain kind of honesty—a brutal kind. The truth sometimes hurts, but the Archers are blissfully unaware of this, when their indignations are flashing. It's useless to expect these people to stifle their Jupiter integrity, but they might try diluting it a bit.

SAG: Why are you so upset, just because I told you that you're pigeon-toed and you walk with a waddle? I think it's kind of cute. Why are you frowning as though you hated me or something? What did I do wrong? I thought you liked me.

TAURUS: That's right. Everybody likes you, because you're so warm and friendly and enthusiastic. You're also a clumsy klutz, verbally and physically. There. See how the truth hurts?

SAG: Okay, so I'm a clumsy klutz. But what does that have to do with your being pigeon-toed and walking with a waddle?

It's no use, a dose of their own medicine won't work with Sag, because truth never cramps Jupiter's breezy style. Most Archers will accept it cheerfully, philosophically—and are genuinely bewildered when others get uptight over hearing the plain facts, whether the sharp arrow of honesty is aimed at themselves or at another victim. A Sagittarian (or a person with the Moon or Ascendent in Sag) is the one who chirps happily, "Was that your husband's brother I read about in the papers, who forged those checks and got caught? Listen, it's all in the family! I have a sister who was picked up twice for shoplifting. She's in therapy now. But it still hasn't cured her kleptomania."

The broken twigs on their own family trees don't bother the Archers in the least, so why should you flinch over yours? That's Jupiter's sunny, but sometimes exasperating, outlook.

Sagittarians take life and people literally as they skip around, spreading their jollies and blasting out truth with their jovial Jupiter vibes. When the Bulls get hit between the eyes, they can get their backs up, but they're normally placid, patient souls. Unfortunately, the qualities of placidity and patience often annoy the more impulsive Archers, when they're exposed to it for long periods of time. It sometimes seems to Sag that the dogmatic and cautious Bulls are as slow as a herd of snails.

Nevertheless, if these two decide to take a gamble, and combine the Jupiter luck and logic with the Taurean shrewdness and common sense, they stand a good chance of making lots of money together. M-O-N-E-Y. That message will reach both of them loudly and clearly. Taurus likes to keep it in the bank. Sag likes to keep it in circulation.

☆ ☆ ☆ ☆ ☆ ☆

TAURUS *Woman* SAGITTARIUS *Man*

Michael was ready: he wanted to see how long it took him to do a billion miles. But Wendy hesitated . . . .

There he is, bouncing happily up and down, like a typical Jupiter rubber ball, thinking he has a great new friend to pal around with, and since she's a female, well, who knows? It could mean a beautiful love affair, or even better, maybe a life-long, platonic friendship. Since Sagittarius likes the truth so much, this is about the time he should face up to it. If she's a Taurus girl, she's not mentally casting herself either as his pal or as the helpless half of a casual affair. She has another role in mind for herself.

An Archer reading this will probably feign shock, and murmur to himself, "What does that mean?" What does he mean, what does that mean? It means marriage, that's what it means, and he shouldn't be so surprised. For a man who prides himself on his honesty, a Sagittarian male can be pretty shifty about romance. He may think he'll always win the game he plays called "Love now, leave later," but if his partner is a Taurean, he'd better be prepared to lose—either the game, or her.

A Taurus woman falls in love with a Sagittarius man for perfectly good reasons. He's an idealist, a cheerful companion when she's blue, an intelligent conversationalist, a dreamer, a philosopher, an astute businessman—and a little boy who needs looking after. You certainly can't expect a Taurus female to resist the impact of a man like that. No wonder, even when he told her plainly the first night the way things were, she didn't hear him. Her head was in the clouds, somewhere up there where he scatters all his enthusiasm. An Archer's excitement is contagious. But sometimes he forgets he's a Fire Sign. You know what fire does? It flares up into flames. And more flames. He'll have to cool it if he doesn't want to get burned by his own sparks—or be buried beneath her earthy anger, which can pour down on him like an avalanche when he ignites her love, then fails to put out the blaze.

The very least a Taurus woman will settle for when she's in love is the status of permanent mistress or common law wife, though she won't like either situation, and she's only biding her time in any case. What she won't stand for is to be part of an Archer's harem. She isn't illogically jealous, as a Leo or an Aries girl might be. She is, however, possessive, which means that her idea of love is based on exclusivity. This woman would never have accepted a proposal from Brigham Young. A female Bull won't be suspicious of her man without good cause, but neither will she give him yards of rope with which to string her along.

Actually, this man is capable of being very loyal to a woman he really loves. His problem is in making the wrong choice, which causes him to lose the right partner. At first, his frankness and his outspoken manner will seem genuine and wholesome to the Taurus girl. So will his lack of hypocrisy. She won't waste a moment of her time on a liar or a phony, so she'll admire his honesty. That is, she will until the day (or night) he demonstrates it with painful clarity to her by saying, "Baby, we can have lots of fun knocking around together, if we level with each other from the beginning. Like, yesterday I ran into this old girl friend, and she wants me to spend the weekend with her on Squaw Mountain. You know how I love to ski. Can you find something to amuse yourself with until I get back?" When the Archer gets *that* honest, she's liable to amuse herself by cracking him over the head with one of his skis.

Although a Sagittarian is governed by sincerity in romance, it isn't always accompanied by a sensitive regard for his partner's feelings. Still, if she can try to overlook his stinging arrows of frankness, she may discover things about him that a female with a quick temper and less patience will never know. When an Archer finds a woman who understands him enough to love him and trust him, his nature will expand to its highest level. No one makes a more enthusiastic lover and devoted husband than a well-loved and *trusted* Sagittarian. He's like a big, friendly sheep dog, a little clumsy maybe, but warm, happy and faithful, and who could question his playful sincerity? He needs a woman who will believe in all his dreams, not one who constantly pops his balloons with the needles of doubt and nagging.

He needs a cheerful companion to take hiking with him, someone who challenges him with her own independence, who can bounce stimulating ideas with him, who gives him plenty of freedom and also smothers him with plenty of affection. It's a large order for any female, but a Taurus girl can probably fill it, except perhaps for the part about bouncing ideas with him. She's smart (maybe even too smart) but she's a better listener than a brainstormer. It takes Taurus some time to mull over wild ideas before she can work up an excitement to match his and she's suspicious of ideas that bounce. But her practicality and common sense provide an excellent balance for his reckless tendency to throw the dice for double-or-nothing. He should appreciate her down-to-earth approach, and not expect her to continually match his own frenetic creative drive. Besides, it's good to rest once in a while against a soft pillow of purring femininity. He can play bounce with the fellows, and enjoy other pastimes with her.

A Sagittarian man who feels restricted may seem to submit, because he's inclined to make the optimistic best of an existing situation, but it will eventually lead him into becoming irritable and sarcastic, and then the union will be far from happy. If she has the Moon in a Fire or Air Sign, or he has the Moon in an Earth or Water Sign, they could have a circus together. Otherwise, their relationship may be somewhat rocky at times. He's looking for a mental companion to roam the hills with him. She needs a dependable, predictable man to sit by the fire and hold her hand. Not that a Taurus woman wants to spend her life in the kitchen stirring the noodles, but neither is she the type to want to spend it spinning around on a Ferris Wheel or munching lichee nuts. This girl is faithful and warm-hearted. She's patient and self-controlled, good-hearted and jolly. Her nature is humorous, hospitable and easygoing. She seems too gentle, too kind, and far too tranquil to be capable of anger. But goaded beyond the point of her endurance, she'll erupt into an irrational fury, lacking all logic and reason. Sagittarius is not the least likely sign to arouse her to such a rare display of temper. The Archer ranks close behind Leo, Scorpio and Aquarius in the ability to aggravate the Bull into earthquaking action.

She'll have to be on guard against the Archer's method of teaching her (and learning himself) by the method of conversational inquiry. He's an expert at it. Sag can pull out your deepest emotions and your most private opinions by this method of careful questioning. Taurus doesn't always want her deepest emotions and most private opinions exposed to light.

She doesn't pry into other people's affairs. Why should they pry into hers? So the Sagittarian burning curiosity, which is a natural outgrowth of his brilliant and logical mental process, will not always please her. Nor will his clever method of casual cross-examination delight her when she has a secret she'd like to call (and keep) her own.

It's possible for their physical relationship to be a good one, if they both try to understand each other's different natures and sexual needs. When a woman enhances his highest opinion of himself (and a Taurus woman can) an Archer's desire for her increases. Her earthy emotions are deeply stirred by his fiery ones, and he'll feel a sense of pride from her obvious feminine pleasure in sexual submission. But he seeks an emotional experience somewhere above and beyond the actuality of passion. Since he's not quite sure what it is himself, she may never guess his yearning, and they both could be aware only of a vague and nameless dissatisfaction.

She's a warm and sensuous woman, yet it isn't easy for her to express the emotions she feels so strongly. She can only show her love through the sense of touch. To her that should be enough, and silence is golden when she's making love. But the Sagittarian idealist wants to analyze, then express, both physically and verbally, the miracle of fulfillment. He may feel he's caressing the Sphinx, and she could decide she's being loved by the actual legendary Centaur, half blazing with animal passion and half abstracted in thoughts which are beyond the horizon of reality.

An Archer is consumed with mental activity, and so seeks and needs the democratic freedom of companionship with men and women of every walk of Life, not unlike his Aquarian brother. He's defiant of public opinion, uncompromising in his honesty, rather indifferent toward domestic life, and detached from his own parental family ties.

A Taurus woman is the opposite of all these things. A marriage between them, if their mutual Luminaries are in negative aspect, can be as full of both devotion and irritation as the union between Socrates and his wife, Xantippe, who dutifully created a warm and comfortable home for the philosopher, but who found him so frustratingly impossible to live with that she periodically emptied the household slop jar over his head. It may not quite come to that, but the Archer will be impatient with the Bull's lack of enthusiastic reaction to his spontaneity, while she is driven to the edge of fury by his scattered dreams, procrastination and thoughtlessness. This is a man who whistles before breakfast, and this is a woman who is positive that means he'll cry before supper. They translate Mother Goose somewhat differently.

Only if she's willing to thaw her frozen silences when he needs her understanding—and only if he's willing to curb his fiery temper when he can't get his own way—can they find happiness together. And they should *both* remember *this*: Like the forces of Yin and Yang, false pride opposes true love.

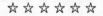

TAURUS *Man* SAGITTARIUS *Woman*

———◄◆►———

Again Tink replied, "You silly ass."

Peter could not understand why . . . .

Like forcing a square peg into a round hole, trying to blend the Taurus tranquility with the Sagittarian exuberance gives the Bull and the girl Archer the symbolic appearance of a ruptured Tinker Toy.

On the other hand (there's always a Libran trying to get into each chapter of this book to start an argument), on the other hand, it's not necessarily the greatest thing in the world to mate with a mirror image of yourself. It's more fun to team up with someone who has crooked ears to balance out your twelve toes—or someone who has a soft heart to compensate for your hard head—things like that. Mix and match, and make up for what you lack with what the other person has in excess, and wants to give away, if only he or she can find someone who needs it—and who will take it. It develops character. Or something.

We may need an example. The two of them are walking along the street, window shopping. That is, *she's* window shopping, *he's* counting to ten, making a determined effort to control his growing annoyance.

SAG: Oh, WOW! That really rips it! Look at that string bikini! I'm going in and open up a charge account, so I can buy it right away, and wear it to the beach tomorrow to look sexy.

THE BULL: Silence. Absolute, ominous silence. He can't decide what bugs him the most—her lack of maidenly modesty, her hollering slang right out on the street, that caused everyone to stare curiously at them, or her extravagance in insisting on buying things when she doesn't have the cash, and furthermore, has no idea when she *will* have it—which he suspects probably means that she'll try to borrow it from him when the bill from the store arrives, and she's still broke. (He's right. She will.) And so, for the moment—silence from the Bull.

(or . . . to switch scenes)

SAG: Honey, let's get a St. Bernard to keep Lady Macbeth, our sheep dog, company, and name him Merlin. Wouldn't that be a scream? Or maybe we could change Lady Macbeth's name to

Elizabeth, and name the St. Bernard Robert, after the Brownings. Do you think dogs understand poetry? I do. They certainly understand it better than you. You wouldn't know Solzhenitsyn from Sasquatch. Do you think they would mate?

THE BULL: Solzhenitsyn and Sasquatch?

SAG: No, stupid. The dogs. The sheep dog and the St. Bernard. How could a Russian poet mate with Sasquatch? You probably don't even know that Sasquatch is the name of Bigfoot . . . the one they keep tracking in the High Sierras. Of course (she muses, thoughtfully) they don't really know if Bigfoot is male or female, so I suppose they could, but . . . .

THE BULL: Bigfoot. That's you, baby. You're always sticking your big foot in your big mouth. I'm going to call you Sasquatch from now on.

SAG: Do you suppose the puppies would be retarded or something?

THE BULL: Solzhenitsyn's—or Sasquatch's?

SAG: Stop trying to be funny. Did I tell you I think our cat, Maybelle, is going to have a litter of kittens in a few weeks?

THE BULL: Listen, Sasquatch. I am not a dog breeder. I am also not a cat midwife. Once and for all, get this through your marble head. I do not enjoy having furry little creatures climbing all over me in bed when I'm trying to sleep. This place is beginning to resemble the ASPCA Annex.

(or . . . to switch again)

SAG: Why don't you want me to march in the ecology protest parade? We only have ten years left on this planet if somebody doesn't do something right away. Do you want to suffocate in ten years because there's no more oxygen left in the air, because the plankton that makes the oxygen, which grows in the ocean, is gone—because of pollution of the water, caused by greedy industrialists like you?

THE BULL: I am not a greedy industrialist. I own a small Orange Julius stand. And I don't care which Chinese Communist-inspired "cause" you march for on your own time, but I just got home from work, and I haven't been fed. I'm hungry. Stifle yourself, and feed me.

SAG: Say, do you think you own me? I'm not your slave. You act like you expect me to punch a time clock around here. Go out and get yourself some egg fu yung tonight. I'm not cooking.

THE BULL: You see? Now you're even pushing Oriental food. You're a sucker for Karl Marx.

SAG: Listen, if you're so jealous that you've decided to lie, and make up stories about me, don't pick a German Nazi name like that. Who said I was seen talking to this Marx guy anyway? The only man I've spoken to all week is the intern at the blood bank, who . . .

THE BULL: Shut up.

SAG: *What did you say?*

THE BULL: I said shut up.

SAG: Well, I don't have to take *that*. I'm leaving.

THE BULL: (yawning) Where are you going? Your mother won't take you in. You haven't written or called her in five years.

SAG: I have no intention of going home. That would be worse than living with you. I'm going to move in with my old boy friend, Kevin—*that's* where I'm going.

THE BULL: (no longer yawning, now alert and snorting) Over my dead body you will.

SAG: It's okay. Don't get any nasty ideas, Lumpy. Kevin is married. His wife won't mind. I'll call them first.

THE BULL: (now furious) What do you want to bet his wife *will* mind? WHAT DO YOU WANT TO BET? Or maybe you're planning a *ménage à trois*. IS THAT IT?

SAG: Stop shouting. Your face is red. I thought you didn't approve of gambling. Now you want to make a bet with me over some smutty suspicion you have. See how changeable you are? I thought Taurus men were supposed to be steady and dependable. That's the only reason I married you, because my astrologer told me you were steady and dependable. All astrologers ought to be arrested. What's a *ménage à trois*? If you're going to insult me, at least insult me with slurs I can understand. You know I don't speak Russian.

THE BULL: I GIVE UP! I GIVE UP! Come on Sasquatch, I'll take you out to dinner, and maybe a play afterwards. It's our wedding anniversary, but I don't expect you to remember anything so trivial as that.

SAG: Oh, Buttercup, Sweetheart! Really? Can we see *Man of La Mancha*? And can I call Kevin and his wife, and see if they'd like to go with us?

It kind of goes like that, with variations. And don't let the mix-up over Karl Marx influence you. If she has a Ph.D. in political science, and speaks several languages—which many girl Archers do—she'll be even *more* indignant. Sagittarians are just as fiery and self-righteous when they're well informed as they are when they don't know what they're talking about. Since Sagittarius rules higher education, among other things, the chances are she will have a degree or two. Either way, she'll find tons of topical and tangled issues of the day to analyze with her cool logic and brutal honesty. Then she'll attempt to straighten them out with her Jupiter optimism. It makes breakfast with the morning newspaper a lively meal. Her scintillating discussions make up for burned toast and un-sectioned grapefruit (a degree in cooking she probably does *not* have).

Their political views will differ somewhat, to put it mildly. *He* thinks the *Chicago Tribune* is an underground newspaper and Barry Goldwater is a flaming liberal. *She* thinks John Lindsay is an uptight conservative who's a secret member of the John Birch Society because he was so stuffy about nudity in Central Park when he was Mayor of New York. But she voted for him anyway, because, after all, Lindsay is a Sag himself, so his intentions were probably good. As for the Bull's choice for Mayor of Manhattan, Ronald Reagan or William Buckley—she thinks they would make a worse mess of the job than Lindsay.

At this point, Taurus will shout, "The only possible way that anyone could make a worse mess of governing Manhattan than your friendly Archer John Lindsay did would be to formally declare war on the city!" But the stalemate isn't altogether hopeless. There's an outside chance they both might agree on Jerry Brown and the revival of the *Saturday Evening Post*—for different reasons, of course.

The Sagittarian girl's ebullient spirits help her snap back from most misfortunes like a rubber band. She looks on the bright side of things, and her sunny disposition makes the Bull smile indulgently at the idealism and naivete behind it. But she doesn't recover as quickly from a broken heart as she does from smashed ambitions, a fractured dream, or a period of poverty. Unrequited love (meaning love she gives freely to a man who abuses her trust) gets her down, and sometimes keeps her there. But the gentle understanding of a patient Bull could heal her emotional scars and, at the same time, teach her that not all men are fickle phonies who break promises. It's not uncommon for these two to fall in love while he's playing Big Brother, and drying her tears over a broken affair. His dependability soothes her, and his steady faith in her calms her troubled soul. So she may decide this is the man she's been shooting for and missing since she first aimed her bow and arrow toward the stars and reached for an impossible dream. He may be. Then again, he may not. If the Sun and Moon in their mutual charts are friendly, they can build a relationship which, although it will certainly never be dull, might be snug and satisfying. With a negative Luminary vibration between their horoscopes, they'll need courage.

She is fond of argument. The Sagittarian girl enjoys crossing swords with a good antagonist. Because her swift flashes of logic give her a sharp insight, she's a skillful debater, and painfully honest. The trouble is, a Taurus man is not fond of argument and debate—or even of overly long friendly discussions. She may then invite packs of assorted friends over to camp out, hang around, and keep her wits sharpened. But that will only make things worse. The Bull does not like to see his castle cluttered with noisy strangers, and it will take a good deal of emotional elasticity to ease the tight tensions.

The subjects on the double bill of many of their comic-tragedies will be his stubbornness—and her extravagance. As for how long the quarrels last, it depends on her awareness of his Venus-ruled nature. She'll forget her own anger quickly. He can pout for days unless she knows the secret to his heart. With a Bull, one hard squeeze, and one gentle kiss, will tear down all his obstinate defenses.

That brings us to their sexual harmony. It could be an exciting meeting of Fire and Earth that gives them enough mutual pleasure to soften all their other differences. The initial physical attraction is strong. Her frank, wholesome approach to sex will incite the Bull to open up his heart to her, releasing emotions which may have been stifled within him for fear of rebuff. She'll respond naturally to his affectionate gestures, and his air of tender protectiveness. He makes her feel totally loved, not just passionately desired. Yet she may fulfill his physical-emotional needs more completely than he fulfills hers.

The Sagittarian woman often clings to her phantom lover, the one who promised to carry her off into the clouds in her adolescent fantasies—so there may be times when the Taurus man will vaguely sense that she isn't entirely consumed by abandoned passion during their intimacies. If he does, he should remain silent, and not start one of those Sagittarian arguments. She might zing out one of her truthful arrows at a crucial moment, and damage his Taurean masculinity permanently. The possibilities of this happening are too numerous and embarrassing to mention. Still, despite her daydreams or nightdreams, or whatever, she's not likely to chase her phantom lover anywhere but in her restless mind. Not when she has a real live, warm, kind and cuddly Teddy Bear to take to bed with her. He'll replace the stuffed one she used to sleep with when she was lonely and lost, and despairing of ever being "really truly loved."

A Sagittarius woman is quick to reach out for love, if the hand she grabs and holds tightly also offers friendship. She's impulsive, excited by mental qualities—and loyal, once she becomes sincerely attached. So is he.

But he won't eat egg fu yung in a restaurant forever. To the Bull, a woman's place is in the home, with strong emphasis on the kitchen and the bedroom. If that's where she's happiest, and willing to spend a reasonable amount of time with him, their contentment could be lasting. If she'd rather be out tumbling with the clowns, well—Lumpy and Sasquatch will just have to find some sort of compromise. Real love can always find one.

If she calls him Buttercup (but PLEASE, not in front of others) he'll call her Honey-cakes—if she tickles his *oreille* and scratches his head, he'll grow ecstatic, docile and sweetly manageable. And if he stops telling her to shut up, and tries a little harder to understand her honesty, to take a genuine interest in her opinions and excitement, she might blunt her arrows a little—and maybe even cook some egg fu yung for him herself . . . at home, where she belongs.

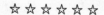

TAURUS

Earth — Fixed — Negative
Ruled by Venus (also by the
Planet Pan-Horus)
Symbol: The Bull
Night Forces — Feminine

CAPRICORN

Earth — Cardinal — Negative
Ruled by Saturn
Symbol: The Goat
Night Forces — Feminine

The **TAURUS-CAPRICORN** *Relationship*

> *It would be an easy map, if that were all; but there*
> *is also first day at school, religion, fathers . . . . .*
> *verbs that take the dative, chocolate pudding day,*
> *getting into braces, say ninety-nine, threepence for*
> *pulling out your tooth yourself, and so on . . . . . .*

The shining virtues of solidity and dependability surround the Taurus Bull and Capricorn Goat with an aura of earth-colored sureness. Life to Taurus and Capricorn is not all grey and brown, nor black and blue. But you'll seldom find useless pastels, optimistic yellows or extroverted reds in their personal halos. When these two animals meet at the zoo, the ground shakes with the vibrations of destiny. Who knows what successes lie ahead when a Bull and a Goat get into harness together? They do.

Neither is in any doubt as to where he (or she) is going. To the top. In a large city or a small town, all the way to the top—to the place where it's peaceful, quiet, financially comfortable—where they'll be isolated from silly dreamers who muck up the air with foolish illusions, fantasies, and the doomed failure of misguided idealism.

The Bulls and Goats are both modest and reserved, and they both use moderation as an inner alarm, or security system, to warn them of any wayward emotions which might short circuit the smooth mechanism of their ambitions. Now, that's not to say that these people are dull, stodgy, humorless and unimaginative plodders. (Taurean Shakespeare, a plodder?) As for Capricorns, nearly all Goats have some sort of creative or artistic talent. Many of them draw as well when they're only doodling as professionals do when they're working, and some of them do actually become successful painters or writers. (Capricorn novelist Henry Miller is both.) As for the Bulls, they have music in their souls, regardless of all the common sense in their heads. Many Taureans are famous singers, musicians or composers. Others just piddle around on the piano, hum into a harmonica, or pluck a homemade zither. Nearly every one of them sings in the shower when they're sure no one can hear. In the humor department, Taurus is the original Falstaff, or court jester, full of throaty chuckles and funny one-liners. The average male or female Bull will slide into a comic monologue with little urging, in the living room or at the office.

The Capricorn Goats also possess a dry and droll sense of humor. Their keen observations on the comedy of life are amusingly clever, even though they normally make their remarks with a straight face, which only makes them funnier. When something really turns these people on, they can weave funny, whimsical tales of dry humor that would be the envy of a professional comedian. So you see, a combination of Taurus and Capricorn can be warm and amusing as well as steady, stable and steadfast.

Still, you shouldn't expect the Marx Brothers. Each was born under a negative Earth Sign, which does not provide fertile soil for frivolity. Goats and Bulls *are* funny, but they're not hilarious, and they won't lose an inch of dignity while they're cutting up. You won't find many of them dancing wildly in noisy disco dives. A nice quiet evening at home, watching movies of the family's vacation at Yellowstone National Park, is more their speed. Taurus and Capricorn constitute what has been called the "Backbone of America."

Since theirs is a 5-9 Sun Sign Pattern (see the back section of Volume II) the areas of romance, children, religion, travel, education and show business are, percentage-wise, the probable pastures where the Goat and

Bull will find a common interest. From there, they may engage in an endeavor which will unite them in a glorious strength of effort and purpose (if their mutual Luminaries are harmonious) or which could result in a hopeless locking of horns and total boredom (if the Sun and Moon Signs between their horoscopes are unfavorable). However, even in the latter case, they can always use the natural sympathy of all 5-9 vibrations to bridge their difficulties. It's difficult for any two people who are influenced by this Sun Sign Pattern to remain angry or opposed for long. The path to reconciliation is always easy, and visible to them, when they desire to find it.

You might see an occasional Capricorn wearing a feather headdress and love beads, smoking peyote in the park and openly flouting convention, but if you do, you can be sure that he (or she) is a lost and lonely soul, trying desperately to prove something—heaven knows what. It's not a natural state of dress or behavior for the normally staid, formal Cappy, and there's certain to be a mild neurosis, or a dissatisfaction with Life, lingering in the smoke trailing out of the peace pipe.

You may also run across a rare Bull who drives a flashy yellow Stingray to the bank and shakes a pink tambourine while he makes his hefty cash deposit, but he's probably just trying to get the attention of a female teller to satisfy his sentimental Venus yearnings. It's really best in the long run to know who and what you are and be true to your own Sun Sign image. A Ram shouldn't try to be docile and meek. A Virgo would be miserable trying to be careless and casual. A Bull and a Goat should not try to be wild gypsies. It doesn't become them. It often becomes Aquarians, but not these two.

One area these Sun Signs are highly unlikely to be involved in together is the drug scene. Most Taureans don't really need the extra kick of a high, because their senses are so acutely tuned in on their environment. The Bulls can sniff a sweet pea or a zinnia, in pure ecstasy for hours, contemplating its form and color and scent—until they get stung by an angry bumblebee. As for the typical Capricorns, they wouldn't dream of indulging in recreation against the law, and certainly not one that might delay or obstruct their Saturn-directed, ambitious climb up the mountain—or cause a scandal.

The Goats want, above all, to be accepted and respected by their friends, relatives and neighbors, and by society at large. When scientists get around to taking their noses out of their test tubes and seriously investigate astrology, they'll find an amazingly small percentage of Taureans and Capricorns in "halfway houses," or in drug and alcohol rehabilitation centers, as compared with the number of other Sun Signs. There are, of course, occasional exceptions that prove the rule, but very few.

I know a Capricorn jeweler in Cripple Creek, Colorado, named Steve, who has mapped all the spots where the wild strawberry grass (a mystical herb) grows the greenest, in the hills behind the small mining community. He gathers it, dries it, dips it in gold or paints it—then uses it to make abstract pictures of Western scenes to sell the tourists in his "Crucible." You can always count on Cappy to find a practical angle for anything. This particular Goat wears modified sideburns as his concession to the Aquarian Age, but somehow, on him, the sideburns only add to his dignified, Dickens-like appearance, and he still doesn't quite fit the picture of a mod swinger.

Speaking of jewelry, many Capricorns and Taureans share with Leo a love of precious gems and metal. The flamboyant-type Leos like to wear them, the flashier the better. The Bulls like to dig them out of the ground, creatively stirred by the excitement of discovery, as they burrow deep into the bowels of the earth for turquoise, gold, silver or diamonds. Capricorn likes to mold them into practical art objects, and the Goat often satisfies those secret artistic yearnings while burnishing the brass and leaning over the Bunsen burner. However, the final objective of both the Taurus Bull and the Capricorn Goat is to find the vain Lions or Lionesses to buy their wares, so they can make Money, which is spelled S-E-C-U-R-I-T-Y. By the way, Steve Mackin, the Colorado Cappy jeweler I mentioned, doesn't always buy his metals from a Taurean miner. He finds many of the materials he turns into jewels fit for a pharaoh—in junk yards. What more appropriate place for a billy goat to roam and nose around in? The great talent of the Saturn-ruled lies in finding hidden treasures, buried among the discarded trash, twisted tin and broken glass of Life. Both literally and symbolically.

Capricorns become adults somewhere around the age of two or three. Taureans decide on the scope of their future financial empires at around the same age. So it doesn't matter how old or how young these two are when they team up. Their goals will be identical. Both the Bull and the Goat are wise to the ways of the outer world. It's their own inner worlds that give them trouble. Each is brimming over with a sentiment he or she won't show—and each is deeply in need of affection and appreciation for which he (or she) won't ask. So there they stand like two mountains, side by side, starving for human comfort and closeness, each stubbornly resisting the other's timid overtures of friendship or demonstrations of open affection.

Children are tiny persons who see, and demonstrate with simplicity, the magic their elders have forgotten as they've passed through Life's sobering experiences. Since Taurus and Capricorn have spent so little time as children (having grown mature at the age of two or three) they may have missed some magic tricks along the way. How can they make up for those lost years of childhood? Easy. Taurus can say to Cappy, "Let's go skinny-dipping in the creek, and the last one in is a rotten egg!" Then Cappy can say to Taurus, "Let's go down to the junk yard and shoot off some fireworks!" While they're there, they can climb an apple tree, play Frisbee with a frog, smell the sweet peas and zinnias, swing in an old tire, and then—ONE-TWO-THREE-GREEN-LIGHT! They're both home free.

☆ ☆ ☆ ☆ ☆ ☆

TAURUS *Woman* CAPRICORN *Man*

————◆————

Will they reach the nursery in time? If so, how delightful for them, and we shall all breathe a sigh of relief, but there will be no story. On the other hand, if they are not in time, I solemnly promise that it will all come right in the end.

They would have reached the nursery in time had it not been that the little stars were watching them . . .

I believe we should devote a major portion of this section of the Taurus-Capricorn chapter to a lesson much needed by all Earth Sign men and women. A lesson, yes . . . but also, perhaps, a kind of karmic warning.

Did you ever notice how people forget things, then try to pretend that what they forgot wasn't very important anyway? A Taurus woman will seldom resort to such pretense. She doesn't forget much, and everything is important to her. All Bulls possess powerful memories.

She certainly will not forget the very day and hour she meets a Capricorn man whose Moon or Ascendent was in an Earth or Water Sign at birth, especially if her Moon and Ascendent were in one of these same elements when she was born. Adding that sort of Luminary harmony to the powerfully compatible 5-9 Sun Sign Pattern, it will be a rare Bull and Goat who don't instantly recognize the soft, humming sound of future happiness together. It's like hitting a romantic jackpot with your last quarter of faith, when you've gambled and lost too many dreams to count, an especially heart-warming win for Taurus and Capricorn, since they both gamble so rarely. On anything.

Because Earth Signs don't talk a lot about their personal lives (both these lovers were born into the Earth Element) lots of people believe the awesome experience of the intertwined destiny of twin souls happens only to those who are born under the influence of the Fire, Air or Water Elements. Not so. Such fascinating appointments with Fate also occur between Bulls and Goats (and Virgo Virgins) leaving them just as profoundly moved as any Earthlings who are swept into a sense of trembling wonder by the realization that their meeting was planned, and inescapably so. To prove this to all the Taurus women and Capricorn men reading their own chapter, or any other curious Earth Sign couples, I offer the following example.

I know a Goat named Steve (not the Cappy jeweler mentioned elsewhere) and a Bull named Debbie (not the same Steve and Debbie pair referred to in the Libra-Aquarius chapter). The surname of these two is Atwell. Capricorn Steve and Taurean Debbie Atwell were married in the fall of 1977. To the average person, Steve and Debbie appear to be just a normal, ordinary, happy and contented young married couple. They are happy and contented, certainly, but their relationship has been more paranormal than normal, more extraordinary than ordinary. From the moment each of them was born, a cosmic plan was formed to draw them magnetically together—as happens with many lovers in the 5-9 vibratory experience, whose Luminary and other planetary aspects are also harmonious.

It's never easy to convince two Earth Sign people that their love—or anything else—is fated. Taurus and Cappy usually believe only what they can hear, see, smell and feel, tangibly. Yet, the Higher Angels of any two who are cosmically programmed to join, are quite persistent, and never stop their efforts until the starry mission has been accomplished.

Pretend you're living on Venus (ruler of Taurus)—or on Saturn (ruler of Capricorn) looking down upon the following events below, on Earth. Capricorn Steve is born, a baby boy Goat, in Woodland Park, Colorado. Near the same time, Taurean Debbie is born, a baby girl Bull, in Milwaukee, Wisconsin. (Like parachuters and astronauts, twin souls sometimes miscalculate, and land a few miles away from the astrally scheduled spot.)

Venus is troubled, but Saturn intones wisely—*wait*. A couple of decades pass, as the lovers grow, miles apart, from boy and girl into man and woman. Then, in 1967, Venus guides Steve, the Goat, to Milwaukee, where Debbie, the Bull, was born and lives—to enter college there. Now, surely, the two of them must meet, and read Life's meaning in each other's eyes. But no . . . stuffy, restrictive Old Man Saturn delays their union still longer. He influences Taurean Debbie's parents to move, with their daughter, in 1969, to Woodland Park, Colorado, where Steve, the Goat, was born.

Like love letters crossing in the mail, now the Goat has found his way to the city where his future wife was born—and she has found her way to the town where her future husband was born. Yet they are still separated as before, except that their separation has reversed itself geographically. So Venus steps in, determined. With her gentle powers of persuasion, she guides Steve, the Goat, in 1971, back to his birthplace—to Woodland Park, Colorado—where Debbie, the Bull, unconsciously awaits him, growing lonelier by the hour, and wondering wistfully, "What's the use of wishing on stars? The stars don't have the power to make wishes come true." She's wrong. They do. For Venus has added a clever twist. She has sung a lovely song into the sleeping ear of Steve, the Goat, haunting him . . . and persuading him to accept a job with the County Road Commission, working for Debbie's Cancerian *father*, Les. Surely, now, the star-crossed lovers must meet!

Alas, no . . . Saturn is ready to impose his cruelest karmic test. After delaying the meeting between the two for nearly another year (how was Steve to know his boss was his future father-in-law?) Saturn influenced Steve to leave. The Goat, whose wanderings had brought him so near the end of his heart's seeking, heeded the command of Saturn, became dissatisfied with his job and resigned (after the proper Capricorn notice, of course) to accept a job as a logger, many miles away. Saturn even tried to convince Steve at this time to move permanently to Alaska. But he was foiled by the free-will choice of the Goat's own Higher Self, in conspiracy with Debbie's Venus. Steve struggled with his strange restlessness (Earth Signs are normally, nearly *never* restless) and at last submitted to the melody Venus sang to him in his dreams at night. He moved *back* to Woodland Park, Colorado, in 1972, and once more went to work for Taurean Debbie's father. Love's victory is in sight!

No. Not quite yet. Cautious Saturn has decreed another three years of waiting in blindness for the lovers, causing Venus to weep in frustration, but then she dries her tears, and cleverly begins to influence the vivid dreams of Debbie's Cancerian father, Les (with the help of *his* ruler, the romantic, sentimental Moon).

At last, as Earth time grew near the mysterious Christmas season of 1975, Debbie's father, while discussing with Steve the approaching holiday party for County Road Commission employees, "just happened" to mention that his daughter didn't feel like attending, because she had no escort (Venus had arranged *that* quite nicely), and since Steve had no date for the party either, he offered to take her (Goats and Bulls, you know, are very circumspect regarding social convention)—as if he had a choice in this karmic drama, which he had not at all, of course.

Then Debbie's mother, Pat, invited Steve to dinner a few days before the party, where he finally met the Taurus girl who was the other half of himself. That evening, Saturn gave only one, final, half-hearted gesture of discipline, as he drew a veil across the eyes of the Goat and the Bull, so they didn't recognize each other at all, except as ordinary people, exchanging ordinary conversation, in an ordinary way.

Then, came the magical night of Christmas Eve, and the party. It was time. Near midnight, the Bull and the Goat looked deeply into each other's suddenly familiar eyes, and *knew* . . . . . . as they were swept into one of those shining moments in eternity.

Yes, it was time. *"Two shall be born . . . . the whole wide world apart . . . ."* sang the Higher Angels of themselves, in joyful unison . . . as trillions of tiny, twinkling stars caroled in space . . . . . . the Moon smiled, behind a single tear . . . . . even Old Man Saturn grinned . . . . and Venus lay herself down on a soft cloud, to rest for a while, exhausted.

It's really a wondrous experience to look down upon events below, on Earth, from the higher vantage point of the stars . . . and watch destiny unfold its silvery-gold wings. An esoteric astrologer, carefully studying both horoscopes, could have predicted that unexpected Christmas Eve for the Goat and the Bull, when he was born, in Colorado—and when she was born, in Wisconsin. It's what makes astrology such a happy art and science. For, we have no real free will at all, any of us, on this level of awareness—except in our choice of *reaction* to Life's destined dramas. Only our Higher Selves possess complete free will over the control of events, which we may attain . . . touch briefly . . . only when we make contact, and thereafter communicate with—the *Super*conscious. I trust this true example will loosen somewhat the esoteric sensoriums of Taurus women and Capricorn men everywhere who have this odd notion that they may exert some sort of sensible, earthy control over their love—its alpha and its omega—without heeding their dreams, which are the true reality, and listening carefully to the symphony of the stars.

The natural chemistry between the Goat and the Bull, as with all 5-9 influenced lovers, makes it appear that their romance will be velvety smooth and free of static. But that's not necessarily true. The 5-9 blessing merely bestows the gift of a relationship which can bear more strain and stress than most, because of the mutual sympathy of the Sun Signs. Tensions may be more easily resolved with less bitterness, the occasional hurts interchanged are less painful, and reconciliations are usually more frequent and successful. They'll have their share of problems, but it takes really serious trouble to create a permanent break between two who are graced by the 5-9 Sun Sign Pattern, once they've committed themselves to each other in earnest.

Taurus and Cappy are each motivated by the same thing—security. Emotional and financial security. Unless the Moon or Ascendent of either was in an Air or Water sign at birth, these two normally don't possess the soaring imagination considered by poets and dreamers to be an absolute necessity for romance. Yet, they do share a quality between them which is profoundly necessary to the strength of any human relationship—the quality of patience. And patience is a virtue which nearly always gives birth, eventually, to triplets—Devotion, Faith and Loyalty, those three magic wands of words that can turn a casual infatuation, based on chemistry alone, into the deeper and enduring emotion of love.

Another ingredient the poets and dreamers deem to be a requirement for the flourishing of lasting romance, is—sentiment. At first glance, the Taurean girl may not appear to be brimming over with sentiment, but there are, nevertheless, sparkling wells of it within her for the right man to discover. Despite her surface practicality, it shows clearly in the strong attachment she has for home, her material possessions, old love letters, her children and her husband. She will resist any major change stubbornly, even when she *seems* to agree. Nor does she easily adapt to minor changes in personal habits. For what is a desire for change but a lack of sentimental attachment to what already exists? Therefore, her resistance to it means the opposite—an excess of emotion for what is already, and what has been. And this is the quality of which sentiment is made.

All right, so sentimental she is. Soft-hearted too. But she is not soft-headed, this lady. She knows what she wants, and will pursue it, in her own determined, yet outwardly unhurried and quiet way. The Taurean woman is perfectly willing to wait, and not push things prematurely, a trait the Capricorn man finds irresistibly feminine. It embodies the ultimate in female sexuality—passivity—which hints to him of the subtle mystery of submission to the dominant masculine force. This will never fail to both please and emotionally "turn on" the always slightly chauvinistic male Goat. And so, he may not notice the hardness of her head when he's been so entranced into seeing himself as the virile conqueror by the softness of her ways and the gentleness of her manner. Not to mention by her deep, throaty, musical voice—and her intriguing curves, all nicely rounded in the proper places, and designed for cuddling. Besides all that, this lady is usually a superb cook, and she has a marvelous sense of humor.

Sometimes it may seem that these two are so alike, you can't tell them apart. But there are ways an astrologer can tell them apart. Here's one. The Taurus girl will seldom burn up her carefully conserved energy in seeking either public acclaim or private approval. When she's made up her mind that she's right about anything, all she asks is that she be left alone, and not pushed by those who think differently. Tell the typical Taurus female that people are whispering about her, or that someone dislikes her, she'll simply shrug and say, "So? Have they nothing better to do than live my life for me? Have they no lives of their own? They must be very frustrated and lonely." Then she'll continue doing whatever it is she is doing, content in her *self*-respect.

Conversely, the Capricorn man cares quite a lot about both public acclaim and private approval. Secretly, he wants to reach the top of his goal or dream, then move into a position of power, far enough away from the clamorous crowds not to be annoyed or contaminated by the childish behavior he observes all around him. The quieter the Goat, the more intensely he inwardly yearns to get there first—with the most. Tell him that someone disapproves of him, and Cappy may shrug, like the lady Bull. He may even murmur the same kind of "I couldn't care less" reply. But *privately*, he will frown, perhaps even frustrate himself into a good toothache or stomachache over it, crack his knee cap several times a week, or break out in nervous bumps. He'll try to raise the opinion of himself held by those disapproving ones, as soon as he can do it without arousing the suspicion that it bothered him. Respect and admiration from business associates, friends, relatives and neighbors is vitally important to the Goat. Taurus appreciates any posies of praise thrown her way too, but unlike her Capricorn man, she won't be crushed when she receives an occasional onion of criticism or a mud pie of gossipy disapproval. She may guess his secret, but she's too kind and tactful, normally, to ever let him know the pain she's aware that he feels when he is not fully appreciated by others. Many emotions pass between this man and woman silently . . . unspoken, but no less deep and binding . . . . communicated in ways the heart hears.

In their sexual relationship, she may sometimes unconsciously project a faintly condescending attitude toward him. The Taurus woman is better prepared for the intimacy of sexual union than the average Goat, because her highly developed senses of hearing, seeing, smelling, tasting and touching, in all areas of existence, also increase her ability to express her love physically in subtle ways. She's also more adept than he in being able to show her affection through sentimental words and gestures (though she won't overdo it) and there could be some scattered occasions, in the beginning especially, when her superior talent for pure erotic sensuality may cause the Goat to feel inadequate as a lover. His physical expression of love is intense and direct, and can cause the Capricorn man to be quick and unrestrained in his sexual desire, with little delicacy. He tends to seek passion, without any frills, and though he doesn't lack tenderness, it may now and then *seem* to her that he does. But tenderness can be taught when it's latent, as it always is, in Capricorn. It may be buried beneath tons of his earthy nature, yet it's a treasure well worth digging for, with perseverance. If she uses her great reserves of patience and gentleness to lead him, he'll be anxious to learn how to fulfill, through their sexual Oneness, all her needs, which are no less intense than his. The Goat never finds it easy to express his strongest yearnings. A Taurus woman, when she follows her instincts, can help him free the emotions he shyly feels, and so very much longs to release.

One of the unfortunate quirks of many Saturn-ruled, Capricorn people (of both sexes) is their tendency to expect love to be sad, somehow . . . . . . because of early romantic disappointments. Since his physical desires are as strong as any man's, this can cause an occasional Capricorn man to separate sex and love, in what, to him, is a practical attempt to satisfy the flesh urges of the former, and avoid being hurt by the latter. Because she is ruled by Venus, it's the responsibility of the Taurus woman to teach her shy, funny, affectionate Goat the eternal truth that these two needs cannot be divided if both are to be completely fulfilled. Sex without love leaves the body cold. Love without sex leaves the soul empty.

Now and then, it happens that there's a Capricorn man who seems to be made entirely of the earthy materials of selfishness, coldness, practicality and ambition. Now and then, it happens that there's a Taurus woman who seems to be made of the earthy materials of common sense, stubbornness, ambition and stale habit. But in both cases, these are simply façades to keep love at a distance, which is just the way they like it.

Why should they openly display their hearts, or offer them for sale to the highest bidder? This man and woman place too much value on their hearts to toss them casually upon love's auction block. But when the Taurus girl comes along to tenderly touch his hand, and gaze deeply into his eyes, quietly . . . the Goat will give his heart away, willingly, to her. Just as she will hand him her own, when she discovers he has guessed her

most closely guarded secret (as closely guarded as his)—that she's a romantic dreamer too.

The Goats and Bulls reading this chapter have, I trust, learned not to
scoff at Destiny and Fate, simply because they are intangible, unseen
forces. To refuse to tune into one's higher consciousness can cause the
path of destiny to take a wrong turn, sadly, somewhere along the way.
And this is far too frequently the fate of dogmatic Earth Sign men and
women, in following the road to happiness. Maybe it would help them to
meditate on the *entire* verse Steve and Debbie's Higher Angels of themselves were singing on that magical Christmas Eve, in Colorado . . . . .
first channeled by Venus, long ago, through the sensitive awareness of a
poet name Rossetti.

> *two shall be born . . . the whole wide world apart*
> *and speak in different tongues . . . and have no thought*
> *each, of the other's being . . . and no heed*
>
> *and these same two*
> *o'er unknown seas, to unknown lands, shall cross*
> *escaping wreck, defying death*
> *and all unconsciously*
> *shape each act, and bend each wandering step*
> *to this one end . . .*
> *   that one day, out of darkness*
> *they must meet*
> *and read Life's meaning in each other's eyes*
>
> *and these same two*
> *along some narrow way of Life shall walk*
> *so nearly side by side*
> *that should one turn, ever so little space*
> *to left . . . or right*
> *they needs must stand acknowledged, face to face*
>
> *and yet . . .*
>
> *with wistful eyes, that never meet*
> *and groping hands that never clasp*
> *with lips, calling in vain, to ears that never hear*
> *they seek each other all their weary days*
> *and die unsatisfied*
>
> *   . . . and this is Fate*

☆ ☆ ☆ ☆ ☆ ☆

TAURUS *Man* CAPRICORN *Woman*

"I won't go to bed," he had shouted, like one who
still believed that he had the last word on the subject.
"I won't, I won't" . . . . . . then Mrs. Darling had come in,
wearing her white evening-gown.

The practical side of a Taurus man will respond, with excitement (as much excitement as a Bull can arouse) to the practical side of the Capricorn girl. He'll admire her self-sufficiency, and her air of well-bred, dignified reserve will intrigue him, not to mention her quiet beauty. Taurus doesn't like anything to come easy, including love. This girl's love never comes easy. Since the Bull believes nothing is worth much if he doesn't have to work hard to get it and keep it, Cappy will interest him right away. Her affections are difficult to capture, for she does not yield her inner self lightly, or quickly. Obviously then, she's a prize the Bull deems it worthwhile to pursue.

But he may not respond with the same fervor of excitement to her apparent lack of sentiment. Despite his feigned disinterest in mushy declarations of love, Taurus is the most sentimental of all the Sun Signs. He doesn't wear his heart on his sleeve, but it's in the right place, however well hidden from view. It beats faster when he plays their favorite song, smells her perfume unexpectedly somewhere, or hears a laugh that reminds him of hers.

The female Goat is not quite so bowled over by nostalgic memories when a love affair is over, nor by the daily reminders of it while it's still alive. That's not to say she isn't capable of a deep devotion. Her loyalty, in fact, is unmatched by any other female on the astrological wheel, once she finds a man she thinks is worth loving wisely and well. She can also be tender and funny and gentle and comforting, all those lovely, feminine things. After all, Capricorn is a feminine sign. But it's also a negative Earth Sign—and Cardinal too—which means she doesn't want a man to dominate her completely, and she's not about to submerge herself in sentiment that might cloud her judgment or cause her to make a mistake she'll have to live down.

You notice I didn't say a mistake she'll regret. Cappy doesn't waste time on regret, which she considers a useless, maudlin emotion. But she does feel obliged to live down an action not based on good sense. It's the yoke of punishment Saturn places on her shoulders when she goofs, a stern reminder not to goof again. To her, "living it down," means taking her medicine straight, without whimpering.

This pretty, feminine woman is as tough as a gold miner's old boot, although she can have exquisitely tender feelings for those nearest and dearest to her, and she's quite capable of being faithful, if her mate was chosen by both her heart and her head. When she occasionally slips up, and allows her heart to rule alone, her head does not quickly forgive her. She must be somehow self-punished, according to Saturn's stern discipline. But she's not burdened with the kind of idealism that causes people to mask unpleasant facts behind a veil of sentimental evasion. She corrects her mistakes, then plods right on, along the rocky trail, seldom looking back. This girl is enormously practical, and imbued with a great deal of common sense. For example, very few Cappies become hookers or call girls, but their choice has little to do with sentimental morality. I once had a conversation with a female Goat about prostitution. She was decidedly contemptuous of women who sell their sexual favors in the market place, not because of moral or emotional objections, but because, in her precise words: "the profession involves so many middlemen that the prostitute ends up a financial loser, as well as a social outcast—and she can work for such a limited number of years. Then what does she do? It just isn't *practical*."

So, back to what we first discussed. The Taurus male will admire her common sense and practicality, because they match his own, but will probably be shocked (or hurt) at her lack of sentiment. It can put him in a twin dither of STOP and GO urges with her. But since their chemistry is so right, he'd be wise to swallow his shock and hurt with patience (another quality they both possess in abundance) until she's made one of her combined head-and-heart decisions to love and marry him. After that, she'll probably be as sentimental with him and with their family (including her parents and siblings, whom she'll stick to like a burr) as he could possibly desire. Married to the right man, no one makes a better wife and mother than Capricorn. She may appear snobbish and cold and a bit of a social climber to the rest of the world, but her husband, children and relatives will know only her warmth and love.

Jealousy will probably not be a large problem with these two. Neither the Bull nor the Goat is as mortally wounded, in an emotional sense, by an isolated act of infidelity as a Fire or Water Sign would be. With these two, it's more as if someone has robbed them of a valued possession. A Taurus man will become just as furious if an intruder steals his wife's affections as if he had stolen his car or his checkbook, about which he is more or less equally sentimental. A Goat Girl will be as coldly angry if a woman flirts with her Taurus husband as if she had caught the vixen trying to steal her mother's heirloom bedspread, or her father's antique clock.

When you comprehend how painful it is for both the Bull and the Goat to give up cash, or material things, I suppose you might say that unfaithfulness is no more pleasant for them than for the more emotional Sun Signs. But neither he nor she is inclined to throw away a secure relationship or a marriage over a single act of infidelity. Bulls and Goats have little desire to tamper with or to destroy an existing situation. When they do, which will be a rare occurrence, you can be sure of three things: (1) they will never forgive, (2) they will never forget, (3) they will never turn back and start again, with fresh hope in a new beginning. What's lost is lost, what's gone is gone. Finders may be keepers, but losers are never weepers, when they are Taureans or Capricorns.

Although they don't turn on the spigots of tears or hysteria, rejection or failure can, nevertheless, hurt them both deeply. But a Goat and a Bull will not sniffle in front of nosy neighbors. They'll brood in dismal melancholy privately, until finally, after weeks, or months, or years of inner sadness, they decide that the continuation of grief over spilled buttermilk is just not *practical*. Then they'll brighten up a little. Since this is a 5-9 Sun Sign Pattern, it will take a really major catastrophe to break a tie they have cemented together with sincere intentions.

Sexually, they are firmly and comfortably mated, because the physical relationship is usually—not always, but usually—more satisfying when the man is the Taurus, and the woman the Capricorn, than when the team shifts sides. He is a quietly sensual lover, full of the erotic ability to stir her passions, yet capable of also expressing himself with honest affection, combined with the kind of respect for sex (and for her womanhood) that she demands. She's not a girl who will expect long hours of preliminary romancing, and sentimental whisperings before their physical Oneness. Nor will she require her lover or husband to spend another several hours murmuring drowsy endearments, after the passion of their love has been fulfilled. The natural, silent feeling of closeness following sexual union contents her, and gives her a feeling of completeness. Why gild the lily? It's no wonder this woman can lure a Bull more successfully than a flaming Fire Sign female (who might frighten him away) or a changeable Air Sign lady (who might drive him into confusion).

However, the sentimental Bull may require more than five minutes to demonstrate *his* devotion to *her*. Since Cappy is no more inclined to shirk her marital or love responsibilities than any other kind of duty, she'll usually respond beautifully, by genuinely trying to match his more leisurely

Taurean lovemaking pace herself, and they'll become happy romantic, as well as sexual, lovers—so that, by the time they reach their Golden Wedding anniversary, they'll have the whole Sex-Love relationship bound up together in a lovely, warm unity. An occasional Capricorn woman may tend to separate sex from love, due to bitter memories of youthful hurt. The Bull may have fallen into the same pattern, unconsciously, and for the very same reasons. (Both Goats and Bulls have incredibly long memories.) But together, they can teach each other how well these two needs blend, and she'll awaken, through his tenderness, to the childhood dreams and innocence she lost through the premature growing-up all Capricorns experience—while he'll gradually forget his painful memories of the past, as she gently replaces them with warm and loving images for tomorrow's remembering.

The typical Taurean is rather uncommonly devoted to his family, which is a good thing, because it will help him tolerate the Goat Girl's obsession with hers. A Capricorn's devotion toward family ties can be summed up briefly, with Milne's poem:

> James James Morrison Morrison
> Weatherby George Dupree
> took great care of his mother
> though he was only three

The verse is appropriate to the Saturn-ruled, whether the Goat is male or female. In the latter case, just change the name to Jane Jane Morrison Morrison Weatherby Elizabeth Dupree, and *know* that she, also, "took great care of *her* mother, though she was only three." Not only that, she'll take good care of her family when she's past one hundred, and her parents are pushing the second century mark. Unless some traumatic and tragic experience in youth has left a neurosis of bitter rejection—between these two, and their mutual families, holidays will never be lonely and guest rooms will always be filled. The Bull will benignly approve of his Goat Girl's attitude toward both her own and his relatives, unless his mother is a Cancerian, and then it might get a little sticky. (Or if his Moon or Ascendent is in Cancer.) It could create anything from a mild emotional tremor, now and then, to a full scale earthquake on occasion.

A Cancerian mother is intensely possessive of her son, and a Capricorn wife is intensely possessive of her husband. (Jealousy and possessiveness are not quite the same thing.) It's possible that such a situation could cause the Goat Girl to feel tugged on from both sides, until she decides (figuratively) to butt her tough horns against one side or the other. But the Bull has horns too, and it's only fair to warn Cappy that the odds are stacked against his using them against Mama. For either a Capricorn woman—or a Bull with a Cancer Moon or Ascendant—to be forced to choose between love and family ties, is like being condemned to the horrors of a Tchen-type Oriental torture chamber.

They are good for each other, in so many ways, the Goat and the Bull. After a while, they can even read one another's thoughts, so closely attuned can Taurus and Capricorn become, throughout their years of togetherness.

HIM: Would you like to . . .
HER: Yes, if we can get there in time for the first feature. Shall I . . .
HIM: No, don't call them. Let's go by ourselves. Remember . . .
HER: . . . our first anniversary, when we couldn't afford to go anywhere, so we stayed home, and . . .
HIM: You wore your white evening gown anyway, and I . . .
HER: . . . spilled grape juice on it, and I . . .
HIM: And you laughed. Most women would have cried. Then I . . .
HER: Then you said you were glad of me . . .
HIM: Wasn't that a . . .
HER: A silly, sentimental thing to say? Yes, but I've never forgotten it. Look at the time! If we don't hurry, we'll miss the first feature. Do you . . .
HIM: Still want to go? No. Let's stay home tonight, and . . .
HER: Yes.

☆ ☆ ☆ ☆ ☆ ☆

TAURUS

Earth — Fixed — Negative
Ruled by Venus (also by the
Planet Pan-Horus)
Symbol: The Bull
Night Forces — Feminine

AQUARIUS

Air — Fixed — Positive
Ruled by Uranus
Symbol: The Water Bearer
Day Forces — Masculine

The **TAURUS-AQUARIUS** *Relationship*

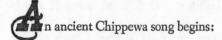

> . . . . . *they knew it was make-believe, while to him*
> *make-believe and true were exactly the same thing.*
> *This sometimes troubled them, as when they had to*
> *make-believe that they had had their dinners.*

An ancient Chippewa song begins:

> *as my eyes search the prairie*
> *I feel the summer . . . in the spring*

These words were surely chanted in the Garden of the Gods, at sunrise, by an Aquarian Chippewa. They express so clearly the essence of the Water Bearers, who feel the summer in the spring—and the winter in the fall—always a season ahead of everyone else. Their Uranus vision, spanning the years, the decades, and even the centuries, gives them the benefit of an extra dimension or two, which accounts for the vague expression in their eyes.

The rare ability to gaze into the world of Tomorrow, while remaining acutely conscious of the world of Today, involves the *Intelligence*, the *Instinct* and the *Imagination*, functioning together as a trinity, smoothly and simultaneously. When Pisceans peek into Tomorrow, they often ignore Today—and the brief glimpses into the Future that Sagittarians occasionally experience are just that—brief moments of prophecy. Scorpios become too intensely involved in whatever dimension they're floating within, to pay heed to any others at the same time. Only the Water Bearers can juggle the *Intelligence*, *Instinct* and *Imagination* as a triplicity, allowing them to form a three-dimensional image of Past, Present and Future, which is perfectly synchronized. Now do you see why Aquarius is called the "Sign of Genius"?

Some Aquarian men and women enjoy it so much out there in Tomorrow, or Yesterday, however, that they forget their synching talent, and decide to visit there for a while, in their astral bodies, leaving their flesh bodies behind them to manage as best they can during the absence, walking around zombie-like, neither hearing nor seeing, and speaking in an unintelligible mumble. Do you see why Aquarius is also called the "Sign of Insanity"?

Ah, Genius and Insanity! They go together, like pickles and pumpernickel, and every single Aquarian who has ever walked the Earth is the first, while also being harassed, from time to time, by the second—or accusations of it. From Mia Farrow Previn to Lewis Carroll, from Abraham Lincoln to Tallulah Bankhead, from Ayn Rand and Telly Savalas to Vanessa Redgrave and Charlie Brown's dog, Snoopy (alias Joe Cool and the Red Baron) Aquarians are well aware that they possess this half-and-half nature, and they are all rather marvelously untroubled by it, happily admitting their quirks, like Aquarian astrologer Carroll Righter, who cheerfully quipped, when his mother called him "an odd duckling"—"*Well, quack quack!*"

Grand Ole Opry star Minnie Pearl tells about a man in her home town who isn't very bright. After he's opened his mouth and said, "Howdy!" he has told you everything he knows, claims Minnie. She shouldn't judge him too hastily. He could be an Aquarian, out there on one of his extended trips into the ethers. The mechanism on his Time Machine which he carries in his noodle got jammed somewhere, perhaps in another century, caught in a Space Warp (a kind of hole in the sky) and he hasn't returned yet. But he will. Or *she* will. Water Bearers always count-down from Tomorrow, and reappear brighter than when they left in their mental capsules. The Aquarians who keep an even keel between all dimensions more often than they get lost in a Space Warp, are the prophets, visionaries, creative brains and inventive geniuses of mankind and womankind. They gather the Waters of Wisdom and Higher Truth from the deep wells of Tomorrow, and pour it out in a continuous flow, in their weird guises of pixilated scientists and inventors, musicians, artists, writers, politicians, cab drivers, barbers and Chippewa Indian Chiefs and Squaws. That's sort of "where it's at" with Aquarius, "it" being their consciousness, and "at" being the triple dimension of Time and Space they visit.

As for the Bulls, we can sum up their position in Time and Space very quickly. Taurus exists in solid, tangible form in the Here and Now. Never mind the Heretofore or the Hereafter. One dimension is usually more than satisfactory for both the male and the female Bulls. As far as these men and women are concerned, there are quite enough problems to be solved on this level, in the Present, without flying around looking for trouble on other levels in the Past or Future. Tomorrow was made for some, perhaps. But to Taurus, Tomorrow may never come. Take care of Today. Even the very rare, "psychic" Bull, such as Taurean Peter Hurkos, is glued to Earth. Hurkos may take a swing out into the Future, or back into the Past, due to other planetary positions in his birth chart, but when he returns from his brief, un-Taurus-like flights, he wants his dinner, and he wants it on time. He also pays his bills, minds his business, and expects others to mind theirs. Besides, the only reason a Taurus psychic scatters any predictive pearls, is to convince people they should behave in a *sensible* manner right *now*, and they should be prepared, in a *practical* way, for any emergencies the Bull may have glimpsed in the Future.

Unlike Aquarius, Taurus is neither weird nor pixilated. Taurus personifies Norman Rockwell's paintings—all of them. The Bull's eyes do not contain the Aquarian's vague expression. They are soft, serene—and sometimes beady, when the Bull is in a fury (which occurs most infrequently, but when it does, makes up for its rarity with intensity). However, Taureans do often mumble, like Aquarians, in unintelligible monosyllables, at times, like "Yep"—"Nope"—"Uh-Huh"—"Huh-Uh"—and "Grmmmpphhff." So in this respect, there's a faint resemblance between them. These two were both born under a Fixed Sign, giving them also in common a certain Fixity of purpose (you might prefer to call it obstinacy). Outside of these similarities, they're as far apart as two humans can be, and still recognize one another as being from the same planet. (It must be admitted here, in all honesty, that sometimes Taurus and Aquarius do *not* recognize one another as being from the same planet.) Taurus desires to retain the status quo. Aquarius desires to change it.

Picture these two, eyeing each other across a room, or across the street. Aquarius, the Bouncing Crystal Ball—and Taurus, the immovable, but lovable Lump of Earth. It's difficult to imagine their conversation, if they should decide to draw closer, isn't it? I mean, after all, what does an immovable, but lovable Lump of Earth say to a Bouncing Crystal Ball? "Grrmmmpphhff"? And what, in heaven's name, does a Bouncing Crystal Ball say to an immovable, but lovable Lump of Earth? "Howdy!" ? ? ? Well, let me tell you that, regardless of what the folks in Minnie Pearl's home town might believe, this mutual greeting will definitely never convey all that either of them knows.

Taurus is not inclined to be a chatterbox, blabbing all his (or her) knowledge to strangers. However, the practical facts and common sense the Bulls have cautiously accumulated, and carefully stored in their heads, are nonetheless powerful mental tools, when they choose to sharpen them and go to work building a house, a financial empire, a career—or a firm approach to love and friendship. "Grrmmmpphhff" is assuredly not all Taurus knows. But it may be all the Bulls are willing to tell an Aquarian on short acquaintance, until they've had time to decide if the Water Bearer is worth the energy required for any further chit-chat.

As for Aquarius, the Uranus-ruled men and women always know far more than they spill carelessly out of their little brown jugs. They receive their kicks from life by playing W. C. Fields, speaking in Sanskrit, underwater . . . sometimes varying this by switching to Peter Lorre or Boris Karloff, whispering through a megaphone, while chewing bubble gum underwater. When they're on dry land, they use a word scrambling device (invisible, of course) that makes their Uranian conversations often sound like a tape being played backwards, at high speed. Even when their remarks are clear enough to sound like a tape being played forward, at slow speed, there are usually lots of blank spots, where the tape has been erased. Haven't you noticed that? Taurus has noticed it, frequently, and gives a disgusted grunt or "Grrmmmpphhff," refusing to try to cope with such nonsense. Or . . . do the Water Bearers perhaps just flip off their switches now and then, when they want to splice out a thought, an idea, a feeling or a concept too far advanced for the ordinary mortal to comprehend? Whatever, the point is that Taurus and Aquarius will communicate with one another exactly in the same manner they each communicate with the rest of us—in their own time, and in their own way.

This is a 4-10 Sun Sign Pattern, which means that compatibility and comprehension between these two is achieved only with effort—and is rewarded with that good feeling of having accomplished something worthwhile, when it *is* finally achieved. Assuming they've broken the ice with "Grrmmmpphhff" and "Howdy!" how do they then break down the bashful barriers of Taurus, and the detachment of Aquarius, to get into action as a unity? It depends on many factors. To begin with, Taurus has a great deal more reserve of manner than do the typical, friendly, gregarious Water Bearers. Even the timid Aquarians count everyone as "friend," from the postman to the President (the President of the local Anti-pollution League, or the President of the United States—Aquarius hardly knows the difference). It's all they can do, these people, to keep themselves straightened out on the difference between girls and boys, top and bottom, up and down, black and white, cold and hot, and all that. A typical Aquarian is not prejudiced in his or her choice of buddies. "Buddy" is a term Uranian folk use to describe lovers, husbands, wives, cats, dogs, squirrels, children, neighbors, dolphins, muggers, pickpockets, relatives and so on. They are all "buddies." Sometimes this is varied with "my pal," "my old buddy," "my good buddy," "my friend"—but never "my *best* friend." Aquarians are no more partial to friends than they are selective of them, so no one ever becomes the Aquarian's "best friend."

Taurus is just one of the crowd. The Bulls may bring along their empty cups if they wish, and the Water Bearers will fill them. But Uranus-ruled men and women (and children) have little patience with the Bull's long silences and pouting spells. There are too many thirsty people out there who need their time and attention, and a long drink from the waters of Uranian Wisdom.

It takes the average Taurean several years to make a friend—a real friend, not counting relatives and casual acquaintances. It takes Aquarius approximately only five seconds to say, "Howdy, Buddy!" Then you've been told, you believe, all he (or she) knows, in Uranus Sanskrit, of course, or maybe in Aquarian hieroglyphics—so now you're friends, right? Taurus is suspicious of friendships made quickly, taken lightly, and so loosely defined.

If these two work through a harmonious Sun-Moon-Ascendent relationship between their birth charts, they'll eventually begin to speak the same language, and be able to communicate. Even without help from a favorable Luminary and Ascendent exchange, and other such harmonious aspects in their horoscopes, they'll learn many valuable lessons from each other, and the mutual education could be fun and firecrackers, as well as mentally and emotionally stimulating—causing their souls to stretch. Souls need exercise too, just like bodies. That's the purpose of the 4-10 vibration.

With a square or opposition between their mutual Luminaries, and Ascendents, these two Sun Signs may have to learn to protect themselves in the clinches. The Bulls will balk at the airy nonchalance of the Aquarians, who may seem to be looking down and patronizing them, from up there in the clouds. The Water Bearers will need a firm grip to keep from slipping over the wobbly line between Genius and Insanity, when the earthy Taureans make them feel they're pulling the dead weight of the Bull's disapproval behind them on their trips into outer space.

Although there's a rumor that a lone cow once crashed the scene in a grand leap, it's difficult for a Bull to jump over the Moon, for all his (or her) splendid strength—as hard as it is for an Aquarian to be confined by a barbed wire fence, in a peaceful, but monotonous pasture. But if it's true that "the dish ran away with the spoon," why can't a Bull frolic happily with a Water Bearer? In the realms of tolerance and joy, cats can play fiddles, and—Hey-diddle-diddle! a Bull *can* jump over the Moon! I just checked my notes, and several of the astronauts were Sun Sign Taureans. What do you know? Life is full of surprises, as any Aquarian can tell you. Even if you don't ask.

☆ ☆ ☆ ☆ ☆ ☆

TAURUS *Woman* AQUARIUS *Man*

◀━━◆▶━━▶

*"Wendy, Wendy, when you are sleeping in your silly bed
you might be flying about with me saying funny things
to the stars."*

"Oo!" . . . . . . *She was wriggling her body in distress.*

Very little comes as a surprise to an Aquarian man, considering his intuitive nature. Still, he may not be prepared for what happens after he knocks around with a Taurus girl for a spell. Here he is, a man with a firm set of ethics (they may be peculiar, but they are his own, and they are firm—or rather, Fixed). He has a great feeling for humanity. He's interested in everybody, he has no prejudices against the female sex, the male sex, or people of any other sex. Yet, look at the hurt he's caused her, all unawares. How can he have hurt her? They had so much fun together at the zoo. He was just trying to be her big brother. Her friend. Her pal. Her buddy.

A Taurus girl was formed for romance by Mother Nature, and this is not a female who argues with Mother Nature. Where he made his mistake with her was back at the beginning. The first time he found himself concentrating his fitful, but flattering attention on her, asking her shocking questions of an intimate sort, and pulling on his ear sympathetically when she cried, he should have made a special effort—to notice that she's a woman. She's certainly aware that he's a man. She noticed it right off. And to her, the romantic arithmetic then became quite simple. One male plus one female equals ecstasy—on several levels, not the least of which is the sensual gratification of touching.

Aquarians reading this may need an interpretation of the word "touching." It means kissing, hugging, holding hands, and all sorts of things. It means, like—well, human bodily contact. Flesh-to-flesh. Human bodily contact is something which not all, but many Water Bearers, fear as they fear the black plague. (The black plague is what you get if someone uses your towel or toothbrush. Or the white plague. Either one. Both deadly.) It isn't that Aquarians are against touching itself, but it leads to—what do they call it—two becoming one? Or some nonsense like that. Aquarius feels safer when two remain two. That way, he's sure of where he stands. Alone. Free of obligations, and in no danger of losing his individuality. If you're going to go around touching people, especially girl-type people, who knows what you're letting yourself in for? Especially if she forgets to bring her own towel when they go swimming. Maybe even the black or white plague!

Perhaps he was devoting himself to her for the purpose of taking her apart to see how she ticks or tocks, with the same fascination he has for all forms of experimentation. But she didn't realize she was only a guinea pig for his curious mind. When he invited her to bring her own pizza and cream soda, and watch the Macy's Thanksgiving Day parade from his roof, she thought he was, well—to be honest—a little crazy. Still, it was a wonderful kind of crazy, and when she considered it carefully (as Taureans always do) she decided he wouldn't invite just any old girl to hang around on his roof with him. She then concluded it meant he loved her.

Maybe he did. But an Aquarian man has a way of switching love-at-first-sight into friendship, as a sort of test of its deeper worth, then letting it rust there. To a Taurus girl, such neglect of mutual emotional needs is a sure way to become a real-born-loser. She believes that genuine love doesn't strike but once (sometimes not even that often) in a lifetime. Why risk missing it by not recognizing it, and giving it a chance? She's astrologically right. Real love (meaning the twin soul union) is a rare and beautiful experience. It's a sad thing to miss it, and have to catch up with it in a future incarnation. Even though Aquarius is the natural ruler of the eleventh astrological house of "karmic love," many Aquarians do miss it. They rank right alongside Virgos and Sagittarians in their inclination toward bachelorhood, and in their desire to avoid confinement in the institution of marriage. Of course, there are compensations. They also avoid mistakes. That's a good thing to avoid with this Sun Sign combination, considering it's a 4-10 vibration. If it should happen to be a mistake, and they get married, it won't take much strain to unravel the knot.

There are exceptions, but the average Taurean girl who is unhappily involved with an Aquarian male is more vulnerable to being devastated by it than he is. Once she falls in love, she intends it to last forever-and-three-days. That would be his original intention too, except for his proclivity for eccentric action, which she may not anticipate, because he can't even predict it himself, and heaven knows he can't explain it. He's a Fixed Sun Sign, so it is conceivable and even possible for him to remain contented with the right woman for a lifetime. But when he's not contented, his Uranus vibes will make the final split much easier for him to bear than for her.

Aquarius adapts smoothly to change, when it's necessary (sometimes even when it isn't), despite his Fixity in daily, personal habits. Taurus does not. To her, change is frightening. It means the new, the strange, the untried and the unfamiliar. She feels emotionally safe, secure, protected in her lover's arms, once there's been intimacy between them. She's used to him. Like she's used to her hair style, her faded jeans, her old records, her broken-down coffee pot, and her broken-in tennies—with much more depth of feeling, of course. Even if living with him is full of friction, to the point of being unbearable, she'll postpone ending the misery through separation or divorce as long as she stubbornly believes there's still hope. You have to admire her staying power. But when and if she does finally make up her mind to leave him, she'll go. And nothing will bring her back. That is, if she was serious about leaving, and not just trying it as a last, desperate resort. If it's the latter, her faith and efforts may be rewarded, because the temporary break provides a change from monotony, and forces him to take a fresh interest in the changing scene. It's a strategy some Taurus girls use successfully, even going so far as to feign a love affair with a handsome gigolo type, which often has the effect of jerking Aquarius back from his world out yonder, and waking him up to the possibility that he's losing more than a comfortable friendship. He may start having nightly hot flashes and cold chills, as he remembers the funny way her nose wrinkles when she laughs, the way she sings off key in the shower—(and uses her own towel)—the sleepy-soft look in her eyes on Sunday mornings, her blueberry pancakes, the little feminine mooing sounds she makes when she's been well loved, her wacky jokes, her shiny hair, her scented skin, her—well, maybe she was *more* than just another buddy. She was so great at pulling splinters out of his toes, massaging his back, having faith in his visions, making things cozy, making poverty fun, making his headaches disappear, making potato soup, making money stretch, making love—yes, she's something more than a pal. She's really something else.

So, he pedals his bike to her pad, brings her a pet mouse as a peace offering, shoves a bunch of ragged dandelions in her hand, gives her a lopsided grin, and asks shyly, "Hey, sexy! You want to play house again?" However, if she's not using the walkout as romantic strategy—if it is, instead, the result of her careful deliberation—he can stuff the mouse and the dandelions back in his pocket. A Bull once gone, is gone. He could move a mountain more easily than he could sway the Taurus woman into trying again, once she decides it's really over between them.

Without a favorable Sun-Moon aspect between this (or any other) 4-10 Sun Sign Pattern, the slightest breeze may rock the boat, and cause a shipwreck. Because his Uranus reflexes are quicker than hers, he may sail away before she realizes what happened, and she'll be left floating around in a sea of emotions without a life preserver, and she's of the Earth element, not Water. That's why Bulls are in more danger than Water Bearers when love goes on the rocks. With planetary assistance from a harmonious Sun-Moon aspect in their mutual charts, however, they can survive the storms and knit a bright crazy-quilt of living and loving, stuffed with soft feathers of compassion and affection, to keep them warm and toasty while they fight and kiss and make-up periodically.

Their sexual relationship may be frustrating and unfulfilling, unless she caters to his need for change by matching his madness. If he surprises her by wearing a Donald Duck face mask to bed, or letting their pet mouse loose under the blankets to nibble her toes, she shouldn't pout stubbornly, or sleep in the guest room. She should shock him right back with her own little surprises, like wearing his dandelions in her hair at night—making a bedspread out of old Union Jacks, wired with a music box that plays "God Save the Queen" when she presses the button—or maybe painting the ceiling with luminous stars and galaxies, like the one at the Hayden Planetarium, so he can lie there and try to spot the Big Dipper while they're making love. Anything to vary the scene.

He'll have to take the time, and have the patience, to understand and fill her deep hunger for affection, and for the sensual in lovemaking. She needs expressions of love at times other than their sexual union. But this man can be a sensitive, considerate lover, if the Taurus girl-woman tries a little harder to be tolerant of his little sexual, emotional and romantic idiosyncrasies. She'll have to realize that his Uranus passion is mental, as well as physical, and find imaginative ways to blend his abstract desires with her more centered and traditional sexual needs. It's a constant challenge to arouse this man to the point of pure, sky rocket passion, but worth the effort, because Aquarius can bring to sexual Oneness an unexpected magic, that turns on the heart and soul, as well as the physical senses.

One word of warning. The pet mouse he may use as a conciliatory gesture when they've quarreled—he'd better make that a gerbil. Taurus people are very closely related, not to just bulls and cows, but also, on a different, but equally powerful vibration, to the elephant. You know what elephants do when they see a mouse. She's liable to do the very same thing. Scream or trumpet chillingly, toss her trunk in the air wildly, in great fright, and leap across the room . . . into his arms. Oh, I see. *That's* why he *brought* the mouse! Hmmmm. Never underestimate the canny calculations of an Aquarian male. He always knows exactly what he's doing, however daffy he may appear while he's doing it.

These two are different. She's a girl. He's a boy. She'd like him to treat her as a woman, he'd like to be treated as a man. She deserves it. He may not. (But men are dreary sorts—boys are more fun.) She likes thick carpets and plush, plump furniture. He'd just as soon sack out in a tent. She likes to scrub her skin with a scented back brush, in a tub of water, filled with perfumed oils. He likes to beat his skin with bamboo leaves, Japanese style, in the shower. She's tuned in to peace and quiet—which he calls boredom. He's tuned in to excitement and controversy—which she calls bedlam.

She may eventually lose her normally well controlled temper and patience, and tell him to go get someone else to pull the splinters out of his toes. Still, if he can teach her how to fly a little, and she can teach him how to get it together . . . . . . well, who knows? "If" is a little word, with a big meaning. But "love" is a four letter word, with infinite power.

☆ ☆ ☆ ☆ ☆ ☆

TAURUS *Man* AQUARIUS *Woman*

An Aquarian is a very special kind of woman, who needs a very special kind of man. Then again, there are those who would say she is a weird kind of woman, who needs a super patient kind of man.

Most of those people would be Bulls, plugging themselves by reminding you that *they* are super patient sorts, along with their other virtues. The feminine Water Bearer's personality is unique, and to most of us, unique means special. To an Earth Sign, however, unique normally means weird. Strange. Not-to-be-believed. It's simply a matter of definition. The important thing for the Bull to remember is that this lady is different. She intrigues the masculine Taurean because she's mysterious. It's not the mystery he senses around a Scorpio woman—the mystery of wondering if she's evil or pure, if she's cool or warm. With this Uranus lady, it's the mystery of wondering if she's for real. It fascinates him. And well it might.

She has a delightfully vague air about her. That's only natural. She was born under an Air Sign. It's hard to define. Like, when she begins a sentence, and leaves it hanging there, in mid-air . . . . when she stares off into the distance, while he's saying "I love you" . . . . has trouble remembering his name. Things like that. Later, the Bull will discover that she was only too clearly present and aware at those times when he thought her attention was wandering. She didn't miss a nuance. Her seeming vagueness is merely a signal that she's mentally floating around, waiting until the scene catches up with where she's already gone—ahead. It's such a bore when a man can't travel on her electrical circuit, so she instinctively fades away or tunes in to a different channel. An Aquarian female can be here—or she can be there—but here or there, she's always very far out.

Since she's as much of an individualist about romance as she is about everything else, this lady makes up her own rules about love as she goes along. Whatever they may be, whether puritanical or permissive by other people's standards, she's true to them, and to herself. It's this very quality of self-honesty and integrity that attracts the Bull to the girl Water Bearer like a magnet, and causes him surprisingly often to tolerate her romantic rules, even when they rub against his grain and grit. He clearly sees her as one of the few really honest people left in the world. One of the few ethical, reliable, dependable . . . . . oh, now, wait just a *minute*. Hold it right here. Honest and ethical she is. But you are inviting trouble, Taurus man, if you start out by expecting this woman to be reliable and dependable.

It's true that she's Fixed in purpose and intent, being born, like the Bull, under a Fixed Sign. She's also an excellent organizer (for all her deceptive fuzziness of manner) and like him, she likes to save and accumulate things. Not because she's economical, a scavenger, or a pack rat—or for any of those sensible, practical (to Bulls) reasons. She saves and accumulates things that just happen to strike her fancy. Like the tassel from Robert E. Lee's baby bootie she bought at an auction down south—or the tiny clapper from the bell on the desk of her fifth-grade schoolteacher. She leans toward antiques (the Bull leans toward breaking them) and she saves all sorts of nonsense, like her old Mousketeer cap, her father's shaving cup, the nude picture a friend took of her when she was soaking up the sun one summer. Stop pawing and snorting, the friend was female—and most Uranus-ruled girls are not modest in the company of their own sex, in the woods, when there's no one around. Some of them are not overly modest in crowds either, but let's not talk about those Water Bearers—the Bull has not fallen in love with this type, you can bet your baby bootie tassel on that. Her fondness for antiques (if she's a typical Aquarian) may annoy the Bull to the point of great frustration, and huge exasperation. (Everything Taurus does is great or huge, never petty or teeny-tiny.) This man may enjoy the tradition of the past, and well made furniture, created by craftsmen to last more than three weeks, but he won't go for those fragile, dainty antiques that fall apart when you sit on them. Many a Bull has fallen plumb through an eighteenth-century chair his Aquarian mate has purchased—while he's reading the stock market reports in the evening paper. And I tell you that a Bull, who has fallen through the seat of a chair on his backside—hard—can be quite bearish about the whole matter. He's capable of picking up the offending chair and smashing it into splinters, while smashing her feelings at the same time, by shouting, "KEEP THESE @@ ## !! % ¢ & ** (expletives deleted SILLY PIECES OF JUNK OUT OF MY WAY! YOU SPENT ENOUGH MONEY FOR THAT @@ ## !! % ¢ & ** THING TO BUY A WHOLE HOUSEFUL OF SOLID, SENSIBLE FURNITURE. I WANT A LA-Z-BOY RECLINER IN THIS ROOM, IN THIS VERY CORNER BY TOMORROW NIGHT—AND WHEN I COME HOME FROM WORK, IT HAD BETTER BE THERE,

EVEN IF YOU HAVE TO CARRY IT HOME FROM THE STORE ON YOUR BACK, WOMAN." (Taurus men are always boss in their homes.)

And what does his Air Sign Aquarian "woman" have to say about her Bull's furious rampage about the chair? She could quite likely ask him, "Listen, Jumbo, what's a four-letter word that rhymes with truck?" (She's working a crossword puzzle in the part of the newspaper he wasn't reading.) In his angry state, he may supply her with a most rude and uncouth, vulgar answer, such as—"schmuck." (Especially if he's a Taurean of the Hebrew persuasion.) Suddenly, her face will light up, and she'll say, "I've got it! *Luck!* I have to use an 'L,' because vertically, it has to spell Lixivate —up and down. I was going to use Buck, but the 'B' wouldn't work, going the other direction, where I needed another 'L' for Lithoid. Thanks anyway, but I don't need an 's,' and besides 'schmuck' has seven letters, and I told you I needed four. By the way, do you know what the word 'lithoid' means? It means: made of stone, resembling a stone, or a stony structure. That's cute. I think I'll call you that from now on, instead of Jumbo. Lithoid."

He stares at her in silence, at a total loss for words. Then suddenly, without warning, a bolt of Uranus lightning strikes, and she tosses the newspaper in his face, yelling, "Carry your @@ ## !! % ¢ & ** chair home on your own back, Lithoid. I'm going on a camping trip tomorrow, by myself—and I'll be gone a week or more. Don't call me, I'll call you if I feel like it, which I probably WON'T!" She slams the door, jumps in the station wagon, guns the engine and takes off, speeding down the street, on her way to nowhere—to "calmly" think things over. That's the sort of thing you can expect when two *Fixed* personalities have a disagreement, and one of them (her) is susceptible to those sudden, unexpected Uranian outbursts.

These two, let us remember, are governed by the tense 4-10 Sun Sign Pattern influence, and are often agitated by this troublesome vibrational energy, into confrontation. They should both be aware that each of their tempers may explode when least anticipated. The Bull always surprises and shocks when he becomes really angry, simply because his rages occur so seldom. The Aquarian is also prone to shock and surprise her lover or husband with her anger, simply because she's ruled by Uranus, and most everything this planet incites her to do is done without warning. She'll come home in fifteen minutes or so, her anger cooled, and bring him a gift, a peace offering—perhaps a puppy she found wandering around, homeless. If the puppy is warm, soft and cuddly, her Taurus man will probably melt, squeeze it—and her—and say they can keep it, but only if she promises to housebreak it. She'll promise, sweetly . . . and peace will be restored again. But it may be a temporary truce, unless their Suns and Moons and Ascendents are in harmonious aspect between their birth charts. If they are not, they're both going to need to acquire some self-discipline, and realize that "volatile" is *not* an eight-letter word that rhymes with happiness.

Let's return to their mutual inclination to save things. (The 4-10 explosion has a way of causing trains of thought to leap off the track.) Like her, the Bull is fond of saving old memories, in the form of junk, although he'll claim, bashfully and stubbornly, that they have some sensible use. They don't, but she should let him *think* they do. (Crabs like to save things too, but for different reasons. Partly sentiment, yes, but mostly because they get their claws stuck, and can't let go.) All right. She and he are both Fixed, therefore, they are both good organizers, and they tend to accumulate. However, when it comes to the quality of dependability, Aquarius is the black sheep of the Fixed family. (Black sheep is not a negative term—they're the sheep that have the gumption to be different, you know.) The other three Fixed Signs, Taurus, Leo and Scorpio, are duly dependable, but this is the place where Aquarius jumps off the boat.

She'll try like blazes to keep a promise, and put forth a Herculean effort to be on time for appointments. She'll seldom retract anything she's said, if she felt it deeply when she said it, and this is all admirable. But her eccentricities of dress and manners, her sudden Uranus zigs and zags of behavior, her unexpected switches, and the surprises she delights in giving you, cannot be described as dependable. They can only be described as unsettling.

The Taurus man is generally conventional, his behavior predictable, he neither likes to zig, nor to zag, and even his worst enemy could never call him eccentric. The Bull is a conformist at heart, which is why the Aquarian Age throws him into a quiet, but despairing tizzy. Who can cope with these crazy young people, the sexual revolution, riots, protests against our government, people running around naked, and women having the temerity to think they're equal to men, when any good anatomy course proves how ridiculous *that* is? So Taurus sits patiently, wondering and privately worrying, protecting his property against wild eyed, anonymous maniacs out there on the streets, and searching desperately, like Diogenes, for an honest man. At the very least, an honest woman.

Along comes the Aquarian girl, with the courage of her convictions carried high and shining, and he thinks his search is over. But what about her eccentricities? Those funny clothes she wears, her peculiar hair style, her odd statements and her sympathy with those dangerous, wild-eyed maniacs? Is it because she's a mere female that she doesn't have enough sense to be alarmed by what's happening in the world around her? Maybe she needs him to protect her.

I won't deny she may need protection. But the reason she's not alarmed is because, after all, the Aquarian Age is *her* age, and being an Aquarian herself, she knows there's never any need to conform to anything, unless you *want* to. She's always been content to live by the seashore, without knocking folks who prefer the mountains. She's always worn her hair the way it pleased her, whether her friends were bald or pigtailed. What's *wrong* with going to church on Sunday, then having lunch with an atheist afterwards? If she could only make him see that he doesn't have to get so uptight about what's happening—that it's just the beginning of a glorious new era of being yourself, conservative or liberal, barefoot or booted, long hair or crew cut. It simply means to live, and to let live.

Now, that last part Taurus will understand. He's perfectly willing to live and let live, as long as he can grumble a little when things don't suit him. They're both inclined to "let it be," but they should apply that philosophy to themselves, as well as to the world, and not ridicule each other's personal convictions. As with all 4-10 couples, each cramps the other's style somewhat, and it pinches.

Her Aquarian inclination to the abstract extends to her sexuality, and since there's nothing whatsoever abstract about the Bull's sexual needs, this can instigate a little insomnia. She's not a woman who is obsessed with sensuality and eroticism, although she may be quite curious about it. Her approach to lovemaking is airy and complicated; his is simple and earthy. Physical desire never runs as strong or as deep in Aquarius as it does in Taurus. Yet, there's something in the Bull's warm, affectionate nature that touches her heart, and makes her want to please him. And there's something about her off-beat passions, so honest and direct, that brings out a gentle tolerance in the Taurus man, a sort of surge of protectiveness, which certainly won't dilute his manhood.

She may overwhelm him with her fierce love hunger one night, then seem to float away from his touch the next. He may not be aware that her physical desire can be aroused by the funny way he whistled while he was clumsily peeling an orange for breakfast (hours before bedtime)—excited by the frosted fairyland scenes etched on a winter windowpane—and dampened by a newscast she heard, just before dinner, about how many millions of babies and children, all over the world, die of starvation every single hour. And *she* may not be aware that her Bull needs more than a few pats and hugs to keep him contented. He needs his head scratched (literally), his hand held, his nose kissed and his ears filled with gentle, baby-soft, tender words—on a very regular basis.

However much love surrounds this man, he's always greedy for more of it. Yet, however much she may be devoted to him, the Aquarian girl is compelled to share her love with her friends, and with all of humanity, in general. Sometimes, it may seem to these two as if there's just not enough love to go around. There never is, when you're taking it. Only when you're giving it. An inexhaustible supply.

TAURUS

Earth—Fixed—Negative
Ruled by Venus (also by the
Planet Pan-Horus)
Symbol: The Bull
Night Forces—Feminine

PISCES

Water—Mutable—Negative
Ruled by Neptune
Symbol: The Fish
Night Forces—Feminine

The **TAURUS-PISCES** *Relationship*

*Thus sharply did the terrified three learn the
difference between an island of make-
believe and the same island come true.*

Yes, there are three of them, for Pisces is a sign of duality symbolized by the two Fish, swimming in opposite directions. In one sense, this symbol represents the powerful polarity of Piscean spiritual and human qualities, struggling for control. In another sense, it suggests the temptation of Pisceans to swim effortlessly downstream, with the current, rather than making the more difficult journey upstream, toward the mountains of enlightenment.

Pisceans aspire beyond the limits of earthly knowledge, because they were born under a Water Sign, and Neptune (their ruling planet) flashes into their souls the light of the spiritual vibrations of the Universe. The

Piscean drug addict, alcoholic, genius and saint are all striving for the same thing. What separates them is the degree of experience each is able to wring out of life.

Taurus can be a great help to Pisces in obtaining experience in a practical way, through the reality of the tangible. Until they know each other better, however, the Bull may think the Fish is a foolish creature, swimming around in watery illusions, his head wrapped in cotton, pursuing futile daydreams.

The Fish may think the Bull is a dangerous animal, stomping around through the corn, his head full of obstinate opinions, pursuing filthy lucre. Filthy, because money is (at least subliminally) a dirty word to most Pisceans. They resent having to concentrate on how to earn it, keep it, spend it, distribute it, budget it and save it. They'd be much happier if someone else handled the cash flow, and just kept them supplied with food, drink, dreams, tickets to shows and concerts, a couple of sarongs, and holidays sailing on the bright blue water—allowing them lots of free time to work on inventions, artistic creations or scientific research. Anything left over can go to the orphans' home, the animal shelter, the actors' relief fund, Greenpeace, taxes or whatever.

The typical Fish doesn't see the point of letting excess cash gather dust under a mattress, or in a bank. Pisces normally worries about money only when he or she doesn't have it. Then it becomes a frightful necessity for the continuation of their changeable, dreamy, multi-faceted existence. Otherwise, it annoys the Fish. Subconsciously, they sense that a wealthy man's fortune is all on paper. The whole concept of currency exchange puzzles the average Piscean, and when a Fish discusses money with a Bull (who comprehends the monetary concept perfectly) the conversation can sound like Antoine de Saint Exupéry's Neptune-guided Little Prince talking with the Bull-like businessman, who is busy counting his assets, the stars, which he figures belong to him, since no one else ever had the common sense to claim them.

"Five hundred and one million, six hundred twenty-two thousand, seven hundred thirty-one . . . . . . I am concerned with matters of consequence . . . . . ."

". . . . . . you own the stars?"

"Yes . . . . . ."

"And what do you do with them?"

"I administer them. I count and recount them. It is difficult, but I am a man who is naturally interested in matters of consequence . . . . . ."

"But you cannot pluck the stars from heaven."

"No, but I can put them in the bank."

"Whatever does that mean?"

"That means I write the number of my stars on a little paper. And then I put this paper in a drawer, and lock it with a key."

"And that is all?"

"It is enough."

The Little Prince sighs, then. *"It is entertaining . . . . . . but it is not a matter of any great consequence."*

On matters of consequence, the typical Piscean has ideas very different from the average Taurean. For, like the Little Prince, the Fish, too, is from a far-off planet, where there exists the most beautiful rose in all creation, which he has seen, and loved with his whole being, remembers with tenderness, misses painfully . . . . . . and to which he longs to return. (Or to *whom* he longs to return. The male or female Fish who wistfully longs for such a reunion isn't certain of the pronoun. Is it a person? Or merely a concept . . . a dream?)

Piscean Cleve Backster, who sneakily, in Neptune fashion, swims and glides silently, almost unobtrusively, in and out of the pages of this book, so that you never know in which chapter he's going to pop up and wiggle his fins—is certainly typical of his Sun Sign's instinctive disdain for material matters. In 1970, a major New York publisher wanted to place Cleve under contract to write a book about his world-famous work with plants, eggs, spermatozoa, yogurt, and all manner of cellular life, which is proving the genesis of Oneness—that all life forces are interconnected, and inseparable. Suddenly, an editor at the publishing house had an innovative idea of his own. He asked a professional astrologer to calculate and interpret Backster's horoscope, hoping it would reveal the extent of his reliability and potential as an author, thereby reducing the publisher's risk.

The editor then visited Cleve in his research laboratory to bring him the awful truth. Silently and sadly, he handed the Fish the neatly typed astrological analysis to read. Among other things, it stated that Backster must "always be associated with an organization around him, for he can't bear the entire responsibility on his own shoulders"—and that "his business sense is absolutely nil."

"I'm sorry to be the bearer of such bad news," the editor commiserated, "but I felt you should know the worst." Cleve's elfin ears wiggled in pure pleasure, and his visitor was shocked to hear him say, "That's amazingly true! It fits my character perfectly. I've always suspected astrology is an accurate science, and now I'm even more convinced. May I keep a copy of that analysis please?" The poor editor was nonplussed. It was obvious that Cleve's delight was genuine. A few years later, when Backster was considerably overdue in turning in even the first chapter of the proposed book about his work, the publishing house wrote him a stern letter, which Cleve promptly answered. "Remember," Fish Backster wrote cheerfully, "you people were the ones who had my character analyzed in the beginning, not me. I never claimed I enjoyed responsibility or had any business sense."

I know a Pisces banker, with a Capricorn Ascendent and a Taurus Moon Sign, who carefully counts copper and silver and paper all day long, but he frowns as he counts, and wonders why he's cursed with aching feet and asthma. As a Fish he's allergic to currency, you see, but the earthy influences in his horoscope won't let him chuck it overboard and swim away.

I also know a Taurus musician, whose Pisces Moon Sign and Ascendent cause him to leave huge tips on the bar, and squander his money at the race track. But he has a few extra gin and tonics each time he loses, to quiet his guilty Taurean Sun Sign conscience.

It's important to be true to your Sun Sign, whatever conflicting planetary influences pull on your inner psyche, because each of the twelve signs has its purpose in human evolvement. An idle, extravagant Bull is always an extremely unhappy person, just as a sober, mercenary Fish is always a pathetically sad, neurotic human being. If these two join forces, they could then each do what comes more naturally.

Pisces could show Taureans more imaginative ways to make money, and teach them the joys of sharing it with others, along with the truth of the infallible Universal Law that the more you give, the faster it multiplies.

Conversely, Taurus could teach Pisces the proper respect for minimal security, that it's wiser to save at least a few dollars, even if you give away a hundred or so, in case there are a few lean days before that Universal Law goes into effect. It's such a drag to have to sit on the corner in the rain, holding out a tin cup. The very idea gives the Bull nervous palpitation, and makes his hair stand on end.

There are, of course, Pisceans who are forced by circumstances, and memories of childhood poverty, to worry and fret about having to take a turn with the tin cup, so they pinch their few pennies, but privately hate themselves for being so miserly. Yet, when they stop pinching, the money to replace what was spent appears like magic from unexpected sources. If these Pisceans would listen to their own hearts, they'd get over their tin-cup traumas, and end their poverty at the same time.

An odd and interesting difference between Taurus and Pisces is a fact as simple as their names. Very few Bulls have nicknames, and if they do, they usually don't like them. As for changing his or her name legally, a typical Bull will balk, even if the name is Percival Perriwinkle or Clarestine Clapper. They may suffer as children, but by the time they're adults they will have convinced themselves their names have a good, solid sound, and anyone who doesn't think so can go sit on a tack. Remember the true story about Ms. Hogg, who named her three children Ima Hogg, Ura Hogg and Hesa Hogg? Since I've never heard or read that any of the three ever changed their names, I suspect they all had Taurus Sun Signs, Moon Signs, or Ascendents.

As for Pisces, almost every Fish you meet will either already have a nickname, or secretly longs for one. After a while, if their friends don't oblige them, many Fish will adopt an alias on their own. A Pisces girl or woman named Catherine will flirt with the idea of spelling it *Kathryn*—a Pisces boy, or man, named John, will doodle it as *Joshua*, or toy with the idea of legally changing it to a more romantic *Jonathan*. Anything to make life more exotic, and to keep your identity hidden from snoopers who pry into your personal life.

Pisces can't stand direct questions, or being pinned down to a positive stand. It's the nature of the Fish to glide in and out and around a situation, looking at all sides, and absorbing its various implications—or glide away quietly from a controversy that chops up the waters around him, and threatens his equilibrium.

None of that sneaking away for Taurus. What is there to be faced, he faces, with open courage, and he will remain standing there stubbornly, until he proves his point. If he can't prove it, after much effort, he turns his strong back and leaves, but he doesn't glide away. He stalks off heavily back to where he started from, with his original opinion clutched tightly in his arms, across his beefy chest.

That's more or less what happens when these two get into an argument. There's seldom a satisfactory or final settlement. But the day can be saved by laughter. The Bull has a rich, delicious, absolutely marvelous sense of humor. It's not the bright, brittle, sophisticated comedy of caustic wits, but a warm humor that stems from the colorful reality of everyday living, the kind that spilled over in the musical *Fiddler on the Roof*. Since the very bright, sometimes super-intelligent Fish has a fine appreciation for humor —somehow, between the grins, they'll either forget their differences, or resolve them through the compromise of their Earth and Water elements, which are essentially, in astrology, as in Nature, compatible. As mentioned elsewhere in this book, Water enriches Earth, and Earth provides a home for Water, but the wrong blending of these two can create mud or quicksand.

Because this is a 3-11 vibratory pattern, the meeting of the Bull and the Fish is seldom accidental, or a "first incarnational encounter." Like all 3-11 Sun Sign Pattern people, the two of them are guided by Fate to insure the return, the even exchange of devotion or hurt given, one unto the other, in past incarnations—sometimes the former, sometimes the latter—but more often a combination of both. Like those people whose *day* of birth (not including month or year) adds to the number 4 or 8, will be bound firmly to the lives of other 4 or 8 persons, like it or not, pleasant or unpleasant— those under the influence of this Sun Sign Pattern will find they have no choice in deciding to meet, or when to part.

They're magnetically pulled together, in order to carry out the karmic balance of action and reaction, under the direction of the Higher Angels of themselves—the Supraconscious of each. Numerology and astrology are sisters or brothers—whichever you prefer, the relationship of these two arts and sciences being one of the very few situations thus far not initially labeled as masculine by male chauvinist pigs, nor later challenged and switched to the feminine gender by female chauvinist sows. Help yourself.

Taurus and Pisces will have, like all other 3-11 influenced people (and also like all those born on a *day* which adds to the number 4 or 8), abundant opportunities for happiness and harmony in this present existence together, if they're willing to accept the duties and responsibilities of past karmic obligations to one another—i.e., bear the frequently tense aspects of their association, from time to time, as well as each other's weary burdens. The rewards for uncomplainingly assuming the duties, however, are great indeed. An example of a Taurus-Pisces, 3-11 fated Sun Sign Pattern, including both the light and shadows of necessary mutual sacrifice . . . and mutual ecstasy . . . is the destined relationship of poet and poetess Robert Browning (Taurus) and Elizabeth Barrett (Pisces). There are thousands, millions of others—including, of course, the Bull and the Fish reading this chapter.

Basically, Taurus and Pisces are tolerant of one another's weaknesses.

But Taurus is deeply concerned with the need for facing reality—even those occasional Master-Avatar Bulls, who now and then pass among us (yes, also *now*), such as the ultimate-enlightened, and esoterically aware alchemist, the very Taurean Count de St. Germain. These particular Masters are here to teach the necessity of the "reality trip" for human evolvement, however spiritually advanced they may be themselves.

Pisces is here on a totally different teaching trip. The Fish are all very old souls, whether they're swimming upstream or downstream. Pisceans have journeyed past horizons of such unearthly beauty they tear at the Neptune heart when he (or she) revisits them in dreams. And so, the Fish cannot bear to face reality, as it appears to be on Earth. They know the *real* "original sin" is in seeing, in recognizing sadness and ugliness, when our co-Creators conceived and manifested only harmony and beauty. In his or her subconscious, Pisces hears the ancient cry of the Tibetan monks whose chants echo across the vaulted ceiling of their monasteries: *This is the world of illusion . . . . . this is the world of illusion.*

To Taurus, the Bull, the recognition of a different kind of sin is necessary for the soul's enlightenment and final salvation. Therefore, the Bull feels compelled to force the Fish to confess his (or her) guilt of self-deception and fantasy—to see things as they are—and the clear, sparkling streams of Pisces visions are forced back to the rich, stable Earth by the practicality of the watchful Taureans.

"Jonathan (Kathryn) *that is not your real name.* You are make-believing and fantasizing again," scolds Taurus, never suspecting that the tears of the chastised Piscean then are not for Neptune's transgressions against Taurean reality . . . but for all the lost and lonely souls in this "world of illusion."

"Jonathan (Kathryn) are you not terribly sorry?" persists the Bull.

"Oh, yes . . . oh, yes," replies the Fish.

TAURUS *Woman* PISCES *Man*

◆━━◄◆►━━◆

*To Michael the loneliness was dreadful. "If only
something would make a sound!" he cried.*

*As if in answer to his request, the air was rent by the most
tremendous crash he had ever heard . . . . . the roar
of it echoed through the mountains. . . .*

Both the silence and the roar of the Bull are an experience known, sooner
or later, to every "Michael" who has the Sun, Moon or Ascendent in
Pisces, in an association with Taurus. But especially to the Sun Sign male
Fish.

When the Taurean girl plays romantic marbles, she shoots to win, and
to keep all the aggies. But when she forgets her common sense, she'll find
herself playing "Blind Man's Bluff," and that's a game she could lose, unless she cheats a little, and peeks out from under the hanky tied over her
eyes. She might as well, if she's playing with a Fish. He'll certainly cheat
a little, by peeking out beneath *his* blindfold, to see where the relationship
might be leading him.

If it looks like it's leading him into the hook of a permanent attachment, he could be a poor loser, and scoot away before he gets caught. But
that's only his protective Neptune reflex action, and he'll be back. His instinct to return may be guiding him well, because there's lots of hope for
lasting happiness inherent in a love affair between this man and woman.

The Bull and the Fish both like peace and quiet. They both believe in
letting sleeping dogs lie. Why ask for trouble? There's enough of that falling in your lap every day, unsolicited, without chasing it, is her feeling.
The Pisces man agrees wholeheartedly. Whistle for trouble and it will
zoom right in on you, is the way he sees it. So, don't whistle where Lady
Bad Luck can hear you, or she'll be sure to pop open the lid of Pandora's
Box, and you'll have no one to blame but yourself. Well, that's not quite
right. Piscean misfortunes are rarely their own fault. The Fish just naturally gets tangled in other people's torments, because he's such a good listener.

Another thing these two Sun Signs often have in common is that, after
all the care they take to avoid sticky seaweed (in the case of Pisces) or
barbed wire and brambles (in the case of the Bull) they both stand a good

chance of falling into the grip of the gloomies anyway, thanks to their mutual inclination to brood, and their tendency toward pessimism. But the Taurus girl is often more patient, and more certain of the final outcome, than the inwardly restless Pisces man. She doesn't mind setting a bear trap for something or someone she wants, then waiting without a murmur of discontent, as long as necessary, for the jaws to snap shut. In fact, she may even enjoy waiting for people when they're late, because it gives her a chance to practice her calm in emergencies.

It's not a bad habit for her to possess, if she plans on becoming seriously involved with a Fish, because most Pisces men have never been on time in their lives. Unless they have a Virgo or other more stable Moon Sign or Ascendent. There are some Pisces men who are late for work, for the movies, for dental appointments, for New Year's Eve (mostly because they start celebrating it in November) and for their own weddings (sometimes even missing them altogether).

The Pisces man may wonder what his true image is to the Taurus girl. He won't really care, but he may wonder. A Fish usually doesn't work up a lot of anxiety symptoms when he's in love, at least, not on the surface. He may fret mildly about the rent money, what life really means, what the future holds and such, but to Pisces, romance is a natural state of being. This bright, gentle, poetic man, if he's a typical Fish, is very much at home in romantic waters, where he probably learned to swim and dive at a shockingly early age. The Taurus girl was still swooning over Deanna Durbin films, or cracking up over Howdy Doody (depending on her age group) while he was planning his first seduction (or being seduced himself, which is more likely). Love, or the fulfillment of it, comes late to the average Taurean female, which is perhaps why she appreciates it and values it more than women born under other Sun Signs. It's the waiting that makes things seem special and exciting, whether it's Christmas, Groundhog's Day or your first kiss.

Whatever his image may be to her, I hope she tries to halfway understand him. I say halfway, because she'll be lucky if he doesn't baffle her completely in the beginning. He's so absolutely different from every other man she's ever known that she can't help being secretly excited by his mysterious elusive quality, even though she normally doesn't trust a complicated or changeable personality. It's because of the magnetic 3-11 vibration between them, a Sun Sign Pattern implying a karmic tie, which is responsible for the strong feeling of compulsion in the relationship. A Taurus woman may feel a strong attraction toward certain Scorpio men too, but it will be mostly physical. With a Pisces man, it often goes deeper than that, and it's not so easily explained. Besides, he so obviously needs someone to cook for him, believe in him, comfort him and love him, all talents in which she excels.

She may occasionally give in to moods of self-pity and dark forebodings. But when her perspective returns, she'll submit to the gentle influence of Venus again, and slip back into her old, comfortable ways. When she's herself, a Taurus woman is firmly convinced that anything can be cured with a tub full of warm water, a cup of hot soup, some cool reason and a few jokes. And that includes everything from trivial upsets to major tragedy. The Pisces man's complicated depressions may need somewhat more extensive and intricate, less prosaic therapy, but he'll enjoy her treatments. She has an undeniably calm and relaxing influence upon his spirit when he's troubled.

Sexually, these two relate well to each other. His Neptunian approach to sex can be described in two words: sensuous and romantic. So can hers. Both of them are determined to feel every possible shade and tone of sensual experience it's possible to know while confined in the flesh, so there will probably be an excellent rapport between them physically. The Pisces man lives almost entirely in and through his psychic nervous system. In his sexual behavior, as in all his activities, he yearns to escape into an ever-higher heaven . . . . . . *"anywhere, anywhere out of the world!"*

The Taurus girl instinctively "feels" through her senses. She has a serene charisma, a soothing aura, an exquisitely tender touch, and an instinctive desire to blanket the man she loves with warm affection—to tickle him with soft feathers of humor. Combine that with her throaty midnight whispers, and her soft Venus curves, and you can see why they usually vibrate to the same emotional rhythm. Her feminine tendency to gently submit to, and not attempt to dominate her man, is enormously satisfying to the Piscean male, who may have been through some romantic nightmares with more aggressive females. Taurus and Pisces know how to clearly communicate their mutual desires to each other, as well as how to fulfill them, so their physical union can be a beautiful experience of both earthy passion and unearthly ecstasy.

However, their total happiness together depends on which kind of Fish he is, the kind who sinks (by choice) or the kind who swims rapidly upstream. If he's the sunken kind, lurking among the conch shells at the bottom of the ocean, hoping to find the lost continent of Atlantis down there —or maybe just meditating an abstract scientific theory in the cool, green quiet—he may be immune to all the mermaids, however alluring. That is, unless he finds one with two strong feet planted on firm ground, who's willing to support him both emotionally and financially until he reaches his dream. A Taurus girl may be willing to fill that double order for a while. But after a time, the Bull's slow anger will be aroused. If he leans on her patience too long with what she regards as a lack of good sense and a disregard for security, she'll explode into one of her rare, but violent rages, and when the thunder dies away, the Fish will have quietly disappeared. But she won't notice, because once she makes up her mind, this girl doesn't look back. She read about someone who did that, who was turned into a pillar of salt for her weakness.

Even if he's an active, swimming Fish, with stronger fins and tougher scales, she may still not comprehend how it is with him, what he goes through in coping with everyone's tears and troubles, and touches for cash. A Fish can be wonderfully clever and creative, in clear water. But if she constantly muddies it with her earthy stubbornness, and others keep polluting it with impositions on his time and sympathy, he may turn to the solace of a few rainbows on the rocks at the corner bar. Then she'll start to frown or pout. And that's the beginning of the end.

The three-part formula for breaking a Taurus girl's heart is: false promises, deception and idle drifting. The triple formula for healing it is: honesty, fidelity and dependability. If he remembers that, it could be the beginning of the end of his loneliness.

If she accepts his need for periods of isolated contemplation to relax his jangled nerves, he'll always return to her serenity, for a few jokes, a warm bath, a cup of hot soup—and those throaty midnight whispers. And that could be the beginning of a love as special, and as worth waiting for, as Groundhog's Day or Christmas morning. Beneath the passion they feel is the warm foundation of the 3-11 vibration of true friendship . . . . . which never fails to deepen love, when it has passed the test of Time.

TAURUS *Man* PISCES *Woman*

◄◄●►►

*He was often thus when communing
with himself on board ship in the
quietude of the night . . . . .*

*She was not a little girl heartbroken about him;
she was a grown woman smiling at it
all, but they were wet smiles.*

Remember when, as a child, you used to watch a magician, and marvel at the way he made white rabbits, silk roses and colored ribbons disappear in front of your eyes? A Taurus man who falls in love with a Pisces girl, and who doesn't study the magic of astrology, may get an opportunity to relive that experience. It may take her months or years to master the disappearing act. And she won't announce it in advance when she does, because a Pisces hates to get involved in sticky controversy, or get tangled up in hollering and endless recriminations. It could happen on a day—or an evening—like hundreds of others, when she says gently:

"Darling, I've been invited to attend a poetry reading tonight. Could you drop me off, then catch a film, and pick me up later?"

"No. I don't want to go to the movies alone."

"Then would you like to come along with me, because . . . ."

"No, I wouldn't. You know I don't mess around with that mystical stuff."

"All right. I won't go to the poetry reading. I'll go to the movies with you. Do you like my new dress?"

"It's too short. You look like a stripper, ready to pull her last zipper. Put on something else, and let the hem down before you wear it again."

"Yes, dear. I will. But everyone is wearing . . . ."

"Sure, and everyone is also going nuts with sex and drugs and riots and revolutions and female liberation. Does that mean the woman I love has to copy them?"

"No, of course not. You're right, darling. I just thought . . . . ."

"You shouldn't think, since it obviously mixes up your brains, and gives you fuzzy opinions. Just stick to your female functions. Come on, we'll be late for the . . . . hey! Where are you? Where did you go?"

She has disappeared, as suddenly and subtly as the white rabbits, silk roses and colored ribbons. She's finally had enough of his blindness to her sensitive feelings, his stubborn refusal to meet her halfway, and his obstinate opinions that leave no room for compromise. Maybe she just slipped away to reflect alone for a period, and she'll return refreshed, ready to submit again, if she really loves him. There's just a slight touch of masochism in all Neptune-ruled women. But there's also a chance that someday she'll disappear forever, especially if she has an aggressive Moon Sign or Ascendent—so the Bull should anticipate the possibility, since he's so big on the practicality of being prepared for trouble in advance.

Naturally, not all Taurus-Pisces couples are so widely polarized by his obstinate masculine superiority and her timid feminine acquiescence. That's just a warning to the Bull and the Fish who have a conflicting Sun-Moon aspect between their horoscopes. If their Luminaries are harmonious, they can have a rare and satisfying love relationship, because they are compatible in many ways, a deep comfort to one another when life gets too noisy and frantic for him—or too harsh and ugly for her. Every man appreciates a sympathetic ear to listen to his troubles, especially when it's attached to an attentive, geisha-type female with a soft voice and gentle manners. But human nature being what it is, every man will also try to get away with as much as he can, when a girl is so tolerant and understanding. A Taurus man is certainly no exception to that rule. And so a Pisces girl who falls in love with a strong Bull must toughen up her ego, if she wants to learn the magic trick of turning him into a lovable Taurean Teddy Bear.

She has one thing going for her, however, that's kind of cool. Behind her sweetly compliant exterior hides a very quick, bright and highly perceptive mind. She'll catch him up when he least expects it, if what he thinks he's getting away with is a flirtation with another woman, although she may forgive him almost too quickly, at least the first time. It's when he's trying to get away with submerging her dreams, and bending her fluid nature to his own rigid one, that she needs practice in toughness.

Not that all the problems between them will arise from his overemphasis on male dominance. Some of them may be caused by her procrastination (oh, let's worry about that later . . .)—her exasperating elusiveness—(I don't know exactly where I'm going, or just how long I'll be. Do you have to pin me down?)—her secrecy—(I can't answer that. Please don't pry into my personal feelings)—her exaggerated dependence—(I can't decide what to do by myself)—or her lack of self-confidence, accompanied by waterfalls of tears—(I'm not pretty enough, or smart enough for you). He can tell her a thousand times that she's perfect for him, but if she's a girl Fish with an afflicted natal Sun, or an also Mutable Ascendent and Moon Sign, she'll still privately worry and wonder, and suspect him of humoring her.

A Taurus man will find it easier to understand a Pisces girl, if he remembers that she not only reflects *back* all the emotional vibrations in her immediate vicinity (including his own), she also *absorbs* them inwardly, like a sponge, through her Neptunian sympathy of spirit. How would *he* like to be forced by a ruling planet to go around mopping up everyone's tears, sopping up their fears, reflecting and absorbing everything from hilarity to hysteria? It would make anyone a little unsure and shaky at times.

Lest you conceive of every Bull as a rough and tough, insensitive male type, it should be remembered that American film actor James Mason is a Taurean—the very epitome of polished, drawing-room manners and sophistication. (But he's stubborn.) And lest you conceive of every girl Fish as a weeping willow tree, frightened and timid, lacking aggression, it should be remembered that Taurean James Mason's legally former and astrally current wife, Pamela Mason, is a Piscean—the very epitome of a lady who will not be pushed around, by Bulls or anyone else, and who most definitely knows her own mind! (But she's gentle and dainty and compassionate.)

One of the things which may disturb the Taurus man is the Neptunian approach to truth of his Pisces woman. She sees truth as what she feels at the moment, and what she feels at the moment is always vulnerable to suggestion and susceptible to change, as the people, the situation and the viewpoint either dilute it or strengthen it. Pisces does not see truth as a static, but as a constantly altering thing, depending upon many interpretations.

The Bull sees truth as a fact, eternal and unchanging. Now, that's what you call a polarity of opinion. Which one is right? Actually, they're both right, at different times, depending on what kind of truth they mean. Some truths are universal, eternally unchanging. Others are many-sided and individual. Still others are in a continual state of flux, since they relate to people's feelings and emotions of the moment—or public opinion of the moment. And some truths, based on indisputable *fact*—such as: Were you in the shower an hour ago?—clearly have but one answer, yes or no. Since everything in the cosmos is relative, why should truth be an exception? The shower question involves the immediate past. Questions of fact involving the more distant past, such as: Was Lincoln assassinated? Did Napoleon lose his final battle? and so forth . . . fall into a deeper esoteric and metaphysical-spiritual category, relating to the heavy Einsteinian Time question. If Past, Present and Future *are* simultaneous, and *not* separate, as "abstract Al" suspected—then, considering that one may change the Future by actions of the Present, should not one also be able to change the Past, through actions in the Present? This sort of truth belongs to the study of *meta*-physics, not physics—and the answer lies buried in the riddle of "how *far* back in time?"—and the use of the singular, as in: "can *one* change the past by . . . . ?" and so forth. But it's much too heavy to discuss further here and now, far too deep a subject for merely one compatibility chapter, and will have to wait for a future book. Still, the entire issue is an interesting one for Taurus-Pisces lovers or mates to exchange thoughts about with each other.

Truth, in its various states and forms, won't matter so much to this man and woman in their sexual expression of love. This is an area where the only truth is the peace of fulfillment they bring to one another. Barring severe Luminary afflictions between their birth charts, or other mutual planetary-aspect difficulties to overcome, the sexual harmony between the Taurus man and his Pisces woman should be a thing of undeniable truth and beauty—the strong attraction of Earth for Water, and vice versa. These two, especially if the Sun-Moon relationship between them is strong and positive, can exist almost in a world of their own, held together by a communion of the senses surpassing anything an Air or Fire sign could imagine. Few human experiences of sharing are more comforting than the physical demonstration of love between a Bull and a Fish, who have surrendered themselves to one another, without questioning their mutual need, only desiring to answer it. It's not the explosive passion of other Sun Sign couples, but the rare tenderness and affection which is so warmly given, and so quietly received, that makes their union so complete and peace-restoring an intimacy. There's always a hint of mystery hovering over and around the sexual relationship between Taurus and Pisces, and they're usually both content to leave it be, perhaps sensing that to expose the silent unknown would somehow dim the excitement.

If he tries to force her love into a definite shape, she may wander away, or worse, wander *around*, inciting the Bull's anger, and arousing his Taurean possessive instincts. He may cause her to feel lonely at times, when he's too busy or preoccupied to share with her the things she feels, and hears, and sees. But Water enriches the Earth, and Earth welcomes Water into the soil of security, so they can grow through their differences, while finding solace in their sameness—if she gives him enough solid, tangible signs of affection—and he loans her his steadiness to lean on when her dreams elude her, and her longings sadden her. Some night, they may be outside together, walking home from somewhere, and she'll look up into the sky, and whisper to him: "Listen . . . . . ." Then he'll ask, "Listen to *what?*"

"To the stars! Listen to the stars coming out . . . . . . don't they sound beautiful?"

Instead of frowning with puzzled annoyance at her confusing sight and sound, he should just hold her closer, and *listen* with her. For they do make beautiful music . . . . . . the stars coming out, snowflakes falling, someone's arms around you when you're unsure . . . . a special smile . . . and Pisces can teach Taurus to hear it.

GEMINI

Air — Mutable — Positive
Ruled by Mercury
Symbol: The Twins
Day Forces — Masculine

GEMINI

Air — Mutable — Positive
Ruled by Mercury
Symbol: The Twins
Day Forces — Masculine

The GEMINI-GEMINI *Relationship*

They were going round and round the island, but
they did not meet because all were going at
the same rate.

Before we get tied into mental pretzel knots, trying to analyze this 1-1 Sun Sign Pattern association, let's get the arithmetic straightened out. A Gemini and a Gemini equals a group of four bright, active people (two sets of Twins) tossing ideas, dreams and challenges back and forth between themselves and the world at large.

They may occasionally block each other's view of life, because they tend to see it in different magnifications, through the wide-angle zoom lens of their Mercurial vision, and sometimes they walk or run at varying speeds. Yet, in one sense, they all four travel at the same rate of speed, in that they all understand one another's need for freedom. Their vibrations radiate from the same frequencies, and their broken rhythms are usually in tune. A broken rhythm may not be orthodox music, but it makes great jazz. The trouble is, while they're jazzing around, they might miss each other in the swiftly passing scenery.

When two Geminis merge and get their vibes, rhythms and mental perspectives working in a parenthetic pattern, the four of them can use each other as a reassuring tie to reality. From the home base of their mutual empathy, they can run out and seduce the world—return briefly to be understood—then set forth once again on a new mental seduction. Do you understand this page? If you do, you're a Gemini yourself, because it's all astrologically accurate but complicated Mercury double-talk. If you don't understand it, and you're reading this to learn to comprehend a Gemini team, partnership or couple you know, stay with us, but be prepared to exercise your mental muscles—and don't forget your parachute.

Philosopher-astrologer Alan Watts defined "Man" (he didn't include women, but that was before ERA made all male animals aware that we're people too) by explaining that the individualization of the Creator, expressing His total Being through the multiple millions of souls on Earth, can be conceived of as *"God, playing hide-and-seek with Himself."* It's long been my favorite esoteric definition of Man and Woman's relation to the Universe, since I've always suspected that Man and Woman and their co-Creators are a unity, after pondering the Genesis riddle that the latter created the former in Their own Image. However, I really must correct one flaw in this otherwise very deeply perceptive definition. I'm sure the late, both kindly and brilliant Alan Watts will forgive us if we re-phrase his words as: *"God and His Mate, playing hide-and-seek with Themselves."* Now it is perfect. But anyway, the point I was trying to make is that, in the case of Gemini, our co-Creators are playing hide-and-seek with Themselves at high speed, with many more hiding places, and probably surprising Themselves more than They do with ordinary mortals, who are confused enough with the challenges of being just one person. There is, of course, another side to all this, the *individual* side, and the integrity of each unique soul.

The Yogi-Buddhist Nirvana concept is grossly distorted. All this business of permanent "blending with the Great All" is nonsense, metaphysically unsound, and quite literally impossible. We are part of both the *fused* and the *separate* bodies of our co-Creators—in a *symbolic sense*, Aries people being near Their "heads," Gemini being near Their arms, hands and fingers, Leos near Their "hearts," and so forth. (That's admittedly an oversimplification, but will suffice for this particular book, because it will be covered in more detail in a forthcoming one.) Now, a nose is not a mouth (when did you ever hear of a nose that ate corn on the cob?), nor is an eye a hand, nor is an ear a heart. (Who ever heard of an ear-beat?) In other words, you are You. *The unique you-of-you is now, ever has been, and ever shall be*—your individual self, and *consciously so*—not just during those periods of time when your blindness separates you from our co-Creators, but also after you blend with Them, from time to time, and even *while* you're at one with Them.

The secret of the latter condition of perfect peace, wisdom, and power is contained in the *polarity* of power—humility—expressed through the word "atone" (at-one). Not until you truly atone, and fully comprehend the meaning of the word, may you be *at-one* with God and His Mate. However, although the achievement of experiencing such *at-one-ment*, periodically and repeatedly, is a glorious thing, you need not (indeed you *should* not) remain at-one with Them on a permanent basis. That would be dreadfully boring for the individuality, just as being inseparably blended in the ecstatic embrace of sexual union, however pure the love between the twin souls might be, would be dull and boring if it were to be an eternal, constant state.

Such a concept removes the very core of existence, which is light and shadow . . . the perfect Libran balance of each . . . the stimulation of controversy, equally balanced with peaceful agreement—with no murders please, within the necessary controversy syndrome—no murder of sex, people, animals, or anything else. That's against all the rules of the cosmic hide-and-seek game.

Well, let's see . . . I began discussing Man's and Woman's relationship with God and His Mate, then went on to an explanation of your individuality, so you'll all be aware that your own sacred and holy, personal "egos" can never be destroyed by blending in a nirvanic *forever* with *anyone's* concept of "God"—all in a few paragraphs. The Gemini essence is extremely contagious. Actually, I'll level with you, although my remarks were all made quite seriously, and are reflective of ancient esoteric truth, I deliberately strung my words together on a chain of quick subject changes —each different, yet all consistently leading into one another—to give you a brief idea of the necessity for remaining alert when you're involved in any sort of discussion with a Gemini, let alone two of them, which is really four of them.

You see, sometimes Gemini double-talk is an aid to superimposing two apparently polarized opinions into a stereoscopic wholeness of third-dimensional depth, the third dimension added by the perceptive recipient of the words. Are you with me? You're simply going to have to become accustomed to word games if you expect to play verbal Pong-Ping with the

Twins, and Pong-Ping is the same as Ping-Pong when you're gazing into the Gemini mirror. Now, is it reflecting back to you more clearly?

Each Gemini contains a twin mirror image of himself (or herself), in reverse, the positive and negative poles of his or her personality. This is because each Gemini symbolizes the soul, on its trip around the astrological, karmic wheel, experiencing the toddler stage of awareness that it's not alone in the Universe, realizing also that there are two distinct sides to the character of each man and woman, which must be brought into harmony before it's possible to relate to others. The trouble is, Gemini seldom knows which of his (or her) split personalities is the real one. If anyone asked (or if our co-Creators asked this portion of Their individualization), "Will the real Twin please stand up and be recognized?", two separate people would pop up, and the game of hide-and-seek would begin all over again.

Naturally, then, when a pair of Twins decide to tangle their temperaments, things can get pretty crisscrossed. There are few Geminians who can sort themselves out from the myriad disguises and conflicting desires of their natures. Gemini is ruled by trickster Mercury, the planet of lightning speed (though not quite as capable of speed as "Swifty" Uranus), who forces this man, woman or child to try on a thousand faces, then discard them, in a restive search for personal identity.

The purpose of the masquerade is what separates the men from the boys, the women from the girls, and Scorpio from Gemini—in case you've been wondering. Scorp changes false faces for an entirely different purpose—to deliberately keep you in the dark, whereas Gemini is just trying to make up his (or her) mind which face belongs there. No, that's Libra indecision. Let's try again. Gemini is trying on masks in an effort to find the true person he or she really is. Indecision has nothing to do with it, in a really detailed analysis. Did I already say that? Yes, I did. I just realized. I said the same thing at the end of the last sentence in the previous paragraph.

Well, get used to it. Geminis often repeat themselves—say things twice. Like, they'll say: "What time is it?" . . . wait a second or so, and repeat: "What time is it?" before you've had time to answer that it's half past anything or a quarter till, which makes it difficult to converse with them in any sort of synchronized way, sometimes. But not always.

Since Gemini is a mental Air Sign, these people are driven to spinning their brains almost continually, even in their sleep, thinking, theorizing, figuring, projecting, condemning, endorsing, discarding, sorting and analyzing the cold, hard facts—at the very same time that they're chasing their visionary dream. You can see why they're all human jigsaw puzzles.

The Mercury-ruled roam the world, either mentally or physically, or both, in search of an elusive ideal of perfect truth and happiness, then often return home again, to listen to a bird singing in a tall tree—the same bird, the same song, the same tree they knew as children. After traveling all over the mental continents of their imaginations, they sometimes, if they're lucky, realize, at last, that their truest dreams were dreamed when childhood's perception was clear and uncontaminated by adult logic and cynicism.

Any 1-1 Sun Sign Pattern combination brings with it the special and unique satisfaction of association with a person enough like one's own self that there's little fear of rejection of personality—although there's always a danger of an overbalance of the similar characteristics. A double-Gemini relationship is especially comforting to each of the four of them, because it's always reassuring to have a pal, relative, neighbor, business associate, lover or mate who's as messed up as you are yourself. It saves a lot of tiresome explanations and apologies. But it can also be wearing on the nervous system, because of the continual frustration of attempting to fool someone who anticipates all your maneuvers and rationalizations.

At least these Sun Signs, when doubled up, can recognize one another somewhat more easily than an outsider would recognize either of the four of them. Yesterday, Gemini was a gentle soul, shy and self-effacing, somewhat detached, quiet and reflective, with occasional spells of wistfulness and longing. Today, the very same Gemini is cynical, sarcastic, irritable, insulting—and acutely alert. Tomorrow, he (or she) may be calm, steady and conservative to the point of being downright stuffy. Then, without the faintest warning, Gemini will turn into a will-o'-the-wisp, sprinkling dreams like lemon drops, scattering ideas like confetti, restless, yearning, as physically active as he (or she) is verbally communicative and emotionally restless. It's terribly puzzling to the rest of us, but even more so to the Gemini himself—or herself. Especially if he (or she) is involved in a close tie with another Gemini. Then, of course, the puzzlement is twinned and twice as tormenting.

The trickster aspect of Gemini's ruling planet, Mercury, is always hiding behind the sharp Gemini intellect, revealing itself in all manner of minor and major ways. An excellent example is Gemini Bob Hope, the comedian with the rapid-fire, speedy delivery of jokes, which nearly tumble over one another in the telling, they're delivered in such machine-gun style. Did you ever pay really close attention to one of Hope's longer comic routines? The kind where he does a monologue for fifteen minutes or a half hour, not his on-again, off-again stabs at the audience at the

Academy Awards. On a lengthier routine, Mercury's delight in tricking and fooling people is very evident.

Approximately every two minutes or so, the Gemini Hope will make a remark that when analyzed, means essentially: "Get ready, Folks. I'm about to close my act, and sign off." *But then he continues.* A couple of minutes (or even one minute or a few seconds) later he tosses out another one-liner, indicating again that his routine is coming to a close. *Yet, he continues.* Listen closely next time. You'll see that this is a consistent pattern with Bob Hope's Gemini comedy patter. Mercury drives him to try to *trick* his audience repeatedly—which is rather astute of Mercury, because it makes Hope's listeners pay strict attention, being led, as they are, to believe that each joke is his last for the night.

Bob Hope's reputation for possessing the finest comedy timing in show business is deserved, a talent that's directly inherited from the influence of his Sun ruler, Mercury. Comedienne Bea Lillie's repartee is equally sharp and staccato, her sense of comedy timing as exquisite as Hope's. Both born in England, Bea and Bob have startlingly similar noses, both are famed for entertaining the troops—and both were born the same month, day, year, latitude and longitude, within a few minutes of one another. *Astral twins.* More about that in a future book.

A blend of Gemini and Gemini has the advantage of creating an atmosphere of freedom of thought and movement, so that their combined intellects can click into action unhampered by petty jealousies, suspicions and restrictions (allowing, as always, for a more conservative Moon Sign or Ascendent). Even then, the emotional climate between them will be comparatively free and easy, allowing them to accomplish lots of tricks and capture many a dream together. These two will sharpen their wits on one another, usually forgive and forget quickly—and boredom will rarely be a problem.

But there are also disadvantages to their association, which they'll have to face, and find a way to erase, between them. Lacking the stability of the more prosaic, less complicated Sun Signs, Gemini and Gemini can tempt each other to scatter their talents to the four winds, neither one willing to hold down the other or able to provide the necessary patience and dependability for success, either on an emotional or on a material level. They may remind their friends of two brightly colored balloons, filled with a blend of happy helium and hot air, having a gay and marvelous time floating through the clouds, but not going anywhere in particular. With this combination, their Moon Signs will write the ending to the story. If the Moon Sign in either birth chart is unfavorable in aspect to the Gemini Sun Sign of the other, they can create lovely poetry or jazz, paint the clouds silver, or paint the town red. But few of their dreams and schemes will take off, or if they do, there could be a crash landing. Or, their balloons might take off too fast, then fly away out of sight, because they weren't grounded. They can still make it all work out harmoniously, but in order to do so, they'll have to be more cautious and less casual.

With a favorable Luminary aspect between their Suns and Moons, however, the sky is truly the limit for creative breakthroughs, scientific discovery, intellectual attainment, material security—and even spiritual perception. As for emotional happiness and harmony, well . . . it's really their own choice. Geminis manufacture their own emotions to sell, keep or give away. What do these Mercury Birds seek on the wind out there? Whatever it is, it's something beyond what is visible and tangible. One Gemini might ask the other, but the answers they get will be exactly the same as if the Twins had asked themselves.

GEMINI: What is it you're looking for?
GEMINI: I'm not sure. But when I find it, I'll know what it is.
GEMINI: And just where do you think you'll find it?
GEMINI: Where? Why, most anywhere, I guess . . . .

And yet, too often, the last place the Twins will look is in their own backyards, where the miracle they're searching for may have been waiting all the time.

Author's Gemini Postscript:
Because it has not yet been corrected in any
current or past editions of my first book,
SUN SIGNS, I would like to say that the mention of
Marilyn Monroe in the Gemini Woman section of
that book was intended to be an accurate description of Marilyn's
Gemini Ascendent and her natal Mars-in-Gemini.
Certain investigation has indicated that Marilyn was
actually born a Sun Sign Aries. Birth certificates
are not always infallible sources of information,
as any professional astrologer well knows.

GEMINI *Woman* GEMINI *Man*

"Well, then, we could go on," said John.

"That is the awful thing, John. We should have to go on, for we don't know how to stop."

This man and woman—although it would be more fitting to call them boy and girl, whatever their illusionary chronological age—are sometimes drawn together for no more reason than that it's fun to have someone to cross the street with you at the corners. Then you can, if that person is a Gemini, trade fast bets with each other about whether you can make it on GO before the traffic sign switches to STOP. Like when the light at an intersection is green, and you don't know how fast it's going to turn to red. It's exciting. Dangerous, but exciting.

Sure, it sounds dippy, but switching from street corners to living rooms, offices or classrooms, it's a fair example of the sort of mental checkers and chess games Geminis play with themselves and with each other. When you're alone a lot, you can think up bushels of crazy ideas. Geminis don't seem to be lonely, but they are. It's a lonely thing to wonder and wander, mixing with frightened, preachy people, to whom the only important game is the one you win by simply surviving. Especially when you know there are so many more important things to be fascinated by than merely staying alive. In fact, many Geminis wholeheartedly agree with Mercury-ruled Peter Pan that "to die, would be an awfully big adventure," perhaps the greatest adventure of all!

If you're a Gemini, your entire life is spent searching and learning, so why should death be any different? Like the elusive something you've been trying to pin down, express or define since you were five years old or so. True, Geminis seldom reveal their inner loneliness. But I wouldn't be surprised if that's not because they're barely aware of it. A person can get good at being lonely, with enough practice. It's like riding a bicycle. It requires concentration in the beginning, but after a time, you don't even notice your own balance or pedaling—you're just aware of the motion and the wind blowing your hair.

Because all typical Geminis are naturally glib, bright conversationalists, when two of them first meet, both may talk a lot, and it seems like they're not thinking of one another seriously. Yet, behind all the chatter, they are —more seriously than either will admit to the other. The dialogue between them will normally flash with wit and sparkle with imagination. It gives each of them time to study the other, when all those little ribbons of speech are rippling all over and around them. But they never say *every- thing* that's on their minds to each other, these two, not even years later when they've been in love long enough to know they can trust one an- other. There's always something held back.

"It's funny," she may think privately, "when you love someone so much, and you've been so intimate, that you have to hold back and remember there are things not to tell him, things you really can't share all the way." Well, when there's all that that he doesn't know about her, it's only right there are things he won't tell too. Do you imagine that, when Geminis chatter, everything they feel is spilling out in a cascade of words? Oh, no. If you think that, you don't understand this man and this woman —this boy and this girl.

A Mercury-ruled female, in love with a Geminian Twin male, should maybe know about something showman Mike Todd once said. Todd, the most prolific talker on record—anytime, anywhere, under any condition— was being interviewed by a perceptive reporter, who asked him, "Mike, do you know why you talk all the time? To keep from saying something. That's how I have you figured."

"Yeah?" Mike was suddenly quiet, quickly on guard.

"What bothers me," the reporter continued, "is—well, I'm curious. What *is* that something you talk so much, and so fast, to keep from saying? That's the real story behind the pitch, isn't it?"

Mike just smiled the three-cornered Gemini smile and answered, "Lis- ten, buddy, when I stop talking, we all stop eating."

It was true, of course. Without the Gemini talent for expressing ideas in vivid verbal images, people would be exposed to a lot less magic in this dreary-grey world, a lot less money would change hands, and fewer dreams would be dreamed—or come true. But the important thing for the Gemini girl to remember is that Mike avoided answering the reporter's *real* inquiry, with the typical mental adroitness of Mercury.

Since no one can say for certain exactly when Mike Todd was born, I've been asked why I call him a Gemini (although any girl in love with a Twin would know why). He gave approximately five different "official" dates to the press and disagreed strongly with his family about several others, all ranging between June 18th and June 23rd. How do I know

Mike was a Gemini, then? By his blarney and his magic. But most of all, by the way he fenced with his birthday, fighting middle age as though he was sure he'd win. At any given time of his life, he looked twenty years younger than he was, whatever he was, and he never really grew up. Only a Gemini could have parlayed a patched-up sack of old hopes into the Giant Twin Jackpot of "Around the World in 80 Days" *and* Elizabeth Taylor—a double win that ended that Gemini's restless search for completeness. Shortly afterwards, his Libra son, Mike Todd, Jr., remarked, "Dad, you're spending money now as fast as you did when you didn't have any." Mike never saved for a rainy day, so for him, it never rained. Well, maybe a few very brief drizzles. A couple of spring showers, that's all. Mike Todd didn't discover the Neverland. He invented it. Like Peter Pan, the eternal Gemini, he guarded the secret of his age from curious chronological-minded "grown-ups"—and a few more secrets besides.

At least 75 percent of all Geminis have a nickname, a pseudonym, an alias, or in some way bear more than one name during the course of their lives, and Mike had two names also. Born Avrom Hirsch Goldbogen, he named himself Michael Todd one day, impulsively, and for no really special reason. His son had already been born and had been named Michael. So Gemini Mike Todd actually named himself after his own son and became his son's namesake, instead of the other way around. Trust Geminis to turn things inside out and backwards, in both small and large ways.

As for Mike's "secret" the reporter guessed correctly he held within himself, the Gemini man or woman isn't secretive in the same manner as Pisceans, Cancerians and Scorpions are—or for the same reasons. It's just that there are some soaring thoughts they're unable to catch and express in speech, for all their Mercurial verbal dexterity. What words could describe an inexpressible longing to literally discover Shangri-La?

"If this is so beautiful," they each think, "then there just *must* be something even *more* beautiful out there, somewhere. Will we be able to find it together? Or can you only find something that special by yourself?" Each loveliness that two Geminis touch, Mercury allows them to drink in and enjoy for but a fleeting moment. Only until his (or her) secret Twin Self whispers seductively, "Ah, yes! But what else might there be to discover, which is even more perfect? This present glory you're experiencing is merely proof that a greater glory exists out there . . . a glory more true, more thrilling, more fulfilling, if only you have the courage to pursue it. How do you know what may be around the next corner, the next kiss, the next dream, the next promise? Don't stop now, don't turn back yet! Go on . . . . ." It's a call more alluring than the song of the Lorelei, and it haunts all Mercury-ruled hearts.

Most of the time, a Gemini girl laughs. Once in a while, less frequently, she weeps. When she does, it's because the lump of loneliness within her has grown so choking that it must turn into tears, or maybe she would simply die from the feeling. Ah, Twin Self! Where are you now, when you're needed? Off chasing the stars and playing tag with the wind? The Gemini man will tenderly understand her brief touch of *Weltschmerz*, with a delicacy of perception surprising in one who's always being accused of being so cold and detached. For all of his curious, inquiring nature, he won't ask questions when he senses the Gemini woman he loves is languishing from her inexpressible and unexpressed (even to him) terrible loneliness because her Twin has temporarily deserted her. He'll probably pretend not to notice, masking his concern with a light remark, like . . . . . "Let's throw *ourselves* into a wishing well, instead of tossing in pennies, and see what happens!" Or perhaps . . . "Come on, we'll buy two round tickets to Ireland, and make love on the Blarney Stone!" Then he'll kiss her cheek softly and say, very quietly, *"It's all right. I'm here."*

Yes, it's partly because he understands the sudden panic his Gemini girl feels when her Twin has disappeared and left her alone to cope, like half a person, because his own Twin pulls that trick on him too. But his finesse and tenderness at such times are prompted by more than just knowing how it is with someone born under your own Sun Sign. It's his . . . the right word just came to me. Gemini never *fumbles*. Whatever the situation with the loved one—joyous or tragic, loose or tight—the typical Gemini can, when he (or she) wishes, carry the ball with easy grace, handling embarrassment, fear or anger, with an incredibly light touch. It's like a magician's sleight-of-hand, and many Geminis actually are professional magicians (along with Aquarians, Pisceans and Scorpions). There are, percentagewise, however, more Gemini magicians, because these people are amazingly multidextrous with their hands. They're also multidextrous with their minds—and as for the Gemini heart, it contains many little secret rooms, in which are hidden compassion, gentleness, surprises, humor, hope and sunshine. Some of them are kept locked for a lifetime, and only another Twin holds the passkey.

Two Geminis in love might ask themselves, each about the other—do any of those rooms hold a quality called "faithfulness" or "fidelity"? Yes. But the door to that particular room in the Gemini heart is tightly sealed, and it takes more than a passkey to open it. It takes trust. And it takes time. Two kinds of trust: the complete trust each must give to the other—and the trust required to believe in *yourself*, that what you love is really what you *need*, and all you'll *ever* need. (That's what takes the time.) But time is free. They can both use as much of it as they like to find that answer within themselves . . . . . and once it's been found and the door unlocked, Gemini will be loyal and true forever after.

Nevertheless, it's probably asking too much to expect either him—or her —to permanently stop flirting, charming, teasing, persuading, or just talking with members of the opposite (or the same) sex. Yet, Gemini lives on the mental plane, essentially existing within the realms of the imagination, and, therefore, may be frequently content to keep human relationships on the same plane. And so, it's sometimes easier for these two to be technically true to one another than to avoid periodic fantasies. Yet, the girl in his fantasies may really be she—and the boy in her fantasies may really be he. It's fun to make believe sometimes, that's all. The more versatile they are as individuals, in their personal lives or careers, the less need they'll feel to imagine, "What would it be like, I wonder, if she would . . . . ." or . . . "What would it be like, for a change, if he would . . . . . ."

If she would what? If he would what? Anything. Anything at all. Some Geminis even fantasize hurt or anger, then split up because they wonder what a break would feel like. When they find out, they streak back to each other again to rediscover the reality of love. No, it wasn't a dream. WOW! What a mind blower! Love is *real*. It's *really real*. You can really, nearly trust it. Yes, you nearly, really can! Such a discovery might not stun the average person's mind, but you must remember that the Twins spend their entire lives separating the possible and the probable from the sure things—and love gives them an exhilarating glimpse of Shangri-La.

These two relate to one another physically, through sexual love, in the kind of kaleidoscopic pattern you might expect, when Air unites with Air, chaperoned by the changeable Mercury. It's light, often stormy, sometimes whipping love into hurricanes of passion, sometimes calming it into quiet, gentle affection. The ways in which they express their love on a physical level are as multiple-faceted, sensitive and changeable as the ways they express it on the mental and emotional levels, and that can take their sexual behavior from acrobatic embraces on the Blarney Stone to making love underwater or in a helicopter. Whatever desire one Gemini may have, the other can fill it, with the cool touch of a spring breeze or the hot, tropical wind of a monsoon. To comprehend the potential of their physical compatibility, two Geminis who are pondering a relationship will just have to use their imaginations. About the only words which won't apply to their possible patterns of sexual experience are deep—earthy—and sensual. But Gemini and Gemini can dream up some satisfying substitutes together. Magical is one.

Some Gemini women are as pathetically wistful and lost as Gemini Judy Garland, following a rainbow that forever seems to elude them. Others are as bright and hopeful as Frank Sinatra's Gemini daughter, Nancy. Some Gemini men are as disoriented, and inwardly insecure, as Mercury-ruled actor Errol Flynn—others as bold and confident as Geminians Mike Todd and Al Jolson ("Folks, you ain't heard *nothin'* yet!"). It's not easy to tell them apart, because the wistful, lost Gemini girls have their bright and hopeful moments . . . just as the bright, hopeful ones have their wistful, lost and lonely moments. The disoriented Gemini man can switch suddenly to stability . . . and the confident ones can feel occasionally insecure.

I'm afraid astrology doesn't have a final answer. Perhaps the Gemini boy and girl who are in love will just have to forget about that romantic togetherness formula of "becoming one," because there will always be four of them. But that also quadruples their chances for happiness. So the odds are good if they cover their bets with the double collateral of lots of trust . . . and lots of patience.

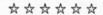

GEMINI

Air — Mutable — Positive
Ruled by Mercury
Symbol: The Twins
Day Forces — Masculine

CANCER

Water — Cardinal — Negative
Ruled by the Moon
Symbol: The Crab
Night Forces — Feminine

The **GEMINI-CANCER** Relationship

"Mind you, I am not sure that we have a drawing-room,
but we pretend we have, and it's all the same. Hoop la!"

He went off dancing . . . . . and they all cried
"Hoop la!" and danced after him, searching for the
drawing-room; and I forget whether they found it,
but at any rate they found corners, and they all
fitted in.

There's a party in progress. Over near the canapé table, loaded with sliced cheese, stuffed munchrooms (the best kind), and other goodies, a voice is heard, rich and warm, punctuated with cackles, attracting a crowd of people . . . . . (a female voice).

". . . . . and the first day I was there, I decided to go horseback riding, up in the mountains. Since there was no one to see me, I removed my shirt, because I wanted to get a tan all over, you know? There I was, perched on this palomino, as naked as Lady Godiva from the waist up, and you know how modest I am. It was a riot. Well, after a couple of hours, I was as red as a lobster, and I figured it was time to ride my horse back to the stables, where I'd rented it. But when I reached for my shirt to put it on, it wasn't there. It had slipped off the saddle horn somewhere in the woods. Can you imagine me riding back, and facing all those men at the stables, in that seminude condition? Naturally, I burst into tears from embarrassment. I knew I just couldn't do it. So, I said to the horse, half hysterically. . . . ."

At the same time, from over near another table, loaded with Perrier water, fruit juices, and several bottles of red and white wine, comes another voice, clear and sparkling, with perfect emphasis and timing, as a second crowd gathers . . . . . .

". . . . . so this guy in Indiana comes home drunk every night for years, until finally his wife threatens to leave him. Because he's really in love with her, he straightens out for a few months. Then this one night he falls off the wagon, gets soused on stingers, and forgets where he lives for three days and nights. Now he's afraid to go home, because she may not forgive him this time. So he has a brainstorm. He goes to a pay phone, drops in a dime, dials his home number, and when his wife answers, he *screams* into the receiver, "Oh, Helen, it's so good to hear your voice! I thought I'd never hear it again. Now listen carefully. I'm in Arizona, and I'll be home tomorrow, but get the police to tap the phone as soon as I hang up—and if they call before I get there, DON'T PAY THE RANSOM MONEY—I JUST ESCAPED!"

They're both good talkers, Gemini and Cancer. The Crab's ability to remember details and to tell a story with sensitive perception, laced with the Lunar imagination and humor, can hold a crowd spellbound. If there's also a Gemini in the room, weaving tall tales with wit and charm, and maybe doing a few card tricks on the side, the bystanders won't know which of the three rings to watch at the circus. (One ring for Cancer, two for Gemini, the Twins. Two of everything for Gemini.)

Before the party's over, either Cancer or Gemini (or both) may whip out a camera and start snapping. Gemini and Cancer share a love for photography with Leo and Pisces, the four Sun Signs most likely to be professional or amateur photographers, each for a different reason. The majority of top photographers were born under one of these four signs, or have the

Moon or Ascendent there—and between them, they have the camera market pretty well cornered.

Another similarity between the Crab and the Twins is that their auras are colored with many shades, because they're both so moody. Cancer dips from the deep blues of depression to the rose of sentiment, sloshes around in the brown of crankiness or the muddy lime greens of fear and hypochondria, then crawls back up to lavender-hued nostalgia and soft pink laughter.

Gemini flits from bright yellow cheer to the indigo of despair, experiments with the shimmering silver of dreams and the gold of hope, then plunges down into the grey of despondency, from which he-she quickly leaps into glistening white childlike faith.

When their auras mix, every color of the spectrum is represented, from transparent etheric to ultraviolet . . . and a few more tones and shades that have not yet been perceived, let alone named.

They're both dreamers, and both expert in the art of getting publicity (although the Crabs pretend not to be interested, he and she fool no one—they adore attention). They also both have vivid imaginations, and they're both inclined to laugh in public and cry in private. So you may think it's difficult to tell them apart. It is not. It's as easy as telling a bird in the air from a crab on the beach. One flies with the wind or an errant breeze, flapping its wings, its bright eyes darting to and fro quickly. The other crawls carefully along the shore, near the water, in the moonlight . . . backwards, sideways, slowly and deliberately. Both are frequently amusing. Both change their dispositions without warning.

Regardless of their matching behavior at times, in their basic natures, as with all other 2-12 Sun Sign Patterns, Gemini and Cancer are as different as night and day, as positive and negative as the north and south poles—and, in this case, as different as Air and Water (which are very different, you must admit).

The Twins are Mutable; consequently, they prefer to dash around, here and there, communicating ideas and dreams, to being the Big Boss and running the show. The Crabs are Cardinal, they definitely do not enjoy communicating (especially their own secrets) and prefer to run things—not necessarily out front, with a brass band, but still very much in charge.

Being influenced by the 2-12 vibration, Gemini senses (because Cancer is the sign ahead of Gemini on the karmic wheel) that he or she has much to learn from the care and caution and secrecy of the Crabs—the ability to sit and wait patiently, and the tenacity to stay with an idea long enough for it to develop from a misty into a solid form. Because Gemini is the sign behind Cancer, the Crab is wistfully conscious of a faint soul memory of how it was to be driven by the multiple yearnings of Mercury, searching the world over for a place to settle, yet reluctant to linger too long in one spot, for fear of missing something more exciting. The Crabs remember, ah! they remember . . . and so, ruled in this present existence by the fluctuating Moon, they are periodically consumed by wanderlust, and at the same time held back by fear (springing from the same karmic soul memory) of losing, in Gemini fashion, what they already possess. That's why Cancerians usually remain by the hearth, flying (normally) only through the imagination, under a Full or New Moon, safely secure during such imaginary flights near the home nest. But because they do understand, the Crabs often tolerate the restlessness of the Twins better than most other Sun Signs are apt to do.

In friendship, business, love relationships, Gemini is not inclined to cling. If anything, they hold too lightly and casually, let go too quickly and sometimes discard too soon. Cancer hangs on for dear life (barring those Twins and Crabs with Moon Signs or Ascendents that strongly conflict with their natal Suns, and even then, the conflict is merely periodic and temporary). The typical Crabs fear that if they should loosen their grip, they'll be left without an anchor, in strange, new waters, bereft of the comforting and the familiar.

Of course, some Crabs will deny this trait with vehemence—the ones whose birth charts contain an Aries, Gemini or Sag Moon or Ascendant. Even so, don't be overly impressed with their denials—especially their claims that they don't save things or hang on to things. The tenacious quality is always there. It just takes some subtle forms in each individual Moon Child. If you search long enough, you'll find it.

A Gemini psychiatrist, whose office is on the ground floor of a building where I used to live, told me about a Cancerian patient he once treated for a mild neurosis. The Crab is completely cured now, happy and well adjusted, no longer weepy. On the first visit to the psychiatrist, there was so much emphasis on nostalgia and financial security, the secretive patient's Sun Sign peeked out. After a couple of hours of listening, the Gemini "shrink," although fascinated, began to fidget from sitting in one place so long, so he switched on one of his fast Mercury subject changes and remarked, "I'll bet you were born under the sign of Cancer."

"Yes, I was," replied the surprised patient. "It's very clever of you to have guessed that, since I have absolutely none of the typical Lunar characteristics. Astrology claims that Cancer is clinging and tenacious. Not me. I'm not like that at all. And I'm not in the least possessive. I don't save things, and I never hang on."

"Well," mused the Twins, glibly, "maybe it's your Moon Sign. Now, let's make an appointment for next week."

CRAB:	You want me to go, is that it? You want to get rid of me, because I bore you as a patient, and you think I'm too far gone for even you to help. That's what you're trying to tell me.
THE TWINS:	No, no—of course not. Not at all. It's just that I'm due in Chicago tonight for a speech, and if I don't leave for the airport within fifteen minutes, I'll miss my plane.
CRAB:	I see. And you want me to leave. You're hinting for me to leave. Isn't that right?
THE TWINS:	No. I mean, yes. Well, it isn't that I *want* you to leave. But I'm afraid I'll miss my plane, that's all.
CRAB:	Could I maybe ride along with you in the taxi to the airport? And if you'll be back tomorrow, you could come over to my place for dinner. I make a really tasty meatless spaghetti.
THE TWINS:	I'd love to, but . . . I've already made another engagement for dinner tomorrow night, after I return.
CRAB:	(weeping) You hate me. I can take a hint. I'll go.
THE TWINS:	Please don't cry. You're wrong. I'm not trying to get rid of you. I wish I could take you to Chicago with me. I enjoy your company. Honest.
CRAB:	(brightening considerably) You do? Okay, then can I make an appointment for the day after tomorrow instead of next week?

The funniest part of the story is that the Cancerian patient was a female Crab, a Moon Maid, who is now happily married to the Gemini psychiatrist. I trust this little story will illustrate to Geminis of any sex, age or profession, who are involved with a Cancerian in any way, that the quick can be tripped up by the quiescent—whether in romance, across the table in a card game or in a business deal, not to mention running around the family circle.

Crabs are impressionable, sensitive men, women and children. They tend to be periodically contrary and sullen, brooding over slights, real or imagined. But the Twins can usually sweet-talk or double-talk them into crawling back out of their shells. Gemini is the mental (or actual) wanderer, a lonely drifter, cut loose from ties, emotionally (and sometimes literally) homeless, lost and seeking . . . the eternal child. A Cancerian is the eternal Mother (or Father), protective, warm, tender and coaxing. It's little wonder these two are drawn to each other . . . part . . . then return . . . then part again.

The element of Water, when it saturates Air with enough moisture, causes a shower that clears the atmosphere of fog, smog—and misunderstanding. Consequently, Cancer can make Gemini pour out those Twin desires, shed some truthful tears, and pause a moment, now and then, to remember the things that really matter.

☆ ☆ ☆ ☆ ☆ ☆

GEMINI *Woman* CANCER *Man*

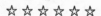

"Do you think I could be a twin?"

"No, indeed," replied the twins; "it's awfully difficult to be a twin." . . . . .

"I hadn't really any hope," he said.

A Cancerian man lives in his sensations, emotions, and imagination. He loves history and likes to read about the glory of bygone ages, from the Byzantine, through the Medieval and the Renaissance. But he's rather romantic about the past (his own and that of other historical characters), and he doesn't like to be reminded that the Knights of the Round Table may have possessed some flaws, that the horses they rode had burrs in their tails—they wore sweaty shirts under their chain mail (the knights, not the horses), ate with their fingers, and may have occasionally slept with comely wenches on dirty straw.

In the Crab's sentimental mind, a knight has impeccable table manners, and he rides a snow-white steed, with a fluffy, carefully brushed tail. He returns from his great crusades unsoiled and unperspiring, to claim the scented hanky of his lady fair. Now there's nothing wrong with a Crab treating a Gemini girl to his sense of chivalry. But *she* should be aware, even if he's not, of the historical fact that many a knight of olden days, after tucking that scented hanky under his shining armour, reached into his visor for the key he carried to the iron chastity belt of his modest lady fair—and sometimes pulled out the wrong key.

That is to say, the Crab, like the real or legendary knight, has more intimate things planned than pocketing a hanky, no matter how slow and courteous his initial approach may be.

A Gemini girl could get emotionally carried away by the romantic scene his gallantry conjures up in her own imaginative mind. With her predilection for daydreaming, she can easily envision herself wading impatiently across the moat, then running through the clover to meet him, her long, golden hair (or raven-black tresses) flying behind her. Then she gracefully curtsies before her Cancerian knight, sitting up there on his snorting stallion. It's almost real. She blushes, then timidly hands him her perfumed . . . . . . *look out!* By this time, the Crab may have grabbed her dainty hand with his firm grip, and isn't about to let go.

When Cancerian possessiveness crosses swords with the Gemini insistence on freedom, the clash can cut into their dreams cruelly. After the Cancer man discovers this girl is really two women—one content to nestle happily beside him in the tower room of the castle—the other determined to roam around on the slopes, playing with the antelope, chasing the hounds or whatever—he may pout. He may snap at her. Or he may retreat into crabby seclusion in the dark, damp dungeon, waiting for her to trip down the stone steps and entice him out again. If there's something else on her mind, he'll have a long wait down there.

Gemini girls have been known to forget mundane responsibilities like lovers locked in dungeons when they've been caught up in a fitful flight of fancy or a mental whim. Not that she doesn't have an excellent memory, but other interests take priority, sometimes even over love, until she gets lonely. Then she'll trail back, looking for forgiveness and comfort. So their story could have a happy ending after all, since a Cancerian man is about as comforting as they make the male animal. No one can be more tender, gentle and understanding to a lost and mixed-up Gemini girl than a Crab. Not even a sweet, gruff, protective Bull. If they have a harmonious Luminary aspect between their birth charts, we can leave them there on the stone steps, as the sun sinks slowly in the West, astrologically confident of their continued bliss—knowing she'll always wander and he'll always pout—but she'll always return, and he'll always pet and forgive her.

If the Sun-Moon aspect between their horoscopes is not harmonious, we can't desert them quite yet. They'll need some help, to keep from falling into the moat and drowning—or disappearing over the hills, in different directions, on different horses.

They can find their share of happy together, but it will take patience on her part and some adaptability on his. It won't be easy, since her ruling planet, Mercury, doesn't send out patient vibes. And his ruling Luminary, the Moon, changes too frequently to count on any one phase remaining for long. He'll pass through a mood of reckless abandon to match hers, then return to his hard shell before she's even had a chance to enjoy it. It takes practice and devotion on both sides. Although the shifting moods they have in common may not be their only problem, they'll form the basis for all the others. When you take a Gemini girl and a Cancerian man, each subject to sudden switches of disposition, and throw them into close contact, no one quite knows whose fault anything is at any particular time.

Here he is, all jolly and full of fun and chuckles, but she has just changed into a somber, contemplative period. So she makes a loving effort to match his hilarity. However, by the time she's reversed gears into a high, he's already turned off the funnies. Now he's obeying the call of the three-quarter Moon, pulling on him magnetically to be quiet and reclusive. So he makes an equally loving attempt to match her new amusement. Except that, by the time he has synchronized himself to the Full Moon, and turned into a laughing Looney Bird, Mercury has tormented her into a mental knot of sarcasm and cutting criticism of his jokes. This deeply wounds the Crab's feelings. So she makes another loving effort to . . . well, it could go on and on—all the way to a mutual nervous breakdown. They'll have to blow the whistle, stop, and take stock of their mood schedules. There are several solutions.

They can both return to the starting line (say, on a day when their planets are working in rhythm) and try to match their changing moods to each other's. That's one way. Laugh together, cry together, mope together, hope together—and cope together. If they can't swing that, because their stars are coming in on different wave-lengths, they can at least stop fighting their crossed purposes and make this promise to themselves: If he's high while she's low—he'll cheer her up instead of letting her pull him down; if she's calm while he's stormy—she'll soothe his worries instead of snubbing him and driving him deeper into his shell. When Gemini is happy, why should she let the Crab's crankiness turn her off? He needs sympathy, not cold rejection. When Cancer is placid, why should he let her jumpiness annoy him into retreating? She needs petting, not pouting. If they keep that promise, they can gradually train their moods to slide into the same grooves, although they'll still have some periodic impasses.

Since this is a 2-12 Sun Sign Pattern, the Cancer half of the team will usually be tolerant of the twin Gemini faults of restlessness and detachment—and the Gemini half will probably try to imitate the Crab's virtues of patience and sensitivity, sensing that she needs to learn them. One lesson she may shy away from learning from him, however, is how to be more cautious with cash. Unless she has a more conservative Moon Sign or Ascendent, she may think he's a tight combination of Scrooge and Shylock. Most Geminis scatter money like birdseed. Most Cancerians hoard it like Midas. Somewhere in between there's a middle road to financial agreement. But it won't be found at the extreme ends of his stinginess or her capriciousness with cash. The Crab's tendency to hang on to money is motivated by his fear of being hungry someday and his need for security.

The more his hunger for affection is satisfied, the less fear he'll have of starving. *If he has enough emotional security, he won't need as much financial security.* As for the material possessions the Crab likes to accumulate, Gemini may fear they'll tie her down. Her tendency to get rid of money is motivated by the feeling that she'll find more excitement in spending it than in saving it. When she has sufficient emotional freedom and mental challenge, she won't be compelled to buy these basic Mercury needs with cash, so she'll be less extravagant. Gemini is gregarious and must be either mentally or physically active, preferably both. She likes to eat out a lot, for a double reason: she's not overly fond of cooking—and she needs a frequent change of scene. The Crab may prefer to eat at home, because it's reminiscent of the coziness of his childhood—or eat at his mother's, which is even *more* reminiscent of the coziness of his childhood. That can put a few kinks in the Cancer-Gemini relationship, unless the partners iron them out by drawing certain lines clearly at the beginning.

Since both of them live in a world of fantasy and dreams, their sexual rapport can be stimulating for her and fulfilling for him. He supplies the sensual sensitivity and the affection—she supplies the imagination and the variety. A Gemini girl is one for having sudden ideas. She may have some changeable ideas about passion. But the Crab is perceptive enough to match his own desires to hers, and he'll probably have a few romantic notions of his own, off the beaten path of boredom. Their lovemaking will seldom be repetitious. It will vary with the Moon's waxing and waning, as they respond to the ebbing and flooding tides of their emotions. She'll notice something warm and protective about the way he approaches their sexual union, and her "lost child" heart will be solaced when his arms are around her. He'll notice there's always something indefinably delicate and gentle about the way she seeks his affection.

Often, a Cancerian man respects the Gemini lady he loves so much he can't seem to abandon himself to total passion with her, as if he believed her so fragile, he might be harming a flower. But she isn't as fragile as he thinks, never mind her delicate, gentle manner, and her airy, light touch. She needs, seeks and wants . . . to be treated as an adult woman, not as a charming child. When she's near him, in the dark, she'll cling to him, and her fears will melt away. Many Gemini girls dislike sleeping in total darkness—but with this man, she may be willing to try.

Many Cancerian men equally dislike sleeping without a night light. But with her close beside him, he'll find darkness a friend. The nightmares that haunt him so frequently will seem far away when he can feel her head on his shoulder. Her restless head . . . but she'll be calmer, quieter, more at peace with him, herself and the world . . . after they've experienced physical Oneness together. Visibly so. Sometimes, for days and days. Until her Twin calls to her again, and she gets that distant look. That's when he needs to grab her, before she floats away.

The male Crab, with his shy smile, enjoys parties and people, music and dancing, though he may be reluctant to admit it. This is just the woman to coax and wheedle and tempt him out of his reclusive hermit act into the bright lights. She may talk him into going dancing, hiking, horseback riding, sailing . . . cross-country skiing, or touring Europe with her, visiting ancient ruins, trying to recall when they perhaps once lived in a bygone civilization . . . and maybe drank a toast to each other from this very cup . . . . did she wear the necklace behind glass in the British Museum when they fiercely loved in Egypt?

The Gemini girl can talk the Crab into most anything, but her easiest persuasion will be to seduce him into traveling. Places like ancient ruins and old museums secretly magnetize this man. He lives in yesterday, and to revisit it with her is perhaps the deepest dream of all, from which he'll hope he never wakens. With her, he may not. Gemini lives on the wind, where dreams are reality . . . where reality itself is a dream. He'll probably learn that, wherever they go together. Nearly always, she'll be streaking ahead of him, her hair flying in the breeze, not even looking back over her shoulder to see if he's still there. She doesn't need to look back. She *knows* he's still there. She knows his love is steady, he is devotion unwavering, and that's what she's been seeking all her life—a pair of eyes that say *"Come home."* He's been seeking a pair of eyes that say *"Let's run through the stars!"*

And so, each sees the unspoken wish reflected in the other's eyes, from the very first time they look at each other, across a crowded street . . . or room . . . and their gaze locks tightly, unexpectedly. For years and years afterwards, they'll tell each other about that night and remember together the sudden tears they both felt, inexplicably, when their eyes first met . . . and they didn't even know each other's names. But that didn't matter. Silently, through a half-forgotten strain of music, they called out to one another by the secret names their hearts knew.

Once they've declared their love, she may shower him with a silvery stream of gifts, and at first his cautious nature will be aghast at such impulsive extravagance. Yet, when she's not looking, his eyes will fill with Lunar tears of pure delight, to be so loved and cherished. He'll timidly, yet proudly, display her gifts to friends. It proves, you see, that he is loved, and with her instant, flashing intuition, she senses this about him. She longs to make up to him for all the times he was disappointed as a child on Christmas morning. How does she know? He never told her. She knows. Because she loves him. Love is funny like that. After a while, she just may perform a magical transformation in the Cancerian man's nature. Then he'll relax . . . and wrap some bright blue and silver or lavender and sunny-yellow ribbons around some special surprises for her, too. When a Crab is snugly loved, the reciprocal affection is boundless, bottomless, returning a thousandfold—and he'll cry, unashamedly, from sheer happiness.

He'll always treat her like a lady. She'll be thrilled at such lovely make-believe of a gentler time and usually behave accordingly. To her, he is a gentleman, a gallant gentleman, who touches her with occasional glimpses of the little boy within. Then *she* cries, because he is so vulnerable to hurt, despite his hard, outer shell of impassiveness. For he is a poet, and she's the very first one who ever guessed it. Geminis are great at guessing, and they always win the jar of jelly beans.

A Gemini girl-woman is a realist, despite her changing masks . . . first whimsical, then cynical, always fascinating to the Cancerian man, whose own facial expressions she loves to watch herself, as they reflect the various colors and tones of his Lunar emotions . . . joy or sadness, tranquility or worry.

Whatever the feminine Mercury Bird's chronological age may be, she's ever youthful and yearning, thoughtful and tender . . . her skin and eyes as crystal clear as a child's . . . filled with misty dreams, yet driven relentlessly by logic. Some of her dreams she carelessly loses along the way, others she forgets, in the sparkle of some new excitement. The deep, sacred ones, she keeps locked up inside herself. A persistent Cancerian man can coax her to share them with him, if he moves quickly, before she spins out of his reach. But it may take him some time to be certain—and Crabs can wait too long. She'll be chattering and charming him one day, then suddenly notice how quiet he's become.

"What's the matter, darling? Did I say something wrong?" she'll ask, vaguely troubled.

"No. It's just that . . . I think I might love you. But I'm not sure."

She won't understand what he means. To Gemini, you can't be sure of anything in this life, especially love. Not until you reach the very end of the trail. There's little enough time before that moment comes. Why waste any of it?

☆ ☆ ☆ ☆ ☆ ☆

GEMINI *Man* CANCER *Woman*

———◄◆►———

He ceased to look at her, but even then she would
not let go of him. He skipped about and made funny
faces, but when he stopped it was just as if she
were inside him, knocking.

Normally, a Gemini man is able to analyze people quickly, with a swift, sure insight. Normally, a Moon Maiden is acutely perceptive of human nature. Together (along with Aquarius and Pisces) they make a great sleuthing team, and it's no accident that almost all Geminis and Cancerians enjoy detective stories. (Scorpios do too, though they lean more toward murder mysteries and ghost tales.)

Yet, for all his cleverness and mental agility, and for all her talent at worming secrets out of people, the one puzzle Gemini and Cancer can't seem to solve is each other. There's always a piece missing. Ask a Gemini man what disturbs him most about the Cancerian girl he loves, and he'll tell you:

"I never know what she's *thinking*."

Ask a Cancerian girl what troubles her most about the Gemini man she loves, and she'll say:

"I don't know what he *wants*."

That's the way it is with these two lovers when they meet, and that's the way it will be when they part, in friendship or in anger—through any kind of earthly separation—and that's the way it will always be, if they remain together. Her secretive manner, her way of clamming up and refusing to talk when she's hurt, will drive a Gemini man wild, which is not a natural state for the casual Twins. From time to time she'll tell him what's on her mind, but just as frequently, she'll snap her Crab shell on his questions, leaving him frustrated and feeling totally helpless to bring her out of a mood he has no idea how she managed to get into. It will do no good to poke at her with accusations and sarcasm. She'll remain inside herself until she's good and ready to come back out—and then she'll claim she's forgotten what it was that made her blue and cranky. She hasn't, really. She just feels safer when she retains her secrets. Sometimes a girl Crab will weep, and pour out her apprehensions, but even then he won't get to the real, rock-bottom reason for the anguish. There are no whys and wherefores. Gemini isn't content until he untangles every snarl and sees into every motive, and so her cryptic behavior leaves him with a continued feeling of vague uneasiness. How can he solve this mystery of her moods if she keeps the clues locked up in her attic, hidden inside her trunks of jokes and tucked behind the corners of her silent fears? Perhaps it's because he can't solve it that he often returns, again and again, to try. But he may never know what she's really thinking between her sobs, her giggles and her serenity—just the bits and pieces he picks up when she lets him sneak into her heart's attic to help her look for an old memory she's misplaced, from long ago, in her childhood.

As for her, she would give him the Moon if she could. A Cancerian girl in love desires only to cherish, to protect and lavish affection on her man (though his portions of her devotion may be abruptly cut in half when their children crawl into her heart). She'll stuff him with food, wash him with sympathy, and distract him with her wacky Lunar humor. But how can she cook up a complete dream that will satisfy all his hunger when he keeps changing the recipe for his happiness? The elusive way he switches the subject, just when she thinks she's caught what it is he's longing for, drives her into tears and tantrums. She may never discover what he really wants, because *he* doesn't know, and even if he did, he'd share it only with his Twin Self.

It's not that he doesn't trust her. But only his Twin can decipher the complications of his Mercurial dreams and translate them into one single goal. Since a Moon Maiden is so reflective, so emotionally absorbent, she'll soak up some of his strategy, just from being around him. She'll know everything about his mental tricks—except how to perform them. That's because these two are set at different speeds. Hers reads: slow and cautious—despite her outward show of busy motion. His reads: fast and reckless—never mind if he's one of those Geminis who appears cool and calm on the surface. His mind is jet-fueled and ever ready for instant takeoff.

This is a 2-12 Sun Sign Pattern, with Gemini the sign behind Cancer and Cancer the sign immediately ahead of Gemini. So, she'll secretly understand his restive nature, from an unconscious soul memory of what it was like to be careless and casual and free of strong emotional ties. In fact, the memory may haunt her to the point of turning her to its opposite—a desperate clinging to security, preferably emotional, and if it's lacking—financial. Gemini will half consciously realize she can teach him an approach to life he's never experienced, and since he's such a quick study, he'll grow in wisdom around her in many ways. But not without a few growing pains.

The typical Gemini man keeps nothing for which he has no further need, from torn ticket stubs and dull razor blades to human relationships which have outlived their usefulness. He can't understand her need to hang on to things. You'd think she had lived through the horrors of some great famine, the way she saves soup coupons and stocks up on canned food that would feed her whole family for months if we were ever under siege by Space people.

What he doesn't understand is that, with a Cancer girl, an interplanetary war is always a possibility. *Anything* is always a possibility, and she wants to be prepared for it. The crinkled money she keeps under the box springs eases her fear of a leaky roof on a future rainy day. But the old ball gowns she packed away in mothballs are back in style, and if she cuts off the tops, she'll have a new wardrobe of evening skirts without spending any of those crinkled bills. Neither is she as hasty as he is to throw away old friendships or ties.

Gemini's more casual attitude toward human relationships puzzles the Cancerian girl. It's not the *usefulness* of any close relationship that matters to her. It's the familiarity, the comfortable feeling it gives her of the past—yesterday, when the world was young and gay and safe and secure. She feels similarly about the deeper relationship called love. A Lunar girl's love has no foundation in reason or logic. She's helpless to destroy it. Other loves can be wished away, willed away, angered away—talked out, or thrown out. Hers has to *wear* out, and it can take many years. Even then, she'll sew a patch on the worn spots and try to somehow make it do. It's one of the most valuable lessons her heart can teach his mind.

You may know a Cancerian girl who is fickle and promiscuous, but don't you believe her. It's a pose. Somewhere under her tough Crab shell is an old, faded love, tenderly darned and folded with care, that she's wistfully hoping will come back into style . . . be *needed* again. The fictional image of the sentimental prostitute with the heart of gold, who "babies" or "mothers" her gentlemen callers, is a picture of a haunted Moon Maid, still waiting, in her fashion, for "him" to return.

To the Gemini who is on a romantic holiday, it's always time to move on, and lugging the memory of old loves slows a man down. He seldom packs any torches in his suitcase. He travels light. He doesn't belong to anyplace or to any person. Not even to his relatives. He knows they love him, but still he feels, somehow, apart—not only from them, from the world—until he finds a woman who knows how to hang on to his heart. Hanging on is a Cancerian talent, but her Crab-like possessiveness will turn him off—and away—unless she disguises it as tender tolerance and makes it stretch to give him room to wander. Then it will lure him and warm him when he's cold and lonely. If she learns to let go, and to let love be the only tie that binds them, she'll discover that, with this man— free can mean faithful.

In their sexual relationship, pure physical sensation will be less emphasized than the passions of the mind and a kind of emotional eroticism. Her affectionate tenderness and vivid imagination are a good balance for his delicate touch and his sensitive sexual nature. When they're expressing their love on a physical level, they may even find that missing piece to be the puzzle of each other they're always looking for, and become whole . . . for brief moments. Because she needs constant, tangible proof that she's really needed, not just routinely desired, his airy embraces could sometimes cause her to wish he would hold her more closely—and longer— just so she can be *sure*. Their most ideal sexual fulfillment together may frequently be experienced during the Full Moon, when she seems to possess a strange, magnetic power to gently reach into the secret corners of his Twin heart and draw him away from his dreams back into the intimate mystery of their union . . . the deepest dream of all.

He'll become impatient with her ingrained economical streak if she tries to transfer her financial fears to him. Then she'll ask, "Do you know how it feels to be poor? It's a nightmare. You'll find out what it's like if you keep throwing away your money and never saving it. Didn't anyone ever tell you that waste makes want?" But Gemini will simply shrug and reply, like archetype Geminian Mike Todd—"I wouldn't know about that. I've been broke, but I've never been poor. Being broke is temporary. Being poor is a state of mind."

A Moon Maiden will understand this man better if she realizes that, however he may appear to the world, to himself he's eternally a young boy, who, in some magical way, has managed to pilot a plane high in the sky. He diverts himself now and then with sudden dives and spins, fascinated by finding a prettier cloud, discovering a more beautiful sunrise or sunset . . . all the while excitedly aware that the great Universe and its glittering galaxies lay enticingly unexplored before him . . . beckoning. If she truly loves him for keeps, she'll cheerfully be ready to pack up and move on when his free spirit grows restless, turning each new rest stop, however temporary, into a warm and welcoming, gracious haven, as only a Cancerian woman can. Somehow this lady can cause each new place she lives to seem like a garden, filled with the fragrant flowers of tradition. And this is the very thing Gemini needs—to be able to wander, yet never leave home. Gradually, she'll tenderly implant herself inside his own longings, until finally . . . . anywhere he hears her lovely Lunar laughter becomes home.

The Gemini man may linger past the sunset in the sky until the Moon comes up. If he stays a little longer, he might unveil the mystery of his Cancerian woman. And wouldn't it be funny if her secret turned out to be that—in a changing world of changing truth, fleetingly glimpsed, then hidden by clouds of passing time—each soul must find its other half, to know —to see—to *be*? The very same Twin secret as his own.

GEMINI

Air — Mutable — Positive
Ruled by Mercury
Symbol: The Twins
Day Forces — Masculine

LEO

Fire — Fixed — Positive
Ruled by the Sun
Symbols: Lion & Shy Pussycat
Day Forces — Masculine

The GEMINI-LEO *Relationship*

"Back, twins . . . ."

As Gemini calculates the sunny but sometimes insufferable antics of the Lion, the Twins wonder: "Does the Big Cat actually possess such complete self-assurance? Or could Leo only be trying to prove that the *reality* is as infallible and fearless as the *image?*"—a typical Gemini mind trip.

As the Lion or Lioness lazily studies the Mercurial Gemini Twins, he (or she) has a similar thought: "All that mental and physical activity must be a compensation of some kind. Survival alone isn't sufficient reason for so much unnecessary maneuvering. Is Gemini trying to span East, West, North, and South all at once to hide the fact that he (or she) is lost in the woods with a broken compass?"

They've both guessed the truth about each other. Yes, Leos are trying to prove to themselves and the rest of the world, through a show of arrogant bravado, that Lions and Lionesses are as brave inwardly as they outwardly seem. And yes, Gemini *is* trying to prove to the Twin Self and everyone else that he-she is racing straight ahead, in the right direction, and not really running around in circles.

Because their two Sun Signs are sextile, creating a 3-11 vibration between them, they're intuitive about each other, are inclined to friendship, despite any differences between them from time to time, and they have a mutual talent for whistling in the dark. When they whistle a tune together, in harmony, it's easier to convince themselves that all is well. Unlike Scorpios (except for the Grey Lizards), who are deeply and unshakably certain of their superiority, the Lion and Lioness believe that if they roar loudly enough, no one will suspect that they tremble with apprehension over their private fear that they may not be completely equal to every occasion that may arise. The King and Queen of the jungle pride—or of any kingdom, classroom, office or home—must never lose face before their adoring subjects, who respect and worship the monarchy, only because their rulers are capable of handling any minor or major emergency with majestic finesse, regal dignity and wisdom. It's the quintessence of royalty to project nobility of spirit and strength of character to the weaker masses. Strangely, and rather wonderfully, in pretending to be all these things, Leo actually *becomes* them, rediscovering through every human crisis (to his or her secret surprise and delight) that the Leonine courage really is as powerful and awesome as the Lion's roar insinuates.

Geminis have the same sort of good fortune with their apparent self-deception. While the Twins are selling others, they're simultaneously selling themselves the validity of their own dreams. Gemini tells stories, flavored with excitement, always amusing, some of them with a double-switch O. Henry ending, instilling enthusiasm and inspiring more cautious, practical souls. With the brush of imagination, Geminis paint marvelous word pictures of nonsensical things and somehow manage to make them seem real and logical to sane people, as well as to themselves. By so believing, Mercury dreams eventually materialize and manifest.

Because Leo inwardly senses that Geminis are telling the truth *as they see it,* the large Leonine heart goes out to the Twins in sympathetic recognition of a soul brother—or sister. Of course. Leo understands. It's like the song from *The King and I*—"make believe you're brave, and the trick will get you far. You can be as brave—as you make believe you are!"

What hurts and perplexes the Gemini Mercury Birds is the way others, who are less sympathetic than Leo, interpret their talent for conjuring up imagery. They can't fathom why it is, when other people do the same thing, they're called creative, imaginative—astute traders, or shrewd businessmen. When the Twins do it, they're called con artists, liars—or, at the very least, deceptively slick and quick with the facts. Geminis think they have the world and everyone in it analyzed down to the last nuance. That is, until they bump up against the exceptions to the rule and finally come to the conclusion that the world may consist entirely of exceptions. It figures. The Twins themselves are.

From childhood, Geminis have been acutely aware that illusion is the most dependable of all riches. No Broadway stage is as packed with drama and color as the "theatre of the mind." And so, the Twins cast themselves in all roles, from the character actors to the ingenues, from the stars to the lowliest bit players, sometimes slipping into the part of the stagehands or musicians. Why not? They've also decided they're the producers and directors, so they can be whatever they choose to be.

However, when playing the boards with the Big Cats, the Twins best be cautious about grabbing off the plum titles of Star, Director or Producer. If there's any kind of show going on, anywhere, at any time, actual or make-believe, you can bet your greasepaint and footlights that Leos are going to insist on directing it and producing it—and most definitely will star in it. No one successfully outshines a Lion or a Lioness for very long, let alone upstages a King or Queen.

That's usually just fine and dandy with the airy, detached Geminis. The Twins are, if the truth be told, actually far more interested in changing the scenery than in hogging the encores. They appreciate press notices as much as Leo, and they're equally if not more adept in the art of getting heard about or written about. But they'll normally, if they're typical Mercury Birds, move gracefully aside and allow the vainer Leos to take most of the bows before a live audience.

Is it because Gemini is a Mutable Sign? Not necessarily. The Twins have another "method to their madness." When you're out front, headlining the show, you see, you're vulnerable to being inspected by a bunch of curious strangers. It makes many Geminians in the entertainment field uncomfortable if he-she can't wear the many-colored cloak of multifaceted identity, which is so handy for disguising a Twin—or even Triplet—personality, who's pretending to be one single entity.

It's been said that inside every plump person is a skinny twin, longing to escape. That's especially true of the chubby Geminis, who have gained weight in an unconscious effort to hide their secret selves—to stop running so fast—because they were bored into eating by a lack of opportunity for physical activity and mental challenge—or through some hidden guilt and frustration connected with their tangled emotions. Gemini fatties, however, are rare, since the skinny Twin is normally the more insistent one, because of being aware that the ability to flash around, thin, and therefore less noticeable, is a more effective means of masquerading. This is the real reason why the few plump Mercury Birds are so very much more miserable than people of any other Sun Sign (except Scorpio and Pisces) who have gained weight. They don't mind the burden of extra pounds so much, and they're not unduly concerned over their health—it's just that it makes them so *visible*, spoiling all their fun and games.

The difference between the Geminian and Leonine natures regarding visibility and public exposure was rather gloriously demonstrated when I was giving a talk in Washington, D.C., in May of 1971, before a very large crowd, consisting mainly of the press, at a banquet honoring Martha Mitchell (who provided them, undeniably, with some of their most colorful copy).

When I asked how many Leos were present, hands shot up all over the place instantly—and they *remained* up, as high as possible, many of them waving frantically in an attempt to be noticed. When I followed that request by asking the Big Cats to please stand and be recognized, heads started bobbing, right and left, as all the Lions and Lionesses present in the ballroom of the Hotel Shoreham that night rose grandly to the occasion. Then, while the audience loudly applauded, all those Leos, as if on cue, immediately began bowing quite formally, graciously accepting their rightful homage—even the Shy Pussycat Leos, who saw their chance to finally be on stage and take a few curtain calls. It was truly, astrologically and otherwise, hilarious. My tape recording of the event clocks the resulting roars of laughter from the other Sun Signs present at a full three minutes, during which time the applause grew louder and louder, as the Big Cats kept bowing repeatedly.

As a sort of test, a few moments after the general uproar had died down, I invited all the Geminis present to raise *their* hands. "Come on," I urged, "let's have a show of hands from all the Twins here tonight." Not one single hand was raised in the entire, huge ballroom. Quickly, a ripple of whispering passed among the audience, as everyone wondered why the Geminis weren't answering the astrological roll call, especially since I had just pointed out that there are, statistically, in several countries, including the U.S.A., more June births than any others. Obviously, percentagewise, there should have been at least *one* Gemini in that large crowd.

The audience had no idea what was happening, but I did. Any astrologer would have known. The Twins prefer to observe, without being specifically identified themselves. Geminis are seldom anxious to be recognized by a crowd. Also, some of them were undoubtedly present at the banquet after telling a friend, mate or relative that they were going somewhere else, following which they changed their minds—and they didn't want to get caught by those present later remarking on their presence because they had become publicly visible to the entire group. The rest of them were reluctant to expose themselves for as many assorted reasons as there are individual (or dual) Geminis.

I made all these remarks aloud to the audience—and repeated my invitation to the Geminis. Very slowly and hesitantly then, only about three or four hands were partially raised in the packed room. Suddenly a wave of laughter burst forth from everyone, as heads turned toward the rear of the ballroom, where what resembled a conga line of a dozen or more Geminis were attempting to sneak out the door without being noticed. As the laughter rose, and people began calling out to the departing Geminis they knew by name, they all began actually running past the astonished doorman. Everyone present, myself included, completely broke up.

And thus did I discover by sheer accident what turned out to be a most enlightening, as well as hilarious, way to prove the validity of Sun Signs to a large gathering of skeptics and believers.

I can't say whether it had any bearing on the hasty departure of the Mercury Birds, but perhaps I should note that the late FBI Chief J. Edgar Hoover was seated on the dais that night, making one of his extremely rare public appearances. Mr. Hoover was, quite clearly, intently interested in the exodus, and I received the distinct impression that he desperately wanted to signal someone to check out the identity of the guests who sneaked out rather than be recognized—maybe even have them followed home. But, being a Capricorn, he was, of course, aware that one does not so behave thus improperly at a social function. It would be against the rules.

The twin Mercury gifts of charm and glibness make the typical Gemini an expert Lion trainer, cleverly cajoling Leo to docilely jump through his (or her) double hoops. For example, Leo might ask Gemini, "What am I really like? I mean, how do I appear to people?"

And Gemini will answer, "Well, you're incredibly egotistical and arrogant. But you're also open-minded, friendly and generous." (With Leos, you let them have the painful truth near the beginning, then quickly slam in a compliment at the close.) But the Lion or Lioness may persist, stroking his (or her) vanity and demanding, "Do others see my virtues as clearly as you? If so, then why are they always underestimating me?"

Gemini: "Of course they do. Everyone knows you're a fantastic person, a little conceited, and stuffed full of yourself, but you're a terrific organizer. It's obvious that you have a wiser head and cooler emotions than the average person. Anyone who doesn't give you credit for it is jealous, and not worth concerning yourself about."

You see how it works? When you're conversing with a Lion, you sandwich the cold facts in between thick slices of warm flattery. There's a Mercurial technique to it—like, grovel while you're leveling with them.

Actually, Leos *are* excellent organizers, expert at delegating authority, and Fixed enough to wait out with composure the final success of their grandiose schemes and promotions. But they may not show as much patience with Gemini's changeability. The Big Cats can become indignant over the Twins' tendency to speed through life, discarding former convictions like yesterday's newspaper, tossing away homes and jobs and friends with minor flaws, too soon, with absolutely no reflective retrospection, but simply dashing off blithely to the next fascinating interest. To the loyal, more languid Lion or Lioness, fast is not always best, or right. Then Leo will feel obliged to enlighten Gemini with one of those regal Leonine lectures.

"You're pretty good at dabbling in the dairy and skimming off the surface cream, but it's always turning sour on you. That mental sharpness you think is so great cuts a lot of large holes in your common sense, and they'll trip you up when you least expect it. Someday you'll thank me for warning you."

Leos, the eternal Big Brothers and Sisters, are unable to resist predicting that the people they benevolently guided are going to want to look them up someday and seek them out to thank them for their unsolicited pearls of wisdom. As if Gemini had time to stop and make out a list of such obligations. The Mercury Birds are too busy selling that sour cream as buttermilk. As for the holes Leo cautioned them about, Geminis will simply leap out of them, land on their feet, and skate across the same thin ice again, while Leo pouts and asks petulantly, "Don't you *ever* get caught?"

Well, yes, sometimes Geminis do get caught by their own cleverness. But why worry, when the brave King (or Queen) will pull them out in a splendid, technicolor, last-minute rescue? Then, Leo will blush and bow (modestly) as Gemini sings Leo's favorite lyric of flattery. "Boy! You sure were right about everything you said. Thanks for warning me in time. I don't know what I'd do without you," cry the Twins, quite probably sincerely, who have now managed to have their cake and eat it too (royal protection—plus freedom).

"It was nothing," modestly replies the Lion or Lioness, purring and rolling over happily in the catnip of Gemini charm. "It's the duty of the stronger and wiser to protect the weak and foolish from the folly of their ways. Just remember in the future to do as I tell you, and you'll stay out of trouble."

"Okay, I promise!" cheerfully call out the Twins, as they wave goodbye and dash off. But Gemini knows, deep down inside, that what Leo said is true. Frustrating, annoying, often infuriating . . . but true.

☆ ☆ ☆ ☆ ☆ ☆

GEMINI *Woman* LEO *Man*

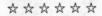

. . she tells him stories about himself,
to which he listens eagerly . . . . .

A Leo man will often deny his superiority complex and try to hide his exaggerated need for respect, but he can't fool the bright Mercury female who loves him. A Gemini woman I know once swore to a group of friends gathered in their living room that her Leo husband had none of the characteristics of his Sun Sign. "Philip is neither vain nor domineering," she insisted. "He's an unassuming person, who doesn't feel superior to anyone."

Modest Philip agreed. "I have no desire to lord it over people," he murmured quietly, "I'm just an average guy." To which his Gemini wife added quickly, "He's more than just an average guy. He's super special. What I meant to say is that he's not at all bossy, and he's certainly not an egotistical show-off."

It fooled everyone in the room. This kind, gentle host, with the courteous manner, was obviously not a roaring Lion. He lounged unobtrusively in the corner, exuding a soft, warm glow and making no attempt at all to command the conversation. Of course, I could have enlightened their guests. But my Gemini friend had cleverly stroked her big Lion into purring so contentedly by that time, I didn't have the heart to break up her little Mercury game.

What do you think this shy Pussycat does all day when he's not languidly relaxing at home, accepting his mate's compliments with a self-effacing air? He's in a tricky, special branch of law—foreign oil leases. He spends a *very* large income, which he earns from spending his *very* valuable time telling *very* large industries what they may and may not do. When you're handing out advice to billionaires and giving companies like Exxon and Standard Oil an occasional tweak on the nose, you don't need any extra outlets for the Leonine ego.

A Lion who is on stage at work, exercising his vanity and passing out his wisdom, can afford to be a little meek socially. Especially when he has a Gemini wife, who knows exactly how to butter him up, by singing his praises so charmingly, there's no need for him to indulge in vulgar bragging about himself.

Gemini and Leo vibrate to a 3-11 Sun Sign Pattern, so there's often sacrifice required in the relationship, some great benefit gained, due to the karmic tie between them—memories of past lives. Like all such 3-11 vibrations, the association is usually a fated one, an involvement difficult to resist, in family or business ties, as well as in friendship and romance. The Leo man feels compelled to teach the Gemini girl things which may truly change her life even more than he feels compelled to instruct others, and that's saying a lot. She can expect more than the ordinary number of Leonine lectures, as this man continually points out her flaws and tells her what she's doing or thinking wrong, from her diet and clothing to her political views and religious concepts. But the same soul memory which prompts Leo to lecture Gemini also brings an unconscious sense of gratitude for former favors received and causes the Lion to also want to protect the Gemini girl. He instinctively sympathizes with her shortcomings, even as he tries to correct them.

Likewise, the Gemini woman is defensive of her Lion. She wants to shield him from the hurt caused by others when they wound his great vanity unintentionally. Something inside her perceptive heart tells her the right thing to say and do, at the right time, to bring out all his warm tenderness and generosity. She looks up to him as a safe, loving haven from a world of skeptics, who don't understand her. Naturally, this flatters the Big Cat's masculine pride, which he possesses in greater abundance than the average male, and makes him cherish her all the more. It can slowly slither into a mutual-admiration society.

However, their basic compatibility won't prevent spells of rebellion on both sides. Her airy nonchalance can fire the Leo temper, which is slow to ignite, but difficult to extinguish, once it's aroused and flaming. Then she may use the quarrel to practice her syntax and sarcasm, which will cut sharply into his Leonine ego. If her multiple Mercury fascinations and outside interests should distract her from daily worship of the Lion, he'll wonder what any other Monarch wonders when his subjects are too busy to line up at the curb and cheer him as he passes—maybe they're no longer loyal to their King? Maybe she's found someone she admires more than *him?*

The poor girl just doesn't realize what she's risking. All the females he loved and left, before her, were simply devastated by grief—as he's told her many times. She'd just better mind her p's and q's or (speaking of the alphabet) Leo will dig out his well-thumbed, fat little black book and ring up a few numbers between "A" for Amy and "Z" for Zelda. Yes, most of his old paramours are married now, though a couple of them joined the convent. But Leo is quite positive that any one of his discarded slaves (including the nuns) would jump—snap!—like that!—if she thought there was the slightest chance of being recalled into the service of His Majesty. *Some* women know when they're lucky.

Because Leo is more Fixed, and therefore more practical than the Mutable Gemini, her erratic behavior could spark some angry sputters from the Lion. She may forget his dinner in her excitement over a new book she's reading, chatter on the phone when he needs an audience, change her mind about going to the theatre after he's already reserved the seats, forget where she parked the car, lose her keys or flood the engine. *He* would never be guilty of such carelessness. (He really wouldn't.) It's aggravating, but Leo is, in truth, enormously capable, a real man's man who handles emergencies with effortless grace, a royal shrug, and the unspoken question, "Doesn't everybody?"

Although the Gemini girl will be delighted with his strength of purpose, his loyalty, intelligence and integrity, she might turn moody and restless on the Lion and distract him when he's trying to work, study, or simply relax. She could also make him feel inferior by begging him to take her on an expensive holiday when he's temporarily too broke to afford it but much too proud to admit it.

He'll roar at all these things but will probably forgive her the minute she flashes her Gemini blarney and pulls off a quick change from the flighty, reckless, bitter Twin to the sensible, womanly, devoted Twin. As for her outside interests, he won't mind if she has a career, studies ballet, takes up jogging, collects mummies, or chases butterflies—as long as none of her jobs or hobbies takes priority over him. But a Gemini girl should never tease her proud Leo man by pointing out to him that the big male Nature cats in the wild jungle permit their mates to do the hunting while they snooze in the sun—or she may be called home from the hunt and permanently retired to the pride.

Besides, that's true of lion-lions, not human Lions. As a Leo, he also has a royal birthright. Would a King allow his Queen to worry about Affairs of State and tangle with the Treasury, back at the castle, while he's out riding with the hounds or getting fitted for a new crown?

Well, yes, he probably would—if she's properly humble about it. After all, she ought to have some worthwhile purpose in life, like seeing that he's happy and contented. Still, a woman who is the King's favorite certainly has her rewards. A Lion is full of fun, generous with his time and money, strong and brave, even gentle, when his ego is stroked softly in the right direction. Last, but surely not least, he's a wonderful lover. Her Gemini talent for imagery will bring excitement to their physical relationship, and if she continues to evoke in him the sensation that he's a sexual conqueror, he'll remain a satisfied and monogamous monarch.

It's possible for a Leo man to fulfill all his romantic promise under the light, nonpossessive touch of a Gemini woman, whose airy approach to sex will fan his more fiery desires, at least in the beginning. However, he may gradually begin to feel something is missing. While he's making love to one Twin, the other is coolly observing the scene. A Leo man can be thrown into a trauma by such partial involvement.

To a warm-hearted Lion, sex is synonymous with both affection and passion. There's something vaguely aloof about Gemini love. He can seduce her emotionally and physically, but her mind refuses to be fully committed to sensual abandon. The inability to conquer completely can destroy a Leo's necessary self-image of virility. Then she'll complain that he lacks interest in lovemaking, when the truth is that her cool detachment and dual behavior has caused him to develop a fear of a possible lovemaking inadequacy, which he's extremely reluctant to expose, because nothing pains a Leo male more than even the suspicion that he may not be the perfect lover. She should remember that this man is a sexual idealist and employ her Mercurial imagination to invent new ways of appeasing his hunger for romance and sentiment as background music for their physical intimacy, instead of using it to fly off on a cloud by herself, when he most needs to know she's close beside him, resting against his heart.

Since Gemini is a natural linguist, she should be capable of translating her Lion's arrogant and regal commands into the language of passion and need.

"You talk too much. Why don't you be still once in a while?" means his vanity has been bruised, because she's upstaged him again, with her twin talents of quickness and cleverness.

"Forget about dinner. I'm going out somewhere and eat alone" means he's been ignored once too often, while she's been chasing interesting ideas and people all day, and his pride needs to be pampered.

"Cancel that party we've been invited to Saturday night. Tell them we can't come. Make some excuse. We're staying home" means he'd rather be alone with the two of her over the weekend than get dressed up and soak up the admiration of a crowd. And lady, for a Leo—that's *love!*

☆ ☆ ☆ ☆ ☆ ☆

GEMINI *Man* LEO *Woman*

"I think it must be a lady . . . a lady to take care of us at last," said one of the Twins. . . .

Every Lioness, quite naturally, you must admit, has an instinctive desire to tame the man she loves, to make him her exclusive property. She needs a mate in whom she can have absolute faith, a man who is clearly stronger than she is, and yet, who will cherish her without reservation. It's a mighty tall order. Especially when she sets out to tame a Gemini.

In the Game of Love, as in the Game of Life and Living, this man is what card players call a kibitzer. He hangs around, with always a few hidden aces up his sleeve, aware of everyone's hand, confident that he could, if need be, pass off a busted straight as a royal flush. He knows a lot about everything, but not quite enough to make a grand slam and end the challenge he finds so intriguing. It makes more sense to Gemini to be a jack-of-all-trades and master of none. Once you become expert at any one of them, you see, people have this annoying habit of expecting you to stay there, doing your thing forever.

Gemini is an Air Sign, driven constantly by the need for change, any kind of change at all, just so it's change, however minor or major, which leads him on to the next traveling dice game with interesting stakes. Unlike the other two astrological gamblers, Leo and Sag, the Twins always want in and out fast, a quick win or a quick loss, then try again. If you deal yourself in for enough games, Gemini figures, you eventually overcome poor judgment and bad luck. No long-term investments in a career, family ties, friendship or romance, for the typical Gemini male—at least, not while he's young. (Of course, you must realize that that may be a long time, because Gemini never grows up.) To the typical Mercury-ruled man, Life is a series of toy dirigibles and fragile bubbles, spent among mischievous children armed with sharp pins. A man must be agile to leap over them, to sail his dirigibles and blow his bubbles out of their range, in the nick of time. And where do the dirigibles, the bubbles, come from? He's never wondered. He only knows they never stop coming. You have to be quick—to pick out the good ones and spot the ones to cut the string on before they fizzle out. The toy dirigibles, that is. As for the bubbles, they're pretty to watch and fun to create, but he doesn't fool himself into trying to make any of them last. Dirigibles are different. They're tougher, and one of them might take him where he's going—if he only knew where that might be.

Take women, for example. Gemini knows—or supposes he does—which one will fly with him and not slow him down by hanging on his sleeve—and the ones to back away from because they think any kind of flying is for the birds. (It is, but that also includes Mercury Birds, like himself.) At first, he'll think the Lioness belongs in the former category, because she certainly won't hang on his sleeve. She has other ways of slowing him down, more subtle.

This is, as the reader may know by now, one of those fated 3-11 Sun Sign Pattern relationships, planned by their Higher Selves long ago. Whether it ends in love or friendship, it is nevertheless pregnant with karmic obligations, often marked for a strange destiny, and always urging each partner on toward either unusual sacrifice or uncommon devotion—or both. Whether the 3-11 vibration (some, of course, involve business or ties with blood relatives) leads to a lasting love or a platonic association depends on many things, among them, the mutual aspects between their natal Suns, Moon Signs and Ascendents—and other planetary exchanges between their birth charts.

If the Leo girl has permanence in mind, she'll first have to tame him. It won't be like taming any of the other male animals in the astrological zoo. It's trickier. A Gemini man is more slippery and elusive. Besides, remember that there are two of him. The escape hatches of the Twins are covered with such charm of speech and gesture that this man can be gone while a girl is still swooning over the wisp of beauty he draped over her, like a delicate cobweb, to camouflage his departure and make it easier for her to bear. (He does have a kind heart.) But the Lioness has a head start on this sort of Mercury chicanery, because a Leo woman doesn't swoon over men. Men swoon over *her*—and don't you forget it.

A more difficult obstacle than seeing through his cobwebs of charm, which she'll have to hurdle in taming him, is that to a Gemini man all females are alike—threats to his freedom, suspicious of his unpredictable behavior, always demanding that he love them exactly the same today as he did yesterday. How can that possibly be, when his emotions contain so many depths and breadths? Sooner or later, a woman will begin to nag you about not having a concrete goal, and who wants to pursue cement? Since the Gemini man is bored by most females, because they all seem the same to him, the Leo girl will have to convince him that she's not like all the others. She'll have to train him, and tame him . . . to listen for *her* step, *her* laugh, *her* voice . . . to recognize that her vibration is individual, making music only for him, that her aura is different from the aura of any other woman in the world. Maybe she can even train him to notice that the golden, tawny flecks in her eyes are exactly like those in a fine piece of amber, so that everytime he sees an amber ring or bracelet on his travels he'll remember . . .

Then amber will always be beautiful to him, because it will bring thoughts of her warm smile, her proud spirit, the glow in her eyes . . . and tug on his heart to return. Not just to her smile and spirit and eyes but to all the other parts of her he misses. Like, there's her bright mind—the way she hikes over the hills beside him with her graceful, Lioness stride, without getting tired—the way she sits tall in the saddle when she rides—jackknifes into the water, swoops down the slopes on her skis, swings a tennis racquet, or smacks a golf ball. Leo women usually excel at one or two outdoor sports, not counting indoor sports, like acting, dancing, romancing, and so forth—and, like Cancerian Moon Maidens, many of them are amateur or professional photographers.

She'll have to seed all these memories in his mind and convince him that she's unique. It's all part of the Gemini taming process. A girl who loves this man must keep up with both his mind and his body, not to mention his two separate personalities and his multiple moods. Eventually, he'll begin to think of her as the most unique woman he's ever known. But he won't be *completely* tamed until he thinks of her as the most unique woman he ever *will* know. There's a definite difference, and a Lioness will comprehend what I mean right away.

Actually, this woman *is* unique. She's a born "lady," and there aren't many of those around anymore. A Leo female can roll in the grass, climb a tree, change a tire, or any number of traditionally considered unladylike things, but her general demeanor will remain as casually gracious and poised as if she were walking down a red-carpeted aisle to be coronated.

(It takes real class for a girl to keep her tiara on straight when she's jacking up a rear axle.) The regal aura is ever present. Let someone snicker, deride her, or make the huge mistake of becoming too familiar when she hasn't extended an invitation to intimacy, and she'll freeze into such a tower of icy dignity that the offender will shrink into his socks—or wish to blazes the ground would mercifully open up and swallow him. Like the typical Capricorn female, the typical Lioness possesses a distinct and unmistakable air of excellent breeding. Whether it's actual or only illusionary, it's tangible and visible. The only weakness in the Leo armour of majestic dignity is the Leonine tendency to be transparently vulnerable to flattery. At any other time, however, the royal blood runs clearly blue, and the manner is aloof, proud, Queen-like. The Gemini man who refers to this female as "babe" or "chick," either by word or implication, will soon learn what the term "lady" means.

He'll have to become accustomed (which he'll probably do rather pleasantly) to allowing her to take most—or all—of the bows in public. She'll get most of the attention, even when she doesn't encourage it. It's that subtle mantle of royalty that hovers over every Leo ever born. No matter how sweetly she speaks to him, no matter how adoringly she gazes up at him, as if *he's* the star of the show—more heads will turn in her direction than in his, however handsome, dashing, witty and intelligent he may be. Something about her bearing, her lazy, confident manner of speaking, the way she carelessly tosses her mane of hair out of her eyes, suggests a royal charisma.

She means no harm. A true, noble, warm-hearted and in-love Lioness never deliberately usurps her mate's status (only everyone else's). She can't help it if the natives are restless and have their eyes fastened on her. Fortunately, a Gemini man is seldom overly or unduly possessive, so he'll probably see her popularity as just another factor in her uniqueness. (You see, he *is* gradually becoming tamed.) He might console himself by remembering that Gemini President Jack Kennedy wryly introduced himself in France as "the man who accompanied Jacqueline Bouvier to Paris." Jackie, as you all must know by now, is a Lioness.

Statistically, the sexual compatibility of these Sun Sign lovers often requires certain mutual adjustments and compromises. For one thing, nothing can so chill the warmth of a Lioness as deception or disloyalty from her mate, and that includes everything from harmless flirting to actual sexual infidelity. The Gemini man will find her Leonine jealousy and fiery pride of possession easier to overlook when the shoe is on the other foot, for then he'll be given a strong idea of what it feels like to be ignored and rejected. He won't like it at all, yet he won't be quite as outraged as she would be in the same situation. Geminis take everything somewhat more lightly than most everyone else—certainly more lightly than an intense Fire Sign like Leo.

However, once she's really tamed him, jealousy may never be a problem on either side. The problem then becomes one of simple romantic technique. A well-loved Lioness is an exceptionally affectionate and loving woman. She's capable of both raging passion and languid sensuality. But a carelessly loved Lioness is extremely susceptible to the symptoms of frigidity. She's not a female who would enjoy being ravaged by a gorilla-type lover (King Kong is not her secret fantasy)—nor is she a woman who would smile indulgently at the clumsiness of a bashful schoolboy, who drowns her in puppy-like adoration. She expects a man to make love to her with finesse. A Gemini man is simply saturated with finesse, charm and delicacy. But his touch may sometimes be so light, his seductive overtures so airy, she feels he might dematerialize, right in front of her eyes, before their physical love reaches fulfillment. To satisfy her deeper needs, which are visibly more fiery than his, he'll have to sweep her off her feet now and then in a dramatic scene of wild and ecstatic surrender.

If not all that, then he should frequently find a way to let her know he can't resist the magnetic sexual chemistry between them. To her, physical union is more than a Mercury mental challenge or an emotional exercise. She still hears the faint call of the jungle. But she'll unfold tenderly under his imaginative approach if he occasionally deepens its intensity—and remembers that she needs to hear how beautiful and desirable she is in order to respond completely. "A woman is beautiful only when she is loved." Especially a Leo woman.

This man and woman are both extravagant with words—and with money. They share exquisite taste, they both adore dressing up, they're equally fond of travel, literature and the arts. They're also both equally adept at getting their own way—she through the lovable quality of expecting it as her right—he, through his irresistible blarney. A Leo girl can tame the Gemini man more easily if she remembers the rules for taming any restless, active, yet curious bird. It requires much patience, and you start by smiling at him with your eyes, at a distance . . . taking care not to move too quickly, for that would frighten him away. In the beginning, silent communion is best, because words, particularly between these two Sun Signs, often contain the seeds of misunderstanding. Then if she moves a little nearer to him every day and never causes him to feel his freedom is threatened . . .

A Gemini man needs to be reminded that there are some things in his changing, Mercurial existence that are very special—and unique—in all the worlds he longs to roam. That's why he'll be happier after he's been tamed by the proud Lioness, if only because of the new beauty of amber he'll never be able to look upon without remembering the tawny flecks in her eyes.

GEMINI

Air — Mutable — Positive
Ruled by Mercury
Symbol: The Twins
Day Forces — Masculine

VIRGO

Earth — Mutable — Negative
Ruled by Mercury (also by
*   the Planet Vulcan)*
Symbol: The Virgin
Night Forces — Feminine

The GEMINI-VIRGO *Relationship*

◄━◆►►

Off we skip like the most heartless things in the world,
which is what children are, but so attractive . . . . we
have an entirely selfish time; and then when we have
need of special attention we nobly return for it, confident
that we shall be embraced instead of smacked.

The playful Gemini Twins may, indeed, seem like heartless children to the more sensible and serious Virgos. Always out chasing cobwebs and mirages, jumping about like grasshoppers, getting caught in summer brainstorms and trying to be in two places at once. To the typical earthy Virgo, Gemini's quick changes of both heart and mind are clearly flaws which need immediate correction.

Perfection is not a quality Geminis enjoy cultivating. They do appreciate, perhaps even admire—and certainly need—the more stable attitude of

Virgo, and are often relieved to find the Virgo relative, friend, business associate, lover, or mate still there, in the same place where they were left, when Gemini flew away for a few hours (or weeks or months or years) to see what was happening on the other side of the mountain. But if they are going to be scolded when they return, they'll just skip off again. Children never like scolding. And all Geminis are essentially children at heart. Not Virgos.

Virgos are possessed of a heavy sense of life's duties, and a mature sense of reliability. They either live up to this essence of their Sun Sign or they feel guilty about *not* doing it and develop hives, ulcers, or hiccups. Conversely, Gemini seldom feels guilty about anything. At least, not where it shows.

With Virgo, most everything shows. Especially secret, nagging worries. Since Virgo rules the bowels, intestines, and solar plexus, these nagging worries, expressed first in a slight frown, then tight lips, can cause actual infection or disability in these areas. The more secret the worries, the more apt they are to manifest into nausea, indigestion or constipation. These people should get it out in the open more often, talk about it, express themselves, say what is on their minds (but not *too* often, or they would be untrue to their Sun Signs).

Gemini is an expert at getting it out in the open—except for those unfortunate Geminis with a Virgo Ascendent or Moon, who would love to cheerfully chatter, and scatter ideas, but who settle down into an uneasy silence instead, staring at their fingers and counting the lines in the palms of their restlessly folded hands. It can be a real conflict. Most Geminis, however, could profitably teach Virgos how to excel in gregarious gab, gleeful glibness and scintillating syntax. Virgo indisputably knows how to spell all those words, but putting them into action is another matter.

The Virgo intellect is as sharp as Gemini's (thanks to Mercury, who likes to pretend rulership of both signs, with his silver cap and winged heels) but not as vacillating and changeable (thanks to the hidden influence of Virgo's true ruler, the as yet unsighted, thunderous Vulcan). Geminis quickly juggle thoughts and create ideas, often it seems right out of the air, which is their natural element, but Virgo seldom juggles or creates. The Virgins are too busy discriminating and distinguishing and sorting facts from fancies, frequently with what may appear to be quite unnecessary preciseness. Explorer-experimenter Gemini seeks the spirit of the law. Purist-statistician Virgo follows the letter of the law.

Most Virgos find it difficult to grasp the concept of a dollar, because it contains such a fascinating number of pennies. They get sidetracked counting all the coins, believing that if you keep track of the bright coppers, the folding green paper will pile up all by itself, with no help.

Gemini thinks in larger sweeps, grander terms, and normally tosses any spare pennies into wishing wells, without counting them. Throw a perfectly good penny into murky water for some silly superstition? There goes that faint Virgo frown again—see it? Just beginning to crease in the forehead over those clear, beautiful eyes.

Now that you understand some of the obvious difference between these two Sun Signs, you can imagine the turmoil which must churn in the breast of a Virgo with a Gemini Ascendent or Moon—or a Gemini, with vice versa and likewise. To face such a methodology variance with a strange companion is abrasive enough, without having to face it in the mirror every morning, lurking within your own character and personality. Send them lots of sympathy cards. Some, as mentioned elsewhere, become human alarm clocks—others sit on a seesaw of indecision, ill at ease when they are talking and twice as uncomfortable when they are silent.

The Gemini-Virgo association is influenced by the 4-10 Sun Sign Pattern, so the relationship between them will never be based on pure frivolity and escapism. Seriousness and respect (or lack of it) will weave in and out of the connecting links between these two, each finding it difficult to fully comprehend the true goals and basic outlook of the other. This must not be taken to mean that they can't create harmonious warmth together. It's just that happy firesides and hearths need lots of stoking with the coals of mutual understanding and tolerance. Peace and compatibility can eventually be accomplished with a little effort, however, because there's often a subtle exchange of loyalty and affection hidden beneath the surface disagreements of these two.

It must be admitted that the average Virgo man or woman does not practice provoking trouble, and does not usually respond to it quickly either, unlike the Geminis, with their constant stirring up of a tempest from a single breath of choppy air, and frequently reacting in hurricane fashion to what seems to them to be constant, critical carping and harping from Virgo. Of course, to Gemini, a quarrel is not really a quarrel, merely an intellectual encounter. With Earth Sign Virgo, arguments go deeper, and the hurt lasts longer. The friendship and other relationships between them can be enduring, in rare cases even intimate, but a community of interests on the business or intellectual level—or in the family or duty-obligation sphere, as with all 4-10 influenced people—is normally what pulls them together in the first place.

Most Virgos seem to be humble and self-effacing, seldom displaying any excessive dignity or pride, yet it would behoove the Gemini to hold his or her sharp tongue at crucial moments, since Virgos are usually quite sensitive about what little dignity and pride they do possess. The more aggressive signs can't understand the Virgin at all, but the Gemini who finds Aries too exhausting, Leo too arrogant, and Scorpio too aloof may very well find the usually sweet and courteous Virgo relaxing to be around, and feel a sense of relief at the lack of need to compete that might be necessary with another Sun Sign.

There's a touching and attractive humility about Virgos, a personal modesty that excites little envy or resentment. But Mercury Birds can still get their feathers a bit ruffled when they learn that, although Virgo may never be able to run as swiftly as Gemini and may seldom beat the Twins to any Grand Prizes, Virgo sometimes manages to grab the plum job without even hinting for it, let alone racing for it. Often those with Virgo Sun Signs, Ascendents, or Moon Signs are chosen as the compromise candidate by party leaders in "smoke-filled" political back rooms on a city, state, or national level, considerably upsetting the more extroverted Sun Signs, who have been blissfully charming the voters out front, confident of victory, until Virgo comes up from the rear—the dark horse chosen suddenly and unexpectedly over the brighter ponies on the track. As an example, Lyndon Johnson was a Virgo, chosen by a clever and canny Gemini, John Kennedy, for calculated reasons.

In any dispute between Gemini and Virgo, Gemini will nearly always win the main point, being faster on the draw and quicker with the cinching retort. But winning a quarrel can't settle everything. It may not settle *anything* for Virgos, who know that what appears to be an absolutely factual statement can still be full or errors and misleading insinuations. The greatest talent of all Gemini Twins is the fascinating ability to twist truth and falsehood in such a way as to weave them together and make each appear to be the other. It fools almost everyone but a Virgo. A Gemini Volkswagen salesman who ticks off too many facts too fast can really "bug" a potential Virgo customer right off the lot. You won't find many Virgos playing speed ball at carnivals or riding the Ferris wheels and carousels on which Geminis love to spin in their circular direction. They don't go much for Mercurial cotton candy either. All sugar and air—no nutritional value whatsoever.

There is an appealing magical quality in Gemini that attracts and excites the more timid Virgins, and this could create enough mystery to make the relationship permanently intriguing. The trouble is, Virgos are never satisfied until they discover exactly how the magic trick is performed, and the whole point of Gemini's existence is to prove something by nothing—to make reality out of pure illusion.

To the practical-minded Virgo, reality can never be illusion, nor can illusion ever be called reality. That's just more Gemini double-talk. Mercury Birds have usually flown and flitted through a dozen occupations by the time they're thirty, while Virgos are often disturbed when they're expected to make a slight change in office routine. As for changing jobs, that's something Virgos normally do with as much serious deliberation as is required for the selection of the President of the United States, in fact, with much *more* serious deliberation than has been the case with the latter in recent years.

Despite their differences and the tensions engendered by the soul-testing tugs of their squared natal Suns through the difficult 4-10 vibration, Gemini and Virgo share a lovely curiosity, an uncommon intelligence, and a certain charming and graceful manner, which allows them to skip happily, side-by-side, through the cornfields of the changeable land of Oz for a few thousand miles. But if they expect to still be together when they reach the presence of the Great Wizard (who is, of course, a Gemini), they may have to adjust and compromise now and then.

Gemini magicians, who are fascinated by all forms of marvels, should remember that the Tin Woodsman who strolled along the path with Dorothy and her friends was a Virgo—a kind and gentle, yet lonely soul, wistfully searching for a human heart. And it was the clever Gemini Wizard who perceived that the Virgo had possessed a heart all the time, without realizing it, hidden inside a suit of cold metal, yet larger than any of the others. *That's* magic!

☆ ☆ ☆ ☆ ☆ ☆

GEMINI *Woman* VIRGO *Man*

> . . . . . *his way was with a pencil and a piece of paper,*
> *and if she confused him with suggestions he had to*
> *begin at the beginning again.*
>
> *"Now don't interrupt," he would beg of her.*

The first problem this man and woman face is the contrast between her gregariousness and his tendency to reclusivity. If he's a typical Virgo male, barring a more convivial Moon Sign or Ascendent, he would really prefer, within his deepest subconscious, to live alone, without the necessity of having a constant companion tagging along beside him—even if she's bright, pretty, soft and squeezable. A man can't spend all his time squeezing a wife. Some hours must be spent in squeezing plans for future security into the proper molds.

Consequently, when the Gemini girl seeks periodic flings of freedom, her Virgo lover or husband may grumble a bit outwardly, but inwardly he probably sighs with relief. Now he can have a little peace and quiet, to figure out how many atoms make up a molecule, what caused the stock market to zip up or slip down last week, adjust his alarm clock, sort his laundry, count his cat's whiskers and ponder the puzzles of the Universe in general, without all that constant chattering and flurry of activity. He may genuinely love his Gemini girl, but his heart contains hidden shelves, where she is not allowed to dust—or even peek. When she's constantly dazzling him with her perfume, her squeezability, quick wit and mental agility, he gets confused and loses track of which opinion he has glued to what shelf, even the particular day and year he stashed it away there. And so, he may not question her whereabouts, so pleased is he to have a period of restful contemplation.

Not that there aren't some Virgo men who display occasional, half-hearted spurts of jealousy. There are a few. But it's a great mistake to become angry with the diversity of a Gemini girl, when you analyze it, and Virgos are past masters at analyzing. Her need to communicate with a variety of people (and men do, after all, make up roughly half the human race) should not be interpreted as unfaithfulness or promiscuity—unless it's certain that this is the case. Sometimes it is. Yet, surprisingly often, it is not. Admittedly, it can become so, if his Virgo criticism, hair-splitting and nagging cause her to feel her wings are being clipped. If there's anything a Gemini female can't stand, it's having her wings clipped, cropped or folded. Birds must fly. Birds in cages constitute unbearable cruelty against Nature's intent.

Still, for a man whose essential attitude and Sun Sign essence points him toward bachelorhood, the Virgo male is capable, when he chooses, of settling down into the groove of matrimony—or a shared life with a woman he loves—with an unexpected grace. Although he's basically a loner and dislikes sharing his every thought with a mate, Virgo is of the Earth Element, and Earth stays where it was placed by Nature, unless an earthquake or a tornado dislodges portions of it. But is that the Earth's fault? There it was, minding its own business . . .

I have thus far referred to their relationship as though it were marbled in matrimony, because most Virgos become uneasy living with a woman without benefit of clergy. Not all. Most. Geminis, however, normally do not find it difficult to sanction and champion free love or free marriage. Gemini is all for anything that has the word "free" in it. Therefore, whether to wed—or not to wed—may be a question of initial contention, once they've both been chemically magnetized into desiring union.

In the necessary confines of love or marriage, as with a business partner, the Virgo man will not ordinarily seek to dominate. He tends to be quite impeccably businesslike about his love affair or marriage, and unless he has an extremely afflicted horoscope emotionally, he will make an excellent partner, insofar as small comforts and conveniences are concerned, attending dutifully and diligently to birthdays and anniversaries, emptying the kitty litter and making sure they don't run out of vitamins. Most Gemini girls would, of course, prefer to have their birthdays and anniversaries observed through the customary process of passionate or sentimental memory, rather than through periodic checking of a date and appointment book with a red pencil. But who is she to complain? Dates are certainly not her own strong point, and she may get mixed up, from time to time, sending him a get-well card on her mother's birthday or buying him a wedding-anniversary gift on the date they bought the house—and while we're on the subject of homes, if they buy one, he will suggest it first, nine times out of ten. The tenth time, if she happens to be the one who initiates a consultation with a real-estate agent, check her Moon Sign or Ascendent. One or both is probably in the Earth Element. The typical Gemini girl likes houses well enough, but prefers apartments, because she can change them once in a while, say every few months or so. Needless to remark, Virgo men normally do not find this sort of musical tepee game feasible or practical. It will pay to remember that practicality—too little or too much of it—will be the true underlying cause for many of their arguments. He has too much to please her and she has too little to suit him, if he is a typical Virgo and she is a typical Gemini.

As for their sexual compatibility, a Virgo can be, with all his innate sweetness, courtesy, consideration and punctuality, an impossible lover or husband for a temperamental woman. Of course, not all Geminis are temperamental. Or rather, one of her Twin selves may be emotionally temperamental—and the other may be detached. Virgo males, you see, are not overly emotional. Nor is the average Virgo unduly affectionate. Legend claims that Narcissus was a Virgo, helplessly in love with his own image. I personally believe Narcissus was a Leo, but aside from all that, it is true that Virgo men are often accused of being cold and self-centered. (Leo can be self-centered, but never cold.)

If the deepest spiritual secret of sex is the mutual abandonment of the self for the mate, resulting in a fusion of minds, souls, and bodies into perfect Oneness (which, as a matter of fact, it is), the typical Virgo has yet to master this esoteric mystery. Unless he's carefully and tenderly taught, or unless he had an early Scorpio sweetheart, it may elude him for a number of years, perhaps for a lifetime. He unconsciously shrinks from the concept of total surrender as he shrinks from the idea of using someone else's Vicks salve. I know a Gemini woman (this is not a fable) who once told me her Virgo husband insisted on labeling the two Vicks salve jars in the medicine chest HIS and HERS. Nearly every Virgo was frightened in the womb by a mean germ (and a scattering of Aquarians were also).

Not only does this man mistrust surrender, sexual or *otherwise*, he's not too hung up on the initial step of conquest either . . . so he may fail to arouse enthusiasm in himself, or in others. This might not go over well with an Aries, Leo or Scorpio female, but it could be the reason the Twins fell in love with him in the first place. Not all, but the majority of Gemini girls feel more secure, in or out of wedlock, whether they realize it or not, when they can play love as a pretend game. Gemini lovemaking is airy and light, delicate ethereal. Since a Virgo man is beautifully adept at the art of light lovemaking, he can succeed with her where other men have failed because they refused to play the make-believe game with her.

Instinctively, she could feel emotionally safe with this man, and they may offer one another a sense of security that forms a foundation for the later development of a deep passion between them—which might never have flowered in her with a more sexually serious male—or with a more passionately demanding female, speaking for his side of the matter. She might find some of his habits, like showering both before and immediately after their physical togetherness, a little disconcerting—but then, he could also find her habit of interrupting their goodnight kiss, or preliminary to an intimate union embrace, with an account of a weird dream she had last weekend to be somewhat dampening and discouraging too. Neither of them will be totally emotionally destroyed if this should happen to postpone their kiss or embrace until the following morning.

Yes, they will have their small differences. Most Gemini girls enjoy sleeping late and are subject to periodic attacks of insomnia. Virgo men suffer from insomnia too, when they're worried about something, which is frequently—but this man would rather be caught wearing red- and purple-flowered Levi's as be caught sleeping till noon, both of these choices of behavior being, more or less, mortal sins to the Virgin. If he's the kind of

Virgo who insists on a neat house and punctual meals, he'll soon learn that this girl won't see the need for absolute perfection in such areas. She's certainly capable of being an exquisite hostess (although he seldom brings anyone home for her to hostess) and when she chooses, she can create a delightful home atmosphere. But it's doubtful that she'll scrub floors with true enthusiasm and excitement—and if she smokes (pray not!), there may be a few dirty ashtrays around. This won't make a hit with him, because most Virgos detest smoking to begin with, and they positively despise the offensive odor of full ashtrays.

Surprisingly, however, the usual, petty, day-to-day irritations may not cause any major quarrels between them. A Virgo man doesn't really demand a whole lot from either love or marriage, except maybe his own Vicks salve jar—and neither does she. He would appreciate, of course, some punctuality concerning meals, at least a semblance of faithfulness. But, in general, a Gemini girl is adaptable enough to cope with things that could cause despair in other females, and he's practical enough not to expect love and marriage to be made either in heaven or in hell, but somewhere in-between. Barring severe planetary afflictions between their birth charts, these two will probably not be overly demanding of one another, compared to other Sun Sign combinations.

Her swift personality changes and many moods could puzzle and annoy him. His quiet spells of introversion, during which he refuses to communicate, could flash her into many an instant, but normally quickly dispersed, thunderstorm. There are times when he'll bore her to tears, and she'll agitate him into indigestion—and it's also possible that their lives together may be one long guessing game of verbal chess and emotional jai alai. Yet, it's equally possible that she'll supply the excitement and the zest for living that this man desires so wistfully and needs so very much—whereas he'll supply the stability of purpose she's seeking, even though she's not aware she's seeking it.

Gemini is Air, Virgo is Earth, and these two elements have little in common. But this is a 4-10 Sun Sign Pattern, and mutual respect may, therefore, be the magnet that brings them together, while duty or responsibility of some kind, related to family ties or career, may hold them together.

A Virgo man is more truthful than a Sagittarian man, more basically honest than even the Archers. To him, telling the truth saves a great deal of trouble. His grandmother used to singsong, "Oh, what a tangled web we weave when first we practice to deceive," and he decided way back then that deception was an unnecessary burden. In no way does he wish to become tangled up in any sort of web. Certainly not one of his own making. And so, the typical Virgo will place the straight facts of any situation right on the table, with no hedging. It's not a habit designed to endear him to anyone, but one of his most admirable qualities is that he doesn't much care if he endears himself to everyone—just to a few close friends. If *they* like him, and if he can serve them as best he knows how, that's enough for him. He doesn't need to win popularity contests to be contented with things the way they are, and make the best of Life. In fact, he often makes much better than the best of Life—and of love—if he's handled gently, softly—and not engulfed in waves of emotion that cause his quiet charm and beautiful manner to retreat into a self-made cave to avoid conflict. When the conflict is something other than emotional, however, he'll press ahead and will rarely turn back from what he believes is the right course.

The path of the Virgo male is seldom strewn with flowers, nor does he stop on the way to pluck posies of praise for his services. Still, his heart will be lighter, and his spirit brighter, if he allows a Gemini girl to dance along beside him and fill those lonely moments with her lovely laugh, her way of catching a breeze in her hands, and phrasing the sound of a cool woodland stream in her voice, even when she's only saying "Good morning, darling." The word "impossible" doesn't exist for her. If something can't be accomplished one way, then she'll think of a new way, a better way. It's a talent he should find beautifully helpful. She's incorrigible, irrepressible—but also irresistible. With a harmonious Luminary exchange between their horoscopes, they can, perhaps, find a familiar country in each other's smiles that will be a wonderful adventure to explore together.

But the Gemini girl is Twins, sometimes even triplets. And a Virgo man has enough trouble coping with just one woman. He wasn't born to be able to handle a harem—or a mate with a multiple personality. To achieve happiness with him, the Gemini girl must first decide who she is, then forever after remain indivisibly his.

GEMINI *Man* VIRGO *Woman*

◆━━◆◆◆◆━━◆

. . . . . and so Wendy, who always liked to do the correct
thing, asked Peter how old he was. It was not really
a happy question to ask him; it was like an examination
paper that asks grammar, when what you want to be
asked is Kings of England.

This is not a love affair that will automatically be draped in clouds of rainbows and blankets of flowers, for these two face the severe test of the 4-10
Sun Sign Pattern influence, with both its trials and its benefits, each of
which can be considerable. They have a rather rough romantic row to hoe.
That doesn't mean they can't raise cabbages together, but it does mean
that their garden of love will need frequent weeding.

It could begin with quarrels about whether the crop they plant should
be roses or veggies. Obviously, veggies make more sense. She is a Virgo,
concerned over possible world famine, termites in the attic, inflation—and
the missing button from his shirt. Veggies are clearly the answer. Not to
the shirt or the termites perhaps, but to inflation and the specter of starvation. What can you do with a rose, when the wolf is pounding on the
door?

Smell it. You can smell it. The Gemini man can inhale the fragrance of
a rose while poverty closes in, in much the same way that Nero fiddled
while Rome burned. Of course, all this gardening talk, as well as Nero's
fiddle tune amid the flames, is merely symbolic. But then, everything is
symbolic, academic or rhetorical, to Gemini. He was born wrapped in riddles, mewing with metaphors and anagrams, and swaddled in analogies.
Also with a telephone in one hand and a telegram in the other. She was
born, he may think at times, of an unlikely union between a computer
and a scrub brush. A self-programming computer. (Is there such an instrument? Never mind, some Virgo with Aquarius rising will invent one,
working with a Gemini partner.)

That's not meant to imply that this man and woman don't find each
other fascinating, only that they also find each other frustrating. Most
Gemini men have forgotten their birth dates, either innocently or deliberately, by the time they reach the age of twenty-one or so on the illusionary
chronological calendar. Counterwise, many Virgo girls have memorized
the exact hour, minute and second of birth—and besides that, they believe

eternal youth is not only impossible, but would be a bore. He finds it both possible and enchanting. You can see that clocks, stopwatches and Einstein's theory of relativity can create one of the chasms between them. There are others.

It's a rare Virgo female who becomes enthralled over the idea of tossing a feather into the air and striking out in the direction it points to as it lands. If she's a typical Virgin, she's not fond of geographical hopscotch. When she travels, she prefers to utilize a travel folder, a travel agent, and the holiday-weekend-family-cut-rate plan. The airlines invented just for Virgos what they refer to as their "chicken-feed" flight (approximately between about 2 A.M. and 6 A.M.), when the world's asleep, but Virgos are alert to economy. As for the Twins, Virgo's Gemini man would secretly like to follow the feather, and as for mode of travel, he's the one those "have breakfast in London and lunch in Italy" posters are designed to attract.

When they first fall in love, often through mutual curiosity, she'll be thrilled with the possibilities of casual, careless living he so charmingly endorses, while he'll be flattered with her rapt attention, her alert mind, and her very feminine manner. But after a time, she may begin to question the wisdom of synchronizing her life to a man who seems to be eternally wandering—either physically, mentally or emotionally—his thoughts and actions no more predictable than the weather. He may later feel her attention is a mite *too* rapt, her mind perhaps too alert to allow him his needed privacy now and then, in which to do his abstract thinking. Then they may become tangled up in the roses-veggies hassle, symbolically. All quarrels between lovers are based on matters which in themselves are not important but have been chosen because they symbolize the deep-seated and *real* problems which are the true cause of the tension between them—some underlying truth that neither wants to face, for whatever reason.

Despite her analytical, razor-slicing mind, the Virgo girl is ultrasensitive and in need of appreciation. A Gemini male may be somewhat unsuccessful in this area, because he's an Air Sign. Although Air Signs are not unsympathetic, there is a certain detachment and aloof coolness about them, which can leave an Earth Sign like Virgo feeling empty, somehow unfulfilled. There are times when he will be truly incapable of understanding both her depth and her strength. Then he'll try discussion and compromise, often failing altogether to touch the source of the trouble. Even so, his combined intellectual ability and charm will enable him to pacify her temporarily, until she's had time to analyze the errors and flaws in his facile arguments.

If she doesn't take him too seriously, their relationship can be mentally exciting, emotionally intriguing, and lots of fun. But Virgo takes everything seriously, and she's certainly not going to make an exception of a lover or husband. Perhaps he should take *her* more seriously. Virgos often give the impression they have committed themselves until "death do us part," then shock the partner with a divorce action as neat and quick (and as unkind) as snapping off the head of a flower. Most everything Virgo does is neat and quick. In that, these two are very much alike. Both can be impatient with routine, and neither of them are sloppy thinkers or dressers.

Sexually, she requires more physical demonstrations of affection than he —and he requires more variety and poetry in lovemaking than she. Not that he expects her to sleep with a copy of Rossetti under her pillow, nor does she require him to conquer her like Valentino, but there are indisputably subtle differences in their approaches to the physical chemistry of love. A Virgo girl does not necessarily want to be treated as a Virgin by the man she loves. True, her sexuality, as a whole, is not dramatically intense or excessively passionate, but she wants to know he is *there*. Not just his mind, heart and soul—*all* of him. Although Virgo women, like Virgo men, can take sexual love lightly, they are somewhat more earthy about it than the airy Gemini. Also, this girl feels more confident and relaxed, and therefore can be a more satisfactory love partner, if she feels some degree of security and familiarity in their intimate relationship. This is not always possible with a Gemini, who is, lest we forget, two-people-in-one (sometimes three or four) and changeable enough to project desire one night and cool disinterest the next.

Such behavior can throw a Virgo girl into a trauma of quiet desperation, causing her to blame some defect in herself as the reason for the change in his ardor. Virgos can be critical of others, but their sharpest criticism is always reserved for themselves. Something will always be held back, in reserve, between these two. Total abandonment and forgetfulness of the self is rarely achieved in their sexual union, and so their physical compatibility, while deeply fulfilling perhaps in some ways, may be somewhat emotionally guarded and controlled.

Mentally, however, very little will be held back between them. Neither can be said to be a slouch in the language department. There are some Gemini-Virgo couples who use words as weapons, with deadly aim. Words hurt. But words can also heal, and these two Sun Signs can use them for better or for worse. No one can tenderly coax a timid Virgin out of her rigid reservations into the blooming rose garden of self-confidence more expertly and smoothly than a Gemini man—and no one can soothe the frequently jangled nerves of this Mercurial male more gently and wisely than a Virgo girl, when they're both motivated by love.

There's no doubt that they'll probably respect one another's mental abilities, yet they may too often stifle open expressions of affection in each other. Neither he nor she may comprehend the need for *depth* in an emotional relationship. She'll attend to all her necessary duties regarding him, neglecting no details. She'll sew on his missing buttons, give him excellent advice concerning his career, if and when he should ask her, seldom or never pressing her opinions upon him uninvited. She'll be a stimulating companion at the theatre or watching television . . . and be able to converse with him most intelligently about the books, magazines and newspapers they read. Still, there may be a hint of "duty" in her devotion, as steady and admirable as it is.

He'll find time to talk with her about all her worries, will probably encourage discussions between them about anything that's on her mind, and allow her lots of room for the free development of her own ideas, ideals and goals. He won't smother her with undue jealousy or possessiveness, but he may cause her to feel boxed-in with his sometimes excessive prying and probing, on a verbal level.

After the first glow of romance has worn off, the Virgo woman could begin to complain to her Gemini man that he's spreading his mental energy too thin. She, too, has a thirst for knowledge, but she's not inclined to scatter it, and it may seem to her that his is a mere craving for continual excitement and novelty. Also, she may not share his enthusiasm for trips and traveling.

Most Virgos possess a strange empathy for children, strange because they are so "adult" in every way themselves. But a child always brings out a Virgo woman's latent potential for loveliness and beauty, an unsuspected talent for imagination, and a great tenderness—an ability to *listen* with genuine interest to all the despairs and delights of a young mind, as well as the wisdom to gently guide it into refreshing streams of thought. Since every Gemini man is a child, a little boy, at heart, these qualities within her can't but appeal to him enormously. However, with him, she must deal, not just with one "child" but with Twins. Repeatedly, she may attempt to teach him the value of discrimination, and find that he has no real desire to discriminate. He may, in turn, try to teach her to be more open, more expansive, to value personal freedom—and to acquire the grace to impulsively follow a dream. But Virgos open up very slowly, like a creaky door, and he's always in such a dreadful hurry. Besides, to her, freedom will never be as valued as security. Conversely, to Gemini, security is often synonymous with a mental San Quentin, restricting all possibility of a change of plans, which is what he feels makes life worth living.

A Virgo woman is the kind to surprise a lover or husband by bringing him breakfast in bed, but, unfortunately, few Gemini men like to sleep late. He's more likely to leap out of bed, shower, bike or jog around the block a few laps or catch the morning headlines before things like toast and cereal occur to him. His sometimes curt or detached reaction to her gentle courtesies may hurt her more than he suspects. Since his Mercury-ruled mind is so analytical, a Gemini man who has been paid the tribute of being loved by an also Mercury-ruled (until Vulcan appears) Virgin should analyze her true nature more carefully if he wants to keep her.

Some Virgo women remain chaste and romantically aloof for years, then risk everything on a single, unexpected and impossible passion that soon dies. And so, she may not be, inwardly and actually, as emotionally cool and controlled as she appears to be at times to him. The Gemini man is equally as likely to find true love eluding him, until he's no longer Peter Pan, and Wendy has grown up to marry someone else, who cared more about her than about his adventures.

Such painful disappointments can cause both Virgo and Gemini to brood alone, tormenting themselves with longing and regret. Or it can cause them to seek a calm, safe and undemanding relationship with each other, which could be what they've both been searching for—if they only looked a little longer into one another's eyes. But instead, they may avoid sustained gazing, fearing the eyes may reveal too much, while she sweeps the floors . . . . and he wanders around the house, whistling his little-boy-blue song . . . each reaching out their hearts, but unable to express what they're really feeling openly.

Because their natal Suns were squared at birth, a certain amount of tension and lack of comprehension is unavoidable between these two. In the electronics of love, tension can short-circuit the emotions into silent darkness. But with a harmonious Sun-Moon interchange between their horoscopes, this man and woman could achieve a lasting affection and contentment through their union. It may never be the turbulent, soaring ecstasy of Scarlett and Rhett, but love need not always be explosive.

Sometimes, happiness can be a calm and quiet thing, a moment of rest upon the wind, that makes sunset less sad and haunting . . . and brightens the sunrise with a gentle promise.

☆ ☆ ☆ ☆ ☆ ☆

GEMINI

Air — Mutable — Positive
Ruled by Mercury
Symbol: The Twins
Day Forces — Masculine

LIBRA

Air — Cardinal — Positive
Ruled by Venus
Symbol: The Scales
Day Forces — Masculine

The GEMINI- LIBRA *Relationship*

◄─◆─►

Sometimes it was dark and sometimes light, and
now they were very cold and again too warm.

Two Air Signs are fun to watch, like trapeze artists at the circus. Their mental gymnastics can be both dazzling and dizzying. Air is intangible, invisible, always moving everywhere . . . . . and nowhere.

Since Librans can never make up their minds, and Geminis are continually changing theirs, it's hard to know what to predict will happen in an association between them, whether they are relatives, husband-wife, friends, business partners, lovers, mates, or what-have-you. Whatever I write may change before it is read or comprehended by either. But I'll risk it, and state that Gemini and Libra constitute a 5-9 Sun Sign Pattern, which usually balances out favorably, no matter in which direction the Libra Scales are dipping, and no matter which one of the Twin personalities of the dual-natured Gemini wants to argue about it.

Lest the sharper, birdlike, alert and calculating Geminis should believe that Librans are nothing but puffy white clouds, I'll remind them that Libra rules China, therefore the Chinese. Since Orientals are the most mysterious people on the planet, it's a mistake to deduce that there's nothing behind Libra's bright smile but soft marshmallow fluff. Of course, that won't intimidate any typical Geminis (who are experts at working Chinese puzzles). So I'll try to warn the Twins in another way. Libra is a Cardinal Air Sign. Gemini is a Mutable Air Sign. Cardinal means leadership. Mutable means communication. A Gemini can communicate beautifully over the airwaves with Libra as long as he or she does not try to lead the discussion or win the argument.

Remember, Libra is Cardinal. Libra must win. Libra must lead. Libra is logical. Libra must always be right. And don't let that lollipop grin, those adorable dimples in their chins, and elsewhere, cause you to think otherwise. These are merely weapons to help Librans get their own way. When they can't do it with their superior intellect, deductive reasoning process, or that oily-smooth voice that sounds like violins blending with harps, accompanied by whispering angels, they will bat those wide, innocent eyes, flash the Venus smile, dimple a few times—and the opposition simply melts away.

Who can resist such a combination of beauty, grace, charm, logic, intelligence, brilliance, and flattery? Gemini can—and frequently does. Gemini is not easily taken in by Libra's coaxing con-artistry. After all, persuading, conning, coaxing and tricking the timid, with a blend of charm and wit, was invented by Geminis. The Twins come first on the zodiac wheel, Libra follows later—so Gemini invented the game, Libra only imitates.

I'm sure all Geminis will agree with me. As for the Librans, I have no intention of arguing the point back and forth, and up and down, with *them*. Instead, I shall sweetly urge the Pollyanna-perfect Librans to bear with me while I continue to tangle and snarl myself up verbally, trying to sort out the differences between them and the Twins.

Air has no particular shape. It just floats around through space, like an interpenetrating ghost. Therefore, when these two Sun Signs team up at home, in the office, on the campus, or anywhere else, it may be difficult at first to see them. It will not be difficult to hear them.

Gemini and Libra will have lengthy discourses on every subject imaginable, and they both have immense imaginations. Sometimes the discussions are friendly, sometimes not. But they will usually remain on speaking terms, since silence for anything but the briefest periods of time is well nigh an impossibility for both of them. These people do like to talk. Neither of them likes to listen.

The reason Libra is symbolized by the Scales is because some Librans have minds so delicately adjusted that no sooner does an idea enter than a contradictory idea is automatically suggested. Can you conceive what it would be like to be cursed with such a mind? Someone says HOT, the computer card flashes COLD. Someone feeds in LONG, you pop out with SHORT. If you hear FAST, you instantly think SLOW. If you hear SLOW, you think FAST. You feel UP, you look DOWN. You feel DOWN, you look UP. Are you still there? Sit down and close your eyes for a moment. The dizziness will pass. Now do you understand why so many Libra people walk around with a dazed look on their beautiful, evenly matched features and a faraway expression in their lovely eyes— half the time? The other half of the time they are doing the exact opposite —staring at you alertly and intently, agitating their air essence into a tornado or making eloquent, impassioned speeches. That's the way it goes (comes!) with these teetering-tottering souls; whatever occurs, they must immediately accentuate the opposite.

In Colorado there is a Libra man named George. One day I was explaining to him certain events in my life which caused me to suspect I was the object of disapproval from a hopefully now extinguished branch of the government, and had been thus persecuted, in subtle ways, for nearly three years. He listened to my brief summary, then dimpled, saying, "I have no doubt that the events which have occurred in your life for the past several years have a *sinister* basis in *provable facts.* However, *on the other hand,* you are a writer, and possess a vivid imagination, so it is entirely possible that the whole thing is actually *innocent.*"

Libran George was not even aware of his own thought process. Now that you have been astrologically initiated and instructed in how the Libra mind works, you can appreciate that no sooner did the word "sinister" pop into his head than his Libra Scales popped up a computer card reading "innocent"—the exact opposite of "sinister." This is the common Libra dilemma. What is truth? Which word should be the final answer? Sinister? Or innocent? The trauma of indecision.

Being an Aries Sun Sign made this particular matter quite simple for me. Sinister. The incidents were based on a situation that was SINIS-TER. However, you see, as a Ram, knowing that they are now behind me, I have dumped the events into yesterday's trash and am no longer concerned. Geminis do the same thing. Toss away yesterday, enjoy the present, and don't recognize tomorrow until it is here. Libra cannot. What if the summary was wrong? Although, of course, it could have been right. But if it was wrong, and thrown away, how recover it to make it right? Sinister or innocent? Bad or good? Real or imaginary? Positive or negative? Polarities, polarities, polarities! Libra is enmeshed in them from morning till night—and dares not discard them, for fear of discarding the only fair conclusion.

Unlike Libras, Geminis juggle polarities and contradictions, not in sequence, but simultaneously, constantly synchronizing their dual thoughts within their Twin selves. Why not? There are always two of him (or her) to handle anything. You can see why these two Sun Signs are not the most reliable people on Earth. If you catch Libra when the Scales are perfectly balanced—fine! If you catch Gemini when he or she has put one Twin to sleep and is displaying only the other for the moment—fine! But most of the time, these two, or three, or four, make quite a crowd. Despite the similarities in the natures of these two Air Signs, there are also a number of ways in which they veer off into different directions. Like making decisions.

Gemini decides quick as a flash, and that's it. No regret, no anxiety, no waiting or wondering—action NOW. Libra balances, weighs, judges, ponders, puzzles, assimilates, and postpones action till tomorrow—and sometimes tomorrow never comes. To Gemini, *not* making a decision can cause the race to be lost. To Libra, *making* a decision can cause a terrible mistake, and Libra cannot, *will* not make a mistake. It must be noted, however, that once the swift Mercury-ruled Gemini has decided, it may mean absolutely nothing. There could be a change of mind and plans minutes later. But once Libra has finally decided, after the delicate balancing act, he (or she) will normally stick by the decision firmly, knowing there are no improvements to be made that haven't already been carefully weighed. Libra is more cautious than Gemini. While the Twins tend to cut ties hastily, Libra never believes in cutting what may be more prudently unraveled, thread by thread. Why make a rash move, when you might subsequently be forced to retrace your steps through the discovery of a failure to take into account some fact or other which was not then known?

Geminis love a mental challenge, and Libra gives it to them. But when the Twins try that Mercurial double-talk on Libra, it doesn't always put them ahead. It can put them somewhere in the middle, occasionally even shortly behind center.

The childish charisma of Gemini can cause the Twins to do very fey and magical things, like speaking the name of a druid twenty-seven times when a star is falling . . . hitching imaginary rides on the backs of friendly squirrels and grasshoppers . . . and looking for diamonds among roses blooming in the snow. Libra doesn't normally care to waste time with such nonsense. In direct contradiction to their optimistic sweetness and their cheerful, sunny-yellow-beaming faces, they are coldly logical.

But there you are again! When you image one face of Libra, it will be fed back to you, through the polarity mentality of the Scales, as its opposite face. What Librans seek is the Golden Mean. Gemini doesn't care at all for the Golden Mean of arriving at a perfect balance. It is the traveling itself, not the destination, that the Twins enjoy. Both Gemini and Libra would be happier with themselves, and with each other, if they would try *feeling* much more and *thinking* much less.

☆ ☆ ☆ ☆ ☆ ☆

GEMINI *Woman* LIBRA *Man*

They are, however, allowed to change, only it must be a complete change.

The fact that the Gemini woman and the Libra man are so much alike is what makes them so compatible and happy together. Also, the fact that the Gemini woman and the Libra man are so much alike is what starts most of the trouble between them.

They know each other only too well, sympathize with one another's dreams and idiosyncrasies, can calmly cope with their mutual chameleon qualities, comprehend each other's various moods, and will usually stick together against outsiders who don't understand the airy mentality. If either he or she has a more sensitive and emotional Water Element or a more stable Earth Element as a Moon Sign or Ascendent, their happiness and bliss is pretty much astrologically insured. Otherwise, these two are still guaranteed a far better than average chance for success, except for small flurries on especially windy days. They can both be a trifle windy, full of both cool breezes and hot air. As a 5-9 Sun Sign Pattern, they are more harmoniously matched than most couples who are trying to fit the jig-saw pieces of the puzzle of love into a perfect picture.

Both of them are aesthetically inclined, moved by beauty, acutely disturbed by untidiness, ugliness, and disorder. Yet, despite this mutual essence, Gemini and Libra, while needing, even demanding loveliness and order, may frequently need a brisk Sagittarian, an energetic Aries, or an efficient Virgo maid to clean up after them. Of course, some Geminis and

Librans are tidy. But even they would prefer to have someone else straighten out their messes—emotionally as well as actually. Since Gemini is quicker, she will often be the one to follow her Libra man around, picking up his discarded socks and banana peels. In return, he will probably not deny her the money (if he has it) to make their surroundings ever more comfortable and beautiful. More often than not, the nest of these two love birds is charming, tasteful, pleasant to the eye, and probably full of books. Even if they live in a tent, it will be well pegged and insulated, with maybe burned etchings on the canvas for decor—and the soft sound of tom-toms beating in the background. Soft, I said. Not too disturbing, because Libra can't stand loud noises, lopsided stools or crooked tent pegs.

When this man and woman quarrel, it will almost always be she who starts it—and he who finishes it. At least it will seem that way to observers. A Gemini female, for all her airy charm and delicate femininity, possesses a sharp, satirical tongue, and she's not reluctant to use it when her fast mind urges her to express her quick opinions. Her Libra lover or husband will have recognized early in Life that rudeness and frank speech is a stumbling block to achieving his true and secret purpose, whether in love or business. So he projects a sort of gentle amiability (most times) and is an expert at hiding his passions and intent behind a smooth smile and a persuasive voice. Yes, she may have started it verbally. But he may be at the *bottom* of it, the real initial instigator of the quarrel—by spending two weeks to make up his mind whether they should take their vacation this month or next, while she had to stall the airlines and coax them into holding their reservations during the busy season . . . . . or something similar. Therefore, regardless of who outwardly starts the fussing, he is seldom innocent.

Libra men are never as innocent as they look and sound, or as they would like to have you believe. In fact, there are times (rare, but they do exist) when his Scales are dipping, and he can be as cranky as a cuckoo bird stuck in the little clock door. On those occasions, however, he probably apologizes so sweetly, overwhelming her with so much sugary Libra charm, that she may forget to remember his grumpiness later. Strangers who gaze upon the Libra man's smooth, even features have no way of knowing about the painfully articulated resolves forming in his mind beneath his cheerful exterior—or the crankiness displayed to his intimates while these are in the formative stage.

A Gemini girl might take a notion to be a dress designer. Then she could become dazzled by the idea of getting a pilot's license and maybe her own Lear jet. Following that, she could take a new notion to translate Sanskrit, study the Dead Sea scrolls, open a pet shop or enroll in law school. But the Libra man can handle all her tangled notions and emotions better than an Earth Sign male, who might erupt like a volcano—a Fire Sign male, who might burn all the oxygen out of her enthusiasms—or a Water Sign male, who might dampen her excitement with a wet blanket.

Libra understands Gemini's wanderlust of the mind and heart, yet is stable and logical enough to control her more erratic impulses before they blow up out of proportion, gently pointing out the pros and cons to her, until she decides to find her bluebird a little closer to home—and to him.

Serene is the word. Libra can be a serene influence on Gemini, except for those occasional cranky-bear spells he charms her into forgetting. Goodness knows the Gemini girl needs serenity. Hers is a restless spirit, a seeking soul. She longs poignantly to know what she wants, where she stands, who she is and why she's going—or coming. The Libra man is the most logical one to explain all this to her. But . . . well, you see . . . a Gemini girl is made up of so many fragments—of honey and spice and everything nice, yes. Yet, she's far more than this. She's all the books she ever studied, a reflection of the ideas and philosophies of her mirror-image Twin, diametrically opposed to her own. She's the swinging rope she skipped in childhood, the plaintive wail of the gulls, and the secrets she whispered to the sandpipers on the beach she once walked along, the memory of her first dance . . . tumbleweeds and tornadoes . . . the flickering candles of a half-forgotten New Year's Eve. These fragments of the Gemini girl make up her private world, where the Libra man who loves her can never freely roam, even though he may guide her through it . . . from a distance.

There's something judicial and cold in Libra's balanced thinking process, despite his charm and sweetness, that doesn't permit him to enter the deep woods of the changeable fairyland where she and her Twin so frequently dwell. He can watch her lovingly, as she removes her shoes and runs through the grass barefoot—he can wait by the gate until she returns from her faraway land, but he can never truly join her. Why? Because he would first have to locate it on a map, see if an airline booked a flight there, learn its population and study its chief industry, before loping off with her. Otherwise, how could he prove to himself logically that such a place really does exist? And if it doesn't exist, why go there at all? There's an invisible veil between this man and woman, for all their many similarities of personality.

Their physical relationship is usually blessed with nearly complete fulfillment, the kind of fulfillment only two Air Signs are able to comprehend (or desire). At night, sometimes lying alone beside her (yes, lying alone beside her) he's grateful when she returns from her make-believe world, back into his arms, often not even guessing that fragments of her are still out there, chasing moonbeams and playing tag with the stars. She *feels* to him like she is there. And, of course, part of her *is*—the one who has vowed to love and cherish him, never to leave him. She can't be expected to account for the other, wayward one—her Twin, who refuses to obey, even when she, herself, pleads.

Their sexual union will not be as all consuming as that between two Fire or Earth signs, but it can be as refreshing as a summer storm, with flashes of thunder and lightning. They are both airy, mental souls, living primarily in the mind, not in the emotions, and so explosive passion may be missing, but the total peace and tranquility of a deeply affectionate blending can be theirs. Sex, as with all 5-9 Sun Sign Patterns, is important to this couple, but not primary for happiness. Romantic love is equally needed, perhaps even more desired, by both, and forms the true basis for the initial attraction between them.

These two will take turns being the aggressive partner in their lovemaking. Both can switch from active to passive, from masculine to feminine, in a strange, mystical way that makes their sexual experiences a constantly changing yet harmoniously blended delight. If they have twin beds, there might be a few discussions about who gets to sleep nearest the window, but aside from such minor adjustments, these two will usually wake up in each other's arms, sharing a good-morning embrace that melts the previous night's disputes, as the Sun disperses clouds.

They may need and complete each other physically, yet it's possible that he may be more in love with her mind and spirit than with her body, and she may have more interest in his intellect and soul than in his sexuality— even though they may be only dimly aware of this. The chemistry between two Air Signs is misty, mental, and variable—rather than earthy, passionate, and sensual. Not all Gemini girls desire children, and very few dream of large families, but when they do, it will often be a Libra man who is chosen to father them. Many Gemini girls who would not have a child with any other man will find motherhood more attractive with a Libra male.

If she marries him, it will be because she likes the way he sings or dances or whistles . . . . . . the way he moves and walks and talks and winks. The way he dresses too. Then, womanlike, she may set about to try to change him afterwards. Ruled by Venus as he is, the Libra man may tolerate this and try to please her, because he loves her—until he finally realizes that, although she thrives on change, too much change affects his own equilibrium. So he'll roar (gently) and put his foot down (softly) to prove he's a masculine Cardinal Sign, return to his old ways—and it will probably be best for both of them.

They're likely to do lots of traveling together, may have either religious or educational reasons for getting together, and may meet on a trip. If he ever gets interested in UFO's, it will probably be because of her. She will inspire him to reach heights he would not have aspired to reach without her. Because they both have wings on their heels—and hearts—they may change residence more often than lovers or mates born under other Sun Signs.

There is little doubt that the Gemini woman will at times confuse and confound her Libra lover or husband. She is, after all, so many women in one. She can be the most talkative when he's trying to think or struggling with a decision, the prettiest when she has provoked him into a spell of rare Libra anger, the most silent when he wants to show her off to his friends, the most energetic at bed time, the laziest in the morning when he's waiting for his poached eggs—but what other woman could be such a kaleidoscope of grief, joy, annoyance, happiness, embarrassment, irritation, delight, and frustration as this twin-packaged mystery of femininity?

True, she can be untidy, lose the car keys, tangle up the checkbook, waste his time and money, destroy his dignity, and try his temper—but just when he's ready to walk out, her little-girl misty tears begin to splash, switching almost instantly into a rippling Gemini laugh . . . . . . and he's lost again, caught between the myriad women bottled up inside this girl, who needs his strength if she's ever going to find her way out of the woods.

As for him, he'll relentlessly try to force her to be more logical and stable, criticize her faults, refuse to help her pick daisies when he has work to do, shatter her fragile nerves, and sometimes behave like a stern judge, pronouncing sentence over her free spirit—but when her dreams are scattered, her house and her hair are both a mess, and she feels like a silly, foolish child, he can make her feel like a woman when he smiles and says, "I don't know why I love you so much, but I do."

Then she realizes that she's the one problem he can never balance on his Scales and make come out even. Being a daughter of Eve, she will privately smile, knowing that the solution to the enigma of herself can never be totally analyzed by his intellect, only by his heart. Yet, also perversely, Eve-like, she'll refuse to share this key to love's Gemini secret with him, wanting him to guess.

One serious level of disagreement within this liaison of Air will be the Libra man's proclivity to weigh and judge things—to see life, people and situations in the proper perspective and balance, coolly and logically, with an odd sort of detachment, void of all whimsical notion. Not only does this facet of his nature clash rather sharply with his own inherent optimism and faith, it will also frequently conflict with *her* tendency to see all these things, not as they are, but as they *ought* to be. She sees what she desires to see, coloring facts with fancy, avoiding delusion (to her way of thinking) by drenching everything with illusion.

If he doesn't make a sincere effort to comprehend her attitude with compassion, she may be forced to tell little white lies to defend her viewpoint. This woman can be frightened of those who demand always the exact, precise, unvarnished truth, with no allowances made for "maybe"— "perhaps"—and "suppose it had been." Then, she could be forced to escape by plunging even deeper into unreality. It wouldn't hurt Libra to add a few sprinkles of Gemini imagination to all the matters he balances so seriously on his Scales. For truth is often not what it appears to be— (Mercury taught her that)—logic can be deceptive and facts can fool.

When the night is frosty and full of stars, who expects a warm summer rain to be hiding just behind Arcturus? The Twins do. She knows that true wisdom is only gained by adapting to life's ever-changing patterns. But he cannot accept today's patterns until he's weighed them mentally against former and future patterns and found them worthy of acceptance. Somewhere along the way, near the center of these polarized points of view, Gemini and Libra will meet, touch lightly . . . . . linger . . . . . and love.

GEMINI *Man* LIBRA *Woman*

He really knew nothing about it; he had merely
suspicions, but he said at a venture, "Wendy,
I ran away the day I was born."

Wendy was quite surprised, but interested; and
she indicated in the charming drawing-room manner,
by a touch on her night-gown, that he could sit
nearer her.

It's a 5-9 astrological fact, and there's no room for argument. A Gemini male is irresistible when he is effortlessly magnetizing a poor Libra girl into deserting her nicely balanced life and pledging her heart to an uncertain future, flying in and out of ideas, towns, cities, and moods with him. Of course, it works both ways. Doesn't *everything* work both ways with Gemini and Libra?

It's just as fascinating to watch an irresistible Libra female spilling clouds of gentle, helpless, femininity all over a poor Gemini man, convincing him that it's his own idea to settle down and do the only sensible, logical thing after falling in love—get married, get a job, raise a family, and stay in one place with one person who can handle both of him—namely her. Who wins this romantic game? It sometimes depends on which one has the stronger Moon Sign, but usually it will be she, not he.

Whoever makes the initial approach, the laws of physics and chemistry soon take over, and these lovers will soon be turning airy dream castles into solid, substantial mortgages, because she smells so good, is so soft and cuddly, while he is so quick and bright and intelligent, and can beat her at chess and checkers.

A Libra woman will seldom glance twice at a man beneath her intellectuality. And a Gemini man will seldom sacrifice his precious freedom for a woman who can't anagram his thoughts and work crossword dreams with him. It's always amusing to watch a Gemini magician get fooled by one of his own magic tricks with a few new twists. Yet, there is a certain poetic justice about it. Here he has spent all his life charming girls, weaving his way in and out of romances, making it seem it was always his partner's fault, never his, glibly charming his way back into being friends again, and, in general, enjoying his enviable ability to handle every situation with a string of words from Webster's accompanied by small-boy innocence.

Now he meets a female who is more than his match at the game of guile, who gives him right back what he dishes out. After he has been led to think he has wooed and won her, after he allows her to harness his free spirit within the confining bonds of matrimony—(let other women play house in the New Age of sexual freedom, Libra females will settle only for a wedding ring)—after all that, he will discover that her gentle, soft, persuasive and amiable manner covers a cool, brilliant mind, a strong will, and a steely determination to get exactly what she wants. This is no fluffy bunny rabbit—this is a WAC field general!

A Libra female will always manage to get her own way under the guise of fairness, femininity and helplessness, but Libra is, in the final analysis, a masculine sign. I keep *telling* you that. She'll be surprised and hurt when he eventually sees through her, which he will, because no one, not even Libra, can fool the twinkling Gemini intellect for long. She didn't mean to be unfair or deceptive. To Libra, all is fair in love and war between the sexes, and the female of the species, in this respect, is more deadly than the male.

Her intriguing mind which so attracted him in the beginning of the romance will later make her a dangerous opponent in a discussion, since she's so skillful at the art of putting him at a disadvantage by arousing him into a display of temper, thereby causing him to lose his cool and poise. Then she has him at her mercy, while she claims tearfully that he is a brute, and his anger is certain evidence that he is wrong. Over and over again, she will outmaneuver him by using his own trick of twisting his statements and intent, leaving him unable to pin down the flaw in her arguments because of her capacity for doing things with such subtlety, and it doesn't seem she is doing anything at all, but fairly and justly defending her position.

A Libra woman is as impatient of constraint as any of the twelve Sun Signs, though perhaps not quite as much so as Gemini, Aquarius, Sag and Aries. For the Gemini lover or husband to attempt to impose any sort of restriction upon her would not be a wise idea. Just remember those Orientals (Libra rules the Orient). They cannot be controlled by other races effectively because, while they appear to be gentle and patient, offering no resistance, they will, nevertheless, always manage to find some subtle way of nullifying the opposition. The Gemini man will never gain a total victory over the Libra woman. Just when he thinks he has succeeded in breaking down all her arguments, she will have slipped around to another tactic or emotional strategy, catching him off guard again. But he should also keep in mind the curious detachment of Libra. She will take infinite pains to win her way, but when she fails, she has nearly the same mental satisfaction in the analysis of the reason for failure as she would have if she had been successful. He should keep this in mind, mainly because the same thing is true of himself. The two of them are much alike in many ways, influenced as they are by the very favorable and harmonious 5-9 Sun Sign Pattern vibration. They are sympatico, and often complement one another even in the areas where they differ.

Essentially, Gemini and Libra are wonderfully compatible, possessing many virtues (as well as vices) in common. They tend to respect each other's mentality, privacy, and freedom of thought and speech—normally. Yet there will be times when he wounds her deeply and is completely baffled by her hurt reaction, by the unexpected violence of her emotions. Any Libra woman in love with a Gemini man will understand why it has been said of the Mercury-ruled male that he is so busy *thinking*, he never stops to *think*.

He has no wish to attack, but his verbal outbursts can be sharp and cutting to the Libra girl, who by nature covers every opinion with the softer blur of tact and courtesy. Still, with his innate Mercurial charm, he'll win her over and make her believe he didn't mean what he said, which he probably didn't (Geminis never mean what they say for longer than an hour or so).

Their physical relationship may not be comprehensible to those born under Fire or Earth signs, but to them it will be enough to fill their hearts with peace and fulfillment. Neither is genuinely passionate, not really capable of love as more intensely emotional people experience it. There will always be something delicate and detached about their lovemaking—poetic and haunting, yes—but sensual, no. Yet the banked fires of the sexual blending between this man and woman are as magnetic and binding to their mutual air natures as the more torrid contacts between other mates and lovers. Romance will eternally be more important to both Gemini and Libra than sex. This attitude will predominate and suffuse their intimacy with a beauty all its own.

These two do not view love as an erotic appetite to be appeased, but as an art to be refined—not as lust, but as mutual pleasure—to be sipped slowly, not gulped greedily or blindly. There's an undeniable air of voluptuousness about a Libra woman, but also an air of refinement. Grossness, coarseness, obscenity and vulgarity offend her.

(Of course, an earthier Moon Sign or Ascendent or a severe affliction between Venus and Mars in her natal chart can dilute this basic part of her Sun Sign nature—but, as always, with all Sun Signs, we're speaking of the typical Libra Lady.)

There's small chance she'll be offended in such manner by the Gemini man, who privately feels the same way she does, although he may need more variety of expression in their physical union than his Venus-ruled wife. Yes, she will eventually become his wife—or leave. Libra rules marriage, you know, and it's a very rare Libran who is satisfied with an emotional relationship other than marital for any length of time.

The typical Libra girl who normally can't make up her mind about love any faster than she can about anything else, may nevertheless feel an impulse to rush into matrimony with a Gemini man before she's taken the time to balance her dipping Scales of decision. The infallible sign of a salesman is his ability to make people fight for the article he's trying to sell, and Gemini is a salesman supreme. When the article he's trying to sell is himself, the Libra girl is no more invulnerable to the Mercury charm and gift of glamour than the rest of his dazzled audience. She's sensible, intelligent, perceptive and all that, but these qualities seem to fail her when she's losing her heart to this gentle man with the bright eyes, light touch and far-out dreams.

Money may be a trifle more important to her than it is to him. Just a trifle more. The accumulation of cash and the manipulation of finances is not the prime motivation of either Libra or Gemini, except for the occasional natives of these Sun Signs who almost accidentally wander into the banking business. To Gemini, money only becomes really important when he doesn't have it—when he desperately needs it. To Libra, money is important because of the luxuries, comforts and beauty of surroundings it can buy. Yet, stinginess and greediness are not qualities belonging to the Air Element, so there should be few disputes in this area, unless the Gemini man throws it away too freely, speculates too often, or gambles on long shots. When he spends beyond the budget, it will usually be connected with some new idea or promotion, a vacation or a change of residence—at the very least, a brief change of scene. When she's extravagant, it's more often lavished on clothes, dancing, singing or music lessons, sculpture, drama or Yoga classes, and the like. Sometimes, home decor and beauty parlors. They're basically alike in their attitudes toward money, as in many other matters, although they may differ in their manner of using it, from time to time. (Naturally, a stingier or more economical Moon Sign or Ascendent may slightly change the picture in either birth chart, but not substantially.)

Their homes will probably be filled with music, flowers, books—and children. Those who love within the vibration of the 5-9 influence often decide to raise a family together, despite their reluctance to have children with members of other Sun Signs. They'll do a lot of traveling, either mentally or geographically, the relatives of each will be prominent in their relationship, and they may find religion or higher education grounds for agreement—or periodic dispute.

If these two are also graced by a harmonious Sun-Moon aspect between their respective nativities, their relationship will be smooth sailing on sparkling water, perhaps punctuated by a few storms and reefs, but, on the whole, like floating downstream on a feather. With a tense aspect between their Luminaries, the air could become humid, muggy, and even smoggy now and then, but there will always be the chance to run back into each other's arms for forgiveness after a quarrel, however serious—to try again.

He'll send sorry flowers, she'll recall the way the lights danced in his eyes, like a small boy, when he was excited, overlook his flaws, melt into his heart once more—and begin all over again to analyze why she loves him. But she won't solve the puzzle until she realizes that he is Twins, two-men-in-one. A Libra woman is compelled to balance any duality she comes across into a harmonious whole, by virtue of her Venus essence. She'll never completely accomplish it, of course, but she may come closer to his magic than he'll ever allow anyone else to come. Except, of course, for the other half of himself.

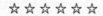

GEMINI

Air — Mutable — Positive
Ruled by Mercury
Symbol: The Twins
Day Forces — Masculine

SCORPIO

Water — Fixed — Negative
Ruled by Pluto
Symbols: Scorpion & Eagle
Night Forces — Feminine

The GEMINI-SCORPIO *Relationship*

+◄─◆─►+

> *All pirates are superstitious; and*
> *Cookson cried, "They do say the surest*
> *sign a ship's accurst is when there's*
> *one on board more than can be accounted for."*

The naturally superstitious Scorpio has every right to conjure an extra person around when he (or she) is dealing with a Gemini, born under the sign of the Twins. Only one person is visible, of course, but this man's or woman's twin (or triplet or quadruplet) eternally hides in the ethers, ready to pop out at the most disconcerting times.

Most people don't know they're dealing with a multiple when they associate with a Gemini, but Scorpio suspects the truth of the matter right away. Scorpio suspects *everything* right away. It's difficult, if not impossible, to fool a Scorpion for long. The suspicious nature of these people prods them to penetrate mysteries like Sherlock Holmes, but they seldom discuss their conclusions with any Dr. Watsons. What Scorpio knows, he keeps to himself (or herself, as the case may be). As I've said before, Scorpio, above all, seeks Power. Knowledge is Power, so why give any of it away? Which brings us to a rather obvious tendency of—not all—but most Geminis: talking. Sometimes, they even go so far as to gossip. At the very best, they usually don't count to ten before speaking, a habit which can upset the more taciturn and reserved Scorpios, even though Gemini words are often lovely bubbles of light and joy.

Not that Scorpios can't be loquacious too, at times. They can be—the rare ones. But most Scorps would rather be seen than heard, and preferably not seen if they can possibly help it. I've mentioned elsewhere that many Pluto-ruled men and women and children have this thing about wearing dark glasses to help keep their incognito status undefiled. Even those unusual Scorpions who chatter have a knack for talking about everything except what is really important. They seldom discuss anything truly personal—about themselves, that is. Anything personal about someone else they will gladly discuss, unless they've promised to keep it a secret. Then their lips are closed as strictly as with the seal of the confessional. It's a rare Scorpio who breaks a promise. Keeping a promise is a point of honor with these people. And so the verbal dexterity of Gemini, not to mention the Geminian childlike attitudes of innocent fun and frolic, can annoy Scorpio, unless he or she has the natal Moon or Ascendent in an Air or Fire Sign. Pluto-ruled men and women not only look askance at a loose tongue, they don't trust childlike innocence either. Scorpio is a lot of things, but "innocence" is not the word an astrologer would choose to describe this Sun Sign.

Scorpios have what can only be called a dominating disposition, ranging all the way from brooding sulkiness to cool withdrawal (sometimes arrogance) when things don't go their way. At other times, Scorpio can be gentle, sensitive, compassionate and fanatically loyal—but never truly *warm*. Gemini is likewise often accused of lack of warmth. (Water and Air Signs both seem cold and detached to those born in the Fire or Earth elements.) As for loyalty, Gemini, as we all know by now, is not famous for loyalty—if the true meaning of the word is unswerving devotion to one person, one idea or one ideal for a lifetime. Gemini does like to swerve! These people have difficulty remaining interested in one topic for a full twenty-four-hour day without swerving and veering into a different direction—let alone for an entire Life-span on the planet Earth. Without periodic variety and changing scenery, however, the average Mercury Bird would suffocate from sheer boredom.

Like all 6-8 Sun Sign Patterns, unless they are born into the same family circle as relatives, or involved in a business association, Gemini and Scorpio might never meet without someone else introducing them. Lacking a Sun-Moon harmony between their mutual horoscopes, these two normally don't have enough in common to feel any pulsing vibrations across a crowded room and usually need third-party intervention to become acquainted. However, once they are accidentally tossed together by some innocent bystander, who has no idea what may result from this mixing of Air and Water, their 6-8 Pattern will invariably cause the relationship, whether friendly, business or emotional, to consist of much service and devotion on one side and an inexplicable magnetism on the other. Incongruously (in an astrological sense), the service and devotion usually flows from Scorpio to Gemini—the magnetic attraction from Gemini to Scorpio. One might say that Gemini represents one mystery Scorpio cannot completely penetrate, and there is precious little Scorpio cannot penetrate. It's indisputably frustrating to the Scorpion, but frustration is sometimes synonymous with fascination when taken in small doses, infrequently. Taken in large doses daily, it can remove a lot of sting from Scorpio and cause some dulling of the childlike innocence of Gemini, ruffling the feathered wings of the impatient Mercury Birds.

Clever, intellectual Gemini is a walking, talking Question Mark (with emphasis on the talking), constantly curious and occasionally spurious. Scorpio is a firm Period, at the end of Knowing, the ultimate punctuation in the power of concentration. Geminis normally have varying degrees of trouble concentrating, their attention span sometimes being as brief as the time it takes a butterfly to hover over one blossom or a bird to remain perched on one branch.

In addition to being intensely domineering at times, Scorpio is also intensely proud and ambitious, in a disguised, quiet and unobtrusive way. As a matter of fact, Scorpio is privately intense about everything. Intensely ruthless, intensely loyal, intensely compassionate, intensely cool, intensely secretive, intensely mysterious. These people do nothing in half measures, never mind how harmless and sweet they seem on the surface. If they are your friends, they are your friends all the way up to heaven and all the way down to hell. If they are your enemies, the same geographical route of extremities and polarities is followed.

If Scorpio does *nothing* halfway, then Gemini can be said to do *everything* halfway (or one to three-quarters). Geminis never devote all—every shred of themselves—to any single person, idea or project. Only small fragments, chips and pieces, occasional crumbs. You see why they might never notice each other in a crowd?

Although these two Sun Signs are different in motivation, character and personality, the differences can be intriguing. Scorpio will never learn all there is to know about Gemini, and cares deeply about the failure. Gemini will never totally plumb the awesome depth of Scorpio, and couldn't care less. Not really. To Gemini, all the fun is over when the riddle is solved. It's the changing dialogue and the fun of guessing the plot that excites Mercury people, not the denouement of the final scene.

Like Virgo, Gemini has a speculative and analytical nature, producing a marked tendency to read between the lines, therefore to often imagine that people mean more than they are saying. Scorpio is no slouch in this department either, although the basic cause is different. With Gemini, it stems from quick intellect, Mercurial curiosity and analytical urges—with Scorpio, from plain old-fashioned fear and suspicion.

Ask Gemini to sit on a particular couch, and he or she will probe your psychological and emotional purposes for choosing that couch, whereas Scorpio will be positive there's a bomb wired beneath it, rigged by computer to explode. There's a slight difference in their attitudes, but the end result is much the same. It's impossible to keep a secret from either Sun Sign, or to retain one's personal privacy around them. When it is Gemini and Scorpio who are suspecting, analyzing and probing each other, rather than one of the remaining ten Sun Signs, it's like watching a couple of pretzels caught in a Chinese chain-lock puzzle. They each create their own individual auras of mystery, and they both like to solve mysteries. But Gemini's mysterious aura is carefree and variable, consisting of unpredictable switches of pastel colors, light and shadow, and rapid changes of thought—while Scorpio's auric ethers of burgundy-shaded mystery are much more complex, with an emphasis on the shadows, lying in far deeper and unfathomable wells, sometimes with a touch of the sinister when influenced by the negative side of Pluto.

Slowness in others is a constant source of irritation to the bright, alert, impatient Twins, the most typical of whom are periodically high-strung and nervous. Scorpios are also periodically high-strung and nervous, but heaven forbid that anyone should ever catch them showing it! The more apprehensive Scorpio is feeling within, the more sure, confident and secure he (or she) *appears* to be outwardly. Since every inwardly experienced feeling and emotion flits across Gemini's features, lighting up his (or her) expressive, fast darting eyes, you should have no trouble deciding where to place your bets to win in a poker game. When the poker game is a relationship of any kind with each other, the stakes can be desperately high for Scorpio, yet it's still only a game to Gemini, whatever the size of the kitty or the pot. If one game is lost, figures the Mercury Bird, there's always another, just down the road. Scorpio does not take losing so lightly. In fact, the Eagles take losing very, very heavily. Losing, to Scorp, is a humiliating experience, degrading, perhaps even cause for inner panic. (Scorp never displays *outer* panic.) Gemini tosses Life's dice with a fine, detached and careless abandon—Scorpio, with cool shrewdness, and then only after carefully calculating the odds. *Life's* dice, that is. In an actual dice game, Gemini calculates rather coolly and precisely himself—or herself. The fast Mercury mind figures the house percentages in a flash.

Let's see if you can straighten out these pretzels of intrigue. They just walked into the room. One of them has glided in noiselessly, almost unnoticed, and stands quietly, while gazing steadily into your eyes. You ask a question, this one remains silent, not answering immediately. The other has skipped, hopped, or flown into the room, perhaps strumming a guitar, tossing a tennis racquet in the air, and dangling the end of a sentence. You ask a question, and this one will jet a convoluted answer in your direction, then quickly head for the bowl of cracked walnuts on the table. Which one is which? Think you know?

All right, the first one described is a Gemini. The second is a Scorpio. Are you confused, mystified? Then you haven't been paying close enough attention to the hints in all the various Gemini and Scorpio chapters of this book. The Gemini was tricking you into believing he-she is cool and poised, using one of Mercury's multiple identities, as smoothly as a seasoned actor slips from one part into another. The Scorpio was wearing one of Pluto's Halloween masks, feigning a casual unconcern and light flippancy to hide his or her quivering intensity. Now, do you understand the problem?

They didn't notice each other at all. Go on—walk over and introduce them, but the responsibility is yours, not mine. If their Moon Signs are compatible, they can create haunting, misty dreams together. After all, isn't a fine mist the result of a blending of air and water, in Nature? But if their Sun and Moon Signs are square or opposed, the result will be fog —and in a heavy fog, Mercury Birds can't fly, while Scorpions make little progress along the seashore.

☆ ☆ ☆ ☆ ☆ ☆

GEMINI *Woman* SCORPIO *Man*

We should start right out by admitting there are some relationships composed of this Air and Water mixture which succeed—some Twins and Eagles who easily manage to find a lasting love, built together on a firm foundation of mutual respect. Not a lot, but there are some.

If the Sun-Moon aspects between them are harmonious, they can find happiness as effortlessly as any other man and woman descended from Adam and Eve, except that they'll have to keep a sharper eye on that sneaky snake than most lovers. Without such an astrological boost, however (if their Luminaries and other planets are in adverse aspect between their birth charts), these particular Air and Water signs might find it easier and safer to remain friends, avoiding the wild winds of passion and the deeper waters of forever vows. Scoring high on a compatibility achievement level is not forbidden to them, but they both must be willing to make a constant effort.

To begin with, "forever" is a word that frightens the Gemini female as much as the word "temporary" frightens the Scorpio male. It isn't that she is unable to remain in love, and true to one man, because many Gemini girls do just that, but such faithfulness and permanency must creep up on her subtly, gradually, one tiptoe at a time, until she's totally involved in the relationship without realizing it. Using the word "forever" too soon, or predicting the outcome of the romance when she'd rather guess, spoils the excitement for her. Conversely, it isn't that the Scorpio man can't cope with "temporary" arrangements as well as the next male creature, but the use of the word itself creates instant doubt and suspicion in his mind, spoiling his sense of power and dominance over the affair.

He'll be initially captivated by her undeniable charm, the champagne bubbles of her voice, her bright mind, her deft conversation and her light touch in every situation. Naturally. He's only a man, after all, regardless of his masked and caped Batman image—and just as susceptible to the attractions of Eve's apple as any other astrological sign. Then, after a while, he'll begin to notice that some of her delightful stories have changed ever-so-slightly the second time around. (Geminis always add a little here, take away a little there, for more sparkle—doesn't everyone?) She may be late for two or three of their dates in a row, or perhaps she'll interrupt his discussion of his very serious plans for their future with the agitated announcement that she left the car keys in the ignition with the engine running. Not only that, but she double-parked and blithely expects him to pay the ticket.

It is at this point, or at some similar stage of discovery, that the Scorpio man will rub some of the stardust from his eyes, take a long and penetrating look at this woman who nearly stole his heart, and cautiously decide to deliberate a bit longer the possibility of his promising to love, honor and cherish her for the rest of his days before a man of God. (Scorpio is secretly very religious, you know.) Once he has given his word, it pains his soul to break it, so he may slow up the courting until he's sure she has no more surprises to spring on him, like one or two marriages and separations or divorces she forgot to remember to tell him about.

It may be that she will hardly note the slight change in his attitude. She's too busy wondering how long she can stand his stifling scrutiny of her personal life, prying into her secrets (nothing bad or necessarily shocking, but just things she'd like to keep private)—and his jealousy. Can't a girl smile back brightly at the clerk in the bookstore or stop to discuss the grooming problems of Old English sheepdogs with a friendly stranger on the street without being accused of promiscuity? What about the way *he* stares at every female he meets, and stares . . . . . . and stares . . . . . . and stares?

She has only herself to blame for her dilemma. Being a Gemini, and having cut her teeth on the dictionary, she should be well read enough to know that a Scorpio male, with his deep, rich, magnetic voice, and steady, wise gaze, possesses the fascination of a Serpent. Formidable as his outward appearance of strength and stillness may be, beneath it is a silent mating call few females can resist.

One of the first things she'll discover about him is his incredible will power. It is simply not to be believed. This man can do anything he sets his mind on doing, literally anything. If he decides to fast for thirty days, he'll live on water throughout the entire period without so much as a whimper of hunger or complaint. If he chooses to become president—of his class, his company or his country—he will attain his goal and become president. If he wants to seduce a girl into being his woman for keeps, she has lost the battle before it begins. He will make her his.

All this can be spooky, Halloween-scary to the bright-eyed Gemini girl, who asks nothing of life but change and excitement, gaiety—and something to challenge the intellect. When she feels those Pluto vibes reaching out toward her, you would think she would run, as she would flee from a panting gorilla in the jungle, who means business. *You* would think so. *I* would not. Because I am aware of the astrological quirk that allows a Scorpio man, at odd moments, to more resemble an innocent, velvet-eyed deer than a gorilla—so sweet, gentle and sensitive, so *apparently* in need of comfort and loyal support, a girl would have to have a heart as hard as bricks to hurt him in the slightest way, like running away from him. The Gemini girl's heart is not as hard as bricks. It may be set at a cooler temperature than the heart of an Aries, Leo or Sagittarius girl with more fiery emotions, but it is soft in all the right spots, and the appeal of an intelligent man, whose burning eyes can see through her soul, hits one of those spots with deadly aim. There is something so satiny smooth about his manner, she forgets that steely gaze he's capable of projecting when he's displaying his tremendous powers of reserve and icy resolve, but he'll give her plenty of opportunity to remember it later.

So much for why and how these two usually fall in love. More is needed about how they can manage to *remain* in love. Since Scorpio is a Fixed Sign, he has an abundance of self-control. He'll need all of it when she tries his patience with her chameleon charisma, her spells of moodiness, absentmindedness and duality of purpose. Since Gemini is a Mutable Sign, she possesses an abundance of adaptability to help her cope with fluctuating scenes and emotions, which she will surely need to call on eventually with this man. She'll need all her ability to stay free and easy and cool when he becomes stubborn or violently emotional over some imagined slight just after he has been an angel of understanding. (It's always difficult to decide if Scorpio is Angel or Devil; they seem to be so at home in both heaven and hell, a foot in each place, but actually existing somewhere in-between.)

She'll have to memorize the lesson that this man wants to know where she is and what she's doing most of the time—if not all of the time. He'll also expect her to remain in one place, more or less (mostly more). He'll frown at her nostalgic tears over her old boyfriends, her casual attitude toward money when something excites her fancy, her whimsical excursions into one hobby after another, from singing-to-dancing-to-painting-to-home-decorating-to-archeology-to-medicine, and spinning around with a travel urge each time the seasons change in Nature—and in her restless Mercury-ruled spirit.

He'll have to be satisfied with fragments of devotion, scattered kisses and temper tantrums, naivete nearly beyond belief (or nearly beyond a Scorpio's belief) along with cool disdain mixed in equal parts with enthusiastic affection, a wandering mind and changeable notions—and not expect her to display anything near the self-confidence and emotional control he has possessed since he was born.

She is surely a challenge to him and to his masculinity, since most Gemini females are full of feminine wile and guile, smelling like cologne, usually dainty and light hearted, witty, talented and clever. But Gemini is a masculine sign, and as for Mercury, the planetary ruler of the Twins changes sex as unpredictably as the wind changes its course. So there will be times when she will offend his sense of manhood, other times when she flatters it. Her intellect will never fail to fascinate him, but he may be disappointed when he discovers that her intelligence is satisfied to skim the surface of most matters, to analyze then discard them, feeling no need to probe the depths, as he does in every subject from sin to sex, from religion to reincarnation, politics to polygamy.

All she needs to know about the Mormons is the name Brigham Young and something about Salt Lake City, Utah. All she needs to know about geology is the difference between turquoise and quartz; that the gold rush took place in Colorado, near Pikes Peak, and may occur again, if America goes back on the gold standard.

He needs to know much more—like Brigham Young's secret reason for wanting to bed down and board with, possess and father children with more than one woman. (Brigham was a Sun Sign Gemini, so let's hope Scorp doesn't probe too deeply. It might really disturb his tranquility regarding his relationship with her if he learned *that*.) As for gold, Scorpio needs more than surface knowledge. He wants to keep up with all the fluctuating gold prices, the details of assaying, the intricacies of sinking a mine shaft—and so on.

When it comes to the sexual side of love, it must always be remembered that, although Scorpio is a strongly sexed sign, the ability to maintain continence, chastity and self-control (as in the religious life of monks, priests, etc.) is equally marked in these males. Assuming he has fallen in love with a Gemini woman, he is presumably not one of the Scorpions who have chosen the rigid discipline of abstinence. He will not, however, look upon sex as a game, as a frivolous pastime or a promiscuous sport. Sex is the Secret of Life itself to him. A woman who understands and fulfills her Scorpio man's deeper desires need not worry about his faithfulness (unless his Sun Sign is greatly afflicted by malefic planets at birth). Normally, a Scorpio male who receives genuine and intense response from his mate will not look elsewhere.

An Eagle is very curious about sex in his youth, but he probably will have satisfied most of his curiosity by the time he marries. His attitude toward the physical mating of love is deeply passionate, overwhelmingly sensual, yet with a certain strain of purity woven through it, amounting to a religious fervor with a few Scorpios.

The trouble is that sex is *not* the Secret of Life itself to the Gemini woman. Her attitude is experimental, and the deeper secrets of sexual union are secondary in importance. Even those Gemini females whose Twin is promiscuous seldom wish to penetrate the mysteries of sex with any real feeling or intensity. It's just a pleasant pastime, that's all. Yet, her very detachment toward physical passion could cause the Scorpio man to find the Gemini woman absorbing sexually, a continual challenge to him to prove to her that sex and God are linked, that all creation is nothing without the blending of Man and Woman. You already know how Scorpio hates to lose (*refuses* to lose is a better way to state it). In the area of their intimate sexual union, he simply *must* win. With a harmonious Sun-Moon relationship between their birth charts, he'll keep trying over and over again, repeatedly, to explain this greatest of all mysteries to his Gemini woman. Lacking such an aspect between their Luminaries—or if other mutual planets in their horoscopes are in conflicting positions, he may do the unthinkable (for a Scorpio)—and become disloyal, rationalizing his breaking of their vows with the reason that he cannot bear the halfway measure of love he's receiving. And that will be truth. An Eagle *cannot*.

It might hearten him to know that, barring disharmony between their natal charts and Luminaries, his chances of achieving physical ecstasy with this lady and successfully teaching her the mysteries of love's total blending are rather good. For Scorpio represents the eighth astrological house of sex (among other matters) to Gemini. Therefore, she really does find him magnetic and compelling, never mind her pretended detachment. He'll just have to keep practicing.

This man's Pluto sense of integrity is difficult for the average or typical Gemini female to comprehend, unless she has the Moon or Ascendant in Scorpio herself. If so, these two can be wonderfully, unexpectedly happy, to the mystification of their relatives and friends, who see only the surface differences between them. Otherwise, the vibrations of the 6-8 Sun Sign Pattern may cause both of them to experience periods of deep unhappiness from time to time. She might feel he's trying to drown her in an ocean of suspicion, or be both frightened and puzzled over his inexplicable, ice-cold retreats within himself.

He may feel she's trying to tear him from his own soul, as a tornado uproots trees. Even so, if Gemini chooses, she's intelligent enough to figure a way to make the relationship work—and Scorpio is intuitive enough to know how to seal each break so it's stronger afterwards than ever before. If they each *desire* to do so. Desire is the key word. To intensely desire to rediscover and retain the brightness they first knew means that they love. And love can cement anything, even hearts that have broken into a thousand pieces.

☆ ☆ ☆ ☆ ☆ ☆

GEMINI *Man* SCORPIO *Woman*

"I daresay it will hurt a little," she warned him.

"Oh, I shan't cry," said Peter, who was already of opinion that he had never cried in his life. And he clenched his teeth and did not cry; and soon his shadow was behaving properly, though still a little creased.

A Gemini man possesses the unusual and uncommonly appealing quality of seeming to remain eternally youthful . . . not rare, I suppose, for one who is reborn each day, but rare enough to attract the normally self-contained and cautious Scorpio female into wondering what makes him scintillate with such multiple colors of the mood spectrum. Now, when a Scorpio girl starts to wonder, there's no stopping her until she's satisfied her wondering with complete knowing. That means coming closer to him —and closer . . . . . . and closer . . . . . . until she suddenly looks around herself with alarm.

Unexpectedly, she is standing between two people, one to either side of her, as different as day from night. Which one is the man she was pursuing closer and closer? Both. They are both the same man. A Gemini male is victim of the Twin syndrome, you know. Maybe she did know. Maybe she didn't. But whichever or whatever, it will upset and topple her natural, cool, poised "I can handle anything at all" auric projection. Can she handle this? Can she cope with this introverted-extroverted soul, this full-of-gladness, filled-with-sadness little boy, this coldly cruel yet sensitive and tender man? He's a maze of non-sequiturs, contradictions, denials and affirmations.

Never mind. She can cope. She is a Scorpio, and she can handle it, solve it, beat it, win it, conquer it—the seemingly impossible situation. Can she? I'm not sure. But *she* is sure. The Gemini man doesn't really care if she does or not. The very thought that this lovely, intense yet poised and womanly creature of depth and mystery is willing to *try* is excitement enough to elate him into whistling a brand-new tune and making a dazzling wish on the first star he sees.

To *guess* the outcome is far more thrilling to him than to *know* the outcome. For a Gemini to know removes all reason for existing. With her, *not* to know removes all reason for existing. Ah, yes! To paraphrase poor tortured Hamlet, "to know or not to know—*that* is the question." That is surely and positively the question between these two at all times, the question which must be answered, finally, before there is any hope of lasting mutual happiness.

You'll have to understand, or rather, *she'll* have to understand that a Gemini male is constitutionally and congenitally incapable of comprehending love as an eternal, searing passion in quite the total way she does. There may be Gemini men who love one woman *totally* forever (in fact, I once knew one myself), but these Twins are extremely few and far between, and even they are sometimes haunted by misty dreams of another face, weaving in and out of the steady love relationship—or there may be a break-up, before he returns to his true Soul-Mate, in such cases . . . or at the very least, he may privately wonder what experiences he might have missed by being monogamous. The more typical Gemini man enjoys the titillation of choosing which of several women to prefer and is shocked when one of his harmless, pretty larks turns out to be an eagle, especially if she turns out to be a Scorpio Eagle. The eagle is a monogamous creature in Nature. So are most human Scorpio Eagles, *by* nature. (Not all, just most. When we're dealing with Sun Signs, instead of with the entire horoscope, we have to consider the averages and over-all percentages.)

Venus is the planet of love, and Geminis are ruled by the planet Mercury, whose influence over Venus in the nativity, causes the emotions to be dispersed and frivolous. Pluto is the ruler of Scorpio, and this planet's effect on Venus is to make her influence deeply serious, powerful—but secret and hidden. You will notice the obvious differences in this treatment of Venus, Goddess of Love. Venus notices it, too, and becomes baffled when these two vibratory forces of Mercury and Pluto mix their rays. The Gemini man and Scorpio woman may not notice it right away, so busy are they being fascinated by each other's strangeness. One thing he will definitely find strange about her is the strongly imbedded Pluto form of jealousy. Scorpio jealousy is sometimes a passion even more consuming than the love which gave birth to it.

Gemini finds all forms of jealousy difficult to fathom. He is, of course, duly susceptible to the normal, small tugs of fear regarding the danger of losing his woman to another, like any average male—but the kind of overwhelming sea storms thundered by a Scorpio woman who feels threatened are incomprehensible to him. When this woman has been hurt, or even suspicions that she *might* be hurt, her Scorpio stinger can strike a deadly blow to the ego of the Gemini man who is innocent of the accusations made against him—or guilty as charged, either way. Most Pluto-ruled women find revenge sweet indeed. Therefore, if she is deceived, or suspects she's been, the retaliation will be swift and cruel, even vindictive, if her Sun was afflicted by major planets at her birth.

Knowing this, the Gemini man, whose nature cannot help being slightly flighty and fickle, should realize just what he could be facing should he make the mistake of attempting a light romance with such a girl, to whom there is no such thing as a light romance, only an all-consuming and everlasting passion. Other than an Aries female, no one can be as jealous as a Scorpion. But Aries has not the same compulsion to get even with the lover or husband as does Scorpio. Taurus and Cancer jealous? No, the word with these Sun Signs is possessive. They cry a lot and hurt inside deeply. But they cause violent scenes infrequently. Possessive and jealous are not quite the same. Any man who has ever loved a Scorpio woman will be well aware of the difference.

This is a 6-8 Sun Sign Pattern, Scorpio being the sixth house to Gemini and Gemini being the eighth house to Scorpio, so there will be a markedly noticeable amount of service and unselfish devotion to duty in the relationship, plus a strong sexual magnetism (felt only when the two people involved are lovers or mates. When the relationship involves relatives, friends, or business associates, different eighth house matters, other than sex, will be emphasized between them). The service will usually be offered from Scorpio to Gemini. The sexual vibration is the attraction Gemini has for Scorpio. Yet, oddly, the very last quality the typical Gemini has to offer is sexuality. Sex isn't an all-consuming interest to this man, unless it's accompanied by poetry, experimentation, far-out ideals, or intricate games of mental chess and checkers. He may exude tons of handsomeness, charm, masculinity, intelligence and romance, but he does not ordinarily exude excessive sexuality (to anyone but a Scorpio). Therefore, it seems strange that she should find him so physically irresistible—and often, he finds her the same way (although that's not so hard to comprehend).

Perhaps it's his elusive air of boyishness, the myriad tricks of his mirror images, changing from one mood into another before her eyes, that make her so determined to penetrate into the core of his heart and soul through their sexual union. He seems to hold a secret, ever so lightly—yet nonetheless, a secret—and an unsolved secret or a mystery which defies solution beckons to Scorpio as a flame entices a moth. She must know him—really, truly *know* him—to satisfy her mind and fulfill her heart. Consequently, the physical expression of their love will magnetize her, sometimes for many years, until she finally realizes that no one will ever know all the facets of this man, not even a Scorpion. About the same time, he will realize that he can never play his favorite game of "guess who" and "guess what I am" with her all the way. She won't discover every sliver of his private dreams, but she will unravel enough threads of his soul's fabric to frighten him into feeling that he is slowly, but surely, being more known than he cares to be. And so their physical blending, although it may begin as a compelling part of their love, could grow from cool to cold, and at last be the undoing of their romance, unless they each are willing to honestly face the things that trouble both of them—to truly *communicate*. Yet, she should not try to overanalyze their relationship.

He may tend to criticize and analyze *her*, since she's so full of silent intrigue, certainly not shallow. Yet, in doing so, he may be floating in deeper waters than he suspects. Scorpio does not take kindly to analysis, and the insistent questioning of the curious Gemini can cause her to retreat in sullen anger—or to lash out with a violent emotional response. Personal privacy is as sacred to her as it is to him, perhaps more so. The two of them should recognize this in one another and not insist upon exploring the things they find puzzling about each other until the resentment between them grows into a high thick wall.

To break down the wall, he'll try his charm, his old jokes, his most imaginative lovemaking, his multiple romantic techniques. She'll try her most sensuous mannerisms, her coolest detachment and most soothing gentleness. They'll both try every trick they have tucked in their sleeves, and that's quite a few tricks between the two of them (the three of them, counting his Twin). Yet the wall grows even higher and thicker. There must be a way over it. (There is.)

Sometimes, the only thing they *don't* try, in attempting to scale the wall that separates them, is to allow a little more space between their hearts so love can breathe free. He's willing, but she may fear a new and unaccustomed space between herself and her mate as she would fear a dark and unknown abyss stretching ahead. Space is made up of air, essentially, and since he is of the Air Element, he feels more at home when there is plenty of space around himself. But she is of the Water Element and must be surrounded with a flowing stream of togetherness or be unable to breathe herself.

It's always sad when the Gemini man and the Scorpio woman who once loved find they've lost the way to happiness, because he believes in things unseen, all magic and wonder, despite his computerlike mental equipment. So does she. She believes in even stranger and more wondrous unseen worlds than he. But the secretive, inexplicable forces of Pluto silence her, seal her lips and heart, and forbid her to speak of them as openly as he does. She will never be able to express her deepest dreams with as much facility as the glib Gemini. And herein lies the sadness.

If only he would not be so impatient with her intense passions, her emotional depths. If only she could find a way to whisper to his wandering spirit that she, too, longs to solve all the mysteries that lie out there among the stars and comets—that she, too, yearns to breathe free, to race the wind, and search for childhood miracles, half-forgotten . . . yet also half-remembered. The cool night air is infinitely more refreshing than the musty darkness of the damp caves of worry, where Scorpions are commanded by Pluto to move about when they are troubled.

Too often, this man and woman reach out to each other, not quite touching. They call to one another, but he hears only the music of the spring breeze—and she hears only the sound of the waves lashing the shore. If they would stop long enough to hear one another's secret cries, they might soar high enough together to see everything from a different perspective, including their relationship.

Their ruling planets can help them, if they *listen*. After all, Mercury and Pluto, along with Uranus, are the ones who taught Merlin all he knew, and also secretly guided Arian Houdini. Surely they can teach Gemini and Scorpio to mix a White Witch's brew of happiness. When your astral guardians are a couple of magicians like these, you should be able to detect illusion from reality—or discover that the two are interchangeable. Whichever.

☆ ☆ ☆ ☆ ☆ ☆

GEMINI

Air — Mutable — Positive
Ruled by Mercury
Symbol: The Twins
Day Forces — Masculine

SAGITTARIUS

Fire — Mutable — Positive
Ruled by Jupiter
Symbols: Archer & Centaur
Day Forces — Masculine

The GEMINI-SAGITTARIUS *Relationship*

. . . not three of them, but four!!

Sagittarians aren't always loud and active, out aiming their bows and arrows to shoot down hypocrisy and falsehood. Some of them are quite timid and introspective, almost owlish, with a decided pacifistic attitude—that is, they are pacifists who sometimes use their fists to put across their points about peace. (Is that a word—*pacifistic*? It is now.) Yet, even these will speak with blunt candor when their opinions are sought. Timid or pushy, all Sagittarians gaze at the world through the measuring eye of truth. What I'm attempting to make clear is that Sagittarius is a double sign, half-horse, half-man. There are two distinct types of Archers: those who take after the front end or *human* half of the Centaur—and those who take after the rear end or *equestrian* half. You may have met both types. I have.

By now, everyone knows that Gemini is also a double sign, symbolized by the Twins, dual in personality, multiple in word and action, myriad in Nature. Do you have any idea of the task involved in sorting out all these identities for the purpose of describing one complex relationship between just two people? The math alone is discouraging.

That Sagittarius friend or neighbor you have, think about him (or her). He-she may have a gift for zinging out the tactless verbal arrow of truth, yet is he (or she) the kind of Sag who acts like Bashful, of the Seven Dwarfs, at a party? All Jupiter sons and daughters are bright and witty, but the rare shy ones may hide it and can be almost self-effacing in front of strangers. Please note that I said the *rare* shy ones.

Now, skip to Winston Churchill, of the merry, twinkling Jupiter eye; John Lindsay, former mayor of New York City (an authentic textbook-type Sagittarian); elfish Mark Twain; the quiet (relatively quiet) Arthur Brisbane, formerly of the *New York Journal;* and, finally, move along to the last friendly puppy dog you saw wagging its tail (all friendly dogs are Sagittarians, by spiritual birthright) and tell me what they all have in common. (Throw in William F. Buckley, if you feel like it.)

All right, I'm an astrologer, I'm supposed to tell you. They have in common honesty, youthfulness, refreshing candor, wisdom and wit—and awkwardness, intermingled with gracefulness. I guess we can take it from there, keeping in mind constantly that although every Archer possesses these qualities, some of them are *extro*verts deluxe and some are *intro*verts deluxe. Be sure you remember that, please, because I'm not going to interrupt the main body of this chapter to remind you again. I don't want anybody to read this and keep interjecting: "But Marvin is so quiet"—or "Mildred is so shy." It has now been established that *some* Sagittarians *are* quiet, timid, and shy. But *more* of them are talkative and outgoing.

I get the feeling we are back where we started in the first paragraph, but we may have advanced slightly. You always face this astrological problem when dealing with the double signs. Thankfully, there are only three: Gemini, Sagittarius, and Pisces. Well, maybe you could throw in Libra. There are two sides to any set of Scales.

As for Geminis, they have no traits in common whatsoever, except the fact that each one of them is a double-mirror image, has two or more dispositions and personalities, which he or she can change as naturally and as quickly as you or I can change from swim suits to sweaters on a day when the wind can't make up its mind.

Gemini is Air, Sagittarius is Fire, and the back section of Volume II will tell you how these two elements mix. Quite superbly, most of the time. Disastrously, at others. But generally speaking, they do get on fairly well.

Gemini can incite Sagittarius into action—both negative and positive—that the Archer would never have taken without being stirred by the Twins. Air always fans Fire into higher flames. Sagittarius can make Gemini feel smothered occasionally, because fire burns out the oxygen in the air, but it can also warm it.

This is a 7-7 Sun Sign Pattern, so naturally, each is slightly envious of the other, because each possesses qualities the other does not have, but would secretly like to cultivate. Gemini needs the Archer's high motivation, ideals, warmth, enthusiasm, and sincerity—and needs also the Sagittarian's ability to travel over more terrain mentally, emotionally, geographically—to shoot for a star, and reach it.

Sagittarius longs for the cool poise and charm of Gemini, the talent for keeping the foot out of the mouth, for remaining cool and detached in the face of most disturbing situations, and especially needs the Gemini verbal adroitness, called *tact*.

When they get together, they have two choices. Each can admire the opposite traits of the other, and try to imitate them, in order to grow and mature spiritually. Or—each can fear and envy the opposite qualities of the other, and try to put them down, robbing each other of all pride in doing his (or her) own thing.

Both Gemini and Sag (pronounced to rhyme with badge) tend to be scintillating, rather than solid—dashing and daring, rather than dependable and enduring. Both have minds capable of high intelligence, but not necessarily designed for achievements of lasting design and construction (unless other planetary configurations in their birth charts give this quality—which, of course, in a number of cases, they do).

The ideas of both are more like shooting stars or comets than steady Suns. What can be accomplished in a few days by Gemini and Sagittarius will often be brilliant, but a project involving longer periods of time and effort may not come off so well, unless there are the just-mentioned supportive planet positions of strength and patience in the nativities. For knocking around together, instant empathy and general compatibility, the glittering Mercury-ruled and the benevolent Jupiter-ruled get along exceedingly well most of the time. But there's always the chance that sly Mercury (Gemini) may be unable to resist tricking sincere Jupiter (Sag) in some way, and the resentment of this may be violent (the Archer being of the Fire Element).

Sagittarians, while excessively emotional at times, are for the most part without guile. The clever, glib Gemini who plays mental chess games with the trusting Archer may later regret the harm done to another human being, however unintentional. According to ancient legends, the gods feel a special affection for these Sagittarian children of the zodiac, watchfully protecting them from those who would harm them. This is the basis for the so-called Jupiter "luck." A word to the wise is said to suffice, but not all Geminis are always wise, just clever—sometimes too clever and the Mercury Bird may, when least expected, trip in his (or her) own trap.

Gemini's quick wit, swift intellect and ease with words can seduce occasional Mercury Birds into becoming con artists supreme, tricky car salesmen and politicians, swindlers, drug pushers, or just plain, old-fashioned crooks. Yet, these very same qualities allow many Twins to become excellent teachers, literary geniuses, creative artists and musicians, clever mathematicians, brilliant scientists, and sincere and convincing salesmen of all manner of things. The Gemini duality calls these men and women in both directions. They're pulled on by both their Twin Selves, between day and night, dark and light, wrong and right—a spiritual struggle that continues, in a mild way, even with the prosaic, "ordinary" Geminians.

Most Geminis are far too intelligent and too fond of their freedom to risk apprehension and confinement by breaking the law, but those who do flirt with antisocial activities lean toward the light-fingered crimes, such as twirling combination locks on safes, forgery and counterfeiting. Seldom will a Gemini be guilty of homicide, although the Twins may be an "accomplice to murder." The Gemini criminal prefers to mastermind the crime and delegate the authority for the action to others, the tendency of all Mutuable Sign people.

There are always a few scattered and very rare notable exceptions that prove this, or any other rule, but only the smallest fraction of those confused souls who commit murder are Geminis. Killing requires more raw physical aggression than most Mercury-ruled people are able to muster. Violence offends the sensitivity of the average or typical Geminian.

All Geminis, of any age or sex, possess active, fertile minds, always operating at high speed, and never mind the quietness and placidity you notice in the surface personality of the *one* Twin who *appears* to be dominant in the Mercury personality. As quiet and placid as he or she may be, the brain is constantly busy, busy, busy. Don't judge a Gemini by his (or her) speech patterns alone. Carefully note the *results*. Somehow, things get done, and they get done fast, when Gemini chooses, however slow-appearing the outward activity may be. The pose of slowness is totally deceptive. The bottom line is what counts.

In fact, many Geminians deliberately choose just such a disguise to fool people. They allow the "quiet" Twin to be the "front" for the Mercury personality, and keep the swift, super-smart, restless Twin in the background at all times, directing the strategy, all unsuspected by the astrologically unenlightened. Notice the *eyes* of the deceptively quiet ones. You'll see a continual "twinkle," a quick darting look, taking in the scope of any situation in a glance. The eyes tell the story.

The essential and basic nature of Mercury-ruled people is very much like that of the Jupiter-ruled people—sunny, cheerful and optimistic (though Gemini is never as naive as Sag, even in youth). Later in life, both become cynical in varying degrees, yet somehow, still retain a certain childlike hope. Yes, I know that's contradictory, but the character of all double signs is contradictory. D-o-u-b-l-e. D-u-a-l. Two things at the same time. Simultaneous non sequiturs.

As for the poor Archers, they are not always quite so persuasive as Gemini, and frequently find themselves in hot water when they blurt out uncomfortable truths. Not that Sagittarians aren't charming. They possess oodles of rain-fresh, dew-drenched charm, but it quickly loses its power when they begin to fling a string of stinging words with very little subtlety or tact. Blunt is the word for Sagittarius, and bluntness doesn't win ball games. At least, not as many ball games as may be won by the verbally graceful and mentally adept Gemini, who often wins on sheer glibness alone. Gemini can be cutting in speech also, but only when he or she chooses to use the weapon of sarcasm.

Sagittarius is usually incapable of sarcasm. The Archer's sharp speech hurts only because of the ring of reality most people don't want to hear. Sarcasm requires a certain kind of *twisting* of the truth to make the truth *clearer* than Sag is normally capable of either handling or comprehending (unless, of course, the Archer's Moon or Ascendent is in Gemini).

It should be pointed out that those rare, quiet Sagittarians and Geminis who are keyed to a lower pitch (outwardly) than the large majority of Archers and Twins are seldom silent when they're together. Gemini has a way, by sheer auric vibration, of fanning the mildest Sag into a flaming spell of an unaccustomed monologue of words—sometimes happy and enthusiastic, at other times angry. In a similar manner, the Archer can stimulate a desire in the meeker (on the *surface*) Geminis to be more loquacious. But after these two have incited one another into conversation, they may not really listen to each other. They may appear to be listening, but actually, one is only waiting for the other to finish talking, so he (or she) can put across a contradictory opinion. A dramatic disagreement between them can get pretty noisy, with the need for a third party to referee. Or— one of the two will completely subdue the other, in which case, the subdued one will seek freedom from such restriction at the very earliest opportunity. In other words, leave. Sometimes, permanently.

Sagittarius tends more to inflict *emotional* blows to Gemini (although the Twins will make an attempt to hide such wounds behind a mask of cool boredom and disinterest) and Gemini is more likely to succeed in bending the Sagittarian *mind* into strange shapes, sometimes causing mental depression in the Jupiter person.

When these two (or four) are in harmony, however, through a positive Sun-Moon interchange between their birth charts, they can be fun to be around. One is always trying to top the other, and they'll also help each other over the rough spots, finding ways to express themselves, and to communicate, which is like a private language between them.

Often, Sag and Gemini will speak to each other's minds and hearts through music, poetry or art—or even body language (which is a very valid form of communication, and can be most eloquent). They reach out toward one another over waves of invisible enthusiasm and excitement . . . dreaming impossible dreams together . . . looking for four-leaf clovers . . . and finding them surprisingly often (thanks to Jupiter luck, and Mercury visual alertness) . . . reflecting, in their eyes, a soul comprehension of the mutual need and desire to imitate which all polarities influenced by the 7-7 Sun Sign Pattern recognize, somehow sensing that they are opposites, seeking to blend into completeness through communion with each other.

GEMINI *Woman* SAGITTARIUS *Man*

----◆◆◆----

*They broke into a bacchanalian dance, which brought
him to his feet at once; all traces of human weakness
gone, as if a bucket of water had passed over him.*

When the Twins (two personalities) of the Gemini girl-woman break into
a dance of delightful distortion and deviousness, right in front of the sincere eyes of the trusting Sagittarian, this man can, at first, feel oddly impotent—mentally and emotionally, if not physically. Then, suddenly, he's
aroused into meeting the obvious challenge of duality with which this female is teasing him.

In many ways, the Sagittarian Archer is a remarkable man. He has extraordinary vision and warmth, he is thoughtful and he is fluent. Hearing
him speak of his ideals, awash in enthusiasm, is a very special experience
to the alert Gemini girl, who simply must be intellectually fascinated to be
able to fall in love. He'll tell her some of his accomplishments (Archers
are never overly modest) and many of his dreams, and he'll always be
frank with her, sometimes mercilessly frank. If he doesn't quite answer all
her requirements for a lover or husband, well—it's only fair to point out
that no man ever does—or ever will.

As with all complex personalities, the Sagittarian man will grow to
know the Gemini girl only slowly. She withholds various fragments of her
multiple nature, allowing him to peek at but one at a time. When he first
meets her, she'll definitely withhold. She'll project only one Twin, the one
capable of charming him, naturally. She could even behave in a rare—for
her—monolithic manner, listening pleasantly, but seldom chattering or interrupting. What a perfectly delightful feminine creature she is! And it's
true. A Gemini girl-woman (it's more accurate to call her girl than
woman, at any age) is perfectly delightful. But as for feminine, we must
always remember that Gemini is essentially a masculine sign in astrology,
although Mercury, her ruler, can change sex in the twinkling of an eye, to
fool onlookers. Still, masculine is masculine, whatever that means today.
With this girl-woman it means she is usually quite determined to get what
she wants—also exceedingly capable of getting it. The trouble is, being
cursed with twin desires and dual motivation, she is never sure exactly
what she wants. What she longed for on Monday may be faded and unat-
tractive by Thursday, perhaps even as early as Tuesday (of the same

week). Often, she's torn between not only two sets of possible actions, but two sets of possible *reactions*. Should she say yes or no? And further—will saying either make her happy—or unhappy? He should have a little sympathy for her. Life is never easy for this woman, and love presents a problem of even greater dimensions. Then, when she does try to explain her many-faceted emotions to the Sagittarian man she has finally decided to trust, she risks being accused by him of insincerity and deception. Is that fair?

Frank, open-hearted, and honest, the Sagittarian man is sometimes intolerant of a female he believes is not all these things herself, never mind the clever Mercurial excuses she offers. Yet she might argue back, quite correctly, that he also has two sides—for he is bold, daring and restless, and at the same time sensitive, impressionable and retiring—or rather, at different times. His two sides manifest themselves in varying moods, his likes and dislikes are very pronounced and he's extremely susceptible to tension or disharmony in his environment, especially in his love relationship. This means he can be a little edgy, easily set off by Gemini airy circumlocution into a fiery Sagittarius explosion. So it's no wonder that she may prefer to keep some things back, and allow herself to be called deceptive, rather than risk walking the plank of his disapproval. When Archers express their disapproval, it can be brutally blunt and to the point, hurtful in the extreme. This sort of thing, after being repeated several times, can trigger her into sharpening the famous Gemini verbal weapon of sarcasm, all of which can cause the love nest to shake a bit, with the Mercury Bird causing the Centaur to become mentally confused, and he, in return, slashing some deep wounds in her fragile emotions.

However, if their Sun-Moon aspects are harmonious (conjunct, sextile or trine) these little differences of opinion and techniques of controversy will almost always end up in poetic (her) and dramatic (him) declarations of renewed devotion. It's all very romantic. But a square or opposition between the Sun of one and the Moon of the other can cause constant bickering and ruffling of feathers, which could grow into more serious confrontation as the years pass. Considering that we're discussing Gemini and Sag, we'd better amend that last sentence to say "as the months pass, even the weeks." These two signs always manage to increase both Life's—and Love's—rate of speed.

Her soaring flights of fairyland fancies can be too intangible and mystical for him. There is little or no impracticality in Jupiter visions. Most Sagittarians are capable of foreseeing and prognosticating the outcome of a plan from its initial inception. Most Geminis are not, and she would do well to imitate those qualities in him which she lacks, among them constancy of purpose and single-mindedness. Being Air, she is cooler emotionally than this man, whose nature is more fiery and passionate. Therefore, he may be the more affectionate of the two in the physical expression of love—more in need of the touching things. She would be happier if their minds touched more often.

Sexually the two of them possibly could reach a rare harmony of mutual experience through their lovemaking, because the ultimate meaning of sex is the fulfillment of an intense desire for each person to blend with —to actually *become*—the other, inasmuch as this is an earthly possibility, in order to achieve Oneness of spirit, mind and body. No two people can be more successful in this than this man and woman of opposite Sun Sign polarity, since sex between them—as with all 7-7 influenced lovers—is always based on their basic mutual need to *become each other*, and therefore, to become a more complete person.

With some Gemini-Sag relationships, a sort of truce is managed, causing very little quarreling to be observed or heard by friends and neighbors. (I won't say by families or relatives, because neither one of them is excessively devoted to blood ties.) When such periods of peace and quiet are observed, it can usually be credited to her Gemini talent for escaping anything unpleasant. Her power to resist obstacles or to push disagreeable people aside is not great at all, but her magnificent sensorium, or network of sensitive nerve signals, often warns her in advance of approaching thunderstorms, so she can duck under a tree and avoid getting wet, or being struck by lightning.

She sidesteps the issues with her Mercury agility, or simply pretends not to understand why he is so upset—and after a while, the typical Archer will give up trying to pin her down to a discussion that actually goes anywhere. It always winds up twisting in circles, which doesn't bother her—she loves circles—but which can leave him mentally and emotionally exhausted. So he could retreat more and more into the newspaper, go out—or go to bed early—and alone—while their communication suffers.

This isn't the best possible state of affairs, of course, but it does make them more desirable neighbors than the type of Gemini-Sagittarius couple who argue all night, expressing every disagreement loudly and clearly. It's seldom that these two will love without some amount of tension, however excellent their Sun-Moon aspects. Their basic natures are not the kind to suffer in absolute, masochistic silence. Since they constitute a 7-7 Sun Sign Pattern, there are always all those opposing qualities which have to be balanced, and balancing is an art which is mastered only after long practice. Ask any tightrope walker in a circus. Of course, so much balancing can wear them out from time to time, but it's better to wear out than rust out, as many lovers do, who have nothing in common at all, not even a mutual desire to adopt each other's different vices and virtues. Gemini and Sagittarius do have some things in common. They both like to read and they both like to talk. But she colors what she reads with her vivid imagination, and he sprinkles his talk with more truth, perhaps, than she wants to hear or dares to face.

She believes the world should be a better place, and her weaving bits and pieces of colorful imagery distorts the truth of existence just enough to make it so for her. Is that wrong? To him it is. He wants the world to be a better place also, but he's convinced that you first have to face the facts square-on before you can hope to change them. *In this, they differ deeply.*

This man and this woman can find much happiness in their relationship if it is also a marriage of mutual endeavor, like a husband-wife team involved in publicity, publishing, the arts, science or medicine. The excitement of the dream will carry them through any minor squalls. When their eyes are fastened on the stars, instead of constantly on each other, they can make a fabulous team, in every way. In Greek mythology, it's said that "Mercury gives joy to Jupiter." Likewise, Gemini can give to Sagittarius—great joy. What can he give her? He can give her the gift of slowing her down, of protecting her with his larger wings, for the Archer likes to fly, too, in his imagination, as high as his arrows. But maybe these lovers should stay just a little distance apart, as they sail the kites of their aspirations. If they stand too close together, on a windy day, the strings may get hopelessly tangled.

The Sagittarian man was born full of *ideals*. The Gemini woman was born full of *ideas*. There is a difference between the two words—the letter *l*, for *love*. An *idea*, when it's nurtured with love, will reach for the higher octave of itself, and become an *ideal*. If they love enough, the Archer can take his Gemini lady's ideas, transmute them into Jupiter ideals, and illuminate her already-bright mind with the light of the difference.

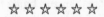

GEMINI *Man* SAGITTARIUS *Woman*

---

*Also he was fond of variety, and the sport that
engrossed him one moment would suddenly cease to
engage him, so there was always the possibility
that the next time you fell he would let you go.*

When a Sagittarius girl falls in love, her whole spirit reaches out like a trusting puppy, hungry for affection, ready to return it in full measure. Only later do the accumulated mistakes of the years cause her to wear the theatrical mask of skepticism and cynicism, which she covers with the bright greasepainted features of the clown. Her innate honesty and refreshing frankness would touch the hardest masculine heart. But sometimes it only tempts a certain kind of Gemini male to test his cleverness by twisting her integrity, her ideals, and even her love, with complex mind-bending games. He courts disaster by doing this. Not his. Hers. Gemini, somehow, always manages to escape in the final reel. It's the sincerely brokenhearted Sagittarian girl who bears the scars of such abusive tactics of the Mercury intellect, sometimes for many moons . . . sometimes permanently.

Before it's over, however, she may call on Jupiter's power of excess, and tear a few jagged holes in the fabric of the Twins' precious freedom robe, with some fiery, emotional scenes of furious passion, which (if he's the type of Gemini we're describing, who has allowed his negative Twin to take control of him) he will probably richly deserve.

This girl is warm, open-hearted, desperately in need of both affection and emotional stability. If the Sun-Moon interchange in their horoscopes is negative, she could be shopping for it in the wrong place, for Gemini can be cruelly detached, cold and unsympathetic when his negative Twin takes over. What happened to the light, gay, tender, loving man she thought he was, the one who wrote such moving poems to her, who raced her to the Moon and back, kissed away her tears with that little-boy-lopsided-grin? He's still there, playing an unkind game of hide-and-seek, somewhere within the multiple-reflected image identities of this complicated man. He can leave her weeping, with an uncaring, bored shrug of his shoulders . . . with not even a backward glance of regret, and the next day, return with a bunch of violets, a new poem and his old gentleness, begging forgiveness and swearing his devotion anew.

It's hardly the thing she needs. A Sagittarius girl is deeply vulnerable. This sort of on-again, off-again romance, ranging from cruel iciness to detached boredom (and frequently outright deception) mingled with beautiful romance, from a man who can charm hissing serpents into docility, may cause her to tremble in her soul, make her unsure of herself as a female, or even as a human being. About this time, he may start his pseudo-psychoanalysis. He isn't the one who needs therapy. It's *she*. He might even manage to convince her of this probable lie. Geminis can convince anyone of anything the first dozen times, until their gullible victims catch on to the trickery. A Mercury-ruled man can commit the most outrageous deeds, then expect the woman who loves him to apologize to *him* as if the misdeeds were her own. You can see why these men make super salesmen. They can sell anything to anyone, and what's more, they seldom get caught when they slip under the line or skip around the alphabet, avoiding the letter of the law of love—or any other kind of law.

Of course, this is only true of Geminis whose natal Suns are severely afflicted by heavy planets at birth. Such Twins deserve to be astrologically exposed to Sagittarian girls who might find a tragic end to romance with this type. The great majority of Gemini men, thankfully, possess far more intelligence and wit than flaws of character.

Still, it must not be forgotten that the negative-type Geminis have broken more hearts and shredded more lives than could be pieced back together with an ocean of Elmer's glue. They have no sympathy coming to them until they become more introspective, and show some compassion for the havoc they caused others through their lack of human warmth, their cruel and curious need to win every game of mental blackjack they play. Unfortunately, even this kind of Gemini is almost irresistible in the act of asking, with apparently innocent eyes (though they are shifting, if you look closely), "Who, me?" Yes, *you*. One can often spot this brand of Gemini male by the number of aliases or pseudonyms he uses. Many positive Mercury people playfully hide behind several names, but *this* type does it for more sinister reasons. Isn't that right, Jim? I mean David—or is it Mel —or Fred? Whatever. By their words and deeds shall ye know them. If only they would truly know themselves.

The more illuminated, charming and near-magical Gemini man has a strong appeal for the typical Sagittarius woman, however—and she for him. Opposites don't always attract, but when they are members of opposite sexes (opposing male and female) they often do. Gemini and Sagittarius are horoscopically opposed, and the powerful pull begins with this feeling each has that the other has qualities intensely desirable of attainment. It's true. Each does possess what the other lacks. Consequently, they can teach one another many marvelous lessons that rhyme with happy. The physical magnetism between them is difficult to resist. So are the mental and emotional vibrations. And so, it is with a haunting wonder that they gravitate toward each other . . . . if they meet under the right planetary aspects, when the stars are smiling on a breezy night, and the Moon is new enough to wish on.

They share an eternal youthfulness of spirit, an inquisitive turn of mind, a responsiveness to Nature and a mutual need for freedom, for space between them, so they can move toward their goals. Both of them like to dream alone for a while, then return to each other's arms for encouragement. But alone is not the same as lonely. Both the Gemini man and the Sagittarius woman seek the gregarious life, surrounding themselves with people, because they have a secret fear of loneliness.

She will almost surely have a pet. A kitten or a dog. And give it odd names. The most precious girl Archer I know named one of her kittens "Frog," the other simply (logically) "Cat." He likes pets too, but may not feel quite the same fierce devotion as she does. Gemini will love a pet only as long as it doesn't interfere with his own pleasures or require money he would prefer to spend on himself, whereas a Sagittarian woman will often sacrifice her own convenience for an animal she loves. There are other subtle differences in their natures. Gemini thirsts for new horizons to soar, and so does she. But she also has need of a warm and steady hand to hold while she's soaring. He likes to hold hands too, but if *she* lets go, he'll wave goodbye more or less cheerily, while she may lose her way if *he* lets go.

Their sexual life is usually where they find solace from their conflicts in other areas, as with all 7-7 Sun Sign Patterns. The strong chemical attraction between them frequently increases as time goes by, and even if it should decrease, it seems to always be there, latent, waiting to be rekindled, to be called upon to mend the cracks in their relationship.

There is a certain passion of the mind between them, which creates a fertile ground for physical consummation. Often, their sexual lovemaking will begin long before bedtime—perhaps at breakfast, through messages spoken by the eyes across the room, a romantic note left where she will find it, the shared intimacy of a familiar smile or special, private nickname which, translated, means: "I love you—I need you—I want you."

The pitfall of the sex between them is that he may use Gemini trickery on her occasionally. A Gemini male is not above inciting a quarrel for the deliberate purpose of increasing emotion or desire in his partner. Anger has a strange way of exciting passion between these two. Then the argument is resolved by physical union—or it should be. But is it? He's capable of bringing it up for lengthy discussion again after their closeness, when it should have been buried and forgotten. To be fair to him, we have to admit that she tends to do the same thing. They should both learn to bury disagreements after intimacy. Why use sex as a weapon against each other? But Gemini and Sagittarius often do. Jealousy is the cause of many of their disputes, with good reason. Neither sign is noted for impeccable faithfulness. Both are too curious, too changeable, too moody and desirous of variety to be snowflake-pure-loyal.

If their Sun-Moon aspects are favorable, or if one has a Capricorn, Taurus or Scorpio Ascendent, they can manage to remain totally faithful as long as they're together. Otherwise, there will be some straying or infidelity, even if it takes the form of only a casual, light flirtation, out in the open, never physically consummated. He is more apt to wander than she. But Sagittarian girls catch on quickly to the various games taught them by Mercury Birds. Then the feathers will fly.

He can be so . . . . . moody. First, the quick blush of happiness, the beating wings of excitement. Then the frown, suddenly, with no warning. The averted eyes. Sadness, deepening into depression. Moments later, the Mercurial quicksilver grin again—and a merry invitation to skip pebbles in the lake or listen to frogs sing love songs at the edge of a magical woodland he knows. First he asks her to make cinnamon toast. Then he's not hungry. With variations, the theme of their romance goes pretty much like that, and she still bravely tries to sing along.

Of course, the Sagittarius woman can have a few moods herself. Being also a dual sign, she can change from sensitive to introspective, then back to temperamental and caustic. If one can manage to stay "up" while the other is "down," and vice versa, they can pull each other through the scary times. Both "up" together would be nice, but then that means they will both be "down" together. Two Biorhythm charts would benefit this man and woman immensely. The name is Biorhythm Computers, Inc., 298 Fifth Avenue, New York, N.Y. (212-239-8422). I couldn't give them a nicer gift than that advice and name.

He'll have to curb his tendency to sarcasm when he's annoyed; and she'll have to curb her tendency to tactless remarks, when what he needs is her tenderness and her understanding. Her blunt truth almost always hurts. So does his sarcasm. The Sagittarius girl, with all her innocent candor, has no conception of the word. It means . . . well, sarcasm usually means saying something exactly the opposite from what you really think and believe, and exaggerating the falsehood for emphasis of the truth, such as—"Of *course* I don't object to a three-hundred-dollar phone bill, darling. It makes me feel important to pay the telephone company all that money, even if it does mean we have to cancel our vacation this summer." You see? Like that. Sarcasm. She'll be both hurt and puzzled. Why doesn't he just say straight out that he's angry about the phone bill being so high, and disappointed that it might mean no vacation this summer? (Then she could say she's sorry, and work overtime, or take an extra job for a few weeks, to make up the difference. As it is, she *won't* say she's sorry, so there!)

Why doesn't he just say so? Because he's a poetic dreamer, a Gemini, dear girl, incapable of saying exactly what he means. To live in any degree of contentment with this clever and marvelously fascinating man, Sag will have to pay attention not to what his lips say but read the truth only in his eyes. Yet, his eyes are forever darting here and there, and are often difficult to read . . . the expression in them keeps changing.

The only thing more stinging than the Gemini man's sharp sarcasm is the girl Archer's blunt honesty. This pair, when they're ill-mated, can verbally slice each other's hearts to ribbons. But there's a lighter side to their relationship. There's always another side, when two double signs get together, for better or for worse—and it *can* be better. They will at least respect one another's intellect, and find their mutual moods more fascinating than the boring sameness of others.

A Gemini man likes to gaze at the galaxies, meditating on the myriad worlds out there in space. Then unexpectedly, he shifts his awareness to himself, and wonders—"Do you suppose there are also myriad worlds within the space of ME, that I might explore?" His ever-present Twin cries, "Yes! There are!" . . . . . and another adventure begins. If the Sagittarian woman wants to hold this man, her labor of love will be to join him on his quest for the Neverland, trying not to resent the third person who must always tag along—his shadow. She might also try, as Wendy did with the Mercurial Peter Pan, to stitch his shadow to him tightly and neatly. So he won't lose the other half of himself so often. That's a kind of riddle, but Jupiter will whisper to her heart the answer, if she listens.

GEMINI

Air — Mutable — Positive
Ruled by Mercury
Symbol: The Twins
Day Forces — Masculine

CAPRICORN

Earth — Cardinal — Negative
Ruled by Saturn
Symbol: The Goat
Night Forces — Feminine

The **GEMINI-CAPRICORN** *Relationship*

The roar of it echoed through the mountains, and the echoes seemed to cry savagely, "Where are they, where are they, where are they?"

hat are these Gemini people trying to do? Where do they stand? Where are they?" cries the honestly puzzled Capricorn, trying to deal with the Twins. "They are nowhere," answers the astrologer. "They are nowhere, yet they are everywhere. It is difficult to tell, without taking into consideration that each Gemini is at least two people."

Do you think for one minute that a Goat is going to stand for that kind of an obtuse answer? No way. It's too ephemeral, entirely too abstract to be a practical solution to the problem. So don't try astrology on Capricorns whose lives are being tossed out of their orbit of set routine by the antics of a pair of Twins hiding within one Gemini. It won't work. I'm not sure just what will work, but that won't work.

You might try explaining Gemini to Capricorn by pointing out that Gemini is an Air Sign, therefore Mercury-ruled people are very much like the wind. The wind is invisible, yet strong. It can be a friend or an enemy. It's more or less neutral (like Switzerland). Sometimes it will uproot entire buildings. Sometimes it will not. There's just no telling with the wind—or with Gemini. The wind is free and unpredictable, and it's impossible to guess in which direction it will blow. It is a question asked only by the foolish; consequently, any astrologer who tries to answer it is a fool. Still, all that won't cut any ice or slice any pickles with the Goat, who will, after all your trouble, continue to demand which way this particular Gemini's wind (or hot air) is blowing. Just tell him North. It is blowing North. Then forget about it. Even if Gemini's emotional wind was blowing South, East, or West at the time under discussion, you can be sure it will be blowing North within a couple of hours. You see? There are always ways to handle these things if you try.

The taciturn Capricorn will not admire Gemini's verbal gift if it becomes too profuse. Although most Goats enjoy listening vicariously to gossip about the famous (those who have achieved, if only in their own communities), they are seldom inclined to partake of it personally. (Gossip, I mean. They are *always* willing to partake of fame.) To Saturn, the ruler of Capricorn, caution is the beginning of wisdom, in speech as well as in action. Symbolically, Saturn is the planet of wisdom gained through long tests of initiation in many incarnations, traditionally the ruler of the Hebrew culture. Also the ruler of exasperatingly bossy employers, grandparents, anyone in authority, including the government—all those people and institutions tending to get their kicks from saying "NO." "Absolutely, NO"—(for your own good, of course). "Yes" is a foreign word to the typical Goat.

Capricorns have trouble even pronouncing it, some of them substituting words like "okay" or "I-suppose-so." I even know a Colorado Goat who substitutes the word "Yippee" (spoken very softly) for YES—an inexplicable habit, but nonetheless typical. So, Cappy does not like to say YES. I think it has something to do with money or financial security. To Capricorns, "no" seems to rhyme more with "dough"—and "yes" rhymes with "less," especially when it's spoken without due and proper consideration. Something like that.

This is a 6-8 Sun Sign Pattern, meaning that Capricorn will attract Gemini for a reason relating to mystery, death, sex, reincarnation, hypnosis, psychiatry—or some bending of the mind, even drugs. One of these areas will be involved in a subtle way or subconsciously. As for the reverse, the Goat will always find some useful purpose for the Twins, and often Gemini will end up by in some way serving the slightly selfish Capricorn. Self-sacrifice of one kind or another is bound to be present in the relationship, whether it be within the realm of the family group, business, friendship or lovers. But then, someone has to sacrifice when two people are as essentially different in character as these two.

Capricorns are clothed in an antique and thoroughly elegant manner, such an exalted aura being only proper as the means of radiating the Saturnine wisdom and skill through experience. The attitudes of some Goats almost whiff of mothballs. Most of them despise modern furniture, leaning more toward the traditional, the old, the *lasting*. Let Geminis pursue the trains of modern thought, deck their homes with plastic and shining chrome. To Cappy, the tried and true seems more sensible. No one can argue the superiority of craftsmanship. I certainly wouldn't. But Gemini might. The Mercury-ruled can argue on behalf of any weak point and make it seem reasonable or feasible. Except to the Goat. Capricorns are rarely the victims of Gemini persuasion. Oh, it happens, but when it does, which is seldom, Cappies will catch on quickly to the manipulative mental game, sense that crooked psychological dice are being used against them, and back away, determined not to be caught twice with their caution down.

There's more than a trace of the magnificence and serenity of Nature in Capricorns, something of the mountain goat's dignified bearing. All this naturally draws the restless Gemini, who seeks repose of the spirit more desperately than is ever shown or admitted. The serious but kindly and gentle Capricorn man, woman or child can supply a stable, calm, and rational basis of emotional security that the Twins find both comforting and necessary, a place to fold their wings between flights. Life moves so swiftly for Gemini, it's often a frightening blur, and on occasion, they need to have the inner frenzy stilled. Capricorn seems almost to be a resident of stillness, of silent, deep-green woods, and can bring many moments of tranquility to the Twins who stop to rest awhile. With Capricorn, Gemini may study the forms of Life and Love at Saturn's more leisurely pace.

There are also lessons Capricorn can learn from Gemini. Innocently self-centered, intellectually independent and curious, Gemini is magically able to temporarily enter the realms of every book ever read, every movie ever seen, every symphony ever heard—to move as naturally and freely in that so-called imaginary world as if it were the kingdom of his or her birth.

Consequently, the Twins can present the Goats with the valuable knowledge of how to be more than just a visitor to the worlds of literature, music, art—for these worlds of make-believe are where they live. Gemini returns to this Earth only by karmic obligation, to re-enter a flesh prison after a long spell of daydreaming on other levels of awareness. Capricorn benefits from this, because it is so difficult for the Goat to comprehend the reality of any place but Earth, Capricorn being so rooted in it, so practical and *down*-to-earth on both a conscious and a subconscious level.

There are, of course, rare Capricorns whose imaginations flash during a summer thunderstorm, whose spirits wonder and wander on a quiet, star-filled night, who display a pixie sense of humor, understand about psychometry, UFOs, telepathy . . . . and the Great Pyramid's mysterious wonders. But the more typical Goat does not waste time pondering anything which can't be taken apart and put back together again by blueprint. When Capricorns fly, they make their reservations early, to be safe. When they go by car, they take a road map, to be sure. But there are no blueprints, no maps to guide the astral traveler. Trips out-of-the-body, into worlds beyond the material or the physical senses, don't require a reservation—only faith.

It must be admitted that Gemini, when investigating other worlds, is not necessarily motivated by faith or spiritual hunger. The Twins are usually motivated by simple curiosity, the kind that killed the legendary cat but doesn't seem to be fatal to Mercury Birds.

A surprising number of Capricorns satisfy their soul hunger in the Saturn-approved method of becoming involved in art. They sometimes collect it, enjoy it, become patrons of artists—or paint, sketch or draw themselves. Some enter the acting profession or become dramatists. A few follow music in some manner. But whatever the Goat is or does, both feet will remain planted firmly on terra firma, and how far can you swing on a star when both feet are on the ground? It requires a bit of stretching to enter other galaxies. Still, any creative endeavor of any kind is akin to a dawning comprehension of an existence beyond the five senses, bearing a hint of a sixth, even a seventh . . . . and more. The ancients claimed that Saturn is a seventh-dimensional planet. We live our daily lives in the third dimension, while Time itself, an eternal Now, as Einstein knew, is the fourth dimension. Surely the seventh must carry a higher wisdom than even Gemini can contemplate. But Saturn guards its secret well, with the usual Capricorn reticence and silence.

Capricorns are inclined to keep their own counsel. Geminis are born and natural communicators. Which is right? Both are—each in his or her own way, as long as neither interferes with the other doing his own thing. Or her own thing. With these two Sun Signs, doing *"their* own thing" is rare. But the dictionary definition of "rare" gives a choice between "uncommon" . . . . or "very beautiful."

☆ ☆ ☆ ☆ ☆ ☆

GEMINI *Woman* CAPRICORN *Man*

—◄◆►—

> . . . . . *the island was looking out for them. It is only thus that anyone may sight those magic shores.*
>
> *"There it is," said Peter calmly.*
>
> *"Where, where?"*
>
> *"Where all the arrows are pointing."*

No matter how brief or long a time these two remain together, the Capricorn man will never be able to figure out why the Gemini girl cannot see clearly what to him is very plain: the consequences of word and action, which are, inevitably, either reward or punishment. Newton's law of "For every action, there is a *reaction"* is obvious to him. Why can she not see it too?

To her way of looking at things, his error is in seeing the material world as reality—and imagination as a separate, amusing pastime. Her own mind is busy probing, dissecting, searching, calculating and wandering on the wind, all at once, which can cause two worlds to fuse as one—the "real" world and the world of imagination, of *possibilities.*

The responses such a mercurial attitude evoke in the Goat are multiple and consecutive. First, he responds with excitement. After a while, excitement turns to apprehension. None of these things she says and does make sense to him, from a logical, practical standpoint. Finally, his apprehension turns to severity—and then he turns off. Once Capricorn has decided a subject is not worth discussing, that's it. He can be abrupt, terse and stern. "We won't talk about it anymore. The subject is closed." No

subject is ever completely closed to the Gemini girl. It is always open for
new argument, fresh points of view. Yet, even with all her charm, she will
have difficulty turning the Goat back on, once he's been turned off.

Gemini's occasional frenetic activity may seem frivolous to Cappy. She
has an apparent lack of attachment in her engagement with Life. But he
will find sufficient cause for admiration in studying the amazing way her
mind works—untangling knots with the greatest of ease, arriving at solutions to intricate problems effortlessly. And she will, initially at least, respect his wisdom—a different matter altogether from her own quick intellect and cleverness. This can create a bond of yearning between them,
which can be both purifying and strengthening. After a time, however,
the essential differences in their natures may become more visible. There
is a certain gravity to Capricorn which can depress her—a curious moodiness in her own make-up which can be disturbing to him. Often, their dispositions, personalities, characters and motivations are miles apart.

Let's take their mutual families. If he's a typical Capricorn, he is very
close to Mummy, Daddy, Auntie, Uncle Hymie—and cousins by the car-
load. No, I didn't forget his siblings. How could anyone forget them when
they are around so much? When they aren't around, he talks about
them. If she's a typical Gemini, she may be genuinely fond of her folks,
even behaving affectionately toward them in an airy, casual way. But she
does not feel quite so cemented to family ties as the Goat. She goes her
multiple ways, they go theirs, and if their paths should cross now and
then—great! If she refuses to allow her own relatives to smother her, obviously she isn't going to be overjoyed about having *his* camping around all
the time and being the main topic of conversation, even in their absence.

Then there's the way they feel about money. They both like it. Neither
of them has a thing against it. But she uses it to spread around, to spend
and enjoy. He uses it as a sort of emotional tranquilizer. As long as he
knows it's in the bank, he can relax and breathe easy, confident in the
knowledge that he's a solid citizen, to whom no unpredictable financial
disasters can occur. Capricorn feels about money the way gold-mining
king Winfield Scott Stratton felt about gold—that the safest place to keep
it is in the ground. To Cappy, the safest place to keep money is in the
bank. The Gemini woman can't comprehend what good it does to have it
just sitting there doing nothing when it could be spent. Interest, my dear.
It draws interest. Then she might say, with one of her sudden Mercurial
twists of mind, "but that only makes *more* money—to leave just sitting
there, doing nothing." What does she mean, doing *nothing*? It's *working*,
isn't it? And it's giving him peace of mind. It's giving *her* a bad case of
frustration.

When the Capricorn man is upset, cross, or out of sorts, he pouts, becomes silent and sullen. When she is in the same state, she can be caustic, bitter and sarcastic. His moods are dark brown, indigo, black and blue, yet they are, to some extent, predictable. Hers never are. One moment she can be as gently exhilarating as a spring breeze, the next, as destructive as a tornado—first restlessly active, then passive and uncommunicative. She smiles, her expressive eyes flashing quicksilver loveliness. Enchanting. Out of nowhere, a frown line appears on her forehead. Now there's a tear in the corner of her eye. Her lips tremble. She is beautiful when she is sad. Suddenly a joyous thought overcomes her, she leaps up, throws her arms around him and plants a kiss on his nose. Her changing moods are as flighty as Tinker Bell's, by turns all frivolous fancy, like a butterfly, then logically concise, one after the other, in swift progression . . . . . first deeply intellectual, then totally abstract, almost mystical. But she does not remain in the dreamy state for long. Gemini is too much of a natural skeptic to be a true mystic.

Now and then, one comes across a Capricorn man who loves to solve mysteries, to answer riddles, and this kind of Goat will follow the Twins down the twisting, turning Mercurial bypaths and shortcuts with overwhelming fascination. She is like the multicolored, scattered pieces of a puzzle, waiting to be put together. Besides, she is dainty and feminine, with a lilting laugh, and she looks good on his arm. Capricorns do enjoy possessing a woman of the type who may be shown off to advantage in front of others. To gain the love of such an exciting creature is assuredly an achievement, an accomplishment of no small order, and the Saturn-ruled have this thing about achievement and accomplishment. The Goat must climb. Capricorn men enjoy the view from the top of the mountain. They like to be looked up to and respected. Displaying a Gemini wife or lover (with him it will probably be wife) who is several women in one, each charming, lovely, talented, bright and feminine—will cause less fortunate males to envy him. Just so he remembers the astrological advice that, regardless of her delightful femininity, her mind is masculine. This will be brought home to him on more than one occasion.

There are Capricorn men who infrequently kick up their heels in a merry dance, especially in later life when they rush to capture what they never discovered in youth, or were too shy to seek, too busy achieving and working to enjoy—just as there are some Goats who are quicker of movement, faster of speech, more careless than cautious. But these are definitely exceptions to Saturn's rule. Most Goats are models of restraint. In fact, his romantic overtures in the beginning are often so tremulous and cautious, so slow and deliberate, that she at first inclines her head to one side, as if she were harkening to a whisper. He'll probably be wearing clothing of subdued good taste, smile at her in a particularly engaging, lazy fashion, his gentleness and soothing stability mingled in just the right amounts to intrigue her into thinking this is one man who will understand her, and not be impatient with her.

He seems happy to please her, touchingly grateful to have a woman to please. It brings him contentment to be in love, and she senses he is not one to be unfaithful to his vows, once committed. It is at this point, perversely, that she may get nervous. It's the word "commitment." Geminis do not like even a hint of commitment. If love is real, it will last. She would like that, of course, but she would not like to sign any long-term leases on romance. Just let it develop. If it turns into a forever thing, wonderful! But to ask for a guarantee—to *expect* a guarantee—is not the way the game is played with Gemini.

In a physical sense, they may surprise each other by exchanging an instinctive understanding of mutual longings. Sex is not something akin to blazing fires of uncontrollable passion to either of them. Both Capricorn and Gemini seek sexual unity as a means of rest and comfort. Normally, they will not make excessive emotional demands of one another. However, there may be infrequent occasions when his need for playful physical and affectionate displays of bear hugs and the like do not find the desired response in her—or when the Gemini woman needs words of love, verbal expressions to excite her into lovemaking, and does not receive them.

Other than such areas of possible discontent and mild frustration, these two could be cozily compatible in their sexual sharing of love. Because their togetherness is influenced strongly by the 6-8 vibration, sex may be a dominant, or at least a most important factor in their relationship, and he will possibly have magnetized her in the beginning in a strongly physical way, which is not likely to fade, as long as they remain together, which will likely be permanently, surprising all their friends (and his relatives)— if there is a Sun-Moon conjunction, sextile or trine between their mutual horoscopes. Even without such planetary help, they will probably remain friends after they drift apart. Not all 6-8 Sun Sign Pattern couples do, but the Twins and the Goat very well may.

Love has a way of melting the ice from a Saturn-ruled heart. Something about this man, when he has melted, will make her tremble with anticipation of the picture of absolute rightness he projects when he's with her —the promise of ultimate happiness through their relationship. Later, it may seem to her that this unspoken promise has been broken, as Life begins to appear drab to the Gemini woman, who feels chained to Capricorn's rather mundane, albeit secure, existence. Still, she should not forget that he's the most likely candidate of all lovers and husbands to be exciting during the golden years, becoming more youthful, turning more free (more like *her*) the older he gets. If she will wait, that promise of rightness may be kept after all.

Gemini is impatient and does not like to wait. But she should make the effort, because if she does, the rewards will be well worth it, and she could discover with him a great secret—that in the halting of restless movement, the true form and shape of love can be discovered, its deeper beauty revealed—and beauty is what her divided heart has been seeking since she was a little girl. Patience. Patience is the key word with this man. She must cultivate it.

There could be a Gemini girl in love with a Goat who reads this and wonders why they should need such advice. They are so very happy—right now. Well, you don't teach someone to swim while they're drowning. You teach them ahead of time—just in case. The word again, Twins, is: PA-TIENCE.

☆ ☆ ☆ ☆ ☆ ☆

GEMINI *Man* CAPRICORN *Woman*

◄◄◆►►

"Keep back, lady, no one is going to catch me and
make me a man . . . ."

She had to tell him.

"I am old, Peter. I am ever
so much more than twenty. I grew up long ago."

"You promised not to!"

"I couldn't help it."

The Capricorn woman cannot help it if she is wise beyond her years, any more than the Gemini man can help it if he is little-boy-irresponsible at times. In our society, until very recently, the man was supposed to be the strong, mature and practical one. A woman was expected to be flighty, somewhat unpredictable and helpless. Now that we have Women's Liberation groups loudly ringing the bells of the New Age in our ears, we might permit him to be sensitive, changeable, and lighthearted now and then—and allow her to be steady and sensible. But before the dawning of the Aquarian Age, they wouldn't have had a chance.

It's a lucky thing for the Goat and the Twins that we've finally recognized her right to be practical and intelligent, along with his right to daydream occasionally, even weep when he is touched by beauty. It's quite fortunate for all of us, but especially for these two. The differences in their personalities are enough with which to cope—who needs the extra problem of trying to fit into the predesigned, prejudiced images of someone's idea of Man and Woman? Not Gemini and Capricorn. They have plenty to keep them busy in the complicated pastime of capturing the harmony of compatibility between their two divergent natures.

The sex of the two Sun Signs is as it should be, at first glance. Hers is a feminine sign, his a masculine sign. That is, well—it's not quite that simple. True, Capricorn is a feminine sign, but it's ruled by Old Man Saturn, who is definitely masculine, all the way. And Gemini is a masculine sign, but ruled by tricky Mercury, the Great Pretender, a planet known for its predilection toward deceiving, capable of switching from masculine to feminine, and back to masculine, in the flicker of a firefly. That's pretty swift. Did you ever try to time the flicker of a firefly? So, there will be problems. Not insurmountable, just on occasion, annoying. Perhaps frustrating would be a better word.

There could be times when he'll accuse her of being callous and unsympathetic—times when she'll accuse him of being fickle and emotionally immature. In a sense, she is those things—just as, to a certain degree, he does possess those traits. Yet, a Capricorn woman can also be affectionate, loyal, and a veritable twinkling rainbow of humor when she feels she's on safe ground, not the shaky terrain of continual change and movement— which may open up and swallow her. (All Goats have a subliminal fear of earthquakes.) Just as a Gemini man can project a truth more glowing than she realizes if he's allowed the freedom of expression he needs, not hounded by suspicions, depressing predictions of the future . . . . . and nagging. Criticism and emotional severity will never bring out the best in the Twins.

The praying mantis is an odd insect, in that the female of the species often chews off the head of the male during the mating act itself. He read about this somewhere (Geminis have read about *everything*), and he's inclined to feel like a male mantis himself when the woman he loves insists on chewing up his self-confidence with rigid, unbending disapproval at the same time she's declaring her devotion.

She may be the one who should handle the money in the family. It will probably *be* a family eventually, if she has any choice in the matter. Cappy seldom loans herself out for romantic interludes of a temporary type. The future intentions are usually firmly understood before she dabbles or dallies. But back to money and the probability that she's the best bet to hold the purse strings. Not that he isn't quick and bright with figures—sometimes too quick and bright. Most Geminis can cause a computer to turn green with envy. It's just that she'll have a way of spending it more sensibly, investing it more wisely, some kind of magic touch in pressing the bank balance higher and higher—whereas he may possess the knack of causing it to sink lower and lower. (Unless, of course, his Moon or Ascendent happens to be in Virgo, Taurus, Capricorn or Cancer.)

Oddly, both these Sun Signs are frequently called "cold" emotionally by astrology—not to mention by their friends and relatives. She, because of Saturn's icy rulership and stern influence over her behavior—he, because of belonging to the always somewhat detached Air Element. But she is, nonetheless, capable of an earthy, even a fierce, love, despite Saturn's iron control over her emotions and his constant admonition against releasing them until she's certain a relationship is genuine, and has a chance of being permanent.

As for him, he's not yet learned, in a spiritual sense, love's true ecstasy —or its anguish. He hasn't, esoterically and karmically, experienced its real depth. Still, he looks forward to it with a special kind of excitement—and is not anticipation magical too? It is, and his enthusiastic searching can cause her own dreams to soar, while her quiet kind of love, like a steady candle flame, lights the way for his search and offers him a soothing refuge during his periods of self-doubt.

Sometimes a Capricorn woman can be almost too good, too perfect, too reliable for a Gemini man to handle. He feels caught in the prison of her very emotional steadiness, inexplicably, as if her devotion itself were an affront to him . . . but only because he suspects he cannot duplicate it, which both frightens and saddens him. And so he may secretly resent her affectional dependability—and run away, perhaps, for fleeting periods, then return to bask in it again—another facet of his twin confusion in matters of the heart.

Due to their natural inclinations (and disinclinations), their sexual relationship may not always be a smoldering volcano of intensity. Yet, strangely, it may fulfill the desire they both have for physical lovemaking, to be comforting and close but not all-consuming. Even during their most intimate moments, he needs to feel his own independence and freedom. So does she, surprisingly enough. A Capricorn woman, considering Saturn's firm hold on her, isn't likely to abandon herself to passion with any-one, not really-truly-all-the-way. Neither does the Gemini man, who is, at the core of his nature, actually two men. One watches the emotional in-volvement while remaining detached from it—the other experiences. This is how the Gemini Sun Sign learns, at the Mercury level of awareness. Still this woman may somehow, in a way he can't explain, attract him physically. To him Capricorn represents the eighth astrological house of sexual mystery, as well as the deeper secrets of life and death.

The typical Goat Girl lives in a serene, traditional world of practical ac-tivity, where wisdom is Queen. He lives in an enchanted world, peopled with myriad fancies, teeming with mental activity, where curiosity is King. It can be a lovely experiment and a beneficial experience for them to visit each other's world, from time to time—not for the purpose of fault-finding and criticism, but as one visits any faraway kingdom, enjoying the strangeness and beauty, yet glad to return home to the familiar.

If they travel a lot he will be happier. She will be less so—(unless her Moon or Ascendent is in Gemini also, or in Aries, Leo, Sagittarius, or Pisces). This is not a woman who can pitch a tent and call it home. Be-cause of her reverse aging process, a gift from Saturn, as she grows older, she'll become more vulnerable to wanderlust, and the mention or thought of a trip may excite her, soften her eyes and lift her spirits—as long as she's sure the trip or voyage will eventually lead back home. Although there are a flock of Capricorn career women, she's still a lady who's essentially more content to sit by the hearth, like a cricket, than lead the life of a nomad or gypsy.

The Gemini man has nothing against sitting and dreaming before the home fires himself, except when his restless yearnings periodically attack him, with little warning. He can go months, years, acting the part of the perfect family man—then, WHOOSH! a spring breeze comes along—or even a winter wind—to sweep him and his dreams into a new adventure, even if it's only a trip to a neighboring city, where he can lose himself for a few days in order to find himself again.

As with many 6-8 Sun Sign Patterns, these two probably met only when someone else introduced them or brought them together in some way. It's seldom that Gemini and Capricorn gravitate toward each other magnetically, on their own—unless her Sun was trining his Moon at birth, or vice versa, or both. Once they do notice each other, however, the 6-8 vi-bration begins to vibrate between them, steadily increasing in strength.

A Gemini man is capable of a great deal of badinage, but it's often only used as camouflage. He feels people would never believe the naked truth anyway. It's too obvious. And so, he disguises it. I know that's confusing, but most everything about Gemini is confusing. A little of this and a little of that. Take Gemini Bert Lance, former director of the Office of Management and Budget of the Carter Administration, who was forced to resign in 1978 under a cloud of scandal involving his former questionable banking practices. During a speech at the convention of the American Bankers' Association in Florida, shortly after his resignation, one of the members angrily remarked that "Bert Lance has done for banking what the Boston Strangler did for the door-to-door salesman."

On the other hand, there are scores of reputable bankers all over the country who adamantly still admire and defend Geminian Lance, for no personal motive or past favors received—but simply because they genuinely believe his professional behavior was always imaginative, creative, courageous, and entirely within sound banking principles. Obviously two different men are being analyzed. Bert Lance. And his Twin, Bert Lance. Geminis are never simple personalities. Take Henry Kissinger. Take Errol Flynn. Take Brigham Young. Take all six of these Gemini men—and what have you? Double images, reflecting every facet of sunlight and shadow . . . . . arousing contempt, hatred, envy, disapproval, awe, admiration, respect and love. This is what Cappy is in for with her Twin lover or husband.

The mercurial truth of the Twins can always be seen from two polarized points of view. But Cappy leans toward total honesty, which allows little or no room for a two-sided truth. Her Gemini man may feel her attitude is too harsh, for the continuation of his free flow of ideas depends upon leaving open ends for individual interpretation, now and then. He doesn't know where the ideas come from, but they never stop, and they are the essence of his very being. To stifle his freedom of thought and expression is not the way to love this man.

She'll want him to seek a profession or a career with some future promise, as well as a reasonable present financial return, and she'll probably insist that they eventually own their own home. Cappy isn't big on antlike apartment dwellings or condominiums. He doesn't really need that sort of security, since roots are not normally a Gemini requirement. He's happier with a million dollars on paper and a hundred in the bank than with a hundred dollars on paper and a million in the bank. The former offers more challenge. She feels precisely the opposite. Gemini feels that his ideas, his imagination, are the most bankable assets he owns. He doesn't understand her kind of security needs, not really—and perhaps he never will. Even the Gemini male with a more cautious Virgo, Cancer or Capricorn Ascendent or Moon Sign will suddenly, someday, without warning, toss away the entire balance in the bank for some new idea, dream, goal or prospect that's popped into his head. (One of his heads.)

If their relationship begins to break apart, it won't be easy for the Goat Girl to let go. After a Capricorn woman gives herself completely to a man, she cannot take back her gift without great pain. She cannot *change* as easily as he. When she loves, she intends it to be a forever thing. But if and when she does decide that her "forever" has come to a dead-end street, there will usually be no hysterical scenes of weeping and accusation, no excessive emotional displays. She will simply turn, hide her tears, walk away and not come back. No Sun Sign can be so unsentimental (on the surface) as Capricorn, when emotional surgery must be performed and there is no other solution possible. But . . . as she walks away, her gentle heart will be breaking, and her torment will be all the more agonizing because she keeps it inside . . . and bears it alone.

The Gemini man cries, with Whittier, "How little I have gained—how vast the unattained!"—then weeps for experiences lost, opportunities wasted, chances tossed away . . . love, unrequited, misplaced, or allowed to drift into emptiness. Yet, swiftly will follow the Gemini three-cornered grin, and Mercury's quicksilver laugh. Tomorrow is a bright, new day of promise! Who knows what magic it may hold? Maybe . . . yes, maybe . . . even a reconciliation—forgiveness from his shy Goat Girl, and the chance to try again, this time treating her heart more tenderly.

Should their love affair or marriage end, Cappy will be slower to smile, and as for tomorrow being brighter—tomorrow will seem to her sad, Saturnine spirit a trillion light-years away. That's why she'll try harder to make the relationship work. With Saturn in her corner, she can build love strong enough to withstand the temporary tornadoes of disagreement.

GEMINI

Air—Mutable—Positive
Ruled by Mercury
Symbol: The Twins
Day Forces—Masculine

AQUARIUS

Air—Fixed—Positive
Ruled by Uranus
Symbol: The Water Bearer
Day Forces—Masculine

The GEMINI-AQUARIUS *Relationship*

The goals are at each end of the rainbow. . . .

Because this is a 5-9 Sun Sign Pattern, and their natal Suns are, therefore, trined, Gemini and Aquarius are ordinarily as cozily compatible as a couple of bugs in a rug or two termites in a totem pole. Now and then, however, depending on other planetary aspects between their mutual planets at birth, they can short-circuit each other's frequencies.

Recently, I received a letter from a young Aquarian named William Dana Snyder, presently employed at the Nuts and Bolts Hardware Store in the Village (Greenwich), where he is clearly very much at home. It was written in the typical Uranus-Sanskrit Aquarians use when they communicate with mere mortals on the Earth plane, and it was signed with the curious phrase: SAT NAM. Beneath this signature, the Water Bearer had helpfully translated the words to mean, in essence: *"There is only one God—and He is Truth."*

Right there you have it. The main current of dissension between Gemini and Aquarians—TRUTH. Gemini continually avoids it, since truth has an intricate web of complex meanings for the Twins. Aquarius constantly seeks it (or stalks it)—lucid, plain, unvarnished with imaginative adjectives, uncolored with personal opinion. To Gemini, truth is a great, rolling ocean, rainbow-hued and glittering, filled with the fish of many-faceted half-truths, maybes, ifs and possiblys. To Aquarius, truth is a great shining drop, shaped like a fact, colorless, transparent, and clearly seen under the microscopic, relentless Uranian eye as itself and nothing but itself, so help it God—which it is, of course. Remember? SAT NAM.

The scene is anywhere. Gemini and an Aquarian are on opposite ends of a telephone. The former had promised to do the latter a favor by mailing a very important letter for him (or her).

AQUARIUS: Did you mail the letter I gave you last night?
GEMINI: Yes, I mailed it. See you for lunch in about an hour, okay?
AQUARIUS: What do you mean, you mailed it? Is it on the way to Saratoga right now?
GEMINI: Well, no—but it will be in a few minutes.
AQUARIUS: Then you haven't mailed it, so why did you say you did?
GEMINI: *The truth is,* I have addressed it, stamped it, and I was on my way out the door to the Post Office when the phone rang.
AQUARIUS: *The truth is,* you haven't mailed the letter yet. Call me back after you've dropped it in the slot. Goodbye. CLICK.

Aquarius is a Fixed Sign. Fixed means stubborn, among other things. If the comments of the Water Bearer seem to ring with undertones of Virgo and Sagittarius truth-seeking, listen again. There is a slight and subtle difference in the Uranus attitude. I'm not sure just what it is, but it's a slight and subtle difference. In everything Aquarius does there is a slight and subtle difference from the way it is said and done by ordinary humans. Water Bearers are not ordinary. They are extraordinary. And flattery will get you nowhere with them. But back to the main issue. Truth is an area where there will obviously be some disputes from time to time between Gemini and Aquarius.

Not everyone understands this Uranian thing about truth, based on fact. Unlike Virgos, Aquarians are not hair-splitters in their quest for truth. Unlike Taurus and Capricorn, Aquarius does not have a closed mind. The Uranus mind is always open to anything, positively anything. If the human brain is capable of imagining it or conceiving it, then to Aquarius it is a possibility, never mind how far-out and ridiculous it may seem to the scientific community and/or laymen. HOWEVER (and I capitalized HOWEVER on purpose), although the Water Bearers accept the possibility of absolutely *anything* with an open mind, they will not accept an existing theory as *final* truth until they have satisfied themselves of the feasibility of the supposition by proving it via visible facts. So you can see they're a curious mixture of fact and fantasy. At least, I hope you see. I trust this has clarified the issue. I am sure it has not. But I tried.

Other than sometimes gazing at truth through opposite ends of the telescope, Gemini and Aquarius, being a 5-9 Sun Sign Pattern, are usually enormously compatible. Shall we say that they are more often than they are not? They empathize, sympathize, philosophize and fraternize on the same electronic wave-length, auric beam, vibratory frequency, or whatever you wish to call it. Normally, they are not shaken by each other's changeable moods, eccentricities, ups, downs, or swoops sideways. Only rarely do you come across a Gemini-Aquarius couple whose mutual planetary positions are severely afflicted by comparative aspects between their birth charts—and who, therefore, either actively dislike each other on sight—or bore one another. It happens with every Sun Sign Pattern, even with the usually smooth 5-9 vibration, but most infrequently.

As I've reminded you many times in this book, in other Aquarian chapters, although Aquarius is pictured in astrology as the Water Bearer, Aquarius is an Air Sign, like Gemini—not a Water Sign. So why are these people represented, symbolized as it were, by a kneeling figure pouring water from a jug, since they are not of the Water Element but of the Air Element? I cannot tell you. I realize it doesn't make sense on the surface of it. It's totally illogical, not to mention contradictory and weird. But then, so are Aquarians—all of those things. Every last one of them is bonkers, to some degree. The Twins are among the few people who notice this right off, because they are known to bonk in and out also. When Gemini and Aquarius bonk around together in rhythm, it's kind of comforting. No one has to explain himself (or herself). It makes life simpler. No, maybe I'd better take that back. Life is never simple with these two Sun Signs. Interesting, fascinating, even magical—but never simple.

One of the most remarkable and affecting or touching sights in the world is a child with the feelings of an adult. Another remarkable, affecting or touching sight is an adult with the feelings of a child. The latter is the case with all Geminis and Aquarians, if they're typical of their Sun Signs. Both of them exist in actuality on planets other than Earth, touching base down here only at intervals, which could range from five minutes to several days. Naturally, they flock together when they have an opportunity, so they can speak to each other in the code of non-Earthlings. The true world of Gemini and Aquarius is called Faërie, the realm or state in which faeries have their being, described by Tolkien as a place which contains "many things besides elves and fays, and besides dwarfs, witches, trolls, giants or dragons; it holds the seas, the sun, the moon, the sky; and the earth, and all things that are in it: tree and bird, water and stone, wine and bread, and ourselves, mortal men, when we are enchanted."

All of us experience fleeting moments of enchantment (with the potential for extending the fleeting aspect of them). But Gemini and Aquarius comprehend and utilize such potential and are nearly continually enchanted, full of the awe and wonder, the curiosity of the true child—Gemini, the toddler, and Aquarius, second childhood—as described in "The Twelve Mysteries of Love" at the beginning of this book. Therefore, they have, more or less, permanent residence in the realm of Faërie. We see them pass among us, of course, but are they really here, or do they not seem frequently to be . . . somewhere else? As a team, these two Sun Signs will mingle and blend at times almost as one, then drift into their own individual ways for a period . . . and float back together again. It's usually a windy, breezy relationship, somewhat detached, and although a controversy between them can create a temporary flurry of excitement, like a summer storm, it normally doesn't last long enough to do any real damage.

Both Gemini and Aquarius understand most subjects and situations thoroughly, in depth, but Gemini can usually transmit this comprehension to others with more clarity than Aquarius, the Twins having been blessed with the gift of both gab and glibness—Aquarians with the gift of genius and insanity, in just about equal parts. They are both, however, masters of the twisted phrase, mind-blowers. Gemini double-talks an atheist by informing him that any scientist can count the seeds in an apple, but only God can count the apples in a seed. Aquarius comments on the restless Gemini behavior by observing wryly that a fly-by-night leaves no shadow, only doubt. How was that again? Listen more carefully the first time. Aquarius does not like to repeat. Gemini cheerfully repeats, but never the same way twice. With their upside-down cakes of phraseology and crisscross alliteration, Gemini and Aquarius would make a great team writing verses for Chinese fortune cookies.

With Sun-Moon harmony between them, they can be a delightful pair, an exasperating puzzle to everyone else, but an open book to each other. Even with a negative Sun-Moon aspect in their horoscopes, because of their Sun trine, they may read the last page of the book first, decide they don't like it, then breeze along their merry, individual ways—possibly returning to pick up where they left off, maybe even to write a different ending, as it pleases them. It's impossible to predict, with these two.

Most people like Gemini and Aquarius despite themselves, rather than for themselves. They're both too complex for the average Earthling. But they usually only annoy with their noise, seldom anger. If their mutual chatter, combined with their speedy head and foot work, could be set to music, the lyrics would surely be haunting but hard to remember. At least, hard for the Water Bearer to remember. All Aquarians are a touch absent-minded. Never mind, Gemini's steel trap of a mind can flip out computer cards of memory fast enough for both of them.

Sometimes they make money together, sometimes they lose it together. Neither is likely to admit which it is, loss or gain, because both are able to substitute one word for another, as they do with all polarities, completely comprehending what many people do not: that any one thing always contains particles of its opposite. These two (who would be perfectly at home, by the way, at the Mad Hatter's Tea Party) are quite likely to have in common some interest in religion, travel to foreign countries and lands, higher educational institutions, astral experience, youth and young people, films, entertainment, artistic or creative endeavor. Or these areas will be, conversely, areas of tension.

Gemini and Aquarius often seem incapable of a completely smooth relationship, despite their innate empathy. If things run too smoothly, they aren't happy. Theirs is an exceedingly strange compatibility. They can frequently be at cross purposes and can get on each other's nerves. Yet, they can also have a barrel of fun together, as they fly around in simultaneous orbit to lace the tired old Earth with flowers . . . tumbling, twisting, turning and tantalizing others who are not so blessed with lightning calculator minds and flashing intuition.

Gemini and Aquarius are as serious as Birth and as joyous as Death—and vice versa. As for the spiritual concept of SAT NAM, Gemini is aware that truth is a different thing to each person, depending on an individual's level of enlightenment at any given time. Therefore, if "God's" name is really truth, then He is a "God" of many faces, a multiple One.

Aquarius is even wiser, takes Gemini's logic one leap forward, and informs the Twins that there is only one truth, which stands high above the multiple truth-Gods of SAT NAM, and its name is LOVE. Not just love between man and woman, although that's the beginning of it, but love of all mankind and womankind for one another and for all living creatures . . . . . in the woods, the seas and the air. "Well then," replies Gemini, brightening, "I see! I see! Then there must also be a Ms. God—two creators—twin souls—from which all this flows down upon us!"

But it took the Water Bearer to open the eyes of the Twins to higher truth. Yes, Gemini, the super-bright, has much to learn from Aquarius, the Water Bearer of Wisdom. In youth, Aquarius may sign letters with SAT NAM. But with maturity, the Uranus-ruled will sign them with EVOL NAM REH-SIH (His-Her name is Love, spelled backwards, of course, in the typical Uranian manner).

The bottomless jug of the Water Bearer contains many such marvelous mysteries, and no one can discover them more quickly than the Gemini Twins.

☆ ☆ ☆ ☆ ☆ ☆

GEMINI *Woman* AQUARIUS *Man*

Now surely he would understand; but not a bit of it.
"Peter," she said, faltering, "are you expecting me
to fly away with you?"

"Of course; that is why I have come." He added a
little sternly, "Have you forgotten that this is
spring-cleaning time?"

She knew it was useless to
say that he had let many spring-cleaning times pass.

Spring has an attraction for all of us, but for the Sun Signs of Aries, Aquarius and Gemini, it holds a special, inexplicable wonder. The Gemini woman, being impatient, can create her own springtime when Mother Nature disappoints her. There will come a year when the icy clutch of winter seems to be endless. She cannot wait for spring another day. And so she flies away to Florida or California, following the elusive Sun, making a miracle by causing spring to come early, at her whim. Long ago, when she was a very little girl, she learned there are many magical things one can do when happiness is slowpokey, and most of those things involve moving around, flying here and there, but mainly—*change*.

No man will understand her preoccupation with that word more than an Aquarian. Oh, Aries, Libra, and Gemini males comprehend it too, at times, but not in the same exciting way as Aquarius. The Water Bearer was born to bring change into the world. But there is a small hitch, which should be noted. He wants the world and everyone around him to change, but not his own basic attitudes—not the essence of himself. His moods and manners may change, but not the Him-of-Him. Remember, he's a Fixed Sign. In the beginning, in the first sunrise of love, he'll cheerfully fly around with her. Later, he'll become more settled in his rut. Granted, a Uranus rut is always more fascinating than others, but to a Gemini girl bubbling with ideas and possibilities, a rut is a rut, and there is nothing more dampening to her soaring spirit than a Water Bearer sitting by the fire in his hut, stuck in his rut. If you know what I mean.

However, just because he can get settled in a residential or geographical way by no means should be taken to imply that this man is predictable. When it comes to his mood, expressions and disposition, to say nothing of his activities, he's as unpredictable as a pair of dice. Actually, it's poetic and romantic justice when a Gemini girl falls into enchantment with an Aquarian man. All her life she's been flitting around like a peripatetic firefly, switching her moods off and on, causing her lovers or friends to moan in frustration over her rather impersonal Mercury style of unpredictability. As soon as she becomes involved with a Uranus-ruled male, she'll be forced to swallow a rather large dose of her own medicine.

He'll invite her to have dinner with him, followed by the preview of a new Steve McQueen or Paul Newman flick (usually typical Aquarian favorites), then after she's brushed her hair and tied on a yellow ribbon, a frog-like creature shows up at the front door, wearing a wet suit and flippers. What is it? It's him. He wants her to go surfboarding? No. He's changed his mind about eating out before the film. He's decided they will eat at her place, and while she's preparing dinner, he's going to go diving for some hermit-crab shells to make her a necklace. They'll still have time to catch the first feature at the theatre, if she'll just hurry up, chill the sprouts and heat up the lentils, so everything is ready to munch when he returns from his scuba search for seashells. "There should be enough of them, deserted, lying around on the ocean floor," he muses aloud . . . as he leaves. "It doesn't take long for a hermit crab to outgrow his cozy house and slip into a new one. Abalone shells are beautiful, but they represent death to the abalone from people who cannibalize sea life to tantalize their greedy taste buds."

What did he say? He'll explain it all to her—the sadness of the food chain—later, after the film. The frog has already disappeared, leaving behind him only the slapping sound of his flippers, along the path to the beach. Life—and love—with this man can be so crazy.

Would there be any way to make other people believe in the craziness, the loveliness of it? No way. It's uncanny the way these two so often find themselves feeling the same things at the same time. Most times she catches on to his tricks almost before he can pull them. Naturally, this is electrifying to him, since Aquarians love to shock people, and the surprise of discovering a female who's hard to shock challenges him insanely. Like a little boy walking on his hands along the top of a wall to impress his best girl—then she yawns and starts walking on her elbows. He continually has to top himself with the Gemini girl.

If they happen to live in the mountains or in the Midwest, nowhere near a shoreline, it doesn't preclude the Uranus shock treatment. Instead of a frog turning up at the door, he'll pick her up some morning in a yellow bug, with Snoopy as Joe Cool stenciled on the hood, and one of those WELCOME UFO's stickers on the bumper. Wasn't his car grey last night? Yes, it was, but this is a bright blue sunshiny day. Time to change colors. He could suddenly decide to grow a beard or a moustache with no notice, or if he's already had one for years, just as suddenly shave it off, pull a wool cap down over his ears, grab her on the street and scare her to death. "Don't you know me, honey? I'm the Jolly Green Giant who loves you!" And like that.

At long last she will understand what it's like to be an innocent bystander recipient of someone else's Ferris wheel of emotions and quick-changing moods. It may even teach her to tone down her own mental acrobatics, to maybe even be on time for appointments. Reliability and dependability are qualities they could both stand to cultivate. Then there's always the chance they won't ease each other into stability at all but will, instead, incite each other into more loop-the-loops. Either way, it will be fun. These lovers constitute a 5-9 Sun Sign Pattern, which means they have a far higher than average chance to discover that they're Twin Souls, especially if there's a harmonious Sun-Moon aspect between their two horoscopes. Even without it, or with a negative aspect between their individual Luminaries at birth, they will find more in common together than they do with most other people they both know.

There's no use denying that she will occasionally annoy and irritate his Fixity with her Mutability. But she can be so easy to forgive. No one has ever lived who can apologize more charmingly than a Gemini. It's really worthwhile for her to do something wrong, just to watch her ask pardon for it. Sometimes he wonders if she knows that. (She does.) Aquarians have a mite more trouble getting the hang of apology. No Fixed Sign (Aquarius, Taurus, Scorpio, Leo) ever finds it easy to say "I'm sorry."

Most of them find begging for pardon about as pleasurable as walking barefoot on hot coals. So she shouldn't expect this male to indulge in such abasement too frequently. It frightens him. What will she expect from him next if he spoils her now with profuse apologies? Aquarian men do not like to be anticipated in any way. I've already told you that. It's advisable not to forget it.

People can become dreadfully bored when there's nothing but sex to interest them in each other. This man and this woman seldom run that risk. Gemini and Aquarius always have something to talk about, so much to teach one another, and the beauty of it is that, half the time, they don't even know they're learning. Sex is usually not a big thing to this man and woman. It's not a small thing either, but it doesn't take first place in their relationship. It seldom occurs to either of them to measure its influence, to count its blessings or curses. Sex is just there, that's all. Most happily mated Gemini-Aquarian couples enjoy the physical consummation of their love as children enjoy wading through puddles, flying kites or chasing butterflies. It's thrilling, exciting—sheer pleasure—uncomplicated, with no dark, mysterious corners—a bright, sunlit room in their hearts. He could be one of those occasional Water Bearers who almost need to be reminded of the rules of the mating game because his busy-bee thoughts are buzzing around happily with other matters, too preoccupied and absentminded to constantly ponder the delights of physical intimacy. And she could be one of those Geminis who finds fulfillment in talking together—through mental union—rather than becoming unduly engrossed in sensuousness or passion. Nevertheless, their lovemaking, when it does occur, is more likely to be satisfactory to both of them than to be a source of tension, however frequently or infrequently they share it.

In a strange way, they anticipate each other's desires, these two. An Aquarian male with Venus severely afflicted in his birth chart can have some pretty far-out ideas about sexual matters—or he can lean toward the platonic love affair, never truly consummated. But once the average Uranian has been spellbound, has given his heart—he knows the language of love, including its physical one, and he can communicate the intensity of his need with a steady gaze, a slight lifting of the eyebrow—or a wiggle of his left ear. As for her, the Twin symbolism of Gemini will be startlingly apparent in her ability to be one special, private woman for him at night . . . and a totally different female the next day.

Speaking of language, as we were a few paragraphs back, the Gemini girl-woman (for she is both by turns) may speak more than one. Geminis are natural linguists. She may also have more than one name, an alias or a nickname, perhaps even more than one husband during her lifetime. This isn't true of every Gemini woman, of course, just most of them. The Twins are seldom satisfied without two or more of everything. Aquarians frequently marry more than once too. (Not always, but frequently.) Not all Water Bearers satisfy their curiosity the first time, although she has the edge on him in the multiple marriage race and is slightly more likely to have tried marriage before than he.

Once the Aquarian man is sure he's not missing anything, he can be purely and perfectly faithful to one woman. His problem with the Twins is that he sometimes feels he's coping with *two* women. I guess he could swing faithfulness to both of her. Gemini females do flirt a lot. They just can't help it. But she'll get away with it most of the time with him, since Aquarians aren't the type, usually, to make a mountain out of a few mole-hills when it comes to jealousy. Light, friendly flirtations may escape his notice altogether. He understands about friendship. In fact, she may wish he didn't understand so well. His friends may cause *her* to be jealous. She'll just have to remember that an Aquarian may find it difficult to sepa-rate love from friendship, but to him, if he's a typical Water Bearer, the physical or sexual aspect of a relationship goes with the former, not with the latter—once he's separated the two by making a commitment (or by combining them, with her).

The one person she has good reason to fear is the girl he first loved. He'll never forget her—never. She'll always be there, buried deep inside his memory, whether she happens to be his first-grade teacher, the girl go-rilla, or the lady hippo at the zoo who winked at him when he was three. It could be more serious, of course, and his first love may be a real, flesh-and-blood, dangerous female, who may pop up someday to make his heart do flip-flops. Even so, except in rare cases, he would prefer the misty, starry memory to all the trouble of picking up where he left off, years ago. Yet, there are those very rare cases.

The one thing this man will demand of her is truth. It's the one thing he may never receive from her. She sees truth through the multiple lens of imagination, colored by her wishes and dreams. It's merely a matter of interpretation. Otherwise, these two share essentially similar vibrations. Their auras blend in a galaxy of moods, synchronized to the same "mother ship" frequency, different only in their individual reflections of the chang-ing seasons of the heart. The differences are subtle, intricate. His reactions are more complex than hers, likewise, therefore, his reflections. She startles him with rainfalls of tears, followed suddenly with sunbursts of laughter. Then he reverses the reflection with rainfalls of laughter, followed by sunbursts of tears . . . . perhaps because Aquarius already knows what Gemini has yet to learn—that there's a reason why Gladness rhymes with Sadness, contained in her yet personally unsensed mystery of Joy and Sorrow, which are in reality Twins themselves, inseparable and interchangeable.

☆ ☆ ☆ ☆ ☆ ☆

GEMINI *Man* AQUARIUS *Woman*

———◄◄●►►———

"So I ran away to Kensington Gardens and lived a
long long time among the fairies."

She gave him a look of the most intense admiration,
and he thought it was because he had run away, but
it was really because he knew fairies.

There are many reasons why these two are sure to notice each other in a crowd, but the main one is that faint chord of music they both hear. The Aquarian girl has always felt that no one truly understands her. Most people judge her unfairly, figure she's playing with only half a deck of cards, full of wild imaginings, a crazy daisy born several hundred years too soon. Everyone but him.

The Gemini man has always felt that no one really understands his dreams. Most people judge him unfairly, figure he's unreliable, sometimes too talkative, at other times too moody, immature—and totally irresponsible. Everybody but her.

The first recognition of kindredship between Gemini and Aquarius always reminds me of the meeting between Saint-Exupéry's Little Prince and the pilot. As a child, the pilot drew a picture of a boa constrictor who had swallowed an elephant, which, unfortunately, resembled a hat. All his life, no matter to whom he showed his picture, people would never recognize it as a boa constrictor who had swallowed an elephant, but would always say, *"Yes, that's a nice drawing of a hat."* It hurts when others can't comprehend your intense efforts, and it's lonely. Then one day, after he's grown up, the pilot meets a strange little man in the desert, who asks him to draw a picture of a sheep. Exasperated, the pilot scribbles the same picture of his childhood—the one everybody always took to be a drawing of a hat. But when the Little Prince gazes at the sketch, he shakes his head immediately, and says, "No, no. *I don't want a picture of a boa constrictor who has swallowed an elephant. I asked you to draw me a sheep.*"

That's the faint chord of music I mean. Without a single word of explanation . . . . . . someone *knows*! Only music, never mere words, can describe the fountain of pure joy that wells up in the soul when after years of lonely, futile searching, one comes upon another being who really (not *nearly*, but *really*) recognizes and comprehends all the secret yearnings and attempts to communicate that others have ridiculed or ignored in the past.

Later, this first faint chord of music from the spheres, as lovely and long-awaited as it is, contains a sour note or two somewhere along the way in the symphony of love between Gemini and Aquarius. But this is a small burden to bear when compared to the broken rhythms and discordant melodies both have been exposed to until they finally found each other. Although no relationship is perfect, a 5-9 Sun Sign Pattern often comes closer to being so than most others. If the Sun-Moon aspects between them are conjunct, sextile or trine, they can reach a rare harmony of living and loving. Even without this planetary assistance, they're better matched than many and will usually remain friendly, whether romance lingers or not.

Sun Signs which are in trine complement each other in ways only the two people involved can appreciate. But one of them is always ahead of the other on the zodiac wheel, on the soul level, in karmic lessons. In this case, it's the Aquarian woman who is somewhat wiser in a subconscious, spiritual sense than the Gemini man she loves. So she'll be the one who will have to do the most giving and be more tolerant. Tolerance comes easily to most Aquarians, who are basically unprejudiced and know well the meaning of the words—"Help thy brother's boat across and lo! thine own shall reach the shore." Uranus incites humanitarianism in Water Bearers, infuses the Aquarian woman with a spirit of brotherhood (and sisterhood). It's possible she may have too many friends, at least too many for men born under other Sun Signs. The Gemini man may not find time to resent the strange birds she gathers around her, because he's too busy being gregarious himself. Only the very rare Geminian with heavy planetary afflictions in his birth horoscope is a loner. The home of a Water

Bearer and a Mercury Bird is seldom quiet. If they're both typical of their Sun Signs, it will be filled with people more often than it's empty.

These two will make many mistakes while trying to love each other for richer and for poorer, for better or for worse. But they'll be interesting mistakes, seldom boring. One mistake he's likely to make is expecting her to put up with his little white lies. She's outraged when he stretches the truth or distorts it. Aquarian women tend to claim they are honest and aboveboard in every way. They do their own thing and never lie about it, whether society approves or not. But the Gemini man is clever and astute enough to analyze her own peculiar brand of dishonesty, which consists of sins of omission. She tells the truth, yes—but sometimes only part of it, only what she wishes to tell, holding back the whole truth, never playing all her cards at one time. When he accuses her of this, she evidences surprise and hurt. He may point out to her that she has other ways of being less than truthful, namely her manner of expressing her true feelings in such a way that only the Red Queen, Tweedledum or Tweedledee could correctly interpret them.

The honesty game between Gemini and Aquarius is complicated, and they are perhaps the only ones who can untangle the knots. Sometimes they do. Sometimes they don't. They will never stop trying. Both of them enjoy mental games and are amateur detectives, instinctively alert to every nuance. This talent is obvious in Gemini, more disguised in Aquarius, beneath the surface mask of "dingbat," wide-eyed innocence and detachment.

The mistake *she* could make is expecting him to mean exactly what he says. Gemini never means exactly what he says. He uses words as blessings to charm, coax, persuade and cajole; sometimes as weapons to taunt, tease and hurt. He makes speeches that magnetize her into rapt attention, then hold her spellbound—or he can break her heart with his mercurial brand of withering sarcasm and sharp comments. It's nearly always a mistake to cry in front of a Gemini man. He can't cope with tears. Intensely emotional scenes frighten him as they would a child. And so, often he reacts with what appear to be cold and unsympathetic words—using them as weapons again, this time to protect himself against the pain that accompanies compassion.

He wants no part of pain, this man, if he can possibly avoid it. The art of satire was invented by Gemini, who weaves words into sentences as the light-fingered magician strings brightly colored beads, pulls another rabbit from his hat, another flowing scarf from his sleeve at the last minute, making his audience sigh and gasp with admiration. Today he is happy, tomorrow miserable, then jolly and exuberant the day after that. His emotions are genuine, they're for real. It's just that they don't last. The

Aquarian girl can usually tolerate his quicksilver moods better than most females, for a very good reason. She hardly notices anything half the time —anything at all. See the cloudy, misty, faraway look in her eyes? That comes from sailing out there among the clouds on her own wave-length, somewhere in the future, momentarily out of touch with Earth and Earthlings, including his twinned moods. He can pass from suicidal to serene before she's aware of what's happening.

In youth, the Aquarian girl drapes her dream-lover with a sparkling halo of impossible rainbow-spectrumed beauty, which could never fit around the head and shoulders of the average male with the usual number of flaws and defects of character. But she learns to hide her vulnerability under the guise of a cool, detached, friendly "let's pal around together" attitude as she settles for something less, all the time secretly treasuring the sentimental illusions of youth. Therefore, the older she is when she meets Gemini, the less apt she is to be wounded by his light attitude toward love. Hers can match his in lightness . . . then. Aquarians nearly all have this strange twist. If they marry more than once, the final marriage will usually occur later in life, when they find someone in need of Uranus wisdom. Then she will turn this man into the astral lover of her teens, finally fulfilling as much as possible her original ideal of a love-friendship combination. The last lover could be a Gemini, who is also desirous of combining love and friendship and is equally as likely to confuse the two feelings as she.

Both the Gemini man and the Aquarian woman have inner fears and doubts about their sex appeal. At some time in the past, they've both privately worried over some problem related to their sexuality, perhaps experienced the humiliation of having been called frigid or at least temporarily unresponsive—especially if either of them have been previously entangled with Fire, Earth or Water Signs.

Together, they can prove to one another the falsehood of these accusations from former lovers. Gemini and Aquarius tend to give only as much as needed and expected, and seldom demand more than what is given, thus often achieving a happy balance in sexual union. Unless one or both of them have a heavily afflicted Venus or Mars in the birth chart, they should find more sexual fulfillment within their physical union than they ever have before with former mates—or probably ever could in the future with new ones. Of course, "probably" is not *definitely*, but it's a stronger promise than *possibly*.

Didn't you realize that as a child, when you asked to go to the circus, and some adult said "possibly" you may go, and your heart sank to the soles of your Buster Browns—or said "probably" you may go, and your heart crawled back up to your knees—or said "definitely" you may go, and your heart flipped right back into place where it belonged, thumping wildly in joy and gratitude and excitement? Both Gemini and Aquarius tend more toward a passion of the mind than of the senses—more emotional intricacies in communicating love than through pure physical abandon to feeling.

Almost always, these two, when there is a break in the relationship, can remain nearly as close, find much of the same affinity as in the beginning. When Gemini and Aquarius are hurt, they both retreat back into the security of a safe, protective, emotionally undemanding friendship. Friendship is a marvelous thing, but sometimes Gemini and Aquarius will sacrifice love for it, because love takes more faith, more courage than a buddy-buddy relationship.

There is a pronounced mysticism between this man and woman, a shimmering thread of light connecting their souls, if they are true mates—as with Aries and Leo, Taurus and Capricorn . . . and all 5-9 Sun Sign Patterns. If they like, they may tug on this thread, to pull themselves back to each other. Not all 5-9 vibrations constitute twin souls, of course, but those that do, allow Soul-Mates easier recognition and more effortless communion than might be granted to true lovers disciplined by other Sun Sign Pattern influences.

As long as he understands that when she laughs, she may be sobbing inwardly—when she cries, she may be inwardly joyous . . . . and as long as she understands that he can fly away today and return tomorrow (or next week, next month or next year . . . but eventually), there will be more pleasure than pain in their loving. Together, Gemini and Aquarius can perform miracles, such as the fusing of several realities into a single, enchanted one. There's such a bond of feeling between them, such shared madness . . . . . and loneliness. They would never see one another's pictures of a boa constrictor who had swallowed an elephant . . . . . as the drawing of an ordinary hat.

And the two of them together could quite probably even convince all boas that it isn't nice or natural to swallow a pachyderm for lunch.

☆ ☆ ☆ ☆ ☆ ☆

GEMINI

Air — Mutable — Positive
Ruled by Mercury
Symbol: The Twins
Day Forces — Masculine

PISCES

Water — Mutable — Negative
Ruled by Neptune
Symbol: The Fish
Night Forces — Feminine

The GEMINI-PISCES *Relationship*

<hr>

> *When their voices died away, there came a cold*
> *silence over the lagoon, and then a feeble cry,*
> *"Help, help!" Two small figures were beating*
> *against the rock.*

There's not much use pretending that Gemini and Pisces are Sun Signs which are naturally as compatible as strawberries and cream, Oliver and Hardy, or Raggedy Ann and Raggedy Andy. Not all, but some of them are as mismatched and antagonistic as the Arabs and the Jews have been over the years, though perhaps not as violent. However, just as peace is possible—and ever more likely—between these traditional foes, a happy compromise is also possible between Gemini and Pisces. If they have a Sun-Moon trine, sextile or conjunction between them, they can get along quite happily, as long as Gemini consents to occasionally swim through Neptune's waters to keep the Fish company—and as long as

Pisces is willing to fly fearlessly, now and then, alongside the Gemini Mercury Birds.

Still, an Air Sign is never completely comfortable in the element of water. There's always the possibility of drowning—just as a Water Sign finds flying without a parachute a little scary. "Could someone please stand beneath me, with a net to catch me if I fall?" Since this is a 4-10 Sun Sign Pattern, should they discover a negative Sun-Moon aspect between their horoscopes, they'll have to remember that mixing air with water must be done carefully, not carelessly. Otherwise, the result could be a dreary fog, or even a dangerous smog. It's easy to see how this can produce a dampening or smothering effect (or both) on a business basis, within the family bosom, in a love affair or among friends. It is, undoubtedly, an unpleasant experience to be dampened (as Pisces can do to Gemini) or smothered (as Gemini can do to Pisces):

GEMINI: You realize that whatever you say will be used against you?

PISCES: That's okay with me. It always has been.

GEMINI: Stop feeling sorry for yourself. Do you plead guilty or innocent? Speak up. You're always so silent. It's called pouting, and you do it to annoy me.

PISCES: Oh, I plead guilty, of course. Guilty of being human, of possessing human needs and desires . . . . even human failings. Isn't that all right?

GEMINI: It depends. You have more failings than most people. You have no sense of deductive reasoning. You avoid the issues, sulk, and refuse to discuss anything. Your mind wanders. Three different times yesterday you ignored me when I told you something I wanted you to do, and you continue to neglect it. You run around listening to everyone's hard-luck stories while your own life falls apart. You're a masochist and a procrastinator. You leave all the important things undone, while you're out chasing bubbles and smelling flowers. Does this make you happy?

PISCES: Oh, yes! No one has ever been happier. Please make sure the jury is told, and the judge too, how happy I've been.

GEMINI: Don't start talking about a judge and jury. This isn't a trial, and you know it. We're just having a discussion.

PISCES: I'm sorry . . . . but you sound like a public prosecutor.

GEMINI: Let's stick to the point. You say you're happy. That's just another of your Neptune lies. You are obviously, at this moment, sad. Clearly depressed. Why aren't you happy right now?

PISCES: Because I'm not making anyone else happy . . . . not even you.

(or . . .)

PISCES: I'm sorry to submit you to a cross examination, please forgive me, but . . . well, I don't trust you. I'm afraid of you. Don't you see how cruelly your words can cut? Are you completely unaware of how unkind and how supercritical you are sometimes?

GEMINI: No more so than others. I'm just verbal enough to express my thoughts clearly, to communicate my feelings. I don't keep everything inside, the way you do. I'm not sneaky, like you.

PISCES: Yes, that's true. You are clever. You can use words ever so much better than I. You're even brilliant, at times. Lots of times. But . . . have you ever been happy? I mean, content with yourself, peaceful. *Have* you been? *Ever?*

(pause)

GEMINI: I . . . uh, well . . . of course. Naturally. Why do you ask me that?

PISCES: I just wondered. What does happiness mean to you?

GEMINI: Happiness? What does it mean to me? It's . . . . . well, it's a number of things you wouldn't understand.

PISCES: Like what?

GEMINI: Like knowing exactly where I'm going, arriving there when I plan to arrive—knowing who I am and what I want.

PISCES: *Who* are you? What *do* you want?

GEMINI: You are deliberately trying to confuse me. I refuse to answer any more questions.

There are some ways in which Gemini and Pisces are alike. Both of them give an overall impression of evasiveness, always sliding just out of reach, with a chameleon's talent for camouflage, as tricky to catch and pin down as fireflies (Gemini) and minnows (Pisces). Their mental and physical maneuvers (both) are quick, darting and elusive, first shimmering in light before you—then disappearing. Where did they go? Well, which one do you mean? The Fish just swam inside his (or her) deep emotional nature, for protection against further questions, more hurt—and the Mercury Bird, for the very same reasons, just soared mentally up into the gathering clouds above your head.

You've heard that Pisceans are very old souls. I've told you that myself, many times. It's true. They are. They've come through the purifying deluge of many incarnations, and they understand everything and everybody —except themselves. The soul cannot reach the Pisces incarnation until it has mastered, at least once, all of the other eleven Sun Signs' lessons. Since some souls remain in (or return to) a single Sun Sign experience for many lifetimes before mastering the *positive* side of that sign's essence, you can see why the Fish is an "old soul." You can also understand why the Piscean faces the most difficult of all karmic testing. For it is here, under Neptune's strange influence, that souls may slip and slide, and forget some of the eleven lessons learned at such expense, either being forced, then, to return to a certain sign (like returning to learn grammar, when you thought you'd passed it) or being reborn into the Pisces vibration itself again and again, until they get the hang of it.

No wonder Pisceans are such a strange bunch. As a group, they seem to contain only saints and sinners, with hardly a normal pilgrim among them. Yes, the Pisces experience is the most vulnerable one, the most tempting to angels . . . the most likely to produce a "fallen angel." A Fish may do nicely in Neptune's school, then one day happen to forget the generosity mastered through the Aries, Sag and Leo incarnations, become stingy—and fall. Or live a smooth life of enlightenment, then some morning (or night), amnesia-like, forget the lesson of Libra fairness, and unkindly judge another . . . . or forget the faint-remembered Taurus patience, and make some impulsive decision, agonizingly regretted, too late. It's not exactly fun, being a Fish. So much more *knowing* is required of these men and women. They're all on the karmic Honor System, and any West Point cadet can tell you how difficult a test of one's worth any Honor System is—deceptively free, yet spiritually and ethically, extremely restrictive.

And so, the Fish float through the complex mazes of their existence, often searching pathetically for their own identities. When they do catch a glimpse of their real images in life's mirror, they are first terrified, then disbelieving. What they see is a godlike self, difficult for the Neptune humility to accept. So they deny it, hide from it, and finally flee from it, into acting or music—often into the escape of drugs, alcohol, or illusion. A few settle into some sort of mundane ambition in the material world, which is entirely foreign to the imaginative Neptunian essence, and therefore, obviously not the Pisces route to happiness. The majority, however (fortunately for the rest of us), flee into creative endeavors, public service, science, religion, healing, teaching—or full-time private devotion to friends, neighbors and relatives.

If the Fish does not understand himself (or herself) the Gemini Twins are only too willing to clear up the mystery. Mercury-ruled people feel they can solve anything, figure out anything, take it apart, see how it works, then put it back together again. But after their cold critical analysis of Pisces, they sometimes leave the pieces scattered around, without putting them back the way they found them. A Fish who has been taken apart by Gemini can flounder helplessly for years attempting to recover his or her self-respect. Gemini is challenged to clear up the perpetual confusion hanging over Pisces with the razor-sharp Mercury mind, but some Twins can't swim deep enough to even get past the seaweed . . . . . like human sandpipers, pecking away at nothing, unable to see the bottom of the ocean or to recognize its depth.

The wiser Piscean will usually look with indulgence, if not with genuine affection, upon the sometimes childlike antics of the Twins. If Gemini lives (and many Twins do) in an enchanted realm of make-believe, Pisces is delighted to visit there too. But Gemini tends to analyze and label all mystical kingdoms, even while frolicking there, and that spoils all the fun for Pisces. A dream is a dream . . . . why come too near, look too closely? Pisces will not stand for personal probing or insistent questioning by the curious Gemini. If pressed too often, the Fish will either glide away to another stream, or take the easier escape of deception, all the way from subtle evasion to outright lying—justified by Neptune as "simple" self-protection from an invasion of personal privacy.

Sometimes the Pisces man or woman will unconsciously get even with Gemini for being continually forced into a position of accommodation, by refusing to show an energetic response to the Twins' exuberance in communicating some marvelous new idea or plan. This may be the beginning of the end, because Gemini cannot long bear to have his (or her) enthusiasms and flashes of inspiration sprinkled with Pisces pessimism, or dampened by Neptune's wet blankets. When they choose, the Fish can be soothingly supportive, full of faith and encouragement. If they don't choose, well . . . . . there may come a time when the Mercury Bird is left out on a limb, singing alone.

There are some things these two can share happily, some ways in which they bear a striking resemblance. One of them is the appreciation of beauty. Most of us don't notice beauty enough, I guess, but Gemini and Pisces are both acutely aware of the transiting loveliness of Nature, the changing of the seasons, sunrise and sunset—and both are usually inclined to bathe their souls in art, poetry or music . . . the spoken or the written word. Pisces absorbs beauty in ecstasy, silently. Gemini grins, in awe and excited wonder. Somehow, beauty brings the Fish and the Twins together, forms a bridge over which they can toss a sunbeam . . . . and perhaps reach the other side of each other.

Another way they're alike is that it's hard to get either of them to pay strict attention to what you're saying, or to get them to look directly at you for more than a fraction of an instant. Gemini's eyes are sharp, alert, sometimes mocking. Pisces eyes are soft, wandering, liquid and full of comprehension when they focus on you, which isn't often. Gemini eyes, too, focus only briefly, then dart restlessly here and there, birdlike. Like their

eyes, the minds of Gemini and Pisces wander also, but for different reasons . . . . . to separate galaxies.

   The reason Pisceans make such excellent sounding boards for the rest of
us is that the Fish have been, in a karmic or a spiritual sense, through it
all. They've learned how to do without constant attention and adulation.
Knowing how to do without, and not complaining about it, is Neptune's
strength, a Piscean weapon against the disappointments of Life. It makes
these people stronger than they seem, much tougher than they appear to
be. The Fish are used to being overlooked, even before they're born.
Geminis, however, are accustomed to being heard and noticed from the
time they're chattering toddlers. Which brings us to one of the main
reasons these two Sun Signs come together, when they do. Gemini must
communicate, needs to express himself or herself—and compassionate
Pisces nearly always finds time to listen with genuine interest to both the
heartaches and the excitements of others. Gemini couldn't survive without
an audience to appreciate the magic of Mercury's beautiful ribbons of
words. And the Fish couldn't survive without feeling needed. But after a
while, the Twins might lose this great gift offered by Pisces, if Neptune's
gentle longings are consistently ignored. There will be signs. Clear indica-
tions. And when they appear, they should be heeded. The best time to
mend a mistake is when it's small.

GEMINI: A magazine just accepted the article I wrote! Isn't that great news?
PISCES: See how reddish the clouds are over there? I remember my grand-
          father used to say, "Red sky at night, sailor's delight—red sky
          in the morning, sailor's warning . . . . ."
GEMINI: Did you hear what I said about my magazine article?
PISCES: I'm sorry. I'm afraid I wasn't listening.

☆ ☆ ☆ ☆ ☆ ☆

GEMINI *Woman* PISCES *Man*

--- ◆◆◆◆ ---

*If you shut your eyes and are a lucky one, you
may see at times a shapeless pool of lovely pale
colours, suspended in the darkness.*

There has never been a Fish who was not slightly uncertain about where
he stood with the Gemini woman he loves. She will give him plenty of occasions to be jealous, or what passes for jealousy with Pisceans, which is a
rather mild form of it, to be sure.

But it won't do him a bit of good, because there's nothing to be done
about the apparent fickleness of the Twins. (I'm assuming you know by
now that every Gemini girl is two-women-in-one. She began flirting when
she was in the bassinet or being pushed in her buggy, blowing kisses to
strangers, grinning at anyone who noticed her, capturing hearts with her
bright, twinkling star-eyes.)

This female will never really grow up. She's like a mischievous, charming little girl, who cries when she's scolded, laughs merrily when she's
pleased, coaxes and teases and wheedles until she gets her own way—and
getting her own way with a Pisces man isn't too difficult. He's essentially a
gentle soul, affectionate and tolerant, not terribly demanding. Of course,
Pisceans can have their irritable, cranky spells, becoming regular cross-
patches when they've been imposed on once too often. But most of the
time he's willing to try his best to answer her needs. He may get confused
when her needs, along with her wishes and dreams, keep changing, but
he'll keep right on trying. For that matter, he's not exactly a tower of stability himself. Neither of these two were blessed with much of the stuff at
birth. The Fish becomes quickly restless after long periods of fighting the
seaweed of obstacles and delays, and as for her—well, Gemini women possess only a thimbleful of patience, if that much. Needless to say, this will
constitute one of the frequent snarls in the smoothness of this 4-10 Sun
Sign Pattern relationship. Patience is the main ingredient called for in any
recipe for happiness and harmony.

The eyes of a Pisces man have the look of being lost. Gemini eyes have
the look of searching for something about to be found. With Pisces,
Aquarius, Scorpio and Gemini—all four Sun Signs—the pattern of the personality and the stamp of the soul is in the eyes.

Her mind is like a house of glass from which she gazes out on life, with a three-dimensional view of every direction her longings may take. Such multiple choice causes many manifestations in the outward personality, but mostly . . . . . moodiness. The moods of Mercury-ruled Gemini are not the same as the deeper oceans of the Neptune moods of Pisces. They are lightning fast, like quicksilver, coming upon her as unpredictably as a change in the wind.

The mind of the Fish is like a house of many windows too, but with no glass panes, no shutters or blinds to protect him from the seasons—or from her moods. A Pisces man is vulnerable and sensitive, not only to the treatment he receives from others, but to the feelings and emotions of those near him, absorbing their own troubles and symptoms in his own mind and body. So you can see that a relationship with the changeable, frequently troubled Gemini girl, who sometimes projects two emotions simultaneously, may at times be somewhat shattering to the Neptune-ruled male.

This woman was born sparking both mental and physical energy like shock waves. Pisces was born tired. It's little wonder that the Fish is a trifle spiritually fatigued, considering all he's seen throughout so many incarnations . . . all the power and the glory, the ugly and the beautiful, the horrifyingly unspeakable—and the ecstatically indescribable. It's exhausting. Especially when you're tempted, in daydreams, to compare it to the present drab and mundane existence. That much at least his Gemini woman will understand. His need to see the world through soft-tinted glass strikes an echoing chord in her own heart. She, too, would like things to be different, lovelier. But her mercurial nature doesn't shrink from coldly and clearly analyzing things as they *are*, while she's dreaming of how she'd *like* them to be—whereas Pisces never wants to admit the awful truth of anything. Her constant tearing apart the fabric of Life to see how it might be more acceptably put back together again alarms him. When she begins this analytical process with love, which Pisces knows deeply cannot be analyzed, lest its delicacy be shattered, it signals the beginning of trouble in River City—Philadelphia, Tulsa, Beverly Hills, Pittsburgh, Belpre, Parkesburg, Denver, Coshocton—or wherever. Gemini-Pisces couples tend to change residence more frequently than any other Sun Sign combination (except Gemini-Sag, double Gemini or double Sag). Actually, this is a decided plus factor, because the excitement of moving doesn't leave as much time for petty squabbles.

Like all 4-10 Sun Sign Patterns, Gemini and Pisces must cope with the vibration of tension. Their natures are so totally different, their motives inexplicable to one another most of the time. Hurtful situations involving relatives, the parents of one or the other, or their individual careers may be the stage for the explosions of disagreement. With a harmonious exchange of the Sun and Moon in their nativities (or conjoined Moons) threads of sympathy will draw them closer together. Without such planetary first aid, each will suffer many wounds, which could take a long time to heal.

She's capable of locking him out of the house all night if he stays too long gabbing with a neighbor. Then he's capable of muttering, "Who needs it?" and drowning his troubles at the corner saloon, which causes her to lock him out of the house again—which causes him to escape into John Barleycorn again—which causes her to . . . . and so on. The one thing a Pisces man cannot bear for long is a barrage of criticism, sarcasm and accusation, and his Gemini woman's negative twin excels in the art of satirical invective. Her angry torrents of words and clever use of subtle nuance can rain on the sensitive soul of the Fish like sharp hailstones of hurt. On the other hand, one thing a Gemini woman cannot stand is silence—or being left alone with no audience—and one thing in which Pisces excels is escape from unpleasant scenes. Sometimes you'd swear these Neptune people have literally mastered the art of de-materialization. Poof! They're gone! Just like that. Then she's left by herself. Well, not quite by herself. She can always fight it out with her other half —her ever present Twin, who surely comprehends her need to express her torments more than does the Fish, who can't see for the life of him why anyone should want to waste so much time in futile verbal contests. Pisces tends instinctively to *feel* his way through trouble. Gemini inclines to talk it away. Even though they may truly love each other, these two sometimes seem like total strangers attempting to communicate with word and sign language, scrambled like a game of anagrams with half the letters missing. Gemini talks—and Pisces won't always listen. Pisces weeps—and Gemini doesn't always sympathize. Yet they both need desperately to be accepted and understood, for neither of them understands themselves. They're involved in a mutual quest for self-identity, each born under the influence of duality, like four people living under one roof, two visibly—the other two locked up inside, trying to escape and make themselves known.

Their sexual adjustment will not be made without effort, although, assuming a positive Sun-Moon aspect or other favorable planetary exchanges in their horoscopes, he can probably satisfy her need not to be smothered or overly possessed, and she can probably provide the variety of affectionate expression he must either have—or become bored. Neither Gemini nor Pisces requires flaming passion for lovemaking to bring them the contentment of true intimacy, and both are capable of adapting instantly to the other's ephemeral whims and wishes. Yet a real depth of physical blending may be missing in their union. Is it because love alone is never enough to satisfy the nameless longings of either Pisces or Gemini? Or is it because Air and Water Signs seldom feel quite the same overpowering urge for sexual consummation of their initial mental and emotional affinity as do Earth and Fire Signs?

Whatever the reason, these two never find it easy to become "one flesh," or to sexually "know one another," in the biblical sense. An ideal man-woman Oneness may not be achieved without unselfishness, a quality as necessary in sex as in other aspects of love and friendship. While Pisces usually comprehends this fully, the more childlike Gemini woman some-times does not. Their intimate moments are likely to be dictated according to her impulsive desires, rather than in answer to their mutual instincts. If she allows him to teach her by example the meaning of unselfish giving—physically as well as mentally and emotionally—their physical closeness will become a repeated renewal of their love, followed by a deeper com-munion than before, because of an exchanging of their inner natures, making him more spontaneous, like her—and her more tranquil, like him.

As I've said, they are similar in some of their attitudes. They both prefer unlisted phone numbers, privacy and freedom—both of them usually enjoy poetry, music, art or dancing. And they each intensely dislike routine. Boredom is a mutual enemy. Not so fortunately, however, they're also both inclined to exaggerate the truth, all the way from tiny white lies to premeditated deception—always rationalized away by myriad excuses. Fre-quently, when Gemini accuses Pisces of distorting the truth (or vice-versa) it's the pot calling the kettle black. A Gemini woman finds Life and Love impossible to comprehend with the senses alone. Her ruler, Mercury, demands that she use her intellect in solving the puzzle. Maybe she could figure it all out if someone would really-truly listen to her doubts and de-spairs, her ecstasies and her ideas. A Pisces man can do this for her if he will—patiently and sympathetically hearing her out, waiting for her to complete her convoluted circles of reasoning and finally locate the right turn in the road toward happiness. After a while, she'll take his hand as they walk along together, and his eyes won't look so lost anymore. How can a man be lost when there are not just one but two charming, delightful feminine companions beside him? Being in love with Twins may be dis-turbing and perplexing at times, but no one ever said it was humdrum.

To the Pisces man, love is just another dream, in which he, the dreamer, joyfully controls the world he's created in his imagination through his intuitive sense perceptions . . . . colored with muted pastels, fragile and changeable. The constantly expressed dissatisfactions of his Gemini lady often tear great rents in his dream—and he tries to patch it, make it like new again. But dreams are not easily mended, once they've been torn apart. They are made of such misty material.

If she will speak softly, move gently . . . slowly . . . she may enter his dream world with him, and see love the way he does—as a thing of calm and beauty. All it takes is putting herself, Gemini-wise, in his place now and then, which will eventually lead her straight into his heart—the very haven she's so long been searching for and thought she'd never find . . . . . that magical garden where roses grow without the need for protective thorns.

☆ ☆ ☆ ☆ ☆ ☆

GEMINI *Man* PISCES *Woman*

> *In his absence, things are usually quiet on the*
> *island. The faeries take an hour longer in the morn-*
> *ing, the beasts attend to their young . . . . . . but with*
> *the coming of Peter, who hates lethargy, they are all*
> *under way again . . . .*

To keep a love affair or a marriage serene and untroubled, the typical girl Fish will do almost anything. She'll accommodate herself, her routine and her habits to the convenience of the Gemini man she loves, even though her feminine-liberation-minded female friends will be scandalized. They'll pity her openly, but she'll just smile and ignore them.

She's not really a masochistic slave to the whims of the Twins. Her sympathetic acquaintances just think she is. They're not alone. Her Gemini man is under the same impression. And that's exactly the impression this sweet, accommodating, soft-spoken lady intends to project to him (and to all her inquisitive friends, neighbors and relatives). She knows what she's doing. She's making life easier for herself. Once she's fallen in love with a Gemini the Neptune woman has enough common sense to comprehend that she has only two practical choices in this challenging 4-10 Sun Sign Pattern relationship. She can decide love isn't worth the demands a Gemini man makes upon her delicate psyche—and leave him. Just slip away some morning when he's not around. Or she can decide that the pleasure and happiness, the contentment and peace of loving him

—and receiving the love and devotion of at least one of his Twin selves in return—are worth a few adjustments here and there in the relationship. If the latter is her choice, she'll simply make it work. It may take some intricate planning, but she'll manage.

Passive resistance is her Neptune secret. She was born with an awesome talent for it, as some people are born with an ear for music or perfect pitch. She knows just when to back off, how far to retreat—precisely when it's a propitious time to advance and how far she can go with him. Actually, she doesn't really know. She *senses* it. It's as though she was equipped at birth with some sort of invisible but sensitive antenna that flashes both precognitive and perceptive signals to her regarding human behavior patterns.

All Geminis are undeniably as mentally quick as can be, always alert and on guard, nearly impossible to deceive. But as clever as the Gemini man indisputably is, he can be blind to the Neptunian strategies of a Pisces girl. If she has things she wants to do, things of which he might disapprove, she won't waste her energies rocking their relationship with insistent demands or tearful pleas. She'll simply do as he wishes when he's there—and as *she* wishes when he's *not* there. What she wants to do that doesn't receive his blessing needn't be anything sinister or sly. It needn't be planning to rob a bank or being unfaithful.

It could be something as innocent and ordinary as sleeping an extra hour. Like all Birds, the typical Gemini is nearly always up and alert quite early, either whistling merrily or complaining crankily (depending on which Gemini Twin arose first), and he can become quite critical of those who lie abed later than Gemini believes they should when there are things to be done. It could be something she wants to read—which isn't necessarily the reading matter he would recommend to her. Perhaps visiting friends when he feels she should be spending her time in a more profitable way. Maybe keeping an appointment with the beauty parlor. Why would he frown on that? Because he thinks she's beautiful just the way she is—and besides, the money she spends on personal beautification could be better spent by the two of them traveling somewhere together. To Gemini, the absolute ultimate of ecstasies is a change of scene—going somewhere—anywhere at all that's different and away from daily routine.

Gemini's cleverness includes an unerring instinct for the expedient. Like, if she made her beauty parlor appointment when he was present, he'd try to talk her out of it, either with his considerable powers of persuasion and charm—or through cranky criticism. But once she's gone and he sees the finished product, he seldom argues the point. First of all, she looks lovely, and he can't find it in his heart to quarrel with her when she's so appealing. Secondly, he knows it's a waste of time to try to stop something after the fact. This man seldom wastes time. He believes time was made to be filled by doing something—every second of it somehow utilized (except for sleeping, a luxury the average Mercury Birds indulge in for only very brief periods). Time is the stuff of which Life—and dreams—are made. To squander it by doing simply nothing is, to him, a sinful thing.

The Pisces woman has a completely different view of time. She feels that it's inexhaustible—there's always more of it tomorrow if any of it slips away from her today. And she believes one of the nicest ways to spend it is doing nothing. Especially after she's depleted her energies with a thousand and one duties of service to others, and her normally cheerful spirit is sagging at the seams. Time is best spent when possible, she feels, in just being herself, simply existing . . . . in the cool, green Pisces waters of calm contemplation. It refreshes her soul.

Living under the always somewhat tense 4-10 vibration with a Gemini man, her soul needs a lot of refreshing. The very qualities that drew her close to him in the beginning may later grow to be extremely wearing and wearying to her more placid nature. His mind is full of little surprises, and this delights her. He's quick, mentally agile, with an instant grasp of everything he sees, hears or reads. His ideas pop out when least expected, and they're nearly always original and fascinating. He seems to be forever busy dreaming, thinking, planning or *doing*—while she is busy just *being*. He can change occupations or careers at the wink of one of his twinkling eyes, and she never knows what to expect around the next corner. It's exciting. It's intriguing and compelling. He's like a mystery she can't completely fathom, and she adores mysteries. But these same traits of her Mercury-urged man, after a while, may leave her longing for solitude and quiet . . . . . for the security of sameness . . . . . a retreat into the soothing stillness of her own slower and softer dreams and goals.

For a time, his wonderful wit, his heart-tugging, little-boy, three-cornered grin, the star-shine in his expressive eyes, his sheer intelligence and his multiple talents will keep the girl Fish mesmerized by his Mercurial spell. It's like watching a living kaleidoscope to see the changes in his moods from affectionate, merry, warmly tender and generous—to irritable, sarcastic, sullen and stingy—and back again (to the dominance of the "good Twin"). When she watches his mental acrobatics from a distance, they're interesting, even electrifying, and certainly stimulating. It's only when she gradually allows herself to become an integral and inseparable part of the many-faceted ups and downs of his unpredictable mental, physical and emotional activity that the wear and tear on her tranquility begins to show.

However much she may try to resist, the Neptune woman can't help being eventually drawn into the nearest vortex of human experience. She absorbs the feelings and emotions around her like a psychic sponge or a sensitive photographic plate (much in the same way that Cancerians and Scorpios do). And because her own aura is keyed to a gentler chord, the percussion of Gemini cymbals and the high notes of the flutes can sometimes jangle her nerves and disturb her poise, leaving her vaguely depressed. Her solution is to swim quietly away from the floods of feeling around her which threaten to drown her . . . . enter the still world of her inner serenity . . . whatever the cost . . . . and return, her strength renewed. During these necessary periods of retreat, the Gemini man who loves her will be puzzled and hurt, sometimes angry.

It never occurs to him that he's adept in the self-defensive tactic of mental retreat himself, an expert at disappearing into aloof detachment when she most needs him to be attentive and concerned. Remember that Pisces is a very old soul, born wise—and Gemini is the symbolic Toddler Child (see "The Twelve Mysteries of Love" in the front of this book). He can't help being a trifle self-centered. Yet, often his insight is surprising, despite the symbolic "Child" charisma. There will be times when he'll display an amazing comprehension of what she's going through, then show her he understands with his Gemini light touch of compassion . . exquisitely tender. Or he senses when the right thing to do is to make her laugh, suggest a trip . . or just a drive or walk together. These are the rare and singing moments of their love.

Frequently, the sexual chemistry between this man and woman is the silent alchemy that brings them closer together in every way—not just physically. Somehow, through the blending of their Air and Water Elements during the intimacies of their sexual union, he becomes more like her— and she becomes more like him. So that, strangely, after their lovemaking, she's more alive, vibrant and aware . . he's more subdued and gentle, less restless and seeking.

When Water joins with Air in sexual Oneness (see "The Blending of the Elements" section in the back of Volume II) Water magically transforms Air into its own element, in the form of life-giving, cooling rain, after which all of Nature is fresh again, drenched with promise and scented with new hope. Enclosed within the circle of each other's arms, the Fish and the Twins often find the elusive harmony they reach for together at other times, and never quite seem to capture. The sexual mystery between them can be a powerful regenerative experience for both, the secret and strong foundation for their continued desire to try to understand one another's vastly different personalities.

Her procrastination, her tendency toward evading issues annoys and frustrates him. But she's an enormously facile subject changer. It's all he can do to keep up with her, swift as he is. His periodic criticism and scattered interests trouble and upset her. Yet she nearly always finds a way to avoid unpleasantness. He'd rather she didn't, because he needs the occasional mental stimulation of debate and discussion to keep his Mercury wits sharpened. She'd rather he relaxed more and worried less. He'd prefer her to relax less and worry more. Well, perhaps not worry—but at least see things as they are, instead of the way she'd like them to be (even though he often succumbs to daydreaming himself). A Gemini man is designed in a mosaic pattern of sudden twists and turns. Just when you think he's critical of metaphysical matters, he'll buy a book about the Great Pyramid. I knew one Mercury Bird who claimed contempt for the occult, then mentioned he'd like a crystal ball for Christmas. He wanted to experiment. Experimentation is the adrenalin Gemini needs to keep going. If something manages to catch his interest, he'll never rest until he's figured out the concept and improved upon it.

The complexities of this man's mind and attitudes will forever both magnetize and elude the Pisces woman. Sometimes his contradictions will increase her admiration of him, moving her to even try to imitate his analytical and intellectual yet occasionally imaginative approach. At other times, she'll despair of ever truly knowing him. For different reasons, he'll also wonder if he'll ever really know her. Because there are two of him and two of her, the game never ends. Gemini and Pisces are both signs of duality. Now and then, when she's mentally, physically and spiritually exhausted, she'll turn icy cold and refuse to communicate, which distresses him more than he ever allows her to realize. But most of the time she avoids a scene by ignoring her own hurt feelings. When ugliness, confusion or confrontation appears on the horizon, the dreamy girl Fish just pretends it isn't there, and for her, then, it disappears. She's learned that if you await patiently, most things resolve themselves. But it's impossible for him to face a problem by make-believing it doesn't exist. He's compelled to analyze and solve it immediately. He can no more resist this urge than he can resist working a crossword puzzle or answering the questions aloud when he watches a quiz show on television (which he always guesses before the person who's being asked). Every Gemini man is an instructor at heart, driven to purify muddy waters with the clearness of reason and logic. Then, too, there's the puzzling contradiction of his daydreaming.

Because Gemini and Pisces are of the Water and Air Elements, they'll never be as demonstrative, warm and affectionate outwardly as people born under the Fire Element. Yet, because of their combined water and air essence, they offer each other a great gift—freedom. She'll seldom question his impulses or his whereabouts, for she is not the possessive type. He'll grant her, likewise, the same freedom of movement. He won't mind where she floats around when he isn't there—but when he is, he'll expect her to be near, for Gemini requires an audience. She's a beautiful listener, and to him, this is her most endearing quality. Privately, he knows this soft-spoken lady of quiet secrets and subtleties is genuinely interested in everything he has to say—and above all, this is his deepest need.

She knows this changeable man of many moods will always need her—and this, above all, is *her* deepest need: to be *needed*. When he's sarcastic, as Gemini can sometimes be, he breaks her heart. But when his charm returns, his eyes twinkle with surprises again, when he projects his wistful three-cornered grin and his Peter Pan yearnings, she knows she's made the right choice to compromise her preferred life style to his. By doing so, she hasn't lost anything really, and she's gained her very own human kaleidoscope, that changes colors, shapes and designs at the slightest touch.

Repeatedly, he'll scold her for being so generous and extravagant. Then one day, without warning, he'll fly all over town, as though Mercury's silver wings were truly fastened on his heels, borrowing money he doesn't have, from two or three banks, to lend to a friend in trouble. For months, he'll make serious plans to enroll in night school to get his engineering degree, then he'll suddenly buy a typewriter and announce he's going to be a writer. He'll come home, tired from doing mental push-ups all day, refuse dinner, inform her he's going to bed, and grumpily head for the bedroom. Less than five minutes later, he'll reappear, wink at her with the old magic, and ask her if she wants to go for a ride to watch the sunset, then have dinner in town and see a play.

While she's changing, he'll nag her to hurry, and irritably complain that it takes her forever to get ready to go anywhere. But when she's sitting in the car beside him, he unexpectedly tells her she's never looked more beautiful. "Do you know I wouldn't know what to do without you?" he asks her. She doesn't reply, she just smiles. She's known that all along. That's why she's still there.

CANCER

Water—Cardinal—Negative
Ruled by the Moon
Symbol: The Crab
Night Forces—Feminine

CANCER

Water—Cardinal—Negative
Ruled by the Moon
Symbol: The Crab
Night Forces—Feminine

The **CANCER-CANCER** *Relationship*

*The little house looked so cosy and safe in the
darkness, with a bright light showing through its
blinds, and the chimney smoking beautifully. . . .*

Did you ever wonder why your parents treated you as they did when you were a child? I mean, do you brood over it a lot? No? Well, Cancerians do, just before they fall asleep at night, and after they do finally fall asleep, they dream about it, or have nightmares about it.

Yesterday—whether it was twenty or a hundred years ago—is very real to the Moon-lured Crabs, which is why most of them know so much about history, a favorite Cancerian subject in school, also a popular hobby with many of these men and women in later years. Lots of Crabs collect antiques.

Unless the parents of those born under this Moon-controlled Sun Sign of Cancer were astrologers, they may not have said "I love you" often enough to these sensitive children. Maybe they discussed how pretty or handsome the siblings were too frequently. Perhaps they gave the little Crabs too meager an allowance, forcing them to go to work cutting the neighbor's grass at the age of eight, because a stipend of a dollar a week wasn't enough to remove that uneasy feeling of financial insecurity (any more than $3,000 a week could take it completely away now). It's even possible that the parents of little Clementine or Clarence didn't kiss the Crabs goodnight, or read bedtime stories to them each evening. (They skipped it on week ends—horrors!)

All these are reasons why the majority of Cancerians grow up lacking a sense of emotional security, causing them to exhibit flashes of moody, sensitive adolescence. It's taxing for other Sun Signs (except for Scorpio and Pisces) to cope with the apprehensions that haunt Crabs, from the persistent spectre of starvation to the lingering dread of loneliness. Only a Cancerian, vibrating on the same Lunar frequency, can find the right words and manner to calm another. Here's a sample of the typical dialogue between these 1-1 Sun Sign Pattern people.

CRAB #1: There you go, diving down into one of your inky moods again. Don't you know all the people who love you wonder why you're so lonely, and why you won't let them help you?

CRAB #2: No one tries to understand me. I had a sad childhood. I keep *telling* you that. And you don't even care. *Nobody* cares.

CRAB #1: Look, first off, try to realize that your parents may not have understood how tender your feelings were. Second off, your friends today have no way of knowing that you feel they don't love you enough, because you clam up and refuse to talk about it.

CRAB #2: Why should I talk about it? People are cold and cruel. I could always talk to my mother, and sometimes *she* understood me, but mother is gone now, and no one will *ever* love me like she did—oh, it's so AWFUL not to have Mama around. No one has made me any whiffleberry jelly since she died. (sob-sob)

CRAB #1: Don't cry. Here, take my hanky. At least your mother tried to understand you when she was alive. *My* mother warped my whole life because she ignored me most of the time. I might as well have been an orphan for all the sympathy I got from *her*. Having a mother who's dead isn't as lonely as never *really* ever having had a Mama at all.

CRAB #2: (deeply sympathetic) It must be an empty feeling.

CRAB #1: Do you know she never kissed me goodnight until *after* she tucked in my baby sister? And once she even stole the dollar the Good Tooth Fairy left under *my* pillow to pay the laundry man for *her* dirty diapers. You may not believe that, but it's true. (sob-sob)

CRAB #2: How dreadful! Don't cry. Here, do you want your hanky back?

CRAB #1: No, thanks. You keep it. I'm sorry I broke down. Anyway, we were talking about you, not me. You're certainly old enough, if you don't mind my saying so, to begin to learn that the best way to *get* love is to *give* love.

CRAB #2: Okay, okay, okay, okay. But even if I do learn how to get people to love me, what good will that do when the whole world is headed for a financial collapse? Probably my bank will be the first one to close, and I'll lose all my money and stocks and end up a pauper.

Note to reader: Should Crab #2 be female, just change the foregoing to: "Harry and I will lose our house and all our savings, he'll probably lose his job, and we'll have to wander around barefoot and homeless or go on public welfare and food stamps, which would HUMILIATE me. I'd rather be dead."

CRAB #1: You're not going to end up a pauper (or wander around homeless) because you have two separate savings accounts, those twelve bags of gold nuggets you buried under the garage, plus your bank account in Switzerland, not to mention the three apartment houses you own. Most people would consider you wealthy and secure.

CRAB #2: *Most* people don't realize that money can be here today and gone tomorrow. What if someone finds out where I buried those gold nuggets?

CRAB #1: *You* should worry! I'm going to lose my business because I can't refinance my loan. My banker hates me. I just *know* he hates me. All my kids need braces and I had to cancel my vacation to Nova Scotia this summer. *I'm* the one on the point of starvation, not *you*.

CRAB #2: Selfish, selfish, selfish—that's what you are, selfish! You don't care at all for my problems, just your own. *We* try to economize here by using margarine, but *you* still use butter. So who's worse off, you or me—I ask you?

CRAB #1: Don't snap at me. I'll snap right back. And we do NOT use butter at our house. We use margarine like you, so there!

CRAB #2: Butter!

CRAB #1: Margarine!

CRAB #2:   Butter, butter, butter, butter, butter!

CRAB #1:   *STOP THAT!* In the first place, it's none of your business what we spread on our bread. That's *my* business.

CRAB #2:   See! You're neurotically secretive. Always afraid people are prying. You should learn to be more direct and out-in-the-open, like me.

CRAB #1:   Out-in-the-open? *You?* HA! That's a howl. You're so secretive you won't even answer a civil question. Everyone knows you're paranoid. It makes people nervous to be around you.

CRAB #2:   Oh! (sob-sob) I *told* you everyone hates me. Now you finally admit it yourself. And you pretended you were my friend. (sob-sob)

CRAB #1:   I *am* your friend. Will you please blow your nose and stop that sniffling? You're not paranoid. I just said that to snap at you because you snapped at me. People do love you. I even like you myself, most of the time. Do you know why people like you so much?

CRAB #2:   Why? (from inside the clothes closet, weeping) Why?

CRAB #1:   Because you're so lovable. Not only that, you're talented, and that makes everyone respect you. People like you because you tell funny jokes, your house is always cozy and warm, you make great chicken soup and you loan people pennies from your piggy bank when they're broke. See how nice you are? You're rich and good looking and smart and popular. . . . . .

CRAB #2:   Am I really? Would you *really* call me popular?

CRAB #1:   Yes, I would. My wife likes you, my kids love you, and . . . . .

CRAB #2:   (peeking anxiously out of the shell) Really? Really-truly?

CRAB #1:   Yes, really-truly, and honor-bright. I swear it.

CRAB #2:   (perking up, opening the shell, and crawling cautiously out onto the warm sands of affection and approval) Say! How would you like a bowl of hot chicken soup? And maybe a slice of toast . . . with butter?

The typical Cancerian wouldn't feel totally secure financially if he or she owned Fort Knox. Nelson Rockefeller, the original John D. Rockefeller and various other assorted Rockefellers are Cancerians. They spend most of their time worrying about how to invest their billions to keep them from shrinking into mere millions, right along with worrying about how to give the whole world a bowl of hot chicken soup. Here they are (they believe) trying their best to solve the problems of starvation and poverty and political confusion, with the few dollars they can spare—and everyone misconstrues their motives and calls them greedy, monopoly-minded capitalists. It's just AWFUL. Nobody understands, nobody really *cares*.

The emotional insecurities which cause many Crabs to snap and be cranky, to withdraw into their shells sullenly and pout, to hoard their cash under the mattress and be fearful and timid about accepting affection, may often best be soothed by another Moon Child. However, sometimes these moody Looney Birds of such deep perception and sharp insight, such gentle manners and graceful ways, need the added dimension of other Sun Sign friends, associates and mates to balance their complex personalities. Two Crabs together will develop strong ties of sympathy, but will they grow? Only when each is wise enough to see in the other his or her own mistakes, thus correcting, instead of compounding them—for compounded mistakes, very much like compounded interest loans at the bank, can be costly in terms of human happiness.

Despite a natural timidity, Cancerians possess incredible tenacity of purpose, frequently losing all fear and reticence when a crisis strikes, and something or someone they love needs their courage. Then they can be amazingly strong, forceful and tough—until their feelings are hurt again—and back they crawl into the protective shell. In any sort of mutual relationship they'll never run out of things to crab about, weep over, laugh at and share.

All Looney Birds are fascinated by antiques, museums and politics. Normally, they're intensely patriotic, and if they're typical Cancerians, they'll be the most loyal, flag-saluting, flag-waving citizens of their country—except for Taureans. Many of them are teachers, scientists, artists and photographers (and bankers, of course, that's understood). The women are usually ideal homemakers, and excellent, though somewhat possessive, mothers. Both sexes tend to collect valuables, as well as totally worthless junk. Crabs are impossibly cranky, touchingly kind and hilariously funny. They're first chatty, then silent, sullen and depressed—sometimes pushy and aggressive, at other times cautious and conservative, blushing with shyness and timidity. They can be gallant, sweet, old-fashioned, motherly or fatherly, protective, scholarly, soothing and gentle. They're highly secretive (but seldom deceptive—there's a difference), graceful, poetic, musical daydreamers, whose raindrop tears are preludes to fits of giggles. Money and food can seduce them into almost anything, yet they're more sentimental at heart than even Leo, Libra and Taurus—and always economical and thrifty. *You'd* be all these things too, if *your* emotions were synchronized to every change of the Moon.

I don't know about your experiences, but all the Crabs who have grabbed my toe—or ear—or heart—on the beach, in the mountains, or in the city, are each doing their astrologically, totally typical thing. Among the Looney Birds I know personally, one owns a supermarket, one is a musician, one interprets dreams—and one is a powerful, wealthy tycoon-politician for whom I have a very high regard, who has, on occasion, requested astrological guidance, and has always thanked me most gallantly and graciously, in writing.

Of course, this tenacious and rock-like Crab is not the first powerful American leader to place his confidence in the wisdom of the planets. Among a number of others, Presidents Abraham Lincoln, George Washington, Thomas Jefferson and Franklin Delano Roosevelt did so—and in fact, the majority of founding fathers of this nation, and the signers of the Declaration of Independence, as well as our Constitution, were themselves either astrologers or serious students of astrology. Each one, including Ben Franklin himself. And if I may be forgiven for letting a Cancerian-type secret out of the bag, because the New Age of Aquarius demands truth at this eleventh hour of our planet's survival, Masonry is based on astrology, as all high-degree Masons are aware. (Most of our founding fathers were Masons, or Rosicrucians, who saw to it that the birth chart of our country was chosen with meticulous attention to planetary positions.)

Don't you believe it's time astrology's detractors should halt their attacks against this ancient art and science? Surely it's time that certain men, who are otherwise intelligent, should cease their futile, yet repeated attempts to assassinate this guide to self-knowledge, which our co-Creators, in Their infinite wisdom, bestowed upon us for both our temporal and our spiritual enlightenment—and which so clearly proves the Synchronicity of the Universe.

The reason so many Moon-ruled Crabs feel rather snugly at home in this country is because the United States of America is perhaps the most typical Cancerian Sun Sign of all, born on the Fourth of July—confused and sidetracked repeatedly by the split-personality, schizophrenic urges of its Gemini Ascendent (preaching freedom, while having denied blacks, women and the American Indians true equality, and so forth). Still, Uncle Sam is basically a Crab, his Gemini Rising Sign notwithstanding, the Lunar qualities subconsciously imbedded in all who live under the Stars and Stripes, whatever their personal Sun Signs may be, for everyone lives three Karmas throughout any given incarnation. Individual, racial and national Karmas equally influence the feelings and actions. And when two Crabs double up in an association within an also Cancerian country, the 1-1 vibration increases in intensity.

Is there a single citizen of the USA (each Crab especially) who doesn't feel an inexplicable heart tug of nostalgic sentiment and secret, if grudging, admiration at the sound of the brisk, clipped accent of "dear old Mother England"—or who wasn't kinfolk proud of the courage of every Britisher, from pub keeper to Churchill, during the World War II blitz bombing of London? Is not our CIA, FBI, NASA, and evidently (judging from the Watergate affair) also, periodically, our Government, unnecessarily secretive? Were we not first to land a man on the Moon herself, our very own Sun Sign ruler?

Are we not, as a nation, continually feeling guilty twinges over our inability to feed the world's hungry—and did we not initiate the practice of sending CARE packages to the needy? (Cancer *cares*.) Like any two Cancerians doubled-up, do we not become unexpectedly Crab-shell tough in a crisis? And—say! Why don't those countries we try to help, by intervening in their private affairs, *like* us more? Why aren't they more *grateful?* Does *anyone* really-truly love us? (sob-sob) Who will dispute America's use of her wealth to buy affection and respect from others, as well as to purchase security and protection against those who might hurt her, and her "children"? Is not the largest defense budget and nuclear stockpile in the world an aspect of undue Cancerian caution? And Heavens-to-Betsy-Ross! Goodness knows we've always fought for and clung to our freedoms—tenaciously.

Now, if we could only get over our Cancerian money hang-up, let go and learn to really *share*, realize that to *get* love, we must *give* love, we might all stop being so crabby and snapping at each other (like any two Crabs, in any sort of an association). Oh, dear, oh, dear, oh dear! Things were so much better back in the good old days . . . . . when we had whiffleberry jelly on our toast . . . . . (sob-sob) . . . . . swinging on the apple tree in the grassy-green back yard . . . . . swimming in unpolluted rivers and streams . . . . . all snug and safe and security-blanketed in the protection of our Constitution . . . . . when our leaders had to be voted into office by the people's choice . . . . . and a simple, honest boy like Abe Lincoln could aspire to become President, without the backing of the multi-billion-dollar interests of modern day, powerful conglomerates . . . . . (sob-sob) . . . . . way back when dear old Patrick Henry said "Give me liberty, or give me . . . ."

Say, you know what? When you really stop to *think* about it, a little Cancerian caution now and then might not be such a bad thing after all. Maybe those "good old days" *are* worth clinging to—tenaciously. Sometimes, the Crab's Lunar fears and nightmares are not imaginary, but very real.

☆ ☆ ☆ ☆ ☆ ☆

CANCER *Woman* CANCER *Man*

◆━◆━◆

"He does so need a mother. . . ."

*"Yes, I know," Wendy admitted rather
forlornly; "no one knows so well as I."*

When a girl Crab and a boy Crab are enticed to peek out of their protective shells long enough to fall in love, emotional security being the important thing it is to each, they'll usually want to marry. Some may make the attempt to tolerate a loosely defined living-together arrangement for a time, but it will be a very short time.

These two really prefer—and need—the warmth and protection of a socially-sanctioned and legally-cemented relationship. It's extremely doubtful that any Cancerian could be comfortable for long under the psychological burden of an illicit union. (What would Mother think?) Only those rare and lonely Moon Children who have been hopelessly alienated from the parental tie, for one reason or another, will successfully adjust to love-sans-marriage, and even they will duck their heads when they pass the neighbors. Yes, there are Cancerian prostitutes, but truly, they're the most unhappy, emotionally unfulfilled females on Earth, except when they're counting their earnings. Nevertheless, every last one of them cries herself to sleep at night.

The casual promiscuity of the Aquarian Age sexual revolution has passed right over the heads of the average and typical Cancer man and woman. Tradition and the sacredness of home life are too deeply ingrained in the Lunar subconscious to be discarded without great uneasiness of spirit, never mind what you may hear from some flippant Cancerian Looney Bird you know who's trying to appear to be "with it." Listen to the stars. They're older and wiser. Watch—wait—and see.

Once the 1-1 Sun Sign Pattern of Cancer-Cancer is planted, and blossoms into the girl and boy Crabs becoming "one flesh," they can surely discover lots of things to do together, based on interests they have in common—like poring over family photo albums, giggling over each other's baby pictures, collecting stamps and old coins, crying on each other's cozy shoulders, visiting each other's homesteads, redecorating the house, gardening, traveling, exchanging dreams and nightmares, reading or writing poetry, singing or listening to music, running along the beach picking up driftwood, scuba diving, making wishes on the New Moon and sharing Lunar madness under the Full Moon. She can cook for him, and he can earn money for her. Or–Cancer being a feminine sign, and the Lunar charisma of both male and female Crabs being what it is–he can cook for *her*, and *she* can earn money for *him*. Either way. All Cancerian men like fine food, and most are good cooks. All Cancerian women like supplemental incomes, and most are good at earning it. And vice-versa, with the boy and girl Crabs.

Emotional crying binges (or pouting periods) will be first on the list of possible problem areas, making Kleenex a big item on the budget. They both sniffle, sob and weep a lot–at sad movies, over real or imagined neglect from the mate, about their lost childhood–and sometimes for no reason at all, except that their emotions wax and wane with the Moon's periodicity.

Food, as already mentioned, will come next in importance, with either happy agreement or tearful argument about which restaurant to dine in (during courtship) or how to cook and serve the artichokes at home (after the honeymoon). Those rare Cancerians who are casually unconcerned with food–with where, when and how they eat–either have the Moon or Ascendent in Gemini, Aquarius, Sagittarius or Aries, or else they were adopted for sure, and were fibbed to about their true birthday. Fabulous food–and enough of it–is a Cancer birthright. It shocks the typical Crabs to think of anyone starving, and it literally *terrifies* them to think of *themselves* starving. Both possibilities will bring tears to their eyes. Some of the most sincerely and tenderly concerned men and women, who deeply yearn to help the hungry masses (especially the children) of the underprivileged countries, are Cancerians (also some of the most frequent purchasers of bathroom scales, although they share this latter distinction with many Taureans and Librans).

After emotional tantrums and food fusses will come babies–raising a family. If one of them has natal planetary positions indicating the lack of desire to have offspring, the other will sulk and pout. If they both want tiny cherubs, they'll find grounds for both agreement and disagreement when the birds are ready to leave the nest. Some Cancerian mothers don't believe Junior is old enough to date a girl or to live alone in his own apartment until he's around thirty to thirty-five. Some Cancerian fathers (and mothers) don't believe a daughter should marry until a potential suitor appears who is healthy, wealthy and wise, who treasures her as a rare pearl of perfect womanhood, whose reputation is unblemished–and who makes over $100,000 a year. (A parent with both the Sun *and* Moon in Cancer might conceivably hold out for President of the United States as the only man fit for such an honor.)

Next on the list of subjects involving the possibilities of both harmony and tension between two Crabs in love—is money. Actually, money comes first in order of Cancerian priority, but sometimes the haze of romance causes this couple to hide their individual financial hang-ups from each other initially, as an unseemly and harsh intrusion upon the harmonics of love. They're right. It is. Nonetheless, they'd best tackle the clash over cash in the very beginning. Separate checking accounts. Definitely, that's what I would advise. Separate checking accounts, savings accounts, stock portfolios, stamp collections and spending money allowances. Then they can each hoard as much lettuce as he or she desires, and practice whatever mild or pronounced degree of stinginess or generosity was implanted by the experiences of childhood, secretly, without the other knowing about it. Cancer is ultrasensitive, and more so about money than about anything else. Keeping their individual finances private could be a futile hope, because these two are *equally* adept at keeping secrets and prying them out of each other.

Last, but surely not least, there's the area of sex. Let's hope they make an attempt to comprehend the peculiarities of their mutual astrological symbol, the Crab. The habit of all Nature crabs, male and female, as I've pointed out before, is to reach a desired objective by first moving backward or sideways, with seeming unconcern, then lunging suddenly forward. If they both memorize this ingrained tendency, she'll be less likely to dissolve into tears of rejection and neglect some night when he casually announces he's going to sleep on the couch to watch the eclipse of the Moon from the front room window. She can instead smile to herself, knowing his *real* objective is to follow her into bed soon, having been aroused by Lunar longings when she kissed him goodnight on the couch, trailing perfume and wearing his favorite nightie. And he'll be less likely to be thrown into an impotent impasse of masculine fears when she coolly turns her back to him on their anniversary, murmuring, "Goodnight honey, don't forget to set the alarm," after her eyes telegraphed to him all afternoon an invitation for a thrilling encore of their wedding night. He can, instead, smile and wait till she signals her *real* wishes by slowly sliding her cold feet over to touch his warm toes—or some similar subtlety. Both of them are inclined to play sexual guessing games, concealing passion for fear of rebuff—or the discovery of a lack of a *mutual* need for union—and so each will often try to trick the other into making the first move. Other than this bedtime hide-and-seek habit, they should find a rare contentment through their physical expression of love.

Neither one of them seeks, or is desirous of handling, a demanding sexual passion. Although they're both enormously receptive to sensuality and capable of a deep response, their need in lovemaking is more for affection than for eroticism. It can crush a male or female Crab if the partner fails to set the proper mood for sex, with preliminary endearments and tender touches—or, even worse, fails to spend time after physical consummation in affectionately reaffirming love. Romance is an integral part of sexual excitement and fulfillment for Cancer. The boy or girl Crab who feels unloved throughout the day will snap sharply at the advances of the mate at night, then crawl into a lonely shell of frigidity, expecting to be coaxed out into desire by frequent reassurances and apologies.

When these two first meet, timidity and caution may color their initial sex reactions. Then suddenly, under a Full Moon, which can act as a strange and mystical aphrodisiac to Cancer, they'll move forward (like the symbolic Nature crab) to do what comes naturally, and it will be a toss-up who seduces whom. Poetry and music never fail to quicken the sexual pulse of Cancerian lovers, but they'll find physical love difficult if not impossible to express when they're worried about finances. A streak of poverty can temporarily halt their sex lives, and a feeling of not being appreciated will also considerably dampen passion. When their physical relationship cools, they don't need a sex therapy clinic or a bag of ginseng cookies. They need lots of money, lots of affection, lots of sympathy—and a Farmer's Almanac. Usually, this man and woman will be faithful. Infidelity is rare between Cancerians. If it should occur, the Lunar possessiveness won't be as likely to create a display of jealousy, as to cause a tenacious determination to wait out the rival.

Secrecy is a trait they'll have to curb early in their relationship. Although Crabs of both sexes like to keep secrets, neither one likes to have secrets kept *from* him—or her. If they work at being more open and direct, less subtle and evasive, much hurt can be avoided. He may think she's hiding a lover, when the real reason she's so quiet and preoccupied is because her mother didn't answer her last letter—or he didn't compliment her on her creamed artichokes, and didn't even notice her new nightgown. And she may think he's seeing another woman, when his real secret is that he's worried about being able to make the car payment—or that she's forgotten to say "thank you for loving me" when they wake up in the morning for three whole weeks. In either case, an honest confession will turn everything rightside-up again, and change tears into laughter—for both of them possess the saving grace of humor, which is always the surest and safest antidote when they're taking themselves too seriously.

More so than with other 1-1 Sun Sign Pattern lovers, the degree of compatibility between the Moon Maid and her gentle Crab will depend on their individual Moon Signs, and the aspect formed between their natal Moons. If this is harmonious, their coziness will far exceed their crabbiness. If not, this man and woman still stand a good chance of becoming wealthy together—and they'll also probably treat one another with more tender, loving care than either of them ever have or ever will receive from anyone else. They may snap at each other under a waning Moon, but when she is waxing, these two will sail away on a sea of imagination into a lovely world of lavender lunacy and pale silver enchantment, faintly scented with Johnson's baby powder. Moonlight becomes them—both.

CANCER

Water—Cardinal—Negative
Ruled by the Moon
Symbol: The Crab
Night Forces—Feminine

LEO

Fire—Fixed—Positive
Ruled by the Sun
Symbols: Lion & Shy Pussycat
Day Forces—Masculine

The CANCER-LEO *Relationship*

"... And I know you meant to be kind ..."

The *Moon Maiden* and the Lion. The *Crab* and the Lioness. *Cancer* and Leo. Is that what you call yourselves? You're making a large mistake. It may seem a small thing, but so is a seed, before it grows into a Sequoia tree. Let's correct it, and start off right. You've no idea how it will help. The *Lion* and the Moon Maiden. The *Lioness* and the Crab. *Leo* and Cancer. A little respectful protocol will go a long way in this association, and never mind the natural astrological Sun Sign sequence on the karmic wheel.

I've already mentioned, more than once, the possible dangers existing between any two persons born into the Fire and Water Elements, when they combine their personalities in the office, school or home, but when we're discussing Leo and Cancer, it's important to remind them again, in case they missed the warning in other chapters—or in the Elements Section in the back of Volume II.

If these two wish, they can exchange as much tolerance and learning in their association as any other 2-12 Sun Sign Pattern people. But if they do *not* wish, in the Fire of Leo and the Water of Cancer each possesses the power to destroy the other—and they may use this power without even being aware that they're using it, until it's too late, and the damage to one or the other (or both of them) has already been done.

For reasons known only to the planets, the 2-12 relationship, when it involves Cancer and Leo—unlike its effect on other Sun Signs in this vibratory pattern—does not cause Leo to be quite as tolerant of the Crab's personality as one might suppose with Cancer representing the twelfth house of the karmic past to Leo. Nor is the Crab usually as anxious as other Sun Sign halves of the various 2-12 Patterns to learn the lessons to be taught by the following Sun Sign, Leo (although it must be admitted that Leo will likely be more than anxious to teach them). However, willing to learn or not, Cancer secretly *knows* (even though the Crab may not ever admit it) that there *are* lessons to be learned from Leo's Sun wisdom, and the longer Cancer postpones the inevitable, the harder those lessons will be to master.

I can image all the Lions and Lionesses grinning and nodding their heads in agreement at this point, and all the Crabs frowning crabbily or sniffling. It's true, Moon Child. You have many things to learn from the Big Cats, and if you've been *unconsciously* trying to teach and overpower, instead of the other way around, you're interfering with your own karmic destiny, and also with that of Leo, which is not a very smart or safe thing to do, and you know how you pride yourself on being both smart and safe. You're only forging karmic obligations into a dreary chain, for future incarnations.

Now the Leos can stop grinning and stroking their vanities because astrology also has a warning for *them*. Have you been less tolerant and understanding of the Lunar traits (annoying as they may be to you) of your Cancerian friend, relative or mate than you have the capacity of being, since your eternal soul so recently experienced the Cancerian essence itself? Have you been pouting, instead of being protective and sympathetic? Or have you become Shy Pussycats, and allowed the Crab to teach *you*, when it should be just the opposite? Let the Crabs teach caution to the sign *behind* them, Gemini—the Twins can use it! You already subconsciously know the need for rain in the soul (Cancer moods) and you're here now to teach the Crabs the value of sunshine in the human heart. Have you permitted some Cancerian to extinguish the fiery rays of your ruling Sun, to crush the proud spirit of your birthright with water pessimism or gentle disapproval—which is, nevertheless, disapproval? Is this what you've done? Shame on you. Where is your roar? Shake your mane (if you're a Lion) or narrow your tilted cat eyes (if you're a Lioness) and behave as your Solar destiny intended you should when you drew your first breath upon this Earth. You needn't go overboard, and completely dehydrate the Water Elements of your Cancer friend, relative or lover with your flames. Crabs can be handy creatures to have around when you need to be hushed and lullabyed and fed chicken soup—and no one else will ever relate such fascinating dreams to you or tell such funny stories—but never allow these people to drown your enthusiasm or drain your adrenalin. Be yourself. You too, Cancer. Be *yourself*, and you'll be much happier. "Be True to Your Sun Sign Essence" is astrology's wisest rule.

There are, sadly, some Cancer-Leo associations in which the Crabs and Lions (or Lionesses) reverse their roles. Cancerians are dear, sensitive souls, but it sometimes happens that the steady dripping of the Water Element over the years will quite literally extinguish Leo's fire—and confidence. It can begin with a Leo who's a Shy Pussycat type, who perhaps isn't tolerant enough of Cancer's markedly different disposition and goals, and who gradually allows his—or her—pouting over not being sufficiently respected and adored to develop into lethargy, to the point where the Leo charisma is completely submerged.

Or it may be the Crab's fault. It can't be said often enough that Cancer is a CARDINAL SIGN OF LEADERSHIP, despite the Lunar surface gentleness and *apparent* reticence. A Crab with a powerfully aspected Sun and Mars in the horoscope can utilize all the Cancerian patience, tenacity, persistence and perseverance to eventually wear down a Fire Sign like Leo into a sort of spiritual fatigue, which is a very sad and serious matter. A long siege of the subtle but determined strategy of an unusually strong-willed Crab can considerably dampen even Leo's proud nature. It's hard to know with which Sun Sign such a role reversal initiates, but usually neither person is aware, on a conscious level, that it's happening. It's seldom motivated by malice or deliberate unkindness on either side, but rather caused by a lack of the constant alertness needed when you're mixing Fire and Water over a long period of time. Nothing is sadder than a Lion or Lioness robbed of pride and dignity, unless it's a Cancerian who is gradually forced into a kind of aggressive self-sufficiency completely foreign to the Crab's softness and sensitivity.

It can work the other way too. Leo can burn out all the beauty of Cancer's deep and normally tranquil emotions. A Cancerian subjected to the arrogant demands of a domineering-type Leo suffers much in silence, sometimes retreating into introversion (in severe cases, into an almost psychotic state), sometimes becoming snappy and irritable, but nearly always escaping in the final reel. (Crabs are expert escape artists.) If the Sun and Moon in their charts are in negative aspect, Cancer and Leo can wound each other deeply, even though unintentionally. Should these Luminaries in their mutual horoscopes be in positive aspect, however, the two of them can become a creative, imaginative and mutually protective pair. The Lion or Lioness will protect the sensitive emotions of the Moon person from the blows of a harsh world, and Cancer will affectionately pamper Leo in return. After all, the Sun and the Moon are their rulers, and *they* manage to exist in peace and harmony in the skies overhead. Due to their combined Solar (paternal) and Lunar (maternal) influences, Leo and Cancer, regardless of personal conflict or tension, often make fine parents.

They must both remember that Cardinal Cancer was born to lead, *however quietly and unobtrusively*, and Leo should permit this (as long as Leo's name comes first over the door). Since Leo is the Fixed Organizer, the Crab should allow Leo to *organize* his (or her) life—which Leo will do most admirably. This will allow Leo to be the sunny person he—or she—was meant to be, and will, in turn, bring out all the lovely Lunar tenderness of Cancer. It will also coax out the Crab's delicious, unsurpassed humor, all of which, when added together, conjures a cozy cradle of compatibility, as Cancer lulls Leo with love and laughter, and Leo's generous heart brings the sunshine after the rain, by understanding and forgiving Cancer's changing moods.

The two of them are bound to clash over cash, now and then. Cancer will privately think Leo is a little wild and wasteful. Leo may publicly think the Crab is unnecessarily frugal. "Waste not, want not," snaps the cautious economical Crab. "Get some new carpeting around this place, or I leave!" roars Leo. Royalty expects top quality as his or her natural right, and the Big Cats become either very depressed or very angry when they are forced to accommodate to shabbiness or to a denial of what Leo considers necessity (which is often what others consider luxury). There are, let us be sure to note, a few Leos (very few) who are careful spenders, even downright miserly, and these rare Pussycats will get along "royally" with the Crabs, if you'll forgive the pun. But the great majority of Leos, whether male or female, child or adult, can't resist treating themselves (and others, for Leo is generous) to the things that money will buy. They have every right to spend what they earned with their impressive talents and organized minds. It's when Leo begins to spend, in a business or marital relationship, what *Cancer* has earned, that the trouble begins.

The typical Crab normally hangs on to everything with a tenacious grip . . . old photographs, old loves, old tennis balls and shorts, old memories, old nightmares, old feuds, old fears, old key rings, old television sets, old bills, stamped paid . . but Cancer is not selective about money. It matters not whether it's old or new, Cancer considers it worth keeping. These people can be touchingly generous with their families and children, and almost never will a Cancerian turn down a friend in real need. But they dislike to throw away or gamble their cash reserves in a frivolous manner. Oddly, they're not frugal when it comes to food. A Crab sometimes turns into the original prototype Big Spender in a restaurant, astounding everyone with the unexpected generosity. Everyone but the waiter. The tip will be adequate, but not cause for celebration. The waiter is not likely to write home to his mother about it. If Leo has been the dining partner, the Lion (or Lioness) may pass the waiter an extra five dollars on the sly. It had better be on the sly, because it's not a good idea to humiliate the Crab in public.

A very strange thing about Leo and Cancer is that both these Sun Signs tend to enjoy photography. Not every single Crab, Lion and Lioness in the world owns a camera, of course, but about 90 percent of them do. Leo will probably own an expensive one, and the Big Cat's fondness for photography, we may as well face it, may in some cases be based on the fact that Leos simply adore to have their pictures taken. If they have a Nikon handy, they can always talk their friends into snapping them, while they pose dramatically. The Crab may own simply a cheap Brownie, although it could be a rare German-made model with high-quality lens, because Cancer doesn't mind investing money in something sensible and practical. To the Lunar person's point of view, a camera is certainly a sensible and practical purchase because it captures Today, so it can be treasured Tomorrow, when Today has become Yesterday. A camera molds memory into permanency for Cancerians, whose very minds are like sensitive film, recording every impression with vivid clarity.

When there is friction between these two Sun Signs, the Lion or Lioness may be incited into ever greater and grander achievement, just to prove his or her superiority to the cautious Crab. When there is creative compatibility between them, the Cancerian's unerring instincts and tenacity of purpose will guide the Lion to successfully launch his grandiose schemes, the Lioness to at last realize her glorious dreams. Either way, Leo can then write Cancer a thank you note.

Dear Crab . . . you made me what I am today, but I like you anyway.

☆ ☆ ☆ ☆ ☆ ☆

CANCER *Woman* LEO *Man*

———◆◆◆———

It was not to receive his thanks, however, that
she hung there in the sky; it was not even to
watch him get into the nest; it was to see what
he did with her eggs.

A Moon Maid and a Lion who have fallen in love face one of three possibilities, assuming they expect their love to result in a lifetime relationship.
(1) After a few years, he will arrogantly domineer her into a trembling,
tearful submission to his royal whims, causing her to become even more
moody than she was when they first met. (2) After a few years, she will
crush his confidence with her gentle, but persistent nagging, causing him
to retreat into sad and sullen silences. (3) After a few years, they'll make
adjustments, compromise their differences, and live happily ever after—loving and laughing and weeping and learning.

Turning the third possibility into a reality won't be a piece of cheese
cake, nor is it a task for the faint-hearted or the selfish. It requires a sensitive awareness of the care needed when you're blending Fire and Water.
He'll have to suffer through her perplexing moodiness, and try to perceive
the root cause of her possessive reflexes. *She'll* have to overlook his ego-
oriented attitudes, and not dwell in self-pity on his sometimes thoughtless
disregard for her feelings. *He'll* have to realize that half her possessiveness
will disappear when she has babies to croon over and wrap in swaddling
clothes and the other half will disappear when he takes the time to calm
her fears and strengthen her sense of emotional security. *She'll* have to realize that much of his arrogance stems from an inner doubt of his abilities
(which increases in exact ratio to his success, oddly) and that she'll get nowhere with him by dampening his pride, yet can almost make him roll-
over-Rover by verbally (and sincerely) appreciating his virtues and allowing him at least the choice of taking the initiative in nearly everything.
But she must be careful to retain her own dignity and individuality at the
same time.

If all this sounds to you like a path to sainthood, you're right, that's just
about what it is. It takes a lot of saintly serenity, love and patience for a
Crab and a Lion to gradually grow to trust their hearts with one another,
for their dreams are very different. Don't be gloomy. There are reliable astrological blueprints for building this relationship into a Forever design,

with a strong foundation of happiness, lit brightly by her Lunar lamps and Solar heated by him. Here's just one example of such a blueprint.

When I first met good friend Eileen Goldman, she was twinkling with her Looney Bird humor. Eileen is married to Bill Goldman, author of a number of best-selling books and TV dramas, also two-time Oscar winner for his screenplays of *Butch Cassidy and the Sundance Kid* and *All the President's Men*. Bill is a Leo, neither a Shy Pussycat nor a roaring Jungle Cat type. He is simply a Lion. A Monarch. A King. He happens to be an exceptionally kind-hearted and generous Leo, but he is a Lion. He is strikingly handsome. She is hauntingly beautiful. She bakes yummy pies. He purrs. (He also growls, of course, but more often he purrs.)

"What is your Sun Sign?" I asked Eileen, a few seconds after our first hellos. (Has it been nearly a decade ago? It has. Time flies.) She gazed at me then, with such an expression of mock sadness in her large, starry-lashed eyes, and gave a gentle sigh of resignation, as she replied, "I'm a Cancerian. I have two Fire Sign children, a Leo dog, a Leo cat, several Leo relatives, a Leo housekeeper and a Leo husband—and I cry a lot."

"I'll just bet you do," I said with an instant rush of sympathy. Of course, I knew she was only joking (about the weeping—the Sun Signs are actual), just displaying her Lunar humor. Still, her remark did indicate in a subtle manner her recognition of the sacrifices involved for a Moon Maiden living with a jungle pride of Lions and Lionesses. She plays her karmic role with the Sun Sign of Leo smoothly, absorbing all the beneficial lessons she's astrologically destined to learn during this present life of servitude . . . . . . I mean, during this present lifetime. Seriously (I was only jesting) this girl Crab is undeniably devoted to her Lion. She respects him, and never tries to upstage him. In return, he has allowed her to wear the glittering crown that designates her as his Queen—and very becoming it is too. But there is no groveling, she's retained her independence as a woman, and she is not a slave (maybe a footman now and then).

Like every Cancerian wife and mother, when her children were teeny-tiny, she fussed over her entire brood a bit much, drowning them in Vicks salve and chicken soup, and smothering them with loving concern and affection in a house awash with galoshes, thermometers, Crayolas and sentimentally bronzed birthday cakes. But after a while, she firmly adjusted her crown, majestically marched forth and formed a partnership with her close friend Lola Redford to found CAN (Consumer Action Now), an energetic and practical concept, which has enormously benefited the ecological movement. In connection with CAN, Eileen has managed to chalk up almost as many radio, TV and newspaper interviews as her Lion. I didn't say *more*, I said *almost* as many. The difference is vital.

In 1974, under her maiden name of Eileen Jones, this Moon Maiden fulfilled another Lunar dream by becoming a sensitive and highly successful free-lance photographer of the theatre and other arts. Wisely, she never allows her own career to interfere with the lavish attention her Big Cat expects and receives. She's a dream as a hostess, even more glamorous and youthful than when they first met, and she has a hundred things to talk about with her Leo that are more exciting than detergent, dish towels and depression.

These two genuinely admire each other's minds, talents and accomplishments, and despite his Lunar Lady's busy schedule, the Lion is properly pampered. If they gave out Academy Awards for Happiness, Eileen would surely receive an Oscar for her supporting role. Not long ago, when a friend of hers was enduring a temporary but agonizing period of poverty and personal tragedy, she appeared every few days, like an angel of mercy, with Cancer CARE baskets, stuffed full to overflowing with fruits, goodies, cash—and loyalty. (But she was always back home in time for dinner, to feed her hungry Lion and her cubs.)

Now you have a blueprint for compatibility between Crabs and Lions, Moon Maidens and Pussycats, Cancerians and Leos. Also for Lions and Crabs, Pussycats and Moon Maidens, Leos and Cancerians. It works with any combination, but may give quicker results with the last three. Leo likes to win all the battles. Cancer prefers to win the war.

The Cancerian girl is powerfully influenced by the combination of her feminine Sun Sign and its also feminine ruler, the moody Moon. Therefore, she personifies the Mystery of Woman, all the complex yearnings and inexplicable behavior of Eve herself. The Leo man is powerfully influenced by the combination of his masculine Sun Sign and its also masculine ruler, the Sun. Therefore, he personifies the conquering charisma of Man, all the wisdom and strength, contrariness and proud spirit of Adam himself. You can see why she's able to tempt him in the beginning, why he's so easily seduced by her home-baked pies. Yet, she's Cardinal, and this makes her a rather bossy Eve. He's Fixed, and this makes him a stubborn Adam. They'll be more at ease emotionally with one another if she doesn't try to compete with his stronger personality, but allows it to bring out all her tender and tranquil qualities. It's natural for the Moon (Cancer) to absorb the brilliant Solar rays of the Sun (Leo) and reflect them back in the form of the softer, more gentle illumination of moonlight.

Imitating Mother Nature never leads *human* nature astray, as long as these two don't overdo their Solar-Lunar roles, and slip into the trap of overemphasizing them. Too many Cancer-Leo couples drift into this sort of danger unaware. There's nothing "natural" about an association with sadist-masochist overtones. But these are the extreme cases. The Cancerian woman and Leo man should strive to temper each other's divergent personalities through a subtle but constant interchange of themselves, and avoid excessive domination on his part, as well as excessive docility on her part. For this sort of balancing act, it will be substantially helpful if the Moon or Ascendent of one or both of them adds a Gemini or Libra influence.

The chemical attraction a girl Crab and a Lion feel when they first fall in love may later ebb and flow. Their physical magnetism is powerful, but it requires a delicate blending of their natures. If he's impulsive, demanding and careless in his lovemaking, and she's too sensitive, passive and elusive in hers—his mind may wander, and her emotions will flee into strange shadows. When physical closeness between them is good, it's very good, for she's beautifully receptive, and he's wonderfully warm and affectionate. Because there's a gentleness and softness in her sexual attitude that complements his intensity, the passion exchanged between them can be very deep. But she can wound him with her moodiness when she's worried, which he mistakenly judges as a lack of response—and he can hurt her with his aloofness when he's troubled, which she mistakenly interprets as indifference.

Tears are often part of their togetherness, but tears can be healing, and with Cancer and Leo they can turn into tears of joy those times when he soothes away her nightmares with the comfort of his familiar nearness. Her dreams are always lovelier when she falls asleep with his arms around her, because it means her heart is safe again for a little while from her subconsciously remembered childhood fear of loneliness. This is when he knows how much he's needed, and then *he* cries . . . but she's not awake, so she doesn't know, and he'll never tell her. She has many secrets, but he has only one. His vulnerability.

The Lion who is enchanted on a summer night by a girl Crab is always surprised when he knows her better. She seemed to be such a helpless creature, seeking his strength . . . . . . as soft as a baby rabbit, and as timid—wide-eyed, needing guidance. He felt a tug of tenderness. Later he learned she's more than feminine—she's *womanly*. Feminine is enticing, but womanly is deeper. She's cozy and maternal, tucking him under her lavender-scented blankets of security . . . . . . and so perceptive she guesses his thoughts and feelings without his having spoken a word. Much later, he'll discover something else, misty, hard to define. It disturbs him, because just when he's sure he's in control of the relationship, she eludes him, makes him feel he's not really the lord and master of this lady after all. Not in the total way he once believed he was. She never defies him, but he suspects she may have a secret place in her mind she escapes to when he's hurt her, when they've quarreled.

He'd like to follow her there to tell her he's sorry, but he doesn't know the way. And so he must wait for her to return, in her own time—from her secret place. She can't be coaxed, and she can't be hurried. He's always glad when she returns and is real again, back to being her normal funny, bright and alert self . . . . . . humming as she bakes his apple pie, stirring him with the fragrance of her hair as she kisses his cheek. It's time to impulsively suggest a trip. Her wanderlust is awakened, she says, "Let's"! And he confidently takes charge of the travel plans. Shall they leave as soon as tomorrow morning? Why not?

Traveling somewhere together is like a fresh wind blowing through the love between this man and woman. She has him all alone then, to herself, the way she likes him—and he can instruct her in all sorts of new lessons. No matter where they go, he'll be an expert on the people, the language, the stores and the surrounding geography. She listens, his gentle Moon Maiden . . . fascinated. And as she listens, she finds herself remembering why she fell in love with him. It was because she could sit curled up beside him forever, just listening to him talk. He knew so much about so many things, and he made them all sound exciting. He had such confidence, he was so sure of himself, the way she'd always longed to be, and couldn't. But . . . something about his sureness bothered her, and for a long while, she didn't know what it was. Then one day it came to her. "If he's so confident," she wondered, "and knows so much, and is so sure he's always right . . . why does he need my constant approval?"

Suddenly, she knew. "He's only *pretending* to be brave and strong and wise. Except when he knows that I believe it. Then he believes it too." The knowing gave her a sharp loving-pain. And she wept the same tears wept by Eve herself when *she* first learned Woman's deepest secret from Eden's Tree of Wisdom.

☆ ☆ ☆ ☆ ☆ ☆

CANCER *Man* LEO *Woman*

---◀◀◆▶◆---

*"Don't go, Peter," she entreated. "I know such
lots of stories."*

*Those were her precise words, so there can be no
denying that it was she who first tempted him.*

The Lioness muses. This Cancerian male is . . . strange. He's a gentle
Crab, a sensitive man, more considerate of her as a woman than anyone
else she's ever known. He's not domineering, he lets her have her own
way most every time they disagree. Of course, there are his moods, but
. . . he worries about her, and he really-truly *cares* about her feelings. He
protects her lovingly and affectionately from the insensitive, rude, crude
and vulgar people who offend her. Truthfully, she's never felt so securely
cherished by anyone in her whole life, except when she was a baby. At
last she's found a man who sincerely appreciates her. Yet, there's something she senses in their relationship that troubles her. Something
indefinable. It causes her to feel a little uneasy somehow, like a whispered
warning. But a warning of what?

That something she senses is the influence of his Cardinal essence. Cancer is a Cardinal Sign of leadership. Over and over, astrologers keep
reminding Fire Signs of this, until they're weary. It means that, beneath
all his sweet gallantry and courteous manner, behind his chuckles and
rich humor, he manages in a subtle way to . . . . well, to *manage*
things, including her life. He never yells at her or flames up in a violent
temper, making chauvinistic demands. She could handle that. A Leo girl
is stimulated, not frightened or confused, by an open and direct challenge.
But she knows, in an unspoken, subliminal way, that she's expected to follow his gentle lead. Whatever small or large Kingdom over which they
preside will be ruled cooperatively. She may attend all the balls she likes,
initiate all the gay celebrations she wishes, dress in queenly fashion, add a
jewel or two to her tiara when she's depressed and needs an extra ruby to
cheer her up—she can even be the one to give all the orders to the milkman and postman and cleaning people in the castle, and decide which
monograms would look best on the linen and silver. On parade days, she
may sit up front, smiling and waving, on a throne bearing her name,

spelled out in roses. But *he* will administer the *real* responsibilities behind the scenes, and it will be clearly understood that, although her whims and fancies will receive his affectionate indulgence 98 percent of the time, his is the final veto power in those matters which make up the 2 percent of the time when her impulsiveness meets in a head-on collision with his caution.

Is it really like that with him? Yes. It is really like that with him. Here she was, expecting this man to personify what she believed were the qualities of the Water Element—kindness, sympathy, mildness, sensitivity, and . . . . wait. He does possess all those virtues. Every single one. Well, yes, but this leadership thing is disturbing. What about that? Your Majesty, the Lioness, dear girl, if you want a man with all the qualities of the Water Element, but lacking the leadership vibration, you'll have to find a Pisces or Scorpio male. The Mutable Fish won't try to boss you, not even in a subtle way, but he's not quite as dependable as your gentle Crab, and although he is also highly intelligent and sensitive, he's emotionally elusive. The Scorpion won't spend his life trying to lead you either. Scorpio is a Fixed Water Sign. He'll just try to organize things for you, but then there's that Scorpio sting if you should happen to tread on his pride or anger him. Your gentle Crab won't sting you. He may pout a little, and crawl under his shell for a few hours or days, but he won't sting you when you're least expecting it.

Think about it. With your Cancerian man you have all the positive and beautiful qualities of the Water Element, plus the security of astrology's promise that he'll never sting you to get even, and the knowing that he's considerably more emotionally reliable than his Neptune-ruled brothers. His actions and behavior are governed by the Moon, so he'll reflect your sunlight softly back to you, and you can surely see the value of having your sunlight reflected. (What Leo wouldn't?) You were born under the Fixed Sign of the Organizer yourself, so why not let him lead, if it's such a big deal with him, while you *organize* his leadership? He won't hide your light. He reflects it, remember? You're the Sun. He's the Moon. You're in charge of daytime. He's in charge of nighttime. I didn't mean to get into the sexual aspect of your romance this soon, but here it is, hinting and peeking at us, so let's discuss it now.

It's interesting, this thing about the Sun (Leo) ruling the day, and the Moon (Cancer) ruling the night. It could mean that the Leo woman will be happy to allow the Cancer man to lead them into the physical expression of their love at night. It probably does mean just that. But it could also mean that her Sun rulership might coax him into realizing the warm surprise, the special kind of intimacy of physical togetherness shared in the daytime, in the sunlight. The combined Solar-Lunar influences created by their relationship could cause them both to enjoy the exhilarating experience of breaking the orthodox, and changing old, tired, meaningless rules in every area of life. Why must night be the only acceptable —or expected—time of lovemaking?

A thought like that can give birth to a hundred more thoughts relating to the confining codes and mores of society, and she'll excite him into worlds of originality and daring he only dreamed of until her Sun blended with his Moon. He only dreamed of traveling, before her. After her—and with her—he'll fasten wings to his heels and his heart, and they'll fly away to new horizons, places he's always longed to blaze through the sky. And this is good. Good for him, and good for her.

In mentioning breaking the orthodox, I wasn't referring to the new styles in sexual promiscuity, such as multiple partners, group massage experiments, or any of those Sodom-and-Gomorrah, Decline-and-Fall-of-the-Roman-Empire, Greek-Acropolis-Drunken-Orgies vibes. That's the road to regret and real emptiness—of both the heart and the body. I meant a mutual discovery that sex between a man and woman can contain newness and freshness, that it needn't be dictated by senseless habit patterns seeded into the subconscious mind. The erotic and the sensual can be mixed with special feelings and memories of barns with sweet-smelling hay, Christmas morning snowflakes, starshine, deep, cool woods, a placid stream in the mountains, covered bridges on sleepy country roads, Easter sunrise, lilies of the valley, horses and chickens, Cub Scout campfires . . . even the way a newspaper smells when it's brought in from the front porch after a summer shower, like ozone splashed on the special scent of newsprint . . . that announces a new day. Or maybe woodsmoke . . . and baby squirrels.

That's what sex is like when it's right and good and special. Physical Oneness between a Cancerian man and his Leo woman can be a moving experience, for his sexual feelings are poetic and perceptive, still and deep —and hers are fiery with intense desire, yet sometimes as serene and calm as an August day. His emotional depth and her emotional warmth can make their union a blissful, peace-restoring moment between them. But they'll have to be watchful of the Fire and Water dangers. She can freeze into frigidity when her pride is wounded, and he can either pout and weep—or grow tough and impassive—when he's made to feel rejected for any imagined reason. Crabs are good at imagining unintended hurt. She's even better at nursing her false pride. They both have other talents they would be wiser to nurture than these. Tenderness is always the cornerstone for intimacy between Cancer and Leo. When it's missing, the peace and fulfillment of their sexual blending is missing.

His changes of mood as the Moon overhead moves through its phases, and simultaneously moves through his mind and emotions, will sometimes worry her, at other times annoy and anger her. But her Leo heart is large and generous, quick to forgive when she loves, and she's not a woman who holds grudges. Unless she has the Moon or Ascendent in Cancer herself, in which case they'll be extremely compatible as lovers, and *both* hold grudges, usually not against each other, but against those outside their circle of love—which could be hard on their friends and relatives. Just so his mother is never the recipient of a grudge, or even the tiniest slight. His mother was—is—and always shall be a saint, whether formally canonized or not. The Lioness would be well advised to keep that in mind. While Leo doesn't ordinarily cling to old injuries, unfortunately Cancer does tend to hang on to them with a fairly firm grip, whether they occurred several hours or several years ago. If the Crab would imitate his Leo woman's magnanimous spirit, he'd be a happier man, and this is one of the things astrology means when it decrees that Cancer has lessons to learn from Leo.

When these two marry, and they likely will, because Cancerians plan for permanency, and the Lioness auditions only for the role of Queen-Wife, never mistress or discarded girl friend—the Crab should know this about his sunny and charming mate: she *must* rule *something*. Or she will try to rule *someone*. Namely, him. (And the children, of course, but what about after they've left home? They might produce a passel of Sagittarian youngsters, and some of *them* leave home as early as ten or twelve.) The Cancerian man who sincerely loves his Lioness—and gracious knows Cancerians never love any other way but sincerely, because they are all so sincere—will encourage her to pursue a career worthy of her talents (the Leo woman has never been born who doesn't possess one or more impressive talents) or allow her to be the absolute, if benevolent, monarch over their home. One or the other. Otherwise, she'll be desperately unhappy, and he'll be a mighty miserable Man-in-the-Moon, frequently scorched by her ruling Sun. Then he might have to resort to the bottle, or other liquid escapes, like swimming at midnight during an eclipse, around the rocks on the beach . . . . . . perhaps even floating beyond the rocks to the next town, and maybe even staying there until she's ready to apologize. Considering Leo's great allergy to apologies, it could be a long siege.

What kind of life would that be, with him sitting in a drab rented room, surrounded by stacks of towels from Woolworth's, a case of soap he found on sale at Walgreen's, and a bottle of wine to drown his troubles—and her bravely trying to hide her heartache wandering around all by herself in the large, comfortable, luxurious and tasteful castle she decorated for him? Then there's the question of property settlement. Who will receive custody of the fluffy eiderdown quilt mama gave him, his Lincoln autograph collection, his old political campaign button collection, his fishing pole . . . her hair dryer, her ruby tiara, her Oriental rugs, her peacock feathers and her throne, spelling her name in faded roses . . their dogs and cats and aquarium, dishwasher and power lawnmower . . . the stereo equipment, station wagon and beach house she gave *him*—and the tiny gold charm shaped like a New Moon he gave *her*? (These two give different kinds of gifts. Hers are larger, lavishly given from her generous heart. His are a mite smaller, yet lovingly given from his affectionate heart.) Last, but not least, what about their joint checking and savings accounts, insurance policies, annuities and real estate holdings? Lord save us from *that* day of division!

It would be much easier for her to swallow that large lump of false pride, and for him to crawl out from his self-protective shell. The Crab and the Lioness are not at home in the ocean, where she feels out of place —nor in the jungle, where he feels out of place. They are only at home together in the sky, on the astral level, where their spirits can commune . . . or in each other's arms, where Fire and Water defy the law of the elements, and blend . . . in the kind of communion that has never recognized any law but its own.

CANCER

Water — Cardinal — Negative
Ruled by the Moon
Symbol: The Crab
Night Forces — Feminine

VIRGO

Earth — Mutable — Negative
Ruled by Mercury (also by
the Planet Vulcan)
Symbol: The Virgin
Night Forces — Feminine

The CANCER-VIRGO *Relationship*

◄◄◆►►

They found the dinghy, and went home in it . . .

When their voices died away, there came cold silence
over the lagoon, and then a feeble cry. "Help, help!"
Two small figures were beating against the rock . . .

You may wonder what a Crab might do with a Virgin—besides snapping on occasion, or perhaps contemplating a firm grip on the Virgin's tempting bare toe. Just as you may wonder what a Virgin might do with a Crab, other then running swiftly away—or maybe deciding to take the Crab home as a pet.

At first thought, it's difficult to imagine that a Crab and a Virgin have anything in common—but technical virgins are, after all, said to be somewhat crabby (unfulfilled, or whatever) and real crabs do possess a certain timidity one normally associates with actual virgins—which brings us a little closer to linking these two. One of them is a nocturnal creature of the sea. The other also tends toward the nocturnal Night Forces, although not especially toward the element of water—unless one counts the still and quiet pools into which astrological Virgins gaze to see their Narcissus images reflected to them, sometimes rippling just a bit but, on the whole, clearly defined. Nevertheless, Earth does contain Water—or lacking it, becomes dry and parched. There's no argument that an association with the Water Sign of Cancer greatly enriches the character and personality of the Earthy Virgo man, woman or child.

Most Virgos are much happier when they're alone with themselves than when they have to bend their somewhat measured and rather precisely patterned life-styles to those of other sloppy, strange, silly and impulsive humans, which makes then nervous and uncomfortable. Somehow, at least in the beginning, the Virgins don't feel this sort of discomfort when they pal around with the Crabs. There's something soothing to Virgo about the Water Element of Cancer. The Cancerian gentleness and mildness of manner often cause the Virgo to feel as though he (or she) is floating on a quiet lake, now and then reaching out, dreamlike, to pluck one of the lovelier lilies, or playfully tease a passing school of mermaids and water babies. Frequently the Virgins feel freer and more relaxed with a Crab, less fearful of being restricted, bossed around, possessed—or of having their own personalities overshadowed to the point of disappearance. (Poor, unsuspecting Virgins.) Also, Virgo is easily enchanted by the Cancerian's marvelous Looney Bird humor, which is not too loud or clownish, not too sophisticated, nor yet too vulgar either—just the right kind of recognition of the ridiculous that allows Virgos, with their exquisite sense of critique and satire, to join in with some amusing observations of their own.

Isn't it wonderful? These two have hopped into their pea-green dinghy and sailed down the river of happiness together, just like the famed Owl and the Pussycat, except that they are a Crab and a Virgin. But no matter, because the whole purpose of the sail in the moonlight in a pea-green boat is harmony, whatever the astrological or otherwise identity of the occupants. You can be sure they'll take along some honey (and honey cakes) for Cancer to nibble on—a small guitar for Virgo to strum while the Crab sings crazy limericks to mournful songs of yesterday—and definitely LOTS OF MONEY—not only to rhyme with honey but also because Cancerians consider a stash of cash—whether "wrapped up in a five-pound note," securely tied inside a paper bag, combination-locked in a safe, buried in a bank or in a sandpile in the backyard—an absolute necessity of life, having a slight priority edge over air to breathe, but not necessarily over things to eat and drink. The latter run a neck-and-neck race with money for the attention of typical Crabs during their entire lifetime. Tagging along as a close third are babies and children of assorted ages and sizes.

The Virgo in the pea-green boat won't mind the mellow mood music. But as for the jars of honey and honey cakes Cancer brings along on any trip these two might decide to risk together, Virgo will probably nag and complain that the space taken by the Crab's goodies doesn't leave any room for Virgo's Vicks salve, Tums for the tummy, Excedrin and Pepto-Bismol—let alone Virgo's vitamins and wheat germ.

They may also quarrel a bit querulously over Virgo's grumbles that honey cakes are not as vital a Life Preserver as pure bee pollen, since the latter is good for anything from promoting no cavities to the prevention of baldness, gaining and losing weight (both) and, in general, for keeping fine and fit in every sense. Therefore, the Crab may have to leave a few dozen honey cakes behind, so there'll be a sizable niche on the dinghy to contain Virgo's "imported" pure pollen from the buzzing Wyeth honey-combs of New England—or the Wilton, Connecticut, Edward Weiss colonies of cheerful, thriving bees, who happily hum on Whipstick Road. Most Virgo pure pollen freaks know about Wyeth and Weiss because, when it comes to such serious matters, the Virgins are more than a mite choosy, even downright fussy about where they obtain the P.P. for their P.H. (Perfect Health). They demand the best. They may be stingy about other things, but not when their own personal well-being is concerned. If they should happen to become ill, they might be unable to go to work, for which inexcusable behavior they'd punish themselves with a heavy fine and six months of solitary. Most Virgos have a sense of responsibility to-ward their jobs that nearly amounts to an obsession (although Crabs are apt to see this fetish as a shining virtue).

However, as already noted, Virgo won't mind plunking the guitar to harmonize with Cancer's serene solos under the Full Moon. Also, despite these few possible squabbles over honey cakes versus the pollen, neither will Virgo object to the Crab's taking along of "plenty of money" any-where they may be heading as a team. In fact, the Virgin will quite likely bring along a few duffle bags of the stuff himself (or herself) because the fear of financial ruin—the specter of poverty—is almost perfectly matched in Cancer and Virgo. It's a toss-up which one of them values money more. Or rather, which one of them values more the assurance that it will never be lacking.

Virgo and Cancer together create a powerful healing vibration. These two, when they join their auras, hands and hearts in any sort of mutual venture, possess the magic cure to many of the mental, emotional and physical ills that plague all Earthlings. Except their own. Alone, both of them are inclined to brood themselves into severe depression or chronic sickness. Together, they can be very helpful by way of preventing and curing in each other such emotional and mental gloominess, as well as all their mutual assorted aches and pains and other complaints.

This is the markedly friendly 3-11 Sun Sign Pattern influence, allowing the Virgin and the Crab, however amusing and odd they may appear to others, to feel perfectly right and natural to themselves, as they stroll along the seashore or through the woods to Grandma's house (Virgo's Grandma —then they'll stop by to chat with Cancer's Mama). The symbolic image is kind of giggly. Imagine the Crab, slightly waddling (all Crabs have a faint waddle to the walk), crawling first sideways, then backward, then skipping merrily ahead, scattering jokes like little berries on their path. Picture then the slim (usually) and modest Virgin, dressed lightly and unostentatiously, clear-eyed, graceful and lithe, humming a lovely melody . . . . . while below, the Crab hastens to keep pace, making funny faces, drawing looney pictures in the sand . . . . . and crankily gripping the Virgin's ankle or leg when the latter goes too fast and the Crab is weary, wanting to rest for a spell.

When the waning of the Moon causes the Cancer man or woman to weep over haunted memories of the past—or nightmarish fears of the future—the tender Virgin (whether male or female) will be sweetly sympathetic and consoling. Virgo will probably have a nice, clean hanky to hand the tearful Lunar friend, relative, business associate, lover or mate—which will be accepted, between sobs, with touching gratitude.

Both these Sun Signs are noticeably dependable and reliable workers. Barring a severe affliction to their natal Suns, or other negative planetary configurations in their birth charts, Cancer and Virgo take their duties and obligations seriously. They both are more inclined to enjoy work than to look upon it as a burden. Virgo enjoys work because a job well done, to the Virgin, is its own reward. Cancer enjoys work because it provides the means to build a large savings account for protecting against such terrible potential catastrophes as flood, fire, earthquake, volcanic eruptions, tornadoes, hurricanes, war, siege, the bubonic plague, a stock market crash, muggers, rapists (even boy Crabs get jittery at the thought of rape), vandalism, socialism, communism and famine. Virgo is no slouch in the savings department either. If there is anything in this world Virgo absolutely abhors, it's the thought of possibly being dependent upon others in some way later on in life. This is why the maternal (or paternal) Cancerian silently projects such comfort to the typical Virgo. The Virgin feels somehow secure within the protective presence of the Crabs, who are so solicitous of Virgo's welfare, so genuinely concerned and affectionate. Likewise, the Crabs feel comfy-cozy floating around in the cool calmness of Virgo, such a haven from the noisy outside streets, all cobblestoned with people, and demanding. Virgo–so clever, bright and witty, so nicely conventional, who can pack such a neat picnic basket, never forgetting the salt or napkins–always remembering a small surprise, like chilled grapes and Brie.

The main obstacle of mounting tension over which the Crab and the Virgin must leap on their way to the cool pool in the fragrant woods is hinted at in the next to the last sentence of the third paragraph of this chapter. I hoped it might stay there, buried in the sand, but it wants to be remembered, and now it whispers to us that Virgo wilts into yesterday's lettuce left out of the fridge at the first clutch of possessiveness and restriction. The Crabs can't separate possessiveness from warm, affectionate caring and friendly concern. Cancerians clam up and won't even tell you when they last stared at the Full Moon and turned into a frog–yet they'll pry secrets out of others as if they were human corkscrews. Virgo is not a can and does not like to be pried open, turning into a walking worry-wrinkle when he or she feels restricted, third or fourth degreed. After a time, the Virgo man or woman may view the Crab's solicitous manner and protectiveness as possession's prison–and courteously (at first) request parole. This is a signal for the Cancerian to step sideways a while, even backward, allowing Virgo to dance ahead, feeling free and living up to the loner image for an imaginary lifetime, lasting a few weeks or months. Eventually, Virgo will return to gently nag the Moon person once again, sugar-coating criticism with politeness, causing the Crab to snap crankily. Virgo will shed one tiny, perfect tear–Cancer will weep a waterfall, and say "I'm sorry." Then Virgo will apologize for the weakness of such sensitivity.

Cancer stimulates Virgo's imagination, stirs Virgo's mind into a creamy whip of promises that will be kept perhaps . . . and Virgo makes Cancer feel that the Crab won't be left alone on the beach, ignored . . . to starve and pine away from loneliness. Earthy Virgo knows and understands, will see that friendship is kept polished and not allowed to rust. These two are lyrically linked by the 3-11 Sun Sign Pattern vibrations, karmically insured of a friendly return to harmony with but the slightest effort. Most 3-11 relationships, even after disappearing, have a way of popping up again to be resumed when least expected.

☆ ☆ ☆ ☆ ☆ ☆

CANCER *Woman* VIRGO *Man*

———◆◈◆———

"What are you quacking about?" Peter answered. "Why don't you let the nest drift as usual?"

"I . . . want . . . you . . ." the bird said, and repeated it all over.

A strong emotional involvement between Virgo and Cancer is multi-layered, an experience of many dimensions. We'll try one on for size. Not fictional, but very real. To protect the innocent (for both players in the drama are indeed innocent of a conscious intent to hurt each other), we'll change the names, geography and such . . . retaining only the thread of truth that could link this Moon Maiden and her Virgo man to you and your own girl Crab—or you and your own Virgo lover. It's much stranger than fiction, truth is, because almost always Life wins the race against man's and woman's limited imaginations.

His name, the Virgo, is Gerald, make-believing. Her name, the Lunar lass, is Hope, for imagery. They met and first miracled somewhere in Illinois, where they fell in love more than a dozen years ago. They are the parents of five assorted beautiful girls and boys, cherished by both of them. They have not yet married. Somehow, they can't live together, nor can they live apart. Following the haunted karmic path of the 3-11 Kismet, they walk along, arm-in-arm, for months of empathy and closeness. Then Gerald's yearning begins, Hope's sighing starts . . . they reach that sad, familiar fork in the road and take different directions, waving good-bye wistfully, before the last, abrupt turn—and the slow walk back alone. Time moves on, but destiny lingers. Sooner or later, there's the memory of her lyrical laugh, her mushroom soup and patchwork quilts of warm affection. His lonely reaches its breaking point just when she's making her wonted wish on the New Moon, and he appears at her door. Then they swaddle the babies snugly within the blankets of their reunion joy, closing out the world of her disapproving, frowning (but long-suffering) parents, and become a family again. Until it's time for him to go, leaving, as always, a part of himself behind . . . to manifest itself nine months later into another living proof of the mutual need that binds them. Five times. Five angels to guide them down that remembered, dreamlike path, through the dark forest of misunderstandings. Next time, it will be six, the number of Venus. It could be different. Venus may have plans to over-come Cancer's inconstant Moon and Virgo's restless Mercury.

That's the way it sometimes is with these two lovers. Especially if the Virgo man is the kind who fears that a deep involvement will cause him to lose his own identity, the common and persistent worry of both techni-cal and astrological Virgins. Especially if the Cancerian woman is the kind who chooses the path of least resistance . . . motherhood and waiting . . . counting on the New Moon magic to weave a spell of magnetic memory to lure back the questing Virgo man who is not quite strong enough to stay, yet is unable to escape the pull of her luminous enchantment . . again and again. Typically, some Moon Maidens believe that babies or money can soften any blow of Fate, anesthetize any kind of pain.

There are, naturally, other kinds of Crabs and Virgins. There's the kind of Virgo man who smoothly adapts to the necessity of adjusting his bach-elor-button antipathy to partnership, of pacing his jogging to someone else's rhythm. He calculates the loss of his privacy against the rewards of companionship, and he remains—asking only for occasional periods of pen-sive apartness, time in which to wander by himself, to refresh his single-minded goals. As priests and monks are required to make "retreats," so are all Virgo men required by their own natures to retreat and meditate alone now and then, returning from their seclusion self-revitalized and freshly sweet. Newly able to innocently believe once more in tomorrow.

The Cancerian girl who understands this need of the Virgo man she loves will take care to walk softly while he's dreaming, find her own re-treat beneath a bristlecone pine that's maybe waited a century or so for a friend to sit beside it, sharing a silent but eloquent communion. Trees know a lot. They listen sympathetically, and they are kind. If trees could walk, they'd never take a cruel knife and painfully carve their names, within a heart, on the arms or backs of lovers. Trees are wondrous teachers of forgiveness.

If the Moon Maid finds her own midsummer night's dream in which to wander, those times when her Virgo man has disappeared somewhere in-side himself to brood or plan—or to heal his worried mind—he'll stay. They can harmonize themselves this way in perfect tempo, their rela-tionship never jolted by the violent percussion of "Goodbye"–"Come back"–"What did I say or do?"–"Don't go"–"May I come home?"–"For-give me"–"Please don't hurt me anymore." It's a matter of calmly floating with the ebb and flow of the tides between them, not trying to surfboard over waves too high and dangerous.

Then too, there are those girl Crabs who are acutely aware of Cancer's Cardinal charisma, those Lunar-ruled females who patiently reinforce the weak or worn corners of the fabric of a relationship with concentration on a career. Her ambitions then become the vivid colors—and a love affair or marriage that wasn't quite made in Heaven but was conceived near enough the stars to sometimes sparkle, becomes the pastel background pattern of her life. It works. It adds strength to their love. They separate each morning, and she goes her tenacious way, while he whistles happily, tinkering with engines, practicing his yoga . . . rewrites the dictionary, draws maps or maybe juggles those odd-shaped objects called numbers, that produce such mysterious results, whether they're dashed and dotted in checkbooks, surveys, charts or graphs. They become sort of friendly strangers who fall in love each weekend. It satisfies her desire for change and his need for time alone to retain his friendship with himself (the person he relies on most). It allows them to love.

When they love in a physical sense, the Virgo man and his Cancerian woman blend quietly into a deep and absorbing union, in the natural way of earth and water in Nature. When the Moon's changeable influence over her emotions is beneficent—and when he is his own normal, tranquil self—their lovemaking is a peaceful consummation of desire for both of them. But when her Moon-madness takes over, when her Lunar fluctuations are waning, causing her to be crablike and moody, she can flood his affectionate intentions with excessive emotional behavior and demands. Just as he can bruise the delicacy of her passion when he's worried himself into irritability during the day and is unable to relax either his mind or his body. Restlessness is a contagious feeling, and they can transfer it to each other without realizing it. Then she may retreat sullenly into her shell, refusing to recognize her attitude as a rejection of his tentative wanting, and he may blame her for a cool response to his own cool advances. This is when his Virgo analytical talents would be very useful, and her Lunar gift of perception would greatly help. Yet, perversely, these periods of sexual frustration may be the very times the two of them neglect to call upon their own best qualities to clarify the breakdown of communication between them.

The Virgo man and his Moon Maiden can walk in sunshine and in rain, and recuperate from the seasonal changes in their love more often than not. They can make Valentines together, cut out cookies in the shape of New Moon Crescents, play anagrams and charades with each other . . . . . because he loves to meditate on words . . and she loves to make-believe she's more than one woman, slipping in and out of her moods like a glittering mermaid, hiding her true mother-of-pearl self in midnight silences and the brightness of noontime laughter. If their seeking is intense enough, together, these two can find whole meadows full of gentle camaraderie together . . . perhaps even dream a vision in the prophet's field of Ardath . . . for theirs is the 3-11 sextiled vibration. In astrology, a sextile is an opportunity, and these lovers will always be showered with as many as they need for tightly mending the occasional chips and cracks in their relationship, like a continual light snowfall of little stars around them, a sextile itself being represented by the symbol of a tiny star . . .

When the girl Crab becomes cranky, her Virgo becomes critical and caustic, and they should escape into the woods, lie down together and take a moonbath, which is different from a sunbath. When you are sunbathing, you may be burned, turn all red and stinging. When you go moonbathing, especially when the Moon is phasing from waning to waxing, near its Fullness, you turn pale golden, lavender and iridescent, like a butterfly's wing. Then, naturally, you can fly.

Another thing Virgo learns slowly but surely from his Looney Bird Moon Maiden. Gazing directly into the Sun can blind the eyes. But gazing directly into Cancer's shimmering Moon is restful, and sometimes makes the miracle of allowing the Third Eye to see things hidden by midnight's mystery from the sunlight. After they've moonbathed together, they can jump into a dinghy and sail away to the ruins of Babylon. Who knows what they might discover? As the prophet Esdras wrote in the Apocrypha . . . *The angel Uriel came unto me and said: "Go into a field of flowers, where no house is builded, and eat only the flowers of the field —taste no flesh, drink no wine, but eat flowers only . . . . and then I will come and talk to thee . . . . . ." so I went my way into the field which is called ARDATH.*

CANCER *Man* VIRGO *Woman*

———◄◆►———

*Presently he noticed as an odd thing that it was
undoubtedly out upon the lagoon with some definite
purpose, for it was fighting the tide, and sometimes winning; and when it won, Peter, always
sympathetic to the weaker side, could not help
clapping. It was such a gallant piece of paper.*

*It was not really a piece of paper. It was the
Never bird, making desperate efforts to reach Peter . . .*

He almost hates them. He really does. They're cruel and unfeeling. The astronauts and the NASA. The whole space program trembled the Crab. But he never said a word to anyone about it. He nursed this awful sense of emptiness secretly, mostly because he didn't quite know how to explain it to people who could never understand why he felt so strangely lost and lonely after the first Moon landing, his self-confidence smothered within the depths of an indefinable disappointment. The second time was even worse.

He wept. When he was by himself, when no one would see. He carried his silent burden throughout all the months and years, unable to share it, because there was no one he could count on to offer the magnitude of sympathy he needed. Until she came along—the Virgin—and they fell in love.

Gradually, he grew to believe that she wouldn't ridicule his secret if he shared it with her. She might even be able to help him lose his appre-hensions, maybe point out to him a heretofore unsuspected happy ending to his NASA nightmares. After all, she's so quiet and calm, like a secret herself, he thought. She's so amazingly intelligent—for a *woman*. (Male Crabs are tinted with more than a tinge of chauvinism, and there's no use expecting them to lose it completely until the image of "Mother" has gone through a complete metamorphosis, which could take more than a few score years.) Besides being so clever, he mused, so mentally quick, she's tender and gentle, soothingly sympathetic—except for those few times when he has noticed her behaving like, well—a little like a virago. A bit cranky and critical. Detached and aloof. But he decided to overlook these rare moments. After all, isn't he moody himself? Who can better understand than he that a person doesn't always mean what a person says when a person is feeling out of sorts? So he gathers up his courage and pours it out into her dainty ears. His sad and scary secret. He confesses his terror, shivers and trembles, waits for consolation. JOY AND WONDER! She *does* sympathize! She *does* understand! She didn't laugh at him; moreover, she *does* have an answer! And a very logical, sensible, practical answer too, surprisingly interwoven with a trace of the esoteric . . . . . and mystical truth. He's overcome with pure pleasure and delight. He made the right decision in telling her.

What it was, you see—he'd been worried and concerned for some time about the Moon landings, for a perfectly rational reason. He's a Cancerian, ruled by the Moon. Down through the ages, mythology and the ancients, the scribes and prophets and poets—not to mention astrologers and metaphysicians . . . have always pictured the Moon as the Lady of Mysteries (the biggest one being what the so-called Man in the Moon was doing there), weaving spells, possessing all the magic of Merlin, the very personification of the magnetic and the hypnotic. It filled him with awe and private longings each time he stared at her bursting into Fullness, then waning, becoming New and lemon-sliced, beckoning him with a wistful promise. He used to wish on the New Moon when he was a boy. Then along came nasty NASA and those blasted, nosy, astronauts, determined to shock his dreams, to expose his lovely Lunar ruler's naked face and body in such a vulgar manner. The magazines were full of their photographed profanity of his Lady of Loveliness. There she was, so pathetically vulnerable, pockmarked with craters, covered by dreary sand and boring rocks, with not a shimmer or a sparkle anywhere to be seen. No magic. No mystery. Just cold masses of dirt, miles of blank nothingness. It shattered his faith in *himself,* in a way he couldn't analyze.

His Virgo woman listened quietly, not interrupting as other women might, until he was quite finished. Then he glanced at her from the corner of his eye to see if she was amused. She was not. She understood perfectly. Her clear eyes reflected a full awareness of his feelings, an unmistakably genuine interest. She told him it was only logical for a Cancerian to emotionally resent such a rude and unexpected tarnishing of his image of his own ruler, with such mundane and prosaic descriptions. It was natural, she said, for people to strongly identify themselves with their personal ruling planets and Luminaries. She pointed out that an Aries man might experience the same loss of self-confidence if forced to listen to accounts of astronauts landing on Mars (ruler of Aries) and reporting back that the Fiery Red Star was populated by rows of Sweet Shoppes, quivering jellyfish and marshmallow trees. MARS? The great warrior, the brave and courageous! The fearless! JELLYFISH AND MARSH-MALLOWS? (He giggled, feeling much better.) Then she confided in him that Mercury is only her foster ruler and mentioned her own secret feelings about her true ruler, Vulcan, soon-to-be-discovered. How she watches the sky, sometimes, and wonders . . . . .

She told him firmly that her personal opinion happened to be that the stories about the Moon's magic and mystery are true. The ground walked upon by the astronauts was not *reality*. Did the rocks and craters make any change in the mystical and still-puzzling-to-scientists power of the Moon to pull the tides in and out, and affect all manner of things on Earth magnetically? No. It did not. And what of Earth? Looking upon this planet from space, she analyzed, one might expect it to be a reasonably sparkling, exciting Star. But when one actually landed on the Earth's surface and saw all the hot-dog stands, smog, pollution, TV sets, greed, cruelty, war, sugar pushers, the poor and the starving, the crimes and drugs and drunks and donuts and insecticides and billboards—the whole ugly mess of it—wouldn't one *also* be disillusioned? (He nodded eagerly, waiting for her happy ending.)

The Moon reflects the Sun, she told him. It is a reflector. It is unlike any other "star" or planet in the heavens, unique in this solar system. It is *still* strange and mystical, and possesses exactly the same powers as before. NASA hasn't explained the Moon's indisputable control over or synchronization with the movement of all water on Earth and all sealife. Even the opening and closing of oysters is precisely timed to the Lunar phases. The real truth of the Moon, she told him, doesn't lie upon its surface, to be seen with the naked eye. The real truth can be seen only with the Third Eye and the heart, combined—by observing the Moon to be the absolute Cause of certain Effects. And perhaps the *whole* truth will be seen later. Then she asked him if he had ever thought that perhaps the Earth, which appears to be such a crazy carnival of noise and nonsense, might not have a strange power *itself*, which we've never guessed . . to change the destinies of entire galaxies? Finally, she ended by quoting to him her favorite truism from her Great Aunt Hester. "Believe only *half* of what you see," warned Aunt Hester. "And *nothing* of what you hear." Tomorrow, the Virgin said . . . she would give him a copy of St. Exupéry's *The Little Prince*, which she promised would clarify it all. (Most Virgos have read and are fond of *The Little Prince*. They are irresistibly drawn to anything with the word "little" in it.)

Nearly always, a Virgo woman can somehow manage to make a boy Crab feel safe and warm and secure. As though everything is crisp and proper and behaving as it should in the world, and within his own orbit. The way he felt as a child. When his mother told him to hush, it was all right. His nightmares were foolish and unreal. Tomorrow will be morning, and the world will still be spinning. Buckwheats for breakfast . . . and the newspaper delivered, as usual. The Virgo woman makes him feel cozy and comfy, like his old bathrobe with its soft, sagging pockets, hanging there beside his bed like a loyal friend. He senses her dependability, her sense of duty and her integrity. All very much like his own. Unless he meets her during a time when she's pulled by Vulcan to stand on her head and run around in thrilling circles for a bit, to change the scene, throwing caution in the corner, where undue caution belongs. Then he may have cause to be nervous now and then. But the typical Virgin in the average situation, when she really loves her gentle Crab, will seldom if ever do anything to really hurt or alarm him. She's so reassuringly predictable (barring those rare Vulcan experiments).

She will wish *he* would be equally predictable. Rocks, craters and all, the Moon continues to rule this man's changing moods, laughter, tears, depressions, elations, pouting spells, jokes, compassion, sweetness, crankiness and just plain contrariness. Still, in her practical, common-sense way, the Virgo girl is able to cope rather efficiently with the Cancerian man's wanderlust, periods of loneliness he can't explain—the fears that make him occasionally stingy—the tender concern for others that turns him suddenly generous. She doesn't mind his cautious nature, for she's cautious herself. She'll also share his dislike for extravagance and waste—his sense of responsibility—and his delicious enjoyment of home life. She'll cook for him, most likely, soon perceiving that he associates good food with emotional security, but she may not be too happy about it. (Unless she has a Cancer Moon Sign or Ascendent herself.) A few of their quarrels could spring from his crablike possessiveness. He may frown if she wants to work or pursue a career, unless her desk is next to his, or they go into business together. He's Cardinal, she's Mutable, and so she'll accept with good grace his tendency to want to make most of the rules and to walk a few steps ahead—if he doesn't overdo it. He's a leader (even if secretly) and she's a communicator. Therefore, she feels no overwhelming need to demand a showy kind of independence for herself, but neither will she stand for her personal freedom to be smothered. He can boss her around, gallantly, and with old-fashioned charm (as he does others, male or female), and she won't be insulted or make a big fuss over it. However, she'll follow up only on suggestions that please her. If they do not please her, she'll frankly tell him so, and proceed to do things her own way. Courteously (like him) but quite determinedly.

Sexually, these two are well mated. With the peaceful affinity of Earth and Water Signs, they melt into each other's arms, hearts and bodies very naturally. To others, the Virgo woman may project a degree of unresponsiveness. But the great sentimentality and sensitivity of the Cancerian man allows him to discover her latent pools of passion. He's often able to cause her to bloom with her own special kind of sentiment, which is pure and fine, like crystal, lacking the heaviness of extreme emotionalism. She may surprise herself then, with a depth of sensitive feelings she never suspected she possessed. Her basic nature may be cool and reserved (especially with strangers), but when she's been stirred inwardly by Vulcan, this woman is more than capable of fulfilling the Lunar man's strong need for both sensuality and affection in lovemaking. She'll respond instinctively to the tenderness and gentleness that are inseparable parts of every Cancerian male. They both approach passion with a respect for its deeper implications and potential. Sexual union is not something either of them normally views as casual or frivolous (barring severe planetary afflictions in their individual birth charts).

Despite his emotional vulnerability and sentimentality (which he hides with practiced success beneath his tough, outer shell), the Crab possesses a steady, watchful intelligence. He's a shrewd business person, and an excellent strategist regarding all forms of human relationships. She'll make it clear that she admires all these qualities. A Virgin cannot love a man who hasn't won her respect, and the Crab will probably do this from the beginning. However, should he be one of the insecure Cancerians who "babies" his groundless fears by turning to drugs, alcohol, daydreaming or procrastination, she'll be extremely annoyed, and she'll soon make her displeasure felt in unmistakable small ways. Like nagging. Polite nagging, but nonetheless, nagging. Little reminders. Tiny frowns. Pouting. A martyrlike resignation. Or she'll just skip off when he least expects it to begin a new life alone, with barely a trace of emotion, once she's decided to leave. (Virgos don't look upon excessive emotion as either sensible or practical.) Because of his extreme sensitivity to hurt—and her natural inclination to criticize—there are dangers inherent in this relationship. But none that can't be overcome by simply being recognized in time, and avoided. He's perceptive enough to sense them. She's analytical enough to detect them. So they really have no excuse for allowing things to go too far.

Her eyes (like the eyes of all Virgos and Geminis, thanks to Mercury's silver gift) are noticeably clear, sparkling with intelligence. Her features, in some indefinable way, are delicate and virginal. Except when her brow is clouded with problems or creased with worry-wrinkles, her expression is sweetly placid. And so . . when she's bathed in moonlight, lying in his arms, the Crab may, for a moment, imagine her to be his lost Lady of the Mysteries, the misty Moon goddess of his haunted dreams.

Once she feels safe with a man, a Virgo girl is transformed into a symphony of fragile femininity. After all, she was born under a feminine Sun Sign, secretly ruled by the powerfully feminine Vulcan. Her crisp self-containment and faint air of aloofness mask her softness, but it's there . . . . . waiting for the patient and persistent devotion of the Cancerian man to warm it into singing. Even should the Virgin and the Crab part company, the strong karmic tug of their 3-11 vibration will nearly always guide them to unexpectedly cross each other's paths again, in ultimate friendship and forgiveness.

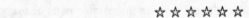

CANCER

Water—Cardinal—Negative
Ruled by the Moon
Symbol: The Crab
Night Forces—Feminine

LIBRA

Air—Cardinal—Positive
Ruled by Venus
Symbol: The Scales
Day Forces—Masculine

The **CANCER-LIBRA** *Relationship*

❖

I don't know whether any of the children were crying;
if so, the singing drowned out the sound. . . .

Cancer and Libra form the squared 4-10 Sun Sign Pattern, through the elements of Water and Air, and like all 4-10 vibrations, theirs is the most interesting and challenging association of all. It's also the most difficult kind to bring into harmony, but that's exactly what makes it so interesting and challenging, because of the great rewards waiting to grace these two when they achieve a soul-stirring victory over their undeniable differences, which are, to be honest, numerous.

The relationship of Libra and the Crab is what life is all about, because it forces them to learn the hard way how to compromise. Mastering that lesson guarantees a much higher level of happiness than can ever be attained by choosing an easier path. For these two Sun Signs to win the battle to understand one another is a worthy goal. Now and then, it's bound to be a bit jaggy and troublesome, to be sure, but Time smooths off the rough edges, if there's sincere effort on both sides, and ultimately, there's the sweet satisfaction of knowing you've succeeded in conquering your own and another's very human natures, and in the process, have come a little closer to the angels. I don't guarantee wings or anything, but maybe a couple of halos (which are only two auras, glowing in the beautiful colors of compatibility).

A halo (or aura) is not something these two will see over each other's heads right away. They're more likely to see imaginary horns and a couple of pitchforks. That's because they aren't trying. They're giving in to human nature, and this particular karmic trip is all about trying to imitate the angels, remember? The first lesson Cancer and Libra must learn is the one so earnestly taught by Francesco Giovanni de Bernardone, of Assisi (known as Saint Francis, but not through *his* humble choice). They'll simply have to stop trying so desperately to be understood, and start trying a little harder to understand. Both of them. It's the only key which will unlock that mysterious barred door between them, behind which lies *Pax et Bonum* (Peace and Good).

As explained in detail in "The Twelve Mysteries of Love" section in the front of this book, Cancerians are experiencing the adolescence of the soul. They sense so much they can't seem to express; their dreams haunt them with a disturbing precognition of the maturing process of both approaching happiness and approaching sorrows, as well as vivid recollections of yesterday. They feel all this, but they can't talk about it, so naturally they're moody, and can't help weeping in nameless dread and depression when the Moon periodically tugs on their emotions, as helpless as the ocean's tides to control the magnetic Lunar pull. Sometimes the Crabs are silent and reflective, at other times they cover their concerns with a crazy and marvelously contagious Lunar humor that frequently fools them right out of their fears, and certainly cheers up everyone lucky enough to be around them when they're feeling funny.

When a Moon Child and a Libran are thrown together, for a while it can be a melodious scene. Librans adore laughter, and the Lunar humor of Cancer becomes a rhythmical lyric to the mellow music of Libra's Venus essence, smooth and restful at times, yet also containing a few crashing chords and sour notes, punctuated by a kind of rocky roll. It's pure entertainment, and happy and fortunate indeed are the innocent bystanders around the home or office brightened by the musical duets of this combo when they're getting along. (The innocent bystanders should enjoy it while it lasts.) I say home or office because Destiny frequently places the

4-10 combinations in a life situation related closely to the home and the career. They seem to harmonize more easily around the family circle as relatives, as business associates, or in a classroom, than as friends, lovers, or mates. (But regarding the latter, don't forget that challenge, and its golden rewards.)

Actually, the Crab and the Libran have more basic empathy to aid them in overcoming their difficulties than some of the other 4-10 Patterns because, although their personalities often clash, their ruling planets—the Moon and Venus, respectively—are sympathetic. Since the Sun rules the personality and the Moon rules the emotions, these two can reach one another more easily through the *emotions* than through the more obvious and outward ways. The problem is that it's never a simple thing to break through a Crab shell to the Moon person's true emotional nature. It's well protected from hurt, and needs much careful coaxing.

Libra is tolerant, and stands a good chance of touching the Lunar person's emotions with a gentle attitude . . and waiting. But unfortunately, the fact that Libra is essentially gentle and tolerant may not be quite enough. For the Moon-ruled man or woman (or child) can be sensitive beyond belief. Despite the innate Libran kindness, Libra, being an Air Sign, is often too intent upon logic, too little aware of the Crab's or anyone else's sensitivity. Librans make excellent lawyers and wise judges, but with few exceptions, as fair as they may be, they make poor psychologists. Libra isn't concerned with the meaning-behind-the-meaning, only with the fascinating game of human action and reaction, on the surface level. That sort of attitude will never get beneath Cancer's crusty shell. Libra will have to practice more in-depth compassion with Cancer, if this man or woman wants to understand what makes the Crab symbolically crawl in such a sideways fashion, instead of being direct and getting to the point.

One of the chief differences between their natures is that Libra is "other-people" oriented and Cancer is "self-oriented." If it sounds as though astrology is saying that Cancer is more selfish than Libra, it *should* sound that way, because that's precisely what it means. The average Libran is demonstrably more concerned about the problems of friends, of a particular business or of the world at large, than about his or her own personal problems, which seem to roll off Libra's back with a shrug of the shoulders and the logical deduction that things can go nowhere from Down except Up. These men and women are outgoing extroverts, whereas the Moon people are more introverted—and protective of Number One. True, many Cancerians are gentle, imaginative, and sensitive folk, often very loving and affectionate; nonetheless, their most intense concentration is upon themselves.

Since concentration upon the self is an unhealthy emotional attitude which never fails to eventually bring on some degree of poor health, the Crabs are ill more frequently than they need be. Libra illnesses are more often seeded in permissive living, an indulgent life style, the tendency to gregariousness, their love of parties, overeating and overdrinking and over-working. All of which causes the Crab to fuss and worry, and inform Libra that he or she is burning the candle at both ends. (How else *could* Libra burn a candle, and still be fair to the candle?)

Money is another area where these two usually see in opposite directions. Librans are not unduly wasteful or extravagant, but money isn't the Big Thing to them it is to Cancer. To the Crabs, financial security and emotional security are of equal and vital importance. Possessing only one of these, and lacking the other, they can be pretty cranky and miserable. Possessing neither causes them to be so snappy and impossible even their mothers couldn't love them, and for Cancer, that's a rare and painful experience. But when Cancer possesses both kinds of security, the Moon person is magically transfigured into one of the most docile, dear, and tender human beings anyone could possibly ask for, including Libra, who sometimes asks a great deal of people, expecting everyone's character and personality pluses and minuses to come out exactly even, and not a micrometer off center.

Despite Cancer's apparent poor health and lack of physical strength, these people are, in the final analysis, much tougher in the art of surviving mentally, physically, and emotionally than Libra. After the deck is shuffled, Libra is the one more likely to give in to mental pressure and suffer a nervous breakdown, be broken hearted over emotional disappointments, or succumb to serious illness when the Scales are out of balance. When Cancer is ill, it may last a long time, true, but only because the Crab hangs on so tenaciously to everything, and sadly, seldom separates the positive from the negative. The Crab reaches out almost blindly, grabs hold, and hangs in there for dear life. Sometimes it takes Libra's gentle reminder to bring a Moon person to his or her senses, to the realization that what is being clung to so fiercely is best released. Letting go is not easy for Cancer, and Libra will have some frustrating experiences trying to pry the Crab's claws loose from bad habits, wrong ideas, and groundless fears.

This kind of tug-of-war is invisibly wearing on the delicate balance of Libra's nervous system over a long period, and can bring on a kind of exhaustion of the spirit, which can, in turn, lead to lethargy and deep wells of unhappiness, not to mention considerably dampening Libra's normal cheerful, affectionate, and optimistic nature. In Nature, as with people, an overabundance of water can make air soggy, foggy, and clammy, just as the right amount of water can make air moist, fresh, and exhilarating.

Libra is wasting time trying to keep a secret from Cancer. The Crabs will use every sly maneuver imaginable to pry out of a person what they wish to know. Cancer asks: "What does so-and-so think of me, honestly?" Libra replies, "I don't think I should take sides." Cancer says, "That's not *fair* of you, haven't I supplied information *you* needed badly, lots of times?" Libra hesitates, then sighs, gives in, and tells the Crab what he or she wants to know, being careful to list all the *good* things said, along *with* the bad. After Cancer hears the sought-for answer, the Crab may snap, "I thought so. I'll never speak to that person again," then leave the room in a huff; also leaving Libra nearly in tears over being forced into the position of agitator, when every fiber of Libra's being is designed in the pattern of peacemaker. Crabs are ultra-ultra-ultrasensitive to the slightest criticism, and very tricky in ferreting out the *whole* truth, then either weeping in hurt or snapping in anger over only *half* the truth—and you know how an emphasis on only half of something drives Libra wild.

The best way for Libra and Cancer to make mellow music together is for each of them to concentrate almost constantly on the very real virtues of the other, even though those traits may be markedly different in each. Libra must remember that the imaginative dreams of Cancer, blended with Cancer's incredible tenacity, are what allowed Moon Maiden Helen Keller to triumph so gloriously over the affliction of being struck deaf and blind at the age of nineteen months. She graduated cum laude from Radcliffe College, learned to knit, crochet, and use a typewriter, to swim, row a boat, and ride a bicycle. Traveling around the world, she gave inspirational talks (when she had so briefly ever heard the sound of a human voice) and wrote numerous books and articles to uplift the faith of others. Likewise, the sensitivity, insight, and perseverance of Cancer allowed Crab Nikola Tesla to use his remarkable memory and inventive genius to conceive of electronic miracles years ahead of his time, to be the first to implement the practical use of AC (or alternating electrical current), to patent 140 inventions of great practical value to Earthlings, one of which made possible the conception of radio broadcasting and receiving circuits used today—and to hang on to his Lunar dreams and visions, despite ridicule, lack of interest, and being cheated out of his rewards for his life's work until after his death. Every Moon Child is made of the stuff of which Helen Keller and Nikola Tesla were made.

Conversely, Cancer might reflect upon what life would be like today had it not been for Libra's desire for justice and need for creative expression—had the world not been blessed with the adaptability and peacemaking talents of Librans such as Dwight Eisenhower, George Westinghouse, and Giuseppe Verdi. Without their Venus abilities to create music for the soul, to be just compromisers who yet never compromised moral values, we might still be involved in World War II, our railroads would not be safe, and the Crab couldn't listen to the soaring sounds of *Aïda* to calm his or her spirit. It was Mahatma Gandhi, the Libran peacemaker, who blended the teachings of Hinduism with the Nazarene's "Sermon on the Mount" —in perfect harmony.

Once Cancer and Libra have learned to genuinely appreciate one another, great magic can result. An excellent example of this is the statement of Cancerian Crab Tesla, regarding Libran George Westinghouse: "If other industrial firms had been as *fair* and *liberal,* and as *just* as George, *I could have offered the world so much more.*"

Cancer and Libra should meditate upon those twenty-four words for a long, long time. They contain a mighty message. For both of them. Equally.

☆ ☆ ☆ ☆ ☆ ☆

CANCER *Woman* LIBRA *Man*

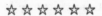

> *She had come to save him, to give him her nest,*
> *though there were eggs in it. I rather wonder*
> *at the bird, for though he had been nice to her,*
> *he had also sometimes tormented her.*

Love has a way of turning a moody, secretive, and sometimes cranky female Crab into a lovely, solicitous, tender, and gentle Moon Maiden. If she should happen to be in love with a Libra man, she'll begin to worry about him right away. He works too hard, he plays too hard, he eats all the wrong foods, he drinks too much, he doesn't get enough rest, he lets other people take advantage of his good nature, he's too easygoing, he'll catch cold if he doesn't stop running around in the rain without his rubbers, and he must stop losing his umbrellas, because umbrellas cost money, and the money spent on just the ones he lost last year alone could buy a new electric juicer to make vegetable juices to dilute the effect of the bad things he insists upon eating and drinking. Cancer *cares*. On his birthday, the Moon Maiden may give him an electric blanket, because she's concerned about his comfort. Actually, it's a hint that sleeping with her curled up beside him would be a much nicer way to keep his toes warm in winter.

Since Libra is a masculine Sun Sign, he will soon set her straight on his determination not to be either dominated or nagged. But he is ruled by the feminine planet Venus, which will harmonize nicely with her fluctuating Lunar moods, brought on by her ruling Moon, making her feel emotionally secure, which in turn will bring out all her sterling qualities of loyalty, patience, and devotion. For a while, all will be peace and tranquility.

Regardless of the rather marked differences in their dispositions and personalities, if he's a typical Libra male, he won't let much time drag by between falling in love and being tempted by the idea of marriage. When a Venus-ruled male is strongly tempted to do something with a female as tempting as this one, he'll mull it over and find a thousand rational reasons why he should, finally deciding that the only way to get rid of temptation is to give in to it. (That's an example of Libra logic when it's distorted by romantic desire and urges of the flesh.)

If he's an evolved Libran, and if the aspect between their Luminaries is favorable (his Sun conjunct, sextile, or trine her Moon, or vice versa—or blessedly, both), he's made a wise decision in proposing marriage to this soft, dewy-eyed creature with the hard shell, this fragile (ha!), sensitive and perceptive (true) Moon Maiden who exhibits such flattering concern for his welfare, and who stirs within him such deep emotions. (You can't blame him for giving in to temptation when you really think about it.) If the aforementioned Sun-Moon aspect between their horoscopes is a square or an opposition, he may still have made a wise decision for the good of his eternal soul—but it could be kind of rough on his mind, body, and emotions. However, we must keep in mind what was noted in the first part of this chapter, that if they're able to harmonize the disharmony, they'll have the sort of love the angels enjoy, and that's worth more than a little effort.

To the Moon Maid and the Libran: Listen, astrologically, I have for you some bad news and some good news. Which do you want to hear first, the good news or the bad?

LIBRA: Give me the good news first.
CANCER: Give me the bad news first.

I guess it has to be the bad news first, because their answers are a perfect demonstration of it—of the vastly different approach these two take toward any sort of situation, outside themselves or between themselves.

No other Sun Sign is by nature more unintentionally but determinedly pessimistic than Cancer (unless it's Taurus, Virgo, or Capricorn, but when the scores are added up, the Crab tops them all). And no Sun Sign is by nature as cheerfully, endlessly (and sometimes maddeningly) optimistic as Libra (unless it's Aries or Sag, but Libra can beat them both to the finish line when it comes to chasing the rainbows).

Looking on the bright side of it, we may play Pollyanna and say that when his optimism and her pessimism are poured out of the same teapot day after day (and night after night), her influence will gradually make his optimism less gullible and more sensible—while his influence will gradually make her pessimism less depressing and a little more hopeful.

Looking on the dark side of it, we must admit that, by the very nature of its Webster definition, optimism cannot be made *less* gullible and cannot become sensible, or it wouldn't be optimism anymore. Likewise, by the very nature of its Webster definition, pessimism can't be made *less* depressing, because depressing is depressing, and degrees of it don't count—and it certainly can't be made hopeful, or it wouldn't be pessimism anymore. Our efforts to help them are clearly becoming snarled in semantics.

We wouldn't want them to solve the problem by trading these ingrained character traits with one another, because a pessimistic Libran would be a dreadfully unhappy man, and a totally optimistic Cancerian woman, lacking all caution, would be untrue to herself. Maybe a touch of anagrams would help. Optimism contains within it the word "mist," pessimism contains within it the word "miss." She might warn him (and beneficially, too) that TOO MUCH (those are the key words) optimism could form a *mist* over reality, which could cause his dreams to fade, when she so desperately wants them to come true because she loves him. He might, in turn, tell her that TOO MUCH (key words again) pessimism will cause her to unnecessarily *miss* a lot of happiness along the way that they could have shared together, a tragedy he wants her to avoid because he loves her so. The solution is Libra *balance*.

Now that we've solved that problem between them, let's go on to the next piece of bad news, and save the good news for last, where it will have more power to cancel the complications.

She is emotionally possessive, and he is emotionally freedom-loving. It seems like an insurmountable conflict, yet it isn't nearly as difficult a situation as each of them may individually talk themselves into believing it is.

Not if they really love one another. *To him:* She isn't possessive because she wants to smother you. It's just her old fears from childhood nightmares, returning to haunt her. She's afraid your love for her is only a mirage and it might disappear someday, leaving her all alone, unloved and unprotected. Surely you can be fair enough to be aware that these very real fears naturally increase when you're out of sight, because she was frightened by the lie "out of sight, out of mind" when she was a little girl. *To her:* He doesn't seek periods of freedom because he wants to plot ways of leaving you—or because he's fallen in love with someone else. He was born into the Air Element, and when Air is confined, it grows stale. Forget that false warning of what happens when the man you love is out of your sight, and realize that it's been proven a million times over that "absence makes the heart grow even fonder." It's a universal law of love that cannot ever be changed. Only if he doesn't love you are you in danger of losing him when he's out of sight—and if he doesn't love you, you're going to lose him anyway, and good riddance, because it will allow your *real* love to enter your life. If he does love you, he misses you more when you're apart than you suspect, and far more than he'll ever tell you if you keep making him think you don't trust him.

A Libra man who truly loves and understands the Moon Maiden who tugs on his heart will invite her to go with him, even when it's a boring business trip he feels would be sooner and more smoothly out of the way if he handled it alone, and really *mean* it when he asks her, remembering that people fall in love to be *together*, and things that keep them apart, that keep them from the constant excitement of discovery together, are enemies to their happiness, never mind the rules of society.

How can they share exciting discoveries together if the only time they see one another is at home, and the only exciting discovery is the baby's new tooth or that the roof is leaking? If he sincerely and impulsively invites her to go with him when it's at all possible, he'll receive a touching surprise. Knowing at last that he really wants her near him, she'll lose every trace of her Cancerian possessiveness, and tell him it's all right, she has lots of things to do while he's gone, just hurry back home—and she'll really mean it, because his wanting her has removed all her Lunar fears. Then *he* may start worrying about why she doesn't *accept* his invitation. These two must learn to quit while they're ahead. Lovers are such strange Earthlings. So contradictory.

There are very few broken Cancer-Libra relationships that can't be mended and glued back together like new if these two see together, holding hands, Neil Simon's 1978 film *The Goodbye Girl*, because the last scene was inspired and channeled by the angels, just for them alone. If they're reading this a decade or two or more from the time I'm writing it, I'd advise them to rent the film from a film library, then rent a projector or a screening room (or watch it when it's on their television) and sit through the *last scene* several times. It contains the complete solution the Cancer woman and the Libra man are seeking—and the only answer they'll ever need. If they don't love, they should part quickly and painlessly. If they do, they should see this film and send Neil Simon a dozen daisies and daffodils every year on their anniversary all the rest of their lives together.

With a little help from Cancerian Neil, who understands the nature of Cancerian females, we've solved that problem. The next one involves money, and here I refuse to be the arbitrator, except to say briefly to *him*: Let her have a savings account and a couple of paid-up annuities to keep her happy—and to *her*: Stop making him feel he's on the verge of bankruptcy, stop imagining poverty or you'll manifest it into reality as sure as God made little green apples, as your grandma used to say—and when you do have cash, LET GO OF IT, give large chunks of it away to strangers on the street, yes, I said strangers on the street and don't faint—and you'll see it return to you three times over sooner than you dream possible. With all your Cancerian caution, you can't change that Universal law of giving. How can you prove me wrong if you don't try it?

The sexual side of their relationship can begin as a gift from the angels too, but it can end with their hearts feeling as empty as they once felt full. The time to prevent such a tragedy is before the curtain rises on it, in the first act of their play. Her seemingly never-ending suspicions may finally drive him into a feeling of futility that can be a prelude to impotence, just as his lack of insight into her deep need for sustained affection and romantic reassurance can drive her into her shell of emotional protection that can harden into frigidity. When they avoid the cause of such a mutually lonely effect by respecting and really *thinking* about Newton's law of Cause and Effect, their physical love can be a beautiful experience of gentle passion, the kind of intimacy that makes them tremble just anticipating it in each other's eyes, and brings them a new peace and contentment every time they rediscover themselves through its ancient alchemy.

Sexual union between a man and woman who love is like a remembered melody of inexpressible longing and silent fulfillment that can be wonderfully healing. Unlike many other couples, these two may use poetry as the language of their love. The typical Moon-ruled woman and Venus-ruled man aren't embarrassed by expressing their feelings in this way, and also music will sometimes intensify the emotional depth of their lovemaking. There are many ways to say I'm sorry . . . I didn't mean to hurt you.

The next time he has to leave her for a few days, he might give her a bottle of *Je Reviens* perfume and a French-English dictionary so she can learn that *je reviens* means *I shall return* . . . or maybe a Raggedy Ann, to show her he knows how it is with her inside, how she treasures yesterday because it seems more real and secure to her than today or tomorrow. She's needed someone to understand this about her since she was a little girl crooning a gentle lullaby to her doll. Then she'll give him a gift beyond measure—her complete trust.

Now for the good news. They are both sentimental. They're both wonderfully imaginative, and they both believe in dreams. She has a beautiful sense of humor; he has a beautiful smile. They're both subject to changing moods, but they're both also touched by tenderness. Last but not least, the angels fight on their side, for having already been there, they're well aware of the sacrifice of self involved in climbing the steep hill to happiness required of the 4-10 vibration, yet ever ready to promise that the view from that height is splendid—not a millimeter off center from beautiful.

☆ ☆ ☆ ☆ ☆ ☆

CANCER *Man* LIBRA *Woman*

*. . . every door in the coral caves where they live
rings a tiny bell when it opens or closes . . and
he heard the bells.*

Libra women are so full of love and loveliness, it really does seem as though bells ring when one is in their presence. Bells ring around most Gemini and Virgo girls too, but they have a more delicate sound. Libra bells are deeper, more like the chimes you hear at Easter Sunday sunrise. It's all part of the music of Venus, and you can just imagine the effect it has on the sentimental heart and sensitive, finely tuned awareness of the Moon-ruled Cancer man. Like the sound of a choir.

To add to the dreamlike quality of the experience, the Libra girl who has enchanted him looks an awful lot like an angel. Venus never fails to bestow upon those who are her children a haunting beauty of feature . . . if not that, then at the very least, a smile that can gladden the weariest soul. Sometimes a Libra female is fortunate enough to have received both of these Venus blessings at birth, and if so, the Crab doesn't have much of a chance. Dazzled by all that beauty, softened by her brilliant smile, and hearing all those chimes at the same time . . . . . . can bring on more than a touch of Moon madness in this man of many moods.

Crabs have a sensational sense of humor, so the first thing he'll do to impress her, shortly after they've met, is tell her a funny story. She will laugh, then . . not just an ordinary laugh, but a laugh very much like the one Peter Pan told Wendy about that breaks into a thousand pieces and creates the birth of faeries . . and he will hear those chimes again. Not only is her laughter musical, but her smile is a symphony, and she has the good taste to appreciate his humor.

Not long after this he'll learn that, in addition to being beautiful and witty, softly fragrant and feminine, and overflowing with the velvet mystery of woman, she's also extremely intelligent and can match his own cleverness in anything from chess to charades. She's capable of being a surprisingly level-headed and creative silent partner in all his business affairs, maybe even an actual partner. She's certainly smarter than all those dunderheads he's used to dealing with who don't laugh at his jokes and have to be told a dozen times how to accomplish the most simple tasks.

While he is being thus enchanted, so is she. Loving parties and people as she does, she's met lots of men over the years, but they've bored her to tears. They're so insensitive, so rude and demanding. They would never ask her advice about their businesses, jobs, or careers, because they think she's "only a woman," so what could she know about such matters? This always infuriates a Libra girl, to whom equality of the sexes is practically a religion. She doesn't have to march in an ERA parade (though she very well might) but equality is equality, and fairness is fairness to Libra.

Now here is this charming man, whose eyes are alive with intelligence and humor, whose manner is so warm and affectionate, who is so reflective and sensitive. He makes her feel so feminine, yet he admires, even encourages her intellect. He makes her feel that he truly needs her, and somehow . . . she feels so safe and secure with him, as though he would never allow anything ugly or gross or upsetting to trouble the new tranquility they've found. There's something just a little old-fashioned and gallant about him, and it lifts her spirits in a strange way, makes her feel pleasantly protected. He understands the swinging of her Scales from lonely to lovely, from happy to hateful, because he's moody too, and that causes him to be sympathetic to her own moods. Mostly, he's so serene and patient, qualities that always appeal to Libra, who seeks the soothing and peaceful.

Why not get married? (She may think of this first.) He may hesitate. Maybe his mother doesn't approve of her, or maybe he's not sure she can replace his mother as The-Woman-Who-Adores-Him-Above-All-Else-In-The-World-Even-If-She-Sometimes-Doesn't-Show-It-But-She-Usually-Does. Maybe he thinks he should concentrate on his career or business until it's financially sound enough to support a wife and family. A Cancer man always looks before he leaps, and seldom rushes into anything. (To the *female* Crab who wants emotional and financial protection, marriage is the ideal answer, but the *male* Crab tends to seek the affection and emotional security he needs just as desperately by lengthening a love affair to its limit before he's willing to contemplate wedlock.) The responsibilities of marriage worry him. Whether he loves her or not isn't the issue. *Of course* he loves her, *but* . . . . .

Her first reaction to his Crablike hesitation and crawling backward may be to become cool to his physical advances—or to torture him by pretending to be interested in other men, hoping that jealousy, fear of losing her—or a denial of physical passion—will overcome his caution. She hopes to convince him of the truth of Samuel Johnson's observation that "marriage may have many pains, but celibacy has no pleasures." If the Sun and Moon in their nativities are in harmonious aspect, her strategy might work. Otherwise, it could only cause him to become snappy and cranky or to retreat into a shell of pouting. She's been exposed to a myriad of his moods, but this may be a side of him she's never seen. It will upset her, although she'll try not to show it. Then she'll turn on her Venus charm again, and begin to gently manipulate him with her soft voice and her dimpled smiles—attempt to win him over with a sort of combination of logic and serendipity. But with his acute perception, he'll sense what she's doing, and perhaps resist it by clinging to his caution even more tenaciously. His mother once told him that its more sensible to be safe than sorry, and that smartness succeeds better than softness in this harsh, cold world. So he's always tried to be safe and sensible and smart. Now here is this beautiful, intelligent woman trying to make him be careless and impulsive . . and free. It confuses him, and makes him even crabbier.

He'll fret privately over her extravagant nature and she'll be annoyed at his unfair suspicions of her innocent friendships with others (but maybe not quite fair enough herself to realize she deliberately incited his suspicions). She'll tell him he's smothering her very soul, and refuse to answer his calls. But she misses him, she needs him, so she'll try to see it his way again . . . . . . and again. He panics a little when they've quarreled, because the moment they're apart, her air of happy optimism and the sheer loveliness of life when they're laughing and loving together—haunts him. It's so like the way he felt in childhood when life was sweet . . . . . . and simple. Will there ever be such beauty again with anyone else? He fears there won't. In fact, secretly he's sure of it, and that's the dark enemy of their love—his secrecy, his reluctance to openly and directly express his feelings and thoughts to her. If he would, if he could, she might be able to help him make some sense of this strange Lunar magic they've discovered, help him find a way to believe in its goodness. But he perversely likes to keep her guessing about what he *really* thinks. It's never as easy for Cancer to be as honest and open as Libra.

When they're making love, they'll say silently to one another, "Let's don't think, let's just feel." And so their physical intimacy makes their troubles fade, for a time. When a Cancerian man submits to pure emotion and feeling, he's being his true self, free of the restrictions of his fears and worries. As a lover, he brings her the kind of peace and contentment he does because of these deep waters of his emotional nature. Sometimes, when they physically experience love, she's reminded of a cool stream, and she's a leaf, floating on its surface. The tenderness and imagination she brings to their Oneness has the same quieting effect upon him, and he relaxes, allowing love to fill his whole being, so there's no room for anything but joy. The way she makes him feel at these moments is not something he'll ever want to lose. But passion comes and goes, and always afterward there are the problems.

This being the difficult 4-10 Sun Sign Pattern, their conflicts and tensions, their impasse over permanency, and their divergent viewpoints aren't easy to overcome. But if he uses his Cancerian tenaciousness to try harder to pull their differences together, instead of using it to pull their love apart—and if she uses her Libra fairness to comprehend his caution with more compassion for his feelings, and less concern for her own, they just might try again . . and maybe this time, they'll make their poem rhyme, somehow learn to sing their song in tune. It's a painful process for Cancer and Libra to reach a compromise, but his need to hear those Easter Sunday sunrise chimes again may cause the Crab to take another chance —and her need to be loved by a man who both cherishes her and respects her may bring her back into his arms to be told again how beautiful she is. While she's gone, it's funny how he still feels her head against his shoulder, now and then, in his dreams . . and last night, he was sure he heard her speak, but her voice was sad. With her wiser heart (for Libra is ahead of Cancer on the karmic wheel of life) he thought he heard her say to him, gently, "You have so much to learn, darling . . . and I hope you never learn it, because it will bring pain, as learning always does, and I can't bear for you to be hurt anymore. That's why I had to go away." When he awoke, there were tears in his eyes, because her presence had been so real, he almost heard the music he'll never quite forget.

The Moon both curses and blesses Cancer with a vivid memory, nearly photographic, sometimes, in its clarity. These two can find their way back home to each other if their need and their patience are both strong enough. But if not, even after the song between them has ended, his Lunar memory will return to him . . . haunting fragments of the lyric. Then he'll regret certain things he didn't say when she was near . . so he'll just think about them sometimes when he's alone . . and hope she hears them, wherever she is . . . . . .

> . . . it's like you told me once
> if we never saw each other again
> it wouldn't make any difference
>
> you didn't say it wouldn't matter
> you said . . it wouldn't make any difference
>
> and did you know I understood the nuance?
> it was so long ago . . but, did you know?*

* From *Venus Trines at Midnight* by Linda Goodman.

CANCER

Water—Cardinal—Negative
Ruled by the Moon
Symbol: The Crab
Night Forces—Feminine

SCORPIO

Water—Fixed—Negative
Ruled by Pluto
Symbols: Scorpion & Eagle
Night Forces—Feminine

The **CANCER-SCORPIO** *Relationship*

Strangely, it was not in the water that
they met . .

The Crab and the Scorpion may meet while they're sunning themselves on a rock somewhere, on a lazy lavender day. They could, of course, meet beneath the briny, but since they are often destined to be drawn together sooner or later, the choice of multiple meeting places is greatly enhanced. A bank is near the top of the list. Or perhaps a United States Treasury building. Maybe a restaurant—a nursery—or in history class. All these areas are sacred to Cancer. Give Scorpio the choice, and it could be any site from an archaeological dig to a church . . . with a strong possibility of Tibet, among the lamas . . . or a library, near the shelves labeled "Sex and the Human Psyche." All sacred subjects to the Eagle.

This is the blessed-by-grace 5-9 Sun Sign Pattern, meaning that these two will almost surely be magnetized together anytime they're within a few miles of one another—not always, but usually. It's not a guarantee—what is, regarding human behavior? But it's an astrological probability that Cancer and Scorpio have a better chance than most people of successfully blending their auras. Anyway, guarantees are boring, don't you think? No. The Crab and the Eagle do not think so. Other 5-9 Sun Sign Patterns, such as Aries-Leo, Gemini-Aquarius, and so forth, may look upon guarantees as boring, but not this particular 5-9 vibe. Scorpions (Eagles) are undeniably fond of sure things, and Crabs mentally visualize the word *guarantee* spelled out in diamond letters, sparkling like the water of an unpolluted stream (a good allegory, since an unpolluted stream is as difficult to find these days as a 100 percent guarantee has always been—and always shall be—to locate).

All right, we'll start over. To the Crab and the Scorpion: You two nice creatures are very, very, very, very close to being certain of achieving harmony together, closer than most anyone you know. That's a promise from the planets and stars, a promise you have the power to transmute into a genuine guarantee with less effort than lots of other people. Does that make you both feel a little more comfy-cozy secure about it all? (Shh! See? Notice. The Crab is now peeking out of the shell, curious . . . and the Scorpion has raised one cautious eyebrow slowly, in interest. Words like *guarantee* and *secure* always have that effect on these Sun Signs.)

An occasional Cancer-Scorpio combination may toss each other up on the beach in an unhappy ending, but the great majority of associations between the Moon-governed (Cancer) and the Pluto-ruled (Scorpio) need never fear such a shipwreck. Their relationship will quite likely still be strong and healthy long after other combinations have given up the struggle. The areas of publishing, religion, space travel, the law, travel, foreign countries, the stock market, young people, schools, and various forms of creativity, including films . . (all ninth- and fifth-house matters) . . are likely ponds where you will find this combination splashing and diving and swimming and floating—or, if they're unevolved types—crawling hesitantly, hiding under protective shells.

The Crab and the Scorpion (or Eagle) have an almost uncanny instinctive understanding of one another. They share, not all, but nearly all vices and virtues. The faults and foibles of one are either possessed by or compassionately comprehended by the other. The lovable traits and talents of one are either possessed by or intensely admired by the other. It's called empathy, and Cancer and Scorpio can always count on this as a supportive influence in their relationship, whether adult and child, business associates, lovers, married mates, friends, siblings, or other relatives.

A child, or children, will typically, in some way, play an important role in their lives, as the relationship grows and endures (and probably it will), either a troublesome and sorrowful or a happy and magical role, almost from the time they first meet. Sometimes, sadly, this takes the form of children one or both deeply desire, but cannot possess, for one reason or another. More often, however, children and young people are a blessing to these two. If not literally children, then the *childhood* of the Crab or the Scorpion (or both) will be, in some strange way, the basis for initial attraction and sympathy. They will enjoy comforting one another concerning a sad past—or laughing and dreaming together over a happy past. Yesterday is always very near to Moon souls, and Scorpio also looks back, secretly, with nostalgia.

Both the Crabs and the Eagles tend to never forget a kindness. Likewise, they mutually share long memories for hurt or injury. Wound either Cancer or Scorpio, and the memory will linger, never fading, occasionally for a lifetime. But there the similarity ends, for the Crab will seldom try to even the score, preferring to cry and nurse injured feelings alone, cauterizing the wounds with liberal doses of self-pity, while the Scorpion will bloody well see to it, in one way or another, that there is returned an "eye for an eye, a tooth for a tooth"—a bruise for a bruise, a dented fender for a dented fender, an insult for an insult, and so on. This is a reaction (though not a very positive one) to the Scale-balancing act Scorpio has already learned from the sign behind—Libra. Making things come out even. But while Libra sorts it all out evenly through logical mental processes, Scorpio balances matters in, shall we say, a more tangible and instant way.

The Crab's hurt seldom, if ever, causes an urge to attack. The reflex action of the wounded Cancerian is to retreat, often remaining mistrustful of that person or situation forever . . . . whereas the word "retreat" is nearly unknown to an Eagle. Scorps may *appear* to give up, to retreat or disappear. But they'll return. Inwardly, these people would almost literally prefer to die than to lose a conflict or come out on the short end of someone else's stick. This goes for love affairs, business deals—soccer and marbles (depending on the age and sex). Yet, the Scorpion does not always *consciously* obtain the satisfaction of revenge. That is, he or she need not necessarily (though some do it deliberately) take an overt action against the offender. The intensity of a Pluto-powered thought alone will do it.

Nevertheless, there is an unearthly sweetness in the Scorpio aura, superimposed upon the determination not to be smashed without teaching the smasher a lesson, and it is this sweetness, this gentleness and sensitivity, which allows the Crab to trust the Eagle.

Since both are of the Water Element, when Cancerians and Scorpions who have heavy afflictions to their individual Suns at birth get together, they can drown in drink, drugs, or other forms of escape, including sexual promiscuity—dragging one another down deeper into the depths, until they've reached the ocean floor. The swim back up is not easy. For these, the extraordinary magnetism of the 5-9 attraction is a trap. Some associations of this type have even become mutual victims of dark arts like hypnotic control, psychic attack, voodoo, and black magic. Scenes like séances with a trance medium are best avoided by either—and especially by both together.

Ah! but the evolved, the emotionally mature, mentally perceptive, and spiritually aware Crabs and Eagles will discover all the joys and pure pleasures of the 5-9 Pattern, feeling and behaving very much like children together—and what could be more wonderful than submission to innocence, excitement, and faith in faeries? This can really be a rainbow kind of relationship, where every small or large misunderstanding is certain to be resolved and forgiven later. Crabs and Scorps don't forgive many people—but they will forgive one another. What is even lovelier, if the Sun-Moon aspect between their birth charts is also harmonious, matching the music of their trined, natal Suns, they'll not only forgive—they'll forget. And that's a true miracle for the Crab and the Scorpion. They can, if they only half try, bring out the best, not the worst, in each other. The trust Cancer has never been able to fully give to anyone will be easily given to Scorpio—and the great gift of forgiveness that Scorpio has never quite been able to give to another person will be painlessly given to the compatible Crab. Cancer and Scorpio, both extremely sensitive, are willing to reveal their vulnerabilities to each other. This is no small matter, for they've both kept their terrible vulnerability hidden beneath their shells for so long, lest the world discover it as a weakness and use it against them.

They tell each other secrets they would ordinarily never tell a soul. No one can pry a secret out of a Crab, if he or she doesn't want it known, but the Eagle just may—and the gentle Moon-ruled Cancerians can sometimes perform the magic trick of accurately reading Scorpio's facial expression of cool detachment for what it really is—a mask. They're both more than a little telepathic, particularly with one another.

When their purposes do clash, it will frequently be over money, because Scorpio is concerned with "other people's money," and Cancer is concerned with—well, with just plain money, never mind whose, just so it's green. Scorpio tends to worry over how to obtain it, Cancer over the dreadful possibility of losing it.

Since all Crabs, of whatever age or sex, as explained in my first book, *Sun Signs*, are "Jewish mothers"—and all Eagles, of whatever age or sex, are fiercely, intensely protective—these two will wrap one another in a very comforting cocoon, which could become a little stuffy unless they allow themselves to come out for air now and then. But oh! that feeling of security. Beautiful. Scorpio can at times be too self-controlled for Cancer's affectionate nature, and the Crab will sometimes snap at Scorpio, ruffling those smooth Eagle feathers, but these are minor tensions with which to cope when the rewards are so solid. After swimming for what has seemed to be eternities, in endless whirlpools of infinitude . . . . . . to be brought together with one who so gently understands your heart's deepest longings . . . . . . is a blessed thing.

☆ ☆ ☆ ☆ ☆ ☆

CANCER *Woman* **SCORPIO** *Man*

> *It was not, she knew, that night had come, but*
> *something as dark as night had come. No, worse*
> *than that. It had not come, but it had sent*
> *that shiver through the sea to say that it was*
> *coming. What was it?*

Although somewhat of an enigma, the Cancer girl is decidedly interesting. Beneath her surface reserve and coolness, she has a delightful sense of joy and humor. She possesses very little ego or vanity, yet she's constantly misunderstood and accused of being cold and self-centered. Mystery attracts her, but she's reluctant to delve too deeply into unknown, uncharted waters . . . . . . unless those unknown, uncharted waters surround a Scorpio man. This particular mystery she cannot resist, and in order to know him better, she'll even discard her innate fears. For the girl Crab to control her fears is no small accomplishment. Give her "A" on her spiritual-evolvement report card for even the effort, let alone success in such a goal. Cancer fears always hover around the aura of the Moon-ruled, so complex, and so deeply submerged in the subconscious, that any attempt to overcome them should be appreciated and applauded.

Being appreciated is her most wistful wish, her dearest desire, though she will seldom admit it. So few people even try to understand her, let alone appreciate her. The Scorpio man will do both. Perhaps that's why she gathers the courage to return his intense gaze. She senses this is one human being on the planet who really *knows* her. She's right. He does.

If any other man attempted to penetrate her secret self with such a burning look, with such an intimate message in his glance, she would shower him with ice water and aloofness. Or snap his head off. A girl Crab can become mighty cranky when someone she doesn't trust tries to pry open her shell. She's always more gentle with other Cancerians, Scorpio, and Pisces, a little less irritable with Virgo and Taurus, sometimes fascinated by the male Goat—but the Aries or Libra man may expect a decided snapping reaction.

Eagles love a challenge, and coaxing the shy but funny Cancerian girl to trust him will be one of his easier ones. Equally as surprising, the normally very suspicious Scorpio Eagle will probably trust her also, from the first moment their eyes meet. It's an extremely rare occasion when the powerful empathy between these Sun Signs isn't visible right away. It can happen, but most infrequently.

Others in the past have accused the two of them of being cold emotionally. There's a good reason for that. They are. After all, they're both of the Water Element; consequently they find it difficult to display their feelings openly. But romantic temperature is a matter of interpretation. What others may call cold, to the Moon Maid and the Eagle can read from warm to hot. Compensating for their undeniable Water Element inheritance of a cooler chemistry, these two are secretly very sentimental, even more so than Taurus and Leo. The Cancer-Scorpio attempt to hide this sentimentality isn't always successful. Tears come to both their eyes easily when their emotions are touched (which is frequently). With her, the tears often spill down over her cheeks, and the secret is out. With him, after the first unbidden misting or faint wetness, a manly gulp and a powerful surge of self-control will dry his tears so quickly most people are none the wiser. Except for her. The Moon Maid saw them. And they caused a sharp loving-pain in her heart. No one in this world can control his emotions as superbly as a Scorpio man. He exercises a continual watch over them, forcing his facial features to assume a neutral position in the midst of any emotion, from surprise or elation to hurt or grief. Nearly always, the Eagle succeeds. When he doesn't, you can be sure the depth of the emotion felt is truly overwhelming, virtually uncontrollable. Others may not sense this, but the Cancer woman does, and it moves her deeply.

So, you see, they aren't emotionally cold at all—it's just that they both find it difficult to show on the outside what they're feeling on the inside. It's not easy for feelings, even strong ones, to break through their shells. For the Crab and the Scorpion each possess a hard shell of self-protection, an extra insurance policy from Nature against the intense degree of hurt always felt by such sensitive, sensitive creatures. This is the real basis for their empathy. Still, there will be times when she'll have to remind herself that what seems to be a coldness and silence approaching cruelty in him can be a mixture of shyness and a reluctance to admit what he's really thinking, until he's sure. He'll have to be aware that her apparent uncaring withdrawal is only her way of protecting herself from possible disappointment, until she's assured of being loved. No one seeks and needs love more than the Moon Maiden and the Eagle. Not an ordinary love, but an all-encompassing love, woven with the strong threads of devotion, gentleness, and loyalty. That last word is ultra, super important to them both.

In direct contradiction to his surface detachment and poker face, this man is an extremist. You'd never guess it from his soft voice, his subtle strategies in his career and personal life. (You'd never guess it, but you'd better believe it!) He can sink into some abysmal wells of depression, and rise to some intoxicating heights of ecstasy. All the while, to look at him, you'd think his days were spent in monotonous fashion, with few, if any, ups and downs, the smooth lake of his personality unruffled by unexpected events. Don't be fooled. (This advice is for other Sun Signs—the Cancer woman doesn't need it. Remember, she *knows* him.) Of course, that cool poise took years of training. He unleashed some pretty sensational rages of fury as a teenager, before he mastered self-control. Ask his mother.

The Lunar lady of his dreams soon discovers that her Eagle lover's chief faults are his suspicious nature, jealousy, and a desire to dominate his mate (and most everyone else), however well disguised—just as he realizes very early in the relationship that her weak points are secrecy, smothering possessiveness, and a quivering vulnerability to hurt, both real and imagined. Imagined hurt, whether emotional or physical, can be as painful as the real kind. Any doctor will tell you that the "imaginary pain" of an amputee, for example, is vividly felt.

All pain begins in the mind, even so-called physical pain—not in the body. And so, when dealing with his Moon Maiden's wounded feelings, the Eagle must first realize how real the pain is to her, how dreadfully her heart aches, even though she only imagined the action which hurt her to be intentional. Then he can tenderly explain to her how medical hypnosis, and many other experiments, have proven that all pain sensations begin in the mind, before manifesting in the body, and therefore, can only be removed through the *source*—the mind or the imagination. The subconscious mind, depositor of all her nightmares and insecurities from childhood, is in absolute control of the body, and of all human emotional reaction. Tell a hypnotized subject the postage stamp placed on a hand or arm is a flame, and an actual blister will rise. Place a *real* flame against the skin, tell the hypnotized person it's an ice cube, and *no* blister will appear. It's as simple and as true as that—and it gives a clue to handling the Cancerian fear fluctuations, when the problem is actually emotional pain, rather than physical.

Sexually, the Scorpion's love nature is more intense and yearning than that of most men. Hers is more romantic and sensitive than that of most women. What each needs most, then, from the other should be obvious: emotional security and reassurance. She needs visible tokens of his affection . . . . . . an unexpected rose or bunch of violets on her desk or on her pillow . . . . . . perhaps a small pet, like the one she had as a child, sitting there with a ribbon around its neck as a surprise some bright morning—things like that. These small things affect her sexual chemistry profoundly.

He needs to know that her lovemaking stems from a genuine desire to be one with him, that it's not, on occasion, feigned to hide a secret boredom. You can't hide anything from him anyway, so why try? If they remain aware of one another's unspoken needs, their physical mating can be a truly transcendental experience. But they both may have occasion to learn that controlled passion is not passion at all. Only when two people trust one another totally in every *other* way can they fully express love through sexual intimacy. The special requirement these two share is the need they each have for continual demonstration of affection away from the bedroom—a demonstration for which they will rarely ask, a need they seldom verbally express, because it's buried so deep. When this mutual need is filled, the happiness they discover in their physical lovemaking will be just about all Earthlings could wish for on this three-dimensional level of man and woman's present awareness—as with all 5-9 Sun Sign couples, barring a negative Sun-Moon aspect between them.

I've said this earlier, but it bears repetition. The two dragons they must conquer together are their most negative traits: her unfounded fears and sometimes smothering possessiveness—his burning jealousy and revenge compulsion—and their mutual financial caution. (Some people call it stinginess.) When they're angry, both tend to retreat into their individual caverns of silence, which is the worst of all possible solutions for these two Sun Signs (although other Fire Sign 5-9 Patterns could profit by a little more of the stuff). What Cancer and Scorpio need, however, is to talk it over, to verbalize their complaints. Burying a resentment in silence won't make it disappear. It only allows what began as a minor irritation to grow into a not-so-jolly green giant which can destroy their relationship. It's always unfortunate when any 5-9 Sun Sign Pattern vibration is destroyed, because they invariably miss each other so very much.

This is a woman who needs a Valentine every February, a hyacinth for Easter, the merry sound of antique sleigh bells at Christmas to match her merry laughter . . . a tiny diamond, or something shining and silvery for the New Year . . . a nostalgic box of sparklers on the Fourth of July . . . lots and lots of time to reminisce about the past on Thanksgiving . . . and no unexpected goblins to frighten her on Halloween.

This is a man who may pretend to ignore holidays, but watch his normally impassive, controlled features light up in sheer delight, should the woman he loves happen to leave a crazy stuffed animal perched on the dashboard of his car, on Groundhog's Day. For a brief, enchanted moment, she'll catch a glimpse of the way he grinned when he was a small boy, before he learned to master his poker face and that enigmatic, mysterious smile.

☆ ☆ ☆ ☆ ☆ ☆

CANCER *Man* SCORPIO *Woman*

Sometimes . . . . he had dreams, and they were more painful than the dreams of other boys. For hours he could not be separated from these dreams, though he wailed piteously in them. They had to do, I think, with the riddle of his existence. At such times it had been Wendy's custom to take him out of bed and sit with him on her lap, soothing him in dear ways of her own invention, and when he grew calmer to put him back to bed before he quite woke up, so that he should not know of the indignity to which she had subjected him.

This relationship works best when the woman is the Crab, the man the Scorpion. Yet, since these lovers are influenced by the 5-9 vibrational Sun Sign Pattern, the sex of the lovers won't seriously impair their chances for harmony. Her ruling planet, Pluto, is stronger, and more intense, than his ruler, the Moon—but then, his Cardinal Sign essence is more powerful in an inter-reactive way than her Fixed Sign essence. Cardinal means to *lead* —Fixed means to *not* follow—which will be one of the more basic problems between these otherwise nicely tuned-in people. Read the last two sentences over several times, and you'll know how the aforementioned problem works out in the final analysis. It takes meditation.

They will share the qualities of gentleness, loyalty, intensity of emotion, and great imagination. Together, they can create all manner of marvelous things—a powerful love, a star-blessed child or children, or a great career. *Create* is the key word. Cancer and Scorpio, when they combine their auras, can become an awesome regenerative force. Sarah and Abraham were surely Cancer-Scorpio mates, never mind which was the Cancerian, which the Scorpion. For Sarah conceived a child, fathered by Abraham, created from the depths of their mutually intense desire, long after they were past what those who follow the illusionary chronological calendar would call the "childbearing age" for her and the "virile age" for him. To prove how illusionary such matters are, each was (literally) several hundred years "old" when their child was born—that alone being a miracle to those who are today brainwashed or soul-washed by the "normal life span" deceptions of insurance companies and the like.

"Is anything impossible unto the Lord?" Abraham was asked. No. Nor is anything impossible unto the *children* of the Lord—(or of our co-Creators)—we who were made in Their image.

Along with Capricorn and Taurus, Cancer and Scorpio share the tendency to longevity. In reality, all Sun Signs have the potential of a life span in the same flesh body of five hundred to a thousand years or so, sans the aging process, but these particular Sun Signs lead the way to enlightenment. Capricorns demonstrate the reversal of age, by appearing younger, as they grow Earth-Time "older"—Taurus shows us how being calm and patient adds less wear and tear to the body, the Bulls retaining their splendid strength long after most others have given up—Cancer exhibits the necessary tenacity—and Scorpio knows, on a still subconscious level (soon to be conscious) the alchemy secrets of cell regeneration which make longevity possible. Naturally, if everyone—or *when* everyone—learns the secret of Abraham and Sarah, such a miracle would appear to create a population problem, in consideration of those new souls being born, simultaneously, as babes. There is a solution to this apparent mathematical problem, but it's too complex to be explored in this book, therefore, it must be delayed until a forthcoming one, in which we will attempt to deal with all these matters in more depth.

Since the Crab and the girl Scorpion have a better chance than most of remaining on the planet for a considerable number of Earth years, it's a lucky thing they're more compatible and harmonious than many other couples. They will surely never bore one another for the first few centuries.

Along with the vices and virtues they share, there are a few traits they *don't* share, and these will be, from time to time, troublemakers. He does not possess her Pluto-propelled intensity of emotion, her near-compulsion to strike back when angered, and this can become a dangerous problem to their happiness, if too many stings from the Scorpion's tail cause the male Crab to permanently retreat into his shell of hardness. Another difference between them, scattered among the smooth similarities of character, which could rock the relationship, will be her inability to comprehend his undue caution, his occasional timidity—and his reluctance to allow fate to guide his destiny. It's difficult for the Scorpio woman to understand his Lunar lack of courage when a challenge demanding direct confrontation occurs— from outsiders, as well as in their personal association. She'll have to remember that all Crabs take a step or two sideways or backward before lunging ahead, giving them time to carefully consider all possibilities, which is why he's a more clever strategist in both material and emotional matters than she may realize. Despite her outward femininity and reserve, this girl fears nothing in Heaven or in Hell (or on Earth) herself—unless her Sun was severely afflicted by malefic planets at birth—therefore, his hesitations will both puzzle and trouble her. Likewise, her willingness to plunge into churning emotional waters and unknown situations which could be dangerous will frighten and trouble *him*.

Much of the time, their conflicts will be quickly dissolved by a wave of his Looney Bird humor. There's nothing as startling—and as refreshing— as the Cancer man's sudden switch into laughter, following one of his dismal, cautious, cranky, and crabby moods. She needs his laughter, for Scorpio is too often deeply engrossed with the mysteries of life to laugh casually. Humor heals. It's a bridge which spans any kind of misunderstanding. The agonizing conflict between blacks and whites in America only began to truly dissolve when comedians of both races had the courage to make fun of prejudice before mixed audiences, whose reactions were at first uncertainty—then finally intense relief, allowing both races comprehension of—and compassion for—one another.

But humor has two sides. The swiftest way to destroy an enemy is not through verbal abuse or bitterness, but through subtle ridicule. The Crab must take care not to overdo his sense of the divine comedy of life to the point of teasing her and making her feel ridiculous. Her sense of self-importance and basically serious nature cause her to be reluctant to laugh at jokes aimed toward herself. She can be offended by excessive teasing or an ill-timed joke. And you know what offended Scorps do—get even. When this woman is really angry (which won't be often, with the emotional control she has developed at great cost over the years) her Cancerian mate will be fortunate to have his crab shell to hide under until the storm blows over, or until the volcano stops spouting lava, whichever image fits the scene.

His own temper isn't anything to scoff or sneeze at either. When his tender, sensitive feelings are hurt, he can pout, snap, or crackle with crankiness for days, weeks, or months—in extreme cases, for years. Not even the powerful force of her ruling Pluto can blast the Crab out of his protective shell when he wants to remain there, nursing his emotional cuts and bruises.

All right, here it comes. I've been waiting to bring up the subject slowly and carefully. Even though theirs is the usually harmonious 5-9 compatibility pattern, there is one HUGE boulder looming between them which must be either gently sailed around—or dynamited at the beginning. A word with seven letters. Interesting. Seven is the number of Neptune, and Neptune rules, among other more positive things, deception. But I'm getting carried away into metaphysical nuances (perhaps not without pertinence). The word is "secrets." Both he and she take perverse joy in keeping secrets—and neither of them can *stand* having a secret kept from them. Do you see the picture? Think about it. Obviously, something or someone has to give—more than an inch. Maybe several yards. Make that miles, depending on their Moon Signs.

True, they'll share more of their secrets with one another than with those outside their personal periphery, nevertheless, there will be times when the Crab will sit on a secret she's burning to burrow out of him; other times when his woman holds back some mystery he's fairly quivering to learn. A Cancerian literally cannot sleep if he believes someone, especially his mate, is keeping a secret from him, however minor it may be— and frankly, however much it may be none of his business. A Scorpio woman is consumed with curiosity under the same circumstances. The difference is that he'll reveal his anxiety by chewing his nails, frowning, or snapping. She'll hide her desire to know behind the cool poise and surface nonchalance that cover her inner turmoil, and will worm it out of him more often than he'll worm mysteries out of her—because she knows how to employ the subtle, sneaky interrogation technique until the secret has popped out unintentionally from her victim. (Victim is the only word.) This will frustrate the Crab, who prides himself on his cleverness in keeping things under his hat, even if he doesn't wear one.

What is my advice, as an astrologer? I'm sorry to say I have none. I could tell these two to level with each other as much as possible, but they won't. So, they'll just have to fight—then go to bed and make up.

I didn't mean that to be facetious, for sexually, this man and woman are blessed with the grace to achieve a beautiful physical fulfillment together. Their auras are color-coded: harmonious, the auric light surrounding them during their mating nearly always shaded in the rainbow hues of love—unless some Sun-Moon static in their charts causes a few muddy tones. Children conceived through 5-9 Sun Sign vibrations, when the Sun-Moon exchange is also favorable, are aptly called "love children." Although this can occur between couples of all Sun Signs, it occurs more often with the 5-9 vibrations. When a man and woman blend sexually, an auric light is sent forth which attracts souls in the astral, seeking a channel for birth. The auric light of love attracts the more gentle, evolved souls into its magnetic stream, whereas mating performed in lust alone attracts the lower evolved or still not yet sensitive souls into a birth channel. Since both kinds of souls must enter the birth wheel of Karma for gradual and eventually certain enlightenment, each at its own chosen speed, even a lust mating has its purpose in the Universal Plan—though a constant attempt to add the tenderness of real love to lust is eternally an obligation to such couples.

The Crab and the Scorpion usually have no need to be reminded of such cosmic responsibilities. Their basic harmony nearly always creates a sexual chemistry which is both aware and inspirational. Cancer and Scorpio instinctively blend the mental and emotional with the physical, which is the secret key to an ecstasy never experienced by those who separate sexual desire from the other parts of their natures, seeking only the sensual. The added dimensions of affection and mental affinity brought to sex by Cancer and Scorpio result in a kind of lovemaking realized by a relatively small percentage of man-woman matings in any particular incarnation. This explains the powerful initial attraction between two lovers of this 5-9 Sun Sign Pattern; their lingering pain when separated . . . . their abundant opportunities for "trying again" after a quarrel.

The Scorpio woman takes her commitment to love very seriously, with an almost religious fervor. But should she find she is not loved in return, she will eventually follow her heart elsewhere, without regret. Let that be a warning to the man who treasures her. The Cancer man is moody, often fussy and exacting. He requires his frequent unconscious and conscious nightmares to be tenderly soothed away in order to be his gentle, funny self. Otherwise, he'll grow crankier and more reclusive, until the soft side of his nature, and his beautiful, romantic imagination disappear entirely, and he crawls away dejectedly—sideways, of course, as is the wont of the Crab—back home to mother, who always understands him. Whether she's still living, or has passed on, she's still the only woman who ever totally understood him. Just ask him sometime. He'll tell you all about her. If he's one of those very unfortunate Crabs who was adopted, or whose mother died when he was an infant, he will dream of her, and sense that she *would* have understood him. The maternal yearning is powerful in Cancer.

Cancerian dreams, like Scorpion perceptions, are very vulnerable, and need gentle protection from harsh reality. These two should cherish one another, true love being as rare as it is these days . . . . . . for no one else will treat the girl Eagle with quite so much reverence as her Cancerian man, and no one else will treat his dreams quite as tenderly as his Scorpio lady—except for his mother. She approves of their union. Believe me, she does . . . . . from wherever she may be on Earth—across the continent, or across the street—or from Heaven—she sends her son's Scorpio mate her secret sympathy.

More than any other man, the gentle Crab will forgive the deceptively quiet Scorpio woman her occasional stormy rages and hurtful words or acts of revenge, because he learned a lesson as a child he's never forgotten. He knows that *the opposite of love is not hate—the opposite of love is indifference.* Whatever he receives from his Pluto-ruled woman, it will never be this. True, she's capable of totally ignoring those for whom she feels contempt, as though they didn't exist—and for her, they don't. Yet, when it comes to the man to whom she's once given herself, once loved, however long ago it may have been—years, or yesterday—her Pluto power deserts her. And this is her well-guarded secret.

Never mind the icy mask she wears to disguise her pain or torment of decision. Her passions may leap from love to hate, and back again—but *indifference* toward the man who has totally possessed her is one emotion this lady will never master. And so, the Lunar man can take it from there.

☆ ☆ ☆ ☆ ☆ ☆

CANCER

Water — Cardinal — Negative
Ruled by the Moon
Symbol: The Crab
Night Forces — Feminine

SAGITTARIUS

Fire — Mutable — Positive
Ruled by Jupiter
Symbols: Archer & Centaur
Day Forces — Masculine

The **CANCER-SAGITTARIUS** *Relationship*

◆━◆◆◆━◆

"Ah, me" one voice said, and another
said, "Oh, mournful day."

So here we have the Crab, hard as rock without, soft as butter within. Extremely sensitive. Oh! very, very sensitive. Acutely aware of the slightest shade of meaning, every nuance of every comment, and extremely vulnerable to hurt.

And here we have the Archer, merry and warm-hearted, essentially kind, but sometimes brutally frank, and possessing only a thimbleful of tact. Make that *half* a thimbleful.

What happens when an ultra sensitive, cautious Cancerian bumpety-bumps around with a carefree, casual Sagittarian, whose specialty is blurting out arrows of truth that sting, however unintentionally? It depends on the phase of the Moon, actually. Since Cancer is ruled by the changeable Lunar vibrations, the Crab could react to the "slings and arrows of outrageous fortune" (and outrageous remarks of Sag) in several ways. By snapping back crabbily or pinching sharply (Crabs do have sharp pinchers). Perhaps by crawling inside the tough crab shell to hide and pout, quivering like a bowl of jelly over the indignity of it all. Or by just sitting there, deeply wounded, shedding trembling tears.

A brokenhearted Crab, with sagging spirits, immersed in murky melancholy from the callous treatment of his (or her) feelings by a thoughtless person, is one of the saddest sights on land or sea. It truly tugs on the soul to see one of these funny, moody creatures reduced to sobs. Even when they bravely try to hide their hurt, their chins quiver pathetically; their soft eyes gaze at you with such reproach you feel like weeping yourself.

That's often the reaction of an Archer who has just realized that he (or she) has inadvertently said or done something to cause a Cancerian friend, business associate, relative, lover or mate to feel the awful Lunar anguish of rejection. Instantly contrite for inflicting such damage through careless speech, the Archer will try to bandage the wound he (or she) caused with "soothing" words. Something like, "Gee, I'm sorry I hurt your feelings by saying you're dumb. Don't cry. So you're not a mental giant. There are lots of things more important than being intelligent. Doesn't that make you feel better?"

Odd as it may seem, frequently the perceptive Crabs will finally see the futility of trying to make the Archers aware of their tactlessness, the whole thing will strike them as humorous, and they'll burst out in hysterical laughter. Actually, a close association with an Archer is often, in the long run, beneficial to Cancer. It may be painful for a while, but eventually, the Crabs will learn the valuable lesson of not being quite so sensitive. Since everything is relative, another bonus is that, after knocking around with Sag, the occasional thoughtless remarks of everyone else the Crab knows will seem like fragrant roses of compliments by comparison, and it all evens out by making life in general smoother for Cancer.

It's sort of like when you've been crying over a toothache, and suddenly you break your leg. You forget all about the throbbing tooth. Or when you've been fussing and complaining about a small bee sting on the end of your nose, and along comes Sag to crack you over the bean with a verbal baseball bat. The only courteous thing to do is to thank Sag for curing you forever of sniffling over bee stings, right? Right. A few stitches, and your head (or self-confidence) will be like new again. Now the Archers will be nodding, thinking these observations are all quite logical and philosophical. Some of them may even be saying, "That's true! Every cloud has a silver lining." (Sagittarians are equally as fond of that Pollyanna truism as Librans.) Admittedly, it's not always easy to view a Sag as any sort of silver lining when he (or she) is aiming the Jupiter bow straight toward your Achilles' heel, but the truth is that the Archers *are* optimistic. Nearly as much so as Libra, but with a touch more skepticism.

There are times when the sensitivity and sympathy of Cancer combined with the direct candor of Sagittarius can be a favorable blend of qualities, resulting in some very clear thinking, whether they're blended through an association between an individual Crab and Archer—or combined within one person, such as a friend of mine, who's a Sun Sign Cancerian, with the Moon and Ascendent in Sag. One day when she dropped by to visit me in my home, she was looking through a current, popular weekly magazine, trying to locate a certain advertisement she wanted to show me. After a moment or so, she found it. "Just look at that," she commanded, her eyes full of Lunar tears, but her voice full of Jupiter anger.

It was a double-page public relations promo for the Martin Marietta Company, the people who make some nice and necessary things, like cement and aluminum, but who are also among the industries we can thank for many of the chemicals that threaten our health and safety, possibly our survival. The ad was plugging a 4-H livestock competition fair in west central Illinois, because the Martin Marietta Company believes that "traditions like this are a basic, enduring strength to our country, for the good of us all, well worth preserving. . . . . to make America better for everyone."

Taking up most of the space in the double-page ad was a color photograph of a small boy named Troy, age eight—posing with bright eyes and a happy smile beside his Hampshire gilt, a blue-ribbon-winning, 236-pound market hog that Troy calls Betsy. The prize hog was velvety soft and plump, a beautiful midnight blue color, with a curly tail, trusting eyes and appealing, floppy ears. In the picture, the little boy was lovingly stroking his gentle friend, Betsy, with so much pure, childlike love and affection in his expression.

"I wonder," said my Cancer-Sag friend, "if they would dare to publish a photograph of little Troy watching his dear friend he'd grown to love as a pet, being slaughtered (which, of course is Betsy's inevitable destiny) so folks can have their morning bacon. Would they dare to publish the terror and shock and agony in the eyes of an innocent child as he watched the Betsy he loved so much being brutally butchered? I suppose children like Troy are just told, after they spend months grooming and learning to love a 'market animal' that 'Betsy' or whoever, has just gone away on a pleasant visit somewhere, and probably won't return—to explain the disappearance of a beloved pet who's been carted off to the slaughterhouse to be murdered when the child isn't looking. They're such sick, misguided hypocrites. If they think slaughtering our animal brothers and sisters is such a beautiful, traditional thing, why don't they have the courage to publish the *end* of the story—show us the expression on a little boy's face when he learns the cruel truth about what adults really plan to do with the animal he adores, his reaction to all the gushing blood and the pathetic squealing and screaming in fear and agony that deafens the ears in a slaughterhouse, not to mention the stench of death that hangs over places stocked with butchered flesh."

After her words had poured out, she was trembling, with a mixture of compassion and fury. Her maternal Cancer Sun Sign was causing her heart to break over the face of the child, while her Sagittarian Moon and Ascendent (Sag is an animal lover) caused her remarks to be blunt and honest, plain-spoken and to the point.

"I know," I tried to comfort her, "and I share your feelings. You're right. Nevertheless, spiritual awareness *is* gradually beginning to grow, as people feel the vibrations of the Aquarian Age. One of the proofs it's growing is that the owners of slaughterhouses have nervously sensed the change, and no longer allow the public to enter and see what goes on inside. The people who work there suffer too, in a different, but maybe equally as terrible a way as the animals, because a recent survey of all occupations by insurance companies revealed that butchers and employees of slaughterhouses are among the groups with the highest rate of suicide—and while that's a sad statistic of subconscious guilt, it's an indication that Earthlings are slowly but surely coming closer to enlightenment."

After a while, my friend stopped crying—about the same time I did myself. I mention this true incident to illustrate the combined essence of Cancer and Sagittarius, but also for another reason, best summed up by borrowing the final words from the Martin Marietta Company advertisement (although my meaning is far different from theirs). The ad ended with the comment: *"This is for Troy, and for the future."*

At various times during this 6-8 Sun Sign Pattern association, the Crab and the Archer will clash over the subject of money, which is always burning a hole in Sagittarian pockets. It seldom burns a hole in Cancer's pockets. It's more likely to tear loose the seams with sheer weight, because the Crabs do enjoy accumulating large amounts of cash, and they prefer it be as near their person as possible at all times. Their fights will be frequent in the area of finances, but they can probably come to some sort of compromise, through friendly mutual agreement. The one astrology would suggest as being the most helpful is for Cancer to maternally (or paternally) keep patching and sewing up the holes that money burns in Sag pockets (training the Archer to be a bit more conservative, in a gentle way) and for Sagittarius to keep Cancer's pockets from bursting at the seams by kindly offering to take some of the Crab's excess cash off his (or her) hands to invest. Archers are startlingly lucky regarding matters like gambling, such as the stock market (the biggest gamble of them all). This will have a dual benefit. It will train Cancer to be more generous and giving, and it will also tickle the Crabs when they gradually learn that Sag has an unexpected way of quickly doubling their money for them— some of the time, that is. Everyone can experience a losing streak, and on such rare occasions (since the typical Sag is too blessed by Jupiter luck to suffer major losses consistently) the Crab must refrain from snapping, pouting and scolding. Otherwise, the Archer will leave in a huff, after causing Cancer to weep by zinging a few pertinent parting remarks about stinginess, and refuse to do any more favors if they're not appreciated.

The Cancerian man or woman will inevitably (even though in the background) be the subtle leader of this 6-8 association between two people who are so very different from each other. Because the Crab is Cardinal and Sag is Mutable. Being Cardinal causes a person to secretly be determined to be in command, and openly resent taking orders from others. There could be some difficulty here, because, although Mutable Sag is not particularly interested in being a leader (Archers would rather gallop around, hither and yon, communicating ideas) Sagittarius nonetheless actively (and outspokenly) dislikes taking orders himself—or herself. The Human end of the dualistic Sagittarian Centaur may be able to accept it cheerfully and philosophically—but the Horse end will kick considerably, and rear the equestrian legs in the air now and then. Sag is half Horse, half Human, you know, both symbolically and literally. One of those double Sun Signs of duality. Although the Human end is quite bright, often highly studious and intellectual, and optimistically philosophical—the Horse end (which is the rear end of Sag) is equally stubborn, contrary, unpredictable . . . and amazingly swift at racing away from problems. Also liable to kick dangerously when freedom is threatened.

Since the Crabs really can't help their inbred trait of possessiveness (which, used in a positive way, can be a warm and cozy virtue of solicitous protectiveness) they'll have to be cautious that they don't unintentionally smother the freedom of the Archers, who need large gobs of it in order to be themselves. (Freedom, that is—not smothering.) Of course, Crabs are naturally cautious by instinct, so all they need do is apply some of their natural Sun Sign caution to being careful not to stifle the free expression and action of Sag. If Cancer can manage to do this—and if the Archers will occasionally at least count to ten or twenty before stuffing their feet in their mouths (hammering on the Crab's sensitive feelings with blunt observations) these two can have a rather jolly time of it together.

In some way, Sagittarius will end up by serving the Cancerian, by being helpful—because the Archers sense some mystery within the Moon-ruled Crabs they're anxious to solve. Sagittarian curiosity being the burning thing it is, there will always be something to keep Sag fascinated, and interested in hanging around Cancer's seashore, beneath the Full Moon, watching the tides flow in and out . . . in-between a few laps around the track when the Centaurs become restless and need some time alone to race against the wind, nearly always winning by a nose. And *this* fascinates the Crabs.

With Jupiter's benign and benevolent good humor, Sag adores playing practical jokes on people, but Cancer might sometimes miss the point. Then the Archer will give the Crab a gentle nudge . . . and finally the Lunar one will laugh, until he (or she) cries. Not over the joke alone. But because Cancer is deeply moved by the naivete and idealism of the brave and optimistic Sagittarian, who keeps clumsily falling, then picking himself up with a bright smile . . . to try once more to reach the winner's circle. Those times when Jupiter allows the Centaur to be victorious, the happy, generous Archer will probably trot right back to the seaside, and offer to share half the good fortune with the Cancerian friend or relative, stuffing the Crab's pockets again with childlike glee. Jupiter rules the huge, the expansive, and sometimes only a Crab really knows how large a Jupiter heart can be. Someday, somehow, Sagittarius will teach Cancer the beautiful rewards of giving, cheerfully guiding the inwardly timid, fearful Crabs toward the Sagittarian religion of *truth*. Then there shall be no more sadness and sighing . . "for God shall wipe away all tears from their eyes." How can you cry when you're laughing at the courageous Archer's latest endearing clumsiness?

CANCER *Woman* SAGITTARIUS *Man*

———◆◇◆———

"Don't have a mother," he said. Not only had he no mother, but he had not the slightest desire to have one. He thought them very over-rated persons.

"Oh, Peter, no wonder you were crying," she said, and got out of bed and ran to him.

"I wasn't crying about mothers," he said rather indignantly. "I was crying because I can't get my shadow to stick on. Besides, I wasn't crying."

The most essential, the most deeply rooted difference between the Moon Maiden and the Archer (other than their conflicting views about money and material security) is often their totally divergent ideas and attitudes toward "family". She leans very much toward devotion and near-worship of family life—usually with more stress on the maternal and paternal than on siblings and other relatives, but nevertheless, this lady burns incense at the family altar with equally as much devout fervor as her Capricorn sisters religiously light *their* family circle beeswax candles (and often, with less resentment than Cappies sometimes feel).

Contradictorily, the Sagittarius man, while he may hold within his large Jupiter heart much genuine affection for his family, dropping by to say a cheerful "hello" every few years or so, probably bringing along an armload of gifts (for the Archer is wonderfully generous) doesn't feel the intense tug of dutiful devotion toward his relatives the Cancerian girl feels toward hers. He may be the very first to help his parents, siblings and other blood ties when they need a friendly boost of the spirits—or a loan of whatever money he may have—but he doesn't believe that a tie of blood should imprison his freedom to roam and search around the world for truth and excitement, perusing his multiple interests and pursuing his idealistic (often gigantic) goals and ambitions. Ties are restrictive. Ties are binding. Blood ties or any other kind of ties. They resemble, to Sag, clanking chains—a rope around his neck, threatening to strangle his individuality. The Sagittarian man can hardly wait to cut the Gordian knot with his family, and be off to the races on his own, obeying the call of Jupiter to dash onward and upward to some great, nameless accomplishment or achievement. The Archer is also quite adept at untying the Gordian knots of problems swiftly and intelligently, and though he sometimes makes mistakes, he's usually shrewd enough not to make the same one twice.

A Moon Maid views "the ties that bind" with respect, if not with downright affection. Ties are cozy. Ties are familiar and comforting. They resemble, to her, softly woven strands of protection and safety. The known, the secure and the comfortable. To cut a tie with friends or relatives, a lover or husband—or with her parents—is something she dreads, therefore postpones as long as possible. This is often the reason Cancerian females are thought of as possessive. It's really not so much possessiveness as the being unwilling to cut a tie, then forced to float around without an anchor. To float without an anchor is as frightening an image to the girl Crab as the image of floating out in the middle of the ocean would be to the Nature crab, who feels much safer in remaining a healthy distance away from deep water.

Astrology can't solve that problem for them. The Moon Maiden and her Centaur will just have to fight it out, hopefully moving closer toward compromise as the years pass, but in the meanwhile fussing and quarreling—arguing (him) and pouting (her) back and forth between them over neglecting Mama and Papa (his fault) or weakening their own relationship by spending too much time with the family (her fault). As time goes by, they'll reach some sort of mutual agreement regarding this difference between them—or one of them will leave the other. But it might not be a permanent separation. For several reasons.

To begin with, it's more likely to be the Archer who angrily leaves the girl Crab (however regretfully) than the other way around. Not always, of course, but usually. It's easier, remember, for him to cut a tie than it is for her, although the knot of love is more difficult for a Sagittarian man to untie than the bond with his own family, for love can make even the normally carefree and nonchalant Centaur reluctant to break away—and once he's left, he may not stay long. Her Lunar madness is hypnotic, and will haunt his dreams at night while they're apart. Because this is the 6-8 Sun Sign Pattern, the Moon Maiden represents to him the 8th astrological "house" of mystery (sexual and otherwise) . . . the unknown. No one is more curious than Sag (unless it's Gemini) and he'll discover his mind is spinning in circles after a while, wondering what she's doing without him. Besides, he's frustrated by the realization that he lost his fiery temper, and left before he had a chance to completely solve her mystery . . . her changing moods, her inexplicable hold over his emotions. There are still a thousand urgent questions she hasn't answered. And so, the Archer who so swiftly and impulsively cut the Gordian knot with his Cancerian lady frequently later returns to tie it up again. Because he finds he misses her more than he guessed he would . . . and because there are all those puzzling questions . . .

Although the Moon Maid will be strangely comforted and flattered that the Sagittarian man she loves regards her as mysterious and magnetic, she rather perversely resents his prying. (She can't have it both ways, but she'd like to, concerning nearly everything.) This woman always has and always will contain within her many secrets, some of which she's not even aware of herself . . . others she is. There's something in the Lunar essence that makes her clam up when she feels someone is trying to probe too deeply into her secret self, even when the "someone" is the man she adores. The girl Crab crawls into a shell of silence automatically, instinctively, the moment he begins one of his questioning routines—even if all he's asking is something as innocent and ordinary as what she thinks about the new neighbors, or what her first boyfriend was like. (Admittedly, that last question might not be too innocent. The Sagittarian male has a temper, and although he's not the possessive type, he is assuredly the jealous type. As I keep reminding you, there is a distinct difference between possessiveness and jealousy.)

As reticent as this lady may be to reveal her own secrets quickly (unless they're drawn out slowly and gently, when she's in the mood to talk about them, not through rude questioning or abrupt and idle curiosity) she's an expert at uncovering her Centaur's secrets—and everyone else's. Somehow, people are unconsciously compelled to pour out things to the Moon Maiden they normally wouldn't confess to others. It's not the same as the confiding everyone does in the sympathetic Pisces listening ear. People confess to Pisces because they want to, without much urging, if any, from the Fish, who simply projects a willingness to listen if you feel like talking about it—and the talker senses the Piscean response will be compassion, which it always is. With the girl Crab, it's different. She's not apathetic or neutral about hearing your secrets. She enjoys learning things about others, and usually employs a conscious strategy to learn them, fully aware that she's digging to see what she can discover. Thanks to her Lunar magnetism (the same kind of invisible force not even the ocean's tides themselves can resist) the other person finds himself or herself pouring out all manner of private confidences, without having initially intended to do so.

The Lunar strategy of the Cancerian woman is even more successful with the Archer. Sag does love to talk, especially about himself, his dreams and his innermost feelings, along with his views and opinions of every subject under the Sun. Carried away by the enthusiasm of his verbal free thought association, he may wander a bit too far conversationally with the girl Crab before he realizes he's caught in an emotional wave that could drown him, by having said more than he intended. That's an astrological warning the Archer will find very valuable, if he heeds it, because there's always the possibility he'll say something that this extremely sensitive, imaginative lady could exaggerate or misinterpret, bringing on the Cancerian suspicion and trembling vulnerability to hurt. It pays the Sagittarian man to count to ten before he speaks at *all* times, but with his lovely girl Crab, he'd be well advised to count to maybe a thousand. It won't be easy for him to refrain from speaking his mind freely, sometimes in an unnecessarily frank way, not just because this is his natural tendency, but also because a Lunar Lady can be mighty tenacious, once she gets the notion into her rather hard head there's something he's thinking he hasn't told her, and she won't give up trying to find out. Not that there's anything he should feel guilty about, it's just that there are things she can take the wrong way and imaginatively dress up, clothing things said guilelessly with her personal fears and apprehensions, until they become threatening to her peace of mind, no longer even resembling their original intent or true meaning.

The time when the Archer should especially allow his actions to speak louder than his words is during their sexual intimacy. The Cancerian woman's way of expressing her many-layered love for him in a physical sense, is sensual and silent. To her, *feelings* are important, not words. She wants their lovemaking to be an escape into an ocean of passion, drenched in fragile moonlight sentiment, its depth a direct result of its delicacy and quiet communion of spirit. She withdraws sexually from demanding desire, able to surrender herself completely only when their mutual need is demonstrated tenderly, gently, even poetically, not fiercely. And if she's been made to feel rejected in some way throughout the day (she literally wilts beneath disapproval, spoken or unspoken) she'll be unable to respond at night in his arms, even though she only imagined the earlier slight to her sensitivity. Making love to a girl Crab is an eternal guessing game—and more successful when her lover or husband consults an almanac before approaching her, for this woman's every emotion is not just symbolically, but seriously and actually—ruled by the Moon's Lunar phases. This part of her sexual nature may at times annoy the Archer as much as it intrigues him, because, being a Fire Sign, his own desire is more impulsive, his need more intense. Finesse in lovemaking is something he has to consciously practice to acquire, especially when he's in love with a Moon Maiden, born into the Water Element.

Strangely, this is a woman who sometimes communicates her wish for Oneness by a misty light in her eyes—like the silvery, promising shimmer of the New Moon's ancient secret. When he sees moonlight in her eyes, he knows it's time to be very still and quiet . . . hold her close until she feels securely protected . . . then gently float beside her out into the mysterious sea that sings remembered songs to her at midnight. He may never solve her feminine mystery, but it will always beckon him to try.

Let's leave them alone now, shall we? If the Looney Bird Moon Maid won't tell her secrets to the man she loves, she certainly doesn't want *us* around when her eyes become misty! Before we go, we'll remind her that, while her Lunar tears fall like raindrops at the slightest hint of a cloud in the sky, his Jupiter tears are hidden and held back . . yet no less profuse than her own. Like a small boy, whistling in the dark, he's too brave to admit he ever cries. But for all his surface nonchalance—he does.

☆ ☆ ☆ ☆ ☆ ☆

CANCER *Man* SAGITTARIUS *Woman*

They talked of Cinderella, and Tootles was confident that his mother must have been very like her.

. . . . Tinker Bell shouted, "Silly ass!" and darted into hiding.

Even though Sagittarius astrologically rules religion (along with Pisces and Scorpio, because religion contains many levels of awareness, not just one)—and even though every Sag, at some time in Life, is deeply concerned about the pros and cons of religious beliefs—the girl Archer may forget, when she's in love with a boy Crab, the most important spiritual advice of all, which is *"count your blessings."*

Quite probably, before she met him, her Jupiter faith and idealism was shattered by the kind of men who treated love casually—and treated *her* carelessly, maybe even cruelly. Except perhaps for the very special boy with the tender eyes, who loaned her his pencils and fought the bullies who teased her at recess in the 6th grade, certainly none of the males she's impulsively loved came anywhere near living up to her private image of a Prince or a Knight who would treat her gently as his "lady fair," awaken her soul with the kiss in his glance that promised to adore her forever and three days . . . sweep her off to his enchanted castle, then sit with her beside the lake, feeding the swans, making her laugh . . . and making her know she was his alone, that his love was loyal and true, faithful and everlasting. She'd just about given up on that particular dream, and was about to settle for either remaining a bachelor girl—or finding a wealthy Arab, who might fall a little short of her image, but who would whisk her away on his private jet to the land of gushing oil wells, in his turban and long nightgown, to feed the camels at sunset. Forget Camelot. Who needs it? Then there was this crazy miracle.

Bouncing along one day, she bumped straight into the surprised heart of a Crab, out strolling the byways and taking his morning constitutional. He was wearing no helmet, no armour, nor was he perched proudly astride a white horse. Neither was he adorned in a turban, and as for a long white nightgown, being a conservative Cancerian, he wouldn't dream of appearing in public clothed in such an unseemly, attention-getting manner. He owned not a single swan, and could introduce her to no camels. But he did sometimes sit by the lake in the park at twilight, he told her, and feed the pigeons popcorn. As for the private jet, after she knew him better, she realized that he definitely had the potential to own a whole fleet of them someday, the way he hung on to his money. I mean, after all, cash *has* to accumulate if you never spend a penny of it—ever. For anything. Except maybe an occasional glass of imported wine or champagne.

Never mind that he wasn't the living, breathing image of Camelot. There was a certain air about him. The kiss in his glance that promised forever was surely not missing. It caressed her, and made her knees feel funny every time he looked at her. And although he might be a trifle stingy with his pencils, not handing them out like potato chips, because after all, pencils do cost money, especially the kind with decent erasers—he still had the tender eyes of the special boy in the 6th grade, and he gave her the distinct feeling he'd protect her from bullies, in the schoolyard or anywhere else—that she was truly cherished as a woman, and that she'd be warmly secure with him forever and three days, because this man would surely keep her safe from all harm.

Well, you can't have it your way to match every nuance, eyelash and brush stroke of your dream image. Goodness knows he had more of those qualities she'd nearly lost hope of ever finding than any of the other gorillas, Casanovas and leering sophisticates who both bored her and let her down with a thump in the past. He might not be exactly Don Quixote, but he did contain his own kind of impossible dreams, behind his shy smile and quiet manner. And so she forgot all about caution, and fell in love with him, head over heels. That's the way Sag always falls in love, or for that matter, does anything. Head over heels. Being a Centaur, therefore half Horse and half Human, this girl stumbles a lot, and is a little clumsy, despite her normally graceful stride that reminds her admiring Crab of a thoroughbred race horse.

The first thing she learned after she shocked herself by loving him, was that she didn't make a mistake in forgetting all about caution when they met. Because this man possesses enough of the stuff to supply, not just her when she runs low on it, but the entire British Commonwealth. An endless source. She'd be happier, she discovers after a while, if he'd forget about some of his own caution—but not all of it. She kind of likes the way his caution keeps her steered in the right direction when she's sometimes tempted to be overly reckless (it's nice to be saved from yourself by someone who really cares about you) but a little of his caution goes a long way with the girl Archer. Too much of it can cause her to feel closed-in, smothered, therefore—restless. It's never a good idea to make the Horse end of a Centaur restless.

Because their relationship is guided and influenced by the 6-8 Sun Sign Pattern, the Cancerian man will hold an inexplicable fascination for this woman, hints of mystery and secrets—in addition to a magnetic sexual appeal. She is curious by nature, so the way he keeps her guessing about his feelings and changing moods is exciting rather than exasperating, as it might be to another female. Most of the time, she'll behave in an unaccustomed docile manner under the spell of the Lunar man. But once in a while, like the times he compares her to his mother (unfavorably) or scolds her for being extravagant, accuses her of talking too much, and never listening—she'll lose her temper. Since Jupiter has a way of expanding everything, the girl Archer does not have a small temper. It is sizable when fully aroused. Then she'll say something pointed and cutting (Sag is seldom or never at a loss for words) that will deeply wound the ultrasensitive feelings of this man. He'll snap back at her, crossly. She'll zing another arrow of tactless truth in answer to the challenge of his snapping, and he'll begin one of his lengthy pouting spells of silence, withdrawing into himself to a place where she can't follow—where even her words can't reach him.

This is when she should take a walk in the woods alone, all by herself (being close to Nature never fails to clear the cobwebs from a Sagittarian mind) and project her astral self back to the way things were before he came along to cozily protect her and make her laugh with his outrageous humor. There was such a vague and lonely longing within her then, that seemed to just melt away the first time he smiled at her with the soft, twinkling eyes of her 6th grade hero, stirring memories of a time when

Life was sweet and simple, and full of warm familiarity. He has his faults, yes. But he's sympathetic, sensitive and affectionate. He's funny and full of fascinating conversation more often than he's grouchy. He's certainly loyal and earnest. He'd never try to deliberately hurt her, or break a promise if he could possibly help it. And he's gradually become more generous, because he wants to please her. He didn't say a word last week when she bought a registered, purebred Old English Sheep Dog for nine hundred dollars, which meant he couldn't have the camera he'd been wanting for over a year. Best of all, he's not a hypocrite. He's sincere and genuine. She can't stand hypocritical people.

After she counts her blessings, she'll go back and tell him she's sorry she yelled at him, and was unkind. Then, if she offers to do something very sweetly solicitous for him, he'll peek out from behind his crab shell and trust her again with his nicest smile. Maybe some stuffed mushrooms, the way his mother fixed them, is that what might heal the hurt, so they can be close again?

No. He'd rather have her than the mushrooms. He has that Full Moon strangeness in his eyes again, because she's touched his heart with kindness. So they make up by making love. Their sexual chemistry is one of the blessings she forgot to count. Her desires are more fiery and passionate than his, but that only has the effect of stirring him with a challenge to teach her that he's Cardinal and she's Mutable. (Cardinal means to *lead*). Then too, there's that haunting mystery of his Water Element, drawing her into its depths, as she learns more about the stillness within the unexplored parts of herself through the slow, gentle way he approaches their mutual need. He leads her to a place where sensuality is a whispering, waiting promise, where trembling enchantment lingers much longer, for all its dreamlike quality, than a flaming rush of instant blending that quickly dies out, leaving no memory of its peace behind it. Fire stimulates and thrills with the hint of explosion. Water soothes and cools . . . remaining. The right amount of each makes sexual expression between Cancer and Sagittarius a strong and fulfilling experience.

But physical love is only one level of a human relationship, so the Crab and his girl Archer must learn to blend their Fire and Water Elements in other ways with the same kind of careful harmonizing. In time, he'll grow to intensely respect her courage—and, yes, even her frankness. Because she's honest. He can trust her to mean what she says, and to be what she is. In time, she'll be grateful for his cautious hand on hers, holding her back from all those deep holes she used to fall into when she wasn't looking. They'll learn to trust each other. And that's the one thing these two very different people had in common, long before they met. The search for someone you can trust to always love you just as you are. Nothing else is important.

CANCER

Water—Cardinal—Negative
Ruled by the Moon
Symbol: The Crab
Night Forces—Feminine

CAPRICORN

Earth—Cardinal—Negative
Ruled by Saturn
Symbol: The Goat
Night Forces—Feminine

The CANCER-CAPRICORN *Relationship*

◆━◆◆◆◆◆◆

*They were the most ordinary questions—"What was
the colour of Mother's eyes? Which was taller,
Father or Mother? . . . (A) Write an essay of not
less than 40 words on How I spent My Last Holidays,
or The Characters of Father and Mother compared . .
(1) Describe Mother's laugh; (2) Describe Father's
laugh; (3) Describe Mother's party dress . . . . . ."*

*By the way, the questions were all written in the
past tense.*

As with all 7-7 Sun Sign Pattern Earthlings, the Crab and the Goat
are 180 degrees apart on the karmic wheel of Life. In astrology—
for that matter, also in astronomy and math—180 degrees is half a
circle or an *opposition*. Now, in human contact, a Sun Sign opposition

need not be negative. It very often is, but it need not be. Will all Crabs and Goats please read that last sentence over several times?

An opposition indicates that two opposing forces are "at war." In this case, those forces are the Moon and Saturn, rulers of Cancer and Capricorn, respectively. It's hard to imagine anything farther apart than the Moon and Saturn. Among other things, the Moon (Cancer) represents dreams, change, movement or travel, memories, reflections, softness, and dependency. Among other things, Saturn (Capricorn) represents realities, stability, caution, waiting, determination, hardness, and self-sufficiency. Like all other blends of the 7-7 vibration, sooner or later (hopefully sooner) a choice must be made by Cancer and Capricorn as to which of these opposing forces, consisting of the Lunar and the Saturnine, will become the dominant force of their association—or the association itself will become a battlefield over which symbolic cannon balls are shot back and forth indefinitely.

And so, the Crab and the Goat must decide whether the Moon *or* Saturn is to rule their *relationship,* even though they may still choose to be *individually* ruled by the Moon and Saturn *both*—and equally.

I realize this all sounds terribly complicated. No one ever claimed a 7-7 vibration is easy to work out harmoniously. But my greatgrandma used to say that "nothing gained easily is really worthwhile." Will all Crabs and Goats please read *that* sentence over several times also?

There is a desirable side to any kind of opposition, which is that opposites do complement one another. Each has what the other yearns for—needs, wants, desires—and is therefore secretly anxious to acquire. Just form a mental image of that, if you will. Two people, each possessing what the other wants. If neither is selfish, if both are generous—if they give to one another and share equally—what could be happier? It's rather nice to be someone's "magic genie" and have that someone be your genie too, at the same time, supplying all your needs, while you supply his (or hers). It's the same with the polarities of anything on Earth. Take a thermometer. You have Hot, and you have Cold. When they meet in the middle, you have Warm—the temperature of eternal Spring. Lovely thought! And that's just what can happen when Winter (Saturn) and Midsummer (the Moon) meet each other halfway.

Yes, Cancer symbolizes Midsummer, just as Gemini symbolizes late Spring and early Summer, Leo symbolizes Summer in full bloom—and Virgo symbolizes Indian Summer. This seasonal Sun Sign conceptual is fully explained in "The Twelve Mysteries of Love" in the front section of this book. But it may be important to remind the Crab and Goat of it again here . . that Cappy means Winter and the Crab means Midsummer.

Despite the opposition of their Sun Signs and Lunar-Saturnine rulers, and in addition to the complementary nuances of opposites being a plus to their association—Cancer and Capricorn are alike in certain ways, as much alike in these ways as they are different in many others. Both the differences and the similarities are strikingly pronounced in this particular 7-7 vibration.

They were both born under the Negative-Feminine Night Forces, meaning that each has a soft inner core, and is rather good at hiding the softness—meaning, too, that the feelings and emotions of both run very deep. They are also both Cardinal, therefore both Cancer and Capricorn like to lead. The Goat prefers to lead unobtrusively; likewise, the Crab tends to lead in subtle ways, and so their mutually shared leadership motivation may be hidden when they first meet. It will not remain long hidden.

It's difficult for an association to contain two leaders of equal stature. Consequently, something will have to give a little. It will more likely be the Crab. For a while, however, it's an amusing scene for the astrologically alert to watch from a distance. Picture, if you can, two "leaders" each attempting—in great secrecy—to lead the other, without letting the other suspect that he or she is being led. Gradually, each of them becomes aware of the leadership motive of the other, never mind how cleverly hidden—and then the quiet, yet intense and determined battle for supremacy between them begins. Truly, it is as fascinating to observe as a movie—*more* fascinating than most films Hollywood has been making recently. (For meditation purposes, Gerald Ford is a Crab; Richard Nixon, a Goat.)

Throughout all these carefully mapped strategies, it would behoove the Crab to remember the Goat's sure-footed reputation—and it would behoove the Goat to remember that the Crab always takes a step or two sideways and backward before advancing straight ahead. It will be a thrilling battle of wills. There won't be as much fanfare as with the Fire and Air Element oppositions in the other 7-7 Sun Sign Patterns (Cancer is Water, Capricorn is Earth) but quiet and steady contests can contain more suspense.

Some of the traits of the Crab and the Goat are neither similar nor dissimilar, but simply supportive of each other. For example, Cancer likes comfort and security in great abundance. Capricorn is intensely ambitious, and since ambition has a way of being one of the quicker routes to all degrees of comfort and security, this is one thing which may hold these two together, as well as attract them initially.

They are both attached to yesterday, the Moon-ruled because of a liking for history in general, plus a sort of personal nostalgia—the Goat because of the lessons to be learned from experiences of the past and a touch of hero worship. (Actually, Cappy admires the achievers of past and present equally, but yesterday's heroes and heroines have more glamour.) They also share a strong attachment to the family hearth and relatives. Cancer leans toward sentiment for the maternal, Cappy leans toward sentiment for both the maternal and the paternal, the whole family tree—especially if a coat of arms hangs from one of the branches. Some Goats are decidedly snobbish about fame and prestige—the whole status trip. It's hard to detect behind the typical Capricorn's shy smile and gentle manners, but it's there.

It's not uncommon to find the combination of the Crab and the Goat involved in renovation of historical landmarks, laying cornerstones, heading a drive to establish a museum, writing history books, building business empires, collecting antiques, or actively engaged in local or national politics. This is a couple often found in bookstores (as the owners, of course) and especially in banks (on the board of directors). As individuals, the Crab may be drawn toward marine activities, near the water, while the Goat tends to climb the highest mountain of achievement in his or her vicinity. Capricorns abound in the jewelry business and junkyards. Goats, you see, have an odd way of finding something practical, something of value, in anything from diamonds to rusty parts of an old car. Strangely, they are also tuned in to art, one of the few aesthetic experiences which attracts them. But the typical Capricorn has no time for pop art like Andy Warhol's tomato cans and tubes of toothpaste. To a Capricorn, art should be solid and substantial. Michelangelo, Leonardo, Rembrandt—these are artists. Picasso and Dali are joking, aren't they? Art, like everything else in life, is a serious matter to the Saturn-ruled. Imaginative Cancerians, although differently motivated, also appreciate the beauty of fine paintings and works of art, including music, and so lots of the people you see strolling through metropolitan galleries and attending concerts will be Crabs and Goats.

If the Cancerian and the Capricorn are children, the same rules apply. They'll both excel in history class, and both Cappy and the young Crab will start early mowing lawns or delivering newspapers to earn money to stash away in their sock drawers.

Many Capricorns are by nature somewhat cold and suspicious, thanks to Saturn's stern influence, and sympathetic, sensitive Cancer can provide a healing balm of love and understanding for the Goat. Cancer's devotion to home and family will please Capricorn, who is equally loyal to family ties.

Unless one or both were born with the Moon or Ascendent in the Air or Fire Element, these two will never burn dollar bills for fun. Very few, if any, Cancerians and Capricorns are found resorting to public welfare or food stamps. Not only are they clever in financial matters, they also share a rather severe Puritan work ethic. They feel alike concerning the subject of money. Both enjoy stacking up lots and lots of it, and both prefer saving it to spending it. If any two people need to meditate on poet Kahlil Gibran's words on the subject of working for material gain, they are Cancer and Cappy. They would benefit immensely from an attempt to comprehend that man must *"work with love"* or it is better that he sits outside the gates of the temple and *"takes alms from those who do . . . . . . for bread baked without love is a bitter bread, that feeds but half man's hunger."*

At first glance, those words will startle both the Crab and the Goat. Work for love? People work for money, not love. If a person also happens to enjoy his or her work, so much the better, but the first consideration is the financial compensation, isn't it? No, it is not. To work with love is the *first* consideration, the cash return is *secondary*. And therein lies the problem. It isn't that the Moon-ruled and Saturn-ruled don't understand craftsmanship and laboring with the heart, as well as with the hands: It's a matter of *priorities*. And these two are charged with the duty to make a strong effort to change them.

One of the most delightful things about the pairing of these undeniably divergent creatures, the Crab and the Goat, is that the outwardly controlled and stern, but inwardly gentle and lonely, Capricorn can find an escape from his or her seriousness in the rich and refreshing humor of the Moon people. Cancerian laughter is contagious, irresistible. There's something about the Crab's sense of the ridiculous that brings a merry twinkle to the eye of the Goat. Cancer clowns—Cappy grins. And the steadfast Capricorn heart, so sadly locked much of the time by the disciplined emotions, begins to warm, then to beat a little faster.

Few people ever guess the true extent of the Goat's wistful longing to escape Saturn's invisible restrictions, for such longing is also—even especially—kept under strict control. The compassionate smile of a Moon Child, who so well understands what it means to be lonely, can be an open door to a new and brighter world for Capricorn.

As for the Cancerian (unless his or her Luminaries are in negative aspect) from the first moment the Crab feels that powerful magnetic tug from his (or her) opposed Suns—in the classroom or office, in the family circle, the circle of friendship, or within the eternal circle of love, the searching Moon Child will search for a safe home, protected by the tough billy goat.

☆ ☆ ☆ ☆ ☆ ☆

CANCER *Woman* CAPRICORN *Man*

------◄◄◆►►------

> *"Ah, old lady," Peter said aside to Wendy, warming*
> *himself by the fire and looking down at her as she*
> *sat turning a heel, "there is nothing more pleasant of*
> *an evening for you and me when the day's toil is over*
> *than to rest by the fire with the little ones near by."*
>
> *"It is sweet, Peter, isn't it?" Wendy said, frightfully*
> *gratified. "Peter, I think Curly has your nose."*
>
> *"Michael takes after you."*

When a Cancerian girl is attracted to a Capricorn man (or to any man), she has the three M's on her mind. Three dreams she has, as she tosses pennies into every available wishing well. Three goals in her hard little crab-shell head. These may vary in their order of importance with each girl Crab, but all Cancerian women will be consumed with one of the six variations of the three M's, which are as follows:

> *marriage—motherhood—money*
> *motherhood—money—marriage*
> *money—marriage—motherhood*
> *marriage—money—motherhood*
> *motherhood—marriage—money*
> *money—motherhood—marriage*

These, in their sextuplet priority variations, are the female Crab's goals.

Her *needs* are slightly different from her *goals*. Her needs are the three S's, and these do not vary in the order of their importance to the Moon Maiden. They're each of equal value to her peace of mind.

> *sympathy—serenity—security*

One of the most endearing things about a Moon Maiden is that, although she very much needs and seeks the three S's in every relationship, and although her goals are always the three M's, she is willing to give her man a soft cradle of emotional comfort in return. She can be the most sympathetic, affectionate, loyal, and protective of women. When she's on her best behavior, the female Crab is devoted—and better still, she's also both adaptable and patient, surely a fine companion for the Capricorn man. A Taurus woman is patient, but not very adaptable. A Gemini woman is adaptable, but not very patient. The Cancerian woman possesses both admirable traits. As for devotion, many women are devoted to the men they love, but none so devoted as this one. The Goat, loving the home fires as he does, will be especially happy about her own deep feelings about "family." Since Capricorn rules the Jewish people, and all Cancer women are "Jewish mothers" (whether they are mothers or not) you can see there are powerful magnetic forces pulling these two together from the start.

There's always something slightly helpless and appealing in the Cancerian female, and the Capricorn man senses it sooner than most. What this woman needs is a strong man to lean on, someone who can smooth away all her worries and calm all her fears—who provides her with a shoulder to cry on now and then. But she's not quite as helpless as she seems. Cancer, I keep telling you, is a Cardinal Sign of leadership. The Moon Maid would prefer to lead by guiding her man's destiny gently, unobtrusively, in the background . . . . . if she's in love. When she is not in love, a Cancer gal can be mighty ambitious in her career, and will do just about anything to get to the top of the heap.

Every Cancerian woman is secretly looking for a good provider, and this the Capricorn man certainly is. He is always ambitious (as much so as she is) and usually successful. In fact, he's often the epitome of everything she would like to be, but cannot—for she is too vulnerable. Conversely, she represents to the Goat all the Lunar qualities he privately would love to call his own, but cannot—for he is not vulnerable *enough*. Therefore, almost from the moment these two meet, there is an unmistakable appreciation of one another, which is one of the strongest foundations for love.

A Capricorn man can be both conservative and domineering to a high degree. The Cancer girl doesn't mind the first quality, since she's rather unduly conservative herself. As for being dominated, she won't stand for that in any association—except love. When this woman falls in love, she'll at first submit to the Goat's dominance out of a desire to keep peace, but gradually she's likely to forget she's playing a role, and slip into the submissive position for good—which is not really bad! Next to Pisces, no other woman so secretly enjoys being controlled and conquered by the male she adores. And if any man can be domineering, tender, and affectionate all at once, it's this one. So it all works out in a favorable manner for both of them, usually. Barring, that is, a more fiery or aggressive Moon Sign or Ascendent in the horoscope of the girl Crab.

It's a funny thing about Capricorn males. However far out they may swing in an attempt to avoid the granite discipline of Saturn over their natures, they'll swing right back again in important matters. In other words, whatever his temporary actions or behavior, a Goat is a Goat. Or—once a Cappy, always a Cappy. Like that. Normally, this man will strongly disapprove of the "open marriage" theory. He's conservative where marriage is concerned, however much he tries to be "with it" in his speech at times. He essentially believes a woman's place is in the home. Even should he permit his wife to work or to follow her own career, when the children appear, he'll frown on a woman who expects someone else to fill the maternal role while she pursues her own activities. If he's a typical Capricorn, he'll believe that a mother's place is with her children, at least while they're very young. He won't be happy about any frivolous or excessive spending of money either, whether it's his—hers—or theirs. Even if his Moon Maiden earns her own cash, he'll probably take it upon himself to caution and counsel her on the subject of extravagance.

Not that he'll have many opportunities to chide her about spending money. She's as careful with a dollar as he is (unless her Moon Sign or Ascendent is in Aries or Leo or Gemini, and then she'll have periodic, minor nervous breakdowns over guilt each time she's wasteful). With this girl, most of his financial lectures will be in the area of how much of their separate or combined income to save, and what would be the smartest investment for any surplus they accumulate. Being an Earth Sign, the chances are he'll believe that real estate property—or land—is the safest thing to own for future security. If she argues with him, he may quote Will Rogers on the subject of whether or not buying land is wise— "They're not making any more of it." That sort of earthy, practical statement wins arguments by closing a subject abruptly, and it's the sort of undebatable observation Cappies are very good at making when they're pressed for an answer.

He'll approve of her habit of saving things. Capricorn believes firmly that a practical purpose can be found for anything at all, and nothing should be discarded until every possible use has been squeezed from it. If she's a typical Cancerian, she'll go along with that philosophy enthusiastically. In fact, unless one of them has a "looser" planetary influence in the birth chart, they might even save old toothpaste tubes in case they ever have a son who grows up to be a basketball player in high school. (He can use them to practice hook shots in the wastebasket.) I (truthfully) know a Cancerian woman, with a Capricorn Moon Sign and Ascendent, who actually washes and rinses out those little plastic Baggies that come on a roll (to cover vegetables, etc.) and reuses them over and over—until they split. She has them hanging out to dry all over the kitchen. One roll of Baggies lasts her, roughly, a couple of years. (Being an Aries, I go through a roll every week or so.) Someone I know recently suggested that the reason Richard Nixon saved those damaging tapes relating to Watergate was because, as a Capricorn, he simply could not discard them, and kept hoping he could in some way make them useful, or serve some practical purpose. No one has been able to come up with a better answer, even Mr. Nixon himself. Only a knowledge of the Capricorn essence provides any semblance of sense to the mystery of "why didn't he burn those (expletive deleted) tapes?" The answer is simplicity itself (to Cappy). That would have been *wasteful*.

A Cancerian woman will adapt more easily than many another woman to the Capricorn man's introversion, his inclination to "take care of business" and do the sensible thing. But she will not adapt so well perhaps to his lack of excitement over change. Ruled by the inconstant Moon, she needs occasional change in her life, and intervals of travel. Convincing him that their life would be richer by not remaining in one place too long or holding the same ideas always, could be somewhat difficult. Because this man will never completely escape Saturn's restrictions over his inner nature, struggle as he may. Somewhere behind the façade of even an *apparently* extroverted Goat is serious old man Saturn. Always and inevitably. The shade of conservatism may be dyed a lighter pastel in some Cappies, but it can never be painted over entirely. He can be lovable, yes. Affectionate. Tender. Gentle. Whimsical and funny. All that. Nonetheless, he is ruled by Saturn, and there's no avoiding it. Beneath the sequins and rhinestones of a Capricorn rock and roll star, for example, is hiding a portrait of grandpa, complete with pocket watch and chain . . . waistcoat . . . and scowl of disapproval for the foolish.

The sex life of a Capricorn man can range from frankly erotic and sensual–to tender and affectionate. If his Sun and Venus are both severely afflicted from the fifth or eighth horoscopic houses, he will indulge himself in multiple experimentation. But the typical Goat's affairs are few, the intent nearly always permanency. Almost the identical thing can be said of the Cancer woman's love life. It depends. However, her inner desire is for a lasting relationship, even if she goes through more frequent trial and error periods than she would like . . to find it. One thing is quite certain. This woman will greatly enrich the Capricorn man's physical enjoyment of love. Although he's capable of a deep and steady sexual expression and physical intimacy (his sex drive is strong, never half-hearted), he may lack the kind of sensitive imagination that makes mating between two people a trembling, ecstatic kind of sharing of themselves. This is a sexual dimension the Moon Maiden will add to their relationship, and the

Goat will be touchingly grateful for the enlightenment. His strength and loyalty, the stability of his kind of Saturn love, will permit her to relax in his arms, without the fear of being hurt she might have with a less reliable lover or husband. He can supply the emotional insurance she needs, while she supplies the delicacy and romance he so needs, and lacks . . . . and after a while, with enough sharing back and forth of this nature, their physical love will become a strong and lasting cord to bind them together.

I know a Cancer woman who is presently separated from her Capricorn husband. Their problems are numerous, but essentially minor . . . none that can't be softened and healed with a little more understanding, a little less selfishness on both parts. Capricorn men can be hurtfully selfish. There's always a tendency, to some degree, to use people, with little regard for the other person's feelings. One of their heartaches was his inability to express love to her physically, after they'd had even the mildest sort of quarrel. He was like a stone, she told me, totally unresponsive to any tender overtures she shyly attempted. And so she would turn away, weeping silently, never letting him know. Recently she said to me, wistfully, "All those times I was so sorry for myself . . crying myself to sleep, retreating further into my shell of hurt. But I've had lots of time to think since we've been apart. I know more now, and I'm sorriest for him."

She's found the magic key to unlock his heart, at last. Now, if she'll only use it. If she goes to him with her new understanding they'll be closer than ever. When a Moon Maiden learns to stop feeling so sorry for herself and to direct her sympathy instead toward the Capricorn man she loves, she'll realize the depth of his inability to release the emotional power and glory he feels within. It's worth the effort of helping him release it. For no love has more grandeur, more endurance, than Capricorn love, which waits at the very top of the mountain to bless those with the patience and courage to climb high enough to experience it. It's a rough trip, with plenty of rocky ledges . . and always the danger of falling . . . . but the view at the top is inexpressible, indescribable. Like a glimpse of eternity. Saturn gives stern tests, but immense rewards.

☆ ☆ ☆ ☆ ☆ ☆

CANCER *Man* CAPRICORN *Woman*

"Won't you play me to sleep," he asked, "on the
nursery piano?" and as she was crossing to the
day-nursery he added thoughtlessly, "And shut that
window. I feel a draught."

A Cancerian male, whatever he may tell you, however much he may deny it, solicits and enjoys being babied and fussed over, and could at times take advantage of the Capricorn girl's strong sense of responsibility. Cappy will try hard to please the man she loves, without complaints or self-pity, but if he requires her to lean too far over backward to cope with his changing moods she'll balk, no matter how much she loves him.

In all fairness, both of them can be more than a little selfish. At first glance, no two people appear less selfish on the surface than the Crab and the Goat. He is normally gentle, considerate, and courteous, almost old-fashioned in his attitude toward women, especially toward his own woman. She is, in a way, his possession, and Crabs value their possessions highly. Nonetheless, he may demand a great deal more than he gives on occasion, expecting every sniffle and every cranky spell to be lullabyed and rocked away, and if she won't do this, she just doesn't love him, that's all—at least, not as much as Mother loved him.

If she's a typical Capricorn, she's probably rather quiet and demure, even self-effacing . . always willing to help out in a time of trouble. (Goats are truly superlative in a crisis. Emergencies are their specialties, and bring out the very best in their characters.) Still, she won't allow herself to be used beyond a reasonable limit, not even for the sake of love. She's sharply aware of all her human rights, and refuses to be anyone's doorstop. For all her attractive and soft feminine ways, she has a strong mind of her own. This is not a lady to flutter her lashes and hint about anything. What she really wants, she will either ask for directly—or go after, tooth and nail. What she likes, she will simply take, what she dislikes, she will remove from her life, in short order. There's nothing pliable or submissive about her. She doesn't noisily struggle against things which upset her. She just tunes it out, then takes care to avoid the person or situation, sometimes permanently. In this attitude, she is much like the Scorpio woman, except that the whole thing takes much less emotional toll of her in the process than it does of the Scorpion, who is always deeply affected, never mind what doesn't show.

The Capricorn woman is not unduly sensitive, and so she may have to be careful with the Crab, because he *is* unduly sensitive, and quite easily hurt. He's not nearly so thick-skinned as she is. If she should criticize or seriously contradict him, he usually won't let the matter rest until she "takes it back," tells him she loves him, and confesses that he has no real faults as far as she's concerned. He'll first try cajoling or being humorous, making little half-hearted jokes about it, then he'll turn to stronger hints, and as a last resort—pouting. He'll have all sorts of reasons to offer to defend his position, for this man will not rest in peace and calm until there is some sort of agreement after a quarrel. If she allows it to go too far, he'll retreat into his shell, and no compromise is possible. Crabs hang on tenaciously to arguments and to their own opinions, as they do to most everything else.

But he's a gentle man, and will blossom under the slightest praise and encouragement. The Capricorn woman who loves him will have to keep reassuring him, until he has no more need to force her to admit what a grand person he is, and how she adores him. Mother did this, you see. She was always telling him what a good boy he was, and how his enemies didn't really understand him. In extreme cases, he'll translate this to mean that anyone who doesn't agree with him is his enemy, even the woman he loves. He wants the same understanding treatment as an adult he received as a child. It's not terribly unreasonable of him. Wouldn't we all like to be understood? The difference is that most of us give up on it early in life. The Crab expects it as his due, and never gives up seeking it. Respect. Understanding. Love. Affection. Appreciation.

The typical Capricorn woman is not an expert at this sort of thing. She's practical and sensible; she feels he should know she loves him, and that if they disagree once in a while, it doesn't mean she hates him. Excessive sensitivity and extremes of emotions make Cappy uneasy and nervous. It isn't that she has no heart, she just doesn't quite know how to react, exactly what to do or say—and she's afraid of doing the wrong thing, so she would rather do nothing at all than to hurt him unintentionally.

She's too modest. She has an efficient mind to aid her in finding answers where others fail, along with a reliable ability to concentrate and meditate on a problem until it's solved, and usually her judgment is sound. So she should try a little harder to apply these talents to her emotional situations. It would make life in general a lot easier for both of them.

His need for her approval and appreciation isn't an impossible obstacle between them. It just requires less sensitive pouting from him, a little more tenderness and compassion from her. Of course, if the truth be told, she needs to be appreciated too, but never in a trillion years will she admit it—and certainly never request it. The Crab is no more an expert at giving pats on the head than Cappy, because he never had to appreciate Mama or pat *her* on the head—he just accepted the goodies, which, I suppose, is why children will always take advantage of doting parents. The very best gift these two can give one another is an extra hug or kiss, a few extra kind words—more frequent smiles. They both need attention equally, the only difference being his lack of bashfulness about asking for it, and her reluctance to either confess to or openly display any undue emotional needs of her own.

The Capricorn woman is inclined to be rather plain as a girl, growing visibly more beautiful as the years pass, one of her ruler Saturn's rare, but solid rewards. Along with her beauty, however, comes a very hard head (also a gift from Saturn). She is no mere fluff of feminine fancy. This girl is fortified with fortitude—and lots of it.

The Crab is inclined to be shy as a young man, growing more confident and sure of himself, and developing a marvelous sense of humor as the years pass. He's loaded with charm, he has a soft way of speaking, and a softly soothing manner—yet his mind is quick and clever, and he, too, possesses a very hard head. It's been said that Cancer has a soft heart and a hard head (which is surely better than a hard heart and a soft head!) but that the Capricorn woman's head and heart are *both* rocklike. That's not fair. Whoever said that probably tried to put something over on this lady, and she wasn't buying his blarney. Her heart is a woman's heart, but she's learned not to wear it on her sleeve, where it's susceptible to every blow. Could that be because it's so very vulnerable to hurt? Yes, it not only could be, but it is.

There's no denying that wisdom, caution, and self-protection are the Capricorn female's inheritances from her ruling planet, Saturn, but she is, for all that, a woman . . . with all the feelings, all the dreams and long-ings of a woman. Femininity needn't be synonymous with culpability. She possesses a timid (therefore, ultra-appealing) sort of sentiment, the kind which is all the more touching because it's not indulged in casually. It's not phony, but very real, and comes from her also very real . . . . . heart.

Cancer and Capricorn take their physical closeness as seriously as they do everything else, yet it's hard for them to let on to each other what their intimacy really means to them. They don't quite know how to say that their lovemaking causes them to take more notice of all kinds of beauty. She'll say simply, "Look at the way that sunbeam touches the top of the pine tree. I can almost smell the needles from here. Shall we take a walk?"

—when what she really means is . . . . after we've been close, I feel so special, and the world looks so much brighter.

He'll reply only, "Yes, let's take a walk. You're right. It is a beautiful morning"—when what he's really saying is, *you're* beautiful . . . I love you. Their physical relationship, especially if their Sun-Moon aspects are harmonious, can be rich and meaningful, the sort of deep experience that results from the powerful pull of those bar magnets of their astrological polarity—the opposition of their Sun Signs. It can be, in fact, so sacred to them, that sometimes they're even uncertain if such passion really happened, or they only dreamed it.

He may wonder aloud about this some morning, lying beside her—and she'll comment in her practical, common-sense, Capricorn way: "Well, when you can't *believe* a thing, I guess that means it was something special and good, because when it's something bad, you don't have to wonder —you're only too sure it actually happened." Then she'll snuggle closer to him, and murmur: "I'm not certain about last night. Do you suppose it really did happen?"—with one of her quiet little smiles. It's like a secret code between them. He'll answer her then, in a way that removes all doubt.

Both of them are, to some degree, wistful about yesterday, although his nostalgia may tug a little more frequently on his heart than hers does . . . . even making him wish, at times, he could go back there to live. If only there could be, somewhere, he sighs, a real estate agency that sells houses on a long-ago street, complete with all his memories of the past, come to life again. The Goat Girl is sensible enough to realize that yesterday always appears more beautiful in dreams than it was in actuality . . . . . so she's more interested in creating a *real* present, which is the way yesterday only *seems* to have been, a solid improvement over the past. After all, the past didn't include their discovery of each other. But the present does, and so, now, will the future. When she turns his vivid Lunar imagination around from yesterday toward tomorrow, they'll be traveling in the *spiral* direction of the Circle, wherein is contained the alpha and omega answer to the riddle of love.

☆ ☆ ☆ ☆ ☆ ☆

Before

LOVE SIGNS